Syracuse University - Drugs and Human Behavior

Tibor Palfai | Henry Jankiewicz

CENGAGE Learning™

Australia • Brazil • Japan • Korea • Mexico • Singapore • Spain • United Kingdom • United States

Syracuse University - Drugs and Human Behavior

Tibor Palfai I Henry Jankiewicz

Executive Editors:
Maureen Staudt
Michael Stranz
Project Development Manager:
Linda deStefano
Senior Marketing Coordinators:
Courtney Sheldon

Senior Production / Manufacturing Manager:
Donna M. Brown
PreMedia Services Supervisor:
Joel Brennecke
Rights & Permissions Specialist:
Todd Osborne

Cover Image:
Getty Images*

* Unless otherwise noted, all cover images used by Custom Solutions, a part of Cengage Learning, have been supplied courtesy of Getty Images with the exception of the Earthview cover image, which has been supplied by the National Aeronautics and Space Administration (NASA).

ISBN-13: 978-1-111-21023-6

ISBN-10: 1-111-21023-3

Cengage Learning
5191 Natorp Boulevard
Mason, Ohio 45040
USA

Cengage Learning is a leading provider of customized learning solutions with office locations around the globe, including Singapore, the United Kingdom, Australia, Mexico, Brazil, and Japan. Locate your local office at: **international.cengage.com/region**

Cengage Learning products are represented in Canada by Nelson Education, Ltd.

For your lifelong learning solutions, visit **custom.cengage.com**

Visit our corporate website at **cengage.com**

Printed in the United States of America

Contents

Preface to the 2006/2007 Custom-Published Edition

CHANGES TO THE CURRENT EDITION

The last official, contracted edition of our book, *Drugs and Human Behavior* (2/e), was published in 1997 by Brown and Benchmark and later, still unrevised, by McGraw-Hill. We have changed hands several times since then, through chains of acquisitions and mergers in the publishing industry, which has delayed our revising process. From 2003 to 2005-2004, we once more published the 1997 version through Thomson Learning's custom publishing division. This was an exact reproduction of the 1997 Brown and Benchmark edition.

The current edition contains the first significant changes to our manuscript since 1997. This text is a partial revision, which means it is now current in some parts, but still not in most. Instructors beside us who use this book should, therefore, be alert to the following changes:

Because we lost access to the digital copies of the text, updated by several typesetters, we have had to reconstruct the digital manuscript from our files and from previous proofs, galleys, and correction sheets. As far as we could, we matched this version of the book to the 1997 version in every detail before we began to revise. But we accept the fact that the match is not likely to be absolutely perfect. Changeovers between software applications have caused problems with typos, punctuation, and font styles, opening the door to small, undetected errors.

In accordance with requests from reviewers over the years, we synthesized some chapters and reduced the original 30 to the current 26. We joined "Administration" with "Absorption," "Distribution" with "Drug Fate," "Dosage and Drug Effects" with "Nonspecific Effects," and compiled the chapters on schizophrenia and its treatments (antipsychotics) into one chapter.

Whenever we have revised or added material, we have always addressed whole sections or chapters. The altered sections are marked with update times in brackets after the title. These are markers of our revision in progress. The affected sections are:

Chapter 5	"Tolerance"
Chapter 8	"The Medial Forebrain Bundle"
Chapter 9	"Dopamine"
	"The Neurobiology of Tolerance and Dependence"
Chapter 15	In its entirety
Chapter 26	Marijuana: "Pharmacological Effects," "Clinical Applications," "Side Effects,"

There are a very small number of nonsubstantive stylistic changes, such as the smoother rewording of sentences, throughout the text.

We have provided original illustrations for the custom publishing edition.

PASSAGES FROM THE PREFACE TO THE SECOND EDITION

In this second edition of *Drugs and Human Behavior,* we have kept to the basic goals of the first. Central among them was the desire to produce a clear and easy introductory textbook about psychoactive drugs that emphasizes science over sociology. As the knowledge of physiology and neurobiology increases and the image of neurotransmitter systems becomes more detailed, this challenge becomes even greater.

In addition, we have preserved the pattern of having the scientific terminology progress in complexity, from simple opening discussions that assume no prior acquaintance, to discussions that acclimatize readers to, and exercise their knowledge of, terms and concepts. Supporting this effort are an index to refer readers to the introductory discussions of concepts, and a glossary. Even so, we have kept discussions simple and in the vernacular whenever possible. The result is a book that comes off as fairly complex, but which we have found to be appropriate in a drug course open to undergraduates of various majors.

The general organization of this edition is fundamentally the same as the first, that is, analogous to that of traditional, higher-level psychopharmacology textbooks. The opening section explains basic concepts regarding the principles of drug action. The second section elaborates on the fundamentals of neurobiology related to drug actions: the physiology of the nervous system, and the workings of neurons and neurotransmitters. The later sections present a pharmacopoeia of psychoactive drugs, beginning with psychotherapeutic agents and the conditions for which they are used: sedation and anesthesia and the central nervous depressants; anxiety and calming drugs; schizophrenia and the antipsychotics; and mood disorders and the antidepressants. The closing sections address drugs, therapeutic and otherwise, that have a prominent profile as abused substances: stimulants, opium, hallucinogens, and THC. Each chapter treats the history, pharmacokinetics, pharmacological effects, clinical applications, side effects, and abuses for each class of drugs. Lastly, the appendices address aspects of human and animal drug research and development.

Perhaps because of the nature of our collaboration, involving a scientist and a writer, and both of us teachers who speak with undergraduates on a daily basis, we are ever-conscious of the struggle between two voices in our work. One reflects the sophisticated conventions of science and scientific language; it echoes the language of the specialized research journals that we read. This appeals especially to the teacher and the scientist, who inhabit this language and rightly want students to feel the force of good scientific work presented well. If anything, our style has moved more in this direction than in the previous edition. However, we recognize from the classroom that this voice may sell the matter to the teacher, but not necessarily to the students. Teachers know this, too. Many of those who stand by the screen or blackboard in front of a technical diagram speak, not in the pristine scientific prose of the journals, but in a colloquial, intentionally lowered register using slang, metaphor, analogy, and humor. This practice recognizes another voice, one that students can identify with and appreciate. So, even as we've stricken some of the more transgressive journalistic turns from our discussions, we've tried not to lose the feel of teachers making such an attempt.

Acknowledgments

Thanks to our illustrator, Adam Felleman. We don't know what we would have done without you.

Chapter 1

Psychopharmacology and the History of Psychoactive Drug Use

Mind, they say, rules the world. But what rules the mind? The body (follow me closely here) lies at the mercy of the most omnipotent of all potentates—the Chemist. Give me—Fosco—chemistry; and when Shakespeare has conceived Hamlet, and sits down to execute the conception—with a few grains of powder dropped into his daily food, I will reduce his mind, by the action of his body, till his pen pours out the most abject drivel that has ever degraded paper. Under similar circumstances, revive me the illustrious Newton. I guarantee that when he sees the apple fall he shall eat it, instead of discovering the principle of gravitation. Nero's dinner shall transform Nero into the mildest of men before he has done digesting it, and the morning draught of Alexander the Great shall make Alexander run for his life at the first sign of the enemy the same afternoon.

Wilkie Collins
The Woman in White (p. 622)

One of the remarkable things about the foregoing passage is that it is not as much exaggerated bragging as it may at first seem. A hallucinogen would be sufficient to do Shakespeare in, in the manner described. And marijuana, some artists have noted, has been capable of making them feel they are in the throes of some magnificent creative transport, only to find later their opus is somewhat incomprehensible. And the other prescriptions called for would be easily filled: marijuana again for Newton, to induce a strong appetite; tranquilizers for Nero; and, perhaps, for Alexander, LSD, a disorienting and unpredictable drug that can distort and intensify emotional circumstances.

What all these drugs—and the other drugs considered in this book—have in common is that they change behavior by acting on the nervous system, particularly the nerve cells of the brain and spinal cord (the central nervous system). They have been referred to as *psychoactive*, *psychotropic*, or *mind-altering* drugs, and they include such agents as sedatives, tranquilizers, antidepressants, stimulants, opiates, and hallucinogens. Non-psychoactive drugs have their primary action in other organs and tissues besides the nervous system. They can affect the nervous system and behavior, but this would occur indirectly as a result of their other actions. For instance, if a drug were to relieve pain by acting on the circulatory system, this would ultimately affect the nervous system and have a behavioral effect, but the drug would not be considered psychoactive because its primary effect was not on nerve cells. What distinguishes *psychoactive drugs*, then, is that they participate directly in the ongoing processes of the nervous system.

Understanding this, one can see how **psychopharmacologists** differ from pharmacologists—in their focus on psychoactive drugs and their actions rather than on drugs in general. Nevertheless, they consider all aspects of psychoactive drugs: their history and early use, their manufacture, their biological mechanisms, their movement in blood and tissues, their effects on organs and the nervous system, their breakdown, their behavioral effects in humans and animals, short- and long-term side effects, even the users themselves—in short, a raft of considerations that involves many other sciences, including chemistry, biochemistry, and physiology.

The word **psychopharmacology** has telling origins. Before 600 BC, in sheds by the main gates of most large Greek cities, a small host of the sick and disabled were housed and boarded on city funds. In times of general afflictions, like plague or famine, the city would appease the gods by casting lots and electing one of these unfortunates to be stoned to death in the marketplace. The chosen scapegoat was known as the *pharmakos*, the medicine or cure for public ills (Latimer & Goldberg, 1981, p. 24). This word later crossed by analogy to the use of herbs and medicines as cures for the body, and the word *pharmakon* came to mean "drug" or "medicine." (Also, it meant "poison," which is not so surprising, since many healing compounds can kill in slightly different doses or circumstances.) From such ignoble origins came our word "pharmacology"—the study (*logos*) of drugs.

Our word *psychology* derives from the Greek word *psyche*, meaning "soul," or "mind," represented in art as a butterfly. Psychology is thus the study (*logos*) of the mind (*psyche*). However, it is important to know that some psychologists reject the term "mind" as a vague and ill-defined concept. For these, the term is more a hindrance to objective investigation than a help. Such psychologists envision themselves rather as examiners of behavior, since behavior (the observable actions of tissues and organisms) is something that can be precisely defined, quantified, and measured. Hence, they prefer to be considered **behaviorists.** Furthermore, when one is interested in the behaviors resulting from drug use, it is convenient to regard behavior as the end product of a series of biochemical changes. This provides a context in which we can see drug actions and behavioral changes as phases of a single process.

Many psychologists object to the behaviorists' mechanistic interpretation, which seems to deny the existence of human will, yet despite its restrictions and in light of its practicality, it is the framework most psychopharmacologists adopt to work toward their primary goals: finding ways to use drugs to treat mental illness and deepening our understanding of behavior and the brain.

It can be seen, then, that the term **psychopharmacology** is a contraction of psychological pharmacology, which we can define as the study of how drugs modify behavior.

Next, we would like to look briefly at some of the salient points in the history of drug use, touching on the development of the therapeutic uses of mind-altering drugs. As for particular substances, their discovery, abuses, and impact on societies, we will consider these in later chapters devoted to individual drugs.

Long before any systematic attempts were made to understand the biological mechanisms of psychoactive drugs, their use was established in human culture. In fact, the ingestion of these substances is probably as ancient a practice as eating. People of antiquity dwelt in a natural world where psychoactive materials were to be had for the picking:

> *Blue morning glories covered the entrance to cave man's abode and a bowl with green seeds of ololiuqui might have stood inside. Amanita muscaria, the brilliant red mushroom with dots of white, grew in shady groves. Yellow-orange fruits of cactus studded arid plains. Red poppies bent their heads when it rained in the spring. Rauwolfia blossomed pink on tropical Himalaya mountains. Coca grew green and wild in equatorial America and so did cannabis nearly all over the world. (Caldwell, 1970b, p. 3)*

Ololiuqui, amanita, the peyote cactus, poppies, rauwolfia, coca, cannabis[1]—all contain psychoactive ingredients that are found in a natural state.[2]

Almost all human societies have used psychoactive drugs. Archaeological evidence shows the use of opium as far back as 4000 BC. The second millenium BC has left evidence of hallucinogenic mushroom use, and about the same time an emperor described marijuana use in China. Records from 1500 BC show alcohol drinking in Egypt, a practice that might really be as much as 10,000 years old. Poppies adorned the tombs of the pharaohs and crowned the statues of Greek deities. In general, the archaeology and mythology of antiquity are rife with drug references. It is important to make the distinction, however, that these drugs were taken in cultural contexts much different from ours. While the biological mechanisms remained a mystery, subjective effects often had important cultural uses (as with oracles or healers), and the taking of potent substances often involved carefully controlled ceremonial practices. These societies had none of our concepts of legislation, free will, and recreational use. In some cases, secular use was more likely to be regarded as an irresponsible involvement with very real and dangerous deities, or as a social affront against powerful and dangerous priests, shamans, or sorcerers. Such holy men and magicians were the closest thing to the psychopharmacologists of the time; they kept and transmitted the secrets of the drugs and how to obtain them; they guarded their ceremonial ingestion, preserved their pragmatic uses, and trained apprentices in how to avoid pitfalls and navigate in the otherworldly realms of altered states.

Many references to psychoactive drug use have survived from early Greek culture. *Kykeon*, a weak relative of LSD, was imbibed during the mysteries of Demeter, and *opos*, congealed poppy juice, during the spring rites of the Eleusinian Mysteries. Wine was central to the rites of Dionysius, and the oracle at Delphi may have fumigated herself with burnt hemp (cannabis) in order to prophesy.

A reference from Homeric literature that has intrigued a number of modern psychopharmacologists occurs in the *Odyssey*. Here Homer named the sorceress Circe as *polypharmakos*, which, in his use, means "skilled in the use of drugs":

> *Circe ushered them in [Ulysses' crew] and seated them on high-backed chairs and thrones and served them cheese and barley meal. She lavished on them Pramnian wine sweetened with yellow honey, but she laced it with vicious drugs that stunned their memories. They quickly grew mindless of home and country, and when they had done drinking, she suddenly whacked them with her wand and drove them into pigsties. There they found themselves to have the snub noses and clumsy bristly bodies of swine. And they wept in the pens, human minds enswined, horrified by their own oinking and grunting. And now Circe threw them acorns, mast, and cornel fruit—a diet for animals who rut in wallows—hog fodder. (Homer, X: 316-326)*

Conceivably, Homer may have based his Circe on real sorceresses who worked magic by warping the perceptions of their victims through drugs. Fighting fire with fire, Ulysses took the advice of the god Hermes, and outdrugged Circe by fortifying himself with an antidote, "a black plant with a flower white as milk" (Homer, X: 408-411).

In another scene from the *Odyssey*, Helen of Troy soothed some morose guests gathered in the palace at Sparta with a nameless cocktail that has long baffled psychopharmacologists—"a drug to drown anger and care, a drug to weather despair" blended into the wine. This compound was undoubtedly a narcotic or tranquilizer, since it came as a gift from Polydamna of Egypt, whose name means "super-tamer." However, if it were opium, Homer probably would have mentioned it by name, and cannabis lacks the exact pharmacological effects displayed by the guests, who lapse into a lucid, untroubled, and receptive story-telling mood. The drug remains a mystery (Caldwell, 1970a, pp. 13-14).

In medieval Europe, psychotropic drugs were still poorly understood but easily had. The ailing were less likely to consult a doctor or priest than an apothecary, herbalist, barber-surgeon, or midwife, all of whom dispensed remedies. Meanwhile, on a more heretical bent, witches and occult sectarians pored over the landscape, prying up mandrakes, flaying frogs, and bursting the berries of the deadly nightshade in search of the keys to diabolic spells, astral flights, and prescient visions.

The uninformed use of mind-altering drugs continued for centuries. Sedatives and narcotics made good potions for abduction, seduction, and Machiavellian intrigue, and the recreational use of alcohol, caffeine, and nicotine spread through Western civilization and beyond, while the medical grasp of drug actions remained rudimentary. Psychopharmacology did not start taking shape as a science until the nineteenth century, when it had spurious beginnings with the introduction of various drug treatments into the insane asylums of that time.

By the nineteenth century, rationalism and the rise of scientific thought had curbed some superstitious notions of drugs as magical potions, and scientists took a more directed and analytical, if somewhat haphazard, approach in applying drugs to the treatment of mental illness. There was a broad conviction that drugs could benefit the mentally ill, but no one had any hard information on what would work, since the mechanisms of both the illnesses and the drugs remained conjectural.

The nineteenth century was a time when the therapeutic and recreational uses of drugs were confusedly mingled. Three important kinds of pharmacological knowledge developed over the course of the century. The first was a growing systematic understanding of addiction and the implications of drug use for the individual. This became the focus of scientific inquiry only after the publication in 1821 of Thomas DeQuincey's

Confessions of an English Opium Eater (1821/1981), in which the author described his drug use and addiction in glowing detail. The compulsive use of drugs by individuals, of course, had been recognized earlier, but often it was attributed to a morally degenerate character. Withdrawal symptoms, too, were recognized, although in some cases they were mistaken for other illnesses, or for the return of the original illness, if one had been taking medicinal drugs. But there was no consistent medical or theoretical recognition of withdrawal as a biological syndrome associated solely with drug use. By the century's end, however, the study of addiction and the seeking of cures were prominent in medicine.

A second kind of knowledge that made long strides during the 1800s was the technological development and the means of mass production that changed the delivery of drugs to the human nervous system. Advances in chemistry brought methods for isolating the active ingredients of plant materials, such as cocaine from the coca plant and morphine from opium, and they brought, too, methods for synthesizing new molecules, such as the barbiturate sedatives and heroin. Developing in tandem with the purer, more potent substances was an understanding of better ways to deliver them, chief among these being injection, made possible by the invention of the hypodermic syringe. Put these together with the Industrial Revolution and its techniques for delivering goods to mass markets, and one can imagine what happened. There were potent, injectable drugs in the hands of most physicians and many patients, who had only a rudimentary sense of the possible consequences.

The third frame of knowledge gained through the 1800s concerned the large-scale social consequences of drug-taking. Western civilization had already had a foretaste of this in the seventeenth and eighteenth centuries when the invention of gin—made possible by the technique of distilling—plagued Europe with a debilitating inebriation for almost a hundred years. In the nineteenth century, however, a whole pharmacopoeia of psychoactive agents was available in the name of therapy, while physicians still had no idea of the physiological mechanisms underlying the drug effects. Furthermore, early on, before a sense of social dangers blossomed, there were no legal restrictions. This meant there was legal access to all these agents, among them hashish, cocaine, opium, morphine, ether, and sedatives. Physicians dispensed morphine freely as a painkiller, the public bought medicaments off the shelves, and quacks and unscrupulous entrepreneurs fueled the patent medicine craze, hawking elixirs laced with cocaine, alcohol, or opium, which masqueraded as medicines. It was the era of snake oil and the medicine show. But as the century progressed, so did the realization that all this home pharmacology, though it may have been what the doctor ordered, was not to the betterment of society. By the turn of the century, addiction was recognized as a medical problem, and opiate addiction cures were doing conspicuous business. Moreover, the moralists had begun to sort out the issues: temperance movements sprang up against alcohol and tobacco, political pressure was building to restrict or ban substances outright, and the early groundwork was being laid for the moral tone that would come to fruition in the 1900s, when bans such as Prohibition went into effect—that addicts were moral degenerates and criminals.

Given the state of knowledge in the nineteenth century, it is characteristic, therefore, that the person considered to be the first true psychopharmacologist was working with a treatment that misses the mark by today's standards. This French psychiatrist,

Jacques-Joseph Moreau (1804-1884), called Moreau de Tours, was the first to use a drug to induce and study mental symptoms and to treat mental illness. The drug was cannabis, prepared in a recipe known as *dawamesc,* a flavored paste of hashish or pure extract, taken with black coffee to potentiate and accelerate the effects and enhance the flavor (Caldwell, 1970a, p. 15). In 1845, Moreau introduced his treatment to psychiatry and published his study, "Du Hashish et de l'Aliénation Mentale." However, as we know today, hashish contributes little if at all to the alleviation of severe mental disorders.

More informally, Moreau ran with "The Hashish Eaters' Club," a small coterie of young Paris bohemians who experimented with then-legal hashish when it was a romantic craze in Europe in the 1840s, easily purchased at the pharmacist's or procurable from travelers. From the club later emerged three major French literary figures: Theophile Gautier, Charles Baudelaire, and Gerard de Nerval. In a memorable portrait, Gautier captures the image of a figure who is very likely Moreau:

> *The doctor stood beside a sideboard on which was a tray filled with little Japanese porcelain saucers. A piece of greenish paste or preserves, about the size of one's thumb, was drawn by him from a crystal vase by means of a spatula and placed beside a vermeil spoon on each saucer.*
>
> *The doctor's face radiated enthusiasm, his eyes sparkled, his cheeks reddened, the veins in his temples stood out, and his dilated nostrils breathed forcefully.*
>
> *"This will be deducted from your share of paradise," said he, handing me my dose. (Gautier, 1846/1977, p. 88).*

Moreau was something of a controversial personality, mixing hashish with business and pleasure. The preeminent mind of the club, Baudelaire came to see hashish as artistically and intellectually limiting, and in a later essay condemned Moreau severely as an evil influence ("On Wine and Hashish Compared," 1851/1958).

The first half of the twentieth century brought a host of treatments with known depressants, none of which proved especially fruitful. In the 1930s, stimulation by amphetamines and tranquilization by rauwolfia alkaloids (a psychiatric therapy used in India at this time) were employed with less than overwhelming success. A similar fate followed the use of chemical shock treatments, like insulin- or Metrazol-induced convulsions, which initially seemed beneficial for certain psychotic symptoms. LSD made its halting start in 1947 as a clinical drug, and lithium carbonate emerged two years later, after reports by J. F. J. Cade of its successful use in the sedation of guinea pigs, and then of humans. Cade's discovery, in retrospect, was really the first reasonably successful psychopharmacological treatment, but his findings, reported in *The Medical Journal of Australia,* went unnoticed at the time.

Until 1951, most psychopharmacological investigations involved shocks, surgery, and experimental attempts to apply existing psychoactive drugs to psychiatric ends, all with feeble results. Then, in 1950, Henri Laborit, a French anesthesiologist looking for a means to reduce shock[3] during surgery, in collaboration with chemist Paul Charpentier, managed to produce a drug with strong tranquilizing effects that did not put patients to sleep. This was the greatest breakthrough up to that point in the history of psychopharmacology. The drug was chlorpromazine (Thorazine), a compound that produced, according to Laborit, "not any loss in consciousness, not any change in the patient's mentality but a slight tendency to sleep and above all `disinterest' for all that goes on around him" (Laborit, 1952). Jean Delay, who used this drug in psychiatry in early 1952, was the first to report its benefits at a conference, and he pushed eagerly for its widespread use and acceptance (Delay, Deniker, & Harl, 1952/1989). The resultant spread of chlorpromazine constituted a revolution in the chemotherapy of mental illness. Over the next three years, it became more and more popular in mental hospitals. Hallucinogenic terrors receded, physical restraints were dispensed with, and many patients recovered enough to return to normal life. Records show that the number of hospital residents in the United States plummeted after 1955, as chlorpromazine was going into general use, and they continued to drop steeply throughout the next twenty years (see Figure 1.1). Thus, the history of modern psychopharmacology really begins with the use of chlorpromazine.

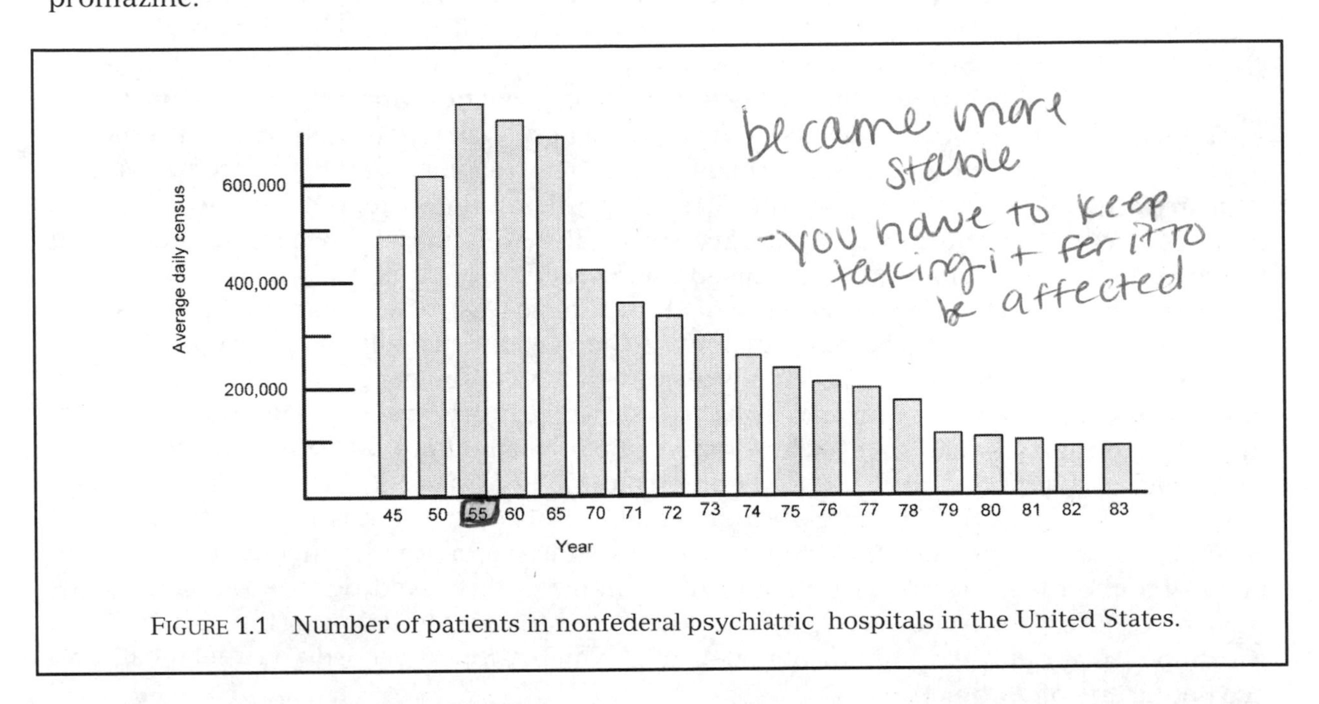

FIGURE 1.1 Number of patients in nonfederal psychiatric hospitals in the United States.

What followed was a boom in the synthesis of drugs. Once pharmaceutical companies got wind of an effective agent like chlorpromazine, their interest flowered in the manufacture of related substances. The fifties were a time of furious productivity in drug chemistry, as researchers methodically altered the structures of molecules in hopes of producing new psychochemical agents. Attention also focused on how chlorpromazine interacted with natural chemicals in the nervous system; such study raised the hopes of more effectively tailoring molecules to obtain specific behavioral effects. During this period, several key modern drugs were synthesized, some only to be shelved until later, when more sensitive screening techniques or the caprices of history would make their significance known.

Between the 1950s and the 1970s, psychopharmacology took on a new air. In the fifties it seemed to consist of a select group of scientists developing specialized medicines for select groups of mentally ill patients. But soon the inventions of these specialists began to have extensive social and cultural implications. Drug threats to society were nothing new, as earlier references to the gin epidemic and the patent medicine craze show. However, societies were no longer quite as naive about new drugs as they had been, and there was a clearer connection between the work of individual psychopharmacologists or research teams and the social impact of their productions. The methods being used also made it clear that researchers were not just poking about on a whim in hopes of hitting on useful pharmaceuticals. They were systematically mining an area of enormous chemical potential; one could imagine hundreds of thousands of molecules that these methods would eventually produce. And who knows what repercussions some of these inventions would have on populations at large?

The first of these modern waves came with meprobamate (Miltown or Equanil) in the fifties, the first major mass-marketed tranquilizer. No one was quite prepared for what happened, because meprobamate was different from previous drugs. It did not fit the established notion of a drug of abuse. No one associated it with minorities, lower social classes, or a criminal underground. Muckrakers could not blame it for stimulating "crazed dope fiends" to acts of violence. Occultists, mystics, and artists seeking mind-benders did not embrace it. Moreover, its medical application was ambiguous. It relieved tension and stress, but when were tension and stress normal and when were they a disorder? Here was a drug that not only did not intrude on daily life, but seemed beneficial to healthy people undergoing temporary stress. Previous mass-appeal drugs had been borrowed from medicine (opium) or used for recreation or thrill seeking (nicotine, alcohol, ether, caffeine). To the workaday world, such drugs were necessary evils, intrusions, escapes, or ornaments. Only marginally were they seen as useful coping drugs. As a result, medical and cultural expectations were not yet schooled enough to handle new agents that seemed to temporarily enhance everyday functioning without much impairment.[4] Tranquilizers, like many drugs before them, seemed at first to be a different animal: mild, relaxing, an aid to work, a relief from the jitteriness of the times, and a friend and pillar of society. These were attributes that established attitudes were not capable of assessing wisely. The result, as you may guess, was widespread dependence and a review of some of the lessons learned in the century before. And despite the experience with meprobamate, tranquilizers struck again with the introduction in the late 1960s of the minor tranquilizers Valium and Librium, which topped records as the most prescribed drugs of all time.

The hallucinogen LSD was another compound that inadvertently made a huge psychopharmacological impact on Western societies. A drug of more curious interest than proven therapeutic value, it left Albert Hofmann's lab to shape history. A little more than a decade after its effects were discovered in 1943, it was international news as a powerful and interesting hallucinogen, for cultural, not medical, reasons. The taking of LSD was politicized by the youth revolution of the sixties as well, so that drug-taking became a philosophical statement, opening up implications beyond the arenas of health, medicine, and drug legislation. The developing craft of molecule-making, it was becoming clear, was something to be reckoned with.

The most significant development in psychopharmacology in the seventies was more technical. Early in the decade, researchers located drug receptors in the nervous system—the structural points where drug molecules attach to nerve cells and interact with them. Whereas before there had been an understanding only of a drug, a nerve cell, and an observable response, more or less as separate entities, now the links in the process promised to become clear, opening the potential for vast advancements in the study of how drugs produce behaviors. The historic discovery revealed that morphine molecules attach to structures on certain nerve cells that seem specifically designed to receive them. But why, researchers queried, would our nervous systems be designed to receive morphine, a substance that has to be processed by fairly elaborate means out of opium poppies? The inference they reached, of course, was that perhaps the body produced some natural substance resembling morphine that used these receptors to get natural, morphine-like effects. If so, it would open up tremendous potential for learning about the body's response to pain, since morphine is one of the most effective painkillers known. As we will see in the chapter on opiates, these hypotheses proved correct.

In the 1980s, psychopharmacology's knowledge of receptors became more detailed regarding their variety, structure, and roles in particular systems. Moreover, the possibilities of drug synthesis have proliferated as organic chemistry becomes capable of finer and finer manipulations. Based on these developments, researchers are now trying to identify new receptors linked to specific drug effects, in hopes of designing more accurate drugs to fit them. For instance, we still do not have a painkiller as effective as morphine or heroin that does not also produce euphoria and addiction. The psychopharmacological ideal would be to isolate and analyze only the receptors that mediate pain (assuming there to be such), and to tailor for them a morphine-like drug that will interact exclusively with these receptors and not influence any other systems, such as those that produce constipation, euphoria, or addiction. We could similarly hope for tranquilization without drowsiness, suppression of psychosis without movement disorders, stimulation that ignores the heart, and more.

The designer drug craze of the mid-1980s was partly a result of this "smarter" chemistry. A drug designer can start with an amphetamine or heroin molecule and alter it in hundreds of ways by attaching atoms or shifting them about. The result can be a molecule with similar, or even stronger, effects than the original. What's more, the modification may make the drug legal, not covered by the restrictions governing the parent heroin or amphetamine molecule. And with all of the ramifications available, the home chemists can move faster than Congress. This has already caused a need for rethinking legal theory to cover such contingencies fairly.

In addition to the synthesis of new molecules in the laboratory, the other chief method of discovering new drugs—searching the globe for plant and animal sources—continues as well (see Appendix A). At present, there is marked concern in this field over areas of the planet, rich in undiscovered species of life, that are being threatened by environmental factors. Among other things, a multitude of undiscovered drugs may be lost with the Brazilian rain forests or certain delicate ocean ecologies.

As we know from the news, the drug underworld and the street trade have kept up with technological advances, manufacturing newer agents and refining some of the tried and true drugs of abuse. Plant breeders of the seventies developed *sinsemilla*, a more potent marijuana. The eighties saw brown heroin, a more potent euphoriant; and crack, cocaine done up with lethal purity.

In the future, we can anticipate the appearance of strange new drugs that raise hot controversies, such as friendly pills to improve memory or reaction time for brief periods. Would it be ethical to take such drugs before a language exam or a driving test? Or how about safe appetite-suppressants for dieters or mild, long-acting euphoriants for the depressed? These are not outlandish hopes—to have specific, nonaddicting drugs that boost human performance in traditionally desirable ways, like a weak cup of tea to make you excel for an hour or two. Because of such clear possibilities, one can easily imagine many of the fattest headlines of the future reserved for psychopharmacology.

Endnotes

1. Cannabis, mentioned throughout this chapter, is the species of plant from which both marijuana and hashish are derived. Consult the glossary for further information.

2. The case of animals and psychoactive drugs is an interesting one. Many animals in their natural habitats are known to ingest psychoactive drugs. Reindeer, cattle, and rabbits eat intoxicating mushrooms. Pigeons eat cannabis seeds. Mongooses eat toads with the hallucinogen bufotenine in their skins, and goats munch coffee plants. Ronald K. Siegel (Greenberg, 1983) reports observing over 2,000 cases of animals self-administering drugs and 300 cases that "suggest that these ingestions are both intentional and addictive." In Tanzania, elephants have been seen breaking into stills and grain storage facilities or munching on the fermented fruit of the *mgongo* tree. Tests have shown that elephants prefer preparations containing 7 percent alcohol, the same as in these fruits (Leavitt, 1982, p. 169).

3. An acute state of weakness and a reduction of many vital functions.

4. In the 1940s, after World War II, amphetamine (speed) may have briefly seemed to be such a drug, stimulating workers with more energy and more productivity, but its adverse effects and addiction potential became quickly evident.

Chapter 2

Receptors

Before elaborating on the various modes of administering drugs, we would do well to consider generally the reasons for administering psychoactive drugs in the first place. To put it broadly, whether we are speaking of social, therapeutic, or recreational motivations, the purpose is to elicit some chemical or physiological change in the tissues of an organism.

Between the taking of the drug and the observed response, there is an intricate chain of biological events. The most important point in the sequence is the place where the drugs contact and produce changes in nerve cells--at the **drug receptors.** Psychoactive drugs are compounds able to interact with drug receptors in the nervous system and cause some change in nerve cell functioning. A neurochemist might say, therefore, that the reason you take drugs is to deliver the drug molecules to the receptors--that a smoker smokes, for instance, to get nicotine molecules onto nicotine receptors. It is from here that the behavioral effects proceed.

Why do some compounds have dramatic behavioral effects and others none? The answer lies in the fact that individual nerve cells (neurons) communicate with one another, not simply through electrical impulses, as was once thought, but through the release of chemicals called **neurotransmitters.** The way a ``message'' travels along a sequence of nerve cells is that the finely branching ends of a stimulated neuron release chemical transmitters; these cross a miniscule gap (the synaptic gap) to attach to **receptor sites,** protein complexes that act as receiving stations on the following neuron. The new neuron is thus influenced at the receptor site to either inhibit the impulse or repeat the process and continue the transmission to yet another neuron.

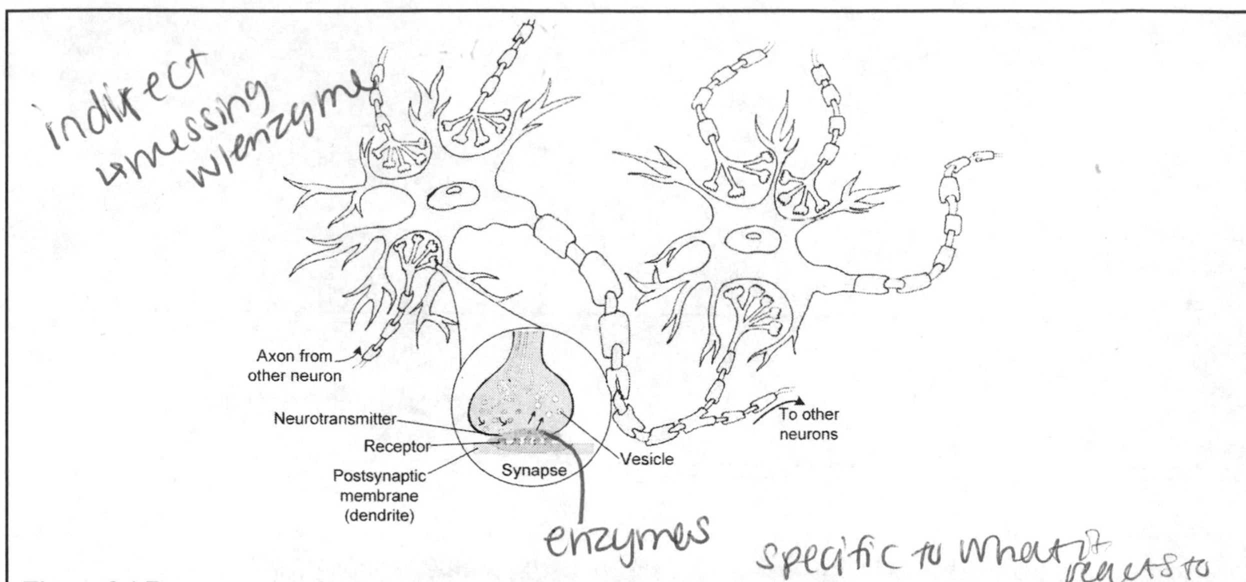

Figure 2.1 Receptor sites in the nervous system are found in the gaps between cells on the outside of the membranes. They are activated by neurotransmitters released from adjacent cells.

Certain psychoactive drugs are able to participate in this chain of events because they are similar enough to a particular neurotransmitter to use its drug receptors. They may have a somewhat different effect on neurons, overdriving them, inhibiting them, or altering their response. This may lead to the range of behavioral effects we are familiar with--nausea, staggering, euphoria, hand tremors, and so forth. Of course, there are other mechanisms drugs may participate in, too; these we will consider later while discussing in detail how neurons work. It is our purpose here merely to acquaint you with the existence of the drug receptor, the target of drug administration.

One note of warning—biologists use the word *receptor* broadly and confusingly. Essentially, it means ``receiving mechanism,'' a term applicable to many situations. For example, there are receptor cells, like the rods and the cones in the retina, or the Pacinian corpuscles, the pressure-sensitive receptors under the skin. These receive environmental stimuli. In discussing drug effects on neurons, however, two uses of the term *receptor* are important. The first, a *receptor site,* (or just *receptor*) which we have described above, refers specifically to the protein structures typically found on nerve cell membranes, into which the neurotransmitters fit like keys in keyholes (see Figure 2.1). The second, *drug receptor,* refers widely to any tissue (or biochemical structure) able to receive and interact with a drug and participate in a drug response. For example, one action of alcohol is to directly affect the entire membrane of a cell, without having to pass as a neurotransmitter and use its receptor site. In this case, the whole membrane acts as a drug receptor. So you can see that the receptor sites are one particular type of drug receptor, and any number of other tissues may serve as well.

In general, to have a behavioral effect, a drug must affect the neurons in some way, either directly or indirectly. It is worth noting also that drugs do not produce completely new or different actions in the nervous system; they alter ongoing processes.

DRUG ACTION

Drug action means simply the interacting of drug molecules with biological tissue. The specific process in any given case is known as the **mechanism of action** of the drug. Morphine acts by attaching to receptors and stimulating nerve cells that are capable of causing analgesia (the blocking of pain). That is one of its mechanisms of action. The **drug effect**, of course--the observed changes--follows from the drug action. Whereas the effects of most drugs are known, many of their mechanisms of action are obscure. For example, beer intoxicates, but the exact mechanism of intoxication is not yet clear.

Many psychoactive drugs have a mechanism of action that mimics the action of neurotransmitters. Receptor sites are constructed of proteins that give the site a specific size and shape and specific electrical and chemical properties that fit it to a particular type of neurotransmitter. A drug molecule similar enough in these properties can ``fool'' the receptor site into accepting it in place of the neurotransmitter. As a result, the drug binds to the receptor with a weak, reversible bond and activates or inhibits the neuron, just as the neurotransmitter would.

When small changes are made in the structure of a molecule, the geometry and electrochemical properties may be altered enough to cause dramatic changes in effects. For instance, small modifications in dopamine, a naturally-occurring neurotransmitter, transmute it into a potent hallucinogen (mescaline). The relationship between the structure of a drug and its action is called the **structure-activity relationship.** Understanding this relationship is important for the synthesis of new drugs.

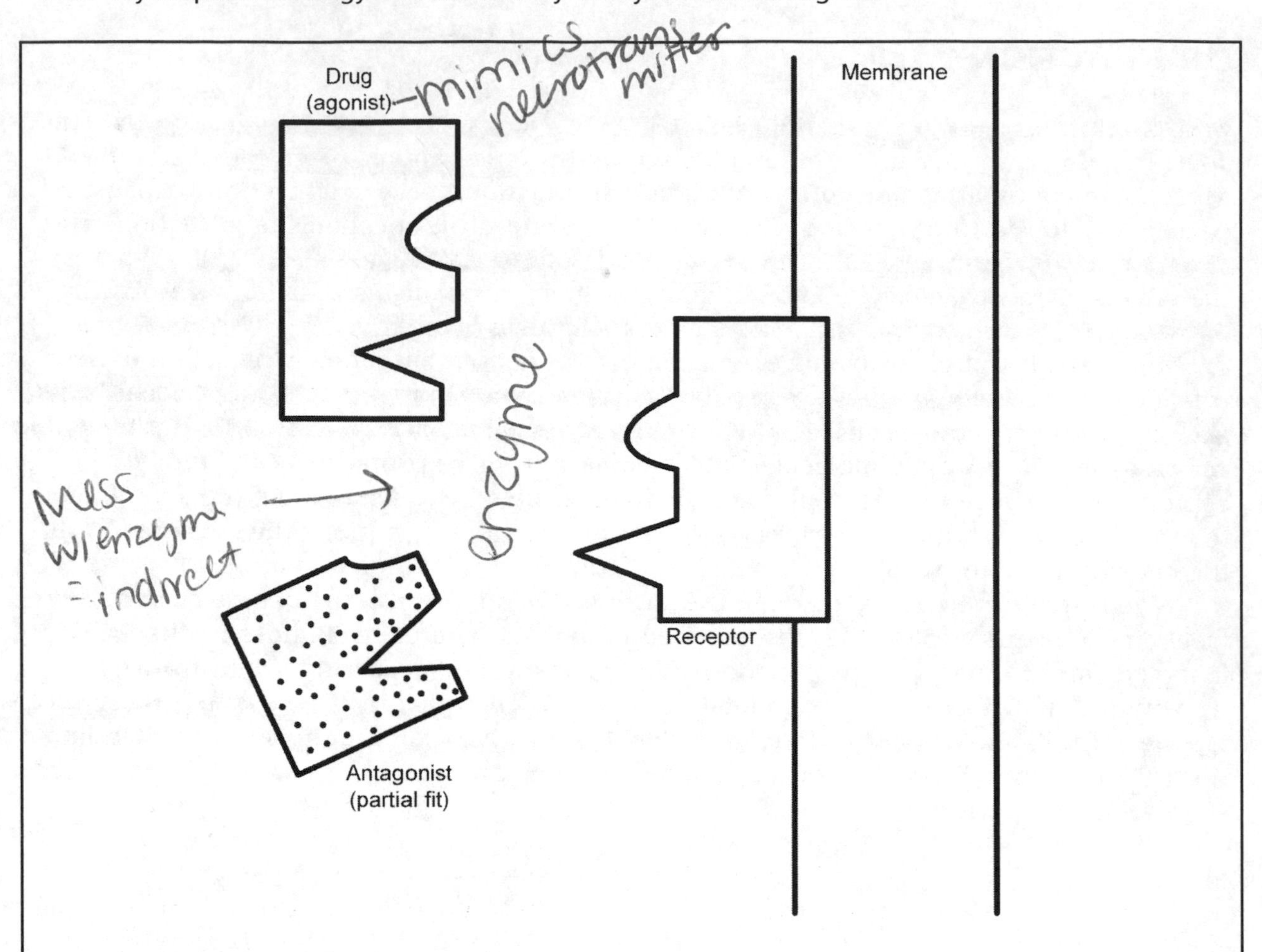

FIGURE 2.2 An agonist fits the receptor and activates it. However, the antagonist in this depiction can partially fit the receptor and prevent the agonist from gaining access (assuming its affinity is high enough).

A drug that can mimic a neurotransmitter and partially or wholly stimulate its receptor is called an **agonist** of that neurotransmitter. Conversely, a drug that interferes with the action of the neurotransmitter is an **antagonist**. For example, a drug may resemble the neurotransmitter enough to occupy the receptor partly, but not enough to stimulate it. Furthermore, the drug's presence may block the neurotransmitter from getting onto the receptor. In this case, the drug would be antagonistic to the neurotransmitter, and the observable drug effect would result from the blockage; a drug that antagonizes the neurotransmitters that mediate movement, for instance, will cause paralysis.

Figure 2.2 shows a schematic diagram of a drug receptor with an agonist that fits it fully and an antagonist molecule that fits it partially. One can see how the access of the agonist to the receptor would be blocked by the antagonist. This arrangement is equally true for a drug blocking a neurotransmitter or for one drug blocking another.

Based on their molecular geometry and electrical attraction, the receptor sites show a preference--or affinity--for some compounds over others. The receptor may accept another substance in place of the neurotransmitter. Such substances, which have the ability to vie with neurotransmitters for possession of the receptor sites, are said to be **competitive antagonists**. For instance, based on its **affinity**, a competitive antagonist may occupy 20 percent of the available receptors, while the neurotransmitter occupies 80 percent, or the competitive antagonist may have a high enough affinity to occupy 90 percent of the receptors, and so forth. An antagonist of equal affinity to the neurotransmitters will occupy 50 percent of the available receptors.

Curare is a poison used by South American Indians to paralyze their victims. It is a competitive antagonist of acetylcholine, the neurotransmitter that works the skeletal muscles. Curare occupies the receptors and stops acetylcholine from using them. As a result, the transmission of movement to the skeletal muscles is blocked, and the victim becomes paralyzed while remaining fully conscious. Eventually, the paralyzing of the respiratory muscles causes suffocation.

A drug related to curare, gallamine, may also interfere with the action of the same neurotransmitter--acetylcholine--but it does so by attaching to a different receptor. Because it is not competing for the same receptor site, gallamine is considered a **noncompetitive antagonist** (Kenakin, 1993, p. 323).

Agonists can also compete for a receptor. The only difference is that they produce an action like that of the neurotransmitter, but maybe not as strong.

Understanding the combined effects of drugs, their agonisms and antagonisms, is essential to the study of drug action. Naloxone and heroin, a derivative of morphine, provide another interesting case. Heroin has an affinity for opiate receptors in the brain; it acts as an agonist for them. But naloxone, an antagonist, has a much higher affinity for the receptors; consequently, it can unseat the heroin, bind to the receptors, and block stimulation. This has profound repercussions for heroin addicts. Addicts given a shot of naloxone suffer immediate withdrawal because the antagonist knocks the heroin off their receptors and prohibits further action, sending them from euphoria into the miseries of prompt withdrawal.

In competitive actions, we have seen that drug molecules attach right to the receptor; that is, they have the same site of action as the neurotransmitter. Such actions are referred to **direct**. Direct actions can tell us something about the shape of a receptor, because we can analyze the shapes of the molecules that bind to it. On the other hand, noncompetitive actions are **indirect**; they affect the activity of the neurotransmitter in some other way. Some antagonists, for instance, can interfere with several neurotransmitters at once by disrupting steps in their synthesis. Another possibility is that a drug may interfere with the enzymes that break down neurotransmitters.

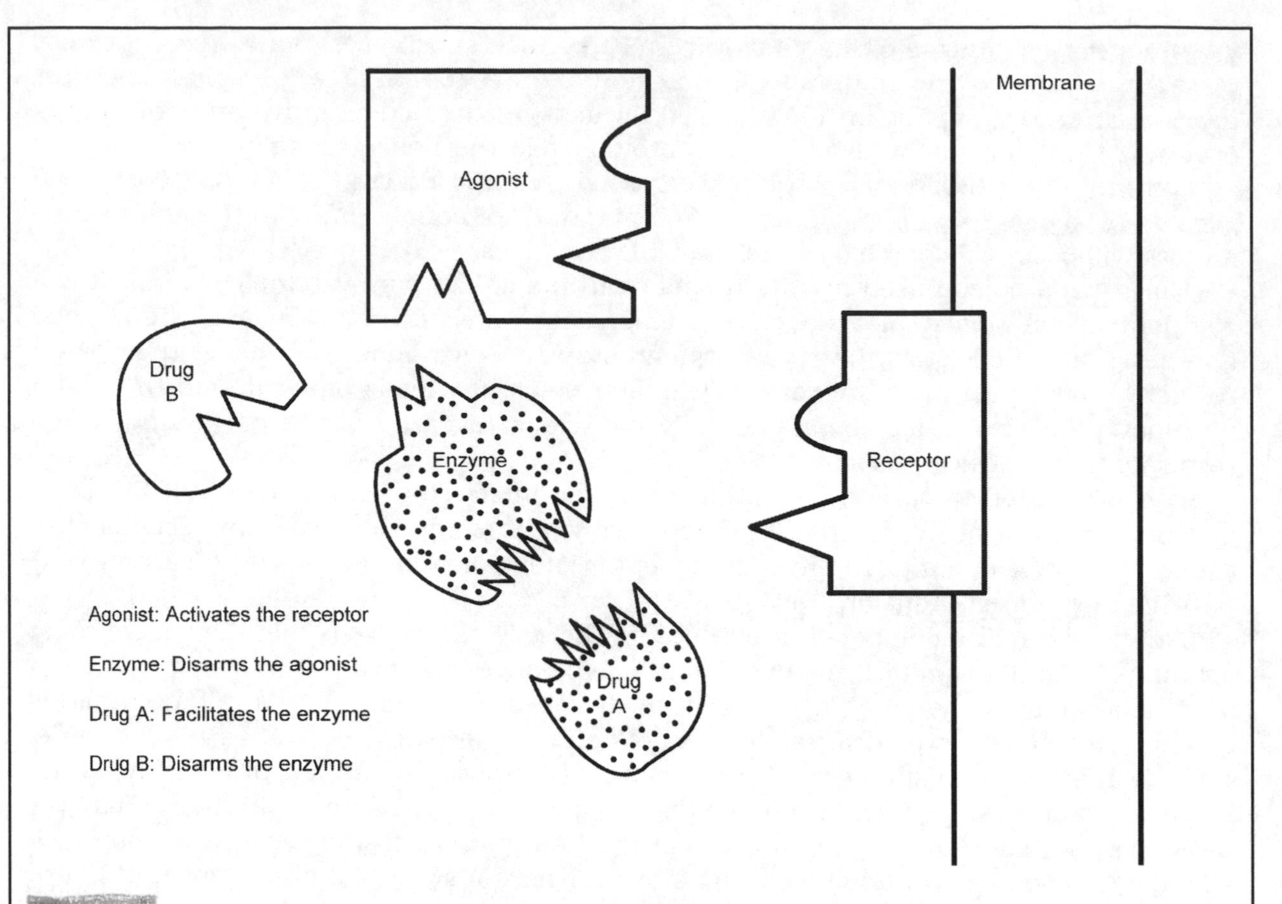

Figure 2.3 Relationship of receptor, enzyme, and agonistic and antagonistic drugs. Both the enzyme and drug A act as antagonists.

In many instances, the action of neurotransmitters is terminated by enzymes. These enzymes may be considered natural antagonists of the neurotransmitters. It follows, then, that if a drug can help the enzyme, it, too, is an antagonist because it helps to stop the stimulation of the receptor.[1] Conversely, a drug that interferes with the enzyme is agonistic because it fosters the action of the neurotransmitter.[2] These relationships are depicted in Figure 2.3.

A practical illustration of enzyme interference is the treatment of certain forms of depression presumed to be caused by lack of the neurotransmitter norepinephrine in the brain. It is sometimes possible to treat depression with a drug that interferes with the enzymes that break down norepinephrine. Inhibiting the antagonistic enzyme increases the supply of the neurotransmitters, activating the receptors and relieving depression.

Most drugs are **specific** in their action on neurotransmitters, enzymes, receptor sites in the synapse, or on other organs and processes. Some drugs have a **nonspecific action**, that is, they alter tissues or chemistry in a more fundamental way, affecting diverse organs and systems. Alcohol, as we have said, can inhibit impulses by acting on the walls of all nerve cells and reducing the excitability of the entire central nervous system.

Although the interplay of agonists with antagonists, and neurotransmitters with enzymes, may at first seem confusing because of the technical terms they go by, the basic relationships are actually quite simple and are essential to an understanding of drug action.

Endnotes

1. From the neurotransmitter's perspective, we may alter the proverb to say, "The friend of my enemy is my enemy."
2. "The enemy of my enemy is my friend.'

Chapter 3

Administration and Absorption

The giving or taking of a drug is **administration.** A drug, we might say, is not a drug until the moment it enters the body. To be effective, it must enter and travel to the place where it can exert its influence. The entry point is known technically as the **site of administration,** and the method by which the drug is administered--by mouth or needle, say--is the **route of administration.** When it arrives at the place where it works, the drug has reached its **site of action;** this may be local or general, depending on which types and parts of tissue respond to the drug.

One must consider many factors when choosing a route of administration. *What are the chemical properties of the drug?* Some routes are better than others, depending on whether the drug is alkaline or acidic, fat- or water-soluble. For example, heroin, if eaten, may have little or no effect because the drug is poorly absorbed from the gastrointestinal tract, and not enough reaches the site of action in the brain, but even a tiny amount injected into a vein has an effect. *What is the proper medium to carry the drug?* Oily solutions, for instance, should not be injected directly into the blood because they clog the vessels and interfere with blood circulation. *How soon should the drug begin to act?* An intravenous injection can deliver a drug to the brain in seconds, whereas absorption through the gastrointestinal tract may take two or three hours. *How old is the patient?* Metabolism and body chemistry change as we age. Elderly stomachs, being more alkaline, have difficulty assimilating common drugs such as aspirin. Babies, on the other hand, cannot swallow tablets. Therefore, occasionally aspirin has to be administered to the elderly and to infants rectally. Other factors to consider are the mechanisms for transporting the drug through the body, and the mechanisms for absorbing, metabolizing, and excreting it. In a word, the chemistry, form, and route of the drug are closely related.

DRUG FORMS AND PREPARATIONS

Forms, or preparations, of drugs are designed for the routes they are intended to follow. The word *drug* itself comes from a fourteenth century French word, *drogue*, meaning "dry substance," an allusion to the fact that most pharmaceuticals were once prepared as dried herbs. When this was the case, the potency of drugs would vary widely from region to region, due to different growing conditions. Modern techniques that extract the active ingredients and standardize the dosages, therefore, have enhanced the uniformity and safety of drugs. Their preparation in the form of salts stabilizes them chemically so they last longer in marketing and storage, but still allows them to dissolve easily in solutions and on mucous membranes.

In **solid form**, designed for oral routes, drugs appear as tablets, crystals, and powders in capsules. Suppositories are a solid form taken rectally or vaginally; these are drug-filled capsules that entirely dissolve in surrounding membranes. In **liquid form**, drug salts are dissolved in a predominantly inert fluid referred to as the **drug vehicle.** Most injected drugs are solutions like this, although some drugs in semisolid form may be made into suspensions and injected. Other drugs may be dissolved or suspended in oily or creamy vehicles, to be applied to the skin as ointments and creams. Finally, **inhalants** are drugs prepared as gases, smoke, or vapor, to be inhaled.

The matching of drug forms to drug routes is not entirely rigid. *Snorting* cocaine, for example, involves inhalation of the drug in solid, crystallized form; it then dissolves on the mucous membranes of the nose, sinuses, and respiratory tract. A tobacco smoker has the option of drawing smoke into the lungs or retaining it in the mouth and absorbing its ingredients through the lining of the oral cavity. Sometimes a single drug can be taken in several forms. Marijuana can be rolled in cigarettes and smoked, it can be brewed as tea and drunk (hence the term *pot*), it can be baked in cakes and eaten, and its active ingredient, THC, can be injected.

BODY COMPARTMENTS

Navigating the route between the site of administration and the site of action is rarely a simple matter for a drug. The body's interior is walled off into sections by various membranes and tissues. Each of these sections is a **body compartment**, more specifically, a continuous area bounded by tissues or membranes; it is possible to travel from one part of it to another without passing through a barrier. So, for instance, the entire bloodstream is a single body compartment, because no barriers obstruct movement from one place to another within the circulation. As a result, a substance that dissolves in the blood permeates the entire compartment; that is, the entire circulatory system. Another body compartment is the **extracellular fluid (ECF)** of the brain, which fills the space between blood vessels and nerve cells and makes up a single interconnected area.

The most important compartments for drug study are (1) the gastrointestinal tract, (2) the bloodstream, (3) the cell interior, (4) the extracellular fluid outside the brain and spinal cord, and (5) the extracellular fluid inside the brain and spinal cord. These last two are partitioned from one another by the membranous barrier that houses the central nervous system. Somewhat less important compartments are the peritoneal (abdominal) cavity, the pulmonary (lung) cavity, the extracellular (interstitial) fluid under the skin, and the area (intrathecal area) enclosed by the sheathings around nerve bundles, the spinal cord, and the brain.

On most routes of administration, at some stage the drug enters the blood. Hence, these routes all end with the same three barriers and body compartments. The drug passes

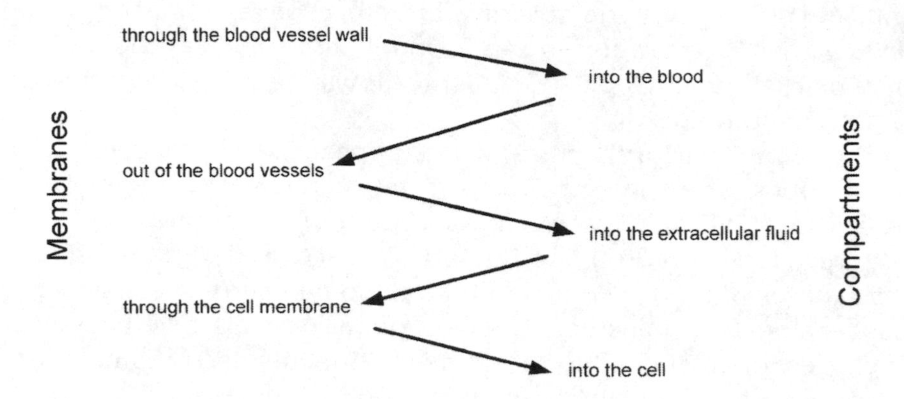

In many cases, especially with nerve cells, the drug does not have to enter the cell but binds with receptors on the outer surface. In the descriptions that follow, it is assumed that a drug entering the blood follows this pattern or part of it to reach the site of action. We will be concentrating mainly on the ways drugs get into the blood.

ORAL ADMINISTRATION

Oral administration refers to the giving of drugs through the mouth. Sometimes the Latin designation *per os* (P.O.) meaning *through the mouth*--is used. Usually, an oral drug is swallowed and absorbed through the gastrointestinal system, but it can also be retained in the mouth and absorbed through the mucous membranes, or it can be held under the tongue and absorbed (**sublingual administration**). The two latter methods are faster than swallowing and can also achieve the desired drug concentrations in the blood. Heart patients who take nitroglycerine tablets sublingually feel the effects within minutes.

Drugs on the oral route face a long, arduous journey to the site of action. They have the most body compartments and membranes to cross. These are, by way of the mouth,

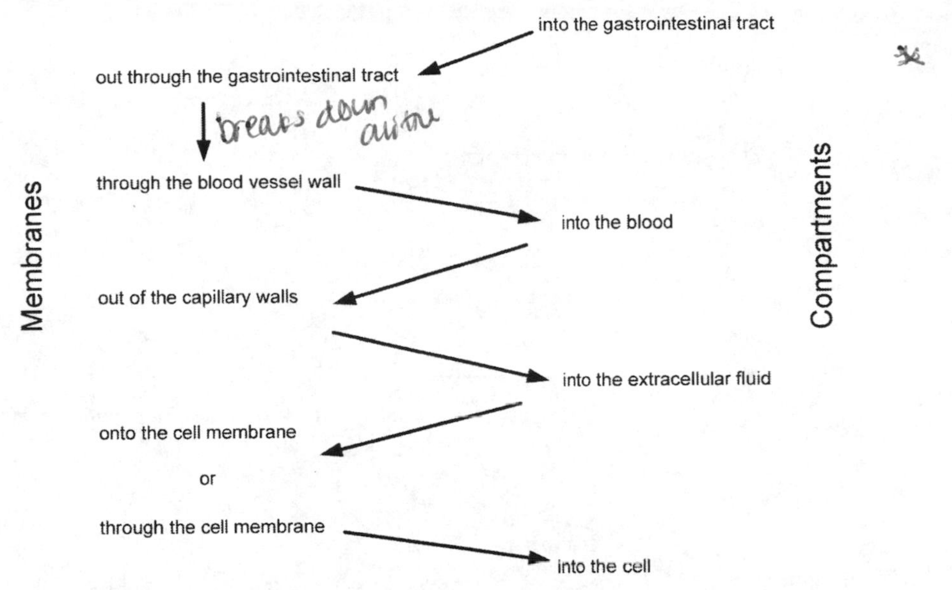

Absorption takes place all along the gastrointestinal tract--in the mouth, stomach, and intestines--although most occurs in the small intestines, which have the largest absorptive surface area (see Figure 3.1). Most drug absorption on the oral route takes place between 5 and 30 minutes after ingestion; total absorption takes an average of 6 to 8 hours, but may vary, depending on the drug.

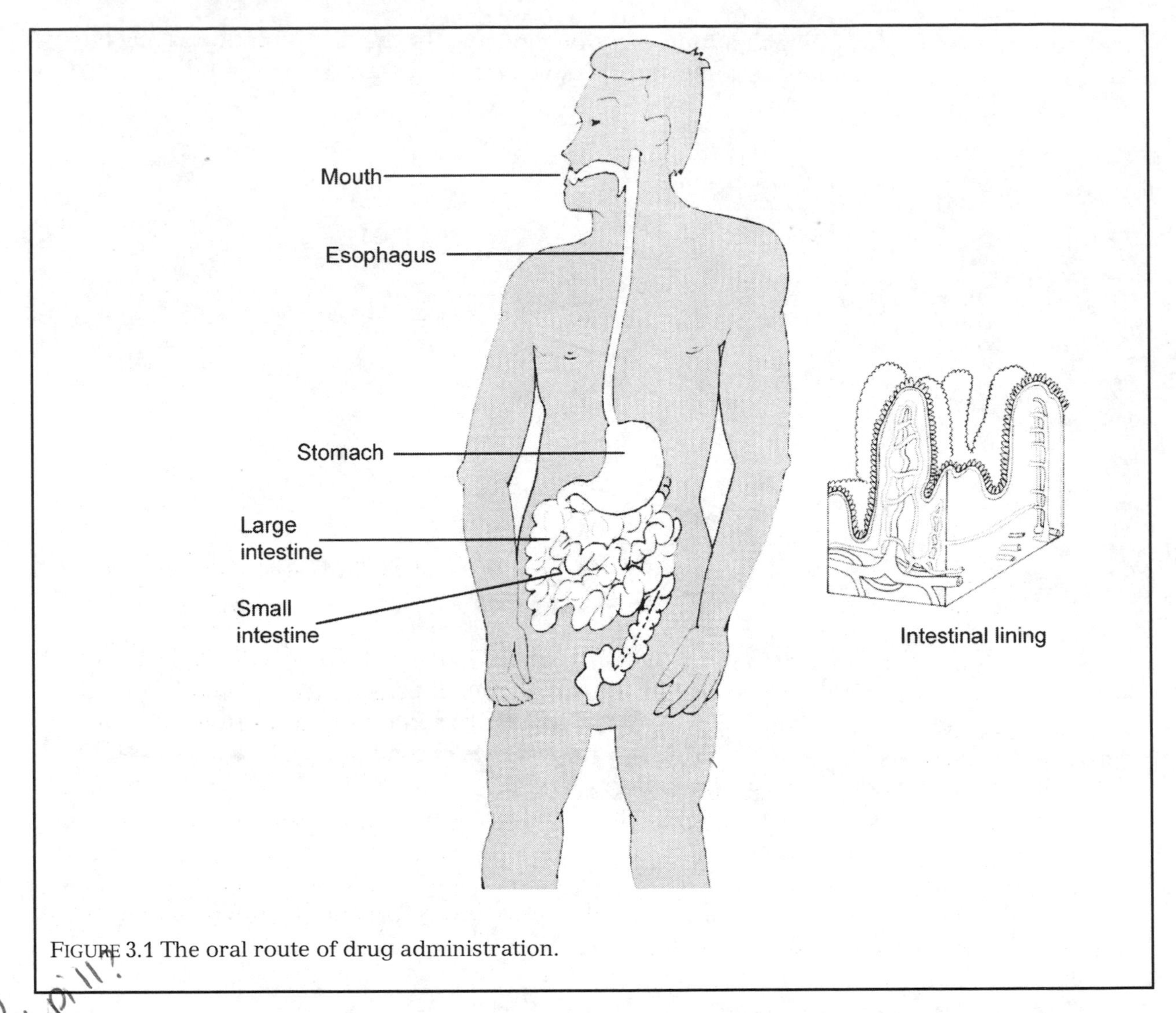

FIGURE 3.1 The oral route of drug administration.

Oral administration is the oldest method of issuing drugs and has many advantages. It is easy, economical, and safe, and consequently is still the means most commonly used. The route through the gastrointestinal tract reduces the probability of allergic reactions, and its slow rate of absorption allows time for response in an emergency. One can readily recall a drug by inducing vomiting, before too much enters the blood. If a patient is unconscious, as might be the case with an overdose of sleeping pills, a doctor can void the stomach with a pump, and the patient will recover, if not too much time has passed and not too much drug has been absorbed.

Oral administration also has many drawbacks, however. If a therapeutic drug turns out to be insoluble in the gastrointestinal juices, it should not be administered orally because it will not cross into the bloodstream; it will be eliminated before it has the desired effect. Other drugs, chemically unstable in gastrointestinal juices, will be digested before they reach the site of action. In addition, the intestinal lining itself is the main barrier to drug absorption; only substances with appropriate characteristics (e.g., the right pH) can cross through it.

The presence of other substances in the stomach also poses a problem on the oral route. Volumes of fluid can dilute the drug and delay absorption. Certain foods and beverages can react with drugs and deactivate them. Calcium ions from milk, for instance, bond with the antibiotic tetracycline and form a compound that is hard to absorb. Furthermore, the presence of food in the stomach slows the rate of **gastric emptying**; that is, the time it takes for food to empty from the stomach into the small intestine, where most drug absorption takes place. Eating can detain a drug in the stomach, where absorption is generally poor. Movement into the small intestine, and absorption, then become irregular and unpredictable. Eating can lengthen the absorption time of a drug from about 10 minutes on an empty stomach to about 90 on a full one. That is why, if you drink alcohol on an empty stomach, you will feel tipsy sooner than if you have eaten first. Alcohol races through an empty stomach to be absorbed quickly through the intestine into the blood; however, it is soaked up by food in a full stomach and detained where absorption is much slower. It then reaches the intestine gradually and diffuses into the blood at a more sober pace.

Another disadvantage to oral administration is that most substances absorbed through the intestine are routed to the liver to be metabolized, and some or all of a drug dose, especially if it is small, may be reduced in effect in this way. To compensate for this attrition in the liver (**first-pass metabolism**), oral drugs usually have to be given in relatively high concentrations. In addition, all these processes--digestion, absorption, metabolism, and excretion--vary widely from person to person, making it more difficult to predict accurately and to control a drug effect.

Oral administration has other disadvantages besides those connected with the route. Irritants that cause nausea or vomiting and foul-tasting medicines are undesirable. (Some medicines are designated to be taken “after meals” so that the food can shield the stomach lining from direct contact with the drug.) Moreover, the consent and cooperation of the patient is needed; if a patient is antagonistic, convulsing, or unconscious, oral administration is impossible. A routine case of noncooperation is found in animal research, where technicians often administer oral drugs through a tube gently inserted down the animal's esophagus.

INJECTION

Of the routes of administration that do not involve the gastrointestinal tract (called **parenteral routes**), injection is by far the most often used. Injection involves the introduction of drugs into the body with a hypodermic needle; the exact drug route and action depend on the entry point. Figure 3.2 shows the plot of blood concentrations against time from administration for several routes.

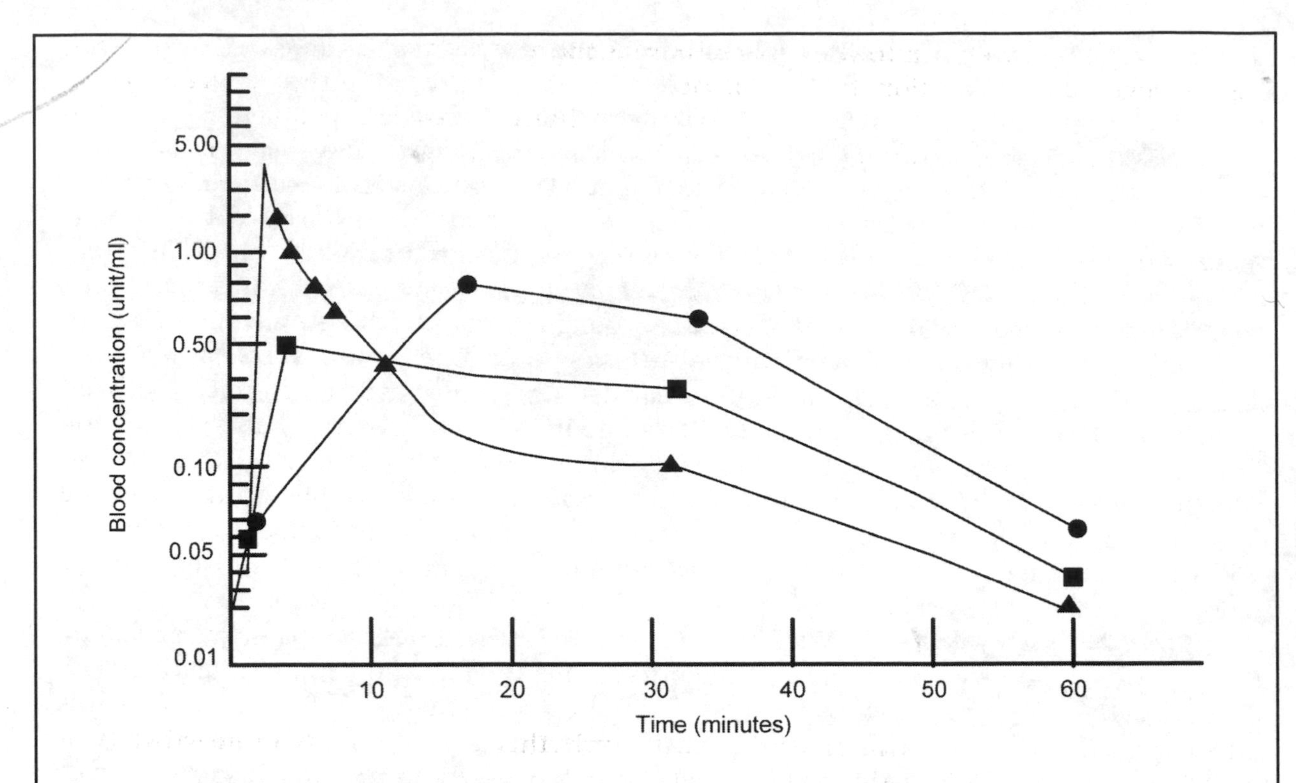

FIGURE 3.2 The effect of the route of administration on blood concentration of penicillin as a function of time, following the injection of 15,000 units. The triangle represents *intravenous* administration; the square stands for *intramuscular* administration; the circle stands for *subcutaneous* administration.

Injection is the usual alternative to oral administration, and many stomach irritants are given this way. Injection has the advantage of providing a more direct route to the site of action; absorption is swifter, and some of the undesirable variables of the gastrointestinal tract can be avoided. With special injections, drugs can be made to bypass the liver and the attendant problem of being promptly metabolized. And injected drugs can be used in cases where the patient is vomiting, unconscious, or otherwise unable to cooperate.

On the other hand, injection has its disadvantages. Needles are needed, and these demand sterile conditions to avoid bacterial infections or abscesses. Some people might have trouble with self-injection, so that a doctor or attendant has to do it. Also, injections can hurt, as any child in the doctor's waiting room will testify. On the whole, a primary disadvantage is that injected drugs begin to act so quickly that they allow no time to respond to unexpected reactions, and even so, there is no way to recall the drug. This is especially true of intravenous injections.

Intravenous (IV) Injection

Intra means "within" and *vena*, "vein," hence **intravenous (IV) injections** go into the veins and follow the route from the blood to the cell, described above.

Putting drugs directly into the bloodstream is the most accurate means of controlling dosage levels, since dilution by the blood is the only factor affecting concentration. Blood levels remain steady and high for a while. There is also a much shorter delay in the onset of effects, and this can be an advantage in emergencies. Generally, a substance injected intravenously disperses in equal concentrations throughout the circulatory system in about one minute, although a shot in the carotid artery of the neck reaches the brain in high concentrations almost instantly.

This promptness can also be a disadvantage, however, and because of it, intravenous and intra-arterial injections are the most dangerous routes of all. If difficulties arise, the drug cannot be recalled. Also, because of the high concentration levels, any adverse reactions are likely to be much more severe than on the oral route. For these reasons, IV injections should be administered only by qualified people. An expert can control the blood levels of the drug by giving the injection slowly and then stopping if reactions manifest; anesthetics, for example, are not given in predetermined doses, but are adjusted to the observed responses of the patient. When the rate of injection is a factor in administration, extra care is needed, because even a recognizably safe dose given too rapidly could shock the heart, dangerously drop blood pressure, or arrest respiration.

A limitation to IV injection is that only aqueous solutions may be used. Insoluble drugs or drugs in oily suspensions may clog blood vessels. Furthermore, care must be taken not to inject air into veins. If a vein in a rabbit's ear is injected with as little as one milliliter of air, the rabbit will die. In humans, **arrhythmia** (irregularity of heartbeat) results from air bubbles in the blood, and they can block blood flow in the brain.

Intra-arterial (IA) injection is similar to IV injection, but is much more dangerous because of the pressure of the heartbeat in the arteries. Hence, it is used rarely and then mostly to either localize a drug effect or dye a particular organ or tissue.

Intramuscular (IM) Injection

The **intramuscular (IM)** technique places the drug into muscle tissue. It then diffuses through the blood vessels supplying the tissue and enters the bloodstream. Most medical shots are given this way. A good dose of drug spreading through tissue that is rich in blood vessels diffuses briskly into the circulation. The rate is faster than on oral routes, but slower than on intravenous routes, although most of the precautions for IV injections still hold. Quickest onset occurs through the deltoid muscle of the arm, from which veins run straight to the heart. Medium onset occurs through the thigh. Slowest onset follows from the buttock, where the blood supply is lower. When injecting drugs intramuscularly, one must be careful to avoid hitting a blood vessel and inadvertently giving an IV injection. Most muscles are fairly safe in this regard, but when there is a doubt, you will see the doctor draw back on the syringe. If no blood is drawn, the shot is safe.

Subcutaneous (SC) Injection

In the **subcutaneous (SC)** method, substances are placed by injection under the skin, a method referred to by drug abusers as *skin-popping*.

From outside in, skin tissue consists of four layers: two layers of epidermis, one of dermis, and one of subcutaneous fat. Beneath these layers lies an area containing a protective membrane, the extracellular fluid, and then the muscle proper. An SC injection disperses through the area of fatty tissue and extracellular fluid, spreading between the skin and the muscle membrane; next, it permeates the membrane and enters the bloodstream through the walls of the vessels that service the muscle. When you skin a frying chicken for dinner, you are exposing the area where an SC injection would be placed. The fatty skin peels off, exposing a muscular surface covered by the moist, milky membrane.

The advantage of SC injection is that it reduces the chance of hitting a vein when that might be a danger, and it is less painful than injecting into a muscle. SC injection is slightly slower than IM injection because there are fewer vessels to absorb the drug on the muscle surface. This can be an asset, because relatively steady absorption rates can be achieved. In both SC and IM administration, absorption can be retarded by injecting vasoconstrictors along with the drug to shrink the vessels and reduce the absorptive surface area. Drugs can also be injected in suspensions, requiring extra time to dissolve first. To speed absorption, **vasodilators**--drugs that dilate the vessels--can be added, or the area can be massaged to draw in more blood. Also, both kinds of administration may be halted by treating them like snake bites--using a tourniquet to block the return of blood to the heart, thereby localizing the problem.

However, peripheral blood vessels and subcutaneous absorption can be influenced by other, less intentional conditions, like temperature. Cold weather delays absorption by constricting vessels, and hot weather speeds it up by dilating them. Alcohol, too, can dilate the vessels and hasten absorption. These influences can be disadvantageous.

There are other disadvantages to SC injection as well. Even though slow and steady absoroption rates can be achieved, variations in the blood supply may make the amount of the dose absorbed erratic and unpredictable. Doses also have to be somewhat smaller than IV or IM doses, because they are limited by the volume of fluid that can be placed under the skin. Irritation may be caused by the formation of bubbles under the skin, as well as by the prolonged presence of a drug being slowly absorbed. Moreover, if a patient is in shock, vital functions are depressed, including peripheral circulation, so that absorption proceeds very slowly.

Intraperitoneal (IP) Injection

The abdominal cavity is a body compartment bounded by the **peritoneum,** a tissue that contains the intestines and other abdominal organs. An injection placed here, an **intraperitoneal (IP) injection**, dissolves evenly in the peritoneal fluid that surrounds the entrails and is absorbed through the networks of vessels that feed the organs and cover the intestines and abdominal wall. This offers a large absorptive area through which drugs enter the circulation rapidly and evenly. The absorption rate is the same as for intestinal absorption, because it uses the same vessels, but from the other side, outside of the intestines.

IP injection is seldom used clinically due to the fairly high risk of infection. Accurate placement of the shot is difficult, and a needle that accidentally punctures the intestines or other organs can release toxic substances into the peritoneal fluid and infect the entire abdomen. A puncture could also produce adhesions, weblike structures that grow over the organs, binding them together and increasing the danger of a rupture.

Liabilities of this technique are few enough, however, to make it the preferred method of injecting lab animals. The thinness and horizontality of their abdominal muscles, different from humans, make abdominal injection convenient. Furthermore, the abdomen offers a large target on a fidgety animal being held by hand.

Intrathecal (IT) Injection

An **intrathecal (IT) injection** (from Latin *theca*, or "sheathing") is placed under the sheathing that encloses nerve fibers, the spinal cord, and the brain. It is used mostly for localized anesthesia (such as that of an arm or leg) and is of little importance in relation to psychoactive drugs.

Intracranial (IC) Injection

The **intracranial (IC)** method is mostly used in animal research rather than for humans, because administration is difficult, and the risk of injuring vital parts of the brain is high. The needle may be introduced into the brain directly, giving the drug direct access to cells, or it may be put into one of the brain's fluid-filled cavities (ventricles), whence it must diffuse into the brain proper.

A problem with IC injection is that drug effects in the brain are not always the same as those in the rest of the body. For instance, curare, which causes paralysis when given outside the brain, produces convulsions when given inside, and Metrazol, a potent convulsant when given intravenously to rats, produces nothing more than sniffing and grooming behavior when administered intracranially.

INHALATION

Drugs can also be inhaled as gases or vapors. (Vapors are liquids that are atomized so the droplets can be drawn into the lungs.) Because the capillary walls of the lung lining are exposed, absorption into the bloodstream occurs instantly; in some cases, the onset of effects is even faster than an intravenous injection.

Inhalation is usually the means of administering volatile anesthetics, as in surgery, or vaporized liquids, as is common in the local application of decongestants and antiasthmatics to relieve bronchial asthma.

The drawbacks of inhalation are that no irritants of the lungs may be given, and dosage control is difficult, since individual lung capacities differ. Inhaled volatile drugs such as ether are not stored by the body; they exit the bloodstream as rapidly as they enter it. When administration ceases, the effect does, too. Consequently, one must inhale the drug for as long as the effect is desired. In addition, as in the case of vaporized drugs, this method can depend on the use of cumbersome equipment.

On occasion, solid drugs like cocaine are inhaled, but not into the lungs; they dissolve on the mucous lining of the nose, sinuses, and other parts of the upper respiratory tract, through which they are absorbed.

Smoking is the most prevalent form of drug administration. It can deliver a drug to the brain faster than an IV injection in the limbs or body, since it follows a speedy route from the lungs to the heart and brain. With smoking, the active ingredients of opium, marijuana, and tobacco are inhaled, not as gases, but as smokeborne particles that dissolve on the lung membranes and diffuse through the capillary walls. Despite our knowledge of the absorption of gases through the lungs, little is known of the absorption of particulate matter by this route, except that it can damage the membranes, as is the case with the tar in cigarettes. This is similar enough to the tar used to pitch roofs and mend roads, so that it can be said that, over the years, smokers gradually and literally pave their lungs.

OTHER ROUTES OF ADMINISTRATION

In **topical**, or **transdermal**, administration, drugs are prepared as creams and ointments to be applied to the skin surface. Ease of administration is the advantage here, but the skin, despite its many pores, constitutes a thick barrier that excludes many drugs. When administering ointments, one should consider that babies' skins are more permeable than those of adults.

A recent development in the topical administration of psychoactive drugs is the nicotine patch (Fiore et al., 1992). Used in the short-term treatment of smoking dependence, the patch is fixed to the skin like an adhesive bandage and delivers a low, controlled dose of nicotine to alleviate withdrawal symptoms and the craving for tobacco.

Drugs are prepared for **rectal and vaginal** routes in the form of suppositories. These are soluble drug salts enclosed in capsules made of an inert material that dissolves on the moist, mucous lining of the vagina or lower intestine, and the drug is absorbed through the capillaries there. These routes are useful if a drug cannot withstand the acid of the gastric juices, or if a patient is vomiting or unconscious. However, rectal and vaginal absorption is somewhat incomplete and unpredictable.

Other membranes offer themselves as drug routes as well. Eyedrops, nosedrops, and eardrops enter through blood vessels in the moist membranes of their respective organs, and some drug is usually lost through drainage. A rarer oral route that does not involve swallowing or sublingual use is placement of the drug in the cheek and absorption through the mouth lining there. *Dipping snuff*, for instance, involves tucking a pinch of tobacco into your cheek. Likewise, it is common usage among residents of the northern Andes, where the coca plant grows wild, to take cocaine by chewing coca leaves or stuffing them into the cheeks. Pre-Columbian statues of Inca figures with cheeks abulge seem to confirm the venerability of this practice.

DEVELOPMENTS IN DRUG ADMINISTRATION

Finding new ways to deliver drugs is a rich area of research. It centers mainly on two problems: (1) delivering drugs in effective concentrations to specific sites without influencing other tissues or systems, and (2) placing time-release forms in the body, so external administration is not needed for extended periods of time.

Extending the interval between times of administration is often desirable. This would certainly be true in cases where drugs might have a life of only hours in the body and have to be administered several times a day, or where they might have to be delivered intravenously at a constant rate, confining patients to the hospital. In some contexts, however, longer intervals between doses are not always an advantage; they can be counterproductive. For example, schizophrenic outpatients may be asked to return for antipsychotic medication at two-week intervals. Since the antipsychotics are used to maintain normal functioning (which is without dramatic effects) and since the interval between drug treatments is long, patients may decide they do not need the medication, or they may forget the appointment and relapse into former symptoms. However, rather than returning to more frequent doses, these patients might benefit from a once-a-year (or longer) treatment with a drug in a safe, slow, time-release form.

As a result of these considerations, many strategies are being tried to place drugs safely at the site of action or to store them in the body for sustained release. Three current branches of research are concerned with transdermal, implantable, and microparticulate delivery systems (Juliano, 1991).

Transdermal systems, patchlike devices like the nicotine patch, which deliver drugs through the skin, can sustain and control drug delivery over a period of hours to days. In addition to nicotine, patches are available for the delivery of hormones (estradiol) and of medication for chest pain (nitroglycerine), high blood pressure (clonidine), and motion sickness (scopolamine).

There are a number of strategies for implanting drugs. One subcutaneous technique involves the surgical implantation of drugs under the skin, in the form of solid pellets or encased in capsules of synthetic material that the drugs can slowly permeate. This technique allows a steady infusion of drug, which can maintain the blood concentration of a substance from weeks to years at a time. This type of implantation has been used mostly in connection with contraceptive drugs.

Another technique that has been tried is the surgical placement of a pump (much the way a pacemaker is implanted) driven by a compressed propellant that forces the drug slowly into the circulation at a precise rate (Blackshear, 1979). The pump can be worn for two or three years and can give continuous delivery of a drug for about two weeks, after which it can be refilled by injection, and drug concentrations can be adjusted (The Network for Continuing Medical Education, 1984). Pump implants have been used for cancer chemotherapy as well as contraception. In general, implantation holds great promise for the treatment of certain forms of cancer, diabetes, high blood pressure, and internal blood clotting. In dentistry, an implant in the form of a small drug reservoir may be attached to a tooth (Langer, 1986).

For the treatment of pain in patients with bone cancer, tiny morphine pumps are now being implanted in the wall of the abdomen and filled with improved long-acting narcotic painkillers that can be released over a 12-hour period (Rosenthal, 1990).

An example of a microparticulate delivery system is liposomes. Liposomes are microscopic beads containing drugs, which can be injected. The beads are actually droplets of oil that biodegrade slowly and may slow drug absorption as much as ten times (Lee, Sokoloski, & Royer, 1981). Because they are formed of essentially the same proteins that constitute cell membranes, they are nontoxic, and they can pass as cell material, eluding the body's immune system with their cargo, and reaching the target tissue in high concentrations, without being diluted or affecting other tissue. Delivered in this way, a drug may be needed in only very tiny amounts, which reduces toxicity (Ostro, 1987).

New means for administering drugs safely and more effectively will undoubtedly be developed, based on an expanding knowledge of the chemical and biological processes involved in the absorption, distribution, and metabolism of drugs, which are the subjects of our next chapters.

ABSORPTION

A drug is said to be fully absorbed when the concentration at the site of action equals the concentration at the site of administration. For instance, alcohol is said to be fully absorbed when brain and stomach levels are equal. Many substances, however, are prevented from entering the brain by the barrier that surrounds it, or they enter only in very small amounts, like LSD; in such cases, full absorption occurs when the concentration peaks at the site of action.

The absorption of all substances into the body is regulated by membranes. Although membranes vary in details and functions, one basic structure is common to all, as are the diffusion and transport mechanisms that move substances across them. There are four significant membranes and barriers to consider regarding drug absorption: (1) the capillary wall, (2) the cell membrane, (3) the blood-brain barrier, and (4) the placental barrier.

THE CAPILLARY WALLS

The bulk of membrane activity occurs between the capillary walls and cell membranes, as material moves out of the bloodstream into tissues. Capillaries service every; needless to say, they are crucial to absorption. The number of capillaries and the drug's ability to penetrate their walls are major factors in determining how well the drug can enter body tissues. Where capillaries abound and the blood flow is rich (the brain predominates in this respect), absorption will proceed at a rapid rate; where capillaries are fewer, as in the bones and joints, it will be slower.

The capillaries consist of one layer of cells rounded into a tube, bound together and supported by a thin membrane. They have pores wider than most molecules, so passage in and out is a simple affair. The only substances blocked are the red corpuscles and blood proteins, which are larger than the pores and are thus confined to the bloodstream. By the same token, a drug in circulation cannot escape the capillaries if it consists of large protein molecules or if it chemically bonds with the blood proteins. Conversely, if a drug has properties that allow it to diffuse easily through the pores, it shows a rapid onset of action and a short duration of effect, since it gains quick access to the cells and their membranes.

CELL MEMBRANES

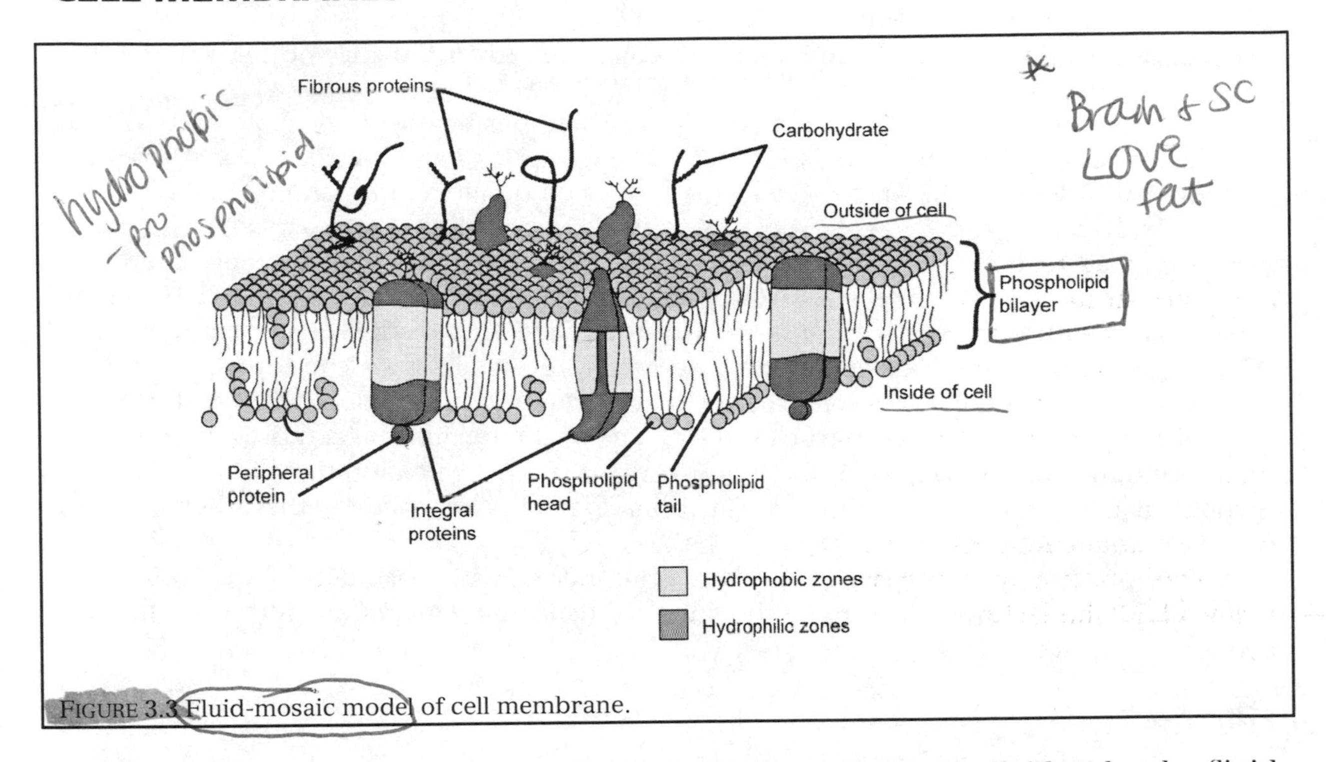

FIGURE 3.3 Fluid-mosaic model of cell membrane.

Cell membranes in the body consist of a double layer of phospholipid molecules (lipid molecules with a phosphate component) (see Figure 3.3). Imagine an upper layer of molecules with heads up and tails down, then a lower layer that mirrors the upper layer. That is how the cell membrane is constructed, with the heads of both layers forming the inner and outer surfaces, in contact with the intracellular and the extracellular fluids. The phospholipid bilayer makes the membrane **hydrophobic**, namely, chemically "afraid of" or resistant to water. The two layers or leaflets are closely bound together but are seen to move relative to one another--sliding around on one another, if you will.

Embedded in this two-layered sheet are large protein globules. Some of these are large enough to jut from both sides of the membrane; others are small and project from one side or the other. Because of these smaller globules, the inner and outer surfaces of the membrane can differ in protein content. The globules float freely about the membrane like dumplings in soup, so that their arrangement on the surfaces changes. The proteins that make up the globules vary in function: some are enzymes, some help transport useful molecules through the membrane, an others play roles in cell-to-cell contact. In the case of nerve cells, these globules sometimes contain the structures (receptors) to which certain drug molecules can attach, on the outer surface of the cell. Generally, cell membranes differ according to their function, to the number and nature of the proteins they contain (e.g., the kind of receptors they have), and to the types of lipids that constitute the core (Campbell & Smith, 1982).

Scattered over the membrane are pores which penetrate it from side to side. These are either structural openings to water-filled channels or momentary openings caused by the movement of molecules. Pores differ in size from membrane to membrane. In the intestinal lining they are narrow enough to admit only tiny molecules like urea and water, but in the capillary walls they are wide and admit all but the largest molecules.

This description of membrane anatomy, called the **fluid-mosaic model**, is currently the most widely accepted hypothesis.

As for functioning, biological membranes are semipermeable: they allow certain substances through but not others. This selective permeability is responsible for the unequal distribution of substances on either side. With this inequality comes an unequal distribution of electrical charges as well. When negative charges build up on one side of a membrane, they tend (have the potential) to flow to the more positive side, where there are fewer electrons. This is called **electrical potential** or **voltage.** The difference between an area packed with electrons and an area with fewer electrons is the **electrical gradient.** When given the chance, electrons flow "down" the gradient to level out the unequal charge. A lightning bolt is just such a flow, but of stupendous proportions. Furthermore, the activity of all the charged particles in the area of the membrane can present a barrier to charged molecules that are attempting to cross. Thus, a small ion that could easily slip through a pore may be held back because its charge is repelled by the other charges gathered near the membrane.

In the process of absorption, there are a number of ways for material to cross membranes. Those of major concern in the study of drug movements are filtration, passive diffusion, and active transport.

Filtration

Filtration refers to the passage of material through the pores and aqueous channels of a membrane. Water flowing through the pores mechanically carries through any molecule small enough to fit, assuming its electrical properties allow it. As a rule, the pores of most membranes are too narrow to accommodate drug molecules. (But the capillary walls, as we have seen, are an exception.)

Passive Diffusion

When drugs move through the pores of a membrane, they observe the principles of **passive diffusion**. These principles also govern the movement of substances capable of passing through the membrane itself. But first, what is passive diffusion?

Molecules moving at random in solution flow from an area of high concentration into an area of low concentration. When a biological membrane separates these two areas, substances that cross the membrane without hindrance are said to be passively distributed across it, and the process by which they flow "down the **concentration gradient**" (from high to low) is referred to as **passive** or **simple diffusion.** Nerve membranes have ion channels that allow the passive diffusion of specific small ions (Koester, 1981a).

The steeper the concentration gradient, the faster the flow of diffusing molecules. Diffusion is fastest when 100 percent of a drug is on one side of a membrane and none is on the other, and the rate decelerates until the concentration reaches **equilibrium** with equal amounts of the drug on either side. At this point, diffusion continues equally in both directions, keeping the concentration levels stable at 50 percent/50 percent.

The term *passive diffusion* is used in our discussion to refer principally to the passage of drugs that can permeate the lipid material of the membrane and diffuse across it. *Filtration* refers to the specific case of passive diffusion through the membrane's channels and pores only.

Active Transport.

Active transport is a form of *carrier-assisted transport* across membranes. Certain molecules that would not naturally cross by passive diffusion are helped across by specially adapted protein globules, which bond with the molecules on the outside of the membrane, then pull or ferry them across and release them inside without altering their chemical structure. These carriers are selective in the molecules they bond with, and they can discriminate between nearly identical substances. When their task is done, they return to their original position and condition, ready to begin again. This process is considered active because the body must provide the energy to drive it, and the membrane participates. Active transport adds two major advantages to the membrane's capabilities. The carriers may usher through molecules (water-soluble) that could not normally permeate the lipid membrane; these would travel in the expected direction, down the concentration gradient. However, active transport can also move material "uphill" against a concentration gradient; that is, from an area of lower concentration into an area of higher concentration, opposite to the normal flow of diffusion.

It is worth a reminder that, in many cases with psychoactive drugs, movement to the interior of cells is not necessary, since drug receptors are typically located on the outer surface of the cell at the synapse (see Figure 2.1). Therefore, a drug does not necessarily have to cross the nerve cell membrane to have an effect.

THE BLOOD-BRAIN BARRIER

Many drugs have sites of action in the brain. But because the brain is such a complex and delicate organ, it is protected from the vicissitudes of the general circulation and sealed off as a separate body compartment by a structure called the **blood-brain barrier** (see Figure 3.4). It helps to understand that this seal is not like a sac wrapping the whole brain. Instead, picture all the blood vessels of the brain branching like a tree, and then imagine that all the limbs and twigs of the tree are taped over or sealed with glue to prevent the sap from escaping. Such is the blood-brain barrier.

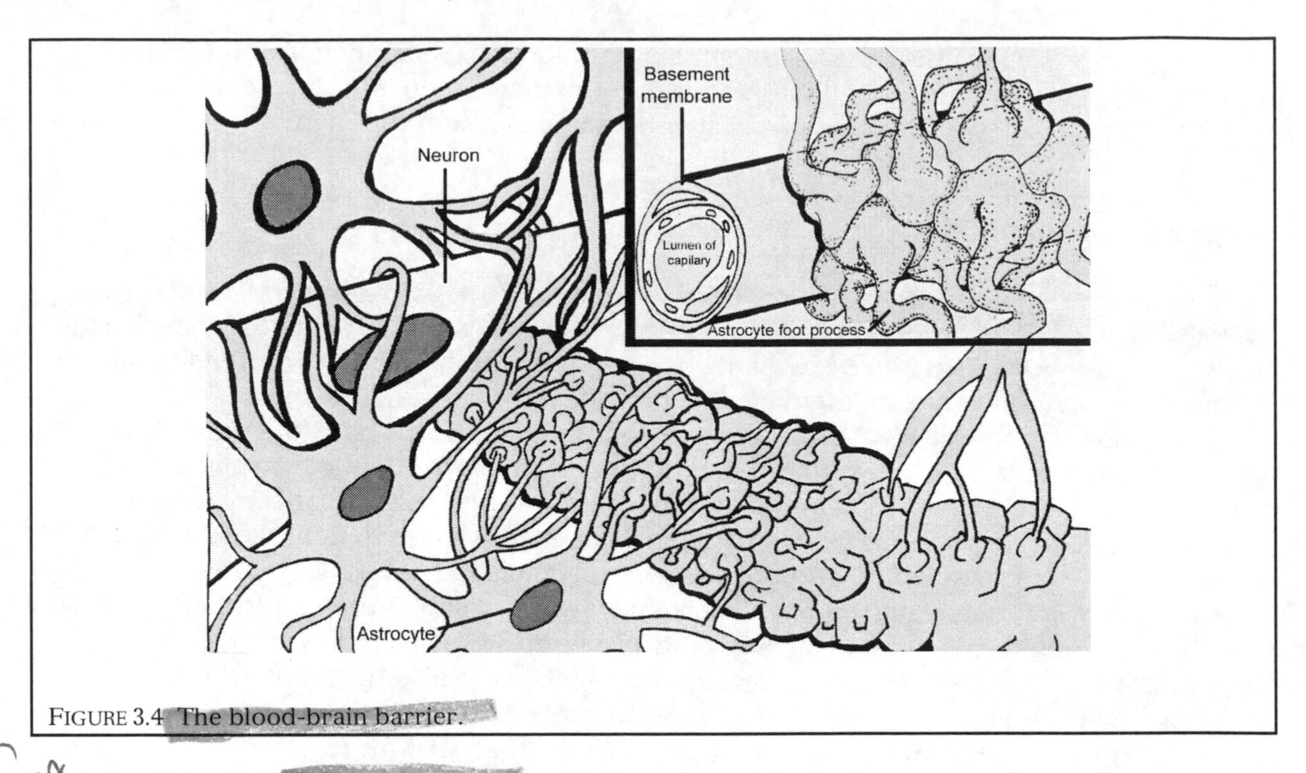

FIGURE 3.4 The blood-brain barrier.

Astrocytes are star-shaped cells whose long processes make contact with several other types of brain cells. They make up part of the glia. Some of their processes end in the glial feet that form part of the seal on brain capillaries. Brain capillaries are ensheathed by the astrocyte foot processes (glial feet). The basement membrane helps to maintain the capillary's tubular form. The lumen is frequently just wide enough for a red blood cell to pass.

Part of the blood-brain barrier is composed of **astrocytes.** Found in the central nervous system, these cells are so-called because of their starry shape (*aster* being Latin for "star," and *cyto* a Greek root for "cell"). Along with other cells and structures, they make up glue-like supporting tissues around the brain cells, called **glia** (see Figure 3.4).

Generally, the cells of the glia serve a number of functions in the brain. They guide the growth and development of brain neurons, and provide a supporting structure. They take up neurotransmitters, remove debris after and injury, and help to control the ion balance in brain fluids. The astrocytes within the glia make up a significant part of the blood-brain barrier. These cells send out filaments ending in foot-like protuberances that pack tightly together around the capillaries, sealing off their entire surface and forming a sheath so tight there is no space nor extracellular fluid to speak of between the outside capillary wall and the glia. About 85 percent of the brain capillaries are covered in this way.

Once it was thought that the astrocytes and their glial feet made up the brunt of the blood-brain barrier, but now it is thought that the primary part of the seal is formed by the capillary walls themselves. The brain capillaries differ from those found in the periphery by the fact that their walls meet in a tight continuous junction, so that the cells are essentially joined, with no gaps or pores to speak of (Goldstein & Betz, 1986). These three characteristics--the glial tissue, the tight junctions of the brain capillary walls, and the lack of pores--constitute the blood-brain barrier, a seal so effective that it can exclude even the smallest molecules. Because of it, drugs cannot enter the brain to have an effect unless they are lipid-soluble enough to diffuse through the capillary walls and the glia. For instance, nicotine is a common drug lipid-soluble enough to clear the barrier effectively. About ten seconds after a puff on a cigarette, 90 percent of the nicotine that has been absorbed is deposited in the brain, which is why a smoker will get a surge of stimulation after one puff, especially if it is the first of the day, following a lapse of smoking during sleep.

When substances are not able to diffuse through the barrier, their absorption is roughly in inverse proportion to their size; the larger the molecule, the less likely its uptake by the brain. Generally the barrier is selective about which molecules may pass. Active transport accounts for the uptake of many useful molecules that cannot enter on their own.

The blood-brain barrier has a number of functions. First, it maintains the brain as a super-stabilized body compartment and separates the brain's extracellular fluid from the haphazard fluctuations of the general extracellular fluid, whose chemistry changes as substances enter the body by various routes. Second, the blood-brain barrier is in part a watchdog, keeping out poisons. Third, it prevents chemicals required by the brain for its functions (for example, neurotransmitters), from leaking into general circulation and being lost. It also screens out similar substances to prevent overloads or chemical interference with brain activity. And fourth, its carrier-assisted transport systems regulate the entry of nutrients and supplies for the nerve cells. For example, glucose is essential for the high-energy needs of the brain. In cases of hyper- or hypoglycemia (too much or too little blood sugar) the blood-brain barrier helps to hold the glucose levels steady (Oldendorf, 1982).

The blood-brain barrier is incomplete at birth and may not function fully in humans for perhaps a year or two. Until then, the fetus or infant is vulnerable to toxic material, and a pregnant woman should consider this when taking drugs. In adults, sometimes the barrier breaks down. Trauma, concussion, or cerebral infection can incapacitate the astrocytes or other tissue and damage the glia. The brain's capillaries then become unshielded and more permeable, allowing unsuitable substances to seep into the brain.

The barrier is not found in absolutely every part of the brain. Substances in the blood have access to the pituitary and the hypothalamus, because these structures need to be in contact with blood contents, since they play an important role in monitoring the blood and secreting hormones as part of a biological feedback loop.

THE PLACENTAL BARRIER

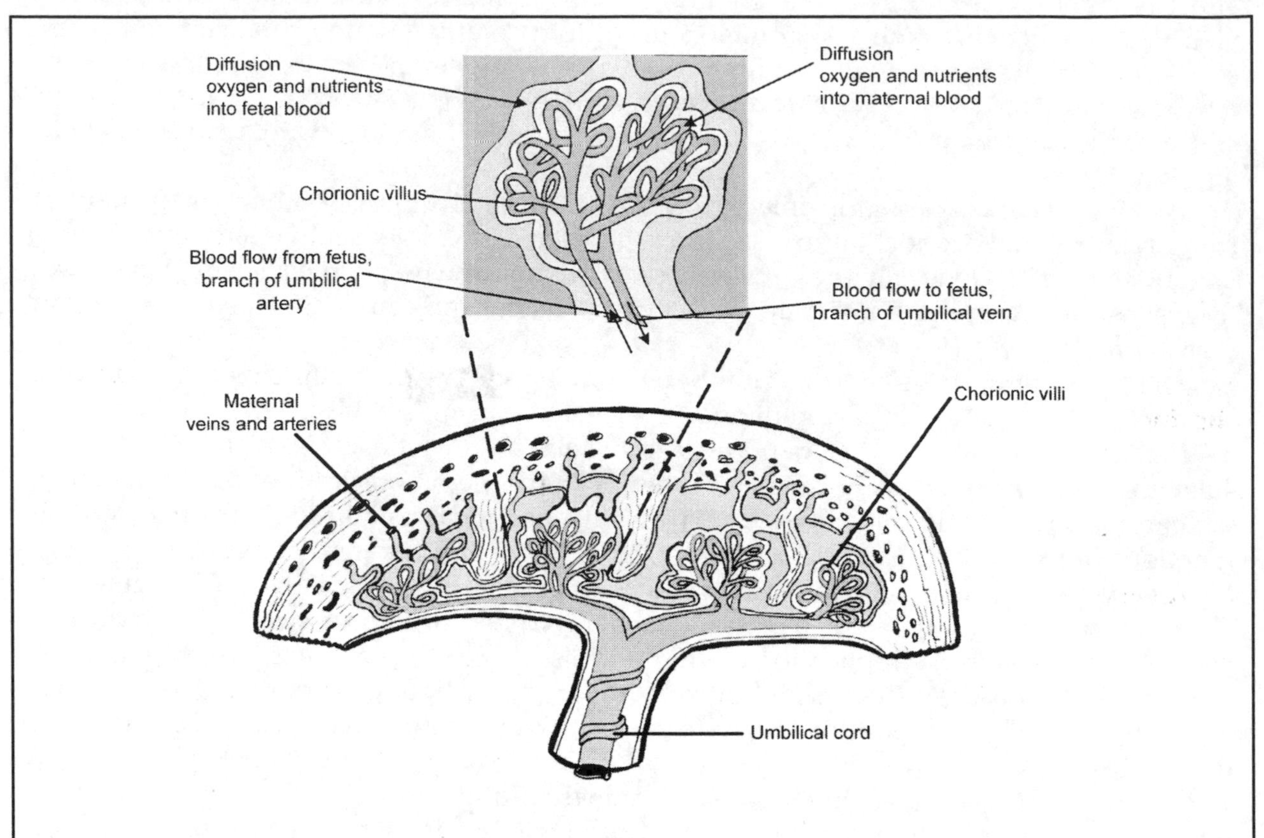

FIGURE 3.5 The placental barrier. Lipid-soluble drugs in the circulation of the mother can diffuse into the chorionic villi and the umbilical cord and enter the fetal circulation.

A fourth barrier important in drug use is the placental barrier (Figure 3.5). The placenta originates from the embryo and forms in the uterus during pregnancy. Named with the Latin word for "flat cake," it is a membranous structure that mediates the exchange of oxygen, hormones, nutrients, wastes, and other material between the fetus and the mother, and it allows the fetus, whose organs are not yet functioning fully, to rely on those of the mother. Structurally, the placenta is a mass of spongy tissue from both mother and fetus. The maternal vessels widen out from the walls of the uterus to form pools of blood. Into these dip fingerlike extensions called **chorionic villi,** which are actually the branching ends of the umbilical cord, containing the capillaries of the fetus. Oxygen and nutrients from the mother's circulation enter the blood spaces in the uterine wall, diffuse into the walls of the chorionic villi and the fetal capillaries, and then they are carried through the umbilical cord to the fetus. Waste material travels the opposite way to be excreted by the mother. By this means, the exchange of materials is provided for, while the circulatory systems of mother and fetus, two genetically different creatures, remain distinct (see Figure 3.6).

The placental barrier is much less selective than the blood-brain barrier. Most transfer is by the passive diffusion of lipid-soluble molecules. Therefore, the fetus is exposed to any lipid-soluble substances ingested by the mother. In the case of most drugs, this is an undesirable arrangement, and particularly so because the fetus lacks many enzymes and its blood-brain barrier is not fully formed; if it absorbs a drug from the mother, the fetal system does not have the capability to metabolize it or screen it out of the brain effectively. Because of this, and because of their vast difference in size, what the mother might consider a small drug dose could have adverse consequences for the fetus.

Most anesthetics and analgesics administered at birth are lipid-soluble and able to permeate the placental barrier. As a result, newborn infants may have high blood concentrations of these drugs. With deep anesthesia (by which the fetus would be anesthetized as well as the mother), an infant may still be depressed from 4 to 24 hours after delivery because it cannot metabolize or excrete the drug readily. Many drugs, including tranquilizers and barbiturates, can cross the placental barrier to the vulnerable fetus. Of recent concern is the number of pregnant women in inner city neighborhoods smoking cocaine in the form of crack and exposing their unborn children. While the children of these mothers for the most part do not seem to be drug-dependent or to show major birth defects, they are at risk for serious complications in pregnancy and for developmental problems (Dow-Edwards, 1991). The children may also show motor abnormalities and seizures at birth, and up to six months afterward (Dow-Edwards, 1991).

Alcohol is another compound that crosses the placental barrier readily. Hard drinking by alcoholic mothers during pregnancy can result in **fetal alcohol syndrome**, a range of disorders from physical deformity to retardation, motor dysfunction, and hyperactivity. The baby may also be born physically dependent on alcohol. There are levels of alcohol consumption that do not seem to pose threats to the fetus; these would be roughly in the light to moderate range for nonalcoholic mothers. However, as yet, the limits on the safe use of alcohol during pregnancy have not been ascertained. Consequently, in 1981, the Surgeon General advised all pregnant women to abstain.

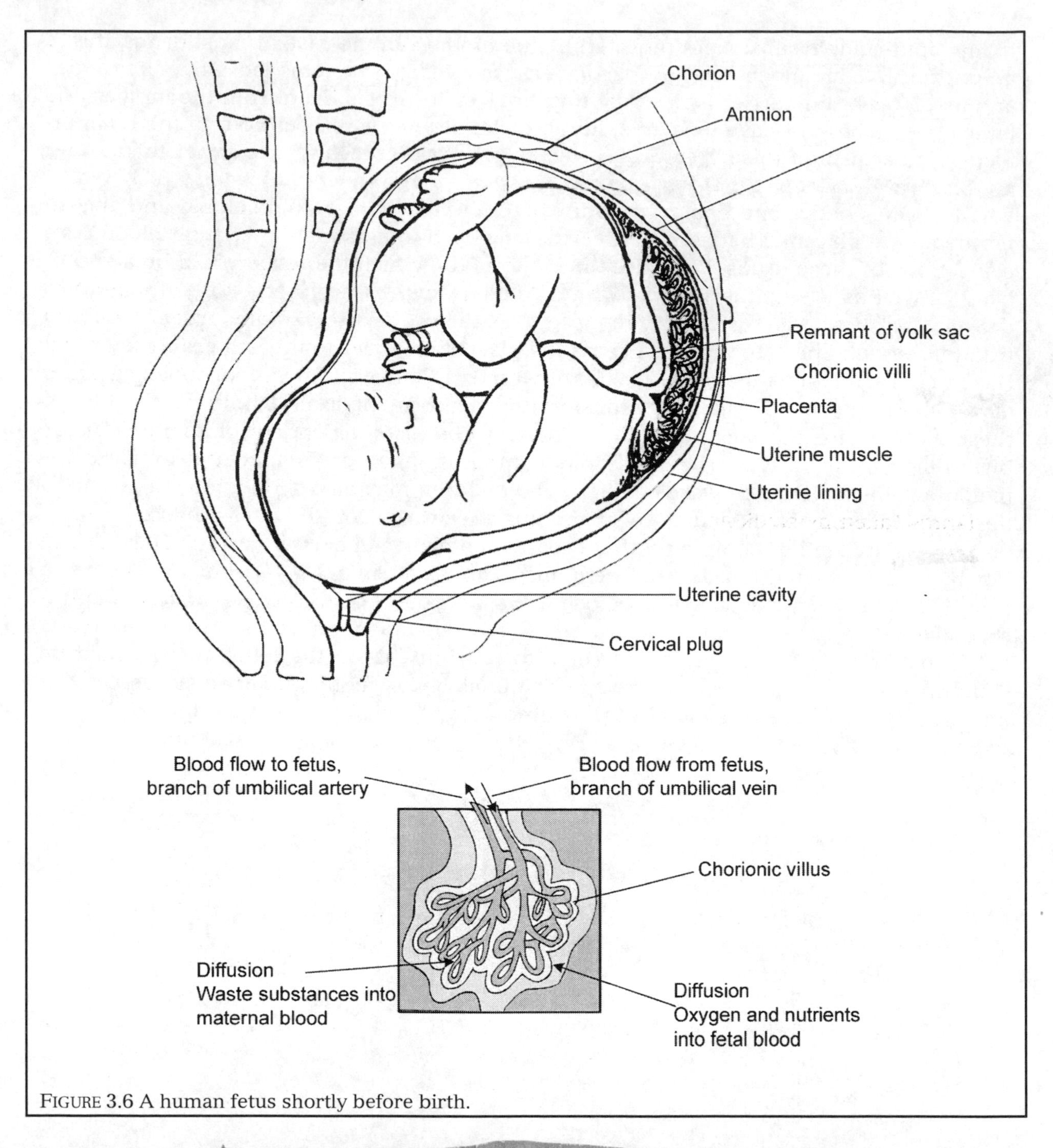

FIGURE 3.6 A human fetus shortly before birth.

Generally, negative drug effects on fetuses fall into two categories: (1) impairment of oxygenation (leading to possible brain damage or suffocation) in middle to advanced pregnancy, and (2) deformity in early pregnancy. In the first case, the oxygen supply to the fetus may be impoverished by substances like alcohol, which can cut down the blood flow through the umbilical cord and lead to damage of the fetal brain cells.

Chemicals that cause birth defects are called **teratogens.** The teratogenic effects of most drugs are still not known, yet it is not uncommon for pregnant women to be using one or more drugs, either by prescription or illicitly. In addition, during the first few months of pregnancy, at two months especially, when the fetus is most vulnerable, many women do not yet realize they are pregnant. Therefore, even if they intend to abstain from drugs, it is already too late.

The most famous incident involving a teratogen was the use of thalidomide in the late 1950s and early 1960s. Thalidomide was then a new and effective sedative. First marketed in Germany in 1958, it spread to Australia, Canada, and other parts of Europe. One of its appeals was its apparent safety. At 14 grams (100 times the dose for sleeping) attempted suicides could still be recuperated. It was not until 1962 that a connection was established between thalidomide and a birth deformity whose sufferers have hands and feet, but no arms or legs (it was named *phocomelia,*"seal-limbed"). By then, about 7,000 deformed babies had been born to women who had used the drug in early pregnancy. The incident caused a good deal of furor and raised many questions about drug use during pregnancy and about the criteria for evaluating and screening drugs. At present, teratogenicity is a major consideration in new drug testing.

Drugs taken by smoking, like nicotine and marijuana, can affect the transfer of oxygen across the placental barrier. Smoking of any kind raises carbon monoxide (CO) levels in the blood. The CO molecules bond with hemoglobin and block the uptake of oxygen. The resulting reduced oxygen levels can cause brain damage to a fetus, or possible suffocation. It has been well-established that a relationship exists between maternal smoking and low birth weights in newborns, and the babies may be shorter. Furthermore, the incidence of death near the time of birth is higher for the children of smoking mothers, although the exact causes are unclear (Longo, 1977).

Much remains unknown about drug effects during pregnancy. Between 1976 and 1982, opinion vacillated concerning the dangers of caffeine to unborn children, and nothing convincing has yet been established. There are speculations, too, about the effects of over-the-counter drugs like aspirin, vitamins, and so forth, as well as about possible toxic chemicals in the general environment--in food, cosmetics, and household chemicals. Even the father is not exempt from suspicion; one report suggests that his drug use may also be significant (Kolata, 1978; Marks, 1979). Also, little is known of drug connections with defects related to later developmental stages of a child's growth, (e.g., cognitive processes), which may not become manifest for years (Vorhees et al., 1979).

In sum, present evidence on the subject of drugs and pregnancy is incomplete and sometimes inconclusive (Rang et al., 1995, pp. 807-811), except for certain thresholds established for particular drugs, like nicotine. It is not reasonable to suppose that all and any drug use may cause injury or that all injury is to be laid to drug use. However, it is known that the fetus is especially vulnerable during the first three months. In light of this, the guaranteed safe course is for pregnant women to avoid all drug use unless it is essential to maintain pregnancy. Some also advise any woman of childbearing age to avoid all drugs except those proven safe by long usage. Heeding such advice is not always possible, though, in which case moderation is good counsel. Ideally, childbirth too would take place painlessly with no anesthesia, but since anesthesia is commonly used, it is better that it be light, so the mother can assist with the birth.

SOLUBILITY

The **solubility** of a substance is its ability to dissolve in a medium. The molecules of the soluble substance form bonds with and disperse evenly throughout the medium. The two types of solubility that are most significant for drugs is their ability to dissolve in water and their ability to dissolve in **lipids** (fats and fatty tissues). Drugs that do not dissolve at all, for the most part, will not cross membranes, and they will be eliminated from the gastrointestinal tract. Injected into the bloodstream, they can remain and cause blockages.

Lipid solubility is of critical importance to drugs. Because membranes have a lipid structure, **lipid-soluble** molecules are able to dissolve in them and passively diffuse through to the other side. A lipid-soluble drug passes through the blood-brain barrier in such fashion.

Anyone who has mixed water and salad dressing knows that oil and water do not mix. Chemically, oil is said to be *hydrophobic*--afraid of water--and, as we have seen, this applies to lipid membranes. They will block out water and any molecules dissolved in it. The only chance these molecules have to pass is to be able to infiltrate the pores. Or, if the membrane needs certain water-soluble molecules, there may be an active transport carrier to ferry them. On the whole, then, it is a prime consideration in absorption whether a drug be lipid- or water-soluble.

To drive this home with an analogy, imagine you are camping in a canvas tent that has been well-treated with oil. When it rains, the rain runs off like water off a duck's back (because a duck's back is naturally oiled, too). This is like water-soluble molecules trying to pass the cell membrane. But now picture it raining oil. The oil, of course, is going to come through the canvas eventually, just as the lipid-soluble materials come through the membrane.

Ionization

Aside from the chemical ability to dissolve in water or lipids, ionization is another factor that affects the solubility of a drug.

To refresh your memory, an **ion** is an atom that has lost one or more electrons to another atom or has stolen them from another atom. By stealing electrons, it acquires a negative charge, because it now has a surplus. By losing them, it acquires a positive charge. Sodium (Na) and chlorine (Cl) furnish the typical example. These two elements are initially attracted because the configurations of their electron shells give them opposite charges. When they meet, they cling together in an ionic bond, forming the compound we know as ordinary table salt. (This type of bond differs from the covalent bond formed by atoms sharing electrons among their shells.)

When table salt is placed in water, the attraction of the water molecules pulls the Cl and Na apart. When they separate, they dissociate into Cl^- and Na^+ ions and form new ionic bonds with the water molecules around them. Thus, table salt is a weak compound that ionizes easily and almost completely as it dissolves.

When drugs enter the extracellular fluid, the blood, gastric juice, or any other body fluid, they may ionize to varying degrees as they dissolve, yielding a solution that contains both ionized and un-ionized portions of the drug. Since the ionized portion of the drug carries an electrical charge, like the Cl^- and Na^+ ions, it generally has difficulty crossing membranes, due to the equilibrium of electrical charges already established on both sides. Therefore, another significant factor in absorption is how much of the drug is in ionized form.

Water-soluble drugs tend especially to ionize in body fluids. It is therefore a rule of thumb that water-soluble drugs are harder to absorb, because as ions they cannot readily cross membranes. Lipid-soluble drugs normally cross through membranes, but if they ionize, the ionized portion loses its lipid-solubility. Ideally, then, to cross a membrane, a drug should be both lipid-soluble and in its un-ionized form. Its molecules must also be fairly small.

Polarity

Another attribute that determines the ability of a molecule to penetrate a membrane is its **polarity**. A bar magnet and the earth are polar objects, having a magnetic field that is positive at one pole and negative at the other. Molecules can be polar in the same way. Water molecules are the smallest polar molecules of biological significance.

Because of their polarity, water molecules display an affinity for one another, since opposite poles attract. By the same token, highly polar substances placed in water tend to ionize; that is, they form weak bonds with the water molecules and dissolve. Generally, the polarity of a molecule is defined by its degree of affinity for water molecules, compared to its affinity for a nonpolar, oil-like medium (Thompson, 1983).

Suppose we fill a beaker half with water and half with olive oil, so the oil floats on the water. Now we add our drug. What proportion of the drug concentrates in the water as opposed to the oil? This ratio demonstrates the drug's water- and lipid-solubility and gives us an idea of the polarity of the drug molecules. Highly polar substances gravitate toward the water, whereas nonpolar substances prefer oil. Moreover, the affinity of a drug for oil reflects its affinity for body membranes, which are lipid. But it is important to understand that a drug, despite its affinity for oil or water, may not completely ionize and dissolve. In other words, its polarity is no guarantee it will dissolve; rather, it marks a tendency to dissolve.

Most psychoactive drugs are relatively nonpolar, which means they tend not to ionize, have an affinity to oil, and can cross a membrane easily, assuming they are small enough.

	cross membranes easily	cross with difficulty
solubility	lipid-soluble	water soluble
ionization	un-ionization	ionized
polarization	non-polar	polar
size	small	large

TABLE 3.1 Factors that determine the ability of a molecule to cross membranes

It should be understood that these properties of drugs do not always operate as extremes. A substance is not always 99 percent lipid-soluble and 1 percent water-soluble or vice versa. The ratio may be 40 percent to 60 percent or 50 percent to 50 percent, depending on the drug's chemistry. Similarly, there are degrees of polarity. It also helps to realize that these properties are interrelated, but they do not strictly determine one another.

Table 3.1 gives a review of which of these properties is most advantageous for absorption. Generally, the ideal drug is made of nonpolar, lipid-soluble molecules in un-ionized form. The chances of crossing a membrane decrease as the molecules become more polar, more water-soluble, or more ionized.

pH

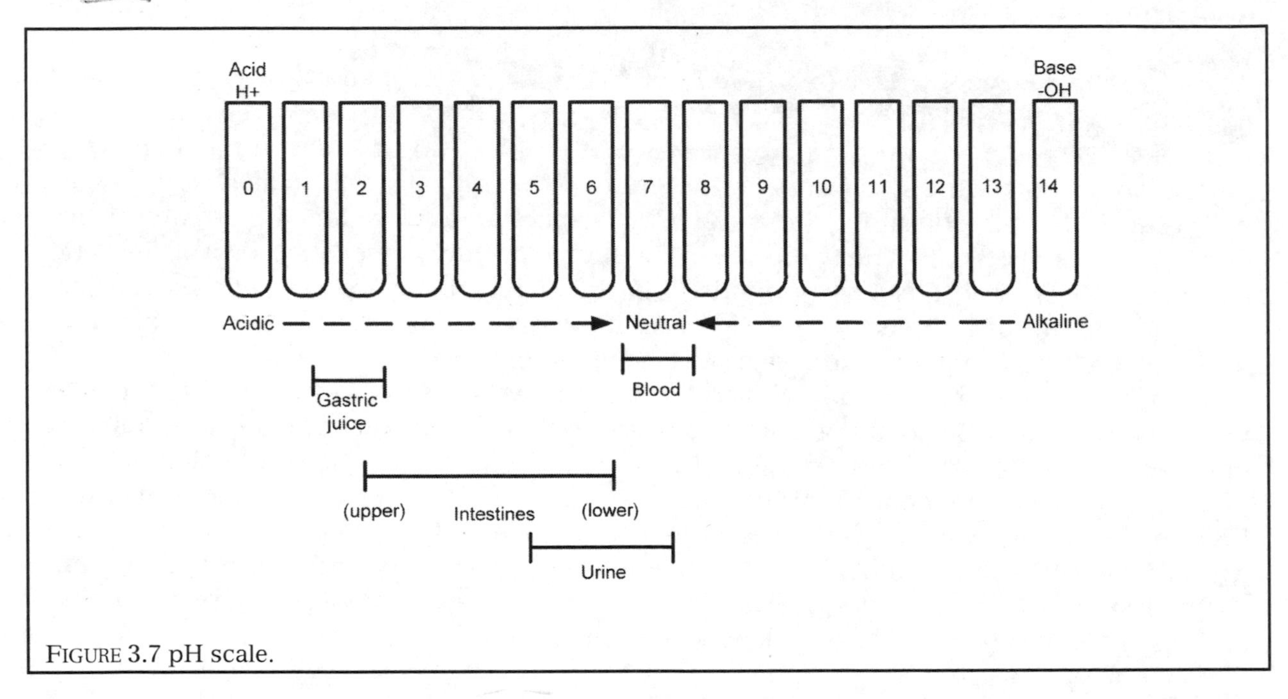

FIGURE 3.7 pH scale.

To complicate matters further, another factor in the absorption of drugs is their pH value. The pH is an index of the relative acidity or alkalinity of a solution, based on the concentration of hydrogen (H^+) ions in it. In chemical terms, an **acid** is a substance that causes the ionization of water to a great degree, yielding a high concentration of H^+ ions. For example, a pH of 1 contains 10^{-1} (one-tenth of a mole of) hydrogen ions per liter. A base is a substance that causes less water ionization, yielding a lower concentration of H^+ per liter. For example, a solution of pH 12 contains 10^{-12} (one million-millionth of a mole of) hydrogen ions per liter. The measurement scale for pH runs from 0 to 14 (see Figure 3.7). The lower the number, the more acidic the solution. Water, found at 7 on the scale, is neutral. Bases fall at the higher pH, the alkaline end of the scale. Most drugs form weak acidic or basic solutions, with a pH ranging from about 5 to 9.

The pH is important because acidic drugs tend to ionize in an alkaline medium and vice versa. The amount of ionization depends on how far apart the drug and the medium are on the pH scale; the wider the difference, the greater the ionization. Thus, the ability

prefer a nutral drug 7

of a lipid-soluble molecule to cross a membrane may be reduced significantly if it is placed in a medium with a different enough pH (up or down the scale) to cause it to ionize. An alkaline drug like heroin, for example, ionizes when it hits the stomach acids after being swallowed. Conversely, acidic drugs ionize if they are injected into the alkaline environment of the blood. As we have seen, this reduces lipid solubility and absorption and leads to weak effects.

The pH values of the different body compartments vary. The gastric juice is extremely acidic with a pH of 1.2, whereas the blood is slightly alkaline at 7.4, and the extracellular fluid is nearly the same. The intestines graduate from acidic to almost neutral as they descend, from 2.0 at the top of the small intestine to 6.6 at the anus. Urine in the kidneys ranges from 4.5 to 7.0. Because of these variations, a drug may face a variety of chemical environments on its travels, some of which might cause ionization and impede absorption. Absorption thus depends on the number of body compartments a drug has to cross and on the distance it has to travel.

Ion-trapping

By causing ionization of a drug, the pH of a body compartment can aid or inhibit absorption (see Figure 3.8). As an example, imagine a simple lipid membrane permeable only to lipid-soluble, un-ionized drug molecules. It is part of the stomach lining, so that on one side there is the acidic compartment of the stomach containing the gastric juice (pH 1.2), and on the other side is the alkaline compartment of the bloodstream (pH 7.4). If an alkaline drug enters the stomach, most of it will ionize in the gastric juices, impeding its absorption, and the remainder will probably have a negligible effect. As the drug proceeds down the gastrointestinal tract, however, it will encounter less acidic territory, favorable to its reintegration and absorption, but chances are good that by then some of it will have been digested or damaged by intestinal enzymes.

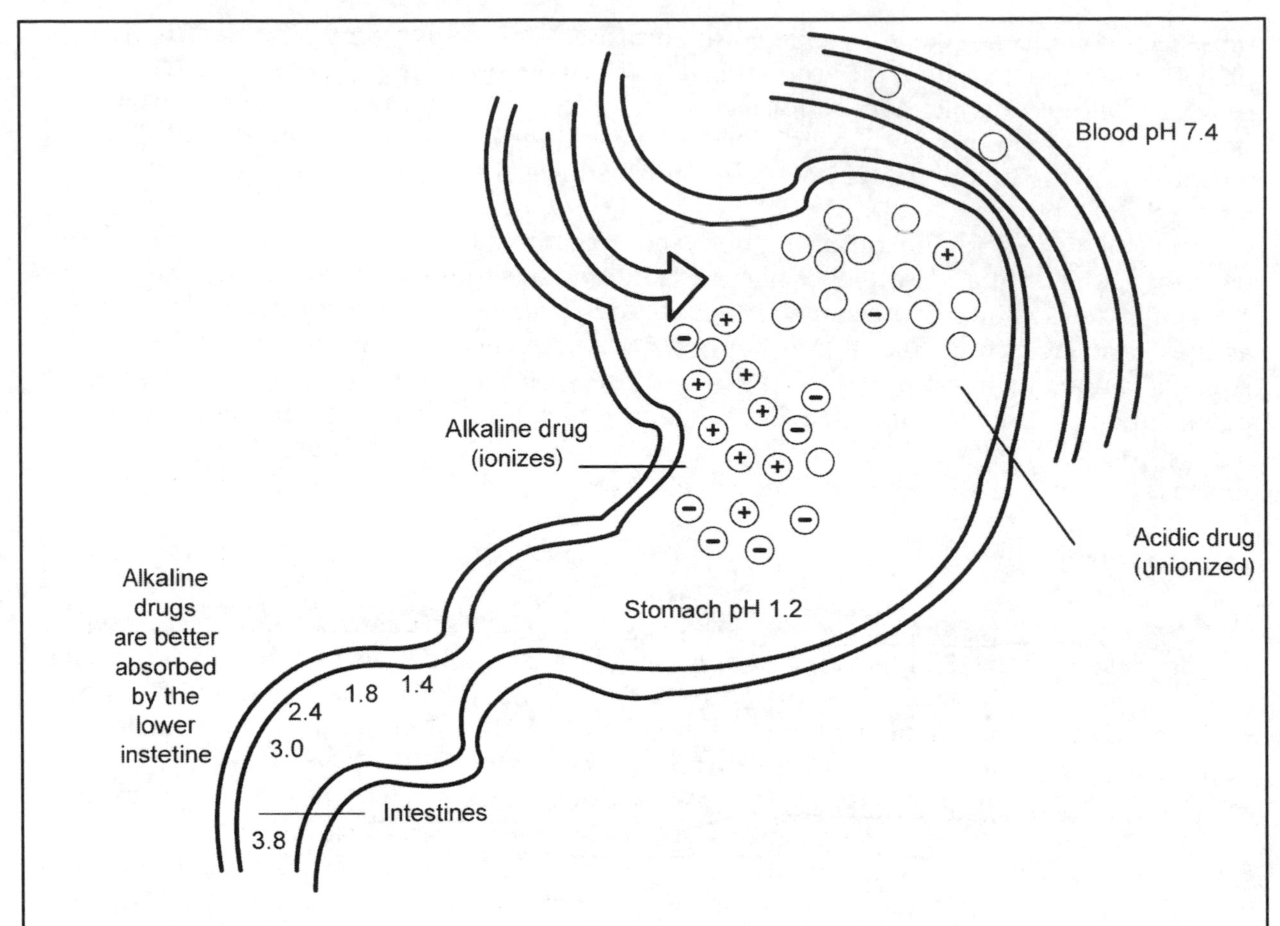

FIGURE 3.8 The effect of pH on absorption. Alkaline drugs ionize more in the stomach, become ion-trapped there, and are poorly absorbed. Acidic drugs remain largely un-ionized and are more effectively absorbed into the blood. (Once there, however, they can ionize more and become trapped.)

The drug of choice for the oral route, then, is acidic. Assume, in this case, that we choose a moderately acidic drug, consisting of a lipid-soluble, nonpolar molecule, a molecule possessing two of the attributes that allow it to cross a membrane easily. As absorption proceeds through the stomach lining (or more likely the small intestines), a harmony of proportions is maintained, based on patterns of ionization and diffusion. Since the drug is acidic, let us assume that only 10 percent of it ionizes in the stomach. This portion loses its capacity to diffuse out through the stomach lining and becomes trapped, while the remaining un-ionized portion diffuses into the blood. Since the blood is alkaline and much more hostile to an acidic drug, we may say that 40 percent of the drug in the blood ionizes and becomes trapped, while the remaining un-ionized portion begins to enter the cells and gets metabolized. The total amount of drug now drops. As this happens, the molecules redistribute in such a way that all these proportions are preserved as the supply of drug gradually depletes. No matter what amount of drug remains, we will always find a 1 to 10 (10 percent) ratio of ionized to un-ionized molecules in the stomach, and a ratio of 2 to 5 (40 percent) ionized to un-ionized molecules in the blood. In addition, the un-ionized molecules will always be seeking a 50/50 equilibrium as they diffuse across the membrane. For these balances to continue, a percentage of the ionized molecules have to return to their un-ionized state.

FACTORS IN ABSORPTION

Understanding and predicting the absorption of a drug is far from a simple matter. The following is a list and summary of the factors that can be used to gauge how likely it is a drug will be absorbed.

1. *Lipid- and water-solubility.* Lipid-soluble molecules diffuse across membranes; water-soluble molecules do not.
2. *Ionization.* Un-ionized molecules will diffuse across membranes. Many ions, as a general rule, will not; they are typically carried across by active transport. Water-soluble molecules convert easily to ionized form. Lipid-soluble molecules tend to remain intact.
3. *Polarization.* Molecules that are attracted to water (polar compounds) may or may not cross membranes, depending on the strength of their charge and on their degree of solubility. Large polar molecules are likely to ionize. Nonpolar molecules, if they are lipid-soluble, cross membranes without impediments.
4. *pH.* Acidic drugs ionize in alkaline body compartments, and alkaline drugs ionize in acidic body compartments. One must be aware of ion-trapping as a factor in absorption.
5. *Molecular size and configuration.* Small molecules are more likely to diffuse through the pores of a membrane; large ones cannot. Large, polar molecules are more unstable than small ones and tend to ionize more easily. Large molecules also enter the brain with more difficulty. As for configuration, certain membrane mechanisms (like carrier transport or the receptor proteins for drugs) are sensitive to a molecule's geometry, and "look alikes" may be absorbed to some extent. If we take the isomer (the mirror image) of the molecule of amphetamine, we find that it fits some but not all of the receptors for the drug.
6. *Route.* The choice of a route determines how many body compartments a drug must pass through and how many membranes it must cross. These in turn influence absorption.
7. *Distance.* If a venomous snake bites your foot, the speed with which it affects the central nervous system will be slower than if it bites you in the carotid artery of the neck. In the first case, the dose of venom is diluted by the blood as it travels, via the liver, the whole length of the body to the brain; in the second case, the brain would instantly take the full dose of the poison.
8. *Size of absorbing surface and number of capillaries.* The richer in capillaries a tissue is, the more access it provides to the bloodstream, and the faster absorption will be. Wider surfaces like the intestinal lining can naturally accommodate more capillaries and absorb more efficiently.
9. *Membrane transport.* Membranes use different processes to transport material. Most transfer takes place by the passive diffusion of lipid-soluble molecules through membranes. In the case of the capillaries, most substances enter and exit through large pores; however, the capillaries sheathed by the blood-brain barrier

have no pores and entering molecules must either be lipid-soluble or use carrier-assisted transport systems.

10. *Drug concentration.* The higher its concentration, the faster a drug will be absorbed, because of the steepness of the concentration gradient across the membranes. A drug will move faster if the ratio across the membrane is, for example, 1000 to 1 rather than 10 to 1.
11. *Transportation in the blood and drug fate.* Many drugs must ride through the bloodstream to the site of action and avoid being broken down too fast and excreted. Both of these factors will be treated in the following chapters.

Chapter 4

Distribution and Drug Fate

As a drug is absorbed, it **distributes** throughout the body in a pattern determined by its chemistry. With some exceptions (eyedrops, eardrops, nosedrops, and sympathomimetic bronchodilators), drugs typically do not follow a neat path straight to the problem area, as many drug commercials on television would have you believe. Usually the drug disperses throughout the entire circulation, even though it produces its effects only from specific sites of action. The collision of drug molecules with receptors, for instance, is a matter of probability, not an inevitability. In some cases, the drug may accumulate more in organs or tissues removed from the site of action. The drug will likewise distribute according to which membranes it can or cannot cross.

TRANSPORTATION IN THE BLOOD

Drugs enter the body by the various routes and then enter the bloodstream. On the average, the human circulatory system contains about 12.6 pints (6 liters) of blood. The heart pumps about 10.5 pints (5 liters) a minute, so that the whole circulation turns over in a little more than one minute (see Figure 4.1). An intravenous injection would thus be found evenly distributed throughout the entire circulation in that short a time. The same is true of any quantity of a drug diffusing in through the capillary walls from the drug routes.

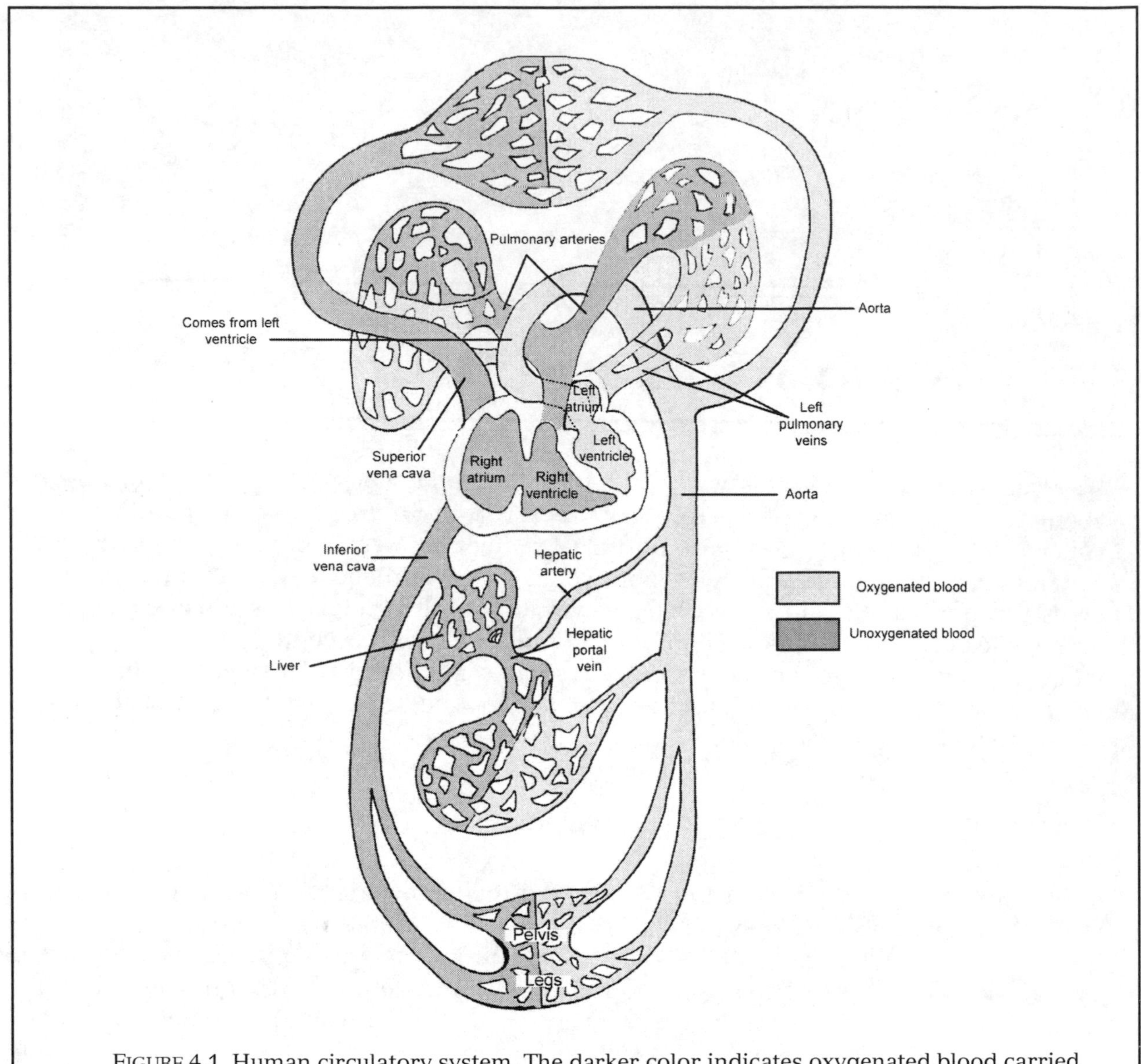

FIGURE 4.1 Human circulatory system. The darker color indicates oxygenated blood carried away from the heart. Note how blood from the gut is routed through the liver.

When a substance enters the capillaries, it is carried into the veins, which return the blood to the right atrium of the heart. From here it is sent into the right ventricle, which pumps it to the lungs for reoxygenation. It returns to the left atrium and is pumped out by way of the left ventricle into the aorta and the general circulation, where arteries distribute it to the capillaries. Every cell is near one of the ten billion capillaries, so that substances in the blood are distributed to every tissue in the body. From the cells and capillaries, blood flows again into the veins, renewing the cycle.

The concentration of a drug at the site of action is difficult to determine, but it depends on the overall concentration of the dose maintained throughout the body. The overall concentration is critical to the intensity and duration of the effect, even though only a relatively small portion of the drug may actually be necessary at the site of action. For instance, most of a dose of LSD might be found distributed throughout the general circulation, but only a little might be at the site of action in the brain. Besides distribution and dilution in the blood, a drug may diffuse further through capillary pores into the extracellular fluid, which then functions with the blood plasma as a single pool of solvent. Water makes up 58 percent of the body weight, so that a 150-pound male contains about 86.6 pints (41 liters). If 12.6 pints (6 liters) of fluid is blood plasma, that makes an extra 74 pints (35 liters) of extracellular fluid able to dilute drug concentrations.

TISSUE AFFINITY

Certain drugs and tissues show a chemical affinity for one another. Some drug molecules bond with the molecules of their "favorite" tissues, which then show up as areas of high concentration in the distribution pattern of the drug. A common example is **protein-binding** in the blood. Many drugs attach themselves to the large protein globules in the blood, particularly to albumin, the predominant protein. These bound drugs are then trapped in the capillaries unable to act, because the capillary pores, wide as they are, are still smaller than the protein globules. Such a drug is in the position of a person chained to an elephant, trying to climb out a porthole. Ninety percent of the antipsychotic drug chlorpromazine (Thorazine) and 99 percent of the tranquilizer diazepam (Valium) binds with proteins. Most drugs, however, protein-bind only in small amounts.

Bound and unbound portions of a drug in the bloodstream balance in a type of equilibrium similar to that achieved by ionized and unionized molecules in body compartments. Different drugs protein-bind to different extents, but the ratio of bound to unbound molecules for a particular drug is a constant.

Chlorpromazine ions will always be found in the blood 90 percent bound to 10 percent free. As the free 10 percent diffuses out of circulation, bound molecules free themselves to maintain the proportion. Hence, chlorpromazine escapes from the blood slowly, at a low, steady level, as the body works on the small portion of the drug available at any given moment. Because of this, protein-binding can be manipulated to control dosage levels and store drugs for slow release. On the other hand, drugs like phenobarbital and alcohol have a low affinity for blood proteins and diffuse wholesale out of circulation.

One method of overcoming the impediments posed by protein-binding in the blood and by other tissue affinities is to administer an initial dose of the drug large enough to saturate the binding site and then give more to provide a satisfactory effect as well. Another technique is to administer a second drug that exhibits more of an affinity for the tissue than the first. This second drug unseats the molecules of the first drug and replaces them in the tissue. The first drug is then freed for action. This mechanism can cause poisoning if a drug is accidentally bumped from its binding site, and blood concentrations suddenly soar to toxic levels.

Besides the blood, other major depots for drug storage are tissues richly supplied by blood, such as the liver, kidneys, and lungs, or tissues with water content, such as muscles. One important qualification to this rule is neutral fat tissue. Fat tissue is a key storage site. It is well-supplied with blood, but because fat cells are larger and have more volume than muscle cells, the ratio of blood and water to tissue tends to be lower than in muscles (Montgomery et al., 1983, p. 453). People vary widely in the proportion of body weight that consists of fat. The range runs from about 10 percent in the starving to about 50 percent in the obese. Women genetically have a higher percentage of body fat than men, and the elderly have a higher percentage than the young.

Large proportions of lipid-soluble drugs will go into storage in various fat tissues, removing themselves from immediate action. Because of their affinity, they are then released slowly. Usually, such a drug has a two-phased effect. First, it distributes evenly throughout the body as the circulation disperses it, which produces the initial effect; then the drug **redistributes** according to its affinities, shifting the concentration pattern and changing the effect. Thiopental (Pentothal), an anesthetic barbiturate, is a good example. Being lipid-soluble, it crosses the blood-brain barrier quickly after administration and has a rapid onset of action. The subject falls asleep. Then the drug redistributes as it enters storage in muscle and especially in neutral fat tissue. The blood and brain concentrations sink and remain low, causing the subject to awaken. Three hours after administration, 70 percent of the drug may still be found in fat tissue. This is then slowly released, metabolized, and excreted, inducing a slight, prolonged depression in the subject.

In contrast, pentobarbital (Nembutal), another anesthetic, which is less fat-soluble than thiopental, takes longer to cross the blood-brain barrier and has a slower onset of action. It redistributes much less than thiopental, so blood concentrations remain high, and the subject remains sedated longer. The action declines only as the drug is metabolized and excreted. Pentobarbital would therefore be preferable for long-term surgery.

THC (tetrahydrocannabinol), the active ingredient in marijuana, is equally soluble in oil and water (50 parts in oil to 50 parts in water). THC first distributes throughout the circulation, then redistributes to storage in fat tissue. Hence, the initial effect is somewhat brief, but blood levels remain low and steady for eight hours or so. Alcohol, on the other hand, a polar compound which is 25 times more soluble in water than in oil, does not store in fat.

The blood-brain barrier makes the brain a special case in distribution. The brain constitutes only 2 percent of the body weight, yet it receives 15 percent of the blood supply (Little & Little, 1987, p. 320), distinguishing it as the tissue richest in blood, but drugs enter it slowly because of the barrier. Once inside, they continue to distribute according to their affinities. LSD, for example, concentrates in the brain tissues governing vision, and the drug is celebrated for producing an array of visual fireworks and lucid hallucinations. The presence of other drugs and even of particular types of stimuli can also affect the pattern of drug distribution in the brain. This has been suggested in studies using deoxyglucose (2DG), a form of glucose that can be labeled and traced. Stimulated neurons take up more glucose as well as 2DG, and the same may be true of drug uptake. Visual systems receiving stimuli may take up more LSD. It is thereby conceivable that the psychedelic laser light shows and concatenating concert rock of the 1960s may not only have given a "tripping" audience something to respond to, but that the very presence of stimuli like these might have enhanced responses to light and sound by absorbing more LSD into the appropriate sensory areas of the brain (Hand, 1981; Sokoloff et al., 1977). The same would be true of the modern-day marathon dance parties known as raves.

There are many other possible sites of concentration for drugs, depending on their affinities. Quinacrine, an antimalarial agent, has such an affinity for liver cell nuclei that, 4 hours after administration, levels in the liver may be 2,000 times those of the blood plasma, and after repeated doses they have been known to reach 22,000 times the plasma level. Thorazine, an antipsychotic tranquilizer, accumulates and stays in hair, to be lost on the hair stylist's floor. The gastrointestinal tract can be used for the storage of weak bases, since they ionize in the stomach and become active only as they are absorbed through the lower intestinal tract. The blood levels of bases following this route are low, steady, and prolonged. Tetracycline, an antibiotic, is stored in bone. Iodine concentrates in the fluid of the thyroid gland. Finally, a number of drugs concentrate in mother's milk, where they can pose additional drug threats to a nursing child.

DRUG FATE

When a drug is administered, the body begins the process of metabolizing and excreting it. This phase of its action, the immediate and long-term disposal of a drug, is known as **drug fate.** Drug fate determines the duration of an effect. Theoretically, if drug molecules could stay unchanged in tissues, their effect would be constant; this is suggested to some extent by the persistence of anesthetic effects in newborn infants, whose metabolic systems are underdeveloped. In fact, however, drug effects end by one of two fates. In most cases, the drug is metabolized, usually ionized so that it cannot be reabsorbed, and is filtered out of the body with dispatch by the kidneys, passing via urination. But the drug may also remain unchanged. This is the case with many water-soluble drugs, which are already largely ionized. Their excretion rate depends mainly on diffusion, as they pass slowly via the kidneys in active, unchanged form. Some of these unchanged drug molecules may reenter the circulation from the kidneys, remaining active and sustaining the effect. In consequence, the percentage of a dose that exits the body unaltered and active is an indicator of a drug's persistence in the bloodstream and its duration of action.

A third and less frequent possibility is that effects end due to the drug's redistribution and storage in fat tissue.

An important concept in the fate of a drug is its **half-life,** which is measured from the time the drug reaches equilibrium during absorption. The half-life (*plasma half-life*) is the amount of time it takes for the blood levels of a drug to drop to half, after equilibrium. If a drug has a half-life of 3 hours, it means that after 3 hours only half of the drug is active and circulating in the blood. The plasma half-life may be a result of distribution as portions of the drug go into storage (*distribution half-life*), or it may be a result of metabolism and elimination of the drug (*elimination half-life*).

The metabolism of drugs may occur at a number of sites. By far, the grand site of metabolism is in the liver. But it may also occur in the blood plasma, or at the site of action, where the same enzymes that deactivate neurotransmitters may act on drug molecules. Metabolism is also seen to occur in the intestines, kidneys, lungs, and skin.

The remainder of a drug's fate, its excretion, occurs by four main routes: the kidneys, intestines, lungs, and skin (in sweat). Lesser paths include the bile, saliva, and breast milk.

THE LIVER

What is the size of a pumpernickel, has the shape of Diana's helmet, and crouches like a thundercloud above its bellymates, turgid with nourishment? What has the industry of an insect, the regenerative powers of a starfish . . . . ? (Selzer, 1974)

The most significant organ involved in drug fate is the liver. The largest organ in the body, it weighs in at about three pounds. Its functions are manifold. Seething with an immense array of enzymes, it metabolizes carbohydrates, lipids, and proteins. It stores iron, vitamins, and nutrients; synthesizes proteins that circulate in the blood plasma; and destroys red blood cells, as well as steroid (sex) hormones. Furthermore, it detoxifies possibly harmful compounds like insecticides, dyes, food preservatives, and drugs.

The liver has a double blood supply. The portal vein returning to the heart brings in nutrient-rich blood from the intestines, stomach, spleen, and pancreas. In addition, about a fifth of the blood supply enters through the hepatic artery (*hepar* is Greek for "liver"), which delivers oxygenated blood fresh from the heart. Between the portal vein and the hepatic artery, the liver receives about 3.5 pints (1 to 1.5 liters) of blood a minute.

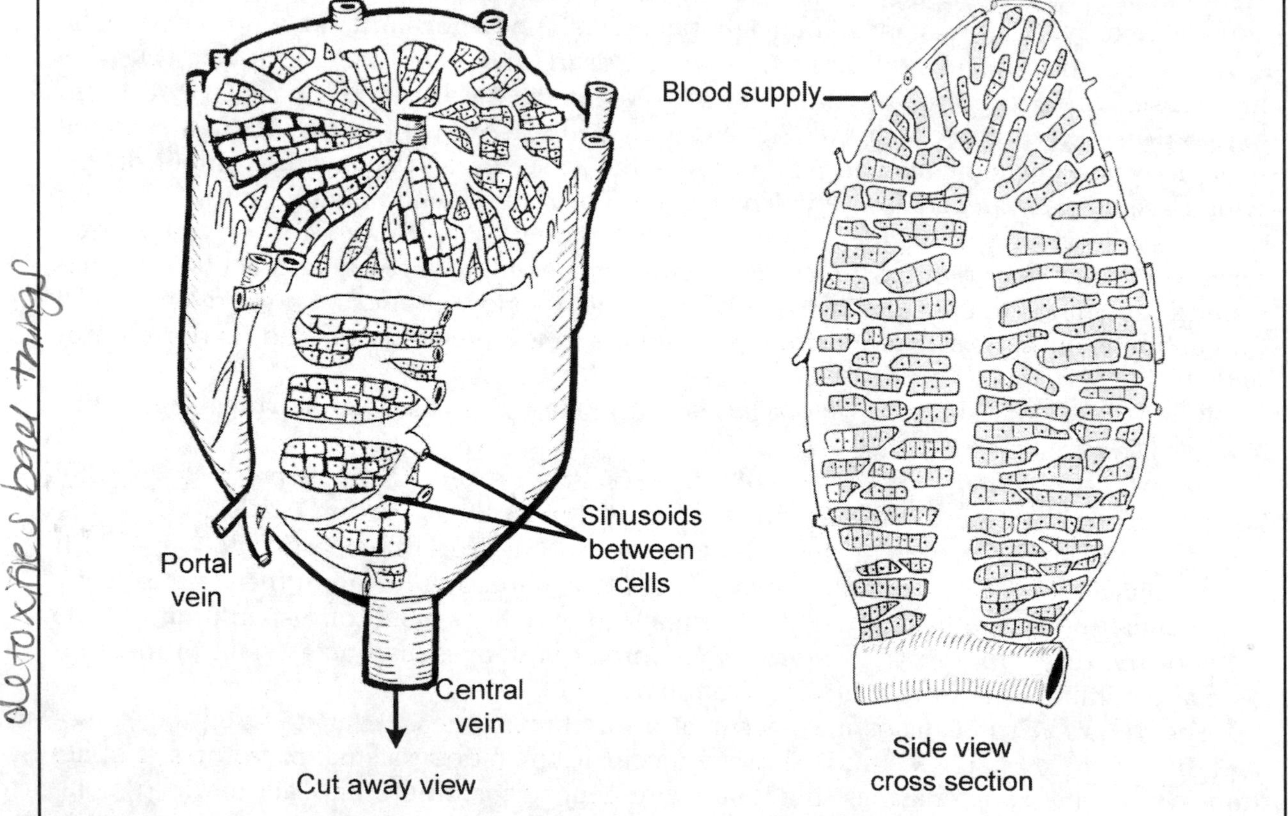

FIGURE 4.2 Liver lobule. In the left diagram, blood flows from the portal vein (or from the hepatic arteries) through the sinusoids to the central vein and out. The right diagram shows the lobule in cross section.

The basic structural unit of the liver is a **lobule**, a group of cells fastened together in a column (see Figure 4.2). The hepatic artery and portal vein branch out more and more finely until their blood runs together into gaps (sinusoids) between the liver lobules. Here the major chemical changes occur; nutrients and wastes are exchanged with liver cells, and phagocytic (cell-eating) cells gobble intruding microorganisms. The blood then drains to the central vein of each lobule and exits via the system of hepatic veins.

Not everything that goes to the liver is metabolized in one pass. If you drink a bottle of beer, the blood concentration of alcohol will rise as your stomach and intestinal capillaries absorb the drug. Your liver will immediately go to work on it, metabolizing and deactivating a portion as it passes through, until the blood level begins to drop. After about an hour, the alcohol will all have been metabolized. For this reason, if the liver is on the route between the drug's site of administration and its site of action, a higher dose might be given to compensate for the metabolism that occurs on the first pass through (**first-pass metabolism**).

BIOTRANSFORMATION

Liver enzymes are situated in the endoplasmic reticulum of liver cells. This structure, literally a "network within the cell plasm," is a system of interconnected, flattened tubes and channels permeating the plasma of the cell and resembling, in electron micrographs, the contour lines on a topographic map. Liver cells sport two kinds of endoplasmic reticulum, rough and smooth: the former is involved in protein synthesis; both appear to be involved in various detoxification processes. In the lab, fragments of endoplasmic reticulum separated by centrifuge from the cell are known as **microsomes**; hence the liver enzymes are also referred to sometimes as **microsomal enzymes**. These account for the metabolism of lipids, steroid hormones, and most drugs (Csaky & Barnes, 1984, pp. 652-655).

Biotransformation, or metabolism, is the process whereby enzymes modify a molecule and alter its chemical properties. Generally, liver enzymes act on drug molecules in one of two ways: (1) they deactivate the molecules; (2) they ionize the molecules to increase water solubility so that they will not bind readily with tissues, cannot penetrate membranes or be stored, and consequently will be excreted by the kidneys. The product of biotransformation, the modified molecule, is a **metabolite**. In essence, this is a new compound differing in properties from the original. Although usually inactive, drug metabolites may be active forms of the original drug, or even of different drugs. For instance, about 10 percent of a dose of codeine is biotransformed into morphine. In one case, a drug company found that the tranquilizer Valium was biotransformed into an active metabolite, so the company marketed the metabolite as a competing drug.

Other patterns of biotransformation include processes that activate an initially inactive molecule or processes that shift molecules through chains of active and inactive phases. It is possible, also, for a substance to react with its own metabolite.

Problems in predicting biotransformation in the liver arise from the fact that most of our knowledge is drawn from animal research and that metabolic rates vary from species to species. Phenylbutazone, an anti-inflammatory drug used to treat arthritis in racehorses, has a half-life of 3 to 6 hours in horses, dogs, rabbits, rats, and guinea pigs, but a half-life of 3 days in humans. Human metabolism also varies widely. For some individuals, it proceeds too fast to maintain a therapeutic dose, and in others it goes slowly enough to cause toxicity.

There are four types of biotransformation: oxidation, reduction, hydrolysis, and conjugation. Most biotransformation is by oxidation. Liver enzymes are unique in their ability to involve oxygen directly in a chemical reaction; to do this they use *heme*, the same iron-containing compound that makes up hemoglobin and binds oxygen in red blood cells. The enzymes involved in this process are called **mixed-function oxidases** because their action is nonspecific; that is, applicable to an array of different molecules. The mixed-function oxidizes, for instance, existed long before any of the modern synthetic chemicals they currently biotransform.

In most cases, the metabolites of oxidation, ionized and unable to be reabsorbed, are destined for excretion. In conjugation, the second most frequent type of biotransformation, the metabolites are almost always inactive; typically, a substance (e.g., glucoronic acid) is added by the liver, which deactivates the molecule or makes it too large to be reabsorbed. For most drugs, conjugation is a second step after one of the other forms of biotransformation, usually oxidation. The process of oxidizing then conjugating a molecule, now used in the metabolism of drugs, originally evolved as a means of metabolizing body substances such as steroid hormones, cholesterol, and fatty acids.

Reduction and hydrolysis are rarer forms of biotransformation. Reduction splits the target molecule into simpler compounds, and hydrolysis modifies a molecule by adding water. A hydrogen (H^+) atom is grafted onto one fragment, and a hydroxyl group (OH) onto the other.

The duration of a drug effect depends on the relative rates of all the biotransformations involved. As more and more molecules are deactivated, the drug effect declines, and the inactive metabolite continues to circulate until the kidneys eliminate it. To maintain prolonged and steady levels of a drug effect, dosages must be accurately timed and adjusted so that the absorption of the drug exactly replenishes the amount deactivated by the liver. To do this, a thorough knowledge of absorption, of biotransformation, and of each drug's unique characteristics is important. Instructions on medicine bottle labels reflect these considerations. If you ignore a typical injunction to take a medicine "one hour after eating," or if you skimp on the dosage, you may not only be altering the absorption characteristics of the medicine, but also its fate. If you procrastinate in taking your medicine, biotransformation may outpace you, the effect may drop, and the absorption rate may shift if some of the drug comes out of storage. In the end, the drug's efficacy is compromised, causing unsteady results.

If a substance cannot be biotransformed, or if the end product of biotransformation is active, it will be excreted in active form.

ENZYME INDUCTION

Cytochrome P450, found in the endoplasmic reticulum of liver cells, is the key enzyme of the mixed-function oxidases. *Cytochrome* literally translates from its Greek roots as "cell color"; it is named this because, in its reduced form, cytochrome P450 (henceforth referred to simply as P450) binds with carbon monoxide and absorbs light most intensely at a wave length of 450 nanometers. Based on this measure, a scientist can estimate the amount of P-450 in a sample of liver extract.

P450 is indispensable for the active oxidation of drugs. It is involved in the metabolism of alcohol, tranquilizers, barbiturates, antianxiety drugs; androgen, estrogen; DDT, PCBs, and a variety of other carcinogens; and other substances as well. A continued exposure to any substance oxidized by P450 causes the smooth endoplasmic reticulum to grow and the plasma of liver cells to expand, resulting in an increased production of P450. In effect, these chemicals are stimulating their own deactivation by P450. Over 200 substances have been found that do this to a greater or lesser degree, among them certain insecticides, lipid-rich foods, and some food additives. The process is known as **enzyme induction**, because a substance is inducing the production of extra enzymes, and it is one form of **tolerance**, the body's compensating for the presence of drugs in an attempt to maintain normal functioning.

The sharing of P450 by many substances seeking to be deactivated causes a broad, fascinating, and sometimes lamentable battery of results. Two significant factors come into play. The first is competition. Because there is only so much P450, many different molecules compete for its use. Hence, drug X can monopolize the available P450, while drug Y, forced to wait, remains active in the bloodstream much longer than usual. The second factor is that one substance can induce P450, and this causes the accelerated metabolism of other substances as well. If the inducing substance is absent and not competing for the P450, the enzyme will occupy itself by metabolizing whatever comes its way. Let's look at some examples of these factors:

Alcohol induces P450, which also biotransforms barbiturates. Suppose an alcoholic man has had an accident and requires immediate surgery. He has been drinking the morning of the operation, so that, despite a liver sopping with P450, the enzyme is busy on the alcohol. The anesthetic then will have an exaggerated effect or will kill the patient, because the liver has no available P450 to cope with it. This is a simple case of competition. However, now let's suppose our patient, because of his injury, refrained from drinking before the operation. In this case, all the P450 normally used for alcohol, a much higher amount than in an average man, will be ravenous and ready to go to work on the anesthetic. As a result, the anesthesiologist will have a surprisingly difficult time keeping the patient unconscious.

A similar case arises for machinists and car mechanics. The PCBs (polychlorinated biphenyls) in insulators and oil, easily absorbed through the skin, induce P450 in the livers of those who handle them. This P450 is also useful for alcohol. It is not so fabulous to hear, then, of employees in a Munich gear factory who can go out on Sundays and down forty beers, enough to kill a worker with clean hands. If the same people drink on the job, however, they will feel the effects immediately, because the P450 is occupied by the oil they are absorbing through their skin. Similar inducers in work environments include lubricants, heat-exchange fluids, plasticizers for paints, plastic compounds, insecticides, and lens immersion oils used in microscopy.

P450 also biotransforms steroid hormones like testosterone. Hence, alcoholics unable to get enough alcohol lose interest in sex, in part because their livers eat up their hormones (Rubin et al., 1976). This factor has also been found to have serious environmental repercussions. If a bald eagle preys on mice contaminated with DDT, P450 is induced in the eagle's liver. If the eagle then feeds on a run of uncontaminated mice, the surplus

P450 occupies itself on steroid hormones. The breakdown of these hormones causes the eagle to lay eggs with defective shells, endangering the survival of the species.

In medical treatment, doctors must attend to the enzyme induction relationships between pairs of drugs. They must be wary, for instance, of one medication occupying the liver while a second goes unchecked. On the other hand, physicians can manipulate enzyme induction for salutary ends. Bilirubin, the pigment that causes yellowing in jaundice, can be eliminated by inducing P450 with small chronic doses of phenobarbital; the surplus P450 then metabolizes the bilirubin.

Research has shown that metabolites may be more toxic or carcinogenic than their original molecules. Benzpyrene, benzanthracene and similar polycyclic hydrocarbons (PCHCs) are among the most widespread carcinogens. They are found in tobacco smoke, car exhaust, polluted city air, and in charcoal-broiled or smoked foods. PCHCs and PCBs in the liver induce the synthesis of a mutant strain of P450 that absorbs light more effectively at 448 nanometers, giving it the name *cytochrome P448*. This maverick enzyme may play a role in the cancerous growth of body tissues.

THE KIDNEYS

The kidneys are our main excretory organs; smaller than a fist, they weigh about a quarter of a pound each. Although the intestines eliminate more bulk than the kidneys, intestinal matter has never been absorbed and has never really entered the body. The kidneys, on the other hand, strain the blood and remove used or useless material after it has been absorbed. They also secrete hormones, help in the production of vitamin D, and regulate the pH balance of the blood plasma.

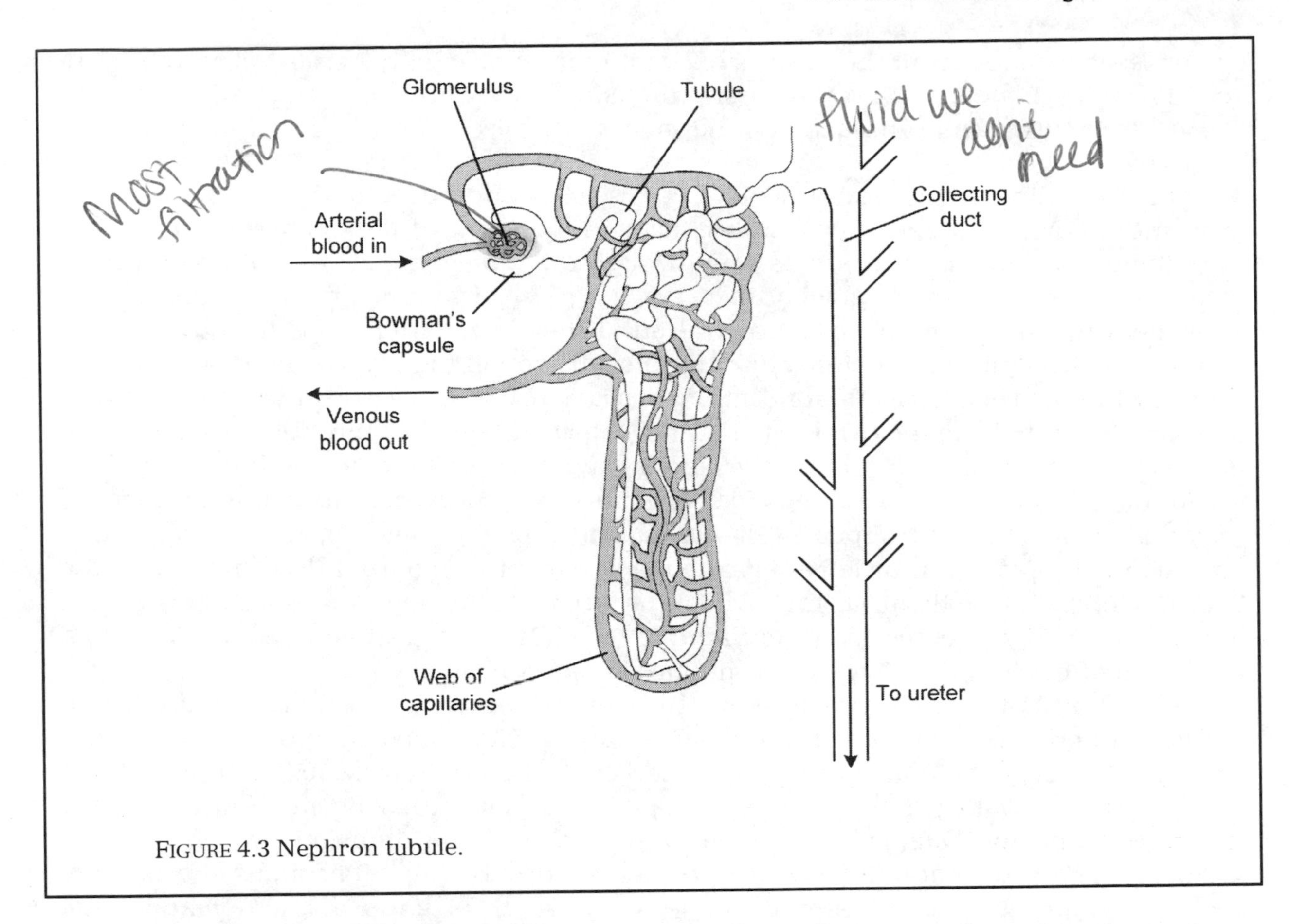

FIGURE 4.3 Nephron tubule.

The basic structural unit of the kidney is a **nephron**, which consists of a looped tubule interwoven with capillaries (see Figure 4.3). Each kidney contains a million or more nephrons. Excretion begins when blood from the renal arteries enters the Bowman's capsule, a protuberance on the end of the nephron tubule. The capsule resembles a round bud, cupping a whorl of capillaries known as a **glomerulus.** Blood entering these capillaries finds the exit from the capsule more constricting than the entrance; as a result, blood pressure doubles inside the glomerulus, and about 20 percent of the plasma is forced through pores in the capsule walls and crosses by filtration into the nephron tubule. This process is nonselective, except for bodies like red blood cells and blood proteins, both too large to fit the pores. The amount of a drug entering the tubule depends on the filtration rate and on the extent of its protein-binding.

Much more material than needs to be excreted is forced out of the glomeruli into the tubules, including nutrients. Such matter is in danger of being lost, so that as the filtrate winds its way through the tubule, most of it has to be reabsorbed into the capillaries, which continue from the Bowman's capsule to weave a net around the tubules. Of about 190 quarts (180 liters) of material pushed daily into the tubules, all but about 2 pints (1 to 1.5 liters) is reabsorbed. This remaining 2 pints is urinated. It proceeds down the tubule to a collecting duct, which becomes the ureter leading to the bladder.

Although entry into the tubules from the glomeruli is mainly by filtration, some molecules, like uric acid, and drugs, like penicillin, are actively separated out by the membrane. Reabsorption from the tubules back into the capillaries generally occurs through active transport, along with some passive diffusion and osmosis (selective diffusion). Because of all this membrane activity, the kidneys require a great deal of energy, even more than the heart.

Understanding the role of diffusion in the reabsorption process is important for understanding drug excretion. Drugs filter through the pores of the glomerulus and enter the tubule. As the filtrate winds its way through the tubule and reabsorption proceeds, water is reabsorbed more quickly than anything else. Draining off water this way is equivalent to raising the drug concentration in the tubule. Moreover, introducing this water into the capillaries dilutes the drug concentration in the blood on the other side of the membrane. This causes a concentration gradient. Now, if a drug is unionized and lipid-soluble, it follows the gradient (and the water) and diffuses through the tubule wall back into the capillaries, rejoining the circulation and remaining active. Because of this, the kidneys alone are unable to eliminate such drugs. However, if the drugs are ionized, they will always be ion-trapped in the tubule and excreted, unless active transport rescues them. Therefore, in order to eliminate lipid-soluble, unionized drug molecules, the liver must first ionize them, so that, when they arrive in the nephron tubule, they can be ion-trapped and prevented from returning to the circulation. Excretion thus is a twofold process that begins in the liver and continues in the kidneys.

Many nutrients are filtered into the nephrons along with blood plasma and are in danger of being excreted. For these, reabsorption is vital. Such compounds fare differently in reabsorption. Water is the most cherished, and it will be reabsorbed first. If the body is shy of water, the capillaries will pull more fluid than normal back from the nephrons and any suitable drug along with it, due to the diffusion process just described. The reabsorption of alcohol is an example of this. One of alcohol's effects is dehydration. Another is that it inhibits the hormone **ADH** (or **antidiuretic hormone**) that signals the kidneys to hold fluid; this increases urination, causing a further dehydration from loss of fluid. As the body dries out, the capillaries draw more fluid back from the tubules, water and alcohol both, to conserve body moisture. This results in a longer drug effect, since alcohol flows back into the bloodstream. It is also the reason you feel parched and thirsty several hours after a drinking spree. The only reasonable way to shorten intoxication is to drink a good deal of water, reducing reabsorption and facilitating the urination of alcohol.

The pH gradient across the nephron tubule membrane is significant too in reabsorption. If the urine in the tubule is acidic, alkaline molecules will become ion-trapped; if it is alkaline, acidic molecules will be trapped. The trapped molecules will be urinated. Despite the pH gradient, however, the overall trend is reabsorption, because the concentration gradient arising from the reabsorption of water has more influence than the pH gradient.

Nevertheless, in certain cases, the pH balance of the kidneys can be artificially upset to speed the elimination of undesirable substances. For an overdose of phenobarbital, a weak acid, one can alkalinize the urine with a dose of bicarbonate of soda, ion-trapping the sedative in the nephrons and blocking reabsorption.

OTHER ROUTES OF EXCRETION

In addition to the kidneys, drugs may also be excreted through the bile, skin, lungs, and in saliva and mother's milk.

The bile serves as an alternate route for substances that cannot be excreted through the kidneys. Many antibiotics follow this route, among them penicillin, streptomycin, and tetracycline. They are metabolized by the liver and secreted by liver cells into the bile, passing down the ducts to the gall bladder and into the upper part of the small intestine. Here, if the drug is lipid-soluble, it will be reabsorbed, just as if it had been swallowed. Water-soluble substances will be trapped in the intestines and defecated.

Volatile anesthetics are excreted unchanged by the lungs. When the anesthesiologist stops administration, the lung concentration of the drug drops and even lipid-soluble drugs diffuse back out of the capillaries into the lungs and are exhaled. Part of a dose of alcohol is excreted by this route. The tainted odor of drinkers' breath is caused, not by the alcohol they have had in their mouths, but by small amounts of alcohol being eliminated through the lungs.

Less common paths of removal are sweat, salivary, and mammary glands. Salivary excretions are swallowed and return to the oral route. Breast milk, being acidic, ion-traps alkaloids, although ethanol (the alcohol that is the main ingredient of alcoholic beverages) achieves the same concentration there as in the blood plasma, regardless of pH. Also, cow's milk may contain antibiotics that have been routinely administered to prevent disease in the cow.

Chapter 5

Dosage, Drug Effects, and Nonspecific Factors

The first cup moistens my lip and throat, the second cup breaks my loneliness, the third cup searches my barren entrail but to find therein some five thousand volumes of odd ideographs. The fourth cup raises a slight perspiration--all the wrong of life passes away through my pores. At the fifth cup I am purified; the sixth cup calls me to the realm of the immortals. The seventh cup--ah, but I could take no more! I only feel the breath of cool wind that raises my sleeves.

Lotung, a Chinese poet of the Tang dynasty,
in praise of tea (Kakuzo, 1928, p. 34)

Although we think of certain drugs as having characteristic effects, these effects can change drastically at different dosage levels, while the mechanism of action may remain the same. For example, alcohol is a nervous system depressant, but a little nip suppresses inhibitory neurons and may induce hyperexcitability for a while, whereas a good wallop suppresses the entire central nervous system, causing sedation, sleep, and possibly death. That is why the proverbial party-goer, tap-dancing on tabletops with a lampshade hat after four or five drinks, can be found snoring behind the sofa after eight or nine. Strychnine, a potent convulsant, has been shown to facilitate learning in animals at low dosages. The list of possible examples like these is endless. The point is, you must know the dosage to predict the behavioral effects of a drug. Even then there is a special problem in that the desired effects may be reduced or enhanced by other factors besides the drug action. For example, tension may be mitigated as much by a stroke of good fortune as it is by a dose of a tranquilizer, and in the final outcome these two factors are indistinguishable. One must therefore be cautious when ascribing effects to a drug.

DOSE-RESPONSE CURVES

The **doseresponse relationship** is the relationship between the amount of a drug and the magnitude of the effect the drug produces. It is influenced by many variables, but primary among them is body weight. A 95pound female is much more likely to be affected by a given dose than a 350pound one. To account for this, standard dosages are usually expressed in milligrams-per-kilogram (mg/kg) of body weight; that is, the amount you would receive if you weighed one kilogram. To get the suggested dose, multiply this factor by the weight of the subject (in kilograms). Thus, a 60 kg (132 lb.) male getting 420 mg a day is receiving 420 mg/60 kg, or 7 mg/kg a day. Framing the dosage this way makes it possible to achieve equal concentrations of a drug (or as close as possible) in the body tissues of individuals of different weights. As it stands, however, animals in laboratories are more often weighed to ascertain the accurate dosages than are people in the clinic. Drugs in solution are measured by the amount of drug per milliliter of fluid (mg/cc, or milligrams per cubic centimeter). **Dose-response curves** are always constructed on the basis of mg/kg.

Other variations commonly seen in this system are gm/ml (grams per milliliter) or μg/ml (micrograms per milliliter) and ng/ml or nanograms per milliliter. A milligram is a thousandth of a gram; a microgram, a millionth; and a nanogram, a billionth.

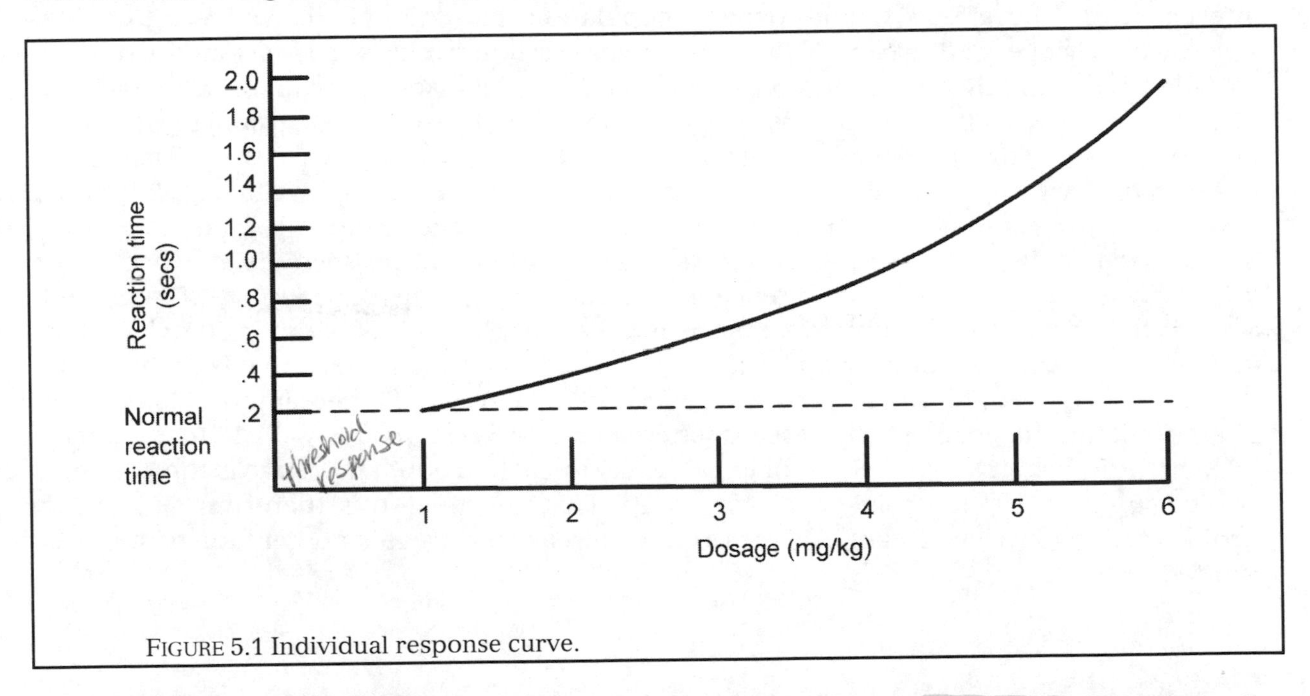

FIGURE 5.1 Individual response curve.

An **individual response curve** graphs the degree of a single drug effect on a single individual at varying dosages. First, a scale for quantifying the effect is established, then this is plotted against the scale of dosages. The resulting curve displays the individual's changing responses as dosages increase. It should be noted that some effects, like sleep, do not happen by degrees. An individual response curve would not be used in such cases (although related measures may be used, like the time it takes to fall asleep or sleep duration time).

Figure 5.1 shows an individual response curve for reaction time as doses of a hypothetical sedative are increased. The curve begins at the **threshold response**, the point where the first measurable effect is observed. The dosage at this point is the threshold dosage. Suppose we arrange a test of reaction time based on how quickly a subject on sedatives can hit a button after a light blinks on. Assuming the individual's normal response time to be about .19 seconds on this task, we see that at 1 mg/kg the response begins to slow as a result of the drug. The trend continues gradually as the dosage increases, until at 5 mg/kg it takes the individual almost a second and a half to respond to the stimulus.

A drug has a dose-response curve for each effect. For instance, an amphetamine has one curve for its appetite-suppressing effect and another for its euphoric effect. Ethanol (ethyl alcohol) has separate curves for excitation, sedation, and sleep duration.

The types of drug responses shown by these curves are unique to every individual and depend on a number of factors: the person's weight, diet, genetics, metabolism, and so forth. Ideally, a physician would work out these factors for every patient, if possible.

On the other hand, dose-response curves are usually not of much use to a researcher interested in drug effects for the general population. For example, if we were to invite several nondrinkers to a New Year's Eve party (all nondrinkers, so seasoned drinkers wouldn't have an advantage) and give them each three glasses of champagne, we would observe an array of behavioral effects as each individual responds uniquely to the same dose of the same drug. Because of this, individual response curves are of limited use to a researcher trying to discover how different dosages affect the general population. A **group drug-response curve** describes this information much better. To get this type of curve, once again a single effect is selected, and a number of test groups are formed. A different dosage of the drug is administered to each group. The dosages are then plotted against the percentage of individuals showing the desired drug effect in each group. For instance, a researcher might want to know what is the dosage necessary (viz., how many drinks are required) to put 10 percent, 30 percent, 50 percent, 80 percent, or 100 percent of a population to sleep. So the researcher creates 4 or 5 test groups with 10 to 15 people in each, administers a specific number of drinks to each group, and records the percentage of subjects that fall asleep in each group. This information is then graphed as the group-response curve. Usually, as the dosage increases, a greater percentage of subjects is affected.

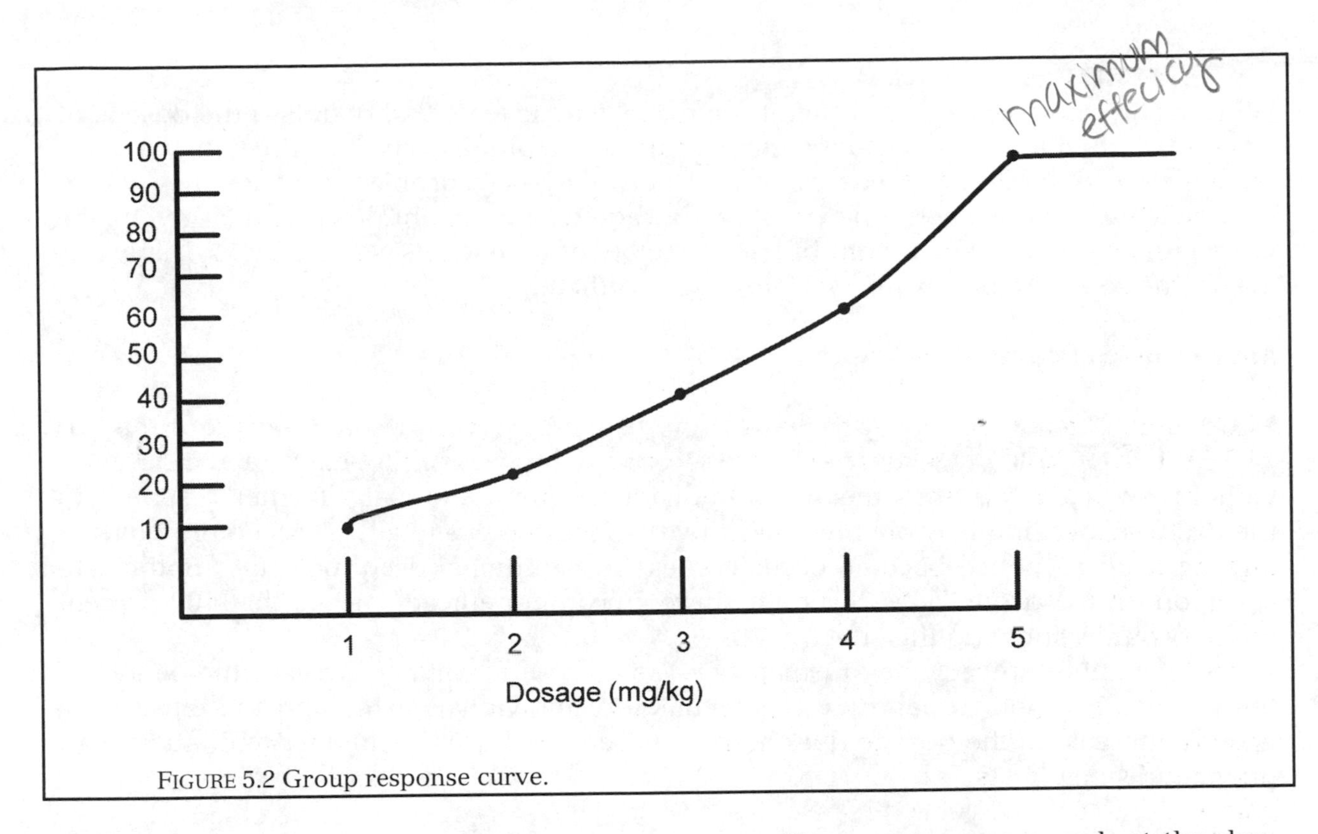

FIGURE 5.2 Group response curve.

Figure 5.2 shows a group dose-response curve. Five groups were used, at the dosages indicated. As soon as any individual in the groups exhibited the selected effect, this person was counted as part of the percentages. Ten percent of the 1 mg/kg group was affected, 20 percent of the 2 mg/kg group, and so forth, until at 5 mg/kg the entire sample showed the effect.

Slope

Three aspects of the dose-response curve are important. The first is the **slope** of the curve. In the individual dose-response curve, a gradual slope indicates that, as we increase the dosage for that subject, there is a gradual rise in the degree of response. This is evident in Figure 5.1. A steep slope at a certain point on an individual response curve indicates a sudden leap in the intensity of effect on a subject, at a slight increase in dosage.

In a group dose-response curve, a gradual slope means that, as dosage increases, the percentage of individuals showing the chosen effect also increases slowly. A steep slope indicates a sudden leap in the percentage of individuals affected, with only a slight increase in dosage. In Figure 5.2 it can be seen that the dosage increase between the 1 mg/kg and 2 mg/kg groups shows only a 10 percent gain in the number of subjects responding, while the same dosage increase between the 4 mg/kg and 5 mg/kg groups shows a 40 percent leap in respondents.

With this in mind, one can see that it is a mistake to assume that doubling the dosage of a drug will double the effect. Depending on the slope of the curve, the effect may quintuple or scarcely budge. Sometimes, steep slopes may be a problem because they represent delicate dosage levels where a slight dosage change might produce a large change in response. Considered in light of the variability of individuals' sensitivity to drugs, this makes the selection of the appropriate dosage difficult.

Maximum Efficacy

Maximum efficacy occurs at the upper end of the dose-response curve where the line plateaus. It indicates the dosage that is necessary to produce an effect fully. In an individual response curve, this means the individual cannot show any further response to the drug; this ceiling is probably caused by the fact that eventually all receptors governing the drug response become occupied, leaving additional drug molecules nothing to act upon. In the group dose-response curve, maximum efficacy means that 100 percent of the group is showing the effect.

At maximum efficacy, any further increase of dosage will not increase the degree of the effect (in an individual) or the percentage of individuals exhibiting the effect (in a group). Increasing the dosage does nothing except increase the number and intensity of unwanted side effects.

Potency

In everyday usage, when a drug is said to be potent, it means that a small amount produces strong or impressive effects. But, technically, **potency** is a relative value. The term is still a description of the amount of a drug but only in relation to another drug. If a certain dose of a drug produces a given effect, and we can produce the same effect with a smaller dose of another drug, the second drug is the more potent. On the dose-response chart, the curve of a more potent drug lies to the left of a less potent one.

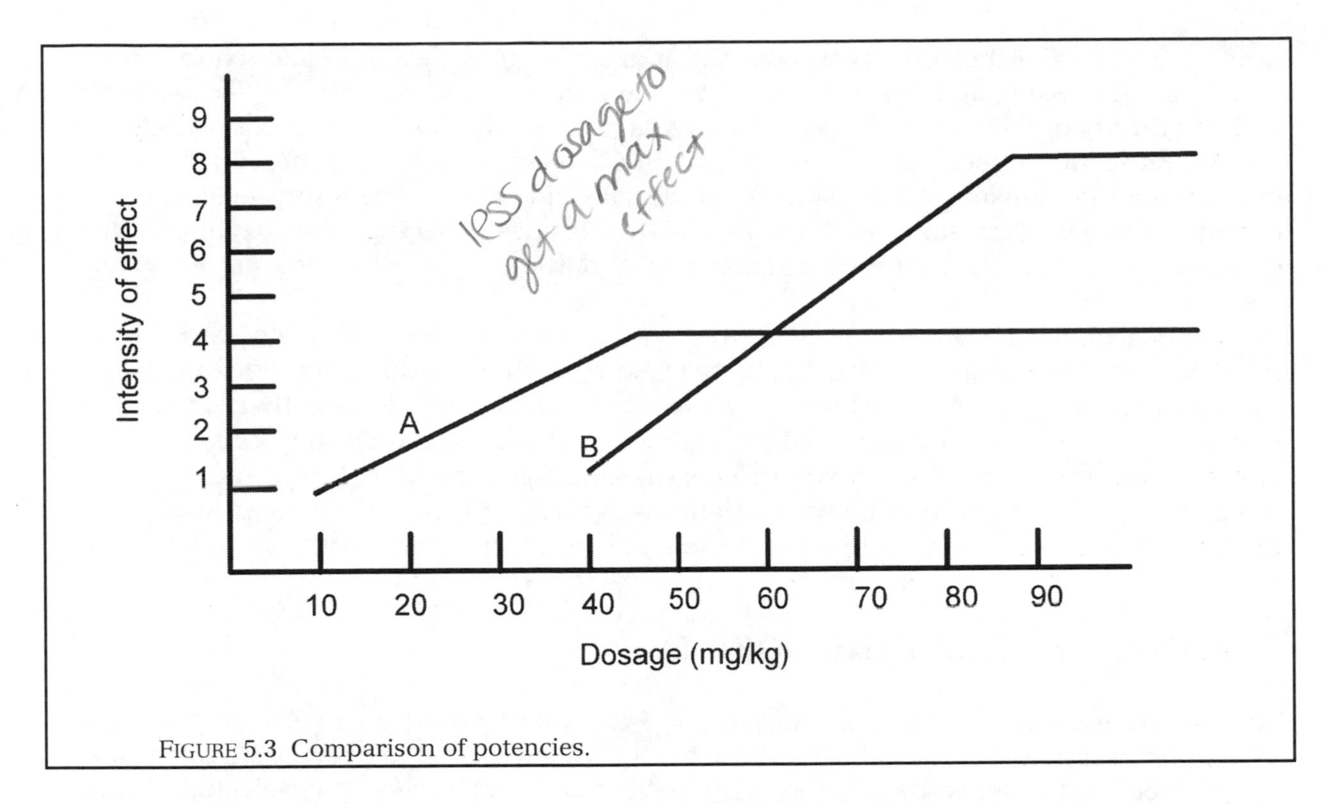

FIGURE 5.3 Comparison of potencies.

Potency has nothing to do with the effectiveness or maximum efficacy of a drug, only with the amount that is required to produce a certain degree of effect. In Figure 5.3, drug A shows a threshold response at 10 mg/kg, whereas drug B does not begin to act until 40 mg/kg have been administered. A is therefore more potent. However, the effect of A levels off at intensity 4, while B reaches intensity 7 before it plateaus. So, even though B is less potent and requires higher dosages to produce the desired effect (to get a 4point effect we need only 40 mg/kg of A but 60 mg/kg of B), B has a higher maximum efficacy. This demonstrates how potency does not describe the effectiveness of a drug, but only gives a sense of the proportion between the desired effect and the amount of drug required to produce it.

Potency is therefore not a factor in the choice of drugs, unless it is so low that an awkward quantity of the drug must be administered to get results. Advertisements touting a product for its potency (``One of our tablets equals two of theirs") are foisting an irrelevancy on the consumer, since the less potent drug may be cheaper and safer, it could have a higher maximum efficacy, and it could even have fewer negative side effects. Simply more of it is required.

SIDE EFFECTS

When one administers a drug, it is always with a selected effect in mind. No drug, however, is a magic bullet that whizzes to the site of action and cleanly relieves the problem;

it often has many other effects besides the intended one. These are called **side effects.** Sedatives, for instance, have been used as sleeping pills and as anticonvulsants in the prevention of epilepsy. If one takes sedatives as anticonvulsants, the induction of sleep is considered a side effect. But if one takes them as sleeping pills, then the anticonvulsant effect would be considered the side effect. Usually side effects are a nuisance, if not an outright danger. Tranquilizers such as Valium, besides relieving anxiety, often cause drowsiness as well, prompting warnings on the bottle like, "Do not operate heavy machinery."

In general, as the dosage of a drug increases, its side effects also increase. In fact, maximum efficacy sometimes cannot be reached because of undesirable side effects. The most common way to eliminate them is simply to lower the dosage. Another is to administer a separate medication expressly to counteract them. But to do this, of course, is to choose a potentially new set of side effects caused by the additional drug. For example, antipsychotic drugs given to mental patients cause tremors. To relieve the tremors, anticholinergic drugs are administered, but these in turn produce dry mouth and thirst.

EFFECTIVE AND LETHAL DOSAGE

The **effective dosage (ED)** is the dosage of a drug that produces a selected effect in a given percentage of people. The ED1 of a drug is the dose that produces the selected effect in 1 percent of a test group; the ED99 is the dose that produces the selected effect in 99 percent of the group, and so forth. Since only one effect is measured at a time, a drug has an ED for each of its distinct effects. The ED99 is used as the standard indication of a full group response, since there are often a few idiosyncratic individuals who do not respond to the drug. The ED1 is the same as the threshold dose for a particular effect.

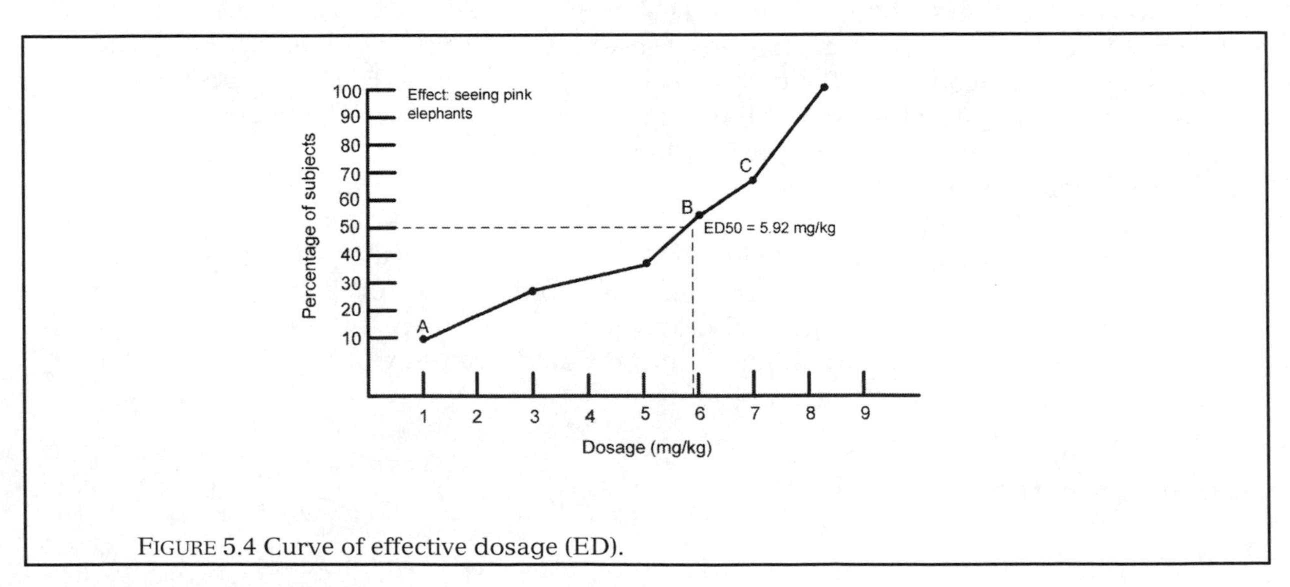

FIGURE 5.4 Curve of effective dosage (ED).

A typical way of plotting an ED is with a group response curve. The curve plots the dosage levels against the percentage of subjects in each test group who exhibit the chosen effect.

In Figure 5.4, 1 mg/kg is the ED10, in that 10 percent of the subjects see pink elephants at that dosage (point A). Seven mg/kg is the ED70 (point C). In most experiments, however, the standard reference point is the ED50, the dosage where 50 percent of the subjects show the effect. This is about 5.92 mg/kg (point B) for the drug in the graph.

The **lethal dosage (LD)** is the dosage that causes death. As with the ED, numbers are appended, so that the LD99 of a drug is the dose that kills 99 percent of the test group; the LD50 kills half, and so forth.

In animal studies, the relationship between the EDs and the LDs determines the safety margin of a drug for humans. At the ED99, we have the dosage that produces an effect in 99 percent of the animals in the group, and at the LD1, the dosage that kills 1 percent of the animals. Ideally the LD1 should be well above the ED99. The perfect drug is one that is selective in its effect, which means it has no significant side effects, treats 100 percent of the population at low dosages, and has a sky-high LD1. Unfortunately, some important drugs do not fall into this category. In fact, drugs almost always involve some risks of toxicity. One could say a drug is simply a low-dosage poison.

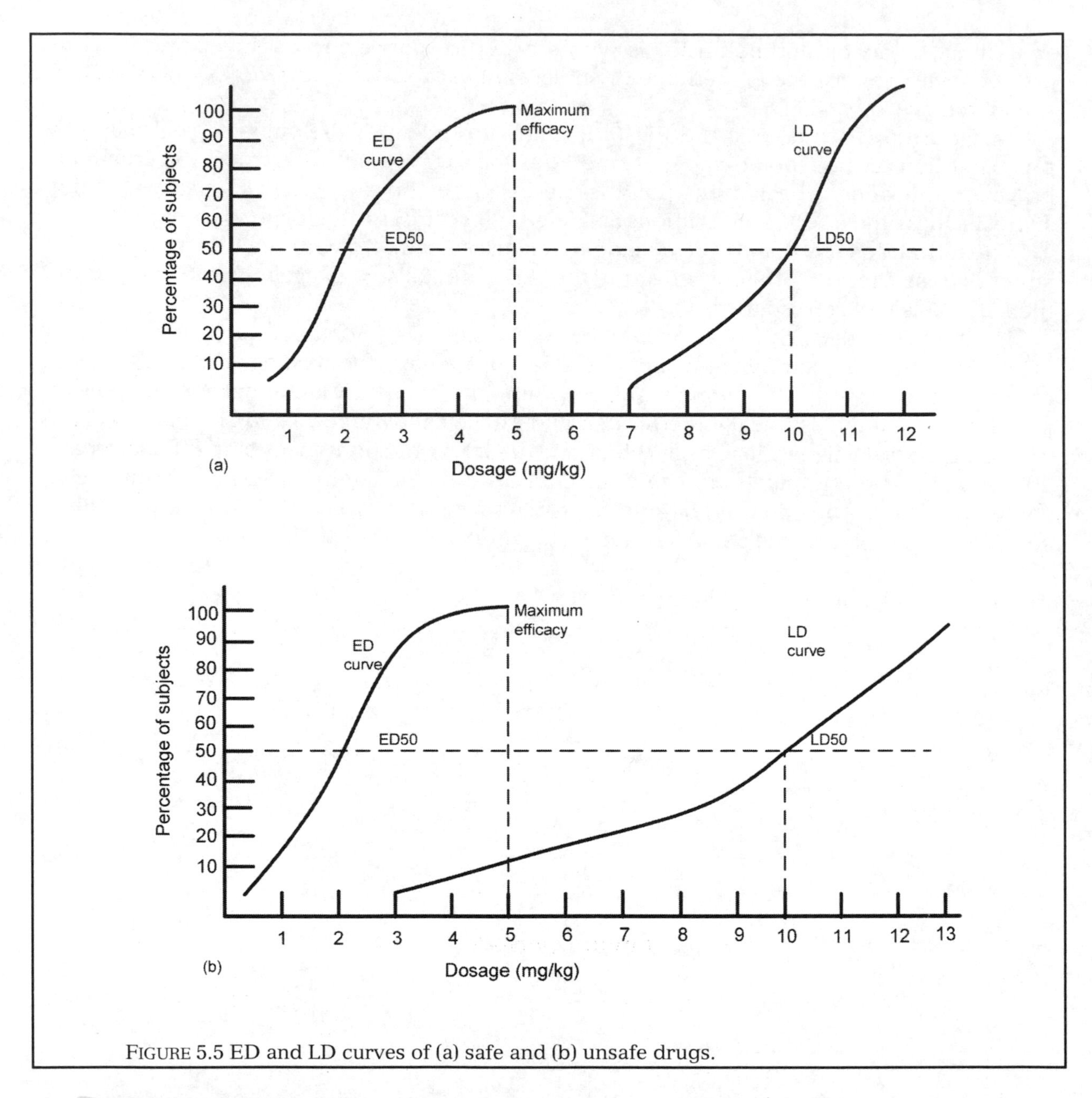

FIGURE 5.5 ED and LD curves of (a) safe and (b) unsafe drugs.

The **therapeutic index** is a measure of a drug's safety. The index consists of the LD50 divided by the ED50. A therapeutic index of 3 tells us that the 50 percent lethal dosage is only three times the 50 percent effective dosage. One milligram will produce the desired effect in half of the test group, but three milligrams will kill half of it. Is this a good risk? To find out, you should examine Figure 5.5, especially the slopes of the curves. Consider the situations in graphs A and B there.

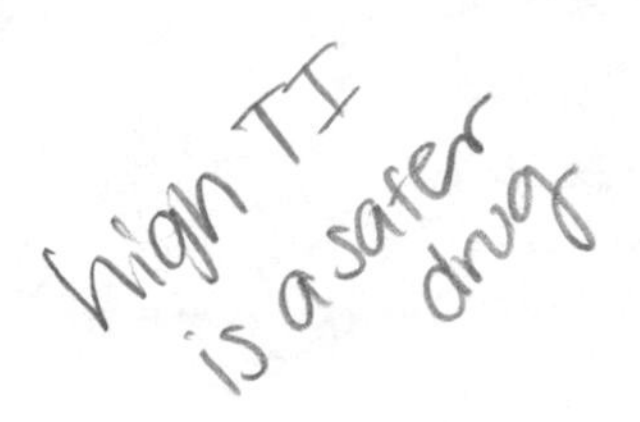

Graph A shows the dose-response curve for a chosen effect (ED curve) and the dose-response curve for lethality (LD curve) for the same drug. The therapeutic index is 5, because, reading along the dosage scale, you can see the LD50 (10 mg/kg) is five times the ED50 (2 mg/kg). At 5 mg/kg, 100 percent of the subjects show the desired effect; this is the dose for maximum efficacy. At this dosage, no subjects die, so the drug is safe. The first death does not occur until 7 mg/kg, the beginning of the lethal dosages. But now look at graph B.

In graph B, we have essentially identical conditions in that the therapeutic index is 5. However, the slope of the lethality curve is different, so that at 5 mg/kg (maximal efficacy on the ED curve), 10 percent of the subjects have died. Surely, this drug is a risky proposition.

In practical terms, a therapeutic index of 20 or more indicates a relatively safe drug, although an index of 100 or more is to be preferred; even that, however, is no surefire guarantee of safety. Marketed drugs typically have a therapeutic index based on the LD1 divided by the ED99. This ratio gives one a sense of the space between the curves—between the peak of the desired effect and the first death. In this case, if the index were 3, one milligram might treat 99 percent of the population, but three milligrams would kill 1 percent.

There is a therapeutic index for every effect of a drug. For instance, sedatives have different ED curves and different margins of safety for sleep and for inhibiting seizures. Generally, the higher the dose needed for therapy, the higher the risk of toxicity.

The parameters for safety in the use of medications vary with the situation. In some drugs used to fight cancer, the ED50 and LD50 are regrettably close. Digitoxin, a heart stimulant, has a dangerously low index; patients using it must be monitored. In this case, there is no safer choice. However, most psychoactive drugs have a safe therapeutic index, and side effects are the primary consideration in controlling dosage.

TIME COURSE

The **time course** of a drug is the time between the moment of administration and the end of the effect. This includes the **latency period,** the time between administration and the onset of action, when the effect has not yet appeared. A common counterculture anecdote of the sixties would recount how someone who had taken a hit of LSD would wait and wait for the effect, decide the acid was bad, and go out to dinner with the family instead, only to discover during the soup course an hour later that the centerpiece had a halo and the trip was beginning.

Slow absorption of a drug means a long latency period. As a rule of thumb, increasing the dosage shortens the latency period and prolongs the duration of the effect. The duration also depends on metabolism, excretion, redistribution, and one's tolerance to the drug.

Figure 5.6 shows the effect on an individual of a single dose of a decongestant over the course of several hours. Superimposed on the course of the effect, from a different graph, is the curve of the blood concentration in milligrams per milliliters (dotted line),

After two hours, maximum efficacy has been reached, but absorption continues and blood levels increase until they peak at three hours. At four hours, both curves are subsiding.

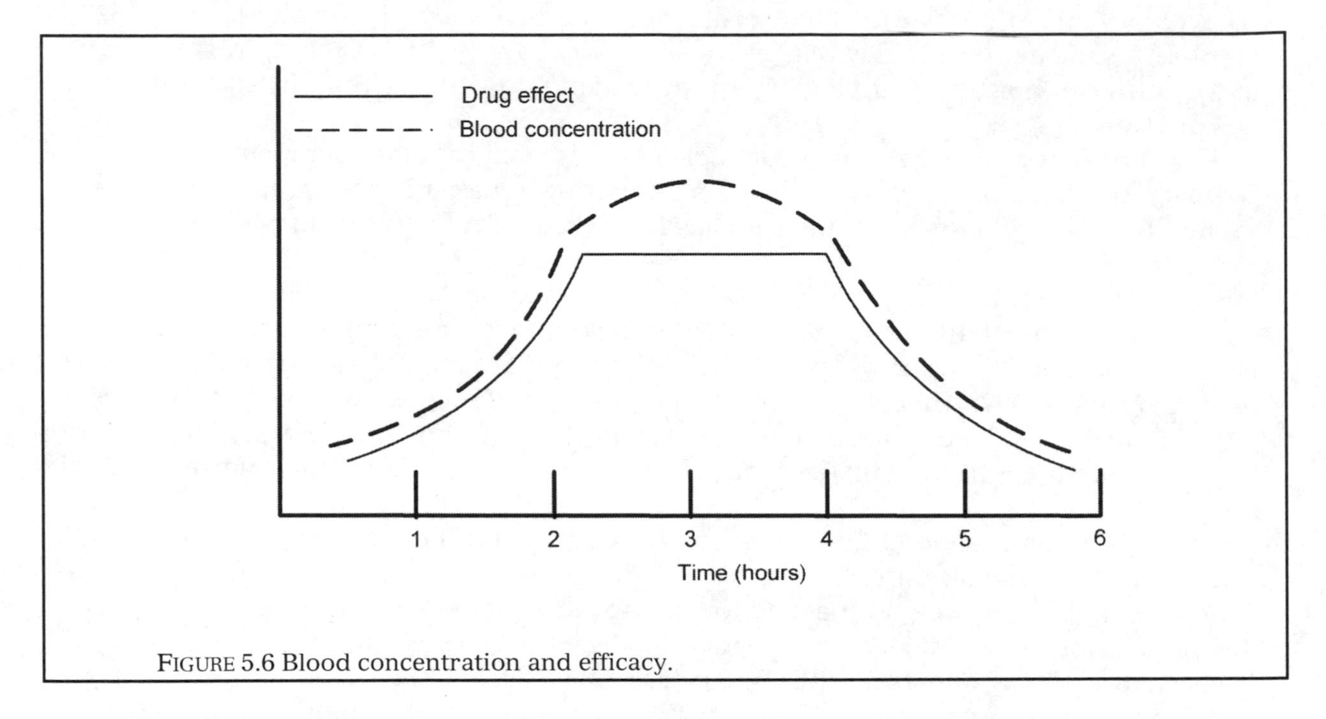

FIGURE 5.6 Blood concentration and efficacy.

The hump representing an extra rise in blood concentration after maximal efficacy here is pharmacologically unnecessary and is to be avoided, if possible. It would be more efficient if the blood concentration and effect leveled off parallel to each other and ran that way a number of hours before subsiding. A device designed to accomplish this is the time-release capsule. It provides a stiff initial dose of a drug to get a good level of effect, then small additional doses to tailor and prolong the effect, eliminating the need for blood levels to soar over the point of maximum efficacy (Ray, 1983, pp. 127-129). Oral time-release capsules have been developed that can maintain the duration of effect for up to ten hours. Some of the surgically implanted devices discussed under subcutaneous administration (see page xx) can maintain desired blood levels of a drug up to several months.

Figure 5.7 shows two more realistic curves of the time courses of drugs, comparing subjective effects with the blood concentrations of alcohol and cocaine.

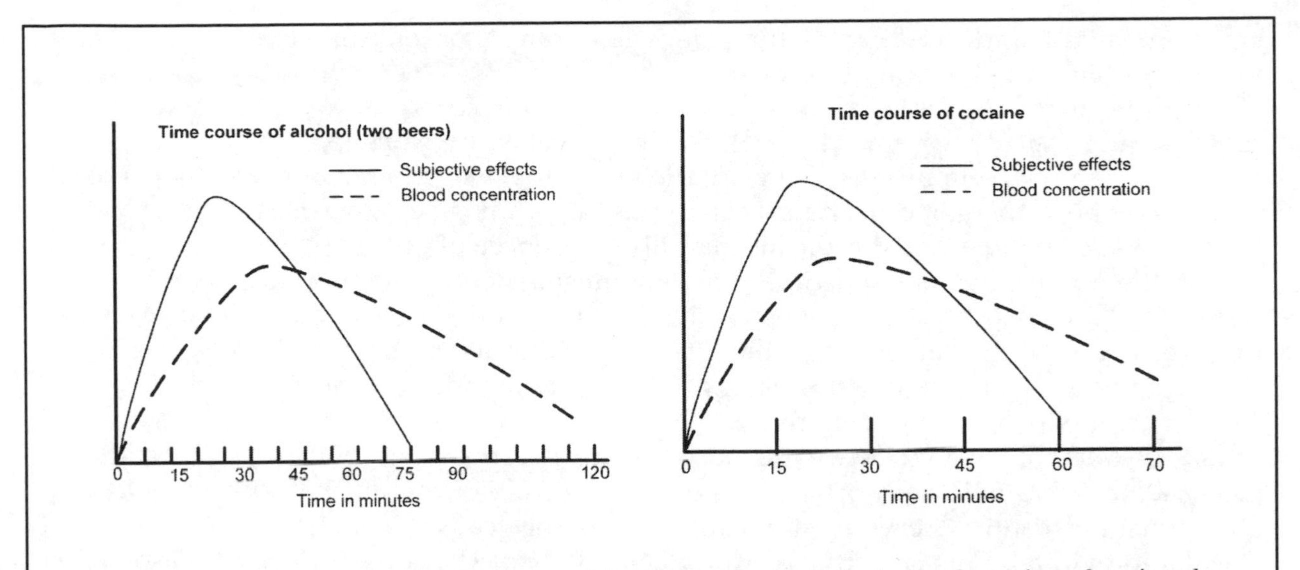

FIGURE 5.7 Schematic representation of the time courses of alcohol and cocaine, showing the curve of subjective effects superimposed on the curve for blood concentrations. Notice that the subjective effects of a dose of cocaine are falling steeply while blood concentrations are still rising.

The time a drug lasts in the body is usually indicated by its half-life, the amount of time it takes for the maximum blood concentration of a drug to drop to half. Usually, the drop is due to metabolism and excretion of the drug, but it can also be due to distribution. Some drugs leave the bloodstream soon after administration for storage sites in tissues. In that case, we refer to its **distribution half-life** to indicate that the drug is still present and active in the body, although it has temporarily disappeared in large part from the blood.

VARIABILITY

Variability, the fourth characteristic of a dose-response curve (along with slope, maximum efficacy, and potency) is a pharmacologist's nightmare. It means that a given dose of any drug will vary in its effect on individuals. A dose-response curve is reliable insofar as it applies to a single individual in a carefully controlled situation or to the average individual in a given population. But the group curve is misleading at best in predicting the effect of a drug on any given individual. In addition, some people or animals may have unpredictable and unique individual reactions.

Unusual responses to drugs fall into several categories. Overreactions to drugs can be of two types. Sometimes individuals respond to doses of drugs that would have no effect on most people. Schizophrenics, for instance, react with psychotic episodes to small doses of amphetamine, doses that would have no effect on the average person. This is called **hypersensitivity** or **supersensitivity.** Allergic reactions may also be considered here; they involve symptoms such as drops in blood pressure, bronchial constriction, hives, and swelling of the skin, membranes, or organs. These same doses would not have an effect on other people.

Another form of overreaction occurs when someone reacts unexpectedly to a normal dose as though it were a very large dose. This is called **hyperreactivity.** Hyperreactive people pose a problem because they are the ones most likely to have severe toxic effects at points where the slope of the dose-response curve is steep; that is, the point where slight dosage changes could radically magnify the degree of the effect.

On the other hand, some people show an unusual degree of insensitivity to a normal dose of a drug. A person under-responsive to one drug is likely to be under-responsive to other drugs of the same class. For instance, a sober alcoholic tends to be resistant to the sedative effects of barbiturates. As we will see in the next section, this is cross-tolerance, one form of **hyporeactivity.**

Idiosyncratic responses are incongruous or unexpected reactions that are unique to an individual and occur at normal dosages. A typical idiosyncratic response would be a case where a central nervous stimulant inexplicably causes depression or sleep in a normal individual. This is also a **paradoxical response,** because it produces a reaction that is opposite to what one would expect. However, paradoxical responses can be general (experienced by many or all users), whereas idiosyncratic responses are by definition individual. Allergies, a form of hypersensitivity, could also be considered idiosyncratic.

Variability in drug response necessitates that, whenever possible, the dosage should be individualized. Too often, this procedure is overlooked for convenience's sake, and patients might take the wrong dosages for weeks. Therefore, prescription drug effects should be monitored by patients themselves and reported regularly and promptly to the attending physician.

TOLERANCE

[8/31/05]

The addict is surrounded with slopes. Impossible to keep the spirit on the heights.

Jean Cocteau (1958, p. 63)

Tolerance is a general term used to describe the observation that an organism may begin to react less and less, or not at all, to the usual dose of a drug. For example, an unchanging daily dose of alcohol or amphetamines will progressively lessen in effect, until the effect is negligible or short-lived, and the user will approach a normal state of functioning again. If the user wants to re-experience stronger effects, like those of first use, the dose has to be increased. A normal effective dose of amphetamine is about 10 milligrams, but an addict can take as much as 1700 milligrams and suffer no ill effects. This is tolerance.

Notice that the term *tolerance* does not refer to any specific mechanism for this adaptation. In fact, several mechanisms may be involved. So far, two main types have been identified: tolerance involving the metabolism of the drug, and tolerance at the level of individual neurons. The first type, **metabolic tolerance**, or **disposition tolerance**, which we have already discussed in detail, occurs when a drug passing through the liver induces the production of the enzymes that metabolize it, and the increased enzyme level means more drug is required to achieve an effect.

The second main type of tolerance involves particular nerve cells altering their functioning to adapt to a drug; this is called **neuronal tolerance** or **cellular tolerance.** A prevailing theory holds that neural systems will act to maintain equilibrium in their normal operations and so will adapt to any disruptions or imbalances, such as the constant presence of a drug visited on them by habitual users. For example, sedatives like alcohol work by depressing neural functions, so, over time, neurons counter by increasing their excitability (they might synthesize more transmitter or increase the number of receptors, for instance). Once the system has accommodated to the new conditions, it takes a higher dose of sedatives to depress it once more and produce an equivalent intoxication. The neurons respond by becoming even more excitable and holding the balance at a higher level, and the situation escalates. From the user's perspective, this simply means that, at a given dosage, the effects decline, and more of the drug is needed to produce the same results as before.

Other kinds of tolerance can be elaborated. **Behavioral tolerance** occurs when the subject, although under the influence of a drug, develops the ability to behave normally. This has been observed in laboratory experiments. A pigeon injected with THC (the active ingredient in marijuana) abandons its feeding regimen. It shows signs of malaise, and its pecking at a button to get corn is disrupted. If we treat the pigeon with the same dosage for several days, after about a week its feeding habits return to normal even though the bird has high blood levels of THC. The bird has learned to cope with the intoxication. In this case, performance returns to normal despite the presence of the physiological effects of the drug.

A special form of behavioral tolerance is known as **conditioned tolerance**. Aside from tolerance based on direct physiological changes, this is a discrete form connected to the user's environment. Suppose that a laboratory animal is given a drug, always within the same environment, and develops tolerance. If we maintain all the drug-taking conditions, including the dosage, and simply move the animal to a new environment, tolerance is reduced (that is, the drug has more of an effect). Therefore, some degree of tolerance is connected to environmental cues. This may have serious implications for human drug abusers. As their tolerance rises in a familiar environment, they may escalate the dose to maintain drug effects. If they move to a new environment, however, tolerance is lessened, and the dose they have become used to can act as an overdose, perhaps a lethal one (Siegel et al., 1982).

Cross-tolerance occurs when the use of one drug produces tolerance for another. Enzyme induction in the liver is one reason for this happening. If one drug raises the P-450 level, tolerance may show for other drugs metabolized by P-450. But not all cross-tolerance occurs this way. For instance, by some other mechanism LSD increases one's tolerance for mescaline. There is a cross-tolerance between alcohol and marijuana, also, which remains a mystery (Newman, Lutz, & Domino, 1974; Newman et al., 1972).

Marijuana has been suspected of producing a **reverse tolerance,** that is, increased rather than decreased responses to identical doses. Beginning marijuana users might not get "stoned" until they smoke a half dozen times or more. Reverse tolerance might be due to the fact that the users learn to focus their attention on the appropriate cues of intoxication as they familiarize themselves with a drug's effects. Or it might have a physiological basis. For instance, a drug like marijuana is slow to metabolize; it may take as long as a week to clear the system. If a second dose is taken while some of the previous dose remains, it would take less of the drug to achieve an equivalent effect. This is an example of a cumulative effect, which will be explained in the following section.

Tachyphylaxis refers to the swift development of tolerance within minutes or hours, often between the first two or three doses. The specific mechanism is unknown, but it is possible that the first dose may occupy all available receptors, or it may release the available supply of some endogenous substance (e.g., a neurotransmitter) leaving a second dose nothing to do.

It is possible for tolerance to vary for one of the effects of a drug but not another. For example, tolerance develops much sooner to the euphoric action of morphine than to its constipatory action. In other words, the effective constipating dose stays low, while the effective euphoric dose rises, so that abusers eventually suffer severe constipation to stay high. By the same token, because such mechanisms are distinct, increasing the dosage might poison the less tolerant system. Those who smoke crack, a purified form of cocaine, trying with higher and higher doses to override a rapidly rising tolerance to euphoria, can threaten the heart, which has a slower tolerance to the effects.

Tolerance may be accompanied by **physical dependence,** which means the body requires the drug to continue functioning normally, and intense physical disturbances manifest when administration is suspended. We described above a situation where an uneasy equilibrium is maintained at an artificially high level as the habitual user depresses the nerve cells, and the cells enliven themselves to counter the depressant activity. Eventually, the presence of the drug is required to keep the cells functioning normally. Withholding the drug upsets the equilibrium, and nothing prevents the overresponsive neurons from firing in excess. This is what happens when alcohol, a depressant, is suddenly withheld from alcoholics; the neurons over-fire, causing seizures and possible death. The physiological imbalance and behavioral effects that result from the withdrawal of a drug are called **withdrawal symptoms;** these are the hallmark of physical dependence, and the degree of dependence can be judged by their severity.

Because of the nature of the compensation we have just described, many withdrawal symptoms show as the opposite of drug effects. Known as **rebound effects,** these are the body's compensations unmasked in the absence of the drug. The alcoholic, whose system has compensated for depressants by becoming more excitable, shows excitement when the drug is withdrawn. Amphetamine users, whose systems have compensated for stimulation by becoming less responsive, fall asleep; their appetites, once suppressed, become voracious. The easy breathing of the cocaine sniffer grows sluggish. The constipated bowels of the morphine abuser give way to diarrhea. The catalog is a long one. Such rebound effects may be considered a type of delayed side effect, and the desire to avoid their unpleasantness has a significant role in keeping users on the drug. After all, they are the exact opposite of what the user experiences by taking the drug, and they are often strongly expressed; the drug may appear in the light of a medicine by comparison.

The liability for developing a physical dependence on psychoactive drugs is well known. However, physical dependence comes from more than just avoidance of withdrawal. Some evidence suggests that tolerance and physical dependence are distinct processes arising from different sites of action, with different mechanisms of action in the brain (Koob & Bloom, 1988). We will take this up in detail in a later chapter.

Many definitions of **compulsive substance abuse** (drug addiction) have been set forth, but most involve some or all of the following five factors: (1) the user feels a compulsion to obtain and take the drug; (2) the user has a tendency to increase the dosage; (3) there is both a psychological and physical dependence on the effects; (4) the drug has a detrimental effect on users, their close relations, and society; and (5) users show withdrawal upon abstinence (Kalant, 1966, p. 78). You might note that addiction differs from physical dependence; for instance, newborns may be completely physically dependent on a drug, but they are not considered addicts. According to the principles above, addiction can be defined to some extent as a set of behaviors.

Probably the closest one can come to an official, standardized definition of addiction is that found in the *Diagnostic and Statistical Manual of Mental Disorders*, published by the American Psychiatric Association. This definition is the one generally referred to by physicians, psychiatrists, and health care professionals for diagnosing, treating, and placing patients within the health care system. The basic criteria of this definition are shown in Table 5.1.

TABLE 5.1 Criteria for the Definition of Substance Dependence According to the *Diagnostic and Statistical Manual of Mental Disorders*.

A maladaptive pattern of substance use, leading to clinically significant impairment or distress, as manifested by three (or more) of the following, occurring at any time in the same 12-month period:

1. Tolerance, as defined by either of the following:
   a. A need for markedly increased amounts of the substance to achieve intoxication or desired effect
   b. Markedly diminished effect with continued use of the same amount of the substance
2. Withdrawal, as manifested by either of the following:
   a. The characteristic withdrawal syndrome for the substance
   b. The same (or a closely related) substance is taken to relieve or avoid withdrawal symptoms
3. The substance is often taken in larger amounts or over a longer period than was intended
4. There is a persistent desire or unsuccessful efforts to cut down or control substance use

5. A great deal of time is spent in activities necessary to obtain the substance (e.g., visiting multiple doctors or driving long distances), use the substance (e.g., chain smoking), or recover from its effects
6. Important social, occupational, or recreational activities are given up or reduced because of substance use
7. The substance use is continued despite knowledge of having a persistent or recurrent physical or psychological problem that is likely to have been caused or exacerbated by the substance (e.g., current cocaine use despite recognition of cocaine-induced depression, or continued drinking despite recognition that an ulcer was made worse by alcohol consumption)

Source: American Psychiatric Association (1994) *Diagnostic and Statistical Manual of Mental Disorders* (4/e) Wash. D.C., American Psychiatric Association

The formation of drug addictions is not well understood; some people can use drugs on a long-term basis, yet not become dependent or addicted. Many factors seem to contribute, such as possible genetic factors; personality characteristics; misfortunes, anxieties and other stresses; euphoric drug effects; and fear of withdrawal symptoms.

COMBINED EFFECTS

Administering two drugs together alters the pattern of each drug's individual effect; the outcome is a combined drug effect. Combined effects fall into several categories (see Figure 5.8a). The effect is said to be **additive** when a second drug simply augments the effect of the first, as though it were more of the same drug. Thus, 10 mg of drug A plus 10 mg of drug B would be equivalent to 20 mg of drug A. In its effect, the second drug appears to be simply an additional dose of the first. A **synergistic** effect (Figure 5.8b) occurs when the combined effect is tremendously enhanced beyond the simple addition of individual effects. In this case, each drug may double or triple the effect of the other. Two sleeping pills (50 mg of barbiturates) and a sixpack of beer, taken within one hour, could be fatal because of their synergistic action. If the effect were additive, it would take about 6 pills and 24 beers in an hour to prove fatal. **Potentiation** is a type of synergistic effect, whereby drug A would be completely ineffective alone, but taken with drug B, it produces a synergistic effect.

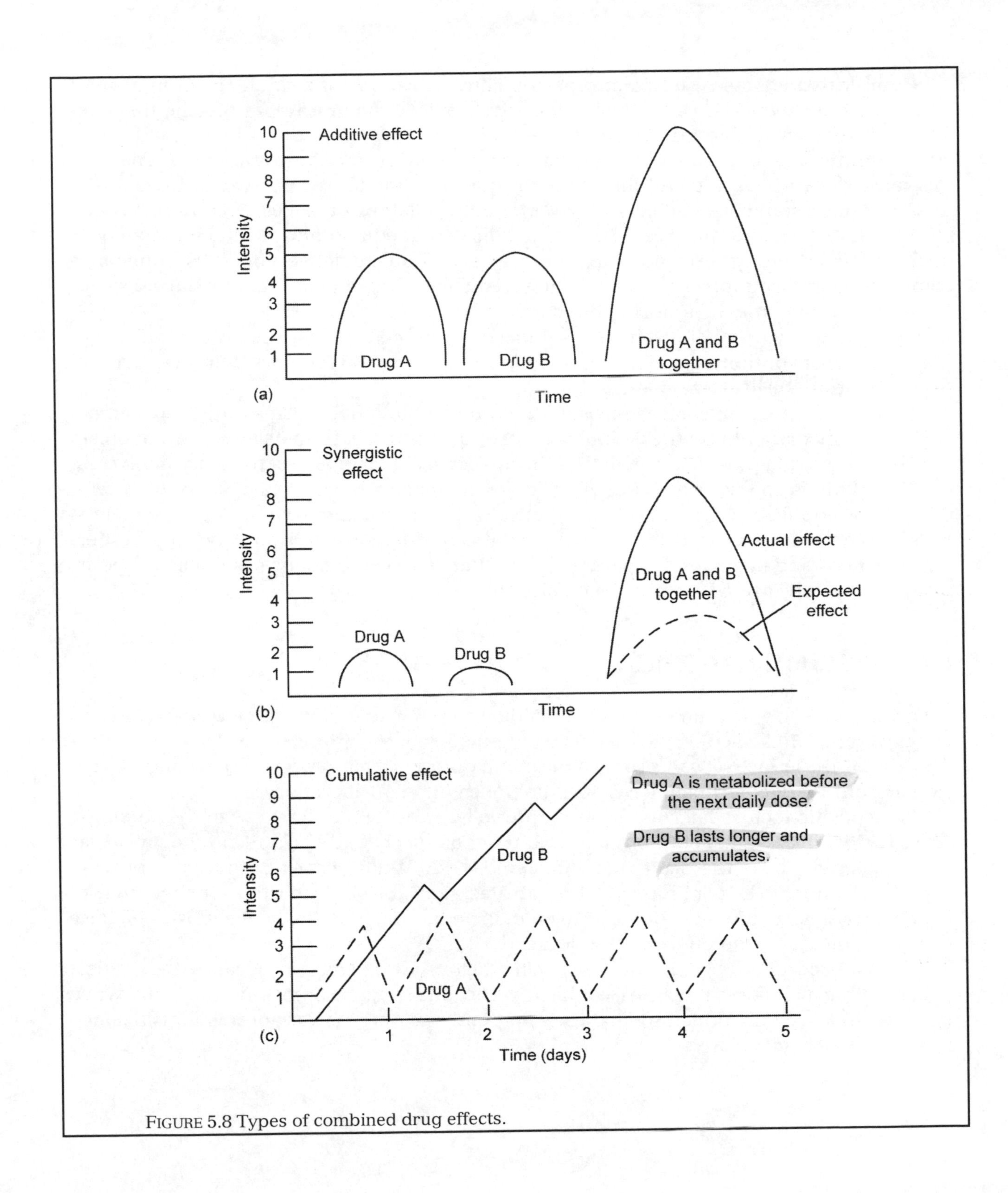

FIGURE 5.8 Types of combined drug effects.

Cumulative effects result from repeated administrations of a single drug, in a situation where the second dose of the drug is given before the first wears off, the third before the second wears off, et cetera (see Figure 5.8c). Here the effect builds until equilibrium is reached between the administration and excretion of the drug. The time this takes depends on the half-life of the drug and on the interval between doses. If the body cannot establish equilibrium, and the accumulation outpaces excretion, toxicity might result. To avoid this, the dose can be adjusted at equilibrium to match the amount being excreted. Long-term administration to achieve cumulative effects is sometimes complicated by drug tolerance, by the inconvenience of taking medications during sleeping hours, or by patients' ignoring directions.

In general, a variety of mechanisms underlie combined effects, among them distribution and redistribution patterns, competition for binding to receptors, and activation of or competition for liver enzymes.

Combined effects may also consist of the reduction of effects. An antagonism can occur when one drug blocks the action of another and detracts from its effect. Antagonism may be of several kinds. It is *chemical* if the molecules of drug A deactivate the molecules of drug B, as is the case with some antidotes to snake venom. It is *pharmacological* if drug A monopolizes or effectively competes for receptors and leaves drug B homeless, as is the case with naloxone and heroin. And it is *physiological* if drug A occupies different receptors and activates a separate system that can overcome the system activated by drug B, as is the case with caffeine and alcohol.

NONSPECIFIC FACTORS

A variety of factors can influence an individual's response to a drug. Those unrelated to chemical and pharmacological actions are termed **nonspecific factors**. Diverse as they are, any of these factors can produce dramatic differences in drug response and can seriously confound experimental results if not taken into consideration.

Nonspecific factors fall roughly under three headings: (1) differences in the condition of individual organisms, both physical and psychological, (2) differences in the particular environments where the drug is administered, and (3) differences in the types of tasks presented under test conditions in the lab (task variables). A fourth category, that of drug variables, could be added; it would include considerations like dose-response curves, combined drug effects, and tolerance.

Some researchers claim that *nonspecific factors* are misnamed because they reflect specific pharmacological actions we have yet to understand. Someday, they say, when drug actions are fully understood, these apparently extraneous variables will be included in a drug's pharmacology.

VARIABLES IN THE ORGANISM

Weight

All other considerations being equal, a smaller organism responds to less of a drug than a larger organism. We have already discussed the weighing of subjects and the expression of drug dosages in mg/kg in some detail in the preceding chapter.

Interspecies Differences

A drug response that occurs in one species of an organism might not occur in another. What is true of animal drug responses might not be true of humans, and some such discrepancies compromise the use of lab animals as models for humans. For instance, a rabbit can eat belladonna alkaloids safely; in humans these produce amnesia, hallucinations, and death. Low doses of morphine sedate humans and most other species, but they stimulate cats, pigs, cows, and sheep (Barnes & Eltherington, 1965). The plasma half-life of caffeine is 3 to 5 hours in humans; in the monkey, it is 3.2 hours; in the rabbit, 1.6 hours; and in the mouse, 0.7 hours (Sawynok & Yaksh, 1993).

Intraspecies Differences

Drug response may vary among strains or races within species lines. The most frequently used subjects for experiments dealing with intraspecies differences are inbred strains of mice. Between strains, the responses of individual mice may vary for drugs, including ethanol (alcohol), pentobarbital (a sedative), and tranquilizers.

In humans, metabolic differences for alcohol have been shown between Asians and Caucasians (Kalow, Goedde & Agarwal, 1986). Chinese, Japanese, and some native Americans show a higher rate of metabolism (Agarwal & Goedde, 1986). (Some Native Americans are in Asian bloodlines, since their ancestors crossed the Bering Strait from East Asia about 30,000 years ago.) Many Asians also show an increased sensitivity to alcohol, manifested by increased heart rates and facial flushing. Data seem to indicate that this is due to a lower level of aldehyde dehydrogenase in the liver, which is an enzyme in the chain of alcohol metabolism (Schaefer, 1986). About 50 percent of Asians show low levels of the enzyme (Goedde et al., 1985). It appears that in these cases, alcohol is metabolized rapidly early in the chain of biotransformations, but the process then stalls at the aldehyde dehydrogenase phase, due to lack of that enzyme, allowing an accumulation of alcohol byproducts to cause the slight adverse effects of increased heart rate and facial flushing.

Sex and Hormonal States

Hormones can also influence drug response. Toxicity studies done by Calabrese (1985, pp. 5-45) have shown male and female rats to respond to drugs differently in a number of areas: protein-binding, excretion, enzyme activity, drug metabolism, and separation of fluids in the kidneys. In 1982, the American Petroleum Institute released findings that exposure to uncombusted, unleaded gasoline caused a dose-dependent renal (kidney) cancer in male, but not female, rats (Calabrese, 1985, pp. 5-45). A similar effect has been noted regarding mercury toxicity. Male rats show kidney tissue damage when exposed to mercury, but if the males are castrated (cutting off the supply of sex hormones) and "feminized" with the female hormone estrogen, this eliminates the effect (Harber & Jennings, 1964). In another instance, a lab disaster at the National Cancer Institute in 1949, during which many strains of mice were exposed to chloroform, revealed that many of the males died from kidney toxicity, while females remained unaffected. Follow-up studies confirmed the effect and showed that castration alone was enough to abolish the toxicity (Russell, 1955; Derringer, Dunn, & Heston, 1953). (It turned out, though, that this had already been documented by Eschenbrenner and Miller in 1945.) Recent studies reveal that women achieve higher blood concentrations of alcohol than men after equivalent doses, and that women develop alcoholic liver disease more readily than men. The metabolism of alcohol in the stomach by the enzyme alcohol dehydrogenase is a factor in this effect; women show lower levels of alcohol dehydrogenase activity in the stomach than do men (Frezza et al., 1990).

Age

Physiologically, children are not just miniature adults, they are practically different organisms. Of course, their lower body weight demands smaller dosages, but they also show other differences, such as a different acid-base distribution in their body compartments and a different rate of metabolism. It has been shown that mild stimulants like caffeine and theophylline, given to treat the respiratory interruptions of apnea, show different metabolic patterns in newborns and are excreted very slowly (Aranda et al., 1981). Moreover, the enzymes and blood-brain barrier of infants may not have been fully formed. All these factors contribute to altered drug responses.

The elderly are sometimes more similar to children in their drug response than to adults. Their acid-base patterns also differ, such as in their stomachs, which are more alkaline than those of younger people, causing many oral drugs to respond differently. (Aspirin is one example; the stomachs of elderly people absorb aspirin more slowly because of increased alkalinity.) Respiration, metabolism, and excretion are naturally slowed in the elderly, and this too can alter drug response. In some instances, drug effects that are temporary in the young can be permanent in the old. For example, in aged animals, reserpine produces unduly long depressions. This is probably because it takes an elderly system much longer to repair the parts of neurons damaged by reserpine. In some cases, permanent damage and depression ensue.

Disease

Diseases of all sorts—of the liver, kidneys, lungs, heart—can retard the circulation, distribution, metabolism, or excretion of a drug, thereby prolonging or diminishing its action. The liver and kidneys are especially susceptible to damage, since so many toxic materials pass through them. Impairment might come from diseases associated with aging, like the reduced blood flow resulting from hardening of the arteries (atherosclerosis). Poor digestion might cause nutritional problems, which can lead to faulty protein synthesis or enzyme functions; these impediments in turn affect metabolic and excretory processes and can prolong the activity of drugs in the circulation, with possibly toxic results. Impairments can also come from drugs themselves, as is the case with cirrhosis of the liver, produced by the overuse of alcohol. In the case of cirrhosis, alcohol gradually gains destructive power by damaging the organ that inactivates it; eventually, an alcoholic with a cirrhotic liver can become intoxicated by a single drink.

Nutrition

Nutrition is another important variable influencing drug reactions. Malnutrition can impoverish the materials needed in enzyme systems. Fasting can shift the rate of absorption. Some foods (brussel sprouts, cabbage, and charcoal-broiled beef) have been shown to alter drug metabolism (Anderson, Conney & Kappas, 1986). Combined drug and food interactions may also constitute a problem, as is the case with cheese and certain antidepressants, which can cause a toxic or even a lethal reaction.

It might also be mentioned that in some studies, what may appear to be ethnic differences in drug response may in fact be due to dietary differences between cultures.

Biorhythms

Biorhythms are natural, recurring cycles of bodily processes and activities over a period of time. They reflect an interplay between an organism and its environment--as in our responsiveness to cycles of light and temperature changes--and this sometimes plays a part in drug response (Moore-Ede, Sulzman, & Fuller, 1982, p. 318-378). Rodents are nocturnal animals; their metabolism is higher at night than during the day. Given a sedative like phenobarbital during daylight hours, rats will sleep longer than if the same dose were given at night, because they metabolize it more slowly during the day. This can cause some drugs, like the stimulant nikethamide, to become toxic (or more toxic than normal). A dose of three hundred milligrams of nikethamide given at 2:00 p.m. kills 67 percent of the test animals, whereas at 2:00 A.M. it kills only 33 percent, because its effect is impeached by quicker metabolism (Carlsson & Serin, 1950). On the average, the human body tolerates alcohol best during the late afternoon and evening and is most susceptible from 3 to 5 A.M. (Bruce, 1977, p. 332). The duration of anesthesia and analgesia (pain reduction) vary, depending on what time of day drugs are given; Figure 5.9 shows the durations of anesthesia and numbness in two dental drugs, varying according to the time of administration (Aschoff & Wever, 1981). Given the data depicted there, you might want to schedule your dental appointments soon after lunch.

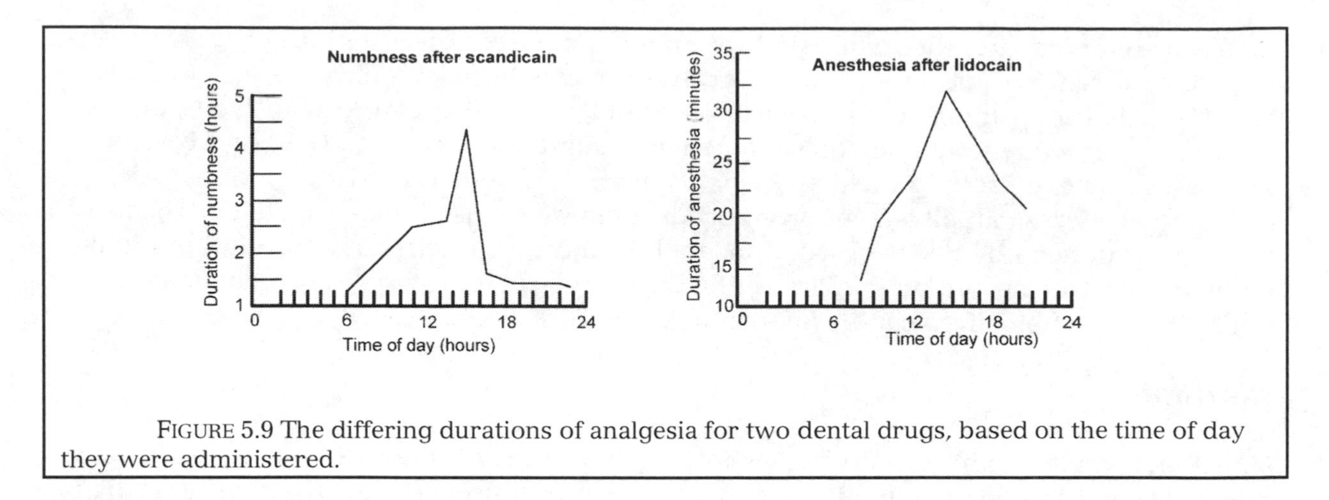

FIGURE 5.9 The differing durations of analgesia for two dental drugs, based on the time of day they were administered.

The two most significant biorhythms are the body's fluctuation in temperature (lowest in early morning and highest in the early evening) and its sleep cycle, which is responsive to the fluctuations of light and darkness (Alper, 1983). It has been found that in many cases of depression these cycles are out of sync, and this could play an important role in antidepressant therapy.

Miscellaneous

A number of other factors influence drug response. Temperature is a consideration because, when the body is cold, peripheral blood vessels constrict to preserve heat. The blood flow is then reduced and absorption slows. This could be of vital importance to people like those who have accidentally suffered **hypothermia** (lowered body temperature) by falling into icy water. Peripheral sites of drug administration are then numbed, almost inactive, and ineffective.

Posture is relevant to some drug actions; ganglionic blocking agents do not affect subjects who are lying down, but given enough of a dose, standing subjects will collapse. Body water content affects the dilution and concentration of drug doses. The use of other drugs, like tobacco smoking, can produce inadvertent combined drug effects; this is a major factor to be considered in detail as we proceed.

PSYCHOLOGICAL VARIABLES

A lie is useful only as a medicine to man.

Plato, The Republic

Expectation: The Placebo Effect

The placebo effect is by far the most ghostly variable the psychopharmacologist has to contend with. The word comes from Latin, meaning "I will please." Hooper's Medical

Dictionary of 1811 defined it as "any medication adopted more to please than to benefit the patient" (as cited in Kornetsky, 1976, p. 22), but today we know it as any inactive counterfeit for a drug that the patient believes to be therapeutic—a harmless decoy. But in fact, placebos have displayed all the pharmacological characteristics of active drugs: time-effect curves, tolerance, side effects, dependence, and cumulative effects in combined drug-placebo use. An experimenter can even produce a dose-response curve for a placebo by varying the number of tablets to be taken daily. Moreover, many of the effects produced are real physiological ones: changes in blood content, constriction of pupils, and so forth, albeit these are effects that can be regulated psychologically.

One of the few incontestable facts established about placebos is that the degree of the placebo reaction correlates with the strength of the patient's expectations about the drug being taken. In most cases, the subjects believe they are taking a real drug when they are given the substitute, but there are cases on record where the effects followed in subjects who knew they were on placebos (Park & Covi, 1965). If subjects given a drug are told to expect a particular side effect, the placebo reactions will be fairly uniform, but if they are told to expect unpredictable side effects, the placebo reactions consist of a motley array of symptoms, apparently fabricated in the psyches of the subjects.

In a typical placebo experiment, inert pills of various sizes, shapes, and colors were administered to patients in place of their normal medications (Leslie, 1954). Superior results were recorded for (1) red, yellow, and blue capsules; and red, yellow, and brown fluids over blue and green ones (some studies even show that medications of the subject's favorite color work better); (2) unusual sizes (large pills probably suggest a large dose, while small pills suggest great potency); and (3) strange and bitter tastes. Odd numbers of drops in a prescription may be more effective than even ones (Leslie, 1954). It has been found that changing the size, shape, or color of a placebo "medication" after a while can renew the effect. For this reason, new and improved drugs hyped by dynamic ad campaigns may have a higher effectiveness until their glamour wears off. In a more dramatic experiment, a man on a placebo reported a full-blown LSD experience, while another man exhibited a lack of response to what he thought was a placebo but was in fact an effective dose of LSD (Reed & Witt, 1965). In another case, a schizophrenic woman being treated with a placebo suffered withdrawal when her physician discontinued its use (Vinar, 1969).

If the placebo effect can result from inactive substances, it follows that part of a real drug's effect must invariably involve the placebo effect to some extent. This suggests an unsettling problem: How are we to measure the true drug effect when it is impossible to distinguish and measure the placebo effect? Some studies have addressed the problem, but no helpful conclusions have been reached. Consequently, the placebo effect is always an unknown factor in the measurement of a real drug effect. The best that can be done is to administer a placebo as part of any drug experiment and compare its influence with the real drug effects. This has become a standard part of testing a drug's effect—judging how superior it is to a placebo.

In some situations, the placebo response may be the only useful effect. One writer claims that the history of medical treatment up to the last seventy or eighty years could be considered the history of the placebo effect. The success of medieval remedies like crocodile dung, pulverized mummy flesh, buns made from granulated spiders, and other unholy prescriptions is commonly attributed to it, and even in modern times (1961), an editorial in the *British Medical Journal* held that 20 percent to 40 percent of prescription medicines really function as placebos (as cited in Kornetsky, 1976, p. 24).

Interestingly enough, there is no correlation between placebo reaction and hypnotic suggestibility. Although the effect does not seem to be related to hypnosis, there is a fair amount of evidence to suggest that the attitude of the physician in handling the patient may be a large determining factor. In light of this, certain types of experiments have been designed to test placebo effects. In a **single-blind study**, only the subjects are ignorant that a placebo is being used; the experimental staff knows the difference. Theoretically, this would still allow an experimenter to unintentionally cue the subject about whether the placebo or drug is being given. It could be something as simple as a slightly more assured attitude on the part of a clinician administering the real drug. To correct for this problem, **double-blind studies** evolved, in which even the experimental staff are unaware a placebo is being given. In **partially blind studies**, the staff knows of both the drug and the placebo, but uses numbered vials or ampoules so that the researchers cannot distinguish between them.

One telling incident of placebo response involved an asthmatic man whose physician treated him with both a drug and a placebo. The drug showed consistently better results. But when the physician approached the pharmaceutical company for a fresh supply of the drug, the representative informed him that the entire first shipment of the supposed drug had actually been a placebo (Wolf, 1959, p. 692). The asthmatic man had thus received nothing but placebos, yet one batch worked better than the other. The attitude of the physician evidently was what made the "drug" appear more favorable. He thought he was running a single-blind study, when in fact, he was involved in an accidental double-blind study. This points up the importance of the physician's attitude even more than a real single-blind study, which involves the chance of a genuine drug effect. It has been shown that a negative attitude on the part of the doctor decreases the effect both of drugs and placebos, and that the use of a true drug by an enthusiastic doctor ensures the best results. Needless to say, the ethicality of giving placebos to patients without their knowledge or consent is a matter of debate, complicated by the fact that the ignorance seems to be a factor that in some cases makes the placebo work as a successful treatment.

It has been suggested that anyone probably has the capacity to respond to a placebo. If it does not happen one day, that does not mean it cannot happen the next. And, strange as it may sound, animals too show placebo responses. This indicates that the environment and conditions of administration may be another factor in placebo response. An animal can exhibit a conditioned response to being injected, which cues it to produce its own drug effect. Of course, this would never happen with the first dose of a drug; the animal has to learn the effect first from previous conditioning.

The drug user's expectations are referred to as **set**. Frequently, a drug does what the user expects it to. When people seek out and eat the hallucinogenic mushrooms of the northwest rain forests of Oregon, they become pleasantly intoxicated, but those who eat them by mistake while foraging for edible mushrooms end up seeking help for poisoning

(Davis, 1985, p. 151). When the FBI tested LSD in the fifties as a possible psychochemical weapon, it produced experimental results that seem inconsistent with the results enjoyed by the hippies of Haight-Ashbury a few years later. Very few of the FBI test subjects had positive, ecstatic, or revolutionary experiences, effects which were later claimed to be pharmacological, but which were undoubtedly partly due to the mental frame (as well as the physical context) in which the drug was used.

Personality

On occasion, an individual's personality may influence a drug effect. For example, introverted individuals have a lower threshold (higher susceptibility) to sedative effects (Eysenck, 1983).

ENVIRONMENTAL VARIABLES

Setting

The physical or social context in which a drug is taken can influence the drug response. For example, mice given a low dose of a convulsant will begin convulsing sooner if an alarm clock bell is sounded. Animal studies also show that social status may affect drug response, because subordinate and dominant animals show different effects. To take a human situation, a person using marijuana in a decorous social situation, such as a family Thanksgiving dinner, is likely to suppress the drug effect.

Similarly, the expectations of a peer group can affect the drug response. If you are given a drug by a group of friends who are sitting around expecting you to get high from it, chances are that you will, even if the dose is not particularly effective.

Lab studies have shown that the manner in which animals are housed influences drug response. Mice housed in groups respond to much smaller doses of amphetamines, and their lethal dose is lower than for mice housed alone (Chance, 1946). Mice in groups also have a lower convulsive threshold, and they show higher degrees of excitement and hypothermia after doses of benzedrine (Shurley, 1970). In human experiments, sensory isolation has postponed LSD and PCP-induced hallucinations from 30 to 150 minutes (Shurley, 1970).

It is worth noting that conditioned tolerance, described in the last chapter, also qualifies as an effect of **setting** on drug effects.

TASK VARIABLES

Task variables are a laboratory effect that becomes apparent in the testing of drugs. Animals exhibit different drug responses according to the types of tasks they are given while under the influence. That is to say, the nature of the test determines the response to some degree. Take as an example pigeons pecking at a button to obtain food. We can reward them after a set time interval, for instance, the first peck after five minutes have elapsed (this would be notated as FI5, a fixed interval of five minutes). Or we can reward them after a set number of pecks, let us say five again (this would be notated as FR5, a fixed ratio of five pecks). When pigeons receive a specific dose of pentobarbital, their pecking is not affected until a specific reinforcement interval is used. For instance, as we extend the interval between rewards their pecking at the button suddenly decreases at FI15. They remain fairly active when we reward them every fourteen minutes, but if we wait one minute longer, the pentobarbital causes them to suddenly lose interest. Conversely, the pecking upswings at FR50. Here we increase the number of pecks needed to produce the reward, until, at fifty pecks, the drugged pigeons suddenly become inspired at the button. In these cases, measurements of the drug response differ solely on the basis of the particular task chosen to evaluate the drug. Pentobarbital is a depressant, and so it appears judged by fixed interval behavior; but, judged by fixed ratio behavior, it appears to be a stimulant. Two experimenters working exclusively with one task or the other would end up with different impressions of the nature of the drug.

CONCLUSION

In light of all the principles we have been considering in the last several chapters, some researchers have put in orders for the ideal drug of the future. It would work quickly to cure or treat a problem. It would be effective in most or all cases. It would work specifically on the problem with few or no side effects and no impairment of cognitive, perceptual, or motor functions. It would be safe, even in early pregnancy, with no tolerance or dependence, no possible lethal overdose, and no interaction with other drugs. It would serve both in and outpatients. Ideal, too, would be a drug with self-limiting effects; that is, when it had reached its therapeutic potential, biological feedback mechanisms would limit further action.

Gains in all these areas are both imaginable and probable in the future, and it is interesting to speculate on what new developments such gains might bring, both in and out of medicine.

Chapter 6

Neurons

In the next four chapters, we will consider the anatomy and physiology underlying drug effects, beginning with the individual nerve cell and progressing to the peripheral nervous system, the spinal cord, and the brain. Finally, we will elaborate on the roles of neurotransmitters in producing behavioral effects; these will figure large in later discussions of how particular drugs work and how their effects are interrelated.

To have a behavioral effect, a drug must affect the neurons in some way, either directly or indirectly. Most psychoactive drugs are therefore intended for neurons, especially the chemical process of transmission across the synapse, where neurotransmitters, their receptors, and deactivating enzymes can be found. In this chapter, we will describe in some detail these processes in which drugs intervene to produce their behavioral effects.

The building block of the nervous system, the **neuron**, or nerve cell, specializes in communication. It is the single most important cell in the body, since all bodily activity depends on the functioning of distinct nerve cells. Neurons number in the billions, but, regardless of shape, size, or function, they all work by the same basic mechanism and use the same structural components. Only their chemistry differs. There is no mechanism for replacing a neuron once it has been destroyed.

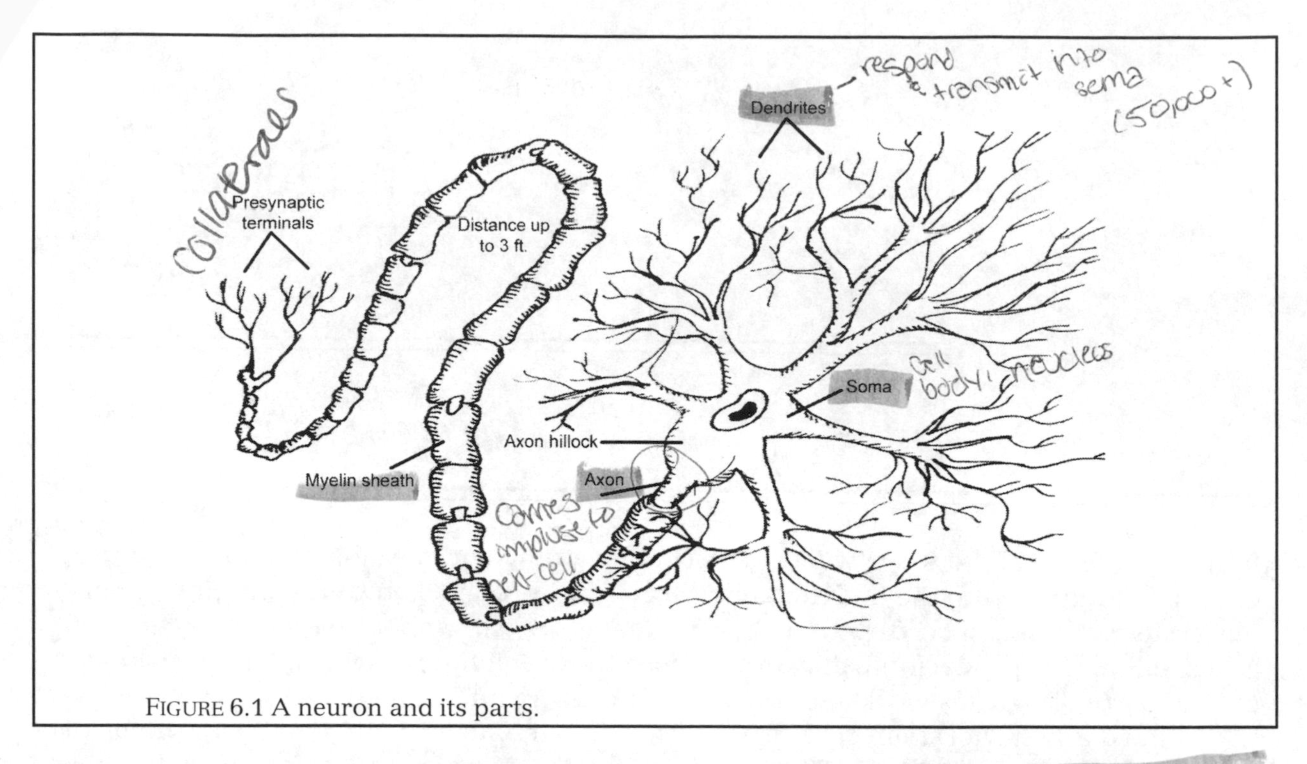

FIGURE 6.1 A neuron and its parts.

A neuron has three parts (see Figure 6.1). The **soma**, or cell body, contains the nucleus. Branching out like tendrils from the soma are short extensions (processes) called **dendrites** (from *dendron*, Greek for "tree"). Their function is to respond to excitations from other neurons and transmit them into the soma, in much the way that a tree would draw moisture from its leaves into a single trunk. Dendrites may have 50,000 or more contacts from other cells.

The **axon**, a single long process extending from the soma, carries the nerve impulse to the next cell. Axons vary in length from those less than a millimeter in the brain to those comprising the 3-foot long sciatic nerve stretching down the leg from the spinal cord to the toe. Offshoots of the axon are known as **collaterals**; both these and the axon may branch into numerous endings that contact other neurons. What we call a nerve is actually a bundle of axons forming what appears to be a single conduit. Most of the large axons of vertebrates are sheathed with **myelin**, a fatty covering interrupted at regular intervals by nodes (nodes of Ranvier), or openings, giving the axon the appearance of links of sausages. This modification greatly accelerates impulses, which leap from node to node.

The thickets of branching dendrites may receive hundreds of thousands of excitations, which the body of the neuron, the soma, integrates into one signal that travels along the axon. The axon can spread the signal through its collaterals and branching ends to as many as 10,000 other cells. This energy always flows one way through the neural circuits: in at the dendrites to the cell body, which integrates them and sends an impulse along the axon to other neurons, which in turn repeat the process. Under normal circumstances, the signal cannot reverse.

A resting neuron is in a condition of electrical tension, holding a charge known as a **resting potential.** It rests like a loaded mousetrap, waiting to be tripped, and, like a mousetrap, the neuron fires either fully or not at all; it cannot partially go off or carry a weaker impulse. This property is called the **all-or-nothing** response. However, it applies only to the axons of individual cells, not to nerve bundles.

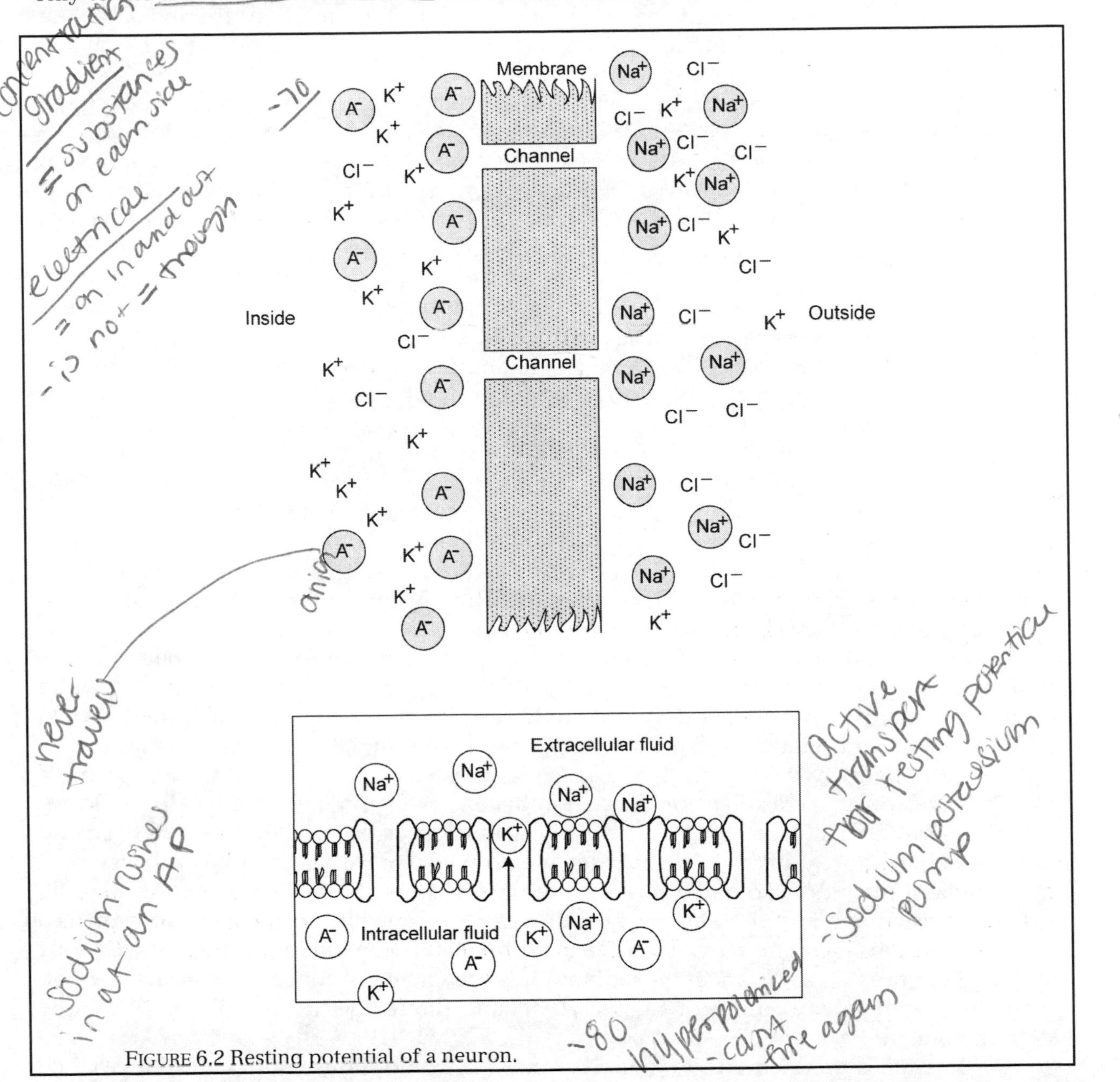

FIGURE 6.2 Resting potential of a neuron.

The source of the resting potential is a complex ionic balance based on the interplay of a number of charged substances. Figure 6.2 depicts four of the key ions involved: large protein ions (A^-), sodium ions (Na^+), chloride ions (Cl^-), and potassium ions (K^+) (Koester, 1981b).

First, held inside the cell by the neural membrane are relatively large proteins, too large to escape through the pores. They carry a negative charge and are designated as A^- ions (anions). Their tendency to diffuse down their concentration gradient and cross the membrane to the outside of the cell causes them to line up along the inside of the membrane, which contains them. That means the membrane has a negatively charged inner lining of A^- ions.

All four of the substances in this ionic drama have two biochemical motivations: one is to equalize across the membrane according to their own particular concentration gradients (e.g., half of the sodium molecules on this side of the membrane and half on that side); the other is to equalize across the membrane according to their electrical gradients, ideally balancing with all the other charged particles in the area. These molecules tend toward a state of equilibrium wherein all substances are distributed evenly across membranes and all charges balance out on both sides. However, the semi-permeability of the membrane precludes this. Already, in our example, the large A^- proteins are a source of constrained negative charges.

The next ion to consider, sodium (Na^+), is in abundance from dissolved salts in the extracellular fluid. It is strongly drawn to the membrane by two forces. First, it is electrically attracted by the negative charges of the A^- proteins just inside the membrane, and, second, it is trying to diffuse in to equalize its concentration across the membrane (until half is on each side). There are gates and channels that could admit Na^+, but for the moment the Na^+ ions are bound up with water molecules, and the gates are shut.

Also present are chlorine (Cl^-) and potassium (K^+) ions, which are likewise abundant because of the dissolved salts in the extracellular fluid. These differ from A^- and Na^+ in that they passively distribute; namely, they are able to diffuse through the channels of the membrane, so they possess freedom of movement.

Let us suppose that Cl^- and K^+ could obey only the impulse to balance their charges and not their concentrations. They would flood the area; the K^+ would enter the cell to be with the A^- and neutralize it, and the Cl^- would remain outside with the Na^+. There would then be equal and neutral charges on both sides of the membrane. Perfect. But that is not what happens.

The concentration gradient of Cl^- is an imbalancing factor. Electrically, Cl^- would remain outside the cell with Na^+. Very little of it would enter because of the already strong negative charge of A^- inside. The charges would balance. But Cl^- also has a concentration gradient pushing it to equalize across the membrane and enter the cell. As a result, extra Cl^- ions move into the neuron, boosting the negative charge there, so that the cell interior becomes more negative than the exterior. You see, no matter how many Cl^- ions stay outside the cell to balance the sodium ions, the chemical concentration gradient always forces an extra helping of Cl^- inside, making the inside more negative compared with the outside.

K+ thus faces an unequal situation. Normally, it would diffuse until half of it reached either side of the membrane, but now, between A^- and Cl^-, there is a huge negative draw pulling it inside the cell, uphill against the concentration gradient. The result is a high concentration of K^+ held electrically inside the cell, with a strong inclination to flow out. On the whole, K^+ has to balance itself according to three main forces: the negative ions drawing it *into* the cell, the concentration gradient urging it *out*, and the accumulation of Na^+ ions on the cell exterior fencing it *in*. When these three forces finally balance, the cell has reached its resting potential. The ions have adjusted, balancing themselves so that the charges inside have neutralized (K^+ and A^-); but because of the Cl^- concentration gradient, the interior charge has neutralized at a higher energy level than the outside, remaining more negative on the whole.

To see this more clearly, imagine that you have two microelectrodes that measure a difference in electrical potential. If you put both into the interior of the axon, they would read zero—all the charges there have equalized. With both placed outside the axon, they would read the same. However, if one were placed inside and one outside the axon, the electrodes would show a difference across the membrane, the interior showing a more negative charge, because there are more electrons in there with the potential to flow out.

For a neuron to fire, the dendrites or soma must collect enough signals from neighboring cells to trip it. It is the sum total of all the inputs, therefore, that determines whether there's enough energy to fire the cell. These inputs enter the soma, where they are integrated. When the net total reaches the threshold, the firing begins. The portion of the axon next to the soma, the **axon hillock** (see Figure 6.1), suddenly becomes permeable to Na^+. The Na^+ rushes into the axon, moved by its concentration gradient and attracted by the negative charges (A^-) inside the cell. The electrical tension across the membrane collapses as the Na^+ ions are freed to resolve their gradients. This is called **depolarization**, because the electrical polarity of opposing charges across the membrane disappears. The negative cell interior even reverses polarity and becomes positive for a fraction of a millisecond, due to the influx of Na^+ ions.

The axon, already containing K^+, is now replete with positive charges. The K^+, piled up against the concentration gradient and able to navigate the pores, immediately rushes out to equalize the charge. This reestablishes the polarity across the membrane, since some of the Na^+ and K^+ has exchanged places.

The influx of Na^+ and the efflux of K^+ constitute the firing of the neuron, more specifically, of the axon. The old idea of the nerve cell as a section of house wiring with electrons flowing through it has been replaced. We now see the firing neuron as a fiber with a spot of depolarization racing along it as area after area becomes permeable to sodium. The front of the spot is marked by the pulse of sodium flowing in; the back of the spot is marked by the potassium flowing out a fraction of a millisecond later. Together, these form the nerve impulse, or **action potential** (see Figure 6.3).

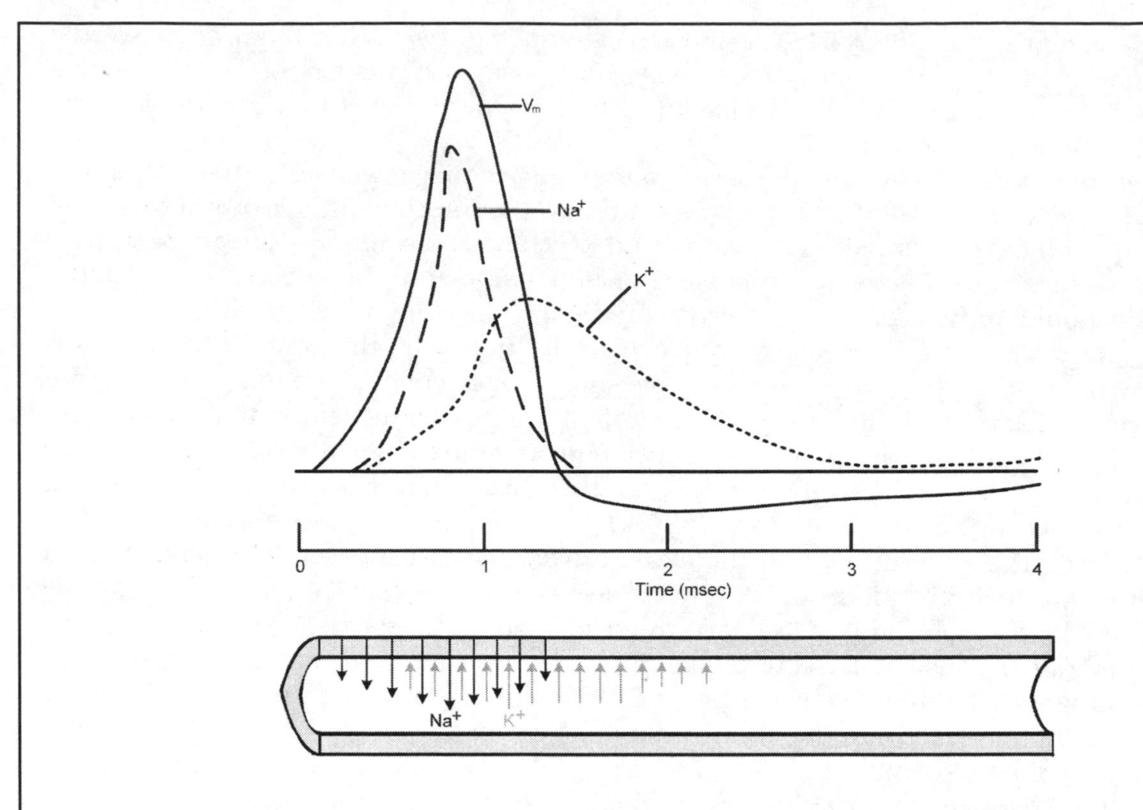

FIGURE 6.3 Action potential V_m is the reading of the action potential, which is the result of the influx of sodium (Na^+) and the efflux of potassium (K^+). The window of depolarization is shown at the bottom.

The process of conducting the action potential has been compared to the operation of a blasting fuse coated with granules of gunpowder. Each granule firing provides the energy to explode the adjacent granule. In the same way, areas of the neural membrane, already in a potential state, receive energy from the depolarization of adjoining areas on the axon. The signal can travel great distances without being reduced, because the axon provides the energy to conduct it. On the average, the action potential takes about 1 millisecond to occur, and travels anywhere from 20 to 400 feet per second along the axon (depending on its diameter and whether or not it has a myelin sheathing).

After firing, the axon must return to its original condition at the resting potential. During the action potential, enough Na^+ enters the axon to reverse the interior polarity from negative to positive, but then so much K^+ evacuates the axon that it overbalances the charge in the opposite direction. For a brief period (3 milliseconds), the interior becomes more negative than when it started out at the resting potential. This is called **hyperpolarization**. During this time, the axon is numbed in the sense that a stronger impulse is needed to excite it. With the efflux of K^+, the membrane again becomes impermeable to sodium. At this point, the membrane is repolarized.

Let's review the situation. Think that a type of window has passed down the axon. At every point, positive sodium ions have jumped through the window into the axon, and in response, positive potassium ions have jumped out. Now the window has passed. The cell has nearly returned to its original polarity because the shifting about has involved positive ions trading places; however, as you can see, these sodium and potassium ions now find themselves on the "wrong" sides of the membrane. How, then, do they get back to where they started from?

The original ionic situation of the neuron is restored by two forces. The first is the patterning of electrical and concentration gradients that set up the resting potential in the first place. The second is an active transport system called a **sodium-potassium pump**. The system consists of large protein molecules embedded in the membrane, which transport sodium and potassium ions in or out of the cell.

Every time the neuron fires, some sodium from the extracellular fluid is trapped inside. Eventually, this buildup would kill off the negative charge inside the axon and reduce the membrane potential. To prevent this, the sodium-potassium pump is constantly at work exporting Na^+ from the cell and importing K^+. Generally, the pump moves more Na^+ out of the cell than it moves K^+ in. Because of this, it helps all along to maintain the negative cell interior and set up the resting potential.

It is only during the action potential at the axon hillock and a little after, a period of about a millisecond, that the neuron cannot be re-excited. Left to its own devices, the axon will restore itself to the original resting potential (about -70 millivolts) in 4 to 6 milliseconds.

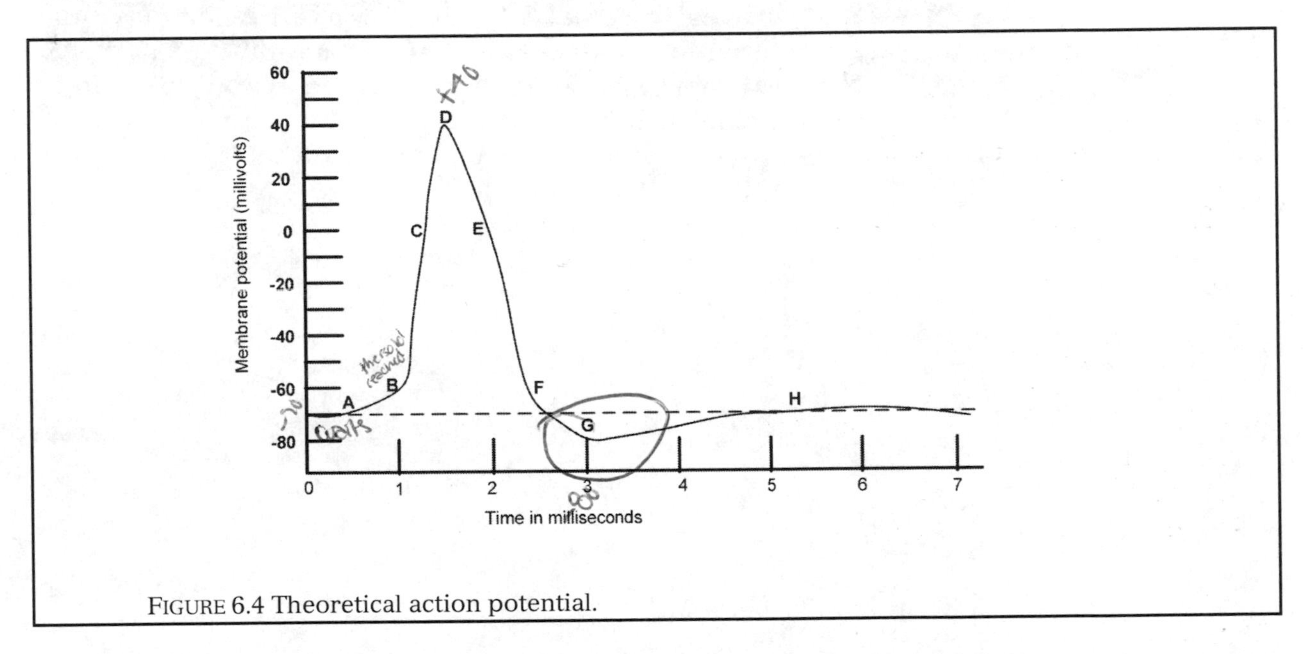

FIGURE 6.4 Theoretical action potential.

Figure 6.4 shows an idealized version of an action potential. The curve represents the changing voltage across the cell membrane, measured by two tiny electrodes (in the giant squid axon), one outside of and one piercing the axon; it shows what happens as the action potential sweeps over the electrodes in one spot on the axon (Eccles, 1973, pp. 13-26). At A, the axon waits at the resting potential, about -60 to -70 millivolts. In the analogous mammalian system, the dendrites and soma then receive a myriad of inputs, which the soma integrates until the threshold potential is reached, corresponding to B in the figure. The axon hillock next to the soma then becomes permeable to Na^+, and the membrane depolarizes. The area (window) of depolarization shoots along the axon. The spike from B to F shows the balance of charges as the window crosses over the implanted electrode. First there is an upswing of positive charge at C, the front of the window, where a predominance of Na^+ is flowing into the cell, and only a small amount of K^+ is beginning to flow out. At D, near the middle of the window, the two flows balance, and **repolarization** begins. The efflux of K^+ then begins to predominate, enough to neutralize the membrane again at E, to repolarize it back to the original resting potential at F, and even to overcompensate and hyperpolarize the axon down to G, an extra -5 to -12 mV. During this period, the membrane again becomes impermeable to Na^+. (When the window of depolarization is occurring at the axon hillock, the neuron is inhibited from firing for about a millisecond.) At G, the original ionic tendencies and the sodium-potassium pump begin to restore the neuron to its original resting potential at H. The whole process as shown takes about 4 milliseconds.

SYNAPSE AND RECEPTOR

When a neuron fires, the action potential travels along the axon and arrives at the **synapse**. The synapse was named by Sir Charles Sherrington near the turn of the century; he derived it from a Greek word meaning "handclasp" and defined it as the mode of connection between neurons. It is used today to refer to the junction of the axon with any part of another neuron (axon-to-soma, axon-to-dendrite, axon-to-axon). Sherrington's coinage came mostly from a studied guess that there was a special mechanism used by neurons to communicate with one another. He had no idea what it was. But we do.

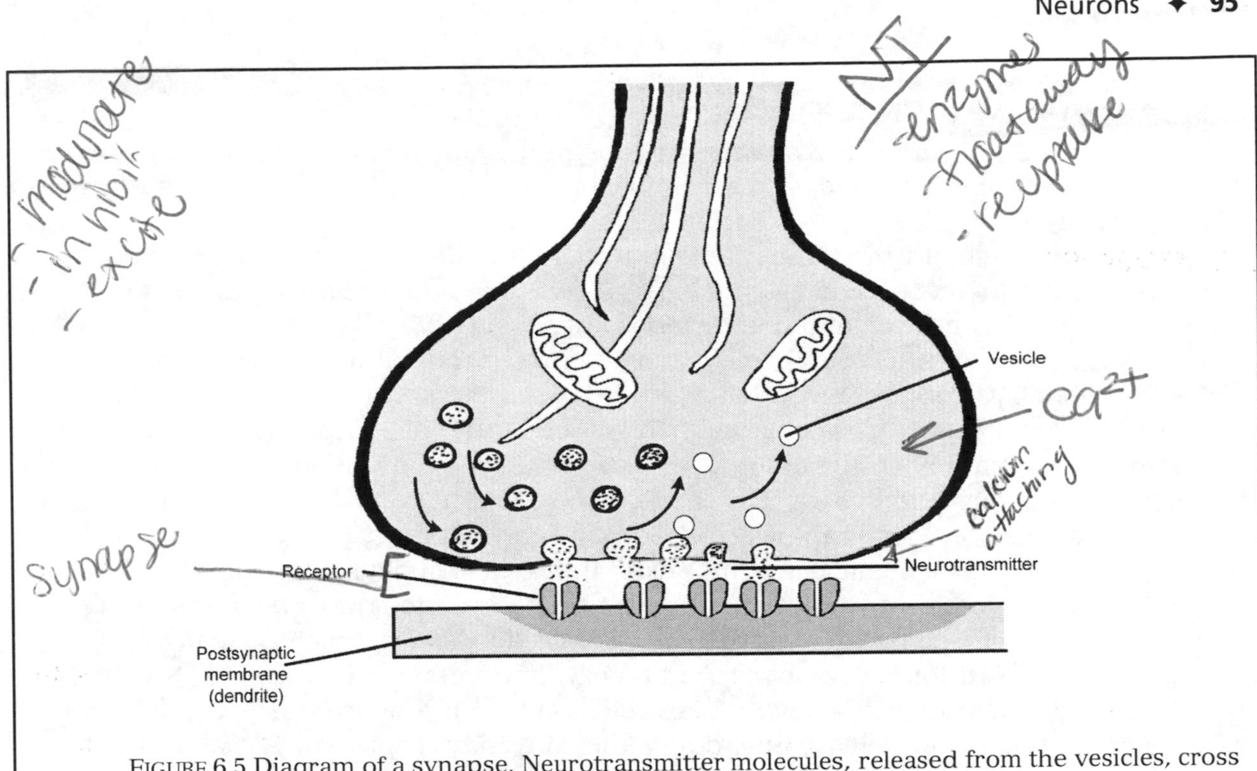

FIGURE 6.5 Diagram of a synapse. Neurotransmitter molecules, released from the vesicles, cross the synaptic gap to attach to receptors.

The end of the axon branches, and these branches end in buttons--the **presynaptic terminals**, or **synaptic knobs**. Between each button and the next neuron is a narrow, fluid-filled space—the **synaptic gap**, or **synaptic cleft**, measuring about 0.00002 millimeters. Across the gap, on the adjacent neuron, is a section of membrane called the **postsynaptic membrane**. This may be located on the soma, dendrite, or axon of another neuron. All these structures taken together—the presynaptic terminal, the synaptic gap, and the postsynaptic membrane—constitute the synapse, a one-way relay station for the transmission of impulses (see Figure 6.5).

When a neuron fires, the action potential travels along the axon and reaches the presynaptic knobs. Inside the knobs are presynaptic **vesicles**, small membranous sacs, each holding a few hundred molecules of a neurotransmitter. When the action potential arrives, it depolarizes the membrane and allows an influx of calcium (Ca^{++}) ions. These cause the vesicles to fuse with the presynaptic membrane and release a set amount of their supply of neurotransmitters (Zucker & Lando, 1986). The neurotransmitters cross the synaptic gap and attach to receptor sites on the postsynaptic terminal with a weak, reversible chemical bond (Cooper, Bloom, & Roth, 1986, pp. 86-105).

When the neurotransmitter attaches to the receptor sites, it alters the membrane of the postsynaptic neuron in any of several ways. First, it can excite the membrane by initiating depolarization. The transmitter molecule attaches to the receptor, which opens a channel, allowing a small influx of Na^+. This slightly depolarizes the membrane; that is, it **hypopolarizes** or slightly reduces its polarization (*hypo* is "below"), hinting to the soma to let the axon hillock fully depolarize and fire the neuron.

Second, a transmitter molecule can inhibit the membrane by attaching to receptor sites that allow a slight outflow of K^+ or an influx of Cl^- (hyperpolarization). This makes the cell interior so negative and polarizes the membrane so much that the cell can't easily be fired. The inhibition of neurons in this way is what keeps all our nerve cells from firing continually.

A third arrangement is that the transmitter can initiate a series of enzyme reactions in the postsynaptic neuron and cause a **slow action**, as opposed to the **fast action** of direct excitation. This may change the membrane's sensitivity to its inputs or alter the firing characteristics of the cell. This type of neurotransmitter action is referred to as **neuromodulation** (Cooper et al., 1986, pp. 106-123).

All the inputs to the cell are partial contributions that are to be compiled and integrated by the soma. When the sum of inputs is great enough, the neuron fires, moving the pulse of depolarization along. Hence, it can be seen that the signal crossing the synapse is not, as was once thought, electrical, like a spark jumping the gap in a spark plug, but it is instead electrochemical, depending on the release of neurotransmitters.

The receptor sites on the postsynaptic membrane are thought to be specialized protein structures that respond to a specific substance--in this instance, the neurotransmitter. In an extreme simplification of current theory, one can imagine the neurotransmitter matched to its receptor like a key to a keyhole; namely, if a neuron uses dopamine, the presynaptic vesicles will release only dopamine, and the receptors that match it will respond only to dopamine or a substance closely resembling it. It is possible, therefore, to classify neurons and neural systems according to the brand of transmitters and receptors they use. It should be understood, however, that a single soma may have receptors receiving inputs from many different types of neurons with different neurotransmitters. To make this simpler, you might think of these neurons as connectors of different colors. A yellow neuron may have inputs from blue, green, and red neurons, but it will convert all the signals to yellow signals and send them all to yellow receptors on other neurons.

Once the neurotransmitter has attached itself to the receptors and affected the neuron, it has served its purpose. If it were to remain, it could cause further uncalled-for actions. Therefore, it must disengage and become deactivated. Usually the change initiated in the postsynaptic membrane by the neurotransmitter is what causes it to disengage. Then there are three ways by which it can become inactive.

First, the neurotransmitter, newly freed, can diffuse away through the extracellular fluid in the synaptic gap. Second, it can be metabolized by enzymes from the postsynaptic membrane. Or, third, it may be taken up again (**reuptaken**) into the presynaptic terminal. This completes the process of the neurotransmitter's action, which begins again at the arrival of the next action potential at the presynaptic terminal.

To summarize, the steps in synaptic transmission are as follows:

1. The action potential arrives at the presynaptic terminal. ← influx of calcium
2. The vesicles fuse to the terminal membrane and release the neurotransmitter.
3. The neurotransmitter crosses the synaptic gap.
4. It attaches to the receptor and alters the postsynaptic membrane by exciting, inhibiting, or modulating it.
5. The reaction of the postsynaptic membrane (the firing of the neuron, for instance) disengages the neurotransmitter from the receptor.
6. The neurotransmitter is deactivated. This may occur in several ways:

a. The neurotransmitter diffuses away.
b. Enzymes metabolize or deactivate the neurotransmitter.
c. It is reuptaken into the presynaptic terminal.

The time needed for one neuron to communicate an impulse to another, proceeding through the first five of these steps, is about a third of a millisecond.

Chapter 7

The Peripheral Nervous System and the Spinal Cord

I believe that much of a man's character will be found betokened in his backbone. I would rather feel your spine than your skull, whoever you are.... I rejoice in my spine as in a firm audacious staff of that flag I fling half out to the world.

Herman Melville
Moby Dick, LXXX

In the chain of biological causes and effects, anatomy and physiology stand between the drug and the behavior. The drug affects particular structures or chemical codes in the brain, for instance, and this causes corresponding shifts in behavior. To understand drug effects, therefore, it is helpful to pursue somewhat the anatomy and physiology of the nervous system, because this is the closest thing we have to a map of where and how drugs work. This study also provides a system to classify drugs according to their mechanisms of action. For example, drugs that inhibit the sympathetic nervous system are called *sympathetic blockers*. Knowing about the physiology of the sympathetic nervous system furnishes a key to the character of these drugs and to the ranges of their effects. For instance, we can classify a new drug as a sympathomimetic (drugs, like amphetamine, that mimic the action of the sympathetic nervous system) by noting the battery of its effects.

TYPES OF NERVOUS SYSTEMS

The nervous system can be divided in several ways. If we go by the location of the nerves, we have the **central nervous system (CNS)**, consisting of all of the neurons housed within the vertebrae and skull (in short, the spinal cord and brain). This whole central nervous system is enclosed within a series of membranes called **meninges** and rests in an insulating bath of cerebrospinal fluid. The **peripheral nervous system** consists of all of the neurons outside the spinal cord and brain (viz., in the periphery), and these branch to every organ and extremity.

In addition, peripheral nerves are classified by the place where they leave the central nervous system. **Spinal nerves** are those that leave the spinal cord, and **cranial nerves** leave the brain.

Another major classification is by function. The **somatic nervous system** (*soma* is Latin for "body") innervates the voluntary muscles, like the tongue and the skeletal muscles that move our bones. These are known as *striated* muscles, because their structure makes them look striped. The **autonomic nervous system** ministers to the organs and glands, automatically maintaining bodily processes and thereby freeing the attention for more interesting activities.

The somatic and autonomic nervous systems are anatomically distinct. The somatic system is characterized by one-neuron links with the spinal cord. If we were travelers on a somatic tour, we would begin at a sensory receptor out in the periphery and then rocket along a single fiber toward the spine. We would pass our soma in a peripheral cluster of somae (a **ganglion**) behind the spine, flying by like a whistle stop on a railroad. Into the rear of the spine we would go, to synapse with a motor neuron and transfer to the outbound line. A single long motor axon would carry us back out into the periphery, in a nerve bundle with other axons, to synapse with a striated (voluntary) muscle. In this manner, both the sensory and motor components are wired right to the spinal cord with single axons. This is the sensory-motor system that mediates all sensations and movements; generally it is used to sense and willfully respond to situations outside the body.

By contrast, the autonomic nervous system uses a two-neuron hookup to connect the spine to the smooth (involuntary) muscles, the heart, intestines, and glands. One effect of this is that autonomic responses are slightly slower than somatic ones. The autonomic nervous system is, so to speak, the Secretary of the Interior. It functions to hold steady the body's internal environment—body temperature, blood pressure, digestion, hormonal balance, and so forth. But it is also able to override these considerations and mobilize the organism in emergency or stress. These two interests are represented separately by the two divisions of the autonomic system, the **sympathetic** and **parasympathetic nervous systems.** These systems, which are both wired to many (but not all) of the same organs, embody opposing functions. Under routine conditions, the parasympathetic predominates, and both systems collaborate to foster a harmonious inner climate. But in moments of stress or excitation, the stormy sympathetic system kicks in to cause an increase in heart rate, blood pressure, respiration, and blood glucose to ready the muscles needed in emotional trauma or panic.

By way of qualification, these calming and excitatory functions as we have described them are only a general rule. Some organs are connected to only one or the other of these systems. And sometimes when they are connected to the same organs, they interact in complex ways. Moreover, the parasympathetic system does not invariably calm organs; it activates the digestive organs, while the sympathetic system shuts them down. In fact, the innervation of the gut is so anomalous that some have entered it as a candidate for separate classification.

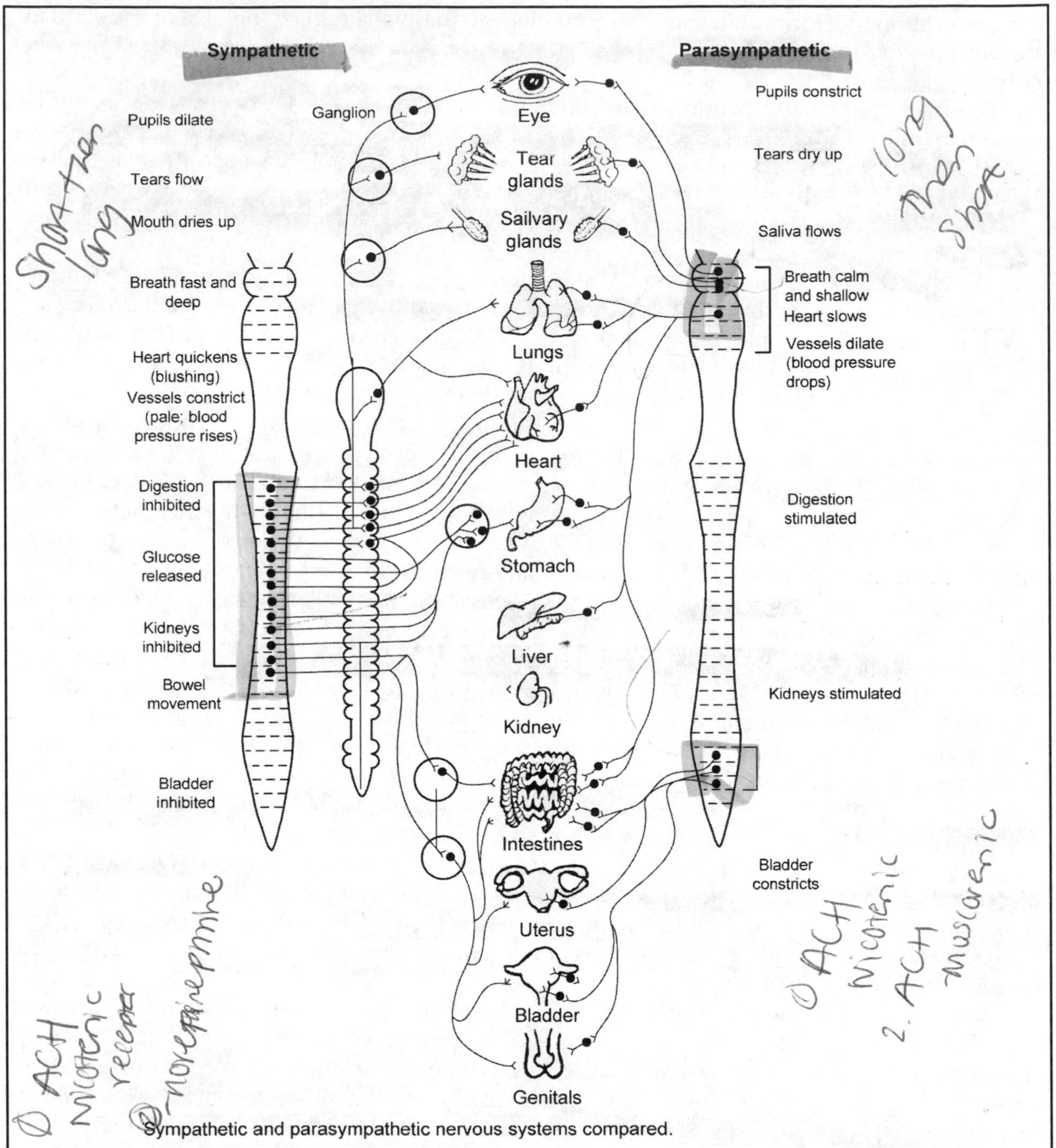

Sympathetic
Parasympathetic
Pupils dilate
Ganglion
Eye
Pupils constrict
Tears flow
Tear glands
Tears dry up
Mouth dries up
Sailvary glands
Saliva flows
Breath fast and deep
Lungs
Breath calm and shallow
Heart slows
Vessels dilate (blood pressure drops)
Heart quickens (blushing)
Vessels constrict (pale; blood pressure rises)
Heart
Digestion inhibited
Stomach
Digestion stimulated
Glucose released
Liver
Kidneys inhibited
Kidney
Kidneys stimulated
Bowel movement
Bladder inhibited
Intestines
Uterus
Bladder constricts
Bladder
Genitals
Sympathetic and parasympathetic nervous systems compared.

FIGURE 7.1 Sympathetic and parasympathetic nervous systems compared.

The parasympathetic nervous system differs from its counterpart in structure as well as function (see Figure 7.1). The peripheral parasympathetic nerves originate from the two extremities of the spinal cord, one at the base of the cranium and one at the southernmost tip (sacral region). Here are found the somae, which send out axons into the periphery. Because it is autonomic, the parasympathetic system uses two neurons in its connections. The first neuron stretches from one of the two centers all the way to the target organ, where it synapses with a shorter neuron, maybe only a few millimeters long, and this in turn innervates the target organ. The neural pattern is thus—long/short. These nerves work to constrict the pupils, dilate the blood vessels, decrease the heart rate, slow and deepen breathing, activate the stomach and intestines, and oversee digestion. On the whole, the parasympathetic system conserves and restores bodily resources.

In the case of the sympathetic neurons, the somae are located in the mid-portion of the spinal cord (thoracico-lumbar region). These somae typically send out short axons to a nearby ganglion, where they synapse with a second neuron. Parallel to the spinal cord on both sides, these ganglia form chains resembling long beaded strings. From here, the somae of the second sympathetic neurons send out long axons to the target organs. So here the neural pattern is short/long, a short trip to the ganglion (the preganglionic portion), then a long trip to the target organ (the postganglionic portion). This is the inverse of the parasympathetic system, where the preganglionic fibers are long and the postganglionic fibers are short.

Sympathetic Reaction

A **sympathetic reaction** is a constellation of effects arising from activation of the sympathetic nervous system. Since many drugs are able to stimulate the system, the sympathetic reaction may figure prominently in their pharmacology.

The sympathetic nervous system causes all the reactions associated with general excitation or emotional arousal—what biologists call the "fight-flight-fright response." Concerned with the needs of today rather than of tomorrow, it preempts the smooth, efficient pace of parasympathetic life and galvanizes the body into action. It steals the blood from the skin and digestive system and shunts it to the brain and muscles, so the body can act quickly in an emergency. It burns the energy resources carefully garnered by the parasympathetic system and gambles them on an act of survival. Under sympathetic influences the heartbeat races, breathing grows heavy and rapid, and pupils dilate. We blush or pale; our hands get clammy, our skin beads with cold sweat while our mouth goes dry.

Some drugs, such as amphetamine, mescaline, and LSD, activate the sympathetic system as part of their initial effects, which greatly influences the psychological quality of the drug experience.

Finally, a major difference between the sympathetic and parasympathetic systems involves the type of neurotransmitters they use to stimulate the target organs (see Figure 7.2). These differences are important because drugs are often classified by their actions on the autonomic nervous system. To start with, the neurotransmitter at the first synapse in both systems is acetylcholine, so this connection is said to be **cholinergic**; that is, responding to acetylcholine. Since nicotine—the active ingredient of the tobacco leaf—can mimic the action of acetylcholine at these synapses, the cholinergic action is referred to as *nicotinic*. In other words, all the preganglionic fibers release acetylcholine, and the second neurons respond to it; hence, they have cholinergic receptors. Again, the action here is **nicotinic**.

At the second neurons, the sympathetic and parasympathetic nervous systems differ. The second parasympathetic neurons again release acetylcholine onto the target organs (e.g., the heart), so these receptors are cholinergic. However, nicotine does not mimic the action of acetylcholine at these receptors; instead, muscarine—an extract of a hallucinogenic mushroom—does. These cholinergic receptors are thus said to be **muscarinic.**

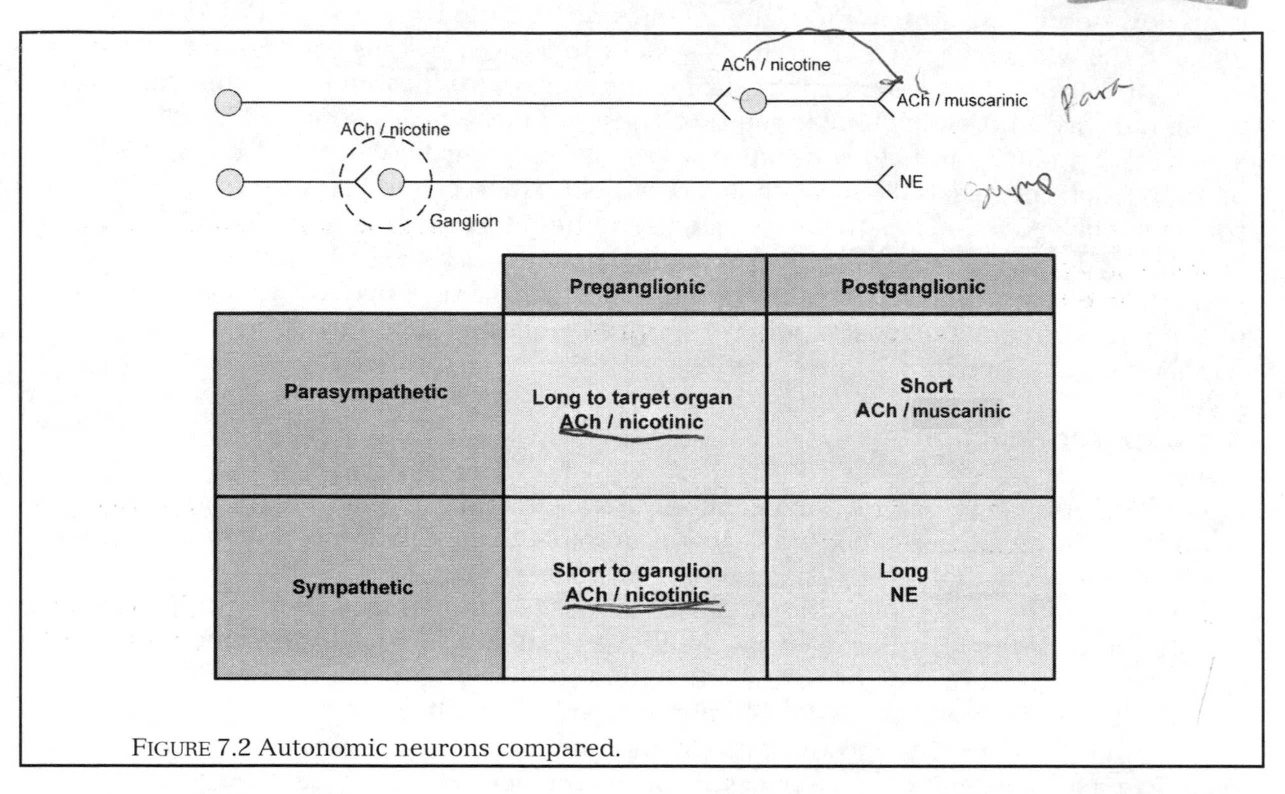

	Preganglionic	Postganglionic
Parasympathetic	Long to target organ ACh / nicotinic	Short ACh / muscarinic
Sympathetic	Short to ganglion ACh / nicotinic	Long NE

FIGURE 7.2 Autonomic neurons compared.

In the sympathetic nervous system, the second neurons all release norepinephrine onto the target organs (e.g., the heart again), as opposed to acetylcholine. Thus, with some exceptions, the target organs increase their activity in response to norepinephrine from the sympathetic system, and they typically (but not always) decrease it in response to acetylcholine from the parasympathetic system.

In summary, the parasympathetic and sympathetic nervous systems display several notable differences:

1. In general, the parasympathetic system calms organs, while the sympathetic activates them.
2. The two systems originate in different centers in the central nervous system: the parasympathetic in the top and bottom, and the sympathetic in the middle.
3. They differ in the lengths of their neurons. The parasympathetic has a long fiber running to a short fiber at the target organ, whereas the sympathetic has a short fiber running to a ganglion near the spinal cord, and a long fiber to the target organ.
4. They use different transmitters at the synapses of their neurons. The parasympathetic goes from a nicotinic cholinergic site to a muscarinic cholinergic site. The

sympathetic goes from a nicotinic cholinergic site to a synapse that uses norepinephrine.

THE SPINAL CORD

Without a spinal cord, the brain would inhabit the skull like a clam shut up in its shell, totally immobile and dead to any form of bodily stimulation. But the spinal cord, as well as keeping the brain's support systems working, empowers it to perceive and act. Accordingly, there are two great tides of information in the cord: flowing inward to the brain is a flood of sensory input, and flowing outward to the muscles, in response to the senses, is a flood of motor output. There are three types of neurons that handle this task. **Sensory (afferent) neurons**, with endings in every part of the body, carry impulses in, and **motor (efferent) neurons** carry commands outward to organs and muscles. A third type of neuron, the **association neuron** or **interneuron**, connects one neuron with another. Interneurons are situated completely within the central nervous system. They form a vast net that may make up as much as 99 percent of all neurons. Ultimately, they integrate all inputs and determine what the output should be. A **nucleus** is a cluster of somae in the central nervous system, analogous to a ganglion in the periphery.

The spinal cord is a white, ovoid cylinder, an eel-like tissue encased by the vertebrae and wrapped in the triple membrane that also protects the brain. Less than a quarter inch in diameter, it descends from the base of the skull about 18 inches and ends in the small of the back in a tassel of nerves called the *cauda equina*—the "horse's tail." Sectioning the cord yields a disc of tissue made of white and gray matter. The whiteness is due to the myelin sheathings on the axons of most of the neurons here. There are also glial cells, but no somae. The fibers of the white matter run vertically in ascending and descending tracts; these are like cables or highways to the brain.

Centered inside the white matter is a butterfly-shaped section of gray matter containing somae (including the somae of the "white matter" neurons), axons, dendrites, blood vessels, and glia. The grayness is a result of the large number of somae, unsheathed fibers, and blood vessels. These are mainly interneurons, oriented horizontally, moving information from the spinal cord to the periphery and back.

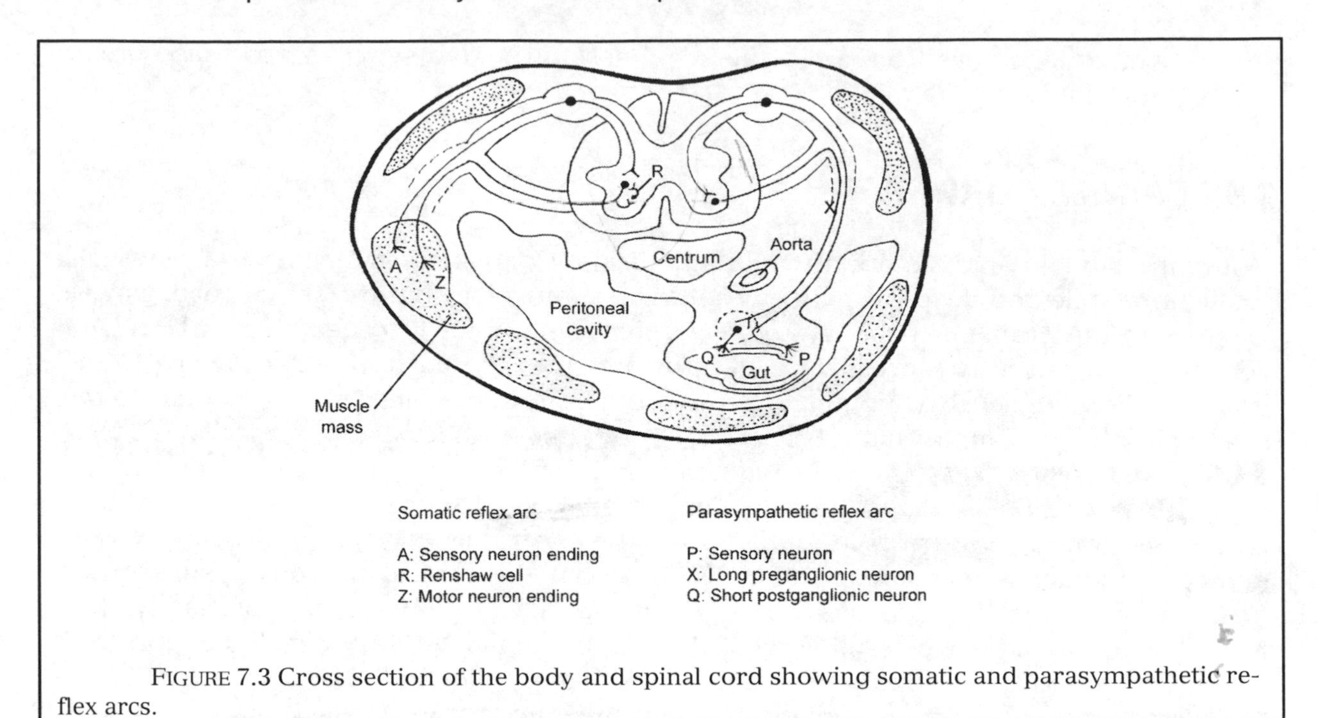

FIGURE 7.3 Cross section of the body and spinal cord showing somatic and parasympathetic reflex arcs.

From each wingtip of the butterfly of gray matter, a nerve root branches out of the spinal column. These four roots then pair off on either side of the spine to form the two spinal nerves at each vertebra. In all, there are 31 of these pairs of nerves leaving the spine to innervate the entire body. Sensory input enters the spinal column through the large butterfly wings of gray matter facing the rear (the dorsal root), and motor output exits via the small wings facing forward (the ventral root). This arrangement can be seen in Figure 7.3.

The spinal cord engages in two main types of activity. The first is the channeling of information between brain and body. The second is reflex activity. A **reflex** is a sensory-motor response that occurs without being referred to the brain. It is a kind of feeling and acting with the spinal cord—the spontaneous leaping of a hand off hot metal or of a foot off a sharp tack. The reaction to the tack can go round-trip to the spinal cord in 1/20 of a second, whereas it takes four times as long to return from the brain. Some other reflexes are the knee jerk, mouth watering, gagging, and erection in men. This braininess of the spinal cord is the reason that the proverbial chicken with its head cut off can keep to its feet and continue to run around the dooryard, flapping its wings in unison. Likewise, beheaded snakes and eels can undulate normally for a while on pure reflex. Such built-in circuits that bypass higher centers are one of the most primal functions of nervous systems. They are, in a manner of speaking, alive without us. They allow immediate reactions and leave other systems free for other uses. The brain, of course, is notified, but only in retrospect. We know that our hand, without our consent, has impetuously dropped a piping hot mug of coffee onto the kitchen tiles, and now we have an instant to wonder how badly we are going to feel the burn.

Reflex arcs, the paths that neural signals follow in the production of reflexes, are rated according to the number of synapses the signal has to cross. **Monosynaptic** reflexes involve one synapse (two neurons); **disynaptic** reflexes, two synapses; and **polysynaptic**, three or more. Monosynaptic reflexes are rare, but one of the most familiar reflexes, the knee-jerk reflex, is of this variety, and it serves as a good and simple example of how a reflex works (see left side of Figure 7.3).

To produce a knee-jerk (patellar) reflex, cross one leg over the other and relax it. Place one finger firmly on the center of your kneecap and slide it down the front of your leg until you feel the hard top of your shinbone. In between you will feel a soft bridge of tendon. Take the hard edge of your hand and chop yourself lightly across this area. Your lower leg will twitch up. This is not a result of the impact, as you may suspect. To prove it, try to arrange it so you can hit the area gently but neatly, and concentrate on relaxing your leg so it will not move. You will not be able to prevent the reflex.

This works as follows: striking the tendon below the kneecap momentarily stretches the thigh muscle and stimulates the sensory neurons there. The impulse follows the fiber to a ganglion behind the spine and continues into the gray matter of the cord (the rear wing of the butterfly on the same side as the leg, the dorsal root). Here it synapses with a motor neuron whose soma is in the front wing of gray matter (the ventral horn), and this sends the impulse along its axon back out to the muscle (via the ventral root), causing the thigh extensor muscle to contract quickly. This jerks the lower leg upward. Reflexes are thus a function of the synapsing of sensory with motor neurons in the gray matter of the spinal cord.

A disynaptic reflex uses three neurons. Its arrangement resembles the knee-jerk reflex, except there is a third neuron, an interneuron situated entirely in the gray matter of the spinal cord, which connects the sensory and motor neurons.

Finally, there are particular interneurons called **Renshaw cells** found in the gray matter of the spinal cord, which are automatic shutoff devices to keep motor neurons from firing incessantly. When the motor neuron fires, it fires the Renshaw cell, which forms a little feedback loop to the motor soma and inhibits it from firing again. Strychnine is a poison that interferes with the action of the Renshaw cell. This causes the indiscriminate firing of motor neurons unable to shut themselves off, a process witnessed as violent muscle convulsions.

The role of the spinal cord and its structures will serve in the understanding of the drug actions to be discussed in later chapters. A number of psychoactive drugs produce a sympathetic reaction, and many have effects on reflexes.

make flashcards of gross description

Chapter 8

The Brain

Scarecrow: Boo! Scared? Boo! You see—I can't even scare a crow. Oh, I'm a failure because I haven't got a brain.
Dorothy: Well, what would you do with a brain if you had one?
(The Wizard of Oz)

Well, Dorothy, evolutionary psychology can offer an answer. We find this elaboration of a central nervous system—a brain—most developed in organisms that move from place to place. It is an exquisite mechanism for rapidly processing complex information and responding to situations in a challenging environment, involving tasks like foraging, hunting, fighting, courting potential mates, and evading predators. Scarecrows, as a rule, do not require one.

Like a great megalopolis, the brain is a super-organized region containing most of the neurons of the central nervous system. As such, it is the most important site of action for many drugs. When a drug produces a behavioral change or psychological effect, we can be assured that it is acting upon the central nervous system and, in the predominance of cases, the brain.

Unfortunately, this organ, which many scientists think of as the crown of evolution, is so intricate and delicate that its workings present a monumental challenge to our understanding. Making up its mere three pounds are about 100 billion neurons, the number of stars in our galaxy, and some of these have as many as 10,000 connections to other cells, providing a possible 100 trillion synapses. It is often remarked that the brain has more potential connections among its neurons than there are atoms in the known universe.

Like the eye, which cannot see itself directly, some researchers hold that the brain has no hope of ever being able to comprehend itself. This sentiment is captured in a famous remark by the author Lyall Watson: "If the brain were so simple we could understand it, we would be so simple we couldn't." Similarly, drug actions in the brain can be understood in only the most indirect and rudimentary ways, although our knowledge in this area is rapidly progressing.

One impediment to understanding the brain is the limit of the methods available. In most eras, the models for the way the brain works have been derived from cutting-edge technologies or other preoccupations—a catapult, a hydraulic system, a clockwork device, a globe mapped into regions, an electric engine, a computer, a neural net. Ultimately, metaphors contribute something to our understanding in this case, but always fall short. They are part of our effort to solve a key problem about the brain—exactly what brain regions and structures are associated with specific activities and functions. Where is the memory loss occurring in Alzheimer's disease? What system or structure is failing with the movement disorders that develop with Parkinson's disease? Is human consciousness centered in a particular location? We have been working on questions like these since the time of the ancient Egyptians, who were alert to the knowledge that could be gained about the localization of brain functions from observing war wounds and associated specific damaged areas with behavioral deficits. This method of observation has continued to the current day.

In the nineteenth century, experimenters extended this principle to the lab, damaging (lesioning) brain areas in laboratory animals and observing the behavioral results. Advances in microscopy and staining methods showed brain structures to be complex arrangements of individual neurons, with connections to the peripheral nervous system. In the 1870s, direct electrical stimulation of the surface of the exposed brain began, when two German scientists stimulated selected spots in the parietal lobes of a dog and observed the resulting contraction of different muscle groups, indicating that the brain contains a motor-oriented map of the body (Hooper & Teresi, 1986).

In the twentieth century, a number of brain-imaging techniques were developed, which answered to several medical and research purposes (for descriptions of several types, see Table 8.1). Techniques that illuminate structure provide anatomical information and help to link visible abnormalities in brain tissue with behavioral traits or diseases. We learn, for instance, that in people with certain types of schizophrenia, the ventricles—fluid-filled cavities in the brain—are enlarged and that certain neural connections are disordered. On the other hand, techniques that reveal activity in brain regions have proved invaluable for showing which parts of the brain are involved in certain tasks. For instance, when a subject is reading a word from a screen, we would expect particular regions of the visual cortex to be activated, but brain scans show a complex of other active regions as well. And timing is a key factor. Ideally, we would like to be able to map activity as it happens. Therefore, one of the measures of the value of these developing technologies is how quickly they are able to capture an image of active brain parts.

Brain imaging has taught us a tremendous amount about the association of brain structures with specific activities. However, it is important to note that, even with a technique as sophisticated as functional MRI, which can "see" almost in the moment what brain regions are active, brain researchers still make inferences about the relationship between what is being measured—increased blood flow or increased glucose or oxygen use—and the significance of a particular part of the brain. By analogy, if we collect data about the traffic flow patterns in a city, we learn a certain amount about the geography of activity, but still have limited information about what the drivers and passengers in the cars are doing, or why.

A common approach in describing the brain is to assign functions to the various structures and districts, as though they were parts of an engine. It is true that in many cases a specific structure plays a key role in a specific function. There are clearly important centers for balance, appetite, language, motor skills and so forth. If these centers are damaged or intentionally lesioned, predictable dysfunctions result. However, we have learned from brain imaging that, when a subject performs a task, like moving a hand, remembering an event, or viewing a photo of a loved one, multiple brain regions are activated. These observations yield two views of the brain. On one hand, when we consider an integrated function like a hand movement, we see that it is not localized in sharply defined brain structures. Each function can be seen as having a team of structures organizing it, and there might be a key brain part that can be envisioned as a conductor who leads the whole orchestra in a particular specialty. On the other hand, when we isolate a given brain structure, we see that it might participate in an array of functions, allowing no simple correspondence between structure and function.

Table 8.1. Developments in Brain Imaging

Name	Description	Measures . . .
electroencephalography (EEG)	Electroencephalography (a word made up of Greek roots for "electric—head—writing") was introduced in the 1920s. It uses electrodes attached to the scalp to record weak electric signals that emanate from brain regions and pass through the skull. These signals provide some information about the instantaneous timing and location of brain activity, but because electroencephalograms record signals from millions of cells at once, they are not very accurate at matching functions to regions. However, EEGs can inform us about seizure activity, tumors, and sleep stages.	activity
computerized axial tomography (CAT or CT)	CAT (also called CT) scanning, introduced in the 1970s, reveals brain structure by registering the density of tissue. Multiple X-rays are taken in an arc around the head to collect a set of two-dimensional images (like slices), and a computer assembles them into a three-dimensional map of brain structures (*tomos* refers to cuts or slices, and *graph* to their writing or recording). Radioactive dye can be used to highlight blood vessels. This technique provides medium-resolution (that is, not very sharply defined) information about damaged areas and functions. However, as with the scrutiny of war wounds earlier, areas affected by hemorrhage, strokes, or tumors can be identified and linked to behavioral deficits.	structure
Single photon emission computed tomography (SPECT)	SPECT scanning assembles a set of two-dimensional images like a CAT scan, but measures activity rather than structure. The scan reveals the amount of blood flow in a brain region. This is done by registering the amount of a radioactive isotope introduced into the bloodstream. When a region is active, its blood flow increases, as well as the amount of detectable isotope. SPECT scanning can localize brain activity, but with a time lag of about twenty seconds.	activity

continued -->

positron emission tomography (PET)	Using a similar technique, based on the radioactive labeling of glucose in the blood, PET scanning provides a more accurate measure of brain activity. Because active brain regions metabolize glucose at a higher rate, this allows the computer more immediately to construct color metabolic maps of specific functions while the brain is performing them. Comparisons of scans can reveal which brain regions engage in processes such as moving, focusing attention on an image, and so forth. Newer modifications of this technique, using the radioactive labeling of other substances, can reveal enzyme activity and the binding patterns of neurotransmitters in brain circuits.	activity
magnetic resonance imaging (MRI)	In the 1970s and 1980s, MRI was introduced and refined. It provides a detailed still image of brain structure. A powerful magnetic field and radio pulses stimulate the protons in the atoms of brain tissue to release radio waves, which differ in amount from tissue to tissue, based on density. A computer then assembles this data into a high-resolution image of brain structure.	structure
functional magnetic resonance imaging (fMRI)	A revolutionary variation of MRI developed in 1993, fMRI applies the same technique, but to activity instead of structure. It uses the detection of magnetic fields to register small changes in brain metabolism, particularly oxygen use. The results are sharp, three-dimensional images that can be collected in series with a mere one-second time lag, and the scans can be compared to accurately associate specific brain regions with particular functions.	activity

A case in point is plasticity. This is the brain's ability to form new synapses and circuits. The young, developing brain grows and shapes its circuitry in response to environmental stimuli, so that exposure to an environment rich in stimuli leads to a brain with more synaptic connections. The brain retains some of this ability, which makes it possible to form new memories, and thus learn, and to create "workarounds" if an area is damaged. For instance, if the speech area is damaged early in development (usually before ten years of age), other parts of the brain can take over, and speech functions will survive intact. In cases of early blindness, part of the brain's "real estate" typically used for vision can be reassigned to hearing. Even older people who suffer brain damage from an ischemic stroke (a blood clot blocking brain capillaries and blood flow and causing a kill-off of cells) often undergo significant recoveries as neural connections are re-established. And there are cases like this to ponder:

> *There's a young student at this university who has an IQ of 126, has gained a first class honors degree in mathematics, and is socially completely normal. And yet the boy has virtually no brain. ... Instead of the normal 4.5 centimeter thickness of brain tissue between the ventricles and the cortical surface, there was just a thin layer of mantle measuring a millimeter or so. His cranium is filled mainly with cerebrospinal fluid.* (Lewin, 1980, pp. 1232-1234)

A fair guess, in this case, is that fluids have slowly compressed the cortical neurons to a remarkable extent, without disrupting their function, or, more to our point, that existing structures have taken over the work of absent ones.

Another dimension of its flexibility is the ability of the brain to function holistically, to act as a whole in organizing input from the senses. It is an impressive integrating organ. Here is a remarkable example: If you watch someone touch your hand, you see it almost immediately, whereas there should be about a half-second lag before you feel the touch come to consciousness, because the visual and tactile signals traverse the nerve pathways to the primary sensory cortex at different rates; however, the brain processes the sight and the feel of the touch so that both seem to occur together (Rock, 2004).

If the brain were as simple as we might once have hoped, we could activate or subtract a brain part and draw a correlation to a new or missing mode of behavior, but even this is not always so. For instance, destroying the subthalamic nucleus in the motor system produces *hemiballism*, where the patient compulsively moves as though throwing a ball. But the subthalamic nucleus does not exist for the express purpose of suppressing hemiballism; this is simply the remaining brain's response to the damage. Thus, loss of functioning in one nucleus can cause a series of complicated disruptions and imbalances in webs of pathways, modulatory circuits and feedback loops. Considerations like these imply a nest of problems for the psychopharmacologist. Eliciting a desired drug effect is not just a matter of letting the circulation carry a drug into the brain. To begin with, the blood-brain barrier prefers certain compounds to others, and this can exclude important therapeutic substances. Another problem is that, once a drug has penetrated the inner sanctum of the brain, there is no way to limit its movements, because the fluid around the neurons occupies one continuous space that includes all the synaptic gaps between them. Hence, a substance diffusing in this fluid has access to the synapses and their receptors. This is not to say it will act at every site, but it could affect certain receptor types in a number of different systems. For instance, if a drug affects dopaminergic neurons, it will affect them in all brain areas that it can reach and will produce not only the desired effect, but many more besides. Another factor is that the different neurotransmitters, both excitatory and inhibitory, may be linked in intricate ways that are not yet understood. For example, the undetected inhibition of one neurotransmitter may lead down the line to the surplus of another. It was discovered that schizophrenia is associated with dopamine overactivity; however, later evidence showed that dopamine was simply the most visible link in a chain of local effects and neurotransmitter relationships. Add to these considerations the properties we have been discussing—the brain's complexity and plasticity, and the fact that impairing a system can produce new, seemingly additional behavior—and you begin to understand some of the hurdles facing psychopharmacologists in their attempts to deliver specific drugs to specific receptors to produce specific therapeutic effects.

DIVISIONS AND KEY PARTS OF THE BRAIN

According to neuroscientist Christof Koch, "the brain is the most complex system in the known universe" (as cited in Rock, 2004, p. 173). It sits in the skull, protected by a three-ply membrane and suspended in a bath of cerebrospinal fluid, a watery cushion that buoys it up for support and keeps us from rattling it every time we turn our heads. This fluid is part of the general, protective system of cerebrospinal fluid that surrounds the spinal column as well as the brain, and presents one route of accessibility for drugs. Complex and vulnerable, about the consistency of oatmeal, the brain feeds mainly on oxygen and glucose, but lacks the capacity to store them. If the blood supply is cut for 10 seconds, unconsciousness follows; lack of blood for a few minutes can cause irreversible damage or death. This is a consideration in the case of abusable drugs like the dental anesthetic nitrous oxide (laughing gas), which, when inhaled, blocks the supply of oxygen to the brain. The

The anatomy of the brain is like the design of an ancient citadel, a vast complex of structures. Instead of being torn down and rebuilt over eons, it has grown through additions and encirclements, expanding in layers, while the old inner edifices are left standing preserving our more primitive heritage as organisms. Evolving over millennia, some areas have shifted their functions, as capabilities such as language and speech have developed. And given the brain's plasticity, changes continue to occur in response to need. If one neighborhood" is destroyed or fails to function, such as through a stroke, others are able to take over to some extent.

The brain is estimated to have about 150 types of neurons, classified according to the patterns of their dendrites, which may be reminiscent of trees, bushes, river deltas and electronic circuit boards. A cluster of somae (cell bodies), which would be referred to as a *ganglion* in the periphery, in the brain is called a **nucleus**. The cells of a nucleus are considered to work in common on a particular function. Nuclei appear as gray matter to the naked eye and come in a variety of forms, small and large. Bundles of axons, which would be referred to as nerves in the periphery, are called **pathways** or **tracts** in the brain. These appear as white matter to the naked eye because they are sheathed in myelin.

The layout of nuclei and their axons is varied and complex. The substantia nigra, for instance, is a small nucleus consisting of the somae of neurons that synthesize the neurotransmitter dopamine, and project axons to a number of other brain areas. Somae in the primary motor area just under the surface of the skull send out axons that project all the way down the spine, to connect with the neurons that work the muscles of the legs. In general, the pathways connect nuclei, running forward and back within brain hemispheres, side to side between hemispheres, and up and down between higher- and lower-order nuclei.

Nuclei are organized into **systems**, which might be devoted to a single function, such as visual processing or motor movements, or into a set of **sub-systems** managing a set of related functions, such as maintaining homeostasis in the body by regulating glucose levels, temperature, the salt content of the blood, and so forth.

The largest scale organization of the brain is its arrangement into symmetrical structures and the overall division of the major part of it into right and left hemispheres, in communication with one another through a huge swath of pathways called the corpus callosum. (Often, as you will see, structures that are found on both sides are referred to in the singular.) In many cases, nuclei in each hemisphere control the opposite side of the body. And although structures mirror one another, they might have related, but different functions on one side or the other. For instance, the hippocampus manages memories, but the left side manages linguistic and autobiographical memories, while the right side manages spatial memory. This means that some functions are localized in a single hemisphere.

The differences in the characterization of the right and left brain are referred to as hemisphericity. The left hemisphere is considered dominant because of its functions relating to language and thought. It appears to regulate routine behaviors, whereas the right hemisphere mediates emotional arousal and rapid responses to unexpected environmental stimuli. Right brain activity is also correlated with experiences of negative emotion (damage to the left hemisphere is more likely to be accompanied by depression, possibly due to a release of suppression or modulation of right hemispheric functioning). Another distinction is that the left hemisphere helps us to focus on local aspects of the environment, while the right handles spatial relations that allow us to take in a whole scene. Dean C. Delis and colleagues demonstrated this in a fascinating experiment in which they asked patients to draw from memory an image of the letter H made up of smaller letter A's, such as this:

```
AA      AA
AA      AA
AA      AA
AAAAAAA
AA      AA
AA      AA
AA      AA
```

Patients with right hemisphere damage (leaving the detail-oriented left hemisphere functions intact) could recall details of the image (viz., that it consisted of A's) but not the overall H pattern. Patients with damage on the left (leaving the global-oriented right hemisphere function intact) could reproduce the H pattern, but not the details (MacNeilage, Rogers & Vallortigara, 2009, p. 63).

The sections that follow contain a whirlwind tour of the anatomy of the brain. The list of sites is daunting; however, consider this your first encounter with a variety of brain structures that we will be re-visiting in more detail later in this chapter when we discuss brain functions, and still later in other chapters as we discuss the layout of neurotransmitter pathways and the sites of action of various drugs.

The Hindbrain - oldest

In addition to its side-to-side hemisphericity, the brain is organized vertically into three parts or layers, which have developed upward and outward over the millenia. The lowest, oldest and most primitive region is the **hindbrain** (see Figure 8.1), a stem-like extension of the spinal cord, less than three inches long, located above the neck at the base of the skull. Through here passes all input on its way to higher brain centers. It is sometimes called "the reptilian brain," because, organizationally, it has not changed much since the development of reptiles. That is to say, the organization of the hindbrain of the reader is much the same as that of a snake.

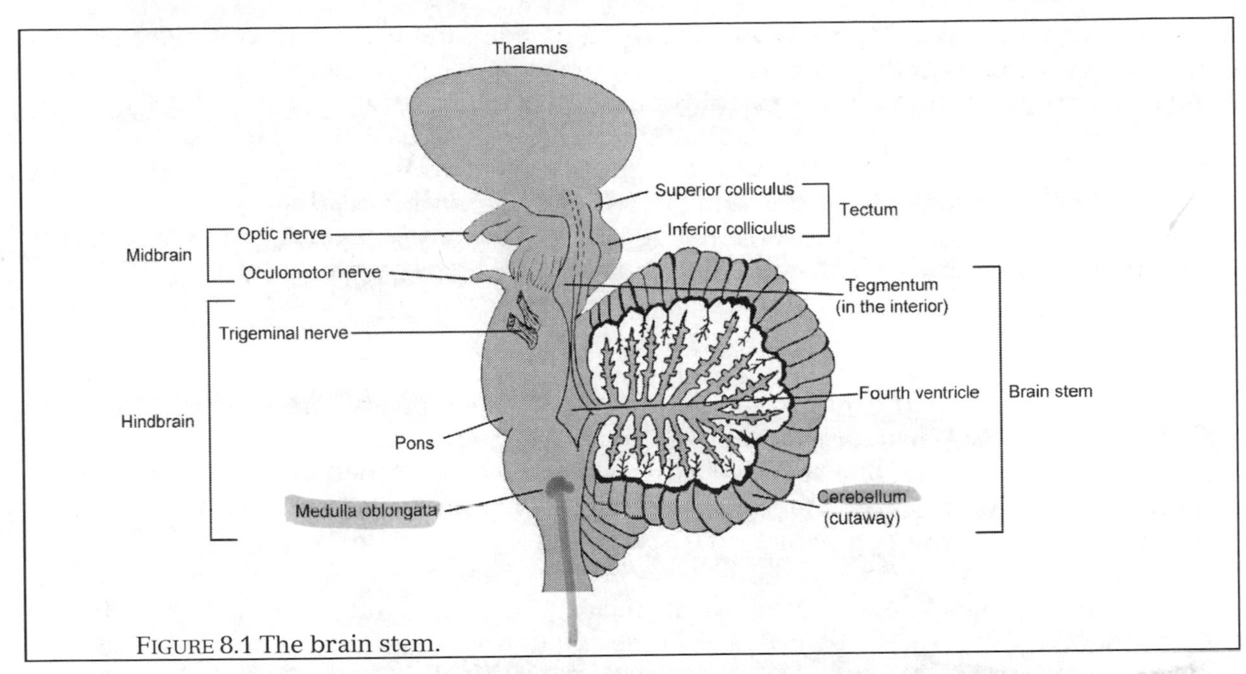

FIGURE 8.1 The brain stem.

Given that this is the most ancient part of the brain, and one we share to some degree with the dinosaurs, it is a site that regulates many simple basic functions. Structures found here include the **medulla oblongata**, which regulates autonomic functions such as breathing and heartbeat, the **reticular formation**, which maintains arousal and wakefulness, and the **cerebellum**, which, among other functions, mediates balance, the timing of movements and the organization of highly coordinated movements.

The pons, or "bridge," is a thick bulge at the back of the brainstem. Through it, sensory neurons pass from the spine on their way up to the midbrain, and motor neurons on their way from the cerebellum to the cortex at the top of the skull. Most of the information passing between the cerebellum and the brain proper crosses through the bridge of the pons. Hence, we might think of it as the bridge to the cerebellum. Part of the network of neurons making up the reticular formation is contained in the pons. Here also is found a grand crossover of nerve fibers from the right brain to the left side of the body, and vice versa.

The Midbrain

The second grand division of the brain is the **midbrain**. This is a short strip of tissue, less than an inch long, above the hindbrain. Together, the midbrain and hindbrain are referred to as the **brainstem**. The midbrain mediates a number of functions, mostly relating to seeing, hearing, and movement. Its two main anatomical features are the **tectum** and the **tegmentum**.

The **tectum** is a brain region made up of two pairs of "little hills" or colliculi. The forward pair (the superior colliculi) governs visual reflexes like blinking, pupil size, eye focusing, and movement. The rear pair (the inferior colliculi) controls auditory reflexes, as in automatically adjusting the ear to volume levels. Combining these functions, the tectum has reflex systems that orient the head and eyes toward sudden sights and sounds.

The **tegmentum** ("covering") forms the floor of one of the large fluid-filled cavities in the brain, the fourth ventricle. It is part of the motor system, passing signals down to the spinal cord and up to the basal ganglia. Located here are nuclei for gross body movements and movement of the eyes. The tegmentum contains two nuclei that are extremely important for drug actions. The **ventral tegmental area** is the key nucleus of cells whose axons make up the main pathway mediating reward and pleasure. The **substantia nigra**, or "black stuff," is a small nucleus packed with the somae of cells that use the neurotransmitter dopamine and which send axons out to other key brain areas (see Figure 8.1). It is an important center for body movements. Damage to this nucleus can result in movement disorders and distortions, like the trembling hands of Parkinson's disease.

The Forebrain

All the structures above the mid-brain are referred to as the **forebrain**. These fall into two sub-divisions: the **old brain** and the **new brain**.

The old brain consists of a set of structures that have developed above the brainstem, in the very center of the brain, near the fluid-filled cavity known as the third ventricle (see Figure 8.2). Many of the behavioral characteristics of birds, mammals and other warm-blooded animals, such as social bonding and caring for offspring, which differentiate them from the reptiles, are mediated by the nuclei and systems found here. In animals that possess them, these structures show very little evolutionary variation among species.

Two key structures in the old brain are the **thalamus** and the **hypothalamus**. The thalamus actually consists of two symmetrical nuclei on opposite sides of the brain (the **thalami**), but together they are usually referred to in the singular as the thalamus. They make up a reception area for the processing of incoming sensory data on its way from the brainstem up to the cortex. The second major structure is the **hypothalamus** (meaning "below the thalamus"), which regulates homeostasis in a number of body systems via the autonomic nervous system, and so is involved to a large extent in maintaining chemical, temperature and other balances in the organism.

The old brain encompasses a number of nuclei that make up the **limbic system**, which is primarily associated with the management of emotion, memory, and motivation.

Just below the cortex in the old brain are the **basal ganglia**, two large nuclei like ram's horns or loosely curled-up tadpoles. They are composed of cell bodies that are part of a secondary motor system that fine-tunes gross body movements—for instance, steadying and smoothing the motions of the hands.

The second sub-division of the forebrain, the **new brain**, forms the outermost layer of the whole brain, enclosing all of the other structures. It is the latest evolutionary addition, mediating functions like learning, judgment and reasoning. Because of its gnarled, barky surface, which gives the brain its distinctive, walnut-like appearance, the new brain was named in Latin the **cortex** ("new bark"). Its underlayer, only three cells deep, is an older evolutionary development known as the **paleocortex**, while the newer, outer part, six cell layers deep, is the **neocortex**.

The **neocortex** forms a thin veneer of gray matter only about 5 millimeters thick, but it contains an extraordinary number of cells. Three-fourths of it is made up of **association areas**. These are areas devoted to neural processes within the brain; that is, they do not mediate interactions with the environment. They include areas that integrate information from several sensory systems, that process information for decision-making, and that create associations between memory and emotion. Receiving most of its input from the thalamus, the gray matter of the neocortex is the stuff of intelligence. Though the layout

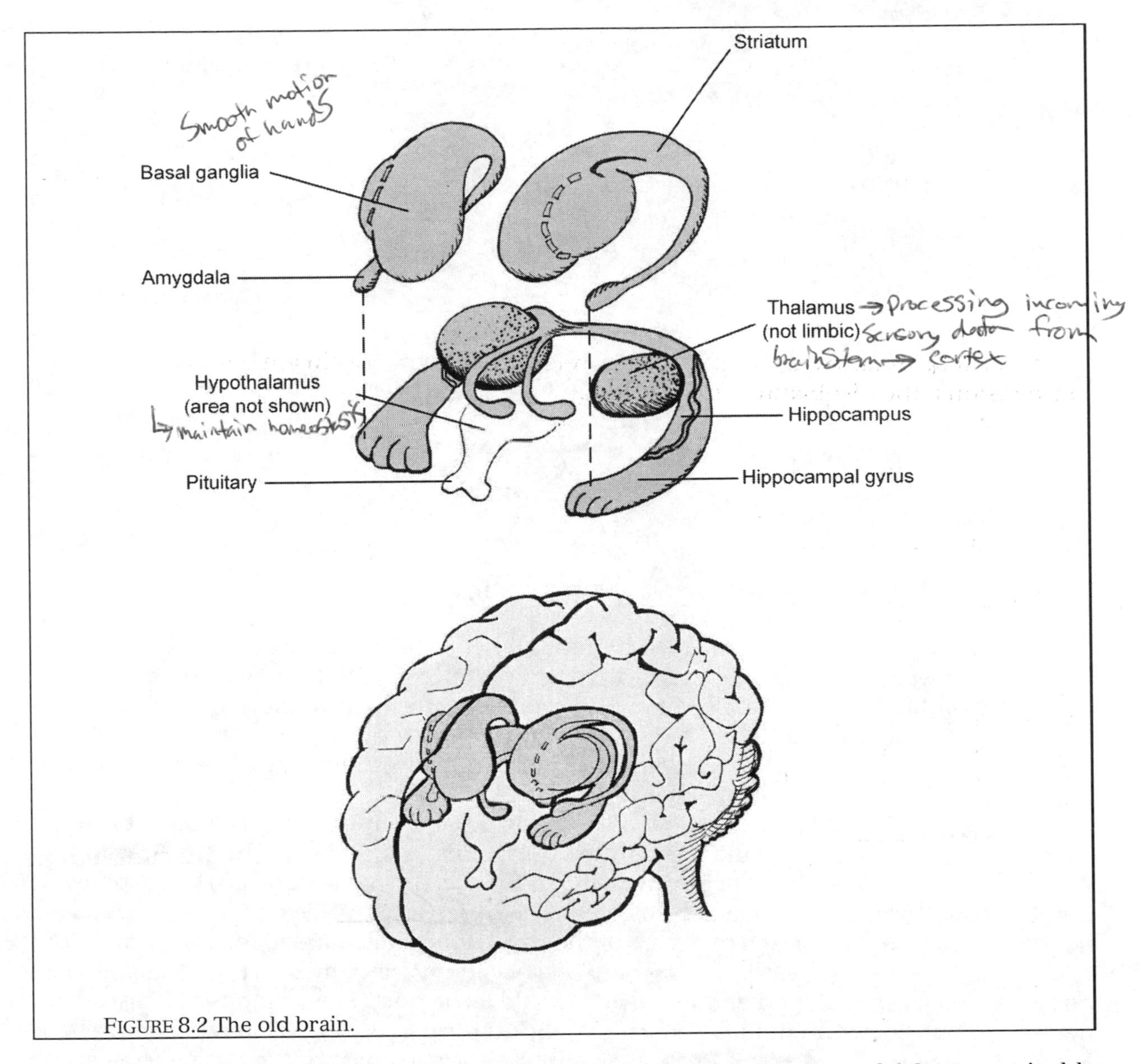

FIGURE 8.2 The old brain.

of its surface is seemingly chaotic, the cerebral ridges and fissures are fairly recognizable from brain to brain. These wrinkles are due to the fact that the surface area of the cortex is much larger than that of the skull, so that it rumples as it grows.

In the cortex are found groups of cells specializing in vision, memory, speech, the sense of body (proprioception), learning, and, one can fairly speculate, an unimaginable number of other complex integrations that fuse all sensory input, decision-making, and motor output into the coherent impression we have of ourselves and the world.

The entire cortex is cloven by a deep fissure into two hemispheres, whose direct connection is a strip of axons bundled together—the **corpus callosum**, or "hard body." Severing the corpus callosum, which is done in a procedure to treat severe epilepsy known as split-brain surgery, cuts off the ability of one cortical hemisphere to communicate directly with the other, although lower brain centers remain in communication.

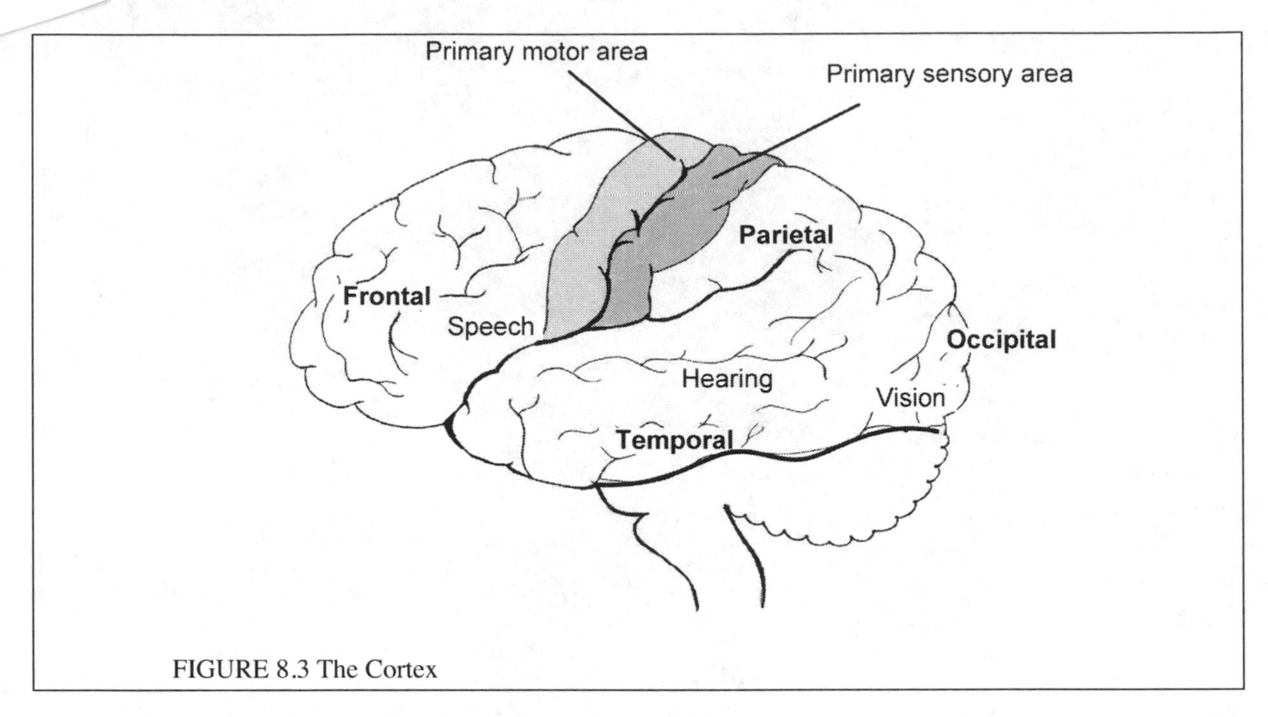

FIGURE 8.3 The Cortex

Furthermore, the cortex is divided into four lobes, whose names derive from the skull bones that cover them. As with many other brain structures, these lobes are found symmetrically on both sides of the brain, but do not necessarily have the same functions on both sides. As anatomical features, they are only a rough indication of the functional division of the cortex. (And like other symmetrical brain features, they are often referred to in the singular.) In a nutshell, these lobes are as follows:

The **occipital lobe**, entirely engaged with vision, is found at the very back of the head. That is why a blow to the rear of the skull makes us see stars. The **temporal lobes,** situated on each side of head below the temples (hence, the name), are largely responsible for auditory sensation and visual memories. The **parietal lobes** lie under the parietal bones, a pair of bones on the mid-part of the roof of the skull, named for the "wall of the cavity" they enclose. These lobes mediate sensory input from the body, such as touch and body, as well as spatial, perception. In addition, a large portion is composed of association neurons involved with cognitive functions, including perception, sentence comprehension, and learning. The **frontal lobes** make up the forward part of the brain. They are the site a number of higher functions, such as spatial organization, the appreciation of experience, learning, intellection, judgment, problem-solving and personality. They are also the key site for decision-making and the execution of motor output. The prefrontal lobe part of the frontal lobe just behind the forehead, is the foremost and most evolutionarily advanced portion of the brain.

In the following discussions, we will briefly explain how the brain mediates certain key functions, keeping in mind that, in producing many of their effects, drugs affect these physiological processes.

REFLEXES AND AUTONOMIC FUNCTION

Housed in the oldest part of the brain, the hindbrain, are several centers that control the basic functions of body organs and systems. The **medulla oblongata**, whose name means "rather long marrow," is an inch of tissue, no more than a slight swelling at the top of the spinal cord, filled with ascending and descending fibers. Primitive and stubbornly alive, it contains reflex centers for the autonomic regulation of heartbeat, breathing, vomiting, blood pressure, the strength of the heart contraction, sneezing, swallowing, and gastrointestinal functions.

The medulla is a major site for a number of drug effects. Sedatives and depressants like alcohol, barbiturates and opiates, at high enough blood levels, can depress the respiratory center to the point of stopping breathing and causing suffocation. This is the most common means of death in drug overdoses. A drug that stimulates the **chemical trigger zone** in the medulla causes nausea, such as heroin when it is first used, before tolerance develops. And the **emetic center**, when stimulated, causes vomiting.[1] The first use of nicotine is usually unpleasant because it stimulates this center. Other drugs influence heart rates and blood pressure through medullary actions.

ALERTNESS, AROUSAL, AND SLEEP

Beginning in the medulla is an elaborate tangle of nerve cells and fibers called the **reticular** (that is, "netlike") **formation**, which controls levels of arousal and alertness of the brain. This system reaches from the hindbrain into the forebrain and sends out a constant flood of signals to form a background of general arousal. Without this, it would always be night in the cortex and the brain would remain asleep. All shades of awareness from unconsciousness to wakefulness are expressions of the activity in the reticular formation.

When sensory input is passing up through the brainstem, the reticular formation is activated by collaterals from the sensory pathways. The reticular formation then sends out impulses to prime the higher centers in the forebrain, arousing them and preparing them to receive the incoming signal. For a sensation to be perceived, therefore, it must reach both the reticular formation and the cortex. If the signal arrives in the cortex, and the cortex remains unaroused by the reticular formation, the signal will remain unperceived.

In the midbrain, where principal centers for sight and sound are located (the superior and inferior colliculi), the reticular formation serves a similar alerting function by mediating the orienting response, the mechanism that causes us to automatically direct our attention to a sudden sound. In general, the reticular formation can be seen as the volume dial of conscious awareness.

The connections in the reticular formation are multisynaptic and especially susceptible to drug influences. Drugs like caffeine and amphetamine ("speed"), which can stimulate neurons in the reticular formation, cause arousal and wakefulness. Laboratory rats stimulated at certain sites in the reticular formation are roused from sleep rudely and thoroughly. On the other hand, drugs like benzodiazepines, which are used as sleeping pills, act by lowering arousal and promoting loss of consciousness.

1. Opiates often cause vomiting by direct gastrointestinal actions.

Sleep

Sleep is not just a time of lights-out for brain activity while nuclei rest, but a highly orchestrated cycle of changes in cerebral functioning that is part of our daily biological (circadian) rhythm. To state it briefly, during sleep, from four to seven times a night, the brain cycles through several stages marked by distinctive alterations in brain wave activity, traveling from waking to deep, slow wave sleep and back. (We describe these in more detail in the chapter on alcohol.) At certain points in the cycle, sleep is accompanied by dreaming and by rapid movement of the eyeballs (REM) under closed eyelids, presumably as we track objects of vision in our dreams. Moreover, so that we do not act out our dreams, certain brain systems disengage our motor circuits. (The failure to disengage results in phenomena like sleepwalking, while an awareness of this disengagement, should it occur, is experienced as paralysis).

It has been theorized that animals developed sleep over the course of evolution to conserve energy during periods of inactivity (for humans, namely, the night-time) and to make it easier to remain hidden from predators. It is clear that, to some extent, sleep is involved in consolidating and storing memories and may play a role in learning. Work by Tonegawa (Alleyne, 2009) has shown that the brain stores most memories in the hippocampus for about a day, but during sleep these are replayed, and certain items are moved into long-term storage in the cortex.

In general, during dreaming, areas of the brain devoted to planning, logical thinking, and self-reflection are turned off, while areas devoted to emotion (the limbic system), memory, and vision become very active. (Interestingly, the primary visual cortex, which constructs perceptions from the environment, shuts down, while the visual association cortex, the higher order visual system that processes visual content internally, becomes more active even than when we are awake. Therefore, if you pry the eyes of a dreaming sleeper open and present an object before them, no perception or memory of this will register, while the dreamer can still vividly see imagery originating from other brain areas.)

Four main sites and nuclei manage the processes of sleep. The forebrain, in conjunction with the **raphé nucleus**, produces the stage of deep sleep marked by the slowing of brain waves. The reticular formation in the brainstem provides the arousal to keep particular regions of the forebrain active. The "blue nucleus," or **locus coeruleus**, part of the reticular formation found in the pons, controls the stage of sleep marked by rapid eye movements, which are most closely associated with dreams, especially complex dreams with story lines. And the hypothalamus puts out connections to all of these other areas, indicating that it plays a modulatory or integrating role among the other sites

BIOLOGICAL DRIVES

Under (hypo-) the thalamus in the forebrain is the hypothalamus, a small but important structure. It is an indistinct cluster of nuclei about the size of a thumb-tip, which regulates the functions of the autonomic nervous system, eating, drinking, sleeping, and body temperature. It is the home of an enormous number of specialized neurons, in sub-systems that serve to maintain various sorts of equilibrium (homeostasis) in the body. For instance, glucoreceptors measure the blood's sugar content and regulate the organism's sense of hunger or satiety. Osmoreceptors gauge the saltiness (osmolarity) of the extracellular fluid (the blood, indirectly), and they control drinking behavior and the reabsorption of fluids by the kidneys. Thermoreceptors sense the body's temperature and initiate appropriate responses like panting, shivering, sweating, and dilating or constricting the blood vessels in the skin. The hypothalamus is also involved in aggression, emotions (e.g., anxiety and anger), and sexual behavior. Steroid receptors check the sex hormones in the blood and register the sex drive. Found here as well is the "biological clock" that regulates our daily rhythms of sleep and waking.

The hypothalamus works closely with the pituitary gland to produce its effects. Lodged almost exactly in the center of the brain, the pituitary is the master gland of the endocrine hormonal system. Its name, meaning "slime gland," is a misnomer stemming from the belief that nasal secretions flowed from it, since it lies just beyond the sinuses, where it seems to hang on a stalk from the underbelly of the hypothalamus. After gauging the state of the organism by monitoring the blood, the hypothalamus signals the pituitary to release the hormones that will instruct the organism to correct or balance the condition. The effects of this variety of hormones are wide; they can suppress the release of urine or stimulate the production of sex hormones or the release of anxiety-causing hormones.

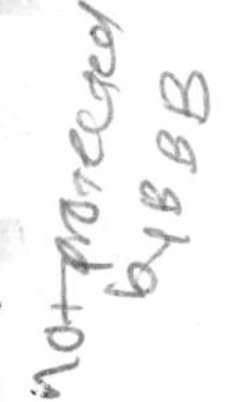

Because the hypothalamus has a rich blood supply and is relatively unguarded by the blood-brain barrier, many drugs influence it rapidly and can produce effects involving the heart, lungs, and gut. By acting on the hypothalamus, stimulants like amphetamine and cocaine reduce the appetite. Opiates like heroin acting here can cause readjustments of temperature levels and a reduction of the sex drive. And nineteenth century users of hashish, a product of marijuana, in high doses, reported that they were seized by an infernal, parching thirst, which suggests hypothalamic actions.

EMOTION

Anything that falls within the orbit of our experience, we can be assured, is mediated by some part of the brain. And this is true of our emotions. These are characterized by neuroscientists as physiological states, recognizable by signs such as elevated heart rate, which are associated with feelings, the subjective appreciation of experience. Our feelings are constructed by an extensive system of complexly interconnected nuclei in the old brain, the **limbic system**, which also mediates memory and learning, and is closely associated with the decision-making areas of the cortex.

The naming of the limbic system originated with the French physician and anatomist Paul Broca, who called it the limbic lobe of the brain (limbic meaning "bordering") because it extends along the margins of the **corpus callosum**, the four-inch strap of tissue that transfers information between the two cerebral hemispheres. It also lies on the border between the old and new brains. However, after Broca, this area was understood not to be a lobe of the brain like the lobes of the cortex, but a vast system of interconnected nuclei.

The limbic system performs a number of functions:

- By producing our sense of emotion and providing the emotional coloring to all of our activities and experiences, it affects how we relate to, and engage with, the world.
- It plays a key role in the reward system, mediating all of our feelings of pleasure and reward.
- Through its interconnections, it provides an emotional dimension to the activities of other systems, associating emotions with what we see and hear. Working with key areas of the cortex, it integrates emotion with decision-making and rational behavior; for instance, it helps to generate the shame or guilt we feel when making what we consider to

be a bad moral choice.

• Because it involves the hippocampus, an important structure for memory located partly in the temporal lobe, it participates in the formation and the emotional coloring of our memories.

• It enables us to compare past and present experiences and the feelings associated with them; for instance, it allows us to anticipate pleasure when repeating an action that gave us pleasure before, and through its complex feedback circuits, it allows us to evaluate ongoing processes and make changes in mid-stream, based on past experiences and our feelings about them.

• It mediates our moods (in the short term) and constructs our temperament and personality (in the long term).

Because of the many centers and the array of functions and connections in this area of the brain, the term "limbic system" is not entirely accurate in describing it. Overall, it is fair enough to say that key centers for emotional experience are found here. In the course of evolution, the limbic system built upon the more primitive functions of the brainstem and added emotional behaviors like those associated with warm-blooded and social animals such as mammals and birds: changes of mood; courtship, mating, emotional bonding and caring for offspring; social bonding; and feelings of empathy, docility and aggression toward others.

As a brain region, the limbic system is not anatomically distinct, but consists of a multitude of nuclei, with projections extending to other areas which can be seen to be activated in PET scans during limbic activity (Lane et al., 1997). Neither is the limbic system functionally distinct; it contains a number of nuclei that are parts of sub-systems with different functions. As a result, this is a very loosely defined topographic region of the forebrain.

Drug actions in the limbic system can affect our emotions and emotional states. We see this in agents that induce euphoria, that cause calming, and that relieve depression. The hallucinogen LSD can cause an oceanic emotional catharsis, and cocaine can exacerbate aggressiveness. The illicit stimulant Ecstasy (MDMA) is remarkable for producing a strong sense of social and emotional bonding with others, so much so that, because of it, some researchers have advocated for a new drug classification named *empathogens,* drugs that enhance empathy.

Among the various structures and areas considered part of the limbic system are the **amygdala**, which mediates feelings of fear and responses to threat; the **hippocampus**, an important nucleus for memory processing, especially short-term memory, and part of the circuitry that forms emotional memory; the **cingulate gyrus**, a brain region underlying the cortex, which is involved in certain emotional aspects of our social behavior (such as those involving fear and aggression); the **olfactory bulb**, part of a complex of nuclei linking emotion, smell, and memory; and the **hypothalamus**, which regulates the hormonal components of emotional responses, affecting organs in the periphery.

We will concentrate in this section on the **amygdala**, the **septum**, and the **cingulate gyrus**, and in the next section on the sub-systems that govern pleasure (reward) and pain (punishment).

The Amygdala

The amygdala consists, in fact, of two bilateral nuclei **(amygdalae)**, named in Latin for their resemblance to almonds, although they are referred to in the singular. They are found in the temporal lobe, at the tips of a pair of nuclei curling through the center of the brain like ram's horns, one at the tip of each horn (see Figure 8.4).

The amygdala has a number of functions. The most important involve the two main tactics associated with self-defense in response to threats: (1) fear responses like freezing (immobility) or flight, and (2) rage, aggression and fighting. Both of these are part of the so-called fight-or-flight response. Projections carrying direct input to the amygdala from the sensory processing centers in the thalamus and from the visual center in the lateral geniculate nucleus, enable it to coordinate an immediate response to a threat before having to fully identify the nature of the source, a process that would otherwise have to be referred to the cortex, causing a dangerous and possibly fatal delay. That is to say, you can be panicked and fleeing almost by reflex, without having to pause to identify what scared you. Connections from the amygdala to the hypothalamus and the extrapyramidal motor system activate the sympathetic and motor responses needed to gear the organism for flight or combat.

Consistent with these observations, when certain parts of the amygdala are activated, fear and anxiety are the characteristic response (flight), while stimulation of other areas produces rage and aggressive assault (fight). Conversely, monkeys lesioned in the amygdala on both sides of the brain show a loss of fear of their human keepers and an overall lack of emotional responsiveness (Kluver & Bucy, 1937). Several of these effects are likewise seen in cases of rabies, a disease that damages and disrupts areas near the amydgala. Rabid animals in the wild show a lack of fear and might approach and attack humans.

The amygdala is involved in learned fears and plays a role in psychiatric disorders that involve inappropriate fear responses, like phobias and the anxiety of post-traumatic stress disorder. Treatment in unlearning these responses relies on pathways extending from the amygdala to the prefrontal cortex.

More broadly, the amygdala assigns emotional significance to sensory input and helps to consolidte memories of emotionally arousing experiences (McGaugh, 2004). Through its actions, we can recognize emotion in other people's voices and faces, which is important in love and friendship. In addition, it has taste and odor connections and is involved in seeking, eating, chewing, drinking, and swallowing behavior. Kluver and Busy's monkeys, lesioned in the amygdala, ate and mouthed non-food objects, and engaged in indiscriminate sexual behavior (Kluver & Bucy, 1937).

The Septal Region

Intimately connected to the amygdala, and located under the front end of the corpus callosum, are the **septal nuclei**, divided by a membrane called the **septum** (from Latin for "partition") (see Figure 8.4). Although they have diverse functions, which are not completely understood, their primary function seems to be inhibitory. Lesioning of the septal nuclei causes hyperactivity, and the inhibition or removal of the septal nuclei results in a (possibly temporary) condition of uncontrollable aggression called *septal rage*. A usually tame animal in this condition becomes wildly irritable; if touched gently with a pencil, it will attack.

The septal nuclei also mediate a number of altruistic behaviors that contribute to the survival of the species—such as courtship, sexual behavior, grooming, and the care and the protection of offspring. It has also been implicated in drinking behavior. Certain sites in the septal region are part of the reward system, connected to other limbic areas and

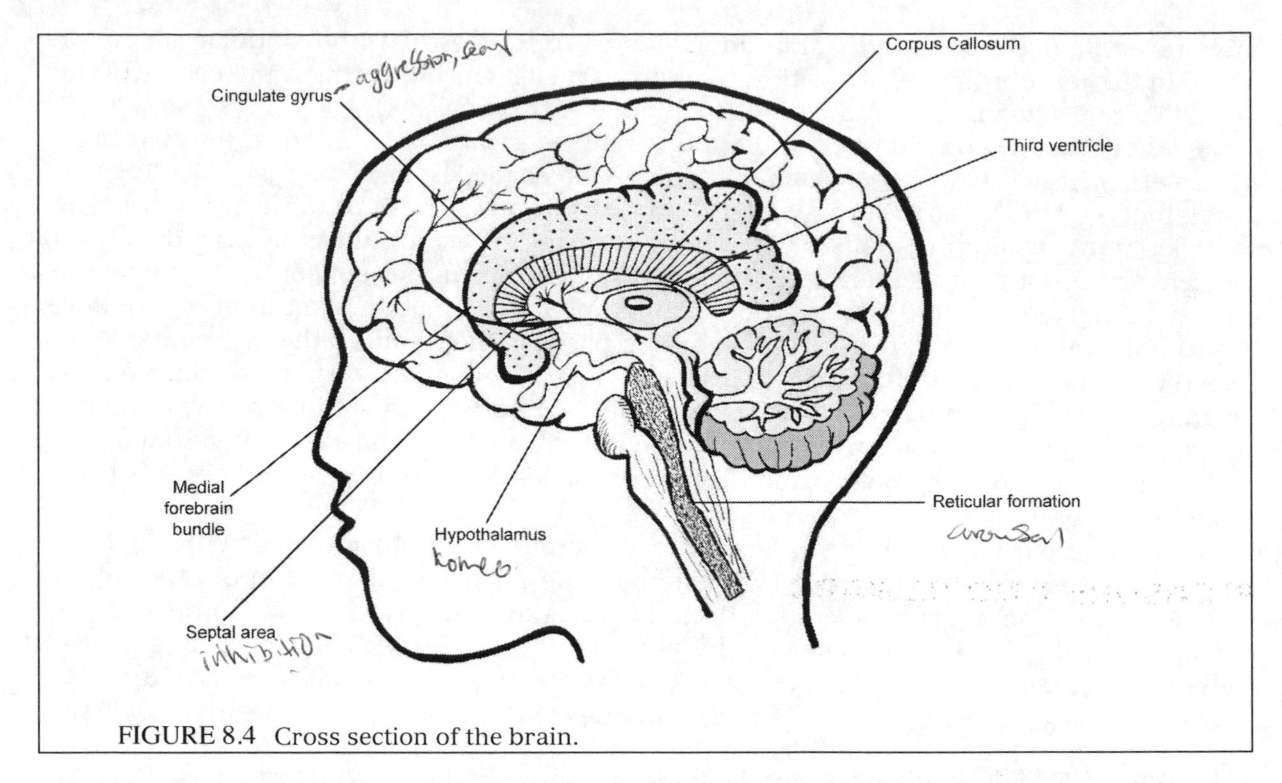

FIGURE 8.4 Cross section of the brain.

reward circuits; stimulation of these sites can produce intense pleasure, manifested as strong behavioral reinforcement (Olds & Milner, 1956), and can cheer depression.

The Cingulate Gyrus

The cingulate gyrus, or "girdling convolution," arches in part over the top of the limbic system; it is part of the older, three-layered cortex. Upon removal of the cingulate gyrus, animals show an increase of docility and a loss of fear, frustration, and aggression, an effect which may fade after six weeks (Grossman, 1967, p. 540). Monkeys with this gyrus removed have been described as follows:

> *Such an animal shows no grooming behavior or acts of affection toward its companions. In fact, it treats them as it treats all inanimate objects and will walk on them, bump into them if they happen to be in the way and will even sit on them. ... Such an animal never shows actual hostility to its fellows. It never fights nor tries to escape when removed from a cage.* (Ward, 1945, p. 440)

Other Limbic Conncetions

Some limbic sub-systems are involved in coloring memories with emotion and in linking memories to smells. Of note is a direct fiber tract to the **olfactory bulbs**. Through this connection, the limbic system can coordinate the experience of a smell that triggers a memory powerfully imbued with emotion. We can imagine a scenario that clarifies the idea that linkages among smell, emotion and memory have survival value: Suppose you are running an errand in an unfamiliar part of the city and become very hungry (that is, your hypothalamus signals that your blood glucose is low). Suddenly, as you walk, you get a whiff of the toasty aroma of baking pizza crust. Rounding a corner, you see a pizzeria. Now, even if you do not have the opportunity to stop and eat, your brain will register a pleasant emotional response to the smell and will form a heightened memory of the place, so that you can locate the shop if you come this way again. That is, you learn by the pleasant associations of smell to map the location of food. This mechanism helps us to negotiate our social landscape as well, because it is important to retain emotional memories of whether others have roused in us affection or repulsion. We do not typically do this with smell, but anyone who has walked a dog has a sense of the role smell plays in the social arrangements of some other species.

Limbic system nuclei are interconnected with the hypothalamus, which influences our bodily responses to emotional states, and with the reticular formation in the brainstem, whose influence on consciousness and awareness is implicated in memory, learning and emotion. Connections also run to areas of the cortex involved in decision-making and moral choice; this underlies the fact that learning, memory and our feelings about certain alternatives influence the choices we make.

PLEASURE AND REWARD

One factor that most drugs of abuse have in common is that they activate reward mechanisms in the nervous system. In evolution, these systems have developed as incentives for organisms to engage in survival behaviors such as eating, sleeping, reproducing, keeping clean, and defecating. Pleasure-giving drugs such as morphine, heroin, amphetamine, and cocaine (crack) are able to exploit these mechanisms and directly stimulate the reward systems, bypassing the necessity of performing the survival behaviors. In other words, you get the reward without doing the work, the "bonus without the onus," as the saying goes. Because of this, at advanced stages of certain addictions, individuals may severely neglect basic needs and hygiene. Why should someone eat, for instance, when their brain is already telling them they have feasted at the table of the master chef? The dangers of such drug intercession have moral implications, and have come to be associated by some with the view that pleasures unearned are sinful gains.

In the 1960s, researchers identified a system of nerve tracts connected with the limbic system, the **medial forebrain bundle (MFB)**, as the brain's seat of pleasure. These tracts extend from the mid-brain, through the hypothalamus, to innervate a number of forebrain sites. In laboratory experiments, researchers implanted electrodes in the MFBs of rats and provided the rats with a press bar, allowing them to stimulate the bundle in the region of the septal nuclei. This proved to be highly reinforcing; namely, it caused the rats to attempt to repeat the behavior and press the bar at any cost. One rat in the early trials astounded researchers by stimulating itself 2,000 times an hour until it dropped from exhaustion (Olds, 1958). Other rats have been known to give up eating, and even starve to death, rather than relinquish the press bar.

Two significant MFB pathways associated with the limbic system have been identified as central to our experience of pleasure and reward. Both project from a small nucleus in the midbrain known as the **ventral tegmental area**, or VTA. One pathway extends from the VTA to a large nucleus in the limbic system, called the **nucleus accumbens**. This is the **mesolimbic pathway**, the key reward circuit in the brain. When this connection is interrupted, rats like those in the bar-pressing experiment mentioned above, who furiously self-administered brain stimulation, completely lose interest in the bar. That is, the mild current no longer rewards them (Brebner et al., 2005). This pathway is crucial to our understanding of addiction and the euphoriant effects of drugs. Brain imaging experiments show that the nucleus accumbens reacts even at the anticipation of pleasure, when cocaine abusers are offered cocaine, or when they see a video of someone using cocaine, or even if they just see a photo of white lines on a mirror, resembling powdered cocaine ready to be snorted (Nestler & Malenka, 2004). In fact, every addicting activity, such as gambling or sexual addiction, involves the nucleus accumbens. The VTA-nucleus accumbens pathway is, therefore, recognized as the critical circuit in our experience of pleasurable, rewarding, and addicting stimuli. In other words, if it feels good, think nucleus accumbens.

The second significant pathway of the reward sub-system, the **mesocortical pathway**, proceeds forward from the nucleus accumbens and projects to two key parts of the cortex. The first is the **orbitofrontal cortical area**. When this region is stimulated experimentally, especially in the left hemisphere, subjects report an increased sense of well-being. More interesting, the orbitofrontal cortex is associated with the development of our understanding of societal rules and, consequently, the development of moral judgment. This has led to the supposition that hijacking the reward system through drug use can compromise good decision-making and moral choice. If this is so, it means that, in a direct physiological sense, drug use has the ability to erode our moral character by disrupting the "moral compass" in the brain (Norden, 2007a). Furthermore, it makes sense that a moral center is included in the reward system because moral behavior can involve empathy toward others, and cooperating with the social mores of one's culture generally produces good feelings of alignment and well-being (Norden, 2007b).

The second significant projection of the reward pathway, the **mesocortical pathway**, extends to the prefrontal cortex. It is most likely that stimulation in certain prefrontal areas provides us with our subjective experience of euphoria when the system is activated.

Other significant functions relating to reward are embodied in the connections that run from the limbic system to other parts of the brain. Connections to the hypothalamus and pituitary mediate arousal and our sense of bodily needs. Motor connections coordinate the movements needed to seek fulfillment. Connections to the hippocampus assist in the recall of events good and bad, and connections to the forebrain enable us to learn how to behave and make decisions regarding the objects of pleasure.

SENSORY PROCESSING

From microsecond to microsecond, from receptors from all over the body, the brain gathers vast amounts of information about the world and our relationship to it. A flood of input—information about the internal and external states of our body, about the positions of our limbs (proprioception), about pressures and pains, as well as the raw stuff of vision, hearing and touch (but not smell)—travels through ascending pathways and converges near the center of the brain in a massive reception area made up of twenty or so nuclei, the two thalami ("antechambers" or `"bedchambers'"), football-shaped masses of gray matter (somae) astride the top of the brainstem. (As we mentioned, these are collectively referred to as the **thalamus**). Parts of the thalamus receive input from specific sensory areas, like the eye or the ear, and relay it to specific areas of the cortex. In this respect, they truly are like antechambers to the higher centers. For the most part, this information is not blended or pooled, but is kept discrete, running in parallel pathways, and is distributed by the thalamus in every direction, to the appropriate parts of the cortex, to be brought into consciousness.

A second set of nuclei in the thalamus integrates sensory information with emotion and memory. It is probably here where the first experience of pain occurs, and where it is associated emotionally with past experiences of pain. "Once burned, twice shy," could be etched on these nuclei. Some parts of the thalami are also considered part of the limbic system, which regulates emotion. A third set of thalamic nuclei are less understood, but they seem to receive impulses from the reticular formation and, thus, play a role in arousal and possibly the conscious perception of stimuli. In general, the thalami are believed to be key generators of much of the synchronized activity in the nervous system, that seen in the brain waves registered by an electroencephalogram.

In many cases, information received by areas in the thalamus travels from there to primary areas of the cortex—that is, the areas that first receive the input. For instance, the primary cortical area for touch and body perception is located in the **parietal lobes**, which extend roughly from ear to ear across the top of the head, where a young girl's barrette or headband would be worn. On their foremost surface is a band of tissue called the **primary somatosensory area**, which receives a large portion of the sensory signals from the body. In fact, this is the place where our sense of having a body is assembled. That is to say, the perception we have of our body does not come from below us in space, but from "above us" in the parietal lobe. All the parts of the body are mapped out onto the brain surface in the primary somatosensory area, forming a schematic model of the body—a **homunculus** ("dwarf" or "little man"). Interestingly, the proportions of tissue dedicated to the homunculus do not correspond to those of the actual body. More sensitive areas like the face, lips, the tips of the fingers and the palms of the hands are allotted more cortical tissue, while the trunk and leg areas are smaller. In certain animals, this brain area shows large exaggerations; the whisker cortex in a mouse, for instance, is remarkably big. From the parietal lobe, we derive our sense of the size, shape, and texture of what we touch.

Stimulation of the primary somatosensory area causes phantom sensations. The existence of the homunculus offers an explanation of how amputees who lose an arm or a leg can continue to feel the presence of a missing limb and experience pain there. They are most likely experiencing activity in the corresponding section of the somatosensory area. For instance, while the physical leg is gone, a patient can continue to experience sensation in the "leg" of the homunculus, which is, in fact, the leg they have always had in their awareness. The homunculus also makes evident how drugs that affect this area can cause perceptions of odd body distortions, like the stretching or elasticity of limbs. Beyond the primary somatosensory area are higher order sensory areas that produce our conscious experience of the various qualities of the incoming signals. The brain interprets these signals to a large extent based on which pathway delivers them. In general, the parietal areas also work to integrate bodily sensations in time and space, and create a holistic sense of the arrangement of our body parts and posture, our orientation in space, our relation to objects in terms of sight, sound and touch, and the direction of our movements.

Damage to the upper part of the parietal lobe results in distortions of body perception. Patients in this condition may be horrified by the perception that half of their body is gone (Blakemore, 1977, p. 82). Some may dress in only one glove, "shave only one side of their face, comb only half of their hair, and they object to sharing their hospital bed with what they feel to be someone else's arms and legs" (p. 82). Subjects asked to bisect a horizontal line bisect only half of it; that is, they quarter the line. Some drugs can cause distortions of body image, the sense we have of the presence, size, and shape of our body. Anesthetics like ketamine, PCP, and ether can produce the sensation that the body is stretching out of shape. Effects like these may be produced in part by alterations of sensory pathways in the thalamus leading up to the somatosensory area.

Seeing

Visual perception is one of the most characteristic functions of the human brain. It is not a simple affair. It involves converting the raw material of light into shapes and edges, colors, shadings, orientations, textures, location and motion. This begins with the cornea and the lens of the eye, which focuses images onto the retina, the light-sensitive tissue on the rear wall of the eyeball (and the only instance of central nervous tissue found in the periphery). Here, photoreceptors convert the energy to neural signals. These are conveyed to the thalamus by the optic nerve, which synapses there with neurons that connect to the **primary visual cortex** in the **occipital lobe** at the very back of the skull. This lobe is entirely dedicated to visual processing, although it is only one of a number of areas involved. Information from the right field of vision in both eyes is delivered to the right side of the occipital lobe, and vice versa. From here, the information is relayed to other brain centers for further processing.

Visual input from the field of vision is kept discrete and orderly, in separate layers, with specific areas of the retina mapping onto specific areas of the cortex. These precise correspondences are illustrated in the fact that slight damage to a precise area of the visual cortex produces a corresponding blind spot (scotoma) in the field of vision. However, a person is frequently unaware of it until tested. (In fact, we all have an unnoticeable blind spot in our field of vision corresponding to the place where the optic nerve enters the retina.) Remarkably, patients with damage to the visual cortex seem to be able to see in the scotoma without knowing it. When a small blinking light is shown there, subjects can often guess where it is, even though they claim to see nothing. Likewise, they can guess with a high degree of precision whether a horizontal or vertical line is being shown (Wieskrantz, 1987). What seems to be happening is that lower visual centers are picking up the information, but it never reaches consciousness. In other words, people with extensive damage to the visual cortex are seeing, but are not aware of it (Cowey & Stoerig, 1991).

A number of other brain areas contribute to our visual functioning. The temporal lobes, part of our memory systems, are important in identifying the objects of vision. Memory comes into play in visual processing because it is one thing to look at and see, say, a passing car, but another to recognize that it is a car, based on the fact that we have seen one before. There are cells in this lobe that become activated only in response to certain shapes or to an object traveling at a specific velocity. Overall, the temporal lobes are concerned with *what* something is, including to some extent *what* color it is, whereas the parietal lobes are concerned with *where* something is. With its motor and sensory areas, the parietal lobe helps us to integrate visual data, locate objects in space, and orient our body movements; for instance, it governs the integration of vision and movement required for any sort of ball game or comparable performance. A midbrain center, the superior colliculus, is important for rapid tracking eye movements. And higher order visual centers in the prefrontal cortex use visual information to produce judgments and decisions.

The primary visual cortex also is capable of producing mental images. Brain imaging studies show that, when people imagine certain images, like large and small letters, particular areas of the primary visual cortex are activated, mimicking or rehearsing the act of really seeing these objects. Activity like this in the cortex and memory systems suggests how we can see images in dreams and hallucinations, without the actual objects being present to stimulate sometimes vivid perceptions.

Drugs can cause a number of visual effects. The hallucinogen mescaline can produce images of elaborate geometric forms in the shape of arabesques, lattices, and tunnels. Effects like these are believed to be related to the organization of our visual systems. More dreamlike hallucinatory effects point to the integration of memories and visual data. According to some theories, the elaborate pseudorealities that may be evoked in the complex stages of hallucinations under drugs like LSD and mescaline are constructed from released stores of visual and auditory memories, in which case the temporal lobe may play a role.

Hearing

> *Yes. I heard voices down along the river somewhere, a man's voice and a woman's voice calling.*
>
> (quote from an experimental subject undergoing electrical stimulation of the temporal lobe in the laboratory)

If you are walking in a dark park or forest and hear something nearby rustling in the underbrush, there are two things you want to know right away: Where is it? And what is it? These are two of the key functions of hearing.

To put it simply, the ear captures sound waves and converts them to neural signals. The primary mechanism for this is deep in the chambers of the inner ear, where thousands of hair-like cells bend like underwater weeds in response to the vibrations of the basilar membrane and the movement of fluid in the cochlea. The bending movement opens and closes potassium channels in a neuron associated with each hair cell. When the channels open, the neurons depolarize and send action potentials to the medulla in the brainstem, from which axons project to many other brain areas, including the **inferior colliculus** in the midbrain. From there, the impulses are routed to the thalamus and finally to the **primary auditory area** in the temporal lobes. Following the spatial logic of the visual cortex, the primary auditory area shows a disproportionate amount of brain tissue devoted to the pitches of human speech. As with visual processing, higher order areas of the auditory cortex contribute to the meaningful integration of these impulses into our experience of sound, locating sounds in space (the parietal lobe), recognizing them from memory (the temporal lobe), appreciating them emotionally (the limbic system), and deciding how to respond to them (prefrontal lobes).

As well as being a center for processing auditory stimuli, the temporal lobe is a storage area for auditory, as well as other, memories, especially visual ones. Early brain researchers found that if they stimulated parts of the temporal lobe with a weak electrical current, they could evoke auditory memories so vivid that some subjects thought they heard a radio go on in the testing room. The quotation at the head of this section came from a woman whose temporal lobe was being stimulated in this way; she also reported some visual recall. Thus, the temporal lobes seem to be largely responsible for auditory and visual memories, and they are closely connected with another structure involved in memory, the hippocampus, which lies partly within the temporal lobes.

Just as seeing images is characteristic of dreams and hallucinations, hearing voices and other familiar sounds is a feature of these states as well. These are likely to be drawn from the brain's memory storage areas and processed through the auditory cortex in the absence of any external stimuli. Auditory hallucinations (hearing voices) are also a key symptom of schizophrenia, one which antipsychotic drugs can successfully suppress.

Pain

Signals relating to pain or temperature, which identify potentially damaging stimuli, work on a system different from other sensory input; it seems that pain can be realized at the level of the thalamus without the need for the cortex to bring it to consciousness. However, the cortex appears to be needed for finer interpretations of painful stimuli. Also, there are sites in the spine involved in the mediation of pain. These structural arrangements at lower and more primitive levels of the nervous system are understandable, because in evolutionary terms, the perception of pain is fundamental to the survival of organisms much simpler than mammals or reptiles.

As the reader is probably well aware, pain also has an emotional component. This is of note because under certain circumstances, the emotional dimension can be separated from the mere recognition of painful stimuli. This happened in cases of the radical surgery known as prefrontal lobotomy, discontinued in the 1950s, where, in order to treat a variety of psychiatric disorders, and especially to reduce agitation and anxiety, doctors severed the connections between the forebrain and the rest of the brain. Lobotomized patients reported being able to recognize the presence of pain, but were completely unconcerned about it. A similar effect is noted with the use of the painkiller morphine.

A key brain center for the experience of pain is the **periventricular (PV) area** (that is, the area "near the ventricles," the third and fourth in this case). Here are found fiber systems that cause fear and pain reactions when stimulated. The PV area works reciprocally with the medial forebrain bundle, which mediates pleasure; that is, stimulating one automatically inhibits the other. Directly inhibiting the PV area has a pleasant effect as well. The tranquil, "passive," high produced by heroin and morphine is partially a result of PV inhibition; on the other hand, an active high results from direct stimulation of the MFB with a drug such as amphetamine.

MOVEMENT, BALANCE AND POSTURE

Much of how we act can be conceived of in terms of four activities: (1) we collect a huge amount of sensory information, (2) we process and integrate it, creating a sense of body, self, and world, including our capacity to learn, remember, judge and decide, (3) we move and act, and (4) we maintain the systems that allow us to do all this. Movement, often referred to technically as motor activity, is a key component here. Without it, we would be all intake and no output. And, as land-dwelling creatures, we would perish from a failure to feed and sustain ourselves.

We engage in many sorts of movement, such as reflexive movements when we are startled or something rushes at our face; gross body movements; facial movements and expressions; adjustments to posture; and fine sequences of rapid, coordinated movements. Movements like these are managed by different motor systems in the brain and spine. In general, there are three main systems: (1) the pyramidal motor system, which is involved in the initiation and execution voluntary and of gross, or larger, movements (2) the extrapyramidal motor system, which fine tunes the activity of the pyramidal system, and (3) the cerebellum, which governs balance, and learned, planned and highly coordinated movements, such as those involved in athletics, dance, or musical performance.

basal ganglia

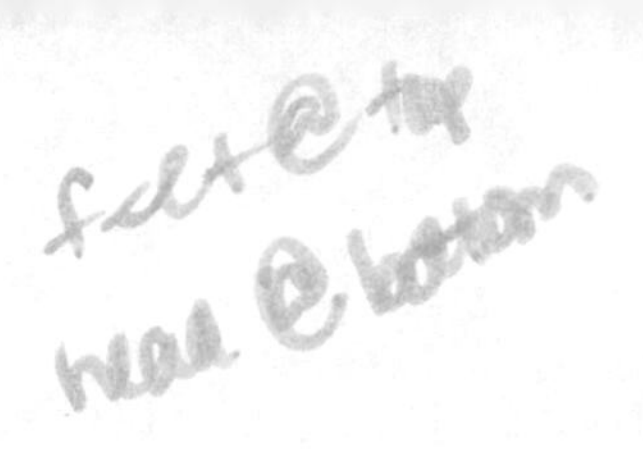

Voluntary Movement

Gross movements and voluntary muscle control are managed by the pyramidal motor system, which takes its name from the pyramidal shape of its cells. Movement is planned and initiated in the **premotor cortex**, composed of higher order motor areas, in the frontal lobe, which presumably integrates incoming sensory data with thought and judgment. It communicates closely with the **primary motor area**. This is a strip of tissue located in the frontal lobe just forward of the somatosensory area in the parietal lobe, separated from it by a deep fissure. The primary motor area stretches across the top of the head like a second "headband" in front of the corresponding region occupied by the somatosensory area, from which it receives sensory data about the location and disposition of the body in space. From other parts of the brain, it receives input about what is happening, visual information that helps us to guide our movements, and auditory information.

In the primary motor area are found the cell bodies of the neurons of the pyramidal system that controls voluntary movement. Many of these neurons send their axons all the way down through the medulla and the spinal cord to synapse with neurons that exit the spine, more or less horizontally, to innervate the muscles in the periphery. In some cases, the pyramidal cells synapse with neurons in other brain nuclei, which then descend through the cord in similar fashion. These indirect connections are responsible for maintaining the background muscle tone necessary for movement.

The primary motor area is configured in the form of a homunculus like the sensory homunculus in the primary sensory area, but in this case it is a motor homunculus, a region of cortical tissue mapping out the muscles of the body. Stimulating the tissue representing the "arm" of the motor homunculus with a weak electric current, for instance, will result in a contraction of the corresponding muscle in the actual arm. Brain imaging shows that just imagining certain movements activates these brain regions. Like the distortions observed in the sensory and auditory areas, disproportionate areas of the primary motor cortex are dedicated to finger movements and speech.

Because of the plasticity of the brain, the constant use of certain muscles and movements results in the corresponding development of connections in certain areas here; for instance, the brain of a musician is recognizable by the widening of a particular gyrus associated with fine hand movements and coordination. And prosthetic devices, like robotic arms, can be successfully operated by will, to a limited extent, through implants that respond to depolarization in appropriate areas of the primary motor cortex (Stix, 2008).

Damage to neurons in the primary motor cortex results in paralysis. And conversely, when a blizzard of uncontrolled depolarization sweeps through the motor area, it causes all the voluntary muscles to contract in the thrashing recognized as an epileptic seizure. For this reason, the primary motor area is a key site for the action of anticonvulsant drugs, which inhibit the spread of impulses by depressing its neurons, and as a result, prevent the muscle contractions that manifest as convulsions.

A recent observation by Rizzolati (Lametti, 2009), based on brain imaging in primate studies, has shown that certain neurons in the premotor cortex, the area in the prefrontal lobe involved in the planning of movements, are firing when the animals make certain movements, but also fire when the animals are observing similar movements. In other words, when one is merely witnessing a movement, the brain seems to simulate the neural activity that would accompany it. Moreover, the same effect is observed in subjects who are simply imagining an action, or who are listening to sounds that accompany an action (like ripping a sheet of paper). Rizzolati, who discovered these effects, called the neurons involved *mirror neurons* and hypothesized that they help us to choose behaviors and understand behavior observed in others.

Associated with the pyramidal system is a secondary motor system, the **extrapyramidal system**, which does not act by synapsing with spinal neurons, but instead is wired to modify signals from the primary motor area passing through the pyramidal system. Generally, the extrapyramidal system presides over the steadying of fine motor movements, the smooth continuous movements of the limbs, unconscious postural adjustments (like those needed to walk on uneven ground), and muscle tonus. It also participates in the production of skilled, trained movements. Whereas loss of the pyramidal system results in weakness and a reduction of movement and motor control, loss of the extrapyramidal system results in movement abnormalities.

Two key sites in the extrapyramidal system are the **basal ganglia** and the **substantia nigra.** The basal ganglia are an important component of the motor system, composed of several nuclei configured like a pair of rams' horns; these are the structures on whose tips the amygdalae are found. They are part of a feedback loop that receives input from the motor cortex (via collateral branchings of the pyramidal systems axons on their descent to the spine), from the somatosensory area and other cortical regions. Thus, they are well informed about movements being initiated. They feed back information to the cortex via the thalamus, and they connect downward to brainstem motor nuclei as well. The basal ganglia seem to play a role in directing the direction and breadth of movement, in guiding movements influenced by memory (Breedlove, Rosenzweig & Watson,2007, p. 341), and in controlling movements of the mouth and swallowing.

Closely associated with the basal ganglia is a nucleus known as "the black stuff," the **substantia nigra**. This dark area is a cluster of somae which is one of the principal locations for the neurotransmitter dopamine in the brain and an important site for regulating movement. Axons extend from here to key motor pathways, including nuclei in the basal ganglia.

When the activity of dopamine in the substantia nigra is eroded or compromised, the result is the abnormal movements of Parkinson's disease. The symptoms of Parkinson's include tremors in the hands or other parts of the body when they are at rest; a stooped, shuffling gait; postural instability; and difficulty in starting to walk, or in stopping. People with Parkinson's exhibit poor coordination and hampered movements, trembling fingers and lips, and a distinctive movement of the hand and fingers called "pill-rolling," which looks like the person, hand with the palm up, is compulsively fingering or rolling a small object between the thumb and forefingers with a small, nervous back and forth movement. Muscular rigidity increases as the condition progresses until the patient is largely immobilized and eventually "frozen stiff," although full cognitive functions remain.

This condition carries the term **Parkinson's disease** when any other causes are unknown. In other words, when the observable symptoms exhaust what we know about the matter, we assume there is some sort of underlying disease process. It is not unusual for very old people to show signs of Parkinson's disease from a slow loss of dopaminergic functioning with aging, but the advance of the disease is typically so slow that the disease often does not have time to progress to an advanced stage. When the symptoms result from a known cause like a brain injury or appear as a drug side effect, they are referred to as parkinsonism. The study of parkinsonian symptoms has provided information about how neurotransmitters and drugs work in brain pathways. And the treatment of Parkinson's disease, in attempts to increase dopaminergic functioning, has challenged researchers in delivering drugs across the blood-brain barrier.

Balance and Coordination

Balance is regulated by several structures in the vestibular system of the ear, which also regulates the sense of our body's location in space and how it relates to our surroundings, and helps us to adjust our body position and posture. Sensory information from the vestibular system travels to the **cerebellum**. This is the second largest, and most noticeable, brain structure after the cortex, and so has received the name "little brain" from the Latin. It does, in fact, exhibit several structural parallels with the brain as a whole (such as its own cortex and hemispheres). Straddling the brainstem atop the pons, it nestles under the overhang of the cortex at the back of the skull. In side views of the brain, it projects distinctly from the rear. Spread out, it would be a fairly sizable organ (47 inches by 6.5 inches, with a surface area equaling 75% that of the cortex), but it is folded up accordion-like into a pair of round lobes, with its pleats so densely rumpled that in cross-section it looks leafy. In fact, it contains more than half of the brain's 100 billion neurons.

The main functions of the cerebellum are to maintain balance and posture; to coordinate the timing of learned, sequenced movements; and to make adjustments to ongoing movements. The movements we mean here are of the highly skilled and coordinated type requiring balance or speed, and which improve with practice, movements such as those seen in gymnastics, tight-rope walking, ice skating, bike-riding, and playing basketball or piano.

Much of the information passing in and out of the cerebellum is routed through the pons, so that, to the extent that the pons is a bridge, it is a bridge to the cerebellum. At synapses in the pons, collaterals from the descending axons of the primary motor area connect to the cerebellum. It also receives signals from the extrapyramidal and sensory systems, including the visual system (for hand-eye coordination). The cerebellum has no direct connections to the spinal cord, but it acts by modulating the pyramidal pathways. It sends output to every major brain structure, much of it via the thalamus.

Damage to the cerebellum results in erratic, jerky, badly timed movements and disruptions of balance and coordination. A sharp blow to the back of head, as seen in a million action adventure films, can knock an unsuspecting enemy down because it shocks for a moment the cerebellum's ability to balance the body. Drugs like alcohol and barbiturates depress the cerebellum, causing drinkers to sway backward on their heels and threaten to topple over. When reaching for something, their hand under- or over-shoots its object. In trying to walk, they wander and stagger, ramming into door-frames and furniture, exhibiting a condition of muscular incoordination known technically as **ataxia**, or lack of coordination. This is the condition targeted by the police when they ask a suspected drunk driver to walk a straight line. In addition, through the cerebellum and the vestibular system of the ear, motion sickness is mediated, presumably involving connections to the nausea center in the nearby medulla of the brainstem.

The cerebellum has other functions as well. It appears to play roles in learning and in emotional growth. Interestingly, this structure is enlarging in our evolutionary development, which suggests a need for finer manipulations and motor coordination as the ages progress.

LEARNING AND MEMORY

Memory is key to our sense of identity and our ability to learn and navigate in our environment. It is not a simple construct. We have several types of memory, which are processed and distributed by the brain in different ways, and stored at different sites. **Declarative memory** consists of our memories of words (**semantic memory**), and facts and events of our lives (**episodic memory**); in other words, material that would often pertain to situations in which we declare "I remember X." **Nondeclarative memory** consists of nonverbal material and motor memory, such as the knowledge of how to do things (**procedural memory**). Also, memory processes are categorized in terms of time. **Sensory** or **iconic memory** lasts about a second. **Short-term memory** tracks events over a span of eighteen seconds and constitutes the first stage of learning. **Long-term memory** moves data involving days or years in and out of storage. In addition, **working memory** actively processes information.

Damage to parts of the brain through accident or stroke can eliminate stored memories or impair the ability to create or access some sorts of memories while leaving others intact. This is because the processing and storage of memories takes place in different brain regions. The prefrontal lobe manages working memory to a large extent. The temporal lobe is a key site for storing auditory and visual memories, and it contains a specialized area of the limbic system and an important site for short-term memory, the **hippocampus**. This part of the brain was named after the "sea horse" by an imaginative neuroanatomist who noted the resemblance. In humans, the hippocampus on the left side is involved in language and episodic/autobiographical memory, while the right side is involved in spatial memory. If the hippocampus in experimental animals is destroyed, they become hyperactive, re-examining their environment continually as if they had never seen it before.

One of the most famous hippocampi in medical history belonged to a man known as H. M. (Blakemore, 1977, p. 94). In 1953, a well-meaning surgeon, trying to alleviate massive epileptic seizures, destroyed the hippocampi on both sides of H. M.'s brain. (It was established practice at the time to remove one side, but this case was particularly extreme.) In consequence, H. M. lost his ability to store new information in his long-term memory. He retained and was able to retrieve most of the information he had acquired up to the point of his operation. However, afterwards, he was able to retain new information for no more than a few minutes, the span of time it resided in his short-term memory. In effect, except for a short fifteen-minute buffer memory, he reached the end of his memory storage, traveling beyond the edge of his past.

H. M. was able to learn simple spatial tasks, but unless he was at work, he was unable to state what he did for his living (as an assembly worker.) Suzanne Corkin, a scientist who studied him for over 40 years, was a stranger whenever H.M. met her, and he could read the same newspaper for years and find the headlines striking. Whenever he was informed of his uncle's death, he grieved freshly as if for the first time. Moreover, he was clearly aware of his shortcomings. The case of H.M., which helped to launch moder memory research, clearly implicates the hippocampus in the conversion of short-term to long-term memories. The discovery in the 1990s that H.M. was capable, to a limited extent, of retaining semantic memories, led to the recognition that the hippocampus is not the only site where memory is processed.

The plasticity of the brain, its ability to produce new neurons and synapses, is crucial to the formation of new memories. The hippocampus is the area which is most active in this respect. Research shows that certain types of learning requiring concerted mental effort commandeer and preserve new neurons continually being produced in the hippocampus.

Besides the hippocampus, some of the other areas involved in the operations of memory are the extrapyramidal motor system, which manages the memory component of habitual movements; the cerebellum, an important site for the learning of skilled sequences of movement; the amygdala, involved in emotional learning; and a number of association areas in the cortex, where long-term memories are stored.

The physiology of memory is of interest of psychopharmacologists because several drugs impair memory function by way of side effects. In studies of rodents, it has been noted that alcohol and nicotine, as well as chemotherapy, reduce the production of neurons in the hippocampus, while exercise, antidepressants, and the consumption of blueberriesincrease it (Shors, 2009). The benzodiazepine tranquilizers and the sedative GHB block the formation of memories for a period of time following ingestion, and this is an especially insidious effect when GHB is employed as a rape drug. A number of natural hallucinogenic agents in use before LSD, substances like atropine and scopolamine, impair learning and memory, so that subjects usually cannot recall the inebriated state. In fact. one of the salient attributes of LSD is that it not only produces complex and vivid hallucinatory sequences, but they can be recalled. Moreover, it is clear that certain types of hallucinations, like dreams, draw from our hoard of stored memories.

Another effect of drugs on memory is known as state-dependent memory. This term refers to the fact that learning acquired in a drugged state can only be accessed again only when one returns to that state. For example, an experimental animal that learns to navigate a maze under the influence of a sedative cannot, when it is "sober," effectively access what is has learned, but only when it is again under the influence of the drug.

HIGHER FUNCTIONS

The higher functions of the brain include such operations as learning, judgment, and decision-making (which is typically referred to as "executive function"). One way to think about them is that they take place between the brain's sensory input and its motor output. They consist of operations that assess information and contexts and determine what motor output, or behavior, is to be. Commonsensically, we would simply say that "I—my self—am the one who does this." Fair enough. We are talking here in some sense about our self-awareness. However, why (in evolutionary terms) we have a sense of unitary conscious awareness, why we experience all these brain processes as a single self, and how the brain manages to produce this experience, are mysteries that remain to be solved. Neuroscientists divide this problem into the "easy question" and the "hard question." The easy question asks, "What are the neural correlates of our subjective experiences?" In other words, what exactly is happening in the brain when we are experiencing X or Y? The hard question asks, "How does the brain produce the conscious self?" (Koch and Greenfield, 2007).

Decision-making

The integration of information and decision-making activity appears to take place in the association areas of the frontal lobe of the cortex. (These are areas where neurons connect primarily to other brain neurons in the same hemisphere and are not engaged in handling sensory input or motor commands, which constitute our relation to the outside world.) Part of the prefrontal cortex is involved in executive functions, the prioritizing of different behaviors, and the ability to adapt to change.

Traditionally, these higher brain areas would be associated with purely rational decision-making. However, recent evidence from comparative neurology points to a close connection between them and cortical areas associated with the limbic system (emotion). MRI brain scans show that when we are making morally charged decisions, the limbic system is very active. This has led to the observation that emotion plays a significant, if not indispensable, role in what we would typically consider our rational judgment. This is not too surprising, since our feelings about previous experiences guide our decision-making, and overwhelming emotion can short-circuit our ability to clear-minded choices.

Emotional functions of the frontal lobes evidence themselves in the results of prefrontal lobotomy, a surgery widely practiced until 1964, but now considered drastic and unnecessary. When the lobe is severed from the rest of the brain, some subjects become calm and detached from emotions and sensations. A similar effect produced by the painkiller morphine can be attributed to its effect on the frontal lobes. As we mentioned toward the beginning of this chapter, the patient under its influence is aware of, but does not suffer from, pain.

A region of the brain called the **orbitofrontal cortex**, located above the orbit of the eye and closely involved with the limbic system, has been identified as a center for impulse control, the inculcation of social mores, and the ability to appreciate the consequences of one's actions (Norden, 2007a). In other words, it serves as a form of "moral compass." In 1848, Phineas Gage, a Vermont railroad worker, suffered a massive brain injury while tamping a blasting charge with an iron rod. The force of the explosion drove the rod, three and a half feet long and an inch and a quarter in diameter, up through Gage's left cheek behind his left eye, and it shot out through the forward surface of his skull. He survived the accident to live another twelve years, exhibiting behavioral deficits associated with limbic and memory systems and frontal lobe functions. But the most dramatic changes were to his personality, which were so profoundly negative his friends no longer recognized him as his former self. He became distracted, moody, and antisocial, lost his moral bearings, and ended up without home or friends, exhibited as a freak in P.T. Barnum's circus (Norden, 2007a; Breedlove et al., 2007). This and other evidence point to the orbitofrontal cortex as a brain region that abstracts a moral code from our cultural environment before we are able to think rationally; damage in this region results in a loss of ability to choose wisely among moral alternatives. The implications for drug abuse are intriguing. If drugs can physiologically compromise the functioning of the orbitofrontal cortex, this suggests that they can, in a purely physical, mechanical sense, induce a loss of moral competence.

Consciousness

Our summative experience of most of the brain functions we have discussed is of a central self, a unitary awareness that integrates all input and directs willful action. For centuries, researchers have tried to locate one nucleus between sensory input and motor output that creates the illusion of "putting it all together," a cerebral headquarters where a chief technician, the "I," processes all the input, makes the decisions, and works all the control panels that generate our behaviors. So far, to no avail.

From various observations, we do know that consciousness is not possible without the participation of the cortex. Two conditions seem necessary. One is that the incoming signals must reach the cortex; the other is that the reception areas in the cortex must be stimulated by the ascending pathways of the reticular formation. It is possible, for instance, to have brain activity without a subjective experience of it. We see this in the case of your morning alarm clock. According to one view (Koch & Greefield, 2007), waking to an alarm occurs when there is a large input from the auditory nerve via the locus coeruleus (part of the reticular formation) and the thalamus, which arouses the cortex. Then, a group of neurons in the auditory cortex and the frontal and temporal lobes, working together, bring you to consciousness. Between the initiation and the perception of the alarm, there is an interval of about eight seconds when you are technically "hearing" the sound, but the cortex has not yet been sufficiently stimulated for you to be aware of it.

There are other demonstrations of this circuitry. When the action of the reticular formation is compromised and unable to stimulate the cortex, the result is a coma. Furthermore, in the case of a scotoma, we saw an example of visual input reaching damaged areas of the visual cortex, which are unable to bring it into conscious experience, although other areas of the brain are apparently aware of the content (such as a blinking light). Subjects with damage to the visual cortex will say they are blind, although they are able to catch a ball. From evidence like this, we conclude that an aroused cortex is a prerequisite of subjective experience.

FOOTNOTES

1. Opiates often cause vomiting by direct gastrointestinal actions.

REFERENCES

Alleyne, R. (2009, July). Brains replay memories while we sleep and store the highlights. *Brain in the News,* 16(7), 3.

Blakemore, C. (1977). *Mechanics of the mind.* New York: Cambridge University Press.

Brebner, K., Wong, T. P., Liu, L., Liu, Y., Camsall, P., Gray, S., Phelps, L., & Wang, Y. T. (2005, November 25). Nucleus accumbens long-term depression and the expression of behavioral desensitization. *Science,* 310(5752), 1340-1343.

Breedlove, S. M., Rosenzweig, M. R., & Watson, N. V. (2007). *Biological psychology: An introduction to behavioral, cognitive, and clinical neuroscience* (5th ed.). Sunderland, MA: Sinauer Associates.

Cowey, A., & Stoerig, P. (1991). The neurobiology of blindsight. *Trends in Neuroscience,* 14, 140-145.

Grossman, S. P. (1967). *A textbook of physiological psychology.* New York: John Wiley and Sons.

Hooper, J., & Teresi, D. (1986). *The 3-pound universe: Revolutionary discoveries about the brain—from the chemistry of mind to the new frontiers of the soul.* New York: G. P. Putnam's Sons.

Koch, C., & Greenfield, S. (2007, October). *How does consciousness happen? Scientific American,* 297(4), 76-83.

Lametti, D. (2009, July). Mirroring behavior. *Brain in the News,* 16(7), 4.

Lewin, R. (1980, December 12). Is your brain really necessary? *Science,* 210, 1232-1234.

MacNeilage, P. F., Rogers, L. J., & Vallortigara, G. (2009, July). *Scientific American,* 301(1), 60-67.

McGaugh, J. L. (2004). The amygdala modulates the consolidation of memories and emotionally arousing experiences. *Annual Review of Neuroscience,* 27, 1-28.

Nestler, E. J. & Malenka, R. C. (2004, March). The addicted brain. *Scientific American,* 290(3), 78-85.

Norden, J. (2007a). *Understanding the brain. Lecture 21: The Limbic System—Anatomy.* [Lectures on videocassette]. Chantilly, VA: The Teaching Company.

Norden, J. (2007b). *Understanding the brain. Lecture 27: Emotion and Executive Function.* [Lectures on videocassette]. Chantilly, VA: The Teaching Company.

Olds, J. (1958). Satiation effects in self-stimulation of the brain. *Journal of Comparative* and Physiological Psychology, 51, 675-678.

Rock, A. (2004). *The mind at night: The new science of how and why we dream.* New York: Basic Books.

Shors, T. J. (2009, March). “Saving new brain cells.” *Scientific American,* 300(3), 47-54.

Stix, G. (2008, November). Jacking into the brain. *Scientific American,* 299(5), 56-67.

Ward, A. A., Jr. (1945). The anterior cingulate gyrus and personality. *Research Publications, Association for Research in Nervous and Mental Disease,* 27, 438-495. As cited in Grossman, 1967, p. 541.

Weiskrantz, L. (1987). Residual vision in a scotoma: A follow-up study of “form” discrimination. *Brain,* 110, 77-92.

Chapter 9

Neurotransmitters

At 3:00 A.M. one night in 1921, Otto Loewi dreamt of an experiment that would prove neurons communicated with one another using chemicals. He awoke and wrote it down. But come morning, he couldn't recall the dream. Not only that, he couldn't decipher his writing.

But at 3:00 A.M. the following night, the dream recurred. Loewi woke with excitement, bolted to his lab, and set up the experiment. He took the hearts of two frogs, bathed in a chemical medium to keep them beating, and he electrically stimulated the vagus nerve of one. The pulsations slowed. This was to be expected, since the vagus nerve normally slows the heartbeat. Loewi then took some of the solution from this heart and applied it to the second. It slowed also. Something had washed from the first heart that also slowed the second. This was proof that the vagus nerve released a chemical when stimulated and that a neurotransmitter existed.

Later research with mammals extended these findings, and Loewi subsequently won a Nobel Prize. However, he was lucky that he had chosen by coincidence one of the few sites on which his experiment would actually work, because of the quantity of neurotransmitter released by the vagus nerve. He confessed later that cold speculation by light of day would have dissuaded him from such an attempt.

Loewi's demonstration led to an arduous hunt for the particular chemicals that were transmitters. Thorough criteria were laid out, which each candidate substance would have to meet if it were to qualify. These five criteria are as follows:

1. The chemical must be present in the presynaptic terminal.
2. The enzymes and the mechanism that synthesizes the transmitter must be present in the cell.
3. One must be able to collect the substance at the synapse upon stimulation of the axon; in other words, the neuron must release the substance when stimulated.
4. The mechanism that ends the action of the suspected transmitter must be at the synapse, and, if possible, the time course of the enzyme action should coincide with that of the transmitter.

5. Receptors must be present on the postsynaptic membranes, and an experimenter should be able to mimic the action of the substance with a known agonist and to block it with a known antagonist of the candidate transmitter.

Up to now, none of the substances accepted as transmitters has met all of these criteria, except at certain sites in the periphery. In the brain, millions of neurons bathe in an elaborate chemical soup, so that ascertaining all of these characteristics is beyond our current technology.

A hundred or more chemicals possessing radically different qualities are currently suspected of being neurotransmitters. Each of these has its own character: some excite, some inhibit; some act quickly, some slowly; some are amines, some amino acids. Physiologically, this variety of transmitters allows a number of neural systems to lie close without quarreling; one system is not going to set another off accidentally. And, as if the structural and functional patterns of the nervous system were not already complex enough, as we examine the specialty areas of each transmitter, whole new maps of interrelationships emerge. Systems unrelated in any other way react in accord to an infusion of the transmitter that triggers them, and drugs produce batteries of effects that relate to the layout of certain transmitters.

ACETYLCHOLINE

Originally referred to as "Vagusstoff" by Loewi, acetylcholine (ACh) is the transmitter he discovered to be released from the vagus nerve. A large number of the synapses in the nervous system are cholinergic (use acetylcholine); they are widely distributed throughout the central nervous system and the periphery. Because of the peripheral sites, which are easier to investigate, ACh was the first transmitter whose action was understood.

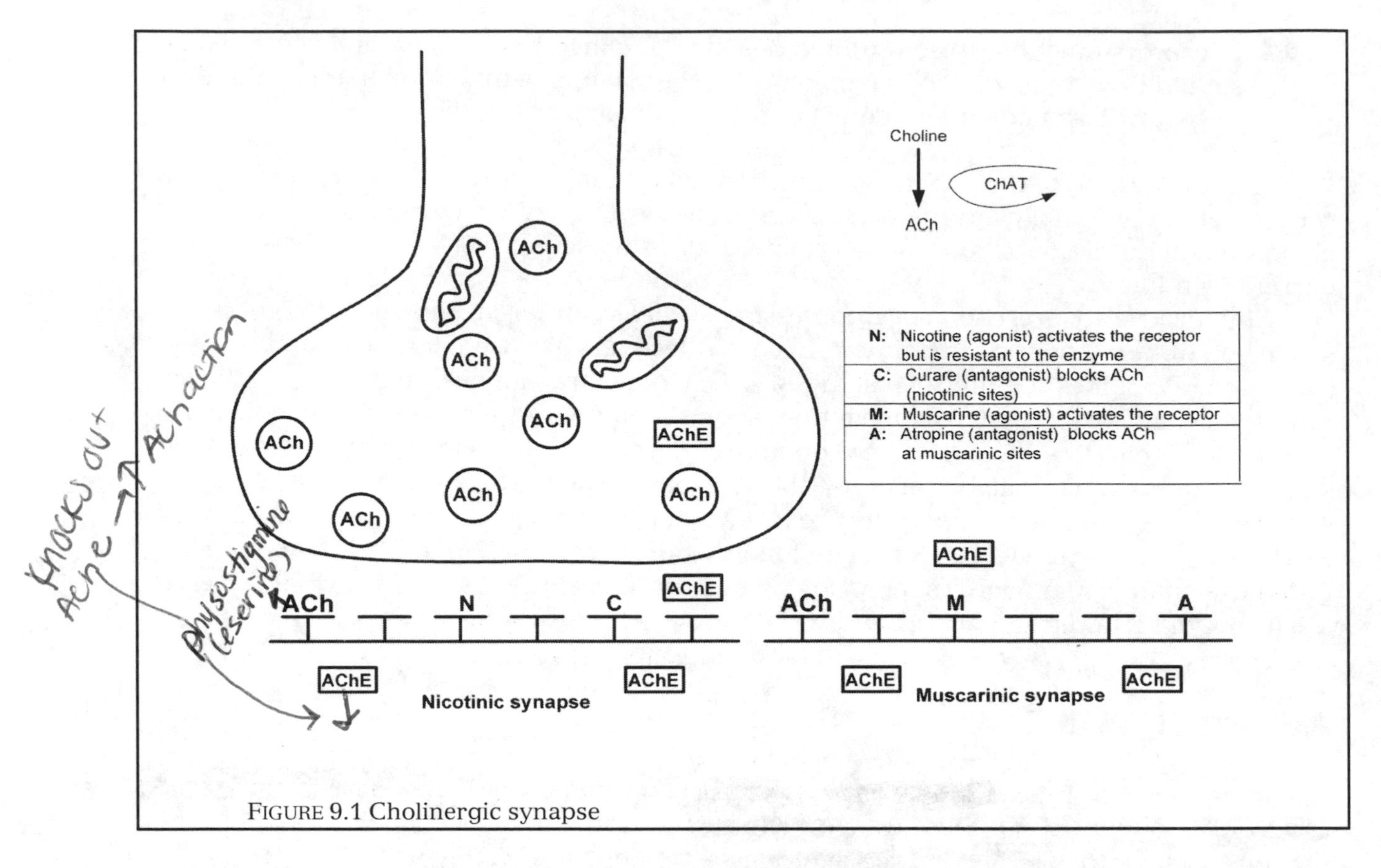

FIGURE 9.1 Cholinergic synapse

The synthesis of ACh can be seen in Figure 9.1. This process is typical of the first five transmitters we will consider: it can occur in the soma, in which case ACh is transported along the axon to the presynaptic terminal, or it can occur in the terminal itself. Choline, a vitamin commonly found in liver, fish, and eggs, is drawn into the neuron by active transport and there, by the aid of an enzyme (choline acetyltransferase, or ChAT), an acetyl group is spliced onto it. The product, acetylcholine, is then packaged in the vesicles and divided into two supplies, one for storage and one for release. Generally, the newest supply is used for immediate release.

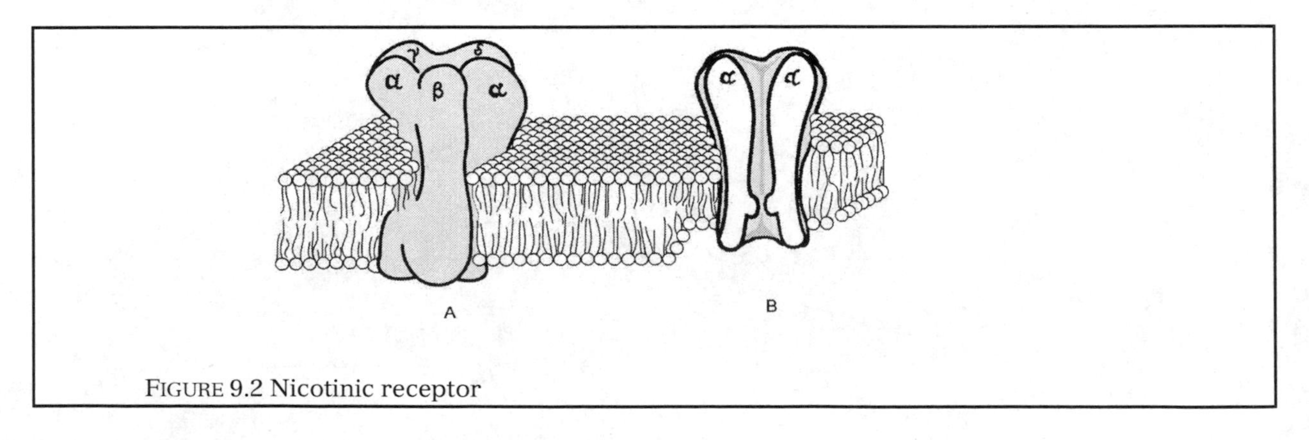

FIGURE 9.2 Nicotinic receptor

Molecular structure of the nicotinic receptor. (A) Subunits of the receptor are indicated by the Greek letters alpha (α), beta (β), gamma (χ), and delta (δ). (B) Shows a cross-section displaying the ion channel.

When an action potential arrives at the presynaptic terminal, vesicles swarm to the synaptic membrane and fuse with it. Calcium ions (Ca^{++}) mediate the opening of the vesicles on the membrane surface, launching ACh into the gap. If you could see this happening, it would look like the bubbles opening on the surface of a pancake as the batter heats, except that in this case, each popping bubble is releasing ACh, which crosses from the presynaptic terminal to the receptors on the postsynaptic membrane. The receptors consist of proteins found in the nerve cell membrane. Each is constructed of five modules arranged as a pentagonal donut, whose hole is an ion channel penetrating the membrane (see Figure 9.2). It appears that the exact binding site for ACh recognizes the molecule by two charges, one positive and one negative, in a specific location on the molecule. The receptor has like charges similarly spaced, so the molecule "locks" on and reacts with the receptor (Ashton & Stepney, 1982, p. 37). This action affects the transfer of ions through the channel, either exciting or inhibiting the neuron. ACh has been found to have excitatory actions at some sites, and inhibitory at others.

ACh attaches to its receptor for only a few tenths of a millisecond, then spontaneously dissociates. An enzyme, acetylcholinesterase (AChE), attacks the ACh in the synaptic gap and by hydrolysis cuts it into acetate and choline. AChE is found in both the pre and postsynaptic components of cholinergic neurons. In the gap, AChE clears the area of ACh, so each action potential releases the same amount of transmitter as the last, and no residue accumulates to casually stimulate the receptors. In the presynaptic terminal, it metabolizes surplus ACh that exceeds the storage capacity of the vesicles. One molecule of AChE can cut thousands of ACh molecules a second.

After ACh has been hydrolyzed into acetate and choline, the choline is taken back into the cell by active transport and resynthesized into ACh.

ACh is the first transmitter for which receptor subtypes were identified. The identification of receptor subtypes is such a visible and vigorous activity of modern psychopharmacological research that it is worth understanding how this is done: Suppose that we have identified neural tissue that to all indications responds to ACh. It is possible to study the binding of other substances to these sites, by choosing a substance with a known affinity for the receptor, tagging it or labeling it (usually with radioactive isotopes), and rinsing the tissue to ensure that it binds with the substance. Through a technique called *autoradiography* (namely, capturing and imaging the radioactive emissions from the tissue on a photographic plate), one can locate the sites where the radioactive test molecules have bound. It is then a careful inference on the part of researchers that this represents the binding of molecules to receptors. To date, no one has produced an authentic three-dimensional image of a receptor site.

In this way, with autoradiography, it was discovered that nicotine binds to some, but not all, cholinergic receptors, and that muscarine binds to others. Why would this be? A logical assumption is that the receptors vary in molecular shape and binding properties, so that all accommodate ACh, some accommodate ACh and nicotine, and some accommodate ACh and muscarine. More study showed even further refinements among the subtypes. For instance, nicotinic cholinergic receptors have been shown to bind differently to other substances, and at least five variants of muscarinic cholinergic receptors have been identified. In general, inroads are being made monthly in the subclassification of receptors. The names and numbers of subtypes for all the receptors we are going to discuss are proliferating, as well as the identification of specific systems in which they participate, making life difficult for authors of basic psychopharmacology books and their readers.

Nicotinic cholinergic synapses are significant in the somatic nervous system as the transmitter of body movements: ACh plays an excitatory role in peripheral locations at the neuromuscular junctions of the skeletal muscles. Blocking the action of ACh at these sites annuls any movement of the skeletal muscles. And because the diaphragm uses ACh, many drugs that antagonize ACh stop the functioning of the lungs and cause death by asphyxiation. In addition, as we saw before, nicotinic synapses predominate in the autonomic nervous system, found at the first junctions of both the sympathetic and parasympathetic nervous systems.

While most muscarinic cholinergic receptors are located in the central nervous system, they can also be found in the periphery, at sites like the pupils (eyes) and on the target organs of the parasympathetic system. In the vagus nerve, where Loewi found it, ACh plays an inhibitory role, acting to slow the heart rate.

ACh is widespread in the brain, with the densest concentration in the hippocampus. It excites neurons in certain areas and inhibits them in others. In studies with lab animals, infusions of ACh into various regions of the brain have shown it to be involved in a range of behaviors that include eating, drinking, movement, emotions, learning, and memory.

A key agonist of ACh is nicotine, but only in small doses. In larger doses, nicotine is a powerful antagonist. This is because, in the early stages of its action, nicotine activates the cholinergic receptors. But because AChE is not adapted to metabolize it, the nicotine remains on the receptor and prevents further activation, in the case of muscles causing paralysis. Therefore, nicotine is a virulent poison. How then, one might ask, do smokers avoid killing themselves? It is because smoking or chewing tobacco does not deliver enough nicotine to the bloodstream to cause these effects. The amount contained in only two cigars, 60 mg, would be lethal if it were all active in the blood at once. Infants usually survive the accidental consumption of a pack of cigarettes because nicotine stimulates the vomiting center in the medulla before too much has been absorbed from the stomach. That is also why first-time smokers "turn green." Although it paralyzes the diaphragm, nicotine kills primarily by suffocation due to depression of the respiratory center in the medulla. Generally, the nerves are much more sensitive to low dosages of nicotine than are the muscles.

Another major agonist of ACh is muscarine, a derivative of Amanita muscaria, the fly agaric mushroom. Some muscarinic actions in the central nervous system are associated with hallucinations and berserk behavior that the subject cannot recall.

Nicotine and muscarine are both direct agonists in that they share a binding site with ACh. But there is an array of cholinergic agonists that act by blocking the enzyme AChE and prolonging the action of ACh on the receptors. Since this action is indirect, it does not depend on the shape of the binding sites and therefore affects all cholinergic receptors. Among the AChE inhibitors is DFP (diisopropyl fluorophosphate), stockpiled as a nerve gas during World War II. This drug blocks AChE, so that constantly acting ACh keeps the muscles depolarized and contracted, which manifests as paralysis and asphyxiation. DFP also causes sleep by increasing ACh in the tegmental reticular formation, where it inhibits arousal.

Many other drugs inhibit AChE as well. Physostigmine (Eserine), a short-acting, reversible AChE inhibitor, produces a range of psychological effects like nightmares, confusion, hallucinations, agitation, memory loss, and the slowing of intellectual and motor functions. But physostigmine has one especially beneficial use, in the treatment of myasthenia gravis. This is a disease in which patients develop muscular weakness, fatigue, and heaviness of movement and breathing. It is caused by the development of antibodies that bind with and damage cholinergic receptors at the muscles, stranding ACh where AChE can metabolize it. Physostigmine (Eserine) relieves the condition by interfering with AChE so that more ACh can act for a longer time.

Curare (*d*-tubocurarine), the drug used by South American Indians (Jivaro) on the tips of their arrows to paralyze their prey, is a competitive antagonist of ACh, but only at the nicotinic receptors, which are mainly peripheral. At a high enough dose, curare will steal the receptors and block ACh in the skeletal muscles and the diaphragm, leaving the victim conscious but paralyzed until suffocation sets in. The meat of animals shot with curare is edible, though, because the poison breaks down in digestion. The Indians of Ecuador and Peru rate the strength of their curare as one-tree, two-tree, or three-tree curare. If an Indian shoots a monkey with a poisoned arrow and it only has time to jump to one tree before it collapses, he has one-tree curare on his arrow—very strong. With a weaker dose, the monkey can escape to two or more trees. Experimenters occasionally use curare to immobilize animals for research, but the animals must be maintained by artificial respiration until the drug effect dissipates.

Atropine is a drug used in eye drops by the ophthalmologist to dilate your pupils so the interior of the eye can be examined. It is a direct antagonist of the muscarinic receptors. Normally, when ACh activates these receptors, the pupils constrict, but the ACh is blocked by atropine, allowing the pupils to relax and open. Atropine is also used as a decongestant because it blocks secretions controlled by cholinergic mechanisms in the nose, mouth, pharynx, and bronchi. But much of the action of atropine is in the central nervous system, where the predominance of muscarinic receptors are located. Larger doses can enter the brain and cause hallucinations.

Indirect antagonists of a transmitter substance have a variety of means to accomplish their ends. An ACh antagonist, botulinus toxin is one of the deadliest poisons known. (As a writer once remarked of prussic acid, "This poison is so deadly that one drop on the tongue of a dog can kill a man.") It works by locking ACh into the vesicles; the result--paralysis and suffocation. Another indirect ACh antagonist, hemicholinium, blocks the uptake of choline into the cell, thereby reducing the synthesis of ACh. Because less ACh is available, synaptic transmission is reduced.

Anticholinergic Syndrome

Some drug actions, by interfering with several cholinergic systems at once, produce a characteristic battery of symptoms, which in many cases are seen as the opposite of cholinergic effects (although simply blocking a mechanism does not necessarily produce an opposite reaction). An old medical school adage names some of the signs as follows:

Dry as a bone,
Red as a beet,
Hot as a furnace,
Mad as a hatter,
Blind as a bat.

"Dry as a bone" because the mouth goes dry and sweating is inhibited. "Red as a beet" because the skin flushes red from the dilation of peripheral blood vessels. "Hot as a furnace" because of high temperatures. "Mad as a hatter" because the subject becomes delirious, disoriented, and agitated and may experience visual and auditory hallucinations, restlessness and anxiety, and thought disorders (delusions). Blurred vision makes the subject "blind as a bat" (remember how atropine works?). Additional symptoms include constipation, urinary retention, dilation of the pupils, motor incoordination, and rapid heartbeat. All of these signs are reflections of blocked cholinergic neurons, and the syndrome can be a problem with some drugs. On the other hand, stimulating ACh sites produces all of the opposite effects: tearing, salivation, runny nose, sweating, paleness, bronchial constrictions, muscle weakness, nausea, cramps, and slowed heartbeat.

DOPAMINE

The next three transmitters to be considered--dopamine (DA), norepinephrine (NE), and serotonin (5-HT)--are all nitrogen-containing compounds descended from amino acids and are referred to as bioamines. These three bioamines may be subdivided on the basis of their chemical structures. DA and NE, closely related in synthesis and structure, both contain a catechol ring (a benzene ring with two hydroxyl groups attached), giving them the name catecholamines. Serotonin (5-HT) has a complex double organic ring called an indole ring, making it an indolamine.

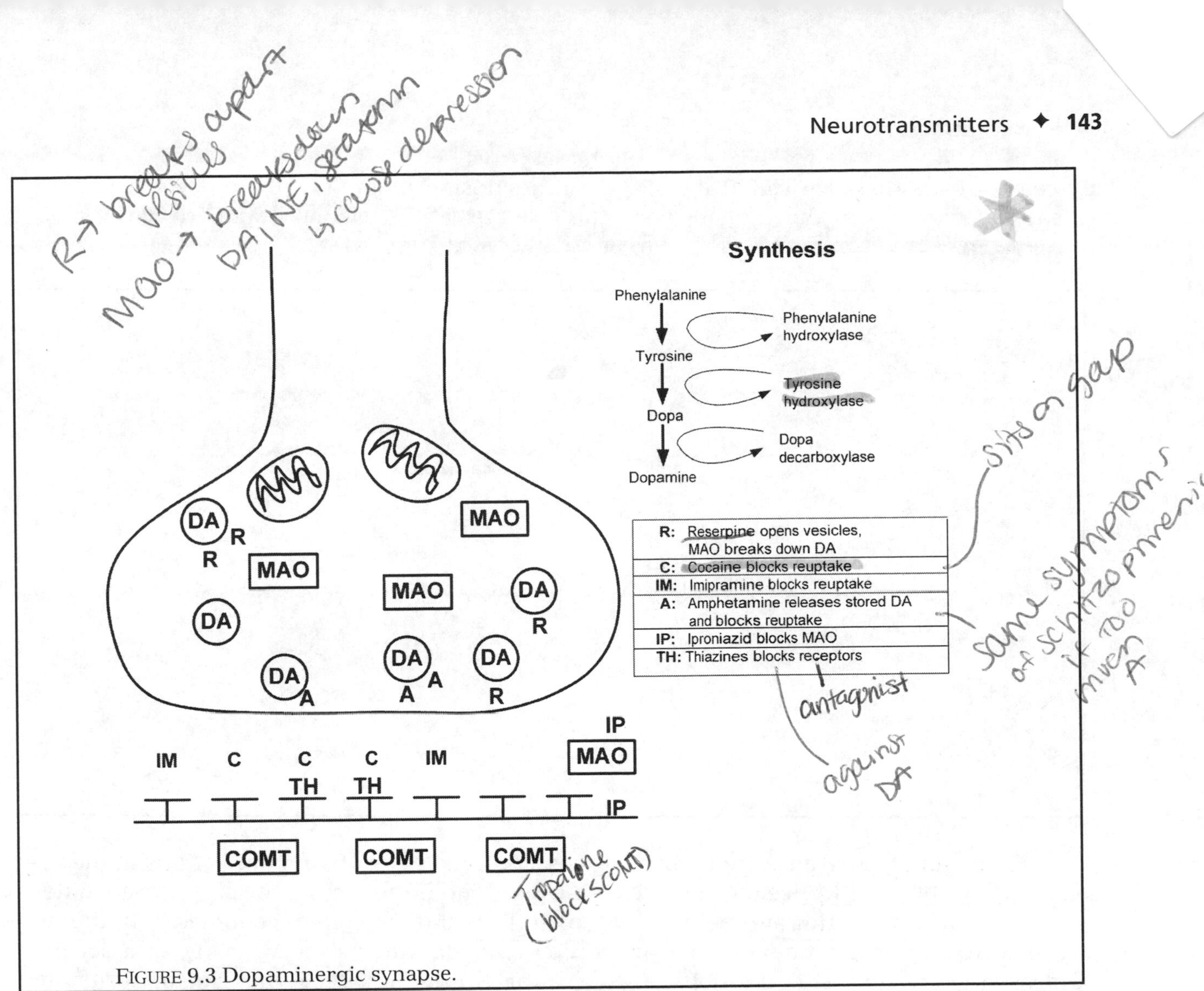

FIGURE 9.3 Dopaminergic synapse.

Dopamine is synthesized from the amino acid phenylalanine, which is found in good supply in cheeses and beer, among other sources. Three enzymes convert phenylalanine into DA through three transformations (see Figure 9.3). Tyrosine hydroxylase, the second enzyme in the chain, is of particular interest because it responds to the amount of its own end products, shutting on and off like a switch to control the amount of synthesis. Since the rate of catecholamine synthesis depends on the activity of tyrosine hydroxylase, this substance is called a *rate-limiting enzyme*.

The action of DA differs significantly from that of ACh in the description above. At its nicotinic sites, ACh alters the permeability of the cell membrane by regulating the ion channels associated with the receptor sites. (At its muscarinic sites, it is more like the action of DA in the description that follows.)

In contrast, when DA attaches to the receptor, it triggers a set of enzymatic changes inside the postsynaptic membrane. Because these changes involve a number of intermediate substances reacting to one another, in addition to the transmitter at the synapse, they are called a second messenger system. For our purposes, we need only a rudimentary idea of second messenger activity. When DA binds with the receptor, it initiates a sequence of chemical reactions inside the cell, producing in the end an increase or decrease of a substance called cAMP (cyclic adenosine monophosphate), which in turn leads to changes in the excitability of the cell. cAMP increase in dopaminergic cells is mostly inhibitory, but is also found to be excitatory at some sites.

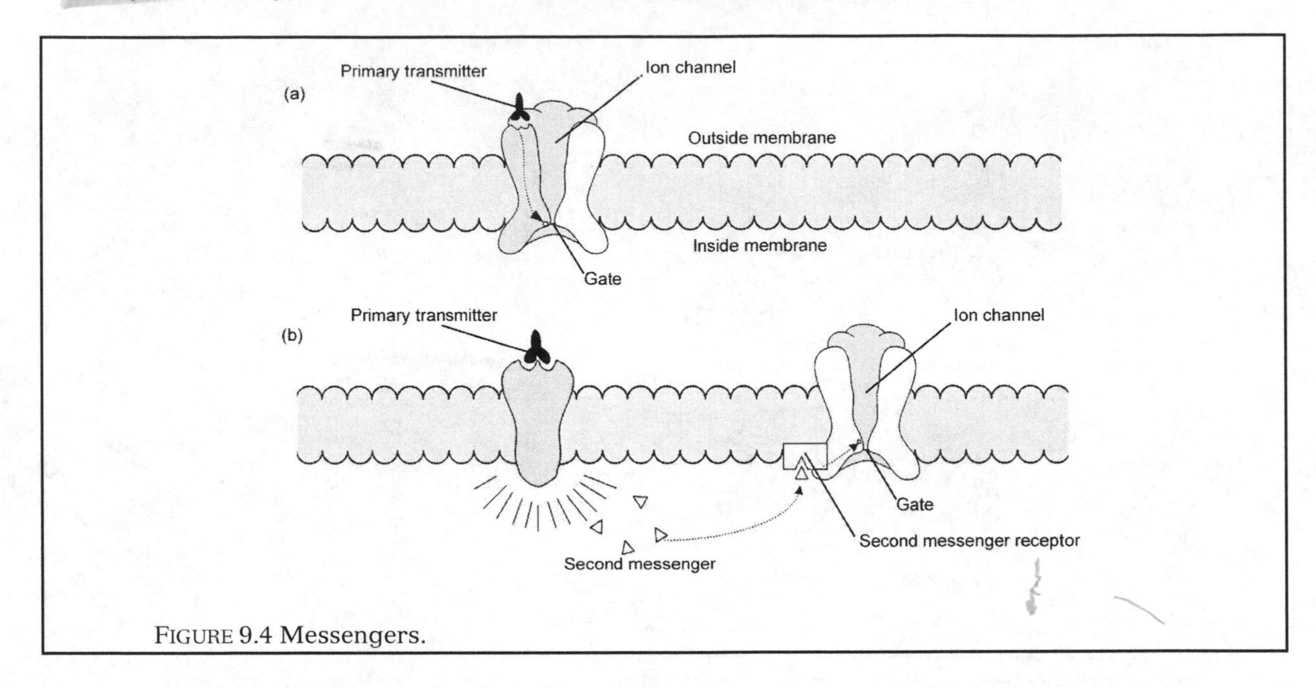

FIGURE 9.4 Messengers.

Given all of the transmitters to be discussed, to date only two main actions at the receptor are of significance (see Figure 9.4). Upon binding to a receptor site, a transmitter either (1) affects membrane permeability by influencing the channel coupled with the receptor (e.g., the nicotinic cholinergic receptor), or (2) affects the working of a second messenger system (e.g., the dopamine receptor). In the first case, the transmitter either hyperpolarizes (inhibits) or helps to depolarize (fire) the cell, depending on which ions the channel admits (Na+, Cl-, K+). In the second case, the object is the triggering of a set of biochemical changes that modulate the firing capability of the cell; in many cases, this is either an increase or decrease in cAMP production.

In general, these two types of action have been characterized as fast and slow. The rapid depolarization resulting from effects on ion channels and membrane permeability can occur in 2 to 10 milliseconds, compared to the slower enzymatic action of second messenger systems, which may take from 20 milliseconds to 10 full seconds. These fast/slow distinctions are not hard and clean, however, since some second messenger systems affect membrane permeability. Moreover, some transmitters (such as ACh and GABA) have both fast and slow action sites. This is significant because the slow sites use similar messenger systems (e.g., involve cAMP), so that agents that interact with these systems can display patterns of effects not necessarily associated with any one transmitter.

Let's return now to dopamine. Unlike ACh, which is deactivated through hydrolysis by AChE in the synaptic gap, the action of DA is terminated largely by reuptake--that is, reabsorption--by active transport through the presynaptic membrane and back into the vesicles. In addition, there are two enzymes active in degrading DA wherever it is vulnerable. The first is monoamine oxidase (MAO), found in both presynaptic terminals and the postsynaptic membrane. The second is catechol-O-methyltransferase (COMT), found in the synaptic gap. Both enzymes deactivate DA and other catecholamines as well. In the presynaptic terminal, MAO deactivates any overabundance of DA. When DA crosses the gap and binds to the receptor, some of it is metabolized by both of these enzymes, and MAO gets more of it on its way through the membrane back into the vesicles. Also, a portion of DA is lost through a third route: it simply diffuses away from the receptor site. But generally most of the transmitter is reuptaken. These mechanisms of termination of DA action are common to both catecholamines (DA and NE).

Although five subtypes of DA receptors (D_1 through D_5) have been identified, two families can be distinguished, based on their effect on cAMP levels. D_1 and D_5 receptors stimulate cAMP synthesis, whereas D_2 receptors inhibit it. The action of D_3 and D_4 receptors is not known.

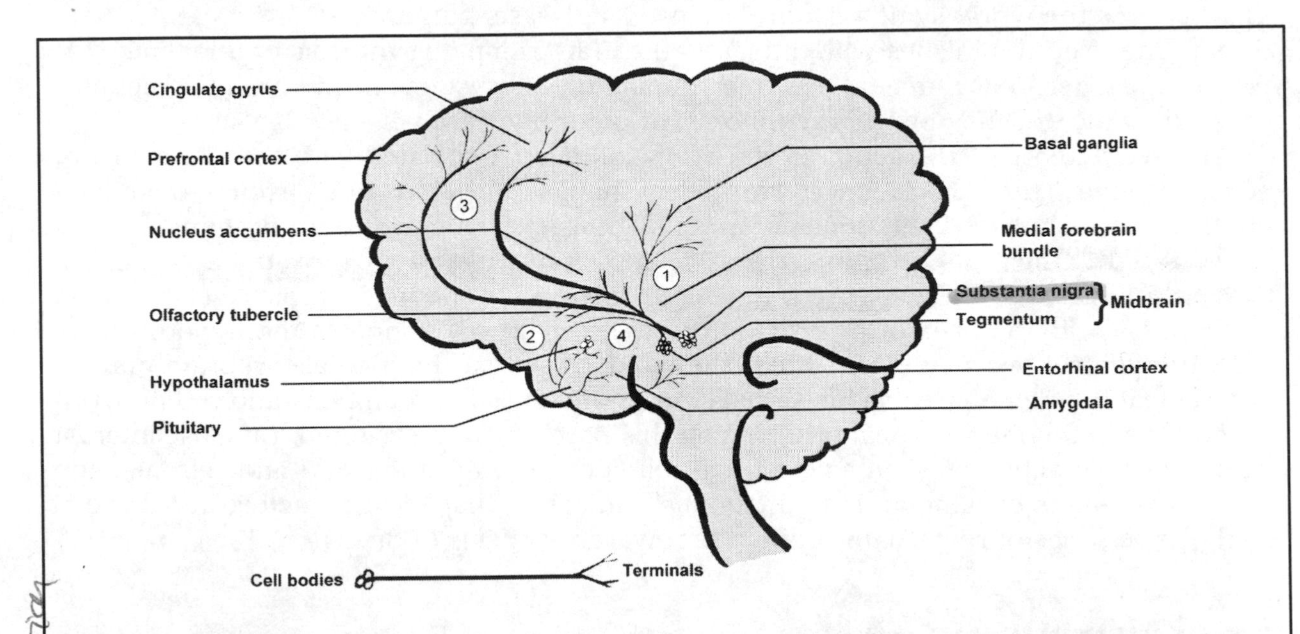

FIGURE 9.5 Four of the major dopamine pathways of the human brain. (1) Nigrostriatal tract. Connects the substantia nigra with areas of the basal ganglia (including the striatal area). It is associated with movement and its degeneration is linked to Parkinson's disease. (2) Mesolimbic tract. Connects midbrain to various limbic structures. The pathway involving the ventral tegmental area (tegmentum), the medial forebrain bundle, and the nucleus accumbens is associated with pleasure, reward, and the reinforcing effects of drugs. (3) Mesocortical tract. Connects midbrain to areas of the prefrontal cortex. Often referred to with the mesolimbic tract as the *mesocortical limbic* tract. (4) Tuberoinfundibular tract. Originates in the ventral tegmental area (tegmentum). Connects the hypothalamus with the pituitary and is involved in the release of hormones.

DA neurons have been found only within the central nervous system. Relatively few in number, they originate from cell bodies in two brain areas (the substantia nigra and the ventral tegmental area) and extend by three major pathways to many other areas. Figure 9.5 shows the distribution of DA neurons in the human brain. The main clustering of dopaminergic cell bodies is the midbrain area known as the *substantia nigra*. From here, connections run up to the basal ganglia and the frontal lobes. The DA map of the brain suggests that DA is important in autonomic functions (hypothalamus), body posture and fine motor movements (basal ganglia), and the regulation of thinking (frontal lobes). It is also of major significance in reward circuits.

One of the key associations of DA is with the movement disorder known as Parkinson's disease. Parkinson's is connected with a degeneration of the nigrostriatal pathway (see Figure 9.5) and a compromising of dopaminergic activity in the area of the basal ganglia called the striatum, where 75 percent of the DA in the brain is found. Similarly, antipsychotic drugs that block DA produce a Parkinson's-like condition (parkinsonism) as a side effect, marked by tremors, rigidity, and the loss of fine motor movements. In treatment, DA is not given because it cannot cross the blood-brain barrier. Instead, its precursor, L-dopa, is administered. L-dopa crosses the blood-brain barrier and is synthesized into DA on site in the brain (though not exclusively by dopaminergic neurons). This relieves the worst symptoms of Parkinson's disease, but, unfortunately, responsiveness to the drug diminishes with time, and the indiscriminate synthesis of dopa into DA, following larger doses, may affect other dopaminergic systems in the brain, sometimes causing manic or schizophrenic symptoms, or other undesirable side effects.

An overactivity of DA action in the brain has been associated with the symptoms of schizophrenia. This was evidenced by the fact that DA-blocking drugs exhibited antipsychotic effects. However, this connection is now not as clear as was once thought.

One of the most important functions of dopamine in relation to drug use is the mediation of pleasure in the reward pathways of the brain. The mesolimbic tract, depicted in Figure 9.5, is the area of primary interest. The pathway connects the hypothalamus with the ventral tegmental area (near the tegmentum) via the medial forebrain bundle; the ventral tegmental area sends signals out to the nucleus accumbens and the prefrontal cortex via the mesocortical tract. When this pathway is interrupted, rats lose interest in pleasurable activities such as electrical self-stimulation of the brain and self-injection of the stimulants cocaine and amphetamine, indicating that these structures are crucial to the experience of reward, including the rewarding effects of drugs.

NOREPINEPHRINE

Norepinephrine (NE), also called "noradrenalin," was first identified as a neurotransmitter in the nerve endings of the liver in 1921. Synapses using NE are called adrenergic synapses, or, more accurately, noradrenergic synapses (Figure 9.6). Chemically derived from DA, NE is likewise both a bioamine and a catecholamine. Figure 9.6 shows how the synthesis of NE matches that of DA, except for one extra stage where the enzyme dopamine-beta-hydroxylase converts DA into NE. It is stored and released in much the same way as DA, and its action at the receptor is similar.

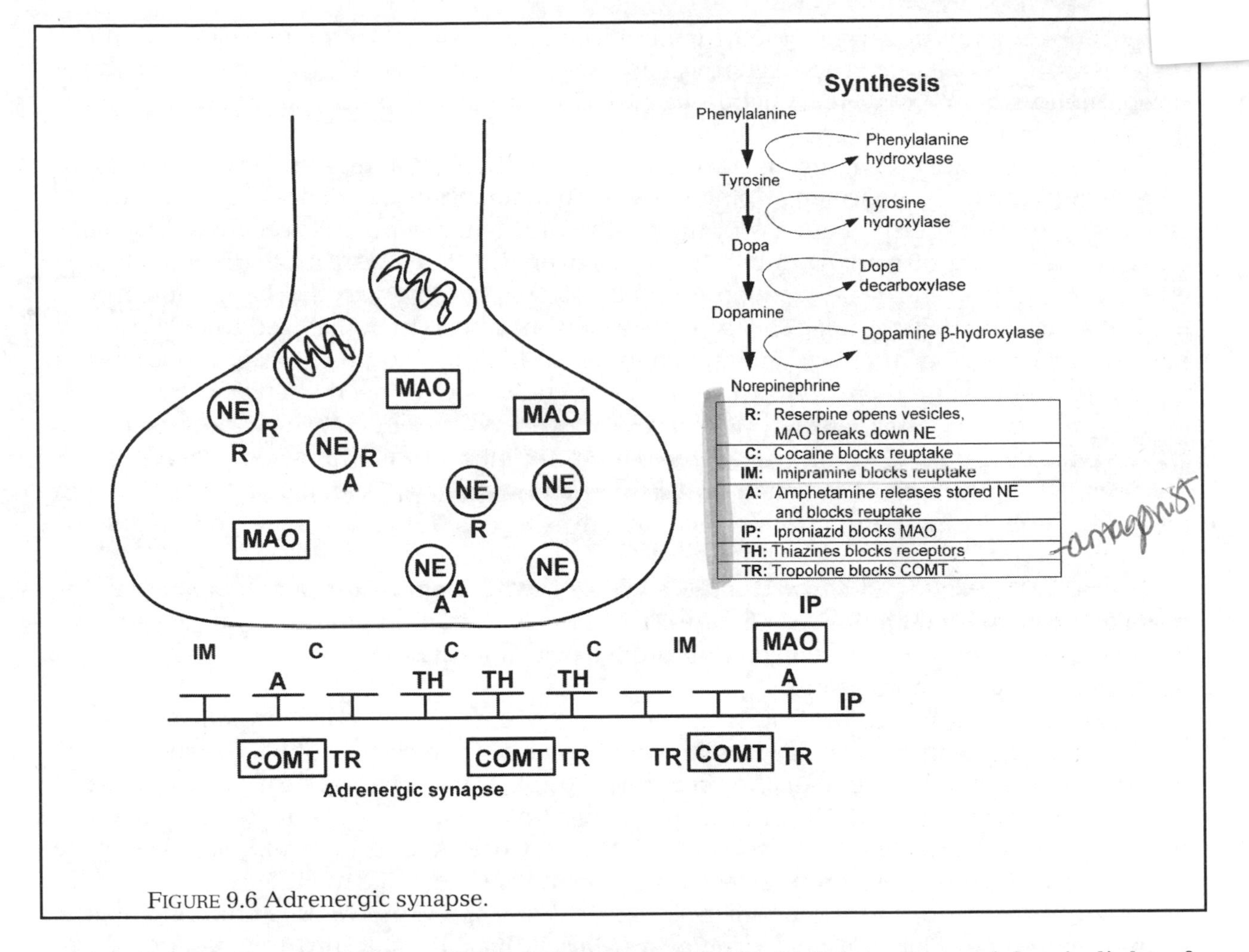

FIGURE 9.6 Adrenergic synapse.

The termination of action of NE is like that of DA, which is not surprising in light of their close chemical relationship. The primary mechanism is by reuptake into the vesicles, and this is supplemented by the degrading enzymes MAO and COMT.

Two major classes of NE receptors have been described. These are alpha-adrenergic and beta-adrenergic receptors. The receptor shapes were first inferred by studying the different binding affinities of NE receptors for three substances: norepinephrine (NE), epinephrine (E), and isoproterenol (ISO). Alpha receptors show highest to lowest affinity in the order NEEISO, while beta receptors bind in order of preference to ISOENE. Subtypes of these in turn have been identified.

In the periphery, adrenergic sites play key roles in the sympathetic reaction (fight or flight response). The adrenal medulla, a gland near the kidneys, releases NE along with adrenalin (epinephrine). The only other peripheral NE sites are at the second junctions of the sympathetic nerves (see page xxx), where it is released by sympathetic neurons synapsing with smooth muscles and glands. Some sympathetic connections are also found at key points in the cardiovascular system. Alpha receptors on the peripheral blood vessels, stimulated by NE, constrict the vessels, increasing the blood supply to vital organs and elevating the blood pressure. Beta receptors on the heart, stimulated by NE, speed and strengthen the beating of the heart, pumping more blood to the muscles. Via these systems, NE-enhancing drugs such as cocaine, amphetamine, and mescaline produce sympathetic side effects. Heart action can be overstimulated by cocaine and can be reduced by adrenergic blockers.

In the brain, most NE neurons have their somae concentrated in the brain stem, in an area named the locus coeruleus ("blue place"). The locus coeruleus consists of two dense clusters of noradrenergic neurons in the region of the upper pons. It receives a tremendous convergence of sensory inputs from all over the body, and it sends connections downward to the reticular formation in the brainstem, and upward to the hippocampus, hypothalamus, and amygdala. The locus coeruleus has been hypothesized to be a novelty detector, responding to environmental changes and mediating other brain responses to them (Aghajanian, 1994, p. 138). Through these and other connections, NE is implicated in a battery of functions, among them arousal, dreaming sleep, and a variety of limbic and hypothalamic activities: anxiety, fear, mood, hunger, thirst, and sex drives. At small dosages, NE has a beneficial action on learning and memory. It can also alter eating and drinking behavior, depending on which sites it is injected into in the hypothalamus or amygdala.

Along with DA, NE is associated with the reward system through its dense receptor population in the medial forebrain bundle. It is likely that, along with DA, it plays a role in the elevation of mood, the mediation of pleasure, and the development of psychological dependence and addictions.

There is a long roster of drugs that can affect every facet of adrenergic functioning, many with stimulant effects. Mescaline and ephedrine, direct agonists, resemble the transmitter enough to stimulate the receptors. Amphetamine induces the slow release of newly formed and stored NE, and at the same time blocks its reuptake, producing a flushed, energized feeling and an elevated mood. Cocaine and imipramine can elevate mood and relieve depression by selectively blocking the reuptake of NE.

A number of adrenergic agonists increase the supply of NE by inhibiting MAO. Tranylcypromine (Parnate) and iproniazid (Marsilid), which fall into this category, can relieve depression by heightening adrenergic action, but they have a much milder action than the rushes of cocaine or amphetamine.

Antagonism of NE generally results in a reduction of excitement. Some antipsychotic drugs act in part by blocking NE receptors in the brain. In a normal individual, they can produce severe depression; however, they allow manic or psychotic people to function more normally. Reserpine, an indirect NE antagonist, is a drug that destroys the protective membrane around the vesicles and releases NE into the terminal; there is an initial excitation before the transmitter is destroyed by MAO. For many years, reserpine was used for sedation and for the reduction of blood pressure, but it has fallen out of use. In normal people, reserpine produces profound depression for several days, until the neurons can resynthesize synaptic vesicles; in the elderly, however, its damage may be permanent. Giving reserpine to aged animals (laboratory rats) depresses general activity severely, and the activity may never return to normal, even after discontinuation of the drug.

Because of the peripheral locations of alpha-adrenergic receptors, which constrict the blood vessels upon stimulation, antagonists specific to these receptors are excellent drugs for reducing blood pressure. Similarly, beta receptors on the heart can be selectively blocked by antagonists like propranolol to stabilize an irregular heart beat. Propranolol (Inderal) may be used as a tranquilizer as well.

SEROTONIN

Serotonin (5HT) was originally studied as a vasoconstrictor present in the blood plasma. Its name thus derives from blood *serum* and *tonus*, a slight, continuous contraction of smooth muscle. The chemical term for it is 5hydroxytryptamine, or 5HT.

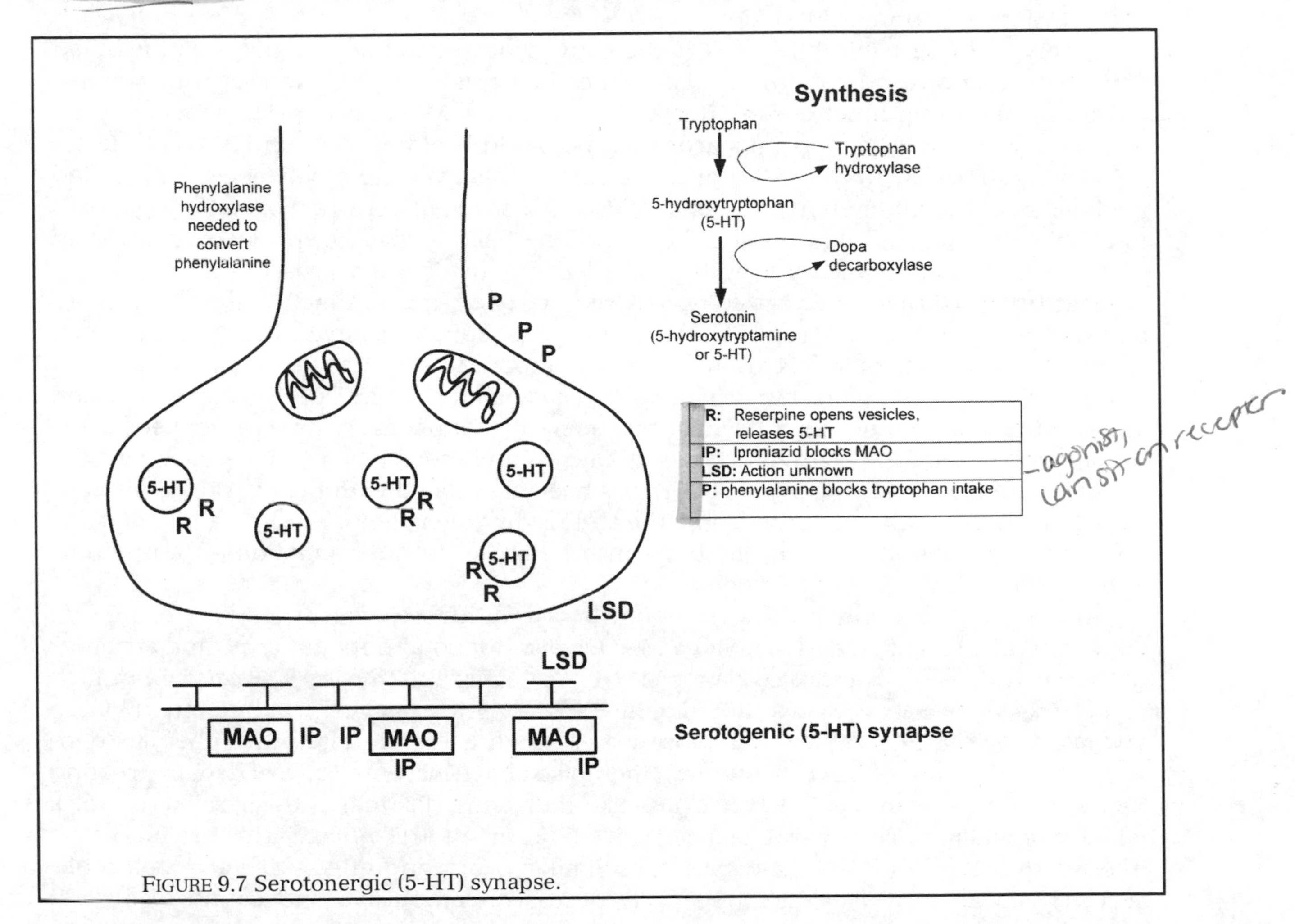

FIGURE 9.7 Serotonergic (5-HT) synapse.

The synthesis of 5HT is schematized in Figure 9.7. It begins as the amino acid tryptophan and is converted by two enzymes. The first is tryptophan hydroxylase. The second is the synthesizing enzyme dopa decarboxylase, which is common to the synthesis of 5HT, NE, and DA in neurons; any influence on this enzyme therefore affects all three systems. In addition, the enzyme phenylalanine hydroxylase figures one way or another in all three systems. In the NE and DA neurons, it is involved in the synthesis of NE and DA from phenylalanine. If this enzyme is lacking, phenylalanine will accumulate. The excess phenylalanine will then interfere with the transport of tryptophan into 5-HT neurons, impairing 5-HT synthesis; this can cause mental retardation in a developing child.

Like NE and DA, 5HT is destroyed by the enzyme MAO. Thus, any of the MAO inhibitors, a class of antidepressants, affects all three systems. In fact, one can't be sure which of these neurotransmitters is involved in the benefits accruing from MAO inhibitors.

Currently, 5HT receptors have the largest number of proposed subtypes, divided into five families ($5HT_1$ to $5HT_5$), with further elaborations thereof. These variants have been linked to different kinds of actions involving ion transfer through membrane channels and cAMP production or inhibition.

Ninety-eight percent of the 5-HT in the body is located in the periphery—in the blood and in the smooth muscles of the gastrointestinal tract, where it causes contractions. Generally, the brain functions are not well understood. Most brain 5HT is concentrated in the pineal gland (which is unguarded by the blood-brain barrier) and most of the serotonergic somae lie in the raphé nuclei, a part of the brain stem between the pons and medulla, near the midline (hence *raphé* for "seam") of the upper brain stem. 5HT appears to be involved in arousal levels and the induction of slow-wave (deep) sleep. As levels of 5HT increase, we tire, and as a result of our sleeping, the levels decrease.

The fibers of 5HT neurons diffuse widely through the brain. An ascending 5-HT pathway projects from the raphé nuclei up through brain areas involving functions such as pleasure (the medial forebrain bundle), temperature control (the hypothalamus), movement (basal ganglia), mood (amygdala), vision (the lateral geniculate body), and sensory perception (cortex). 5-HT neurons innervate almost every area of the neocortex. Stimulation of the 5-HT pathways typically causes inhibition.

In addition to sleep and arousal, 5HT has been associated with the hypothalamic control of hormone release, and with appetite and feeding behaviors. The spreading of serotonergic pathways throughout the brain may be linked to the regulation of biorhythms and the synchronization of functions.

Among the most common 5-HT agonists are antidepressant drugs like iproniazid, which inhibit the enzyme MAO. Since MAO is also found at dopaminergic and adrenergic synapses, these antidepressants stimulate the action of NE and DA as well. In fact, most of these drugs were originally administered with the goal of elevating mood by enhancing the action of NE. It was more or less seen as a side effect that they also enhanced the action of 5HT. However, therapists have recently succeeded in treating depression effectively with newer drugs like fluoxetine (Prozac) and sertraline (Zoloft), which are much more powerful and selective blockers of 5HT uptake. This has increased interest in the role of 5HT in depression. Similar promising effects are also being observed with anxiety disorders (especially obsessive-compulsive and eating disorders) and schizophrenia.

Among the most spectacular serotonergic agonists are LSD and psilocybin, both strong hallucinogens. LSD, whose chemical structure resembles 5HT, appears to work by occupying the receptors and causing a backup of 5HT that exceeds the action of MAO to control it. Although LSD intoxication may last from 6 to 9 hours or more, the majority of LSD is gone after 5 or 6 hours, at which point 5HT begins to flood the receptors (or perhaps they have become supersensitized through blockage); consequently, after about 6 hours, the trip is well under way. It might be, in fact, not an LSD trip, but a 5HT trip.

Similar hallucinatory effects may have been produced in ancient, magical cultures by raising 5HT levels through sleep deprivation. Cocaine, which is not a hallucinogen, may facilitate 5HT action by inhibiting reuptake.

PCPA (p-chlorophenylalanine) indirectly antagonizes 5HT by inhibiting the synthesizing enzyme tryptophan hydroxylase. The result is hyperexcitability and insomnia. In cats, this drug knocks out 5HT completely and irreversibly, and the animals never sleep again; they may survive for about two weeks in this condition. Reserpine, another antagonist, wreaks havoc at serotonergic synapses by destroying the vesicles.

GAMMA-AMINOBUTYRIC ACID

The bioamines (NE, DA, and 5HT) are synthesized from amino acids, yet it also appears that certain amino acids themselves act as transmitter substances. The most prevalent of these is GABA (gamma-aminobutyric acid). It is found only in the nervous system, and mostly in the central nervous system, where it is widely distributed in very high concentrations compared to most other transmitters. Peripheral GABA levels may be very low.

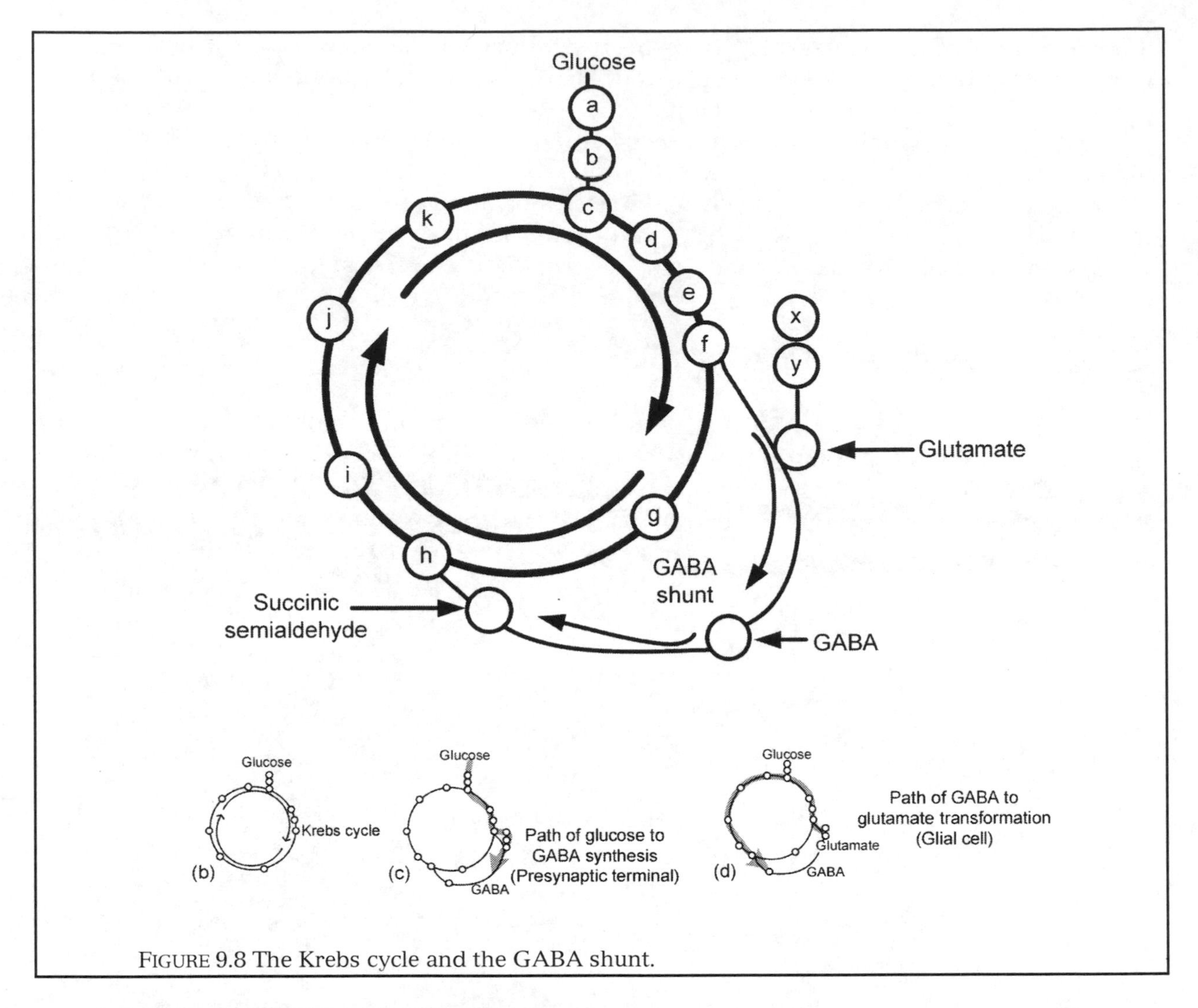

FIGURE 9.8 The Krebs cycle and the GABA shunt.

The synthesis of GABA is complex but efficient, involving a cycle of chemical conversions. The primary source of GABA is glucose, which is essential to all cell functioning. In general, in the mitochondria of a cell, glucose is metabolized to provide energy for ongoing cell processes. This takes place through a round of transformations known as the Krebs cycle. One might think of the Krebs cycle as a chemical engine fueled by glucose, furnishing the cell with energy. However, through one part of the Krebs cycle there is an alternate set of transformations that involves GABA--the GABA shunt (see Figure 9.8a and 9.8b). Because of the GABA shunt, the Krebs cycle is able to make GABA out of glucose in the presynaptic terminals of neurons (see Figure 9.8c).

A second source of GABA is the glial cell. When GABA is released from its receptors in the synapse, the glial cell takes it up and converts it into glutamate (glutamic acid). It does this by two means: through its own GABA shunt (see Figure 9.8d) and through the converting enzyme GABA-T (see Figure 9.9).

Broadly, then, a GABA-ergic neuron gets its supply of GABA through its own Krebs cycle, which manufactures it from glucose, and from the glial cell, which produces it first in the form of glutamate.

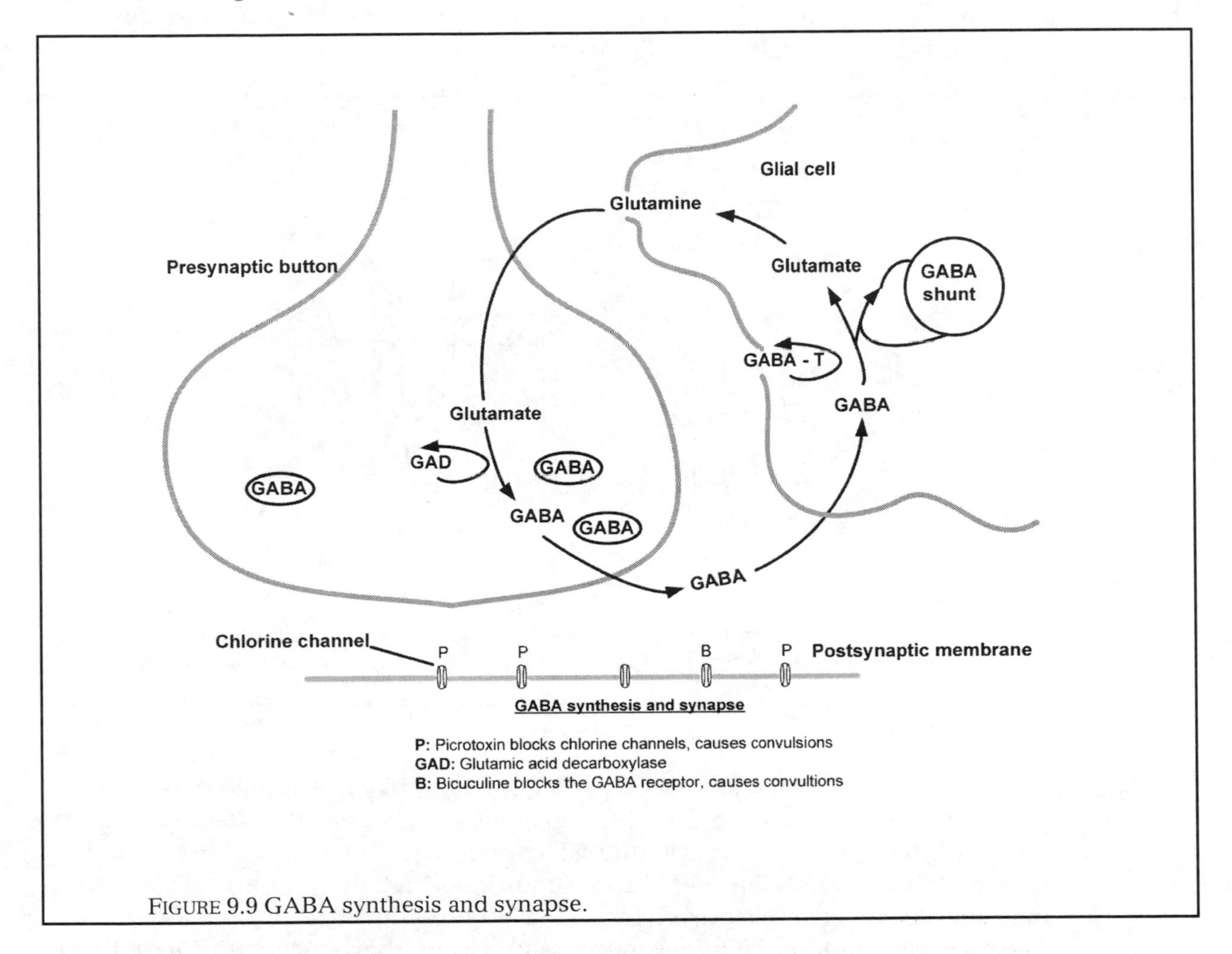

FIGURE 9.9 GABA synthesis and synapse.

Glutamate, however, is unable to cross the neural membrane and reenter the neuron. Consequently, while it is in the glial cell, it undergoes a further transformation into glutamine. Glutamine is then actively transported back into the neuron, through a mechanism that depends on sodium; there it is reconverted to glutamate. In a manner of speaking, glutamate has to be temporarily disguised as glutamine to enter the neuron (see Figure 9.9). Once inside, it is finally changed by the enzyme GAD (glutamate decarboxylase) into GABA and stored once more for release. After its release and dissociation from the receptor, GABA is reuptaken into the glial cell, where the conversion process begins again.

The action of GABA is consistently inhibitory. Upon attaching to the receptor site, it rapidly hyperpolarizes the postsynaptic neuron by admitting Cl- ions through the ion channels, making it more difficult to fire. The action terminates through the reuptake of GABA into both the presynaptic terminals and the glial cells.

Because glucose in the Krebs cycle is an important source of GABA, a low blood sugar supply can cause a depletion of the transmitter. Diabetics, who cannot make use of glucose despite high blood levels, cannot manufacture enough GABA. The resulting deficiency can lead to convulsions, since the inhibitory action of GABA is thus reduced. Insulin alleviates this by making the use of glucose possible.

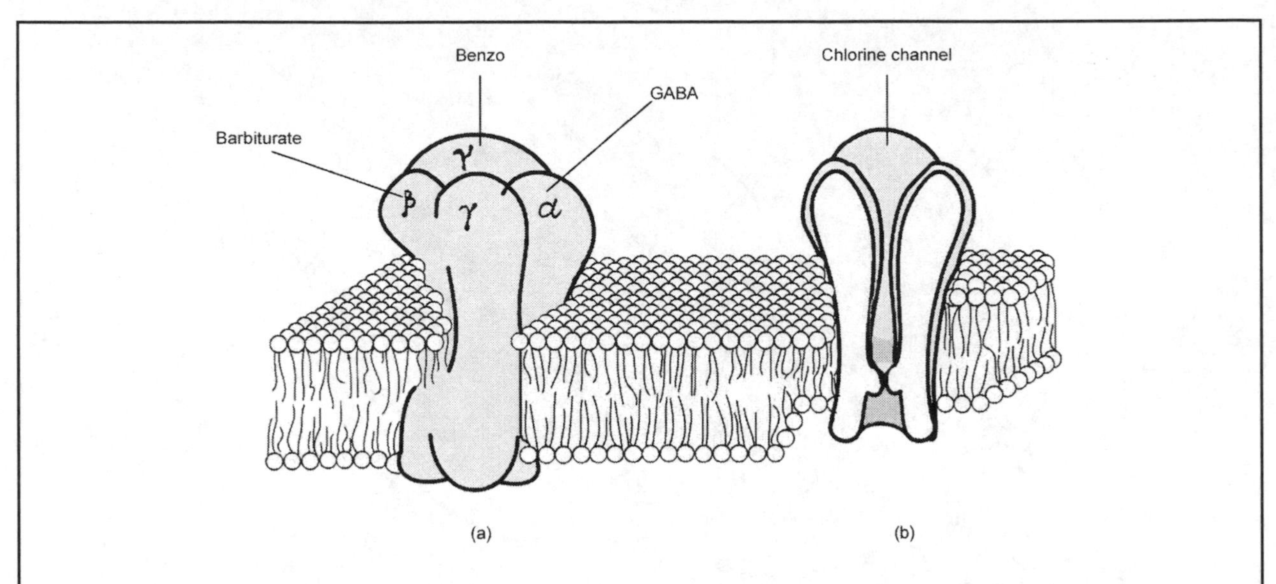

FIGURE 9.10 Structure of GABA receptor. (a) Structure of the $GABA_A$ receptor, showing binding sites for GABA, barbiturates, and benzodiazepines. (b) Cross section of the $GABA_A$ receptor, showing the chlorine channel.

Two distinct classes of GABA receptors have been identified, designated as $GABA_A$ and $GABA_B$ receptors. They differ in their pharmacological properties. The $GABA_A$ sites are associated with an ion channel mediating Cl^- conductance through the membrane—the action we have described above. Evidence indicates that these sites consist of an elaborate macromolecular complex involving separate binding sites for as many as five different classes of substances, including depressant drugs (barbiturates), tranquilizers (benzodiazepines like Librium and Valium), and anesthetic steroids, all of which are capable of influencing cell response (see Figure 9.10). Thus, the protein containing the channel can be envisioned as a complex docking station that allows a variety of agents to attach and affect ion transfer. GABA has its own specific binding site in this complex, and it is GABA that is directly responsible for opening the ion channel. These other substances do not attach directly to the GABA receptor, but bind to associated sites and from there modulate the action of GABA.

Less is known about $GABA_B$ sites. They were discovered because of their insensitivity to important agonists and antagonists of the $GABA_A$ sites. $GABA_B$ receptors appear to be able to affect K+ and calcium transfer (needed to open the vesicles to release transmitter molecules) and can inhibit cAMP production in second messenger systems found at these sites.

About 40 percent of the neurons in the brain use GABA, which points up the importance of inhibition in central nervous functioning. However, most of the transmitter is concentrated in the basal ganglia. The only GABA-ergic site in the periphery is in the retina of the eye, a tissue closely related to the brain.

Because of GABA's important inhibitory role, agonists of GABA make good anticonvulsant drugs, sleeping pills, anesthetics, and tranquilizers. The barbiturates and the benzodiazepines are two families of drugs that have shared these therapeutic uses. Benzodiazepines augment the action of GABA by increasing the frequency of the Cl- ion channel opening. Barbiturates increase the amount of time that the channel stays open in the presence of GABA.

The antagonist bicuculline is a central nervous system stimulant that acts directly and competitively at the $GABA_A$ binding site in the receptor complex. $GABA_B$ receptors were found to be insensitive to bicuculline. Picrotoxin, a powerful convulsant, is a noncompetitive GABA antagonist that acts by binding inside the ion channel and preventing the flow of ions through the membrane.

GLYCINE

Glycine, like GABA an amino acid, is a chief inhibitory transmitter. These two substances, GABA and glycine, account for most of the inhibition in the nervous system. Glycine, however, has also been found to have excitatory actions at some sites. As a common amino acid, glycine makes up 1 percent to 5 percent of the protein in an average diet. And like some other amino acid transmitters, it has multiple functions.

The action of glycine is similar to that of GABA. It is thought to hyperpolarize neurons by acting on ion channels affecting Cl^- movement. Deactivation occurs through reuptake. Glycine is distributed mainly in the spinal cord, in the medulla and pons of the brain, and in the retina.

Unlike GABA, glycine does not appear to be affected by the barbiturates or benzodiazepines. A competitive antagonist is strychnine, which is a powerful convulsant.

EXCITATORY AMINO ACIDS

Glutamate and Aspartate

Glutamate and aspartate are two candidates for admission to the pantheon of neurotransmitters. They have gained slow acceptance over four decades of research. Nevertheless, they still have not met all of the criteria. The identification of antagonists for certain receptor sites, for instance, remains to be seen.

Like GABA, glutamate and aspartate are amino acids, and are found in very high concentrations. This contrasts with what one would expect of a neurotransmitter, since it would not seem advantageous to have large quantities of widely distributed substances that could activate receptor sites on neurons. But as amino acids, these substances participate in other biological processes besides neurotransmission. As a case in point, we have seen how glutamate serves as a precursor of GABA. It seems ironic that glutamate, a key excitatory transmitter, should act as a precursor of one of the key inhibitory transmitters.

Glutamate and aspartate, among the simplest neurotransmitters in terms of their molecular structure, are similar enough in their action that the nerve pathways using them cannot yet be distinguished from one another. As with ACh, the action of glutamate and aspartate at the receptor site opens channels that leak Na+ and other positive ions into the cell and initiate or encourage the action potential. These three substances, ACh, glutamate, and aspartate, are the primary mediators of rapid depolarization in the nervous system.

Both glutamate and aspartate are deactivated by being reuptaken into the presynaptic nerve terminals and glial cells. Supplies are replenished by synthesis out of substances that enter through the blood-brain barrier.

Three subtypes of receptors responding to glutamate and aspartate have been identified: the AMPA receptor, the NMDA receptor, and the kainate receptor. The AMPA receptor (named after alpha-amino-3-hydroxy-5-methyl-4-isoxazole propionic acid, the synthetic analog of glutamate that binds to it) seems to mediate most of the rapid excitatory responses in the mammalian nervous system (Robinson, 1994, p. 112). The NMDA receptor (named after *N*-methyl-d-aspartate) is of pharmacological interest for several reasons. Its activation is unique and complex, involving an agonist (glutamate), glycine, and sufficient depolarization to remove a magnesium ion block in the ion channel. Furthermore, the ion channel contains a binding site for the psychoactive drug PCP and may prove important in understanding the action of drugs that produce psychosis-like effects. The association of the NMDA receptor with memory acquisition and with Alzheimer's disease has raised some hope that it can be manipulated to improve memory and learning (Kozikowski & Barrionuevo, 1991, pp. viii-ix). Investigation of the kainate receptor is still in its early stages.

NEUROPEPTIDES

Peptides are proteins consisting of chains of amino acids. The term neuropeptide indicates those that are active in neurotransmission. In general, the neuropeptides differ from other neurotransmitters in their synthesis and deactivation. The classical transmitters (ACh, DA, NE, 5-HT, and GABA) are synthesized both in the somae and the nerve terminals of neurons; the peptides are synthesized in the somae only. Also, no uptake is involved in their deactivation. As a class, the neuropeptides play an important role in behavior and in the physiology of mental disorders.

In 1973, when morphine, a chemical derivative of opium, was discovered to bind to receptors in the brain, it was assumed that these receptors must exist to respond to an endogenous substance, that is, a substance produced naturally in the body. This substance would resemble morphine and produce morphine-like effects. It would be a natural and powerful pain killer. The search for this compound discovered, in 1975, two proteins, each composed of five amino acids (pentapeptides). They were identified as the sought-after substance and named enkephalins--methionine-enkephalin and leucine-enkephalin.

Like morphine, which is their key agonist, the enkephalins have a powerful analgesic (painkilling) effect originating at multiple sites of action. In the spinal cord, they may influence the transmission of sensations of pain from spine to brain. Limbic system sites my help to mollify the emotional response to pain, which is a known action of morphine. Other sites implicate them in movement and in respiration. Since morphine is capable of producing severe respiratory depression, the enkephalins may have a similar role.

The enkephalins inhibit neurons by hyperpolarization through the promotion of K+ passage through neural membranes. In spinal cord neurons, they block neurotransmitter release by affecting Ca++ (see page 135). Enkephalin molecules are deactivated by the enzyme enkephalinase. This enzyme makes a promising target for drug therapy, since inhibiting it would prolong the action of the body's natural painkillers.

Naloxone is the main antagonist of both the enkephalins and morphine. It appears that methods of reducing pain, like electrical stimulation of the brain and acupuncture, achieve their effects by stimulating enkephalin release. One clue to this is that naloxone blocks the effectiveness of all such techniques. We will consider these more at length in the chapter on opiates.

Recent research has shown that some peptides (such as somatostatin, neurotensin, and CCK) act in very close accord with DA, so close, in fact, that they my in some cases be considered co-transmitters. For instance, CCK, applied to DA neurons in the substantia nigra or ventral tegmental area, is capable of increasing their firing rate (Reisine, 1994, p. 138). In the striatum, somatostatin has been shown to stimulate the release of DA and to facilitate certain DA-induced behaviors (Reisine, 1994, p. 135). Furthermore, neurons have been found that synthesize DA as well as peptides, indicating possible interactions. In the case of DA especially, all of this points to transmitters having companion relationships with peptides, enriching the repertoire of responses of which the cell is capable.

Substance P, a neuropeptide consisting of a chain of eleven amino acids, appears as a transmitter in brain pathways, most notably in the substantia nigra. It is also found in high concentrations in sensory neurons that participate in the transmission of pain sensations from the spinal cord to the brain, and consequently holds promise as a target for pain control. Enkephalins kill pain and block the release of substance P, but it is still a question whether they kill pain *by* locking substance P, since many other possible transmitters are present at these same sites.

CONCEPTS IN NEUROTRANSMITTER ACTION

Probably the simplest concept to understand about transmitter action is that transmitters can stimulate a neuron, causing it to fire and send the excitation through its axon to other neurons. But while we are talking about stimulation here, it is important to remember that some neurons function as inhibitors. For this reason, there can be a drug that is a stimulant, in the sense that its action at the receptors excites neurons and causes them to fire. But when this drug stimulates inhibitory neurons, the net physiological effect can be inhibition. This might be inhibition of other neural systems, or it might manifest as inhibition of behavior. By way of an analogy, imagine an OFF switch that works on an electrical circuit. By activating or stimulating the switch circuit, we trigger the OFF switch, which can shut other systems down.

The opposite can hold true as well. There are systems of inhibitory neurons that act as governors on systems of excitatory neurons. In this situation, inhibiting the inhibitory neurons can result in more excitation in the freed system. Here, an inhibitory action manifests as stimulation. Imagine an electric braking system regulating a large machine. If we inhibit the brake by blocking its power, the other system goes wild.

THE NEUROBIOLOGY OF TOLERANCE AND DEPENDENCE

As we have seen, our brain evolved to reward us with a sense of pleasure for behaviors dedicated to the welfare of the organism and the survival of the species, such as eating and drinking, sex, grooming, and so forth. This experience of pleasure is mediated through the DA pathways in the brain, especially the circuit running from the ventral tegmental area to the nucleus accumbens. Euphoriant drugs are able to affect this system and increase or prolong the DA release that means pleasure. Scientists have hypothesized, therefore, the possibility that all delights might have a single, common biological articulation in the brain, a "final common pathway."

However, with prolonged drug abuse come a number of the undesirable effects we have already mentioned. The system, in an attempt to remain in equilibrium, becomes tolerant, forcing the abuser to increase the dosage. Dependency develops, signaled by a number of very unpleasant effects that present themselves if the drug is withdrawn. And sometimes, long after abusers may have gotten free of the drug, a disturbing craving for their old habit can return to torment them.

One recent initiative in drug research is to investigate how activity in the reward structures in the brain correlate to the behaviors associated with compulsive drug use. Psychopharmacologists have observed for years that key effects (euphoria, tolerance, dependence, craving, and withdrawal) seem to be discrete, possibly mediated by different neural systems. For instance, one can administer antagonists that block drug euphoria, assist abusers through withdrawal, and reduce their tolerance, yet to date no one has found a way to medicate the persistent craving that leads so many into relapse. Ex-smokers may be heard to remark, "It's been years since I quit, but I still get the urge now and then to have a cigarette." What biological changes might account for this? A drug treatment that could eliminate this craving would be a tremendous benefit, as would a treatment that could interrupt the processes causing tolerance and dependence. Recently, scientists have begun to discover cellular changes that reflect the distinction between tolerance and dependence, and that might help to explain long-term effects like the craving.

With what we now know of drugs, the brain, and neurotransmitter systems, let us examine these effects and their distinctions in more detail.

Mechanisms of Tolerance

A quick review: Of the two main types of tolerance (p. XXX), the first is metabolic tolerance, which takes place when drugs passing through the liver induce an increase of enzymes like P-450, which can then metabolize a dose more quickly, so that more of a drug is needed to compensate for attrition in the liver.

The other main form of tolerance is neuronal tolerance, which refers to cellular changes that take place to compensate for the presence of a drug. This will be our main focus in this section.

A neuron functions best when a normal amount of its endogenous transmitter is present. This amount is controlled by various processes, like enzyme actions and reuptake into nerve cells, which are designed to hold the system in equilibrium (p. XXX). Drugs can disturb this equilibrium in a number of ways, such as by acting as agonists on the receptors in the synapse, by impeding the enzyme, and by blocking reuptake. The neuron has several means to maintain equilibrium in the event of these sorts of artificial stimulation or interference.

First, it has been observed that neurons exposed to drugs over a span of time show changes in their number of receptors. These receptors, found in the synaptic gap on the surface of the post-synaptic membrane, are protein structures embedded in the membrane, and are subject to alterations by the cell. They can be created and "decommissioned." In the presence of high concentrations of an agonist, the cell can maintain equilibrium by reducing the number of receptor sites. Some antidepressant drugs that promote transmitter activity at DA and NE synapses can reduce the receptor number in as short a time as half an hour. In the presence of an antagonist, the cell may synthesize more sites, increasing their density and availability on the cell membrane. Changes in receptor number are referred to as up-regulation (increased) and down-regulation (decreased).

A second recourse the neuron has is desensitization. In this event, the number of receptors does not change, but the cell is able to alter the shape of some receptors so that an agonist can no longer bind to them. This is functionally equivalent to reducing their number.

A third rebalancing tactic is for the pre-synaptic neuron to adjust the amount of neurotransmitter it is synthesizing and storing in the vesicles for release.

As can be seen, all of these forms of adaptation depend on feedback mechanisms that help the nerve cell correct for the over- or under-stimulation of receptors. All have implications for drug use. Once these changes have occurred and some semblance of normal cell operations has resumed, a new equilibrium is established, which depends on the presence of the drug and is purchased at the cost of normal cell functioning—leading to drops or rises in receptor number, the desensitization of receptors, or adjustments in transmitter synthesis. This is what we see as tolerance. If a cell down-regulates, it has fewer receptors. It then takes more transmitter to stimulate those that remain, and, similarly, requires a higher dose of a drug to over-drive the system. This increase leads to further down-regulation, still fewer receptors, a new equilibrium, and the need for an even higher dose of the drug.

Recent research (Nestler & Malenka, 2004) has revealed another possible mechanism for tolerance—an inhibitory feedback loop in the VTA-nucleus accumbens brain circuit. Pleasure-giving drugs boost the release of DA from the dopaminergic neurons of the VTA (ventral tegmental area), which synapse onto the cells of the nucleus accumbens. We have seen how, when DA binds to its receptors on the post-synaptic membrane, it activates a series of molecular events in the cell, the second messenger system, which causes increased production of a substance called cAMP (cyclic AMP). We now find, within the nucleus accumbens, that cAMP, in turn, activates a substance known as CREB (cAMP response element-binding protein). CREB increases dynorphin production in certain cells of the nucleus accumbens, which are positioned to inhibit the DA cells of the VTA—that is, they form an inhibitory feedback loop. The more CREB is expressed in the cells of the nucleus accumbens, the more inhibition results from the feedback circuit, and the duller is an experimental animal's response to stimuli. Users would call CREB a "buzzkill," a substance or circumstance that ruins a euphoric high.

All of this suggests the possibility that, if one pushes the VTA-nucleus accumbens pathway with drugs, CREB and dynorphin production can quickly catch up, activating an inhibitory feedback loop that works like an emergency brake on the reward pathway and modulates the response to pleasure. Shortly after a drug dose, CREB activity is high, so that it takes a bigger push and more drug to overcome the resistance of the feedback loop—namely, tolerance. When drug use is stopped, CREB activity subsides with passing time, causing tolerance to decline and restoring the responsiveness of the VTA pathway.

It should be said that the early evidence for these mechanisms is promising; however, these ideas are still hypothetical and await more data to confirm them.

Dependence and the Craving

If tolerance diminishes soon after drug use ceases, what might explain the fact that users become sensitized to drug use and prone to relapse, and might feel stabs of craving for a drug after abstaining for months, or even years? Brain imaging of cocaine abusers shows an increase of activity in the nucleus accumbens if they are merely exposed to cues that suggest drug use, like a photo of white lines on a mirror suggesting cocaine ready for sniffing. The amygdala and areas of the cortex also leap into life. This happens to gamblers, too, who are shown images of slot machines (Nestler & Malenka, 2004). This has prompted a hypothesis about another mechanism in this brain region that might be involved in prolonging the sensitivity to drugs and leading abusers to relapse.

It has been observed that increased cAMP production in the nucleus accumbens not only increases CREB, but another substance called delta FosB. This molecule, like CREB as well, interacts with cell genes and codes for protein production.

If the hypothesis above is correct, a drug user's desire to escalate the dose results from the rapid rise of CREB in the cells of the nucleus accumbens, which damps the reward pathway. Delta FosB shows a different pattern. Data from animal experimentation show that chronic exposure to rewarding drugs causes delta FosB to increase slowly and steadily in the nucleus accumbens and other brain areas, and it persists in its action for weeks or months after drug use. In other words, delta FosB alters cell functions for a prolonged period of time. This makes it a candidate for the mechanism underlying the craving that drug users may feel even after CREB levels and tolerance have subsided. Strains of mice that have been genetically altered to have high levels of delta FosB have shown a tendency to relapse into drug use after a period of withdrawal, offering a possible analogy to humans. This seems to be the case for other types of rewards as well; delta FosB levels rise in mice in response to exercise and sugar consumption. And delta FosB might contribute to another long-term effect that has been observed in the neurons of the nucleus accumbens upon prolonged exposure to cocaine and other drugs of abuse. For months after drug use, these neurons sprout new dendrite-like buds or "spines" that enrich the connectivity among cells. Thus, livelier and stronger pathways develop in response to pleasurable stimuli, like drugs; these can persist for years and heighten the user's sensitivity to drug-related cues (Nestler & Malenka, 2004). This is still only a hypothesis, but if proved true, it means that drug use can alter neurological functioning in key brain centers like the nucleus accumbens over the long term.

The transmitter glutamate is another factor in these scenarios. Glutamate mediates communications between the VTA pathway and other significant brain regions—the amygdala, the hippocampus, and the frontal cortex. The pathway's response to glutamate and to signals from these other regions may be altered for days after drug use, and this change in sensitivity contributes to the build-up of substances like CREB and delta FosB. The increased glutamate response also strengthens memory formation, forging links to highly rewarding experiences that may increase the desire for a drug (Nestler & Malenka, 2004).

Finally, newer studies are beginning to turn up evidence that challenges, or at least modifies, the idea of a common final pathway in our reward centers (Deadwyler, Hayashizaki, & Hamson, 2004), namely, the idea that all our pleasures correlate to a rise of DA in the reward system circuits. There are remarkable similarities in the response patterns of nucleus accumbens neurons to food and drugs. However, it looks as if these patterns occur in different subsets of neurons. In other words, different stimuli (for instance, drugs versus food), sculpt out different pathways among the common pool of nucleus accumbens neurons; once established, these become partitioned so that they do not interfere with one another. If this is so, it can be said there actually are separate pathways designed to recognize different types of stimuli—water or cocaine cell populations. This guarantees that the correct behaviors will be used in conjunction with a particular stimulus.

A final note on the idea of a common final pathway for pleasure is its possible misuse in presenting science to the public. Articles have appeared recently warning readers that marijuana has been found to release the same chemicals in the brain as harder drugs such as heroin and cocaine, referring to dopamine release in the nucleus accumbens. What the articles may fail to mention is that any other number of innocent and pleasurable activities, like eating ice cream or holding one's children, can be seen to do the same, since this is one of the biological correlates of what we experience as pleasure. The writers, intentionally or not, are exploiting the idea of a final common pathway to identify marijuana with harder drugs like heroin and cocaine, a rhetorical move that confuses the issues about differences among drugs and muddles our understanding of the science of pleasure and addiction.

CONCLUSION

The study of neurotransmitter, their receptor sites, and their locations in nervous system pathways is at the heart of psychopharmacological research. It reveals biochemical mechanisms of drug actions and clarifies the relationship among certain effects, as well as the connections between the brain and behavior. Also, it promises breakthroughs in drug treatments for mental and other illnesses. Some researchers believe that discoveries in the field of transmitter research will be as revolutionary as quantum physics was in the 1920s. Eventually, fairly benign drugs could be developed for use by healthy people for cognitive enhancement, like improving memory and learning before tests, or boosting alertness for short periods of time. Such drugs would raise all of the ethical controversies currently associated with issues like the use of steroids in sports. After testing promising drugs of this type, one psychiatrist remarked, "We got the impression that these drugs were more effective than most people would like to admit" (Zinberg, 1985, p. B-1).

Chapter 10

Drug Classification

Every drug has three important names. The chemical name, derived from organic chemistry, describes the molecule. This is not a standardized system, however, and several terminologies are in use. The generic name is the official legal name of the drug for use by the public. (More correctly, this is the nonproprietary name of the drug, and the generic name would refer to families of drugs—equivalent to the genera of animals, like barbiturates, amphetamines, phenothiazines. But misuse by the media has clouded this distinction; here, we will bow to the popular use.) The generic name is assigned by an agency called the United States Adopted Name Council (USAN), composed of members drawn from the American Medical Association, the American Pharmaceutical Association, the U.S. Pharmacopoeial Convention, and the Food and Drug Administration. This name is established so the public has something to call the drug without becoming involved in legalities with the drug companies over registered trademarks. Just as a generic tube of toothpaste would display the name TOOTHPASTE on the front instead of a brand name, so a generic bottle of a drug would carry this generic name, IODINE, SODIUM BICARBONATE, or whatever. This name is never assigned to another drug, and it can be applied only to substances of proven therapeutic value. Except for older drugs, the generic name is also the name listed in the *United States Pharmacopoeia* or the *National Formulary*, both official compendia setting forth standards for the identity, strength, purity, labeling, storage, and therapeutic value of compounds, which help to insure uniformity in quality. Older drugs may also have a separate USP or NF name, like methyl salicylate, a counterirritant, which is known by the public generically as wintergreen oil, sweet birch oil, betula oil, and gaultheria oil.

A third name is the trade name or brand name, which depends solely on the caprices of advertising consultants and drug manufacturers. For instance, the substance known generically as diazepam has been marketed by different companies as Valium, Apaurin, La III, Horizon, Vival, Cercine, Apozepam, Vatran, Sonacon, Ro 5-2807, and WY3467. Each company copyrights and reserves the exclusive rights to use its trade name permanently. Because most prescriptions are written for brand name products, which are more expensive than those marketed generically—one reason being immense advertising campaigns—most states legislated in the early eighties to allow pharmacists to automatically substitute generic for brand name drugs, unless specified by the physician. This saves customers money.

An unofficial name of the drug is the street name, a slang label applied to abused substances by their devotees. For instance, some aliases for marijuana include *boo, giggleweed, mu, hemp, kif, ganga,* and *juanita*. There may be hundreds of street names for drugs throughout different locales, some of which may be misrepresentations--namely, one drug sold as another.

Following are two examples of drug naming:

	Drug I	Drug II
Generic (USP):	methaqualone	*dl*-amphetamine
Chemical:	2methyl3 (2methyl phenyl)= 4(3H) quinazolinone	*dl*-2 amino1 phenylpropane
Trade:	Quaalude	Benzedrine
Street:	ludes	bennies, whites

Frequently, the generic name of a drug carries the name of the acid or base with which the drug was stabilized into a salt. A look at the pH scale will remind you that alkaloids and acids lie at the extremes of the chemical spectrum, and their salts, crystallized in dry form out of solution, are inactive (neutral). Thus, morphine, like most organic drugs an alkaloid, may be neutralized into a salt by using an acid—sulfuric acid—and the product is then referred to as morphine sulfate. Other acids commonly used are nitric, hydrochloric, phosphoric, citric, tartaric, lactic, malic, benzoic, and salicylic, and you may see forms of any of these names following drug names. Conversely, the process known as freebasing consists of undoing the acidification of drugs, using alkaloids (bases) to purify them and strengthen their effects. If you treat atropine sulfate with a base, for instance, it takes away the sulfate and frees up the atropine in a purer form. Crack is a freebased preparation of cocaine (hydrochloride). Cocaine hydrochloride is a salt prepared with an acid; consequently, the cocaine can be freed again in a purer form using a basic solution--in this case, household baking soda and water. Ether also may be used as a solvent, but its flammability and explosiveness make it dangerous.

When an acidic drug is stabilized with a base, the name of the base (calcium, ammonium, potassium, sodium) is placed before the generic name of the drug, yielding names like calcium cyclobarbital or sodium pentobarbital.

Since several companies can market the same substance under different trade names, the prescribing physician must be aware of equivalencies in the drugs' effects. Two compounds are said to have chemical equivalence if they contain identical chemical components and if the molecules of their active ingredients are present in identical proportions. They have biological equivalence if they affect the same biological systems in like degrees, even if they have different active ingredients. Two drugs have clinical equivalence if they produce the same overall effect, like sedation, even if they are different molecules affecting different mechanisms. One can administer phenothiazines or lithium to a manic patient; frequently, the outcome is equivalent with respect to clinical treatment. Yet chlorpromazine, a phenothiazine, blocks dopaminergic action, while lithium may replace sodium and impair the conduction of the action potential (the mechanism is not certain). Clinically, however, their effects are analogous.

It is important to note that clinical equivalence can be seriously compromised if two products dissolve at different rates. In this case, two brands of drugs with the same active ingredients, which would be biologically equivalent under other circumstances, are no longer clinically equivalent. For instance, one brand of aspirin may dissolve quickly and relieve pain, while another brand may clump in the stomach and cause ulcers.

CLASSIFICATIONS

There are several drug classification systems, whose use is usually determined by the goals one has in mind. Amphetamine might be classified by a physician as an antiappetitive drug, since this is of diagnostic interest. The chemist classifies it by its chemical makeup as phenylethylamine. To a lawyer, it is a Schedule II drug, its possession requiring a license. A psychologist classes it with other stimulants for its behavioral effects, and street users do the same, considering it an "upper." The most useful classification for the psychopharmacologist is by behavioral effects and therapeutic objectives.

Categorizing drugs is not easy, because each drug has a range of properties, and some may not rest easily under any one heading. For instance, effects may be different at different dosage levels. Alcohol, a general nervous system depressant, causes behavioral excitation at low dosages by depressing inhibitory neurons, but at higher dosages it depresses the entire nervous system. Moreover, if a drug affects a certain neurotransmitter, all of the systems involving that transmitter may be affected, and the drug then has a smorgasbord of results that do not fall easily into one category. For example, curare given in the periphery causes paralysis, but injected into the brain it causes convulsions, because the cholinergic synapses that it influences play different roles at these two sites. These contradictory effects, then, are not an inherent property of the drug so much as a modification of ongoing processes, more complex in their influences. Therefore, drug classifications serve only as a rough cross-referencing system that can help provide indications of a drug's profile of effects.

Seven categories encompass all drugs of behavioral import, and these are defined by the use and effects of the drugs included:

1. Sedatives. Also known as *depressants* or *downers*, this class of drugs produces drowsiness, sedation, and sleep. Their main clinical uses are for anesthesia, for the treatment of seizure disorder (epilepsy), and as sleeping pills for insomnia. The prototypical drug, representative of the whole category, is pentobarbital (Nembutal), though all of the barbiturates are included, as well as alcohol.
2. Anxiolytics. Known also as *antianxiety agents* and *minor tranquilizers*, these drugs relieve anxiety symptoms. They differ from sedatives in that sedatives cause sleep at larger dosages, but the action of tranquilizers is more specific, relieving anxiety without causing drowsiness. The anxiolytics are used mainly to treat minor mood disorders, anxiety disorders, seizure disorder, and alcoholism. The prototype is diazepam (Valium), and the class of drugs called benzodiazepines are included.

3. Neuroleptics. Also called *antipsychotics* and sometimes referred to as *major tranquilizers*, neuroleptics calm the patient much more than minor tranquilizers, producing catatonia, artificial hibernation, and waking states that resemble sleep. These drugs are used to relieve hallucinations, delusions, symptoms of mania, and, at smaller dosages, motion sickness. Two families of drugs fall under this category. Chlorpromazine (Thorazine) is the prototypical drug of the phenothiazines, and haloperidol (Haldol) is the prototype of the butyrophenones. Both families are dopamine blockers, but, with respect to their basic chemical structures, they differ. In other words, they are biologically and clinically equivalent, but not chemically equivalent.
4. Antidepressants. These drugs are also loosely known as *stimulants*, which we have included below as a separate class. They relieve depression in the depressed, and in normals, they cause excitement and restlessness. Sometimes, they are also used to treat anxiety disorders. There are three major families of antidepressants. The MAO inhibitors relieve depression by interfering with the enzyme (MAO) that degrades NE, DA, and 5-HT. Their prototype is tranylcypromine (Parnate). The tricyclic antidepressants block the reuptake of NE, DA, and 5-HT. Their prototype is imipramine (Tofranil). The selective serotonin reuptake inhibitors, as the name implies, selectively inhibit the reuptake of 5-HT. Their prototype is fluoxetine (Prozac).
5. Stimulants. Also called *uppers, antidepressants*, and *analeptics*, these drugs cause excitation. They are used for bronchodilation (to expand the lung passages for disorders like asthma), respiratory stimulation, and a variety of other applications. Cocaine is used as a local anesthetic. All of the amphetamines, cocaine, caffeine, and nicotine are included, and the prototype is *dl*-amphetamine (Benzedrine).
6. Narcotic analgesics. Also named *opiates*, these drugs can cause drowsiness and sleep, and are used to relieve pain in extreme cases like terminal cancer. All natural and synthetic opiates (opium, morphine, heroin, methadone) are included, and the prototype is morphine.
7. Hallucinogens. Also known as *psychotomimetics, psychotogens*, and *psychedelics*, these drugs cause psychosis-like effects and distortions in perception and cognition. For the most part, they have no recognized clinical use. Because of the diversity of drugs in this category, there is no one prototype. LSD25 (lysergic acid diethylamide) is one of the better-known hallucinogens.

The common procedure in classifying new drugs is to compare their behavioral effects with those of the prototypical drug in each of these categories and to develop a general profile of effects to see where the new drug fits in.

OTHER CLASSIFICATION SYSTEMS

Already in our discussions of pharmacology and neurobiology, we have alluded to drugs by several different classifications. Some of these other possibilities follow (Leavitt, 1982, pp. 4-14).

Central Nervous System Stimulants and Depressants

This method has the advantage of being broad, rough, and simple. There are only three categories:

1. General CNS depressants (alcohol, anesthetics, and other barbiturates) that inhibit the whole nervous system
2. General CNS stimulants (strychnine, caffeine, amphetamines) that excite the whole nervous system
3. Selective modifiers of CNS functions that work on specific nuclei or systems (like chlorpromazine, which, among many other effects, inhibits the vomiting center in the medulla).

By Chemical Structure

When dopamine and norepinephrine are both referred to as catecholamines, or when certain transmitters are singled out as amino acids or neuropeptides, these are chemical designations. The drawback to this system is that structurally similar drugs can have different biological actions, and structurally different drugs can have similar biological actions.

By Synaptic Action

Here we classify drugs by whether or not they mimic or block the action of a particular neurotransmitter. They fall into the same classes as synapses: cholinergic, noradrenergic, dopaminergic, serotonergic, et cetera.

By Autonomic Nervous System Effects

These categories describe the action of drugs at specific sites in the autonomic nervous system and point to the effects produced there. Some examples are parasympathomimetic drugs, which excite cholinergic sites and mimic parasympathetic effects; ganglionic stimulants, which mimic ACh at the autonomic ganglia; and sympathomimetics, which mimic NE in the sympathetic system.

By Sales Status

This system has two to three categories. Over-the-counter (OTC) drugs are those that can be purchased without a prescription, although a doctor can still prescribe them. A second category, prescription drugs includes those which are also called *legend drugs* because of the legend on the bottle reading, CAUTION: FEDERAL LAW PROHIBITS DISPENSING WITHOUT A PRESCRIPTION. The Food and Drug Administration decides which drugs fall into which category.

A possible third category for sales includes drugs sold illicitly on the street. Some prescription drugs fall into this category, also.

DRUG LAWS AND LEGAL CLASSIFICATIONS

The five schedules, or levels of potential drug abuse, are strictly a legal classification of drugs designated by the Controlled Substances Act of 1970. Before describing these, a quick synopsis of the landmarks of drug legislation is in order.

At the height of chicanery in patent medicine salesmanship, the first American drug legislation came with the Pure Food and Drug Act of 1906. This placed no restriction on multitudes of bogus advertising claims, but demanded that drug packaging be honestly labeled. Claims could only be brought against the misrepresentation of ingredients, until 1912, when the Sherley Amendment to the act legislated also against false therapeutic claims. The first comprehensive federal antidrug legislation was the Harrison Narcotics Act of 1914, which was an attempt to control the nonmedical use and marketing of opium and coca preparations; its enforcement, however, amounted to a total ban on these substances. This act still forms the basis of today's drug policies.

In 1938, the Food, Drug, and Cosmetic Act demanded that manufacturers test drugs for toxicity. This followed an incident involving elixir of sulfanilamide, a prescription medicine containing diethylene glycol (a substance found in antifreeze), which killed 107 people, mostly infants. Diethylene glycol fostered another incident in 1985 when it was used as a sweetener in some brands of Austrian wine, causing them to be banned from the American market. However, back at the time of the elixir of sulfanilamide case, Congress could not force the drug to be recalled, since it was properly labeled, so the more stringent 1938 rules were enacted. Companies now had to submit to the Food and Drug Administration (FDA) a *new drug application*, providing evidence that the new drug was safe. The 1951 Humphrey-Durham Amendment clarified the guidelines for designating prescription drugs and created the legend that gives legend drugs their nickname. In 1962, while the first rulings were pending that would require a drug to be proven effective before marketing, the thalidomide disaster struck and expedited their passage. Massive evaluation programs, both private and federal, began testing new and existing drugs and screening them for efficacy.

In 1970, the public law known familiarly as the Controlled Substances Act was passed. This was designed to control the distribution of drugs with abuse potential (controlled substances), and it repealed and replaced previous narcotics and marijuana regulations. All of the legalities regarding the abuse of psychoactive drugs stem from this act, among them that it is unlawful knowingly or intentionally, except as authorized

> to manufacture, distribute, or dispense, or possess with intent to manufacture, distribute, or dispense, a controlled substance; or, to possess a controlled substance unless such substance was obtained directly with a prescription or order, from a practitioner while acting in the course of his professional practice.

The five levels of abuse potential outlined by the 1970 Act are presented in Table 10.1. In addition to these federal regulations, individual states impose their own penalties as well, with varying degrees of severity. Frequently in the news, the federal agency that enforces drug laws, policing interstate drug traffic and illicit operations overseas, is the Drug Enforcement Agency (DEA), an arm of the Justice Department.

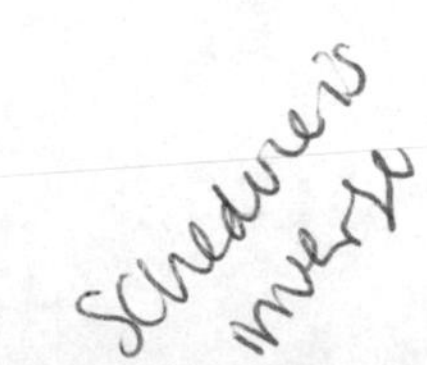

TABLE 10.1 Schedules of Controlled Substances

Schedule	Abuse Potential	Use	Medicinal Value	Prescriptions	Examples
I	High		None; unsafe without proper supervision		Heroin; LSD; peyote; psilocybin; bufotenine; mescalin ; THC/hashish; PCP analogues; methaqualone
II	High	May lead to severe dependence	Yes	Require dr.'s signature; must be typewritten or indelible; cannot be refilled	Opium; morphine; cocaine; codeine; methamphetamine; Benzedrine; Dexedrine; methadone; pentobarbital; PCP
III	Less than I and II	May lead to moderate physical or high psychological dependence	Yes	Six-month limit; can be refilled up to five times	Paregoric; nalorpine; glutethimide
IV	Low	May lead to limited physical or psychological dependence	Yes	Six-month limit; can be refilled up to five times	chloral hydrate; diazepam (Valium); paraldehyde; Phenobarbital; Darvon; other less-addicting barbiturates
V	Lower than IV	May lead to limited physical or psychological dependence	Yes		Preparations containing limited amounts of narcotics, like cough medicines: Robitussin A-C Cheracol

least potential of abuse

Chapter 11

Anxiety Disorders

One of the driving forces of psychopharmacological research is the hope of using and developing psychoactive drugs to treat mental disorders. A growing knowledge of the nervous system and neurotransmission also increases our understanding of the relationship between drug effects and the physiological bases of dysfunctional behaviors. So far, psychoactive agents have been found to be useful in four areas of therapy: the treatment of (1) anxiety disorders, (2) schizophrenia, (3) affective (mood) disorders, and (4) recovery from substance abuse. The last may seem paradoxical in that psychoactive drugs are part of the problem. However, methadone is used to alleviate the craving for heroin, antidepressants are used to reduce the craving for cocaine and crack, and tranquilizers are used to treat the seizures of alcohol withdrawal. This chapter focuses on the first of these categories: the anxiety disorders. It briefly describes the modern classifications of these conditions and discusses what is known about their physiology and pharmacotherapy.

On the long continuum of possible human behaviors, the point where normal behavior shades into abnormal behavior and is diagnosed as a disorder is strictly a question of definition. For example, you might have symptoms of anxiety for the majority of days over a five-month period without being diagnosed as having an anxiety disorder, but if the symptoms persist another month, you would be. The setting of such a clear boundary must take into account complex issues. Since there is a clear need for such a line, mental health professionals judiciously establish one based on some well-defined symptoms and their duration. This definition then becomes standardized and institutionalized. To this end, the key tool used by almost all mental health professionals for diagnosing and categorizing not only anxiety, but all forms of mental illness, is the *Diagnostic and Statistical Manual of Mental Disorders* (American Psychiatric Association, 1980, 1987, and 1994). This is a set of descriptions and guidelines arrived at by the American Psychiatric Association in collaboration with the World Health Organization (which publishes the International Classification of Diseases), and is designed to achieve a uniform standard in the diagnosing of behavior disorders. Each time the manual is published, which is every few years, it incorporates the newest research and theory, and redefines and renames the categories of disorders, in effect reshaping the concept of mental health on a practical level. For instance, the narrators of Mark Vonnegut's *The Eden Express* and Hanna Green's *I Never Promised You a Rose Garden* would currently fit the criteria for schizophrenia, but it is conceivable, and probably to be expected, that definitions will shift so that they may fall under different diagnoses in the future, as researchers articulate the characteristics of mental disorders more effectively, renaming and recategorizing them. At the time of this writing, the fourth edition of the *Diagnostic and Statistical Manual of Mental Disorders* (DSM-IV, 1994) is in effect. The manual can be found on the shelves of workers in mental health fields and of many libraries, especially medical libraries. On it, the following definitions have been based.

THE PHYSIOLOGICAL BASES OF ANXIETY

From the time of Freud until the publication of DSM III in 1980, the anxiety disorders and several modern categories of disorders were known generally as *neuroses*, a term originally coined to describe ailments believed to originate from the nervous system. Nowadays the term is in disuse, and the conditions fall under several areas of classification. Those now considered anxiety disorders have anxiety as a primary characteristic. The symptoms differ from psychoses in that there is no loss of contact with reality.

Where does anxiety come from? It appears to be caused by stress or conflict. To use an analogy, a gale bending a birch is a stressor, an external force, which causes strain—internal pressure or force—in the limbs of the tree. In humans, threats or conflicts—marital quarrels, financial difficulties, change of jobs, tough decision-making, death in the family—are the stressors that cause strain (psychological pressure) on an individual. How an individual deals subjectively with stress determines whether anxiety develops. Anxiety can be defined as a diffuse emotional state resembling fear and characterized by apprehension of a vague future threat. One of its unique aspects is that threats are a matter of interpretation. A traveler who mistakes a wolverine, a reputedly nasty animal, for a dog, suffers no fear or anxiety. But a traveler who mistakes a dog for a wolverine suffers unmistakable apprehension. Although the misperception is a false alarm, the physiological alarm is real. This is a natural, evolutionarily adaptive behavior that contributes to the survival of the individual. But when the anxiety is inflated with respect to the stimulus, or if the stimulus is not one that normally elicits anxiety (for instance, a dish cloth that triggers a panic reaction), or if there is no apparent stimulus, then the possibility for the development of an anxiety disorder exists.

Many causes have been proposed for the anxiety disorders: that they are the result of a possession by spirits; that the behavior is learned and is maintained by some form of reward; that they are based on repressed conflicts (Freud); that they arise from interactions in the social environment that foster stress; or that they are genetic or come from predispositions of personality. The medical explanation assumes that the cause is organic. Similarly, psychopharmacologists are interested in the possibility that as-yet-undiscovered biochemical mechanisms are involved, because these may respond to pharmacotherapy.

For those who treat anxiety with drugs, there are two possible targets: the cognitive component (the recognition of the stimulus as threatening) and the physiological correlates (alarm). Together, these interact to produce the full emotional experience of anxiety. Used for the cognitive component, drugs may lessen the probability of a patient seeing a situation as perilous or anxiety-producing. Used for the physiological reactions, drugs may weaken the response. This weakening in turn reduces the feedback of physiological alarm that seems to justify the recognition of a threat.

Several models have been developed in attempts to understand the physiology of anxiety. One prominent model relates the physiological responses of anxiety to what biologists call the fight-or-flight response in animal behavior. This is the normal alarm response triggered when an animal finds itself in a startling or fearful situation. At the alarm, the pituitary releases the hormone ACTH, which signals the adrenal gland near the kidneys to release adrenaline and glucocorticoids. These hormones prepare the body for action. The heart beats faster, glucose is made available to the muscles, and respiration increases; the classic sympathetic reaction occurs. But whereas in the case of fear the alarm eventually leads to a resolution (fight or flight), in an anxiety disorder the sense of panic and its physiological signs may recur, or persist to a lesser extent over a period of time. And, as we have seen, they bear no intelligible relation to the stimuli that trigger them.

Another physiological model for anxiety focuses on the conversion of glucose into lactate (lactic acid). Under normal circumstances, muscle activity uses glucose and produces lactate as a by-product. This happens more quickly in the presence of adrenaline (epinephrine), which is released in the fight-or-flight response. A buildup of lactate causes symptoms that include shakiness, rubbery legs, faintness, and dizziness. Runners in the Boston Marathon will tell you that when they hit Heartbreak Hill, a steep grade near the end of the run, they experience of all these effects.

Of interest here is the fact that the symptoms induced by lactate resemble the conditions of anxiety. In fact, in anxiety-prone people, strenuous exercise increases the likelihood of a panic attack. Examining connections like these, researchers injected susceptible individuals with sodium lactate (lactic acid) and were able to precipitate panic attacks. Pitts (1969) found that when he infused lactate into the blood of anxiety sufferers, their symptoms worsened; he also discovered that he could reduce the symptoms by infusing glucose or calcium. Evidence like this points to an association between lactate and symptoms resembling anxiety. The exact nature of the connection, however, is not known for certain.

Other clues about the physiology of anxiety are provided by pharmacological treatments and receptor studies. However, it will help in understanding these to know more first about the different types of anxiety disorders.

Despite the term *mental disorders* in its title, suggesting a complete divorce from physical factors, the DSM-IV recognizes that "there is much 'physical' in 'mental' disorders and much 'mental' in 'physical' disorders" (American Psychiatric Association, 1994, p. xxi). The introduction clarifies that

> *each of the mental disorders is conceptualized as a clinically significant behavioral or psychological syndrome or pattern that occurs in an individual and that is associated with present distress . . . or disability . . . or with a significantly increased risk of suffering death, pain, disability, or an important loss of freedom. . . . Whatever its original cause, it must currently be considered a manifestation of a behavioral, psychological, or biological dysfunction in the individual. (pp. xxi, xxii)*

This passage represents a softening of the previous edition's attempt to dissociate the mental from the organic. The problem with such a split is nowhere more evident than in developments in pharmacotherapy, which is beginning to demonstrate how some of the behavioral dysfunctions associated with "mental" disorders can be alleviated by the physiological effects of drug treatments.

ANXIETY DISORDERS

The anxiety disorders are a class of mental disorders that have anxiety as a primary symptom. Of all stress-related disorders, which include more exotic varieties like hypochondriasis and multiple personality disorder, this group responds best to treatments that incorporate the use of drugs. The most-applied drugs are tranquilizers and antidepressants.

Panic disorder involves sudden massive attacks of anxiety that trigger a strong sympathetic reaction without apparent cause. Usually, the attacks recur, and consequently are followed by a period during which the individual suffers apprehension about further episodes. Most of the attacks are unexpected. They may last for seconds or hours. One sufferer writes:

> *When I experience an anxiety attack, I often feel dizzy and off-balance. If the attack is particularly severe, I have difficulty concentrating and understanding things. Words, physical objects, and people may come to seem unreal, almost like in a dream. I sometimes don't know where I am or what I'm doing. The attacks are often followed by profound exhaustion. Shaking and trembling are common and I often feel hot afterwards. (Nemiah, 1980, p. 509)*

Other symptoms of panic attacks include indigestion, dizziness, nausea, shortness of breath, palpitations, chest pain, choking or smothering sensations, feelings of unreality, tingling in hands or feet, sweating, and hot and cold flashes. Individuals often report the conviction that they are going to die or go crazy during the intense fear of the attack and that they are possessed by a desire to flee the scene. The prognosis for panic disorder is good; the symptoms can be medicated with sedatives or tranquilizers, and frequently the threat can be resolved. Antidepressants have been tried with some success in preventing the attacks.

Associated with panic disorder is a phobic condition called agoraphobia. An individual with agoraphobia typically suffers from anxiety, panic-like symptoms, or full-blown panic attacks. In this case, these are associated with a marked fear of being alone, in an inescapable public place, or somewhere where help might not be available. This fear is often a fear that the panic attacks themselves will occur where they cannot be managed well. Other than these general situations, there is no specific stimulus that evokes panic. The condition typically progresses to severe and complicated avoidance patterns that impair normal activities (e.g., shopping or travel). In some cases, a person may become completely housebound. This is represented in the name *agoraphobia*, which means "fear of the marketplace," where the open, communal marketplace stands for public exposure.

In the case of most phobias (states of extreme, unwarranted fear), the anxiety response occurs upon exposure to a specific, recognizable stimulus which does not normally warrant extreme fear, such as mice, snakes, water, high places, bridges, and so forth. These responses are called specific phobias. Sufferers recognize the incongruity of the fear in proportion to its cause; nevertheless, their fear progresses to avoidance behaviors that eventually come to disrupt their daily functioning. This disruption is a key criterion for the diagnosis. For example, a snake-fearing city dweller might not be diagnosed as phobic, since the stimulus is seldom present and as a result is not disruptive. Social phobias are a fear of entering situations in which one will be evaluated by others or might perform poorly and be embarrassed. Two common social phobias in American life are the fear of public speaking (stage fright) and the fear of taking tests. Once again, significant disruptions are implied by these diagnoses, beyond the nervousness that usually accompanies such events.

The anxiety symptoms of phobias can be treated with drugs like propranolol (Inderal). Typical of the agents known as beta-blockers, propranolol suppresses autonomic symptoms by inhibiting beta-adrenergic synapses in the periphery; that is, it blocks a sympathetic reaction.

A current treatment that incorporates drugs in dealing with phobias is desensitization (*exposure in vivo*). With this technique, the patient is put into a relaxed state with mild tranquilizers or muscle-relaxing techniques, and is gradually exposed to the stimulus. Over the course of several sessions, for example, someone with a fear of cats would learn to relax first while thinking of cats, next while viewing pictures of cats, next while viewing cats at a distance, then while viewing cats close up, then while touching a cat, and so on, until the patient is able to tolerate the stimulus with a manageable or negligible amount of anxiety.

Obsessive-compulsive disorder involves two possible modes of behavior—obsessions and compulsions. Obsessions are intrusive, persistent notions that invade consciousness and are found to be senseless or repugnant. In most cases, they are unrelated to actual problems. Some forms involve doubts (Did I lock the door?), horrific or aggressive impulses (Drink from the inkpot; strangle him), fear (I know I'm going to scream obscenities instead of delivering my sermon), and images (Every time I enter the bathroom, I see the baby flushed down the toilet). The most common obsessions concern thoughts of violence, contamination, doubt, and suicide. The reader should note that minor obsessions are normal and commonplace, and usually not intrusive enough to be debilitating.

Compulsions are repetitive and seemingly purposeful behaviors performed according to certain rules or in stereotyped fashion. For instance, one woman felt compelled to walk down the street in the following way:

> *She established a rule that each step on or off the curb at a corner must be accompanied by the thought of some adult she knew, the adult must be a different one for each step on or off the curb, and she must have one clearly ready in her imagining ahead of time. If she thought of the same person twice on the same street something terrible might happen. The provisions of her ritual made a frequent change of street convenient and this obliged her to start work earlier and to shun company, both because talking interfered with preparations for the curb crises, and because her changes of course were hard to justify to someone else. (Cameron, 1947, p. 269)*

In most cases, compulsions are the result of yielding to an obsession or trying to ward it off. Yielding compulsions are evident in people who, like Shakespeare's Lady Macbeth, wash their hands constantly because of the nagging obsession that they are unclean. One woman is recorded as having washed her hands 500 times a day. Another yielding compulsion is shown in the mother who constantly counts her children for fear that one may be lost. Although rituals like these are often designed to produce or prevent some future event, the subject recognizes their excessiveness and irrationality. In some cases, the rationale for the behavior is not clear. It may be years before a sufferer seeks treatment.

The treatment of obsessive-compulsive disorder (OCD) has led to further knowledge about the physiology of anxiety. Psychotherapists have found that the symptoms of obsessive-compulsive disorder, which formerly resisted both psychotherapy and drug treatments, yield to certain new antidepressants (clomipramine, fluoxetine, and fluvoxamine). This action appears to be independent of the mechanisms involved in the relief of depression. And it seems to demonstrate that OCD, as it is called, is a biologically rooted syndrome. Supporting this is the finding that OCD is more prevalent among people with relatives who have the disorder, implicating possible genetic connections, and that 20 percent of the patients display motor tics, which are associated with biological involvement. Furthermore, studies have connected elevated levels of glucose metabolism in the frontal lobe and cingulate of the brain with the severity of the disorder. These discoveries are a step in the linking of mental disorders to likely physiological causes (Rapaport, 1989). Of direct interest to psychopharmacologists is the fact that antidepressants, which relieve the disorder, selectively block the uptake of 5-HT, pointing to a possible involvement of serotonin in obsessive and compulsive behaviors.

Post-traumatic stress disorder consists of anxiety or panic attacks following a traumatic event—war, rape, catastrophe, and such. It usually takes the form of a recurrent reexperiencing, painful recollections, or repeated nightmares reenacting the event. The disorder begins with a period of psychic numbing immediately after the trauma, followed by the onset of anxiety, tension, fatigue, and the avoidance of all reminders of the precipitating event. Stressors include direct physical threats or violent assaults, as well as witnessed events (e.g., a serious automobile accident or explosion).

Acute stress disorder resembles post-traumatic stress disorder. The reexperiencing of the trauma, avoidance of reminders, anxiety symptoms, and social impairment are seen. But two distinctions appear--in the time course and in the experiencing of the traumatic event. Occurring within four weeks after the event, the anxiety symptoms of acute stress disorder are of shorter duration, lasting at least two days but no longer than four weeks. Another distinguishing feature is the experiencing of dissociative symptoms during or after the traumatic event. These may include a sense of emotional detachment or numbing, a loss of awareness of the surroundings, loss of recall regarding the trauma, and depersonalization (discussed below).

Generalized anxiety disorder is a more diffuse state of anxiety that persists for more days than not over a six-month period, and without apparent cause. It may involve a shifting concern about a number of events or activities. The DSM-IV also recognizes categories in which an anxiety disorder can be ascribed to a general medical condition and to exposure to compounds like medicines, psychoactive drugs, and toxins.

Although it is not considered an anxiety disorder, one other stress-related condition (a dissociative condition) is worthy of our attention, since it is related to certain drug states like those of LSD or PCP. This is *depersonalization disorder.*
A 50yearold housewife reports

> *I feel that my legs are moving and I know they are not. I am scared of everything. I feel like my body belongs to someone else. I feel like my body and my mind are detached from each other. (Blue, 1979, p. 904)*

Numerous other symptoms are on record. Sensory perceptions of the external world change: glowing auras appear around things; the environment seems flat, two-dimensional, dreamlike, dead, or strange; objects seem to recede; and sounds become exaggerated. Personal images distort: one's body seems huge, shrunken, hollow, or detached; the genitals may seem to change sexes; patients believe that they are corpses or puppets or trapped in someone else's body, and they may mutilate themselves to prove it is not true. Some feel as though they are floating or flying. There are emotional changes: loss of feelings and enjoyments; blunted sensations; fears of dying and going insane; and some show calmness, while others exhibit anxiety or depression. Time sense may also shift, confusing the past with the future; incongruous memories occur; and time itself may appear to speed up or slow down. And, lastly, there may be distortions of identity: patients think they are someone else, cannot recognize themselves in a mirror, or do not respond to their own names.

These are not delusions, because patients retain their insight into the external world. The symptoms are usually not intrusive enough to interfere with daily activities. In fact, the symptoms may be found to some extent in normal individuals during illness, fatigue, twilight sleep states, sleep, sensory deprivation, and toxicity.

THE RECEPTOR FOR BEHAVIORAL CALMING

The key agents that have been used to treat anxiety are discussed in the following chapters. The two most prominent and useful families of substances are the barbiturates and the benzodiazepines. The barbiturates are a class of general nervous system depressants; the benzodiazepines, the family of tranquilizers and sleeping pills that includes Valium and Halcion. The effects of these agents are characterized by terms like *calming, sedation, tranquilization,* and *depression,* all of which denote states counter to behavioral excitement. As could be expected, the mechanisms of action of these drugs contribute to inhibitory activity in the nervous system, which leads to behavioral calming. Of note is the fact that a common site of action has been recognized for these classes of drugs--the $GABA_A$ receptor complex (see Figure 9.10).

GABA, as you may recall, is an inhibitory transmitter widespread in the central nervous system. The macromolecular complex containing the ion channel associated with its receptor also has binding sites for four other types of substances. Among these are the barbiturates and benzodiazepines. Figure 9.9 shows the layout of these receptors within the complex. From these sites, the barbiturates and benzodiazepines are able to modulate the action of GABA, altering the transfer of ions through the channel and affecting cell response. Evidence shows that alcohol, as well, which is a depressant like the barbiturates, can augment the action of GABA at the receptor. The GABA receptor complex, then, seems to be a key component in the profile of behavioral calming.

CONCLUSION

The anxiety disorders are one of the main areas of application for psychotherapeutic drugs. Knowing their symptoms gives an idea of the conditions under which such drugs are prescribed. The more formal codification of symptoms presented in the DSM-IV is used by physicians in diagnosis, and the descriptions are useful to researchers as well in gauging the effectiveness of new treatments. Future work will continue to develop our understanding of the physiological dimensions of these disorders and of what chemotherapies are possible. This, in turn, will complicate our understanding of the relation between what is considered organic or mental about these conditions and how they should be described and classified.

Chapter 12

Alcohol

And if sometimes, on the steps of palaces, on the green grass in a ditch, in the dreary solitude of your room, you should wake and find your drunkenness half over or fully gone, ask of wind or wave, of star or bird or clock, ask of all that flies, of all that sighs, moves, sings, or speaks, ask them what time it is; and wind, wave, star, bird, or clock will answer: "It is time to be drunk! To throw off the chains of martyrdom of Time, be drunk; be drunk eternally! With wine, with poetry, or with virtue, as you please."

Charles Baudelaire

Alcohol is the excrement of yeast. Yeast, a one-celled fungus, feeds on sugary solutions and can be found airborne wherever plants grow. Thus, the requirements for alcohol production are easily met: yeast, sugar to feed it, water to keep it active, warmth, and a proper pH balance. The yeast eats the sugar and excretes alcohol and CO_2. To the yeast, this is *haute cuisine*, but humans know the process as *fermentation*. When this process is controlled in a fermenting vat, an alcohol accumulation of about 15 percent concentration kills the yeast. Fifteen percent is thus the highest alcohol yield possible in natural fermentation products like beer and wine.

In addition to sugars, starches can be used to feed the yeast, provided there are enzymes to break them down into sugar. So, for instance, the fermentation of beer begins with barley, a starchy cereal grain. Sprouting the barley produces an enzyme that digests starch (in the barley as well as in other grains). The sprouts are then crushed and dried to a powder called barley malt. This is a common additive in the fermentation of many cereal starches. When the dried barley malt is moistened, its own enzymes digest it or any other starches and convert them into sugar. The mixture, or mash, is strained, and yeast is added to convert the sugar into alcohol (about 4.5 percent). A small bit of hops (the dried flower of the female hop plant) gives the beer its bitter bite.

All of the recipes for alcoholic beverages (for some see Table 12.1) are variations on this simple process: varying the species of yeast, the starches and sugars (rye grain, corn, apple cider, grapes), the treatment and flavoring processes (pasteurization, distillation, filtering, aging, spicing), or the mixtures of drinks (fortified wines, cocktails).

HISTORY

Speculation and scant evidence place the discovery of alcohol in the Paleolithic Era, about 8000 BC, when it is likely that hunters or scavengers might have come across a natural product of fermentation, such as puddles of mead standing in a bear's den: the chance encounter of rainwater, ransacked honeycombs, and yeast from the air. Evidence shows the use of beer and wine to date back to the Neolithic (6400 BC), and the first brewery appeared in Egypt in 3700 BC, marking alcohol as the oldest drug to be made by humans. Grape wine was not in use until fairly late (400-300 BC). In these stages of its history, alcohol had a medical or sacramental use. Cults like those of Dionysus centered on the drinking of sacramental wine, and its sacred use continues today in some Christian communion services.

TABLE 12.1 Definitions and Recipes

Ale	Like beer, but it ferments at higher temperatures, using a yeast that floats in the mash. Has more malt, hops, and flavor than beer.
Brandy	Distilled from wine or from a particular fruit wine, like cherry or peach brandy.
Champagne	White generic wines carbonated like sparkling wine.
Dessert wine	Fortified with brandy to raise the alcohol content to near 40 proof. Port and Madeira are most common.
Draft beer	Filtered at the end to remove the remaining active yeast, so the containers won't explode during shipping. Usually pasteurized.
Generic wine	Blends of wines named after regions of Europe: Bordeaux, Burgundy, Rhine wine.
Gin	Distilled from corn and water, filtered through juniper berries to soften the flavor and provide its distinctive taste.
Grain neutral spirits	Flavorless alcohol of 190 proof or above. Used only in research and medicine or diluted in vodka or blended whiskeys to raise the alcohol content.
Lager beer	From German *lagern*, to store. The species of yeast used sinks to the bottom of the mash. The beer is stored to age.
Liqueur	A wine distilled and combined with herbs or other flavorings. Sugar content is high.
Malt liquor	A beer aged like lager, it is carbonated and higher in calories and in alcohol (by 1 to 3 percent).
Rum	Distilled from fermented sugar cane molasses.
Scotch	Distilled from fermented barley malt, cooked over a peat fire, stored 3 years in uncharred barrels originally filled with sherry.

Sparkling wine	A white wine corked before the yeast dies, so that it becomes naturally carbonated by trapped CO_2.
Varietal wine	Over half of the wine comes from a single species of grape.
Vodka	From Russian "a little water" (*voda* is water). Pure, almost 190 proof, alcohol diluted with water, and unaged. There is no difference between marketed vodkas except the proofs, the prices, or added flavorings.
Whiskey	Distilled from rye or corn. *Straight rye whiskey* has over 50 percent rye grain in the mash. *Bourbon* uses over 50 percent corn, and *corn whiskey* over 80 percent. Rye and bourbon are diluted to between 120 and 125 proof and aged in new, charred oak barrels for two or more years. Bourbon gets its name from Elijah Craig, a minister in Bourbon County, Kentucky, who developed this recipe. Congeners that accumulate during the first 5 years of aging make the taste.

Alcoholic beverages remained fermentation products until the invention of distillation, which is attributed to one of two Arabs, the alchemist Gerber (around 800 AD) or the physician Rhazes (around 900 AD). The Arabic word, *alkohl,* meaning "subtly divided spirit," became our *alcohol*. Distillation is simply the evaporation of an alcoholic mash by boiling it and collecting the condensed droplets of steam, usually in coils of metal tubing. Since alcohol boils sooner than water and can be drawn off, the resulting *liquor* or *spirits,* as they were called, might contain as much as 95 percent, even 98 percent, alcohol, compared to fermentation's 12 percent to 15 percent. This was the turning point in the history of alcohol use.

Liquors in the Middle Ages were made mostly from wines. The word *brandy* attests to this, coming as it does from the Dutch word for "burnt wine." These spirits were usually applied as medicines, and from this time come our images of the wine cellars of the Benedictine friars and of Saint Bernard dogs necklaced with brandy kegs, tracking lost skiers and Alpine climbers. Liquors were called *aqua vitae,* the "waters of life"; in Gael, the same, *usquebaugh,* evolved into our word *whiskey*. Fortified wines, like sherry, port, Madeira, and muscatel, were concocted by pouring some of the distillate back into the fermented wine.

The use of distilled spirits spread throughout Europe and started becoming notorious in England in the mid-1500s during the reign of Henry VIII. By 1606, landmark legislation against drunkenness reflected the social problems beginning to arise in England from alcohol use. But the worst was to come.

Around 1650, a Dutch physician made a drink called *junever* by distilling alcohol from a corn mash and filtering the liquor through juniper berries to soften the taste. Called *genievre* by the French and *geneva* by the English, the drink soon became known as "gin." Flavorful, plentiful, cheap, and easily made, gin drenched Western civilization. For almost a century, the "gin epidemic" spread among the poor of Europe at a disastrous rate. When England tried to quell it in 1733, the violent "Gin Riots" broke out. One account claims that around this time

> *. . . cheap gin was given by masters to their workpeople instead of wages, sold by the barbers and tobacconists, hawked about the streets on barrows by men and women, openly exposed for sale on every market stall, forced on the maidservants and other purchasers at the chandler's shop, distributed by watermen on the Thames, vended by pedlars in the suburban lanes, and freely offered in every house of ill-fame, until, as one contemporary puts it, "one half of the town seems set up to furnish poison to the other half." (Webb & Webb, 1903/1978, pp. 20-22)*

By 1747, the British population was beginning to decline as a consequence of gin-related deaths. The pandemonium did not abate until around 1751 with the rise of three new potent influences: coffee, tea, and Methodism.

In the New World, the early colonists consumed huge amounts of liquor. Contrary to popular belief, the colonial Puritans condoned drinking and saw alcohol as one of God's blessings. It was immoderation and inebriety that they abhorred and harshly condemned. Nevertheless, objections after the mid1600s grew when rum and whiskey replaced milder ciders and wines. These liquors, made from the corn and sugar cane available in North America, lubricated the settlement of the continent.

The history of drinking in America contains of the now-familiar ploys at liquor control: licensing, home brewing restrictions, taxation, and the prosecution of drunkards. Around the late 1700s and early 1800s, temperance movements started gaining momentum, marked by the publication of a tract by Benjamin Rush (1784) that received wide attention. Drinking peaked in 1830, about the time when state legislation against drinking began to go into effect. The trend toward temperance continued through to the first decade of the 1900s, at which point it was powerful enough to become a federal issue. Whereas the Civil War had seen a loss in the movement's momentum, World War I strengthened it through the association of breweries with Germany and through the war effort to conserve grains and sugar. Eventually, after much emotional debate between the "wets" and the "drys," the issue climaxed on January 16, 1920, the day when thirteen years of Prohibition went into effect.

During this time (1920–1933), the 18th Amendment put into place a federal law forbidding the manufacture or sale of any drink of more than 0.5 percent alcohol. Minor infractions could draw a $1000 fine or a six-month jail term. Alcohol was so ingrained in American culture and folkways, however, that Prohibition was a hopeless cause. Many who would never have considered lawbreaking now took a naughty delight in flouting the law, and the country eventually had more speakeasies than it had ever had saloons. Among the speakeasies, rumrunners, and moonshiners, it seemed to be as the Wickersham Committee reported: everyone was satisfied, now that "the drys had their prohibition law and the wets had their liquor." Smuggling was such a lucrative business that it brought about the birth of syndicated crime and built the backbone of the American Mafia. Eventually, due to extensive noncompliance, the states voted to end their antidrug experiment, effective as of January 5, 1933.

Today, the control of alcohol centers mostly on problems of alcoholism and drunken driving, and on other forms of alcohol-related mortality. The character of beer and liquor consumption changed throughout the 1980s and 1990s. Light beers, with fewer calories and less alcohol, ruled the health-conscious 1980s. Late in the decade, interest grew in distinctive specialty beers produced by small, local brewing operations called *microbreweries* or *brew pubs*. In response to this trend, the national breweries invented new products such as *ice beer*, which can have as much as 15 percent more alcohol than regular beer and 50 percent more than some light beers.

PHARMACOKINETICS

The chemical formula for the alcohol molecule is C_2H_5OH. Its structural formula looks like this:

$$\begin{array}{ccccc} & H & & H & \\ & | & & | & \\ H - & C & - & C & - OH \\ & | & & | & \\ & H & & H & \end{array}$$

You can see from the structure that a hydroxyl group (OH) is located where a hydrogen atom could be. This is what makes an alcohol; it is any organic compound made from hydrocarbons by substituting hydroxyl groups for an equal number of hydrogen atoms. We will use the term in its more popular sense of "drinking" alcohol. In pure form, this substance is also known as ethanol, ethyl alcohol, grain alcohol, grain neutral spirits, or absolute alcohol. Two other better-known alcohols are methanol (methyl alcohol or wood alcohol), which is toxic, especially to the optic nerve where it causes blindness in the user, and isopropyl, or rubbing, alcohol. Industrial alcohol is poisoned with acetone, wood alcohol, or hydrocarbons to prevent theft and consumption. This is called *denatured alcohol*, undrinkable and unredeemable.

Administration

Most alcohol by far is self-administered orally for recreational purposes (or by personal necessity in the case of alcohol abusers). It is also applied topically as a disinfectant and may be inhaled to help dry up fluid in the lungs.

Absorption

The alcohol molecule is tiny, moderately polar, and soluble especially in water, but somewhat in fat. Because of its small size, it penetrates everywhere. Without becoming ion-trapped, it readily crosses through the blood-brain barrier, so that blood and brain levels become equal. Absorption following the oral route is about 20 percent from the stomach and 80 percent through the small intestine. The rate of absorption depends on how clear the stomach is of food and diluting fluids. On an empty stomach, the blood levels from one drink will peak in 20 to 30 minutes, but carbonation can speed you sooner.

The concentration of alcohol in the beverage is another factor in absorption. The proof of a drink is twice the percentage of its alcoholic content; 86 proof is about 43 percent alcohol. The term originated with British soldiers who used to test the strength of liquor by pouring it on gunpowder and lighting it. If the powder popped in spite of the wetting, it was proof that the liquor was 50 percent alcohol or better (100 proof). The higher the proof, then, the quicker the absorption. Therefore, in equivalent volumes, cocktails will affect you more quickly than wine or beer.

Distribution

Because of its size and solubility, alcohol distributes freely and uniformly throughout the body, though in actuality it tends to be proportional to the water content of tissues. The more water a tissue has, the more alcohol will be found there. This causes a difference in the alcohol content of fat and muscle, since muscle is more richly perfused by blood and water than fat. Lean body mass, containing about 70 percent water to fat's 10 to 40 percent, is thus a determiner of blood alcohol levels. A person with a high proportion of lean body mass will have a lower concentration of alcohol, because the drug can diffuse more widely through the fluids of the muscle tissue, leaving less alcohol in the blood (Vanatta & Fogelman, 1982, pp. 7-10). Generally, women have a higher proportion of body fat than men. Because fat offers less of an opportunity to distribute, blood levels tend to be higher. Thus, women tend to be more susceptible to the effects of drink (Blum, 1984, pp. 237-304). Larger people tend to need more alcohol to feel drunk, because the drug has a larger volume of tissue, blood, and other fluids to permeate.

Metabolism

After absorption, alcohol circulates in the blood until it is metabolized. This is achieved in the liver, which uses several systems to oxidize it. By far the most important metabolic pathway is as follows (Montgomery et al., 1983, p. 453):

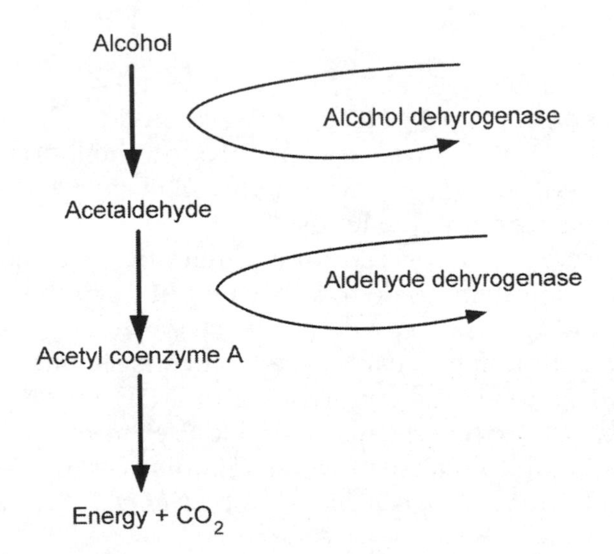

Alcohol dehydrogenase, the rate-limiting enzyme in the chain, controls and limits the amount of alcohol being metabolized. Consequently, it is impossible to speed up alcohol metabolism. It proceeds at a steady rate, unaffected by the blood concentrations. An average (150pound) male can metabolize about 8 to 12 grams an hour; that is, 1/3 to 1/2 ounces, about the amount in one bottle of beer or half an ounce of whiskey. Theoretically, therefore, one could drink 24 beers during a day, one per hour, and stay sober as a judge (Thompson, 1983). In order to become intoxicated, you have to outrace metabolism, so you would have to drink more than a beer an hour. Another factor may contribute, too. There is evidence that the subjective feeling of intoxication correlates with the rising phase of the blood alcohol level, which indicates that inebriation depends on how quickly as well as how much you drink.

One study (Frezza et al., 1990) shows that metabolism of alcohol in the stomach may account for different effects of drinking between women and men. Human males show significant amounts of alcohol dehydrogenase in their stomach linings, which increase the first-pass metabolism of alcohol. This may help to account for the fact that women, after equivalent oral doses and allowing for differences in size, have higher blood alcohol concentrations than men, and it may contribute to the more rapid development of alcoholic liver disease in women. Previous explanations for these effects were based solely on the higher fat and lower water content in the bodies of women, discussed above.

The liver metabolizes alcohol into "empty calories," energy devoid of nutritional value—no vitamins or minerals. When alcohol is taken with food, the body uses the unstorable alcoholic energy first, and synthesizes fat to store the excess from the food. Drinking alcohol along with eating is therefore highly conducive to weight gain, since the meal will be stored over a period of about four hours while the alcohol is being used.

Another significant metabolic pathway in the liver is called MEOS, the microsomal ethanol oxidizing system. This consists of the induction of P450 that we described earlier under drug fate (see pages xx-xx).

Excretion

Only 2 percent to 8 percent of a dose of alcohol is excreted unchanged through the kidneys. A small portion of this may likewise escape through the lungs and skin, but at high doses, as much as 15 percent may go by these routes. The sour breath of drinkers comes from alcohol being removed through the lungs.

The remaining 90 percent to 95 percent, then, must be oxidized in the slow, patient mills of the liver, so there is nothing to do to sober up but flush the kidneys with water to minimize reabsorption, and wait.

Alcohol increases urination in two ways. Most is probably due to the ingestion of the fluid itself. But a second factor is the suppression of ADH (antidiuretic hormone). The presence of this hormone in the blood causes the kidneys to reabsorb water; inhibit this hormone, and the kidneys fail to reabsorb water. That is why the Isar, running through Munich, the beer capital of the world, is said to be the richest of rivers.

PHARMACOLOGICAL EFFECTS

MacDuff: What things does drink especially provoke?

Porter: Marry, sir, nose-painting, sleep, and urine. Lechery, sir, it provokes and unprovokes; it provokes the desire, but takes away the performance.
Shakespeare, *Macbeth* II:3

Folklore figures alcohol as a stimulant, but actually it is a general central nervous system depressant with a reversible effect, although some set it down as a direct toxic influence on the entire nervous system at any dose.

Specific pharmacological actions of alcohol have been shown at the GABA receptor, where alcohol has a distinct binding site associated with the chloride ion channel activated by GABA (see Figure 9.10). By acting at its own receptor, alcohol most likely potentiates the inhibitory action of GABA, which could be the basis of its sedative effects. Distinct receptors for the barbiturates and the benzodiazepines are also found associated with GABA-ergic actions here. It has also been hypothesized that alcohol promotes DA release in the pathways mediating reward and reinforcing effects (the mesolimbic DA pathway).

Dose-Response Relationship

The behavioral effects of alcohol are closely related to the blood alcohol level (BAL), the concentration of alcohol in the blood. Table 12.2 lists the effects with their approximate corresponding BALs.

The misperception that alcohol is a stimulant stems from the disinhibition that occurs near a .04 percent to .05 percent BAL. This in fact results from the depression of inhibitory systems, which has been seen to turn the stuffiest and stodgiest imbibers into loons. As the dosage rises, general depression and sedation increase, with a steady loss of psychomotor function. The rate of alcohol increase in the blood influences the behavioral effects: the faster the rise, the stronger the effects. Performance of all types decreases as the BAL grows. Due to tolerance, although teetotalers may begin to show performance deficits at BALs as low as .05 percent, heavy drinkers may not show them until .10 percent.

General behavioral depression signals that the drinker may be entering the danger zone. After 10 beers in an hour, the drinker is a piece of furniture. The drug now begins to threaten the respiratory center in the medulla. The dosages for sleep and death are only a breath apart, at .35 percent and .40 percent. A sleeping drunk is therefore almost a dead drunk. However, highly tolerant individuals may show only moderate drunkenness at .40 percent, the normal LD50. The *Stiefel,* or "glass boot" of beer drunk at the Oktoberfest in Munich holds the equivalent of 8 American bottles, and some adults can account for 3 in one hour.

TABLE 12.2 Alcohol Dose-Response Chart*

These are approximate consequences estimated for a 150-pound person, drinking on an empty stomach. Danger levels may be lower for certain individuals.

Blood-alcohol level (percent of alcohol in blood)	Effect	Bottles of beer (within one hour)	
		Male	Female
.05	euphoria, disinhibition, loss of motor coordination, overfriendliness, taking liberties	2	2
.10	impaired motor function and decision-making, drowsiness, singing, legally drunk in most states	4	4
.15	reaction time significantly impaired	6	5
.20	drunk, motor depression	8	8
.25	"smashed," staggering, severe motor disturbances	10	9
.30	stupor, breathing threatened	12	10
.35	surgical anesthesia, death may come after 5 to 10 hours of stupor and coma	14	12
.40-.60	lethal dose, near the LD60 or worse	20 (or one quart of whiskey)	16

In the brain, the lowest effective blood level of alcohol first affects the reticular formation, for which it shows an affinity. This in turn means that the cortex is not as aroused as usual. Central effects include a mild euphoria; a loss of discrimination, judgment, and concentration; a loss of fine motor movements; and mood changes. Small, and even moderate daily doses of alcohol cause no permanent mental impairments. This does not apply to some other effects, however.

The effect of alcohol on various components of the limbic system may manifest in aggressive behavior. An untoward number of both murderers and victims have alcohol in them at the time of the crime. Alcoholic aggression may likewise play a role in traffic accidents, increased risk-taking and expressions of anger and violence, lack of coordination, and a reduced sense of consequences. The very act of drinking may serve as an excuse for acting out aggressions. Placebo studies have shown that drinkers adhere to a stereotype of drunkards when they think they are drunk, behaving recklessly and irresponsibly, and blaming the consequences of their actions on the drug (Mello & Mendelson, 1978, p. 262).

Alcohol slows the cortical EEGs and suppresses REM sleep. Of the phases of sleep, this is the one marked by the rapid eye movements (REMs) that indicate dreaming. Alcohol thus cancels dreaming, which can lead to irritability. Generally, when the suppression of REM sleep ends, there is often a "REM backlash" during which the subject spends more time than usual in dreaming sleep. This may occur as an aftereffect of alcohol use.

At low dosages, alcohol, through disinhibition, stimulates the respiratory center in the medulla. However, at high doses, respiration becomes depressed, and death by suffocation ensues. In the event of an overdose, it helps to force breathing by walking or by giving stimulants like Metrazol. Caffeine will do in a pinch, but it is not recommended because, when the alcohol wears off, the nervous system may show a rebound stimulation, and the caffeine could add to it.

Similarly, alcohol reduces seizures, which are the result of storms of electrical impulses in the motor cortex, but when the alcohol wears off, the depressed neurons become hyperexcitable and increase the susceptibility to seizures. People with seizure disorders, therefore, should abstain.

In the periphery, alcohol causes dilation of the vessels (vasodilation) in the skin, sending a warm flush over the user. Because of this, the misconception has arisen that alcohol is a good fortification against the cold, but the opposite is the case. The same expansion of vessels causes heat loss from the extremities, making you more vulnerable to cold. The vessels constrict in the first place to conserve heat, a defense that alcohol undoes. Chronic vasodilation breaks the blood vessels in the upper cheeks of alcoholics and gives them the jolly red nose of Silenus, a classical god of wine and merriment, who may have passed his ripe red schnoz down to the modern circus clown. A characteristic facial flush has been observed after small doses of alcohol in native Japanese, Taiwanese, and Koreans, an unexplained sensitivity believed to have a genetic basis (see page xx).

Taken orally, alcohol irritates the stomach lining and stimulates the flow of gastric acids and pepsin, which is what makes it an ideal appetite stimulant--hence, the custom of taking a drink before dinner.

The sexiness of alcohol is another misperception to be debunked. Alcohol does not enhance sexual performance but impairs it. Moderate doses abolish the ejaculatory reflex in dogs and rats, and in humans penile swelling and vaginal pulse pressure decrease as BALs rise. We might know more about these effects in humans if it were not for the fact that an outraged representative who heard of these studies saw the passage of a Congressional edict that cuts federal funding for any study of the effects of drugs on sexual behavior. We do know, however, that induced P450 metabolizes testosterone in alcoholics, reducing sexual function. Therefore, if alcohol has anything sexy about it, it may be disinhibition coupled with placebo expectations about the drug's action, or it may be that delayed ejaculation in the male prolongs his performance time. The reader is referred to Shakespeare.

In the spinal cord, low doses of alcohol facilitate reflexes, perhaps by first inhibiting the Renshaw cells, which act as a curb on the motor neurons. Moderate to high doses depress the entire spinal cord. Alcohol also anesthetizes minor aches and pains, and this can reach such an extent in the alcohol-dependent that they may burn their fingers with cigarettes and not realize it.

As a muscle relaxant, alcohol acts by inhibiting the motor neurons responsible for maintaining tonus (slight tension) in the muscles.

In summary, when we take a close look at the pharmacological effects of alcohol, we find that it impairs functions of all kinds, except in some cases at very low doses. This drug that we take to stimulate us is actually a depressant. This fortification that we take against the cold actually lowers our natural defenses and leaves us more vulnerable. And this aphrodisiac that we take to enhance our sexual performance ends up impairing it.

CLINICAL APPLICATIONS

Alcohol is not an accepted medical treatment for anxiety disorders, as our inclusion of it with sedatives and anxiolytics would seem to suggest. However, it is by far the most commonly self-prescribed treatment for the prevention and alleviation of anxiety. In addition, alcohol has a long history of medical use, primarily as a sedative and anesthetic. Its anesthetic use was discontinued in the 1800s because the duration of its effect was too long and uncontrollable, and its therapeutic index was too low (that is, the ED for anesthesia and the LD were too close), and because the drug slowed coagulation of the blood. Under protest from the temperance movements, whiskey and brandy were eventually removed from the *U.S. Pharmacopoeia's* standard listing of drugs.

Nevertheless, alcohol still plays an official, if lesser, clinical role than it once did. It works as a solvent for drugs and fatty material that do not dissolve in water. It makes an excellent cleaner and disinfectant, as on the cotton swab with which the nurse rubs you before an injection. It is used as a coolant because it helps to evaporate water, so that people with high fevers benefit by an alcohol rub. Because it draws off water, it is also used to contract tissues and reduce swelling; in cases of pulmonary edema, when the membranes around the lungs fill with water, alcohol may be inhaled to dry them.

In general use, alcohol makes a last resort, home remedy for convulsions and seizures (it may temporarily relieve, then worsen, the condition), and anorectics may use it to stimulate appetite.

As an analgesic, alcohol may relieve angina pectoris, pains in the chest due to arterial contractions caused by NE, although when the alcohol wears off, the contractions become even more severe. In emergencies, alcohol serves as a handy analgesic as well. You may recall two slugs from Westerns, the lead slug in the cowboy's thigh and the slug of whiskey that he takes before self-surgery with a hunting knife.

SIDE EFFECTS

The "wailing of cats," the "cacophony," the "woody mouth," the "workmen in your head," the "anguished hair-roots"--the incurable side effect of alcohol known in English as "the hangover"--is a temporary condition marked by headache, nausea, thirst, fatigue, anxiety, and general malaise. No one is certain of the underlying mechanism. It may be due to the congeners in drinks. These are the additional chemicals found in alcoholic beverages: vitamins, amino acids, minerals, salts, sugars, fused oils, and other alcohols. According to this view, you would be less likely to get a hangover on fairly pure drinks like vodka and light beer (.01 percent congeners) and more likely on gin, wine (.04 percent) or distilled spirits (1 to 2 percent), which accumulate congeners during aging. Other evidence indicates that the likelihood of being visited by a hangover depends on the BALs achieved the "night before the morning after." In this regard, a higher risk is run by the elderly, who have a higher fat-to-muscle ratio and therefore higher BALs.

One culprit implicated in hangovers is acetaldehyde, the first byproduct in the chain of biotransformation. Poisoning by low blood levels of this compound (which run about .001 those of alcohol) may be the cause of nausea and headaches. This is supported by the fact that, if one injects acetaldehyde, it can cause a hangover. A hangover thirst comes from direct cellular dehydration and from the inhibition of ADH (antidiuretic hormone), causing increased urination. The fatigue may be a sequel to the high activity during disinhibition, when blood sugar and energy levels are elevated. An alternate theory holds that a hangover is a slight withdrawal syndrome. Taking another low dose of alcohol, like a Bloody Mary, lightens the symptoms of rebound excitability by slightly sedating them, the remedy known as taking some of "the hair of the dog that bit you."

Drinking too quickly can cause vomiting, if a BAL of .12 percent is reached rapidly. This mechanism protects the respiratory center from an overdose. Slow, steady drinking can therefore be more dangerous.

With long-term use, alcohol is capable of damaging and killing liver cells. This begins with an increase of fat, synthesized and stored in lipid globules, which may eventually break free into the blood, clogging the blood vessels. Another form of liver damage is cirrhosis, from *cirrhus,* meaning "yellow." In this case, fibrous scar tissue forms and begins to mar and cripple the liver. Jaundice and the potential for cancer develop, and impaired metabolic pathways start releasing toxic metabolites that can poison other organs. However, you have to apply yourself to contract it. Drink 3 beers a day (possibly 1.5 for women) for 20 years, and you run about a 65 percent chance of getting cirrhosis to some degree. About 6 shots of whiskey (6 ounces in all) each day for 10 years might do it as well. Still, there are no guarantees. Some long-term drinkers develop cirrhosis and some do not; the reasons are obscure.

Apart from cirrhosis and other liver impairments, inflammation (hepatitis) might also result from chronic drinking. Pancreatitis (an inflammation of the pancreas, cause unknown) and acute gastritis (bleeding in the stomach) are other possible inflammatory effects.

Alcohol is definitely one of the causes of cancer. Heavy drinking increases the risk of tongue, mouth, throat, and liver cancer, especially when combined with smoking.

Surprisingly, of all groups—abstainers, light, moderate, and heavy drinkers—those likely to live longest are the moderate drinkers. This may be because, as some evidence shows, low daily doses of alcohol (up to 2.5 ounces) may reduce the risks of heart attacks and atherosclerosis (hardening of the arteries). Moderate use in general appears to have no serious ill effects, except on driving and pregnancy.

However, these studies have been questioned. For instance, one of them included former drinkers in the light drinker category, which then showed a higher incidence of coronary heart disease. (U.S. Department of Health and Human Services, 1987, p. 64) Other studies indicate that acute alcohol consumption causes functional changes in heart tissue, even in young adults (Lang et al., 1985). Nevertheless, net effects in healthy nonalcoholic individuals appear to be small.

Larger doses of alcohol eventually weaken the heart muscle, enlarge the heart, cause angina pectoris, and predispose the user to coronary artery disease. Hypertension (high blood pressure) and the risk of strokes are further dangers. Arrhythmia and electrical abnormalities in the heart manifest in alcohol-related diseases and even during intoxication.

Malnutrition is another side effect seen in chronic drinkers. Alcohol has about 7.1 calories per gram; therefore, a bottle of beer (14 g of alcohol) yields around 150 calories (with 100 from alcohol and about 50 from congeners like sugar and malt). So four bottles add as many as 600 calories to your normal (2000 to 2500) caloric intake. These are empty calories, with no nutritional value, which the body prefers to food. If you derive most of your calories a day from alcohol, food will be stored and you will gain fat. This will happen somewhat even if you merely drink with meals. Alcoholics can subsist for about 4 years on a diet almost exclusively of alcohol, while their bodies slowly deteriorate. They get a bloated look, flabby muscles, fine tremors, decreased stamina, and show a susceptibility to infections. The depletion of B-complex vitamins gives alcoholics a disease known as beriberi in Asia, where it occurs in those who eat a limited menu mostly of polished rice. Thiamine (vitamin B1) also becomes depleted, and the small intestine loses its efficiency in absorbing glucose, amino acids, water, and electrolytes; furthermore, a lack of vitamin B can cause GABA synthesis to suffer. Since this transmitter is inhibitory, the result is more anxiety and excitement. This might underlie some of the symptoms of those dependent on alcohol.

Korsakoff's psychosis is a behavioral disorder deriving from chronic brain damage caused by the prolonged use of alcohol. It involves confusion, disorientation, hallucinations, suggestibility, and amnesia. This last symptom may become permanent, causing individuals to hide their failings by fabricating stories (confabulation). The behavioral symptoms of Korsakoff's psychosis are often associated in severe alcoholics with Wernicke's disease. This is a CNS disorder involving lesions in the thalamus; it is related to the disease beriberi, arising from a shortage of water-soluble vitamins, particularly thiamine. Together, these two conditions are known as *Wernicke-Korsakoff syndrome*.

Table 12.3 Why Drinks and Drugs Don't Mix

This chart lists classes of drugs that have been reported to interact with alcohol. Some of the dangers that may result from combining alcohol with the other listed drugs are described. It must be emphasized that this chart, or any other like it, represents only the smallest part of the whole alcohol/drug interaction picture.

ANALGESICS, NARCOTIC

(Demerol, Codeine, Percodan, etc.)

When used alone, either alcohol or narcotic drugs cause a reduction in the function of the central nervous system. When they are used together, this effect is even greater and may lead to loss of effective breathing function (repiratory arrest). Death may occur.

ANALGESICS, NONNARCOTIC

(Aspirin, Tylenol, Pabalate, etc.)

Even when used alone, some nonprescription pain relievers can cause bleeding in the stomach and intestines. Alcohol also irritates the stomach and can aggravate the bleeding, especially in ulcer patients. Alcohol may also increase susceptibility to liver damage from acetaminophen.

ANTIALCOHOL PREPARATIONS

(Antabuse)

Use of alcohol with medications prescribed to help alcoholic patients keep from drinking results in nausea, vomiting, headache, high blood pressure, and possible erratic heartbeat, and can result in death.

ANTICOAGULANTS

(Panwarfin, Dicumarol, etc.)

Alcohol can increase the ability of these drugs to stop blood clotting, which in turn can lead to life-threatening or fatal hemorrhages.

ANTICONVULSANTS

(Dilantin)

Drinking may lessen the ability of these drugs to stop convulsions and may exaggerate blood disorder side effects of the anticonvulsant.

ANTIDEPRESSANTS

(Tofranil, Pertofrane, Triavil, etc.)

Alcohol may cause an additional reduction in central nervous system functioning and lessen a person's ability to operate normally. Certain antidepressants in combination with red wines like Chianti may cause a high blood pressure crisis.

ANTIDIABETIC AGENTS/HYPOGLYCEMICS

(Insulin, Diabinese, Orinase, etc.)

Because of the possible severe reactions to combining alcohol and insulin or the oral antidiabetic agents, and because alcohol interacts unpredictably with them, patients taking any of these medications should avoid alcohol.

ANTIHISTAMINES

(Most cold remedies, Actifed, Coricidin, etc.)

Taking alcohol with this class of drugs increases their calming effect, and a person can feel quite drowsy, making driving and other activities that require alertness more hazardous.

ANTIHYPERTENSIVE AGENTS

(Serpasil, Aldomet, Esidrix, etc.)

Alcohol may increase the blood-pressure-lowering capability of some of these drugs, causing dizziness when a person gets up.

ANTIINFECTIVE AGENTS/ANTIBIOTICS

(Flagyl, Chloromycetin, Seromycin, etc.)

In combination with alcohol, some may cause nausea, vomiting, and headache, and possibly convulsions, especially those taken for urinary tract infections. Some are rendered less effective by chronic alcohol use.

CENTRAL NERVOUS SYSTEM STIMULANTS

(Most diet pills, Dexedrine, caffeine, Ritalin, etc.)

Because stimulant effects of this class of drugs may reverse the depressant effect of alcohol on the central nervous system, these drugs can give a false sense of security. They do not help intoxicated persons gain control of their movements.

DIURETICS

(Diuril, Lasix, Hydromox, etc.)

Combining alcohol with diuretics may cause reduction in blood pressure, possibly resulting in dizziness when a person stands up.

PSYCHOTROPICS

(Sparine, Mellaril, Thorazine, etc.)

Alcohol with the "major tranquilizers" causes additional depression to central nervous system function, which can result in severe impairment of voluntary movements such as walking or using the hands. The combination can also cause a loss of effective breathing function and can be fatal.

SEDATIVE HYPNOTICS

(Doriden, Dalmane, Nembutal, Quaalude, etc.)

Alcohol in combination further reduces the function of the central nervous system, sometimes to the point of coma or the loss of effective breathing (respiratory arrest). This combination can be fatal.

SLEEP MEDICINES

It is likely that nonprescription sleeping medicines, to the degree that they are effective, when combined with alcohol, will lead to the same kind of central nervous system depression as the minor tranquilizers (see below).

TRANQUILIZERS

(Miltown, Valium, Librium, etc.)

Tranquilizers in combination with alcohol will cause reduced functions of the central nervous system, especially during the first few weeks of drug use. This results in decreased alertness and judgment, and can lead to household and automotive accidents.

VITAMINS

Continuous drinking can keep vitamins from entering the bloodstream. However, this situation changes when a person stops drinking.

INTERACTIONS WITH OTHER DRUGS

Drug interactions with alcohol may produce a wide range of side effects. Many of the most frequently prescribed drugs contain at least one ingredient that reacts adversely with alcohol. The most common pairing is with anxiolytics (minor tranquilizers such as Librium, Valium, etc.); here the synergistic effects may be prolonged 2 to 5 times the normal duration and cause heart or respiratory failure. With other sedative-hypnotics and general anesthetics, alcohol shows additive effects and cross-tolerance. Combinations with stimulants may be unpredictable; motor impairments and paradoxical coma are possible. Furthermore, alcohol may increase the absorption of some drugs and increase the sensitivity of receptors.

The LD1 of opiates is lowered three-fold by alcohol. This is significant because morphine abusers tend to have alcohol as a secondary dependence. Together, the drugs may cause a catecholamine metabolism problem marked by a sudden high fever, jaundice, coma, and death. Alcohol can interact with other drugs as well. Neuroleptics prolong the half-life of alcohol by occupying the microsomal liver enzymes. Aspirin and alcohol together may cause severe stomach irritation.

Table 12.3 shows the interactions of alcohol with many common families of medications. Still, a great deal is unknown about drug interactions and their mechanisms. Suffice it to say that doctors should be informed of your drinking habits when they prescribe drugs.

Some interest was raised in 1985 over the discovery of an alcohol antagonist, Ro 154513, which can instantly block 90 percent of the effects of alcohol intoxication in test animals. Ro 154513 was first developed when researchers were synthesizing variants of the molecule of the minor tranquilizer Valium (in the class of benzodiazepines). It was noted to be a benzodiazepine antagonist, commercially useless because it caused toxic changes in the white blood cell count and in liver enzymes. It was then discovered to antagonize alcohol effects as well (except at acute dosages). Moreover, in comparison to other known alcohol antagonists, and despite its shortcomings, it was found to be fairly safe. The potential for this was staggering. With further tinkering to modify its adverse effects, Ro 154513 made clear the possibility of a marketable sobriety pill. Partygoers could take it before driving home. Surgeons and test pilots could drink without affecting their performance the next morning. In clinics, it could be used to block rewarding effects in alcoholics, the way methadone is used to block heroin euphoria. However, Hoffmann-LaRoche discontinued development on the project for several reasons. During the time of Reagan's war against drugs, such a pill would seem to sanction more alcohol use—why worry if you can apply the brakes at any time? Also, there was the problem of liability if someone using the pill still had an accident, not to mention that it would disqualify blood alcohol levels as a measure of drunkenness, since BALs can be high, while Ro 154513 simply blocks the molecules from stimulating GABA receptors. This also leads to the most serious concern, that since the drug does not alter blood levels or affect metabolism, people who take the pill and continue drinking could poison themselves with alcohol, even though they feel perfectly sober. Thus, a sobriety pill could be made, but probably won't be (Kolata, 1986; Suzdak et al.,1986, 1988; Hammer, 1986).

Finally, let us consider the two most damaging side effects of alcohol: fetal alcohol syndrome and alcohol dependency.

FETAL ALCOHOL SYNDROME

Fetal alcohol syndrome (FAS) consists of a battery of fetal abnormalities caused by the mother's use of alcohol during pregnancy. It has an estimated prevalence of 1 to 3 cases in 1,000 live births, but it is found only in the offspring of alcohol-dependent mothers, with the degree of symptoms correlating to the stage of alcohol dependency in the mother. Although those as far back as Aristotle were aware that drinking affected the fetus (he advised against drinking on the wedding night), the syndrome was never clearly delineated nor proven until 1973.

Features of FAS include (1) prenatal and postnatal growth retardation; (2) central nervous system dysfunctions: mental retardation, irritability and jitteriness, poor coordination and muscle tone, childhood hyperactivity; (3) skull and facial deformities: abnormal smallness of the head (*microcephaly*), drooping of the upper eyelids, lack of binocular vision due to motor misalignments (strabismus), skin folds over the inner angles of the eyes, arrested development of the mid-facial features, a smooth philtrum (the hollow in the upper lip), a thin upper lip, a short, upturned nose; and (4) defects in major organ systems: eye, ear, and mouth defects, heart murmurs, genital anomalies, birthmarks (blood vessel irregularities), hernias, and bone and joint defects. Furthermore, the children may furthermore be susceptible to minor infectious diseases, such as diaper rash, and to respiratory problems.

These effects may occur partially, depending on the alcohol use, so that mild variations may scarcely be recognized. FAS is the third leading cause of birth defects after Down's Syndrome and spina bifida, and the only preventable one. The risk is clear at a daily intake of 3 ounces (3 drinks), and peak blood levels are a significant factor, more so than the quantity consumed. Some cough syrups and mouthwashes may even contain enough alcohol to be dangerous. The effects probably occur in the first 60 to 80 days of pregnancy, if the embryo is exposed to certain peak blood-alcohol levels. The third week of pregnancy is a time of especial susceptibility to craniofacial and brain abnormalities. However, only 40 percent of the children of alcohol abusers show FAS, for reasons unknown. One theory is that it relates to the degree of disturbance of acetaldehyde metabolism in the mothers. This could explain the correlation between the stage of alcoholism and the degree of damage. Another factor in growth retardation and deformities may be a decrease in zinc absorption caused by alcohol.

FAS has been induced in mice by exposing the embryos to alcohol (ethanol). There is a remarkable resemblance of their facial deformities to those of humans.

ALCOHOL DEPENDENCY

Most drug abuse centers on alcohol. Alcohol abuse involves people from all walks of life, from chief executives and airline pilots to skid row regulars and the homeless--as much as 10 percent of the adult population. About twice as prevalent among men as among women, alcoholism and alcohol abuse are a major cause of arrests and admissions to mental hospitals. They contribute to the battering of women and children and cause half of our highway accidents. They cost billions of dollars in lost work time, health services, medical care, and property damage. Fortunately, the situation shows some improvements. Recent trends include a decrease in the apparent per capita consumption of alcohol, and liver cirrhosis deaths and motor vehicle traffic fatalities have been declining.

The compulsive use of alcohol is referred to as *alcohol abuse, alcoholism,* or *alcohol addiction*. There are a number of symptoms characteristic of the condition that are useful in defining it: (1) psychological complications (frustration due to decreased efficiency, preoccupations with drinking), (2) nutritional complications (heaviness, thiamine deficiency), (3) physical dependence (shaky lips and hands, withdrawal), and (4) loss of control (confabulation, passing out, memory lapses, amnesia, and drinking binges). The AMA first officially recognized alcoholism as a medical problem in the early 1950s, and the government followed in the 1970s. This issue is still not resolved, however, because the "disease" disappears if alcohol is not available. Before the 1950s, alcoholism was regarded entirely as a reprehensible moral lapse.

In most cases, alcohol addiction follows a recognizable progression. It begins with social drinking, which continues for a time while drinkers learn to enjoy the mild euphoria and relief from stress that alcohol affords. This eventually progresses to psychological dependence. In the next phase, tolerance develops, more so in steady drinkers than in bingers. The person may begin to gulp the first few drinks. Early physical signs of the developing dependence include enlargement of the capillaries around the conjunctiva of the eyes, puffiness and flushing of the forehead and face, a red "whiskey" nose, loss of appetite, and hoarseness caused by runniness of the mucous membranes of the nose and voice box. In the phase of physical dependence, the person's behavior becomes more alcohol-centered, and there is a loss of control over when and whether drinking will occur, in part because withdrawal symptoms manifest if the drug is discontinued. As the condition worsens, the person may evince a neglect of proper nutrition and may withdraw from the social environment, breaking ties with former friends and relations, whose relationships to the drinker may already be badly strained. Finally, alcohol takes over completely, and daytime intoxication leads to severe social deterioration, including loss of employment. The drinker goes on binges. Alcohol psychosis and loss of tolerance, possibly due to liver damage, may occur (Jellinek, 1952).

Withdrawal symptoms are triggered in the alcoholic when BALs drop below the intoxication level. This is a relative value with no bearing on the volume or duration of drinking, only on the drinking habits of the user. Not until 1953 was withdrawal seen as an effect of abstinence; it was formerly thought to be a result of poisoning, illness, and malnutrition.

Twelve to 72 hours after the discontinuance of alcohol, tremors, hypertension, nausea, diarrhea, insomnia, copious sweating, and a triphammer heartbeat set in. Between 7 and 48 hours, overt seizures known as the "rum fits" occur if the patient's last drinking spree was prolonged. These are harbingers of the DTs, or delirium tremens. The patient may come out of the convulsions into a state of profound disorientation, nightmares ("the horrors"), delirium, and hallucinations. The subject is jittery, muttering, screaming, tearing at the imaginary snakes, bugs, or rodents titillating the skin, feverish with sweat, and wandering mindlessly. Alcohol abusers in this condition may die—from high fever, hyperthermia, and cardiovascular collapse. The DTs typically start on the second or third day, peak on the fourth, and subside throughout the following week. The subject then falls into a long, deep sleep and wakens with no recollections of withdrawal.

The symptoms of withdrawal are thought to be a result of rebound excitability from depressing neurons so long and continuously with alcohol. The delirium may be a rebound dreaming effect from the suppression of REM sleep. The seizures and cardiovascular collapse could come from low blood sugar levels or from the rebound overexcitation of neurons freed from the depressant. Other central nervous system depressants like pentobarbital and chlordiazepoxide are given to ease these symptoms, but they must be used cautiously to avoid further dependencies.

Factors in Alcohol Dependency

Both psychosocial (environmental) and hereditary factors have been examined as potential causes of alcohol dependency. Psychosocial factors include the family environment, role models, peer pressure, socioeconomic and other stress, and commercial advertising and other media representations of drinking. More attention recently has been given to the possibility of genetic contributions. In animal research, strains of mice have been bred to prefer a mixture of 20-proof alcohol and water to water alone (which normal mice prefer) (Blum et al., 1981). A number of human studies have shown that the children of alcoholics raised by nonalcoholic foster parents have a greater chance of becoming dependent than adopted children with both nonalcoholic parents and foster parents. Concerning prevention, there is a strong research interest in being able to identify psychosocial or genetic markers that would indicate which individuals are at risk of becoming alcohol dependent.

Treatment of Alcohol Dependency

Alcohol dependency is not a simple, unitary phenomenon but a complex one. It may involve the abuse of other drugs besides alcohol, and there may be underlying psychiatric disorders. It isn't possible to represent all alcohol-related problems with a single concept. Because of this, treatment has become diverse, mixing methods, and there is a growing emphasis on matching users to the combinations of treatments uniquely suited to them. The range of available resources includes detoxification, in-hospital rehabilitation, outpatient services such as clinics and day hospitals, family treatment, supervised living services, aftercare (care following rehabilitation), organizations like Alcoholics Anonymous, and pharmacotherapy. Users may be involved with several of these modes of treatment in various combinations.

Alcoholics Anonymous is probably the best-known organization for the treatment of alcohol dependence. Attendance at AA meetings has been shown to have a positive correlation to sustained abstinence. After one year, from 26 percent to 50 percent of the subjects succeed in not drinking, which compares favorably with other treatments. The program aims for total abstinence and puts an emphasis on subjects recognizing their helplessness against alcohol and relying on a belief in a higher power (be it God, AA, or whatever). They are also called upon to atone for the injuries caused to others and to help other alcohol abusers.

Various forms of counseling and therapy are available to recovering alcohol abusers. Marital and family therapy is based on the idea that treating the disrupted family system of the abuser will bring about positive changes, since family life can play a crucial role in an individual's pathology. It seems to benefit certain subgroups of married abusers. Nevertheless, evidence indicates that family dysfunction seems to be primarily an effect rather than a cause of alcoholism. Counseling for persons affected by alcohol abusers is offered by an organization called AlAnon and for the family teenagers of alcoholics by Alateen. *Aftercare* is a term used to describe any program of sustained support after a more intensive course of rehabilitation, such as detoxification (see below).

Behavior therapies have shown little to moderate success. Community reinforcement—helping subjects find jobs, improving social environments, and so forth—has shown some promise. Other techniques include teaching people to monitor and discriminate between blood-alcohol levels to control drinking, and teaching relaxation skills to provide alternate forms of coping.

Pharmacotherapy

It is generally recognized that pharmacological treatments are not very effective when used alone; they serve best as adjuncts to other, longer term and more supportive therapies. There are three major rationales for the use of pharmacological treatments for alcohol dependence: (1) to medicate withdrawal symptoms during detoxification, (2) to alleviate the craving for alcohol, and (3) to cause an aversive effect if alcohol is consumed.

Detoxification is a short phase of treatment—a first small step—designed to get the user off alcohol and through acute (sudden) withdrawal. It may or may not be done in a medical setting. The goals are to keep the subject as calm and comfortable as possible. Benzodiazepines are the most commonly used drugs; they are given as tranquilizers and anticonvulsants to medicate the seizures and rebound anxiety that accompany withdrawal. Detoxification is most rationally seen as a prelude to longer-term treatment.

After detox, drugs may be used in an effort to alleviate the craving for alcohol and to avoid relapse. Naltrexone (ReVia), an opiate antagonist, is one of the more effective drugs that has been tried for this purpose. Bromocriptine, a DA-stimulating drug, has been tried, as well as 5-HT-enhancing antidepressants like fluoxetine (Prozac).

Drugs have also been used in aversive therapy for alcohol dependency. The idea of aversive therapy is to couple the stimuli of drinking (e.g., the sight, taste, and smell of cocktails) with unpleasant stimuli (electroshock or nausea-producing drugs) to condition the patient to an aversion to alcohol. Generally, this kind of therapy is effective only when coupled with other more supportive therapies like counseling. The most widely used drug in this context is disulfiram (Antabuse), which has been found to be of some use as an adjunct to more comprehensive treatment. This drug was once used in the curing of rubber tires; workers who drank and who were exposed to disulfiram became flushed, and their blood pressure dropped. Given orally once a day, disulfiram inhibits the enzyme aldehyde dehydrogenase but allows the conversion of alcohol into acetaldehyde, which accumulates 5 percent to 10 percent more than normal and poisons the body with a horrendous hangover—pulsating headaches, nausea, vomiting, drowsiness, and breathing difficulties. Alcohol users become sickened and discouraged from drinking, and the associative links to the rewards of drinking are reduced. Compliance is one of the key problems with this method. It helps if individuals are highly motivated and in settings where they contract to take the drug and can be monitored for compliance.

Treatment Success

On the whole, treatment success seems to depend more on the participants than on the programs. Those who respond most favorably to treatment are married, stably employed, free of psychological impairments, and are of higher socioeconomic status. About two-thirds of treated alcoholics show some improvement, taking into account that treatment goals vary. For instance, the goal of abstinence has been called into question by some, in preference of controlled drinking. Nevertheless, there is a growing consensus that alcohol treatment programs do work.

CONCLUSION

Although alcohol poses serious threats to millions of people, it has been used by considerably more with success and without ill effects. The distinction seems to lie in the control of its use. Taken on occasion and in moderation, it is certainly one of the safest of psychoactive drugs. Otherwise, it could not have taken such a substantial position in our culture and rituals—so much so that it is considered less a drug than a beverage. A margin of risk, however, comes with the unpredictability of any individual's capacity to manage its use successfully under all circumstances and not to escalate to the point of dependence, especially in an environment where alcohol is so accessible. Furthermore, we have seen how much damage can accrue from its misuse and abuse. It is almost certain that, if alcohol were discovered and market-tested today, it would be a controlled substance.

Chapter 13

Barbiturates and General Anesthetics

Alcohol, considered in the last chapter, and the barbiturates, to be considered in this, fall into a class of drugs known as sedatives. This term refers to drugs that produce calming (sedation), of which alcohol is the prototype. Historically, the barbiturates dominated the sedative market as medicinals from the beginning to the middle of the twentieth century. They were then displaced by drugs with a more specific action for calming—the propanediols and the benzodiazepine tranquilizers.

Although sedation, calming, and tranquilization describe more or less the same behavioral conditions, the term *sedative* connotes a behavioral calming and reduced motor activity associated at higher drug doses with drowsiness and sleep. The term *tranquilizer* connotes behavioral calming and reduced motor activity associated primarily with the reduction of agitation and anxiety. The barbiturates, since they induce sleep, are generally considered sedatives, but not tranquilizers.

The barbiturates show a dose-response profile that is closely associated with their therapeutic use. At moderate doses, they produce sedation that may be accompanied by drowsiness. At somewhat higher doses, they induce sleep. Drugs used for sleep are termed hypnotics (with no relation to hypnotism); hence, another name for these agents is sedative-hypnotics. At high doses, some barbiturates function as anesthetics, inducing deep sleep and an insensitivity to pain. These three effects—sedation, sleep induction, and anesthesia—lie on a continuum of central nervous depression, and they characterize the dose-response profile of these substances.

HISTORY

The sedative-hypnotics take their name from the mythical Greek figure Hypnos ("sleep"). Hypnos came from an interesting family background, rich in metaphorical likenesses. He was the son of the goddess Nyx ("night"), the brother of Thanatos ("death"), and the father of Morpheus ("dreams"). The ancients employed a number of substances for sleep, almost all of which have now been found to contain compounds possessing genuine sleep-inducing virtues. The most common classical prescriptions were the opium poppy, henbane, mandrake, and milk of lettuce. We now know that the opium poppy furnishes narcotics like opium, morphine, and codeine, which have sedative properties. The mandrake contains scopolamine, a drug still to be found in small amounts in over-the-counter sleep medications. Hashish was also used, as was alcohol, the oldest of sleep remedies.

This armamentarium of hypnotics remained much the same throughout the Middle Ages and the Renaissance. The *spongia somnifera,* used for sleep and anesthesia, was a walloping concoction of sleep drugs; it consisted of a sponge soaked in wine, opium, lettuce, hemlock, mulberry juice, ivy, and mandragora. The same ingredients, prepared in various solutions, could be had from the apothecary shop. Prepared in sleeping potions, they served the extramedicinal machinations of sorcerers, intriguers, and seducers.

Alcohol, opium, and cannabis survived throughout the centuries as sedatives and sleep-inducing agents. None of these is accepted as a medicinal sedative-hypnotic by today's standards. Not until the late nineteenth and early twentieth centuries did the synthesis and extensive use of better sedative-hypnotics and anesthetics begin. Ether, although three hundred years old, finally found employment in the 1840s as a surgical and dental anesthetic, and the bromides as sedatives. The anesthetic chloroform was introduced. Chloral hydrate and paraldehyde, synthesized in the first half of the nineteenth century, were eventually put into use as hypnotics in the latter half.

These Victorian sedative-hypnotics became obsolete with the introduction of barbiturates around the turn of the century. The barbiturates' parentage dates to April 12, 1864, the day Dr. Adolph von Baeyer (of Bayer aspirin fame) combined urea (a waste product in urine) with malonic acid (found in apples) to produce barbituric acid. Von Baeyer recognized his creation as a key compound rife with possibilities. To celebrate, he went out to a tavern, and his visit there spawned two speculations about his coinage of the name "barbituric acid." Because the term comes from the name *Barbara,* one story suggests the molecule was named after a barmaid. A second account claims that the name came from Saint Barbara, the patron saint of the artillery, whose officers were in the tavern at the time of von Baeyer's visit, raucously celebrating their patroness's feast day.

Barbituric acid itself has no behavioral effects. These appear only when molecular groups are attached to the compound's central ring. In 1903, Von Mering and Fischer synthesized the first barbiturate (or derivative of barbituric acid), diethylbarbituric acid. Von Mering telegraphed news of the drug's promising properties to Fischer in Verona, Italy, a relaxing city that allegedly inspired the trade name *Veronal.* This started the tradition of ending barbiturate names in *al* (although the British nomenclature ends them in *one,* making America's *barbital* Britain's *barbitone*).

Veronal was replaced in 1912 by the introduction of phenobarbital (Luminal), still one of the best drugs in this class. More barbiturates, with different durations of effect, followed: amobarbital (Amytal) in 1923, and pentobarbital (Nembutal) and secobarbital (Seconal) in 1930. These compounds served so well that they entirely replaced the former sedative-hypnotics, and until 1960, only a dozen other drugs were marketed as their competition. About a half dozen barbiturates now serve all clinical purposes, of over 2,500 synthesized since that first Saint Barbara's Day.

The nonbarbiturate sedatives first appeared with the introduction of glutethimide (Doriden) in 1954. These substances closely mimic the depressant effects of barbiturates, but differ in molecular structure. Glutethimide, instantly popular as a hypnotic, soon proved to be not as safe and nonaddicting as was first thought. However, it provides a satisfactory alternative to barbiturates and remains the most-prescribed drug of this type. Other barbiturate-like sedatives are methaqualone (Quaalude) and methyprylon (Noludar). The infamous thalidomide was also a member of this class of drugs during its brief span of use.

The barbiturates and glutethimide began to fall significantly out of clinical use as sedative-hypnotics beginning in the 1970s, with the development of the benzodiazepine tranquilizers, which proved more specific and effective. These are now the most commonly prescribed calming agents and sleeping pills. The barbiturates have been retained primarily for two clinical uses: they make good anesthetics, and at low doses they can be used successfully over extended periods as anticonvulsants, to mildly depress brain tissue and prevent epileptic seizures.

BARBITURATES: PHARMACOKINETICS

TABLE 13.1 The Barbiturates

Chemical name	Trade name	Class	Onset	Duration	Sedation	Hypnotic effect
barbital	Veronal	long	1 hr	10-12 hrs	50 mg	300 mg
phenobarbital	Luminal	long	1 hr	10-12 hrs	30 mg	100 mg
amobarbital	Amytal	medium	45 min	6-8 hrs	30 mg	200 mg
pentobarbital	Nembutal	short	15 min	3-4 hrs	40 mg	100 mg
secobarbital	Seconal	short	15 min	3-4 hrs	—	100 mg
pentothal (IV)	Thiopental	ultra short	30 sec	30 min	15 mg	10-20 mg
hexobarbital (IV)	Evipal	ultra short	30 sec	30 min	—	—

TABLE 13.2 The Nonbarbiturates

Chemical name	Trade name	Class	Onset	Duration	Sedation	Hypnotic effect
glutethimide	Doriden	medium	30 min	4-8 hrs	—	250-500 mg
methyprylon	Noludar	medium	45 min	5-8 hrs	50-100 mg	200-400 mg
ethchlorvinyl	Placidyl	medium	15-60 min	5 hrs	100-200 mg	500-700 mg
paraldehyde	—	long	10-15 min	8-12 hrs	2-5 ml IM	10 ml IM, IV

The barbiturates are effective oral drugs, usually prepared as sodium salts and administered in the form of tablets or pills. Injecting them can be risky. A solution injected into muscles or under the skin can cause pain and necrosis (death of the tissue) at the injection site. Intravenous injection is used only in anesthesia and in convulsive emergencies when standby respiratory and circulatory equipment is available. Despite the risks, illicit users inject IV and SC anyway. The rectal route is used in cases of infants with high fever who are in danger of convulsing.

Taken orally, the barbiturates are absorbed mostly from the intestine. The more lipid-soluble compounds distribute through all body fluids and tissues, with the liver, kidneys, and heart taking up the drug almost as quickly as the brain. In general, the absorption of these drugs is heavily influenced by binding to blood protein and by storage in fat tissue, although the degree to which these can occur varies significantly from compound to compound. For example, 65 percent of a dose of thiopental binds to blood protein, whereas only 5 percent of a dose of barbital does. The drug effect may be increased in the presence of weak acids like aspirin, which can displace bound drug molecules from blood protein and put them into action.

The lipid solubility of the barbiturates varies from compound to compound; it is the factor that determines the pattern of redistribution in fat tissue and the duration of the effect. A typical redistribution pattern is as follows: The user takes the drug. Blood plasma levels rise as the drug is absorbed, and there may be an immediate effect, such as sleep. The drug then redistributes into fat storage. Fairly early in the course of action, blood levels drop and a redistribution half-life occurs (namely, blood plasma levels fall to half and lower due to binding in tissues). There follows a period of slow release out of storage from fat tissue, which may manifest as a prolonged, low-level effect—a hangover, giddiness, or sense of depression. In this phase, the drug is metabolized and excreted. Eventually, the elimination half-life is reached. This is the point where half of the original dose has actually been deactivated rather than stored. Then, levels continue to drop to zero.

In clinical use, the chief consideration is the duration of action. This is proclaimed in the fact that the barbiturates are usually classed in four categories: ultra-short-acting, short-acting, intermediate-acting, and long-acting. The duration of the effect is influenced by a number of factors: dosage, lipid solubility, the pattern of redistribution, and drug fate. For example, with anesthesia it is important to have a fairly short and well-controlled action. Methohexital (Brevital) achieves this by redistributing. Upon administration, lipid-soluble methohexital passes rapidly through the blood-brain barrier and causes sleep. It then binds in fat tissue, causing a drop in plasma levels that soon wakens the sleeper. In the case of some anesthetics, the stored portion is then slowly released and metabolized, so that, even though you are awake, you remain groggy for hours afterward.

Sedation and sleep induction require a medium duration of effect, from 2 to 8 hours. Amobarbital (Amytal), an intermediate-acting agent used as a sleeping pill, is less lipid-soluble than methohexital. Enough is absorbed to cause sleep shortly after administration, but less of the drug is involved in storage, and more remains in active circulation. As a result, the sedation is longer, and the elimination half-life may not be attained for a number of hours. When the user wakes in the morning, some of the active drug remains, and some stored drug is still being released from tissues. This can cause a mild hangover and impairment of motor coordination, enough conceivably to reduce driving ability. The effects may not trail off until well into the following day. And some of the drug will still be present after 24 hours, so that regular daily doses pose the threat of a cumulative effect.

Anticonvulsants can be as long-acting as safety permits (see Table 13.1). Phenobarbital, used for this purpose, is not very lipid-soluble and for the most part does not go into storage; it stays active in the circulation and is slowly metabolized. Low doses are given so that tolerance develops to drowsiness and sedation.

The lipid-soluble barbiturates effectively penetrate the placental barrier. Consequently, when the birthing mother is given anesthetics, the fetus also receives a dose, and the newborn may have what is called *floppy baby syndrome*, its limbs flaccid and rubbery because it is born stone drunk on barbiturates. And because the infant lacks the ability to metabolize and efficiently excrete the drug, depressive effects may persist for a day or two after delivery.

The metabolism of the barbiturates takes place in the liver and (in small amounts) in the kidneys, brain, and perhaps other tissues. The process of metabolism can be slow. Barbiturates generally follow slower routes out of the body, depending on filtration and diffusion down concentration gradients, especially if they are of a type that is not readily metabolized. Moreover, the more lipid-soluble barbiturates are reabsorbed in the kidneys.

For a number of barbiturate compounds, the clinical use is a function of dosage. Amobarbital (Amytal), for instance, is used as a sedative at 30 mg and as a hypnotic at 200 mg (see Table 13.1). As a rule, hypnotic doses of barbiturates consist of several sedative doses taken in one shot, instead of spread over a day.

PHARMACOLOGICAL EFFECTS

The barbiturates have been referred to as *solid alcohols* because, as general nervous system depressants, they exhibit effects like those of alcohol—disinhibition, euphoria, sedation, loss of motor control, sleep, anesthesia, coma, and death—and they share many other properties as well, including tolerance, physical dependence, and similar withdrawal signs. Barbiturates as intoxicants have the same appeal to users as alcohol, with the assets of being cheaper and less detectable.

Low in selectivity, barbiturates depress all excitable nervous tissue, and they antagonize and reverse the effects of CNS stimulants. The action of barbiturates is believed to occur at the GABA receptor. The molecules bind to a site on the $GABA_A$ receptor complex, increasing the amount of time that the ion channel remains open during the GABA transmitter action (see Figure 9.10). This lets more Cl- ions across the membrane, increasing hyperpolarization and making the cell harder to fire. At higher doses, the barbiturates mimic GABA inhibition, perhaps by activating chloride channels directly.

Peripheral effects tend not to be an issue with the barbiturates. The central nervous system is highly sensitive to them and responds before significant peripheral actions come into play. This may not be the case, however, at doses high enough to cause intoxication and extended depression.

Cardiovascular effects are negligible at oral, sedative-hypnotic dosages. Blood pressure and heart rate drop to levels shown during normal sleep. However, when barbiturates are administered IV at anesthetic dosages, blood pressure may drop precipitously. Therefore, the speed of administration must be gradual and carefully controlled. Only at several times an anesthetic dose is the heart directly affected—namely, in cases of acute poisoning. Even so, death in such cases most often follows from depression of the respiratory center in the medulla, and consequent asphyxiation.

In the brain, barbiturates depress areas in the forebrain and brainstem. They have an affinity for the reticular formation, where they block arousal. This accounts for their ability to cause loss of consciousness. However, though sedatives may help the sleeper fall asleep, stay asleep, or lie still, like alcohol, they decrease REM (dreaming) sleep and effect other alterations on the sleep stages. REM rebound will follow use.

Mood changes caused by barbiturates may be linked to the limbic system. It is probably here that barbiturates at low dosages cause mild euphoria, disinhibition, and a rise in aggressiveness. On the other hand, at increased dosages, the opposite signs occur—emotional withdrawal and depression.

Sedatives affect reflexes, but to different degrees. Reflexes like coughing, sneezing, and hiccoughing are resistant to barbiturates; vomiting survives up to the point of respiratory depression. Spasms of the larynx, a drug-induced reflex, are one of the chief complications of barbiturate anesthesia. Erection in males, another reflex, is severely depressed. Depression of the respiratory center in the medulla is the most common cause of death from these drugs.

In animal studies with barbiturates, the effect known as state-dependent learning has been observed. To demonstrate this, an animal is first trained to perform a task correctly under the influence of the drug. Tested later when the drug effect has worn off, the animal makes errors. Put back on the drug, the animal performs again more accurately. This indicates that what is learned in the drug state can be fully used only in the drug state again. Alcohol produces similar effects. Therefore, a student drinking alcohol when studying for an exam would do well to remain in the drug state during the exam, or recall will deteriorate. Needless to say, the drug would reduce arousal and impair performance, so that, for the best results, no drug at all is recommended. Cross effects between sedatives have also been observed; for example, one could switch from learning on alcohol to recalling on barbiturates, and perform equally well. Still, arousal and performance suffer. At low doses, reinforcement-dependent effects have been noted.

CLINICAL APPLICATIONS

The two most prominent clinical uses of the barbiturates today are for anticonvulsant therapy for epilepsy, and for anesthesia. As sedatives and hypnotics, the barbiturates have been largely usurped by benzodiazepine tranquilizers like chlordiazepoxide (Librium), diazepam (Valium), triazolam (Halcion) and alprazolam (Xanax). In this area, they remain only in minor specialized uses, such as in the sedation of patients before surgery or in lesser medical and dental procedures.

Insomnia

From the turn of the century until the 1970s, the barbiturates were the lullaby drug of choice. It was in the context of barbiturate use that insomnia and its treatment began to be understood. *Insomnia* is a broad term that blankets a range of complaints. It can refer to an inadequate quantity or quality of sleep, to difficulty in falling asleep, to multiple awakenings, to early morning arousals that shorten a night's rest, and to the accompanying problem of daytime fatigue. The causes, too, may vary considerably. Insomnia may follow from breathing problems, from depressive illness, from nocturnal twitching (*myoclonus*), or from disturbed biorhythms (jet lag). In addition, there seem to be subjective values attached to what is reported as insomnia, as opposed to refreshing sleep. One study showed that insomniacs may report a lack of sleep, contradicting EEG readings that show sleep patterns (Monroe, 1967).

The barbiturates proved to be a reasonable treatment for lack of sleep, but far from an ideal one. Wide prescribing practices simply mark them as the best agents available at the time, much superior to the alternatives. At recommended dosages, the barbiturates are safe, and do cause sleep. They have drawbacks, however. Although they help to initiate sleep, like alcohol at moderate to high dosages they suppress dreaming (REM) sleep. (At low doses, dreaming sleep is able to reinstate itself.) Furthermore, the low levels of drug released from fat storage can cause a barbiturate hangover the morning after use. A more serious consideration is the possibility, through intoxication, of protracted use, abuse, and dependence, and long-term treatment at hypnotic dosages is ill-advised. Lastly, because they are toxic in high doses, barbiturates are the drug of choice for suicide. Consequently, when the benzodiazepines were developed, superior to the barbiturates in every one of these respects, they quickly conquered the sleeping pill market.

Epilepsy

Epilepsy is a general term referring to any central nervous disorder marked by seizures (McNamara, 1996, p. 461). These nearly always correspond with abnormal activity in the EEG, which is an indication of storms of electrical discharges in the brain. Typically, the disturbance originates from a single point, or focus, with the synchronous, high-frequency firing of a local group of neurons. This could be caused by a sudden, large depolarization related to the dysfunction of a GABA (inhibitory) transmitter system. Studies suggest that disturbances to the brain (such as infections, congenital defects, a concussion, or lack of oxygen) alter normal neural activity, causing abnormal firing patterns in a certain spot (focus). These may progress over a long interval, like a structural weakness in a building, and eventually become the epicenter for seizures. Some epilepsies may proceed from genetic factors, as indicated by the breeding of highly convulsive strains of mice that suffer seizures if you so much as jingle your keys near the cage.

Although antiepileptic drug actions are poorly understood, most drugs work partly by reducing the excitability of brain neurons so that seizures do not spread from the focus, and some drugs depress the focus itself. Therapy aims at prohibiting seizures without disadvantaging a person otherwise. This is usually achieved through long-term treatment at low doses. Complete control of seizures through drug treatment can be had in half of the cases of epilepsy, and significant improvement in an additional 25 percent (Rall & Schleifer, 1985, p. 449).

Phenobarbital, a long-acting barbiturate with a half-life of 100 hours, is the most frequently prescribed barbiturate antiepileptic medication. It is cheap, low in toxicity, and effective at dosages well below the hypnotic level. The usual adult dose is 60 to 250 mg, with double doses to raise plasma levels for the first four days. Sedation appears as a side effect until tolerance builds, and weeks pass before the proper cumulative dose is reached.

Drugs developed since the late thirties, with high anticonvulsant but low sedative effects (such as phenytoin sodium—Dilantin), suggest two separate mechanisms for sleep and anticonvulsant actions. Newer antiepileptic compounds introduced since 1965 include molecules of different chemical types: benzodiazepines (clonazepam, clorazepate), carbamazepine (Tegretol), and valproic acid (Depakane).

SIDE EFFECTS

The behavioral side effects of barbiturates resemble those of alcohol. In fact, barbiturate inebriation can easily be confused with alcohol inebriation. However, the ataxia caused by barbiturates (the staggering due to muscle incoordination) is exaggerated—so much so that barbiturate drunkards were dubbed *wallbangers* by the drug subculture. In other respects, the barbiturates are cleaner than alcohol. Users popping reds (Seconal) may be pulled off the highway for weaving from shoulder to shoulder, but they can still pass the breathalyzer test.

Drowsiness and nausea are the most common side effects. These may contribute to the hangover that occurs the day after a sleeping pill, which may involve impairment of judgment and fine motor skills that can compromise activities like driving for up to 22 hours after the dose. If residual depression does not show, subtle distortions of mood might. Intellectual performance may also decline, and physiological effects like vertigo, nausea, vomiting, and diarrhea are possible.

Paradoxical excitement is an occasional side effect of barbiturates. That is, in some cases, instead of being sedated, users become highly excited. This is a relatively common response among the elderly. Also, when people in pain are sedated with barbiturates, they sometimes show excitement, restlessness, and delirium. Even normal users may display overexcitement on sedative-hypnotic doses. They may waken the morning after a sleeping pill with higher plasma levels than when they went to sleep, feeling mildly intoxicated, euphoric, and energetic. When incoordination compromises performance during the day, they may grow angry and irritated. Children on phenobarbital can be cranky and hyperactive.

Although the barbiturates, unlike alcohol, cause no apparent liver damage, they do induce the same enzymes as alcohol (P450), leading to tolerance and an increased metabolism of various other drugs. Cross-tolerance, only partially attributable to liver enzymes, shows between barbiturates and alcohol, opium, and phencyclidine (PCP). Liver enzymes do account for interactions with many common agents like antihistamines and antidepressants.

BARBITURATE ABUSE

> *. . . and by a sleep to say we end*
> *The heartache, and the thousand natural shocks*
> *That flesh is heir to. . . .*
>
> Shakespeare, *Hamlet* III.1.61-63

As intoxicants, the barbiturates have the same appeal as alcohol, although it has been said that the maximum euphoriant effects of barbiturates are akin to morphine euphoria. In their time, the sedative-hypnotics killed more people than all other drugs combined, and because the category includes alcohol, they are by far the most used and abused class of drug. The short or intermediate-acting agents, particularly pentobarbital and secobarbital. have been the most prone to abuse. Tuinal, an abuser's favorite, appears on the market as a combination of amobarbital and secobarbital. Barbiturates and alcohol have been another popular combination.

By far the worst side effects of barbiturates are dependence and addiction. Not until 1950, 47 years after their first use, was physical dependence on barbiturates officially recognized, the typical pattern of dependence beginning with insomnia and a sleeping pill prescription. Barbiturate withdrawal symptoms resemble those of alcohol and similarly present a greater danger than opiate withdrawal, because of seizures. Epileptics using barbiturates as anticonvulsants are in especial danger. Susceptible to seizures in the first place, epileptics are doubly at risk when neurons liberated from depressants become overexcited enough to cause convulsions like the "rum fits" even in normal users. For this reason, when any long-term use of sedatives is terminated, dosages must be tapered off through a series of gradual reductions.

An added danger with barbiturate sleeping pills is that they ar the preferred means of suicide, offering the allure of drowsy euthanasia. Included in the death toll are unintentional overdoses resulting from additive and synergistic interactions with other drugs. When barbiturates were widely available, the most common fatality resulted from a sleeping pill taken after a night of drinking. The effect is synergistic. Half of the lethal dose of secobarbital combined with 1/4 of the lethal dose of alcohol can kill in a synergistic double whammy. In another typical pattern of accidental overdose, a person would take a sleeping pill and awaken drugged and confused a few minutes later, annoyed at being aroused. The person would then forgetfully take another pill, or several, from the night stand, and go to sleep forever. This is called *drug automatism*, a good reason not to keep medications within reach of the bed.

At toxic doses, the barbiturates induce slow (or rapid and shallow) breathing, a drop in blood pressure, and pupils that constrict and then dilate from lack of oxygen. Patients may be in shock, with a weak, rapid pulse; cold, clammy skin; severe temperature drops; and fever during recovery. Some may lapse into a coma. When death occurs, it usually follows from respiratory depression and kidney failure.

The best way to deal with an overdose is to keep the patient awake and moving, or, if that is not feasible, to keep the patient warm with feet up. Activated charcoal can be given to slow absorption. Administering stimulants like coffee can be a problem because they may enhance convulsions when the depressant wears off. Hospital treatment involves keeping the lung airways open, conserving body heat, and supporting blood pressure. The patient may be put on life support (respirators, etc.) until the liver has a chance to metabolize the drug. Diuresis (the administration of agents to speed up urination) and hemodialysis (removal of drug from the bloodstream) may also be used.

BARBITURATE-LIKE SUBSTANCES

For all intents and purposes, drugs in this category are similar to the barbiturates, except for slight chemical modifications that may cause anomalous properties in some cases. The CNS depressant effects, classification by duration of action, clinical uses, pharmacology and dynamics, side effects, and so forth, resemble those that we have already discussed. It is even possible that receptors cannot distinguish between these drugs and the barbiturates. Alcohol fits the profile of the agents described here, as do other anesthetics (chloral hydrate, paraldehyde, ethchlorvinyl, and ether). As a rule, these drugs are less known and more expensive than barbiturates, and they are used mostly as alternatives when barbiturates might not be available, in animal surgery, or in cases of brief anesthesia.

Methaqualone (Quaalude, Sopor)

Methaqualone is probably the most renowned of the barbiturate alternatives, because of its reputation as a drug of abuse, going under the street names of "ludes" and "sopors." Synthesized in India as an antimalarial drug, methaqualone proved a better sedative. Following the thalidomide scare, it gained popularity as a safe, nonbarbiturate sleeping pill. In 1965, when it came to the United States as a prescription drug, it had already suffered a stint of abuse in England, Germany, and Japan, and had a reputation as a euphoriant and aphrodisiac, nicknamed "the love drug." The pharmacological reasons for this are not clear, since, like alcohol, it reduces sexual performance. Methaqualone is said to give a heroin-like high without drowsiness. Abuse continued uncurbed until 1973, when it was rated Schedule II, and it has since been removed from the market. Nevertheless, occasional abuse continues.

Glutethimide (Doriden)

Glutethimide was synthesized in 1954. It has an erratic oral absorption, is highly lipid-soluble, and redistributes unevenly. The duration of action is intermediate, with peak plasma levels in 1 to 6 hours and a half-life of 5 to 22 hours. Glutethimide's excretion is noteworthy in that the drug follows the bile duct and reenters the small intestine; from there it is reabsorbed to be conjugated later in the liver. For this reason, overdoses are tough to manage, making this drug more dangerous than barbiturates. Problems can occur in treatment if hemodialysis is used to filter the drug from the blood: As the drug is removed, the blood concentration drops, causing a pronounced concentration gradient in the intestines. Then, even heavier doses flow into circulation more rapidly than before.

The mechanism of glutethimide is unknown, but marked anticholinergic activity (especially dry mouth) occurs with the CNS depression. Side effects, rare at therapeutic dosages, include hangover, blurry vision, gastrointestinal irritation, headache, and skin rash. Respiratory depression is less than with barbiturates. Tolerance, abuse, dependence, and withdrawal are much the same. Some withdrawal signs (shakes, nausea, fever, rapid heart, muscle spasms) occur in regular moderate use or in isolated cases of acute intoxication, without cessation of the drug. Some feel that glutethimide should be dropped from the pharmacopoeia, with so little to recommend it.

Methyprylon (Noludar)

This drug was introduced as a sedative and hypnotic in 1955. At hypnotic dosages it is virtually indistinguishable from secobarbital. It seems to act by raising the threshold of arousal centers. In cases of poisoning, low blood pressure, shock, and water in the lungs are more marked than respiratory depression. Side effects inlcude drowsiness (in sedative use), headaches, and nausea.

GENERAL ANESTHETICS

Anesthesia is one of the clinical applications for which barbiturates have been usefully retained. It is characterized as a sleep state accompanied by muscle relaxation, loss of reflexes, and insensitivity to pain. The stages of anesthesia represent a progressive depression of the central nervous system produced by drugs. In their effects, the anesthetics are essentially the same as the sedative-hypnotics, save for their brief duration of action. The euphoria and excitement they produce in the lighter stages of anesthesia would make them prized intoxicants if availability, administration, and unpalatability were not such drawbacks.

Anesthetics are delivered as inhalants (gases and vaporized liquids) and as intravenous solutions. The inhaled forms are immediately voided unchanged from the lungs, so administration must be continued as long as the effect is desired. The liquid forms act through high lipid solubility and quick access to the brain, followed by redistribution, tissue storage, and later release. Usually a high dose, then lower maintenance doses are given.

A typical and widely employed barbiturate anesthetic is thiopental (Pentothal). It is an ultrashort-acting agent given intravenously. In 40 seconds, 10 percent of the dose is in the brain. In 5 minutes, 50 percent is gone from the blood, and in 30 minutes, 90 percent is gone into other tissues. Thiopental is not analgesic at safe dosage levels, and the patient may react to painful stimuli.

Other barbiturates used as general anesthetics include sodium pentobarbital (Nembutal), sodium secobarbital (Seconal), and amobarbital (Amytal). Some agents used successfully as hypnotics have been found inadequate as anesthetics when used at higher doses, because the duration of action may be long and uncontrollable.

Nitrous Oxide

Nitrous oxide is a general anesthetic used in dental surgery. Its behavioral effects depend heavily on dosage, which a dentist controls by using a pressurized mixture of gas and oxygen. For the drug to be effective, a 50 percent or greater drug-to-air concentration must be inhaled. Typical effects are analgesia and euphoria, and at higher concentrations, giddiness, dreaminess, altered perception, a pounding head, and ringing in the ears. Nitrous oxide is abused for its euphoriant effects, and is known as "laughing gas" because of the giddiness it induces. It went into consistent clinical use around the time of the Civil War (1861-1865), about a century after its isolation and purification. Showmen in the nineteenth century exploited the effects for their entertainment value.

Although it is chemically nontoxic, nitrous oxide can be dangerous when taken in high concentrations, namely, with too little oxygen—20 percent or less. The molecules can mechanically barricade the intake of oxygen into brain cells; at high concentrations, this results in a general depletion of oxygen levels in the brain (hypoxia) and consequent brain damage. Breathing the drug at normal room air pressure, as recreational users do, can result in a risky ratio of gas-to-oxygen, since the oxygen concentration cannot be raised (except by hyperventilating), but the gas concentration can, for instance, by collecting it in a balloon and inhaling it. In the dentist's office, pressurization allows more oxygen to be given, as well as more nitrous oxide, and the mixture can be controlled.

Anesthetic Hallucinogens

Two sedative compounds developed as anesthetics, ketamine and phencyclidine (PCP), are of interest for their hallucinogenic properties, which have also led to their abuse. These are discussed in Chapter 24, with the cholinergic and anesthetic hallucinogens.

EARLY SEDATIVE HYPNOTICS

A number of sedative-hypnotic agents saw their heyday in the nineteenth century, and some survived through the first half of this century. Most now see minor use, if any, but they have not yet been entirely forgotten.

In 1540, Valerius Cordus derived ether from alcohol. As early as the 1700s, it was being used recreationally. It entered surgery and dentistry in the 1840s and brought its recreational use to Britain and America, when "ether frolics" began among the upper classes and spread down the social scale. Its notoriety as a drug of abuse, however, culminated in the Northern Irish counties of Londonderry and Tyrone. At first, it seems, temperance campaigners were turning reformed drinkers over to doctors, from whom they purchased ether as a "legitimate" substitute for liquor—a moral loophole. In 1855, when the British cracked down on the distillation of home brewed whiskey (*poteen*) and raised the tax on alcoholic beverages, "ether topers" sprang up everywhere, even among the respectable classes. An 1878 report tells how the streets of Draperstown, Londonderry, reeked like a doctor's surgery. Tablespoons of ether, a penny each, offered more drunken bouts at the usual cost of one, with no wait and no hangover, although the new drink was said to be difficult to choke down and "highly provocative of vomiting." Still, seasoned drinkers could kill three ounces without a chaser of water. The craze finally subsided with strictures on ether importation from London and a drop in liquor prices, around 1927.

Ether is the prototype of the volatile liquid anesthetics. Anesthesia under this drug is slow and unpleasant with a sickly, sweet odor that irritates the lungs and requires a prolonged recovery. Drunk illicitly, it can be rather distasteful, producing nausea and vomiting. While it has safety as its main recommendation, it is dangerous in another respect. Upon ignition, it explodes.

Chloroform, no longer in use, is similar to ether, but is more potent, easily administered, and nonflammable. However, atropine must be given first to fend off cardiac depression, and liver and kidney damage may result.

Long-acting sedatives, the bromides are mostly encountered today, along with brandy, as a common prop in Victorian novels. Besides that, they are generally out of use, although potassium bromide can still be found (160 mg per capful) in Bromo Seltzer, a headache remedy sometimes abused as an intoxicant, and in Miles Nervine (620 mg per capful). The bromides present significant drawbacks. They are gastric irritants, with a narrow safety margin, and can cause a condition of chronic toxicity known as *bromism*. Since the bromide ion might replace the chloride ion in neural functioning, being of like charge and size, the symptoms of bromism embrace every variety of neural pathology. Table salt is given as a remedy to displace the bromide and quicken its excretion.

Historically, chloral hydrate is used in the notorious "knock out drops" slipped in a drink to make a "Mickey Finn," an anesthetic cocktail used to shanghai sailors to Asia in the 1800s. Alcohol and chloral hydrate have a synergistic effect when used together, so getting "slipped a mickey" really did the trick. All tissues appear to convert chloral hydrate to its active metabolite and hypnotic agent, trichloroethanol. So, although the chloral hydrate has a half-life of only minutes, the metabolite has one of 4 to 12 hours. Since neither of these substances induces microsomal enzymes, interactions with other drugs that induce or are metabolized by these enzymes are not a problem. Chloral hydrate has a rapid onset (30 minutes) and short duration, with negligible cardiovascular and respiratory effects at therapeutic dosages. Also, it is unique among sedatives in that it does not suppress REM sleep. The hypnotic dose is from 1 to 2 grams. The subject wakens easily, usually with no hangover. With all of these advantages, chloral hydrate has recently been coming into use again. Drawbacks are its unpleasant taste and strong irritation, which necessitate its being taken diluted with milk, and its side effects of nausea, vomiting, malaise, lightheadedness, and nightmares. At anesthetic dosages, chloral hydrate has a low safety margin and fairly weak analgesic powers. The other chloral derivative in current use is triclofos sodium (Triclos, Tricloryl).

Paraldehyde (Paral), effective against all types of convulsions, was once used in hospitals and institutions to ease alcohol withdrawal, particularly delirium tremens, but this is no longer the case. An occasional alcoholic may adopt paraldehyde as a substitute addiction. It is relatively safe, shows little respiratory depression, and is rapidly absorbed orally, inducing sleep in 15 minutes. But it has drawbacks. It is a colorless liquid with a strong odor and an obnoxious burning taste, irritating to the throat and stomach, and its partial excretion from the lungs fouls the breath with a persistent fetor. Injecting it, however, may cause nerve injury, pulmonary edema, or low blood pressure. Furthermore, it can react rapidly with certain plastics, and it naturally decomposes to acetaldehyde (the "hangover metabolite") upon exposure to light and air, posing a threat of poisoning.

Chapter 14

Anxiolytics

Anxiolytics are the drugs known by most people as tranquilizers, drugs good for the breaking up (from Greek *lysis*) of anxiety (Latin *anxius*). They may be roughly divided into three categories, each characterized by a different mechanism of action, and each representing a stage in the history of their development. The original group of compounds, used in the 1950s, was the propanediol carbamates, which had meprobamate (Miltown, Equanil) as the prototype. These relieved tension through muscle relaxation, by compromising the action of ACh. In the 1960s came the benzodiazepines, whose prototypes are diazepam (Valium) and chlordiazepoxide (Librium). These work by augmenting inhibition of the central nervous system through GABA-ergic actions. The arrival of buspirone (BuSpar) on the market in the 1990s has signaled another trend. Tranquilizing through serotonergic mechanisms, buspirone points to the involvement of multiple transmitter systems in anxiety and to the possibility of more selective treatments.

PROPANEDIOLS: MEPROBAMATE

In 1947, when Berger and Bradley of the British Drug House in London were searching for new antibacterial agents, they observed the flaccid paralysis of the muscles of mice under the influence of alpha-phenylglyceryl ether. Becoming interested in the possibilities of this side effect, they began a study using mephenesin (Tolserol), a drug first synthesized over three decades earlier. They noted that mephenesin had calming effects at dosages below those for muscle relaxation, and they were able to produce a sleeplike condition from which the subject could be easily aroused. However, the oxidation of mephenesin was so rapid that large continuous doses were needed to maintain calming. For this reason, attempts were made to modify the molecule, and this resulted in more than 1200 substances before meprobamate (Miltown, Equanil) was synthesized in 1951. Meprobamate's taming and calming effect had eight times the duration of action of mephenesin when taken orally. Berger named the new drug after the New Jersey town where he then worked at Wallace Laboratories—Miltown—a name all America was soon to know.

When the FDA released meprobamate to the American marketplace in 1955, barbiturates, barbiturate-like agents, and alcohol were the only resources for sedation. During the first eight months of that year, sales grew by 600 percent, and tranquilizers were on their way to being a mass cultural phenomenon, the most widely prescribed drugs in the history of medicine. At first, the press greeted the new drugs as a panacea (a familiar pattern in drug histories by now), but with their almost preposterous expansion of use in the first year, doubts and suspicion grew. Miltown (or Equanil) became "don't-give-a-damn pills," "aspirin for the soul," and "happy pills." The earlier vision in Aldous Huxley's *Brave New World* of a nation of euphoriant addicts began to take on an ominous and prophetic ring. Wallace Laboratories even marketed a product they named Soma after the coping drug in Huxley's book. The fifties were "The Age of Anxiety," with "nervous breakdown" as its catchphrase, and tranquilizers became the answer. People even dosed their pets on the way to the vet, zoos tranquilized nervous animals, and pigs to slaughter were drugged.

Many factors contributed to meprobamate's rapid rise in use. Among them were its selective antianxiety effects, a large and successful advertising campaign, and the medical profession's desire for a safe, nonbarbiturate sedative. Likewise, within the medical profession, many conditions favored the overprescribing of tranquilizers, which one critic went so far as to describe as "a doctor's disease" (Smith, 1985). There were no established clinical guidelines for the prescription of tranquilizers, definitions of normal and abnormal stress were vague, and physicians tended to "medicalize" normal human problems. There was also confusion in the medical literature about sedation, tranquilization, antianxiety, and antidepressant effects. Patients who clamored for treatment were easily satisfied with a prescription of tranquilizers, which at least visibly reduced their anxieties about being ill and made them more manageable as patients. Many physicians as well relied completely on information they received from drug companies.

By 1959, there were 27 tranquilizer products on the market, compared to 3 in 1955 (Smith, 1985, p. 107). But public opinion had chilled, and the name Miltown had grown so infamous that, if physicians prescribed meprobamate, they used its other trade name, Equanil.

The chief propanediols (see Figure 14.1) are mephenesin (Tolserol), meprobamate (Miltown, Equanil), and the meprobamate derivative tybamate (Solacen). Meprobamate is typical of the class. The dose for sedation (three or four daily doses of 200 to 400 mg) relaxes a person for about eight hours. The drug is well-absorbed from the stomach and distributes fairly uniformly, except for an affinity for the liver and kidneys. The plasma half-life is about 11 hours, due mostly to distribution, but, as a rule, most of a dose is eliminated in a day, predominantly through metabolism in the liver.

Unlike many other sedatives, meprobamate appears to be an AChE agonist, reducing ACh activity at the neuromuscular junctions of the skeletal muscles, effecting relaxation by lessening the normal tension (contraction) in muscles.

One advantage shown by meprobamate over alcohol and the barbiturates is that it only slightly depresses the respiratory center in the medulla. As a result, the toxic dose is high, making suicide difficult, but possible. In most cases, depression of the reticular formation is not significant. The picture that emerges is of a drug that diminishes anxiety through muscle relaxation but allows the user to remain reasonably alert and functional, able to tolerate more frustration and perform better under stress. And physicians could rest on the fact that patients could not abuse their medication by administering a fatal cure for stress.

Meprobamate shows many of the same side effects as barbiturates, albeit not to the same degree. Drowsiness is the most common complaint, and intoxication is possible. By slowing complex reflexes, meprobamate can impair driving ability, and, at higher doses (800 mg or more) it can disrupt motor coordination and learning. Like barbiturates, meprobamate induces microsomal enzymes, suppresses dreaming sleep, and produces tolerance. Dependence has been noted at doses of about 3200 mg a day continued for a month. Withdrawal is similar to that with the barbiturates'. Unlike the barbiturates, however, is the lack of significant respiratory effects.

In 1971, Greenblatt and Shader published a damning review of fifteen years of meprobamate use, claiming it was "no less toxic or more effective on anxiety than a barbiturate," and that, in retrospect, its popularity and notoriety seemed surprising (Smith, 1985, p. 86). Due to the cautionary mood brought on by its widespread misuse, couple with the development of better agents, meprobamate faded into obsolescence.

BENZODIAZEPINES

Although the first benzodiazepine was synthesized in 1933, these drugs did not become significant until Leo Sternbach and his associates at Roche Laboratories first developed chlordiazepoxide (Librium), which is considered the prototype of the class (see Figure 14.1). The discovery of its clinical usefulness was an accident. In the spring of 1957, intense antibiotic work had messed up the lab so badly that the researchers were giving it a thorough cleaning. One worker noticed "a few hundred milligrams of two products, a nicely crystalline base and its hydrochloride," both pure (Smith, 1985, p. 24). Upon testing, the compounds showed promising properties. Then, when the team was attempting to resynthesize the water-soluble salt (the base), they accidentally invented chlordiazepoxide (Librium). Early animal experiments indicated potent taming effects, some muscle relaxation, and anticonvulsant properties. Observation of the taming effects led to clinical trials in humans, and Librium was introduced to clinical use soon after. At that time, all of the known sedatives (including meprobamate) presented problems, mostly of undue sedation, acute intoxication, and physical dependence. Meprobamate had been stigmatized. Therefore, the benzodiazepines looked like a forward leap.

In the wake of the Miltown experience, tranquilizers were getting severe treatment from the press. With all of the new agents coming into being from 1955 to 1960antidepressants, tranquilizers, and antipsychotics--there was a great deal of confusion, even among doctors, over classes of tranquilizers and distinctions between their effects. Nevertheless, nothing stemmed the second wave. Three months after its introduction in 1960, Librium was the most prescribed tranquilizer. And with it amid the uproar, Valium (its name from Latin vale, "to be strong or well") followed in 1963 and eventually rose to the distinction of being the most prescribed drug of any kind.

The Age of Anxiety ended around 1965, when meprobamate was dropped from the U.S. Pharmacopoeia, and America entered a new phase as benzodiazepine use expanded. Flurazepam (Dalmane) swelled the tide with its introduction in 1970. This was a new benzodiazepine sleeping pill that challenged the sovereignty of the barbiturate hypnotics. Despite professional skepticism, benzodiazepine use continued to increase, until it peaked and began to subside in the years 1973 to 1975, and finally underwent a steady decline. In 1975, 104.5 million benzodiazepine prescriptions were written in pharmacies (Smith, 1985, p. 49). In 1977, 54 million prescriptions were written for Valium, 13 million for Librium, and 53 percent of all hypnotic prescriptions were for flurazepam (Dalmane). A conservative estimate says that 8000 tons of benzodiazepines were consumed that year (Tallman et al., 1980, p. 247).

Factors correlating with higher abuse were lower economic status, middle age, and residence in the western United States, with housewives, the retired, and the unemployed ranking among the heaviest users. Significantly higher use took place among women. Many reasons for this have been given, among them that women are socialized to report more neurotic symptoms, that it is more acceptable for women to report themselves ill, that women's assigned social roles are more stressful, and that male physicians misdiagnose female symptoms as psychogenic rather than organic, due to medical school socialization and suggestions in drug advertising (Smith, 1985, p. 141). Only about 1979, the time of the Kennedy hearings on the benzodiazepines, did they begin to see proper management in clinical use.

The 1980s brought a significant discovery in the study of the benzodiazepines, and in pharmacology in general. Studies with radioactively labeled ^{3}H Valium, whose distribution pattern can be easily traced, showed that the benzodiazepines bind with specific receptors in synapses. This finding paralleled events in the 1970s, when researchers identified receptors for morphine, a derivative of opium. Subsequently, the opiate (morphine) receptors were found to respond to naturally occurring substances resembling morphine in the brain. It was but a short step to imagine the same for the benzodiazepine receptors--that there might be a natural benzodiazepine-like tranquilizer in the brain to counter the effects of stress. Although work continues on this front, no such molecule has yet been identified. Currently, about fifteen benzodiazepine compounds are commercially available in the United States.

Pharmacokinetics

It is helpful to keep in mind that the benzodiazepines share several important characteristics of the barbiturates. Varying like the barbiturates in lipid solubility, they show a range of patterns of redistribution and metabolism, from short-acting agents with a half-life of 2 to 15 hours, to intermediate-acting agents with a half-life of from 15 to 50 hours, to long-acting agents with a half-life of up to 150 hours. Like the barbiturates, the benzodiazepines modulate the action of GABA at the $GABA_A$ receptor complex, although they attach to their own distinct binding site. The manifest effects of GABA inhibition are therefore similar and are reflected in comparable clinical applications; namely, for sedation, sleep induction, anticonvulsant effects, and anesthesia.

By far, most administration of benzodiazepines is oral. However, a few compounds, primarily midazolam (Versed), are marketed for injection, the intravenous route being used to medicate severe epileptic convulsions or to induce anesthesia.

All of the benzodiazepines are absorbed fairly rapidly and almost completely through the gastrointestinal tract. Food and antacids can curtail the intensity of a single dose by slowing absorption and reducing peak plasma levels, but because full absorption still occurs eventually, there is no deleterious effect on long-term use. The rate of absorption differs among the various benzodiazepines, and peak plasma levels may be reached anywhere from 1 to 8 hours, depending on the compound. Generally, the benzodiazepines are lipid-soluble. The brain takes them up rapidly at levels almost equal to blood plasma levels, and most bind to a great extent in the blood (diazepam at 98 percent). They display patterns of absorption, redistribution, storage, slow release, and metabolism similar to the barbiturates. The time of the onset of clinical effects also shows a range of variation.

The most significant factors in differentiating the benzodiazepine compounds are not differences in effects, but in their pharmacokinetics. Each drug has a characteristic profile based on the following factors:

1. Its rate of absorption and the time it takes to reach peak plasma levels
2. The time to the onset of effects
3. The amount and the rate at which it redistributes and is stored (its distribution half-life)
4. Its elimination half-life
5. The activity of its metabolites and their half-lives
6. The overall duration of effect

These are the factors that determine the clinical use of most benzodiazepines.

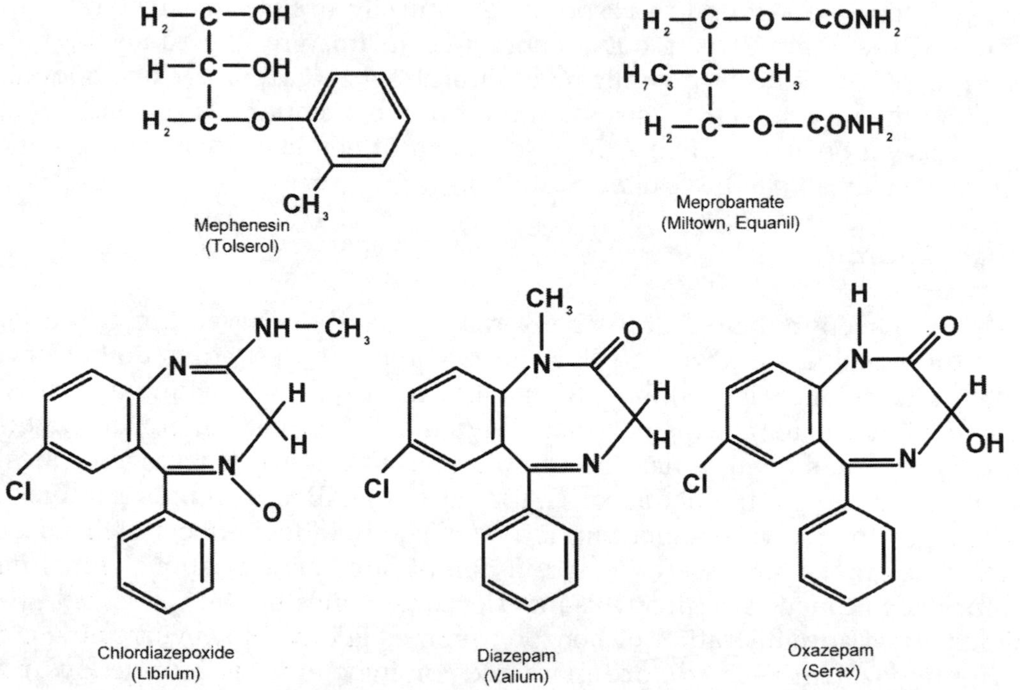

Mephenesin (Tolserol)

Meprobamate (Miltown, Equanil)

Chlordiazepoxide (Librium)

Diazepam (Valium)

Oxazepam (Serax)

FIGURE 14.1 Molecular structures of minor tranquilizers.

The benzodiazepines are metabolized by several different microsomal enzyme systems, but they do not significantly induce these enzymes. Their biotransformation generally yields active metabolites, a factor that is crucial to the profile of the drugs' effects. Several agents—chlordiazepoxide (Librium), diazepam (Valium), prazepam (Centrax), and chlorazepate (Tranxene)—are all metabolized into the same active compound: oxazepam (which itself is marketed as Serax), so that all have more or less the same effect. The action of flurazepam (Dalmane) relies entirely upon the action of its active metabolites; its plasma half-life of 2 to 3 hours is extended to 50 hours or more through its major active metabolite. The duration of action of diazepam is doubled or tripled (from 24 to 60 hours) through the products of biotransformation, which are active at several stages. Metabolism of the benzodiazepines is prolonged in newborns and the elderly, and in the presence of alcohol, disulfiram, isoniazid, and oral contraceptives, resulting in protracted effects and threats of toxicity. Most benzodiazepines are excreted almost entirely in the urine.

Diazepam (Valium) and triazolam (Halcion) illustrate some of these differences. The pharmacological effects of the two drugs are basically the same. Diazepam has a slow absorption rate, reaching peak plasma levels in 4 hours. It binds 98 percent in the blood, and reaches its redistribution half-life in about a day. Biotransformation produces active metabolites, which significantly prolong the action, and it takes about 45 hours for half of a dose to be eliminated. Five to ten milligrams is the sedative dose, while 40 mg may be given to treat alcohol withdrawal. A dose of 120 mg a day continued over two months may cause dependence.

In contrast, triazolam (Halcion) is an intermediate-acting benzodiazepine used as a sleeping pill. Absorption is moderate to slow, with plasma levels peaking in about 2 hours. Ninety percent binds 90 percent in the blood, and it reaches its redistribution half-life in one and a half to five hours. No active metabolites are produced, and half the dose is eliminated in 3 hours. The sedative dose is .125 to .5 milligrams.

Although both diazepam and triazolam have sedative as well as anxiolytic effects, as one can see, the pharmacokinetics of diazepam make it a good anxiety drug, able to maintain its action over an extended time period. The pharmacokinetics of triazolam suit it to sleep induction, able to run most of its course during a normal night's sleep.

Pharmacological Effects

The benzodiazepines act by binding to a specific receptor site located on the $GABA_A$ macromolecular complex (see Figure 9.10). A key site for the modulation of anxiety, this is where the barbiturate binding site is found as well. Whereas the barbiturates, upon binding, increase the amount of time that the ion channel remains open while GABA is acting, the benzodiazepines augment the GABA-ergic action by increasing the frequency of the channel opening. In both cases, chlorine ions enter through the postsynaptic membrane, making the cell interior more negative and raising the threshold for excitation. This hyperpolarizes and inhibits the neuron, with a net effect of reducing excitability in the central nervous system. The benzodiazepines' action also increases the binding of GABA molecules to the receptor.

It is recognized that the tranquilizing action of anxiolytics correlates with their affinity for the $GABA_A$ receptor. This would suggest that GABA imbalances in the normal functioning of the receptor may be a factor in anxiety disorders. It has also been hypothesized that acquired or inherited dysfunctions in the receptor may serve as a biological basis for anxiety disorders. Such connections remain to be seen.

Benzodiazepine receptors are found everywhere in the nervous system, but only in the central nervous system does their presence seem to be of pharmacological importance. Two subtypes of benzodiazepine binding sites have been identified, both associated with $GABA_A$ synapses (LaGenia, Ward, & Musa, 1994, p. 804). Concentrations of BZ_1 receptors have been found in the cerebellum, and of BZ_2 receptors in the hippocampus and basal ganglia. These subtypes may play a role in distinguishing between pharmacological effects like sedation and anticonvulsant effects. Not much is known about actions at the $GABA_B$ sites, but they do not seem to be activated by benzodiazepines.

It is of note that the number of benzodiazepine receptors appears to correlate negatively to anxiety levels (the more receptors, the less anxiety--and vice versa). For example, the Maudsley reactive rat, which has been bred for fearfulness and shows a very high level of anxiety, has significantly fewer benzodiazepine receptors than other rats. Furthermore, environmental exposure to stress has been observed to cause fluctuations in the number of receptors. The results are somewhat unclear, however, since some studies show increases and others decreases (see up- and down-regulation, page xx). Rats that show little fear have been found to have many benzodiazepine receptors. However, exposing these animals to foot-shocks (stress) reduces the number of benzodiazepine receptors, increasing their anxiety. Changes have also been observed for anticonvulsant effects: Seizures induced in rats have been shown to alter the number of benzodiazepine receptors within minutes, and the animals recover within an hour—a process that takes days under other circumstances (Tallman et al., 1980, p. 252). These studies suggest that small changes in the number of receptors may cause behavioral changes, and vice versa. Exposure to alcohol decreases the number of benzodiazepine receptors, as do the natural processes of aging. Accordingly, one could expect a natural increase of anxiety in the elderly.

All of the benzodiazepines display five chief effects, which vary in degree from agent to agent. These are as follows:

1. Anxiolytic effects (reduction of anxiety)
2. Muscle relaxant effects
3. Hypnotic effects (sleep induction)
4. Anticonvulsant effects
5. Amnesic effects (memory loss)

The profile comprising these five effects has implications for the benzodiazepines' clinical applications and side effects, as we will see in the discussions that follow.

The anxiolytic effects of the benzodiazepines are most likely mediated by circuits in the neocortex, where the concentration of benzodiazepine receptors is highest. Although brainstem concentrations are low, circuits involving GABA there appear to mediate the potentiation of fear and the acoustic startle reflex--the automatic jumping at a sudden loud sound. Also implicated are limbic structures such as the hippocampus and amygdala, which contribute to anxiolytic effects and taming effects (the reduction of aggression and conflict seen in animal studies).

Assisting tranquilization are muscle-relaxing properties, which some benzodiazepines have as a powerful and selective action. These are centrally mediated rather than peripheral, but the sites of action are unknown. Humans develop a tolerance to this effect.

The benzodiazepines have several brainstem actions important to their pharmacology. At moderate dosages they block arousal in the reticular formation and cause sleep, hence their usefulness as sleeping pills. After a few days, subjects develop tolerance to this effect. This has two implications: (1) that the benzodiazepines are more effective as sleeping pills in short-term use, and (2) that when benzodiazepines are used over longer periods of time as tranquilizers, the side effect of drowsiness shortly disappears. Benzodiazepines also block the vomiting center in the medulla.

The brainstem action that gave the benzodiazepines their market edge over the barbiturates, however, is really the lack of an effect--that is, negligible depression of the respiratory center, to the point that these drugs have been called suicide-proof. For example, the tranquilizer diazepam (Valium) does not cause a loss of breath until anesthetic dosages, or unless combined with opiates. In a recent incident, a public official on the eve of a scandal breaking tried to kill himself with an overdose of sleeping pills. Such an attempt is understandable for a member of a generation who saw so many in despair use sleeping pills as a final escape from psychological pain. However, this official's vial was filled with benzodiazepines, not barbiturates. His respiratory center survived the assault, and he had to add a lack of pharmacological savvy to his list of public embarrassments.

Sensitivity to the effects of benzodiazepines may decrease with the use of alcohol, and may increase as aging processes alter metabolic functions in the liver.

Clinical Applications

The benzodiazepines are the drugs of choice for anxiety relief, and as such their powers may be too quickly invoked by otherwise healthy people suffering stress of all kinds, from changing homes or jobs to grieving for the dead. In the past, physicians have prescribed tranquilizers uncritically, without a clear diagnosis based on the nature of a particular disorder. The recommended use is for the relief of pathological anxiety associated with anxiety disorders--that is, of such a degree that it markedly interferes with the occupational, social, or daily activity of the patient. The benzodiazepines are most successful for dealing with anxiety of this sort, except that they do not seem to be effective for phobias. Tolerance to the tranquilizing effects has not been shown.

Because of the benzodiazepines' abuse liability, short-term treatment of no longer than a month is recommended, for instance, in cases where they are prescribed to alleviate panic attacks or to treat transitory states of grief and mourning. This assumes that the physician is able to treat the underlying cause of anxiety with other drugs such as antidepressants or buspirone (see below, this chapter), or can recommend other therapies. If longer-term treatment becomes necessary, patients should be monitored.

No one agent is preferable for the relief of anxiety, since all have the same profile of effects. As we mentioned, the differences between compounds sold as tranquilizers, sleeping pills, and antiseizure medication are mostly a matter of pharamacokinetics. The rest is marketing.

The benzodiazepines make good sleeping pills. They show a rapid onset at bedtime, a sustained action during the night, and, unlike the barbiturates, no residual action in the morning; triazolam (Halcion) is especially notable in these respects. The drugs impart a sense of deep, refreshing sleep with fewer body movements. Also, they increase sleep duration, as much as tripling it in short sleepers. Long sleepers may be little affected. For the most part, they delay and shorten REM sleep, but increase the number of cycles spent there. With some agents, REM sleep may be made up later in the sleep session.

Flurazepam (Dalmane), introduced in the early 1970s, was the first popular benzodiazepine sleeping pill, offering several advantages over the barbiturate sedative-hypnotics. It has less effect on respiration and little to no hangover the morning after use. It involves fewer drug interactions, and its better therapeutic index means that suicide is not a problem. Although its abuse liability is probably lower than the barbiturates', flurazepam sleeping pills are not without risk. Tolerance develops slowly, over weeks, and dependence may occur.

Another widely prescribed sleeping pill is triazolam (Halcion), whose pharmacokinetics are discussed above. Its effects fit the profile of the other benzodiazepines, but its popularity was tempered by reports of adverse side effects. Typically, when sleep medications wear off, there may be a mild rebound anxiety and insomnia felt during the course of the next day. In the case of triazolam, some of these reactions appear to be especially strong and disturbing (Cowley et al., 1991). There were reports of acute anxiety and of bizarre and disorderly acts committed by some users, which they were later unable to recall. And in the most extreme incidents, cases were brought against the manufacturer, attributing violent acts and homicide to the effects of Halcion. A number of the problems were associated with marked misuse of the drug, involving high doses taken long after the recommended period of treatment (effects wane after about two weeks). But in general, the incidence of adverse reactions reported for Halcion was higher than for other agents. Since then, the recommended dosage has been lowered from .5 to .12 milligrams, and Halcion continues to be prescribed as a viable sleeping pill.

Another application of the benzodiazepines is in the treatment and prevention of convulsions. Anticonvulsant effects are most likely mediated through the enhancement of GABA-ergic inhibitions, with key brain sites being the cerebellum and hippocampus. As a rule, these drugs do not alter abnormal discharges in the focus of seizure activity, but suppress the spread of the excitation to other areas. Benzodiazepines are used as a temporary measure to relieve the seizures and anxiety seen as a rebound effect in acute alcohol withdrawal.

Benzodiazepines are used as tranquilizers preparatory to anesthesia, usually with thiopental. In higher doses, they themselves can induce anesthesia. They may be given for minor surgeries or for uncomfortable procedures, when patients need to remain responsive to commands. One side effect that is a blessing in such cases is that patients may not recall most of the procedure afterward.

Side Effects

Many of the barbiturate side effects occur with the benzodiazepines, but to a lesser degree. The most frequently reported is drowsiness. As we have seen, this effect is an advantage in short-term treatment with sleeping pills. It is short-lived, however, and usually fades within a week as tolerance develops.

Another evident side effect that soon disappears due to tolerance is ataxia (motor incoordination), which may be of such a degree as to severely impair driving ability. This effect is probably mediated by pathways responsive to benzodiazepines in the cerebellum, the brain center for balance and motor coordination. Both drowsiness and ataxia are milder than with the barbiturates and meprobamate.

Because some $GABA_A$ sites are significant in memory processing, benzodiazepines cause **anterograde amnesia**, that is, a loss of memory for a period of time following administration of the drug. In animal studies, such memory losses disrupt learning.

Confusional states are seen with benzodiazepine use, sometimes with symptoms resembling paranoid and Korsakoff-like psychosis. They may be accompanied by depression and thoughts of suicide. The elderly are especially susceptible to side effects like these. This may be observed in nursing homes, where a significant percentage of the prescriptions is for anxiolytics and sedative-hypnotics, most of them benzodiazepines. The elderly show an increased response to the drug action at the receptor, with more pronounced central nervous system depression (Hoffman & Warren, 1993, p. 643). And, because of reduced liver function, they are not able to metabolize benzodiazepines and their active metabolites effectively. As a result, unmetabolized portions of the drug dose can accumulate and become toxic. Furthermore, an increased percentage of body fat in many elders results in more storage, lowering peak plasma concentrations and prolonging half-lives. These factors result in more drug being available and at the same time being more effective, increasing the likelihood of toxicity. With chronic use, exacerbations of the cognitive deficits seen in the drugs' profile--of memory, thinking, and learning--may be misperceived in older people as a form of dementia. For all of these reasons, particular care must be taken when prescribing tranquilizers (in fact, all sedative-hypnotics) to this segment of the population.

The benzodiazepines are capable of producing euphoria, intoxication, and dependence. Diazepam (Valium) produces gross CNS intoxication at about 100 mg, several times the therapeutic dose for tranquilization. However, while there is no doubt that benzodiazepines are abused for their rewarding effects, they are seldom abused alone. Usually they are taken in fairly high doses as a secondary drug with alcohol, or as a substitute when alcohol and barbiturates are not to be had. In regular medical application, protracted use poses a threat of dependence. For this reason, prescribing guidelines carefully limit the period of treatment for anxiety or insomnia to 4 to 6 weeks, unless there are extenuating circumstances. It has been noted that, after a normal course of treatment, very few users compulsively seek the drug or increase the dosage if they continue to use it.

Withdrawal has been observed with the benzodiazepines (Ashton, 1995), but severe withdrawal is rare. Because of the long duration of the drug action, withdrawal may not appear until 3 to 6 days after discontinuation. The typical course of acute withdrawal lasts 5 to 28 days, usually with symptoms peaking in about two weeks' time, and then declining. A problem arises in assessing the progress of withdrawal, however. Since benzodiazepines are often prescribed to treat anxiety, it is difficult to distinguish the rebound anxiety of withdrawal from the return of the original anxiety symptoms. Symptoms common to both states include anxiety, panic attacks, agoraphobia, insomnia, depression, excitability, poor concentration, dizziness, weakness, muscle pains, and sweating. Symptoms characteristic only of benzodiazepine withdrawal include perceptual disturbances, depersonalization, hallucinations, distortions of body image, tingling or numbness in the extremities (usually the scalp or face), overly acute senses, muscle twitches, and a ringing in the ears. If withdrawal is rapid, the patient may experience psychotic symptoms, seizures, delirium, and confusion. Even within therapeutic dose ranges, withdrawal effects may be a problem. Alprazolam (Xanax) has proved to be especially troublesome. After 3 to4 weeks of alprazolam use, discontinuation might result in REM rebound effects involving bizarre dreams. As a result, a gradual tapering off of the dosage is recommended. Reports on other sleep-inducers--flurazepam (Dalmane), temazepam (Restoril), and triazolam (Halcion)--show this to be less of a problem.

A few users show paradoxical effects with benzodiazepines. Instead of tranquilization, they may experience heightened restlessness, anxiety, irritability, hypomania, euphoria, and rapid heartbeat. Chlordiazepoxide can induce a stimulated inebriation in which a person becomes talkative, excited, and filled with a sense of wellbeing, but also confused and delirious. In other cases, patients show an increase in hostility and rage, or bizarre, uninhibited behavior. Some have claimed that prolonged use of triazolam (Halcion) sleeping pills has resulted in side effects of undue aggressiveness and acts of violence. With the hypnotics, especially with nitrazepam (Mogadon) and flurazepam (Dalmane) during the first week, vivid, disturbing dreams and nightmares may increase. Some anticonvulsants may increase the frequency of seizures in epileptics.

The interactions of benzodiazepines with alcohol, barbiturates, and other CNS depressants may be lethal. Consequently, while the benzodiazepines are safer than the barbiturates, they still are not to be taken lightly.

GABA$_A$ RECEPTOR AGONISTS AND ANTAGONISTS

An interesting point about the benzodiazepine receptor is that three types of actions have been shown to occur there. These are produced by: (1) agonists, (2) inverse agonists, and (3) antagonists.

Benzodiazepine Agonists

It should be said that the benzodiazepines cannot strictly be considered agonists of the GABA$_A$ receptor, because they do not attach directly to the neurotransmitter binding site, as drugs do at other synapses. Instead, they modify the action of GABA by attaching to associated sites.

A fairly new and notable GABA$_A$ agonist is zolpidem (Ambien), a compound of the imidazopyridine class, which is unrelated to the benzodiazepines. Zolpidem is marketed as a sleeping pill to be used in the short-term treatment of insomnia. It has many factors to recommend it. It binds specifically to BZ$_1$receptors and hence is more specific in its action than the benzodiazepines. This specificity may explain the absence of anticonvulsant and muscle-relaxant effects. Given orally in 5 and 10 mg doses, zolpidem is absorbed rapidly, reaching peak plasma levels in one hour. It has a short elimination half-life of two and a half hours and yields primarily inactive metabolites that are excreted in the urine. Both of these factors help to prevent the accumulation of drug with nightly use. Because zolpidem is able to clear from the system in relatively short order, residual next-day effects are minimized, though they may be present enough to compromise performance. Zolpidem also preserves the sleep stages, especially stages 3 and 4, the deep sleep phases.

The most commonly reported side effects for zolpidem are drowsiness, dizziness, headache, nausea, ataxia, and confusion. Like other sedative-hypnotics, it may exacerbate the symptoms of depression, especially suicidal tendencies. Care, too, should be taken in prescribing to the elderly; low 5 mg doses are recommended.

With extended use, tolerance may develop to the hypnotic effects of zolpidem. Seven to ten days is the recommended span of treatment, with a reevaluation of patients before continuing to two or three weeks, with a month cutoff. Zolpidem can produce euphoria. The abuse liability of a single dose of 40 mg appears analogous to 20 mg of diazepam (Valium), but dependence has not yet been shown. The effects on human reproduction and development are not known.

Benzodiazepine Inverse Agonists

The second type of action noted at the benzodiazepine receptor was a significant discovery for psychopharmacologists. Here, a new type of drug action came to light. Consider: Agonists bind to a receptor and stimulate or partially stimulate it. Antagonists bind to a receptor and block or otherwise impede neurotransmitter action. In this case, researchers found substances that bind to the benzodiazepine receptor and produce an effect *opposite* to that of the agonist. That is, instead of enhancing the action of GABA at its binding site, they impede it and slow it down. As a result, they are capable of producing arousal, promoting anxiety, and inducing seizures. Substances that produce opposite (paradoxical) effects like these were named **inverse agonists**. Beta-carboline (FG 7142), among the better-studied benzodiazepine inverse agonists, has been shown to be capable of producing anxiety states in monkeys and humans (Ninan et al., 1982; Dorrow et al., 1983). Inverse agonists have also produced some of the characteristics of depression, which supports the observation that continuous states of anxiety can evolve into depression. Because benzodiazepines can block certain of these depressive effects, hypothetically they could be used to prevent the formation of depression; however, they could not reverse an existing depression.

Benzodiazepine Antagonists

The first commercially available benzodiazepine antagonist that reliably reverses sedation is flumazenil (Romazicon, Anexate). Showing no significant activity of its own (or mild at most), it binds competitively to the benzodiazepine receptor and is capable of reversing the effects of both agonists and inverse agonists. Clinically, flumazenil is of great value in controlling the unwanted effects of benzodiazepine use. It has been shown to alleviate respiratory depression and bring patients out of the coma resulting from a pure benzodiazepine overdose, but its benefits are doubtful for mixed drug overdoses involving benzodiazepines and alcohol, barbiturates, or antidepressants. Because of flumazenil's short half-life, sedation may reappear in one or two hours, and repeated doses or continuous infusion may be necessary to maintain effects. By the same token, flumazenil can trim the lingering effects of benzodiazepines given as an adjunct to anesthesia, but its short half-life limits its effectiveness in getting patients out of the hospital sooner.

Flumazenil has been shown to produce anxiety in panic patients (Nutt, Glue, & Lawson, in press). One hypothesis is that the receptors of these patients are oversensitive, enough to respond to an antagonist as an inverse agonist. This would presume that flumazenil actually has a slight inverse agonistic effect, which does not show in normal people, and that if one's receptors are acutely sensitized, the inverse agonistic effect is felt.

BUSPIRONE: A NEW ANXIOLYTIC

Buspirone (BuSpar) is a newer, nonbenzodiazepine anxiolytic of interest because its effects are mediated through serotonergic rather than GABA-ergic systems. The role of 5-HT in anxiety at one time came under consideration because it is known that benzodiazepines inhibit the firing of 5-HT neurons in the raphé nucleus, and destruction of raphé neurons was linked to the alleviation of anxiety symptoms. It might be the case that these 5-HT pathways play a part in anxiety "further down the line" from GABA-ergic pathways, so that symptoms can be alleviated by addressing them in the larger GABA-ergic systems or in this particular serotonergic pathway influenced by the GABA-ergic ones. The action of buspirone has rekindled an interest in these sites.

Buspirone is a serotonergic agonist that shows a high affinity for 5-HT_{1A} receptors, found abundantly in parts of the brain involving neurons that project from the midbrain raphé nuclei. These projections are implicated in anxiety, judging from the fact that some substances known to bind selectively with high affinity to these sites can produce anxiety. The mechanism of action is unknown, but since buspirone may take one to two weeks to produce an effect, the mechanism is likely to be indirect and complicated. In addition to its influence on 5-HT synapses, buspirone shows a moderate affinity for D_2 receptors as well.

Buspirone is free of sedative, muscle relaxant, and anticonvulsant effects and produces little alteration in cognitive or psychomotor activity. The elderly are able to metabolize it in due course, without prolonged effects or the risk of accumulation. Side effects, which differ from the benzodiazepines', include nausea, dizziness, headache, and restlessness--a relatively mild lot. Because of its long onset, buspirone is prescribed for longer-term anxiety, most commonly generalized anxiety disorder. It is particularly useful for conditions with accompanying depression, since it can relieve that as well.

long term anxiety

CONCLUSION

The history of anxiolytics and their development is like the movement from a broadsword to a rapier in the fight against anxiety. Early sedatives such as alcohol and the barbiturates cut down the excitability of great numbers of neurons and reduce anxiety along with a range of other functions. The move to glutethimide and meprobamate, with affinities a bit higher for anxiety-producing systems, focused the attack more. But even meprobamate was condemned as a faint, if any, improvement over the barbiturates. So, when the benzodiazepines came along, which were even more selective, the advantages were clear. They had a wide safety margin and produced less tolerance, their action endured longer, and they caused less change in sleep patterns and less physical dependence. Today, new anxiolytics like buspirone (BuSpar), a serotonergic agonist with few of the side effects of the benzodiazepines, offer the hope that anxiety-producing mechanisms might be distinct from those responsible for other effects and might be treated more effectively and selectively.

Chapter 15

Schizophrenia and Its Treatments

When I look for food or look for time, the food that comes into my mouth makes a trail. Sometimes one loses the trail of the words that come out of one's mouth. They stick in a tube. And then I look for a trail, but the trail is broken off. There is a trail on the earth--like the path of the sun in heaven. It is as if somebody had been throwing flowers on the earth. And then I lost my mother, but she did not know it. She thought I was at home, but I was with my grandmother. I lost my brain when I put a fork into my hat. If you dust a couch with a duster, then the sun and the rainbow and everything go out--like a pool that stands still. Later my mind was brought back. Once I was so happy that I flew into space. Like the sun. But the food dies in me, like the sun sets in the evening.

N.N., 32-year-old male schizophrenic
(Roheim, 1955, p. 178)

We still know far less than we would like to about mental illness or about schizophrenia in particular. For all intents and purposes, schizophrenia remains less a disease than a recognized set of symptoms. In other words, the term *schizophrenia* is of the same order as a term like *fever*. Not a disease in itself, *fever* describes an observable symptomatic condition that may result from any number of underlying causes. The term *schizophrenia* is of similar status, except that in its case a variety of signs and behaviors are involved, which may be expressed to different degrees and in different combinations. No single underlying cause has been identified for schizophrenic symptoms. They may turn out to be the expression of several diseases arising from several distinct causes.

The word schizophrenia, which has replaced earlier terms such as *madness, lunacy* and *dementia praecox,* remains like its predecessors an umbrella term referring to sets of behaviors. Eugene Bleuler coined the word in 1911 from Greek *schizein,* meaning "split," and *phrene,* meaning "head" or "mind." There is a persistent popular notion that this "split mind" refers to split personality (*multiple personality disorder*). A typical instance is the following lyric:

Roses are red.
Violets are blue.
I'm schizophrenic,
And so . . . am I.

This and other bits of popular lore are entirely in error. The "split mind" of schizophrenia refers more appropriately to the widening gap between internal and external realities, as the schizophrenic withdraws into a private world of personal fantasies and symbols, like a waking dreamer who can neither escape nor control the course of the dream.

SYMPTOMS OF SCHIZOPHRENIA

Schizophrenia comprises a broad range of symptoms that involve thought and perception, mood, and movement. Beginning with the earliest studies, psychologists have tended to differentiate them into groups. Recent practice favors a division between what are termed positive and negative symptoms (Brekke, 1994; Crow, 1980b; Kay, 1991). Positive symptoms reflect the presence of a behavior or function that is normally not there. These include such manifestations as delusions, hallucinations, disorganized thinking, bizarre behavior, excitement, suspiciousness, and hostility. Negative symptoms reflect a loss of behaviors normally present. These include a loss of the experience of pleasure (*anhedonia*), a blunting of emotional responses (*flattened affect*), diminished speech (*alogia*), an inability to initiate or participate in focused activities (*avolition*), and deficits of movement (reduced speech and body motion, and social withdrawal) (American Psychiatric Association, 1994; Kane, 1999). A distinctive cluster of cognitive symptoms, which overlaps with the preceding two categories, has recently been singled out for separate attention. They involve disjunctions in thought processes, like impairments in responding to and processing various sorts of stimuli, impaired verbal and spatial memory, wild leaps of association in speech, loss of attention, and the inability to engage in abstract thought and problem solving. These symptoms, especially, cause much of the impairment that makes it difficult for sufferers to function in their personal and social lives, as well as at work or school, and they respond poorly to drug treatment.

One interest in dividing the symptoms of schizophrenia like this, as we shall see, is that different sorts of symptoms might represent separate disorders.

Delusions, or baseless beliefs, are a frequent positive symptom of schizophrenia. These often involve scenarios of persecution--that one is being followed, ridiculed, or spied upon. Also common are referential delusions, the idea that generally directed events, texts, or gestures apply specifically to oneself. For example, a delusional patient might have the conviction that the TV news commentator is speaking in coded references specifically about her. Delusions are termed *bizarre* if they are based on scenarios highly unlikely or out of keeping with reality. Some patients feel that their thoughts are broadcast from an external source beyond their control. Others claim to feel thoughts being inserted or removed without their consent. In one case, a patient believed that his internal organs had been surreptitiously removed and replaced by someone else's.

Hallucinations are another positive symptom of schizophrenia. Schizophrenic hallucinations are to a great extent auditory, and "hearing voices" is a frequent psychotic symptom. Such voices are usually abusing, criticizing, addressing, or commanding the subject. Mark Vonnegut (1975, p. 106), describing a schizophrenic breakdown in *The Eden Express*, says of these voices, "In the beginning it seemed mostly nonsense, but as things went along they made more and more sense. Once you hear voices, you realize they've always been there. It's just a matter of being tuned to them." Tactile hallucinations have also been reported: electrical, tingling, or burning sensations. Some have reported a feeling of snakes crawling in their abdomens. One patient complained that every time he said a word, he could literally feel that thing stuck in his mouth. When he said "street," he could feel the hard edges of the buildings on his palate.

One of the common and characteristic negative symptoms of schizophrenia is a blunting or flattening of emotional responses (*flattened affect*). The subject becomes unresponsive, immobile, and apparently indifferent to events. With this might come other negative symptoms such as less speaking, a disinclination or inability to participate in activities, and a loss of the ability to experience pleasure. In a severe form of withdrawal, the patient may sit motionless and incommunicative for days.

It should be apparent that both the positive and negative symptoms of schizophrenia constitute a loss of contact with reality, whether through incongruous associations in the content of speech, through an emotional withdrawal from ongoing events, through disorganized behavior, or through bizarre and unlikely beliefs about the structure of events in the world.

A key marker of schizophrenia is disorganization of thought, of speech, and of behavior. Disorganized thinking, as evidenced in speech, displays a loosening of associations that may range from the merely unorthodox (an erratic shifting of topics) to the incomprehensible, as in this example: "I came to the hospital because I--it's my father. The farther I get the only reason I try." (Also, see the epigraph at the head of the chapter.) Schizophrenic speech may display ambivalences, where positive and negative values exist simultaneously. Harold Searles cites the following example: ". . . [A] hebephrenic woman made to me an eight-word statement in which the first seven words were uttered in a tone of heartfelt adoration and, with no pause whatever, the eighth in a tone of equally profound contempt: `You should have the Congressional Medal of Spit" (Searles, 1965). Disorganized behaviors include childlike silliness, unpredictable agitation (shouting or swearing), loss of grooming and personal hygiene, or inappropriate sexual behavior (public masturbation).

The term psychosis has often been used to describe a loss of contact with reality, in association with both schizophrenia and mood disorders. It has been used ambiguously to refer to symptoms as varied as emotional withdrawal and violent and confused actions. The current move is to apply *psychosis* to more severe losses of contact with reality. Signs associated with psychosis by the DSM-IV are:

1. Delusions and hallucinations (including those recognized as such and those mistaken for reality).
2. Disorganized speech and behavior.
3. Catatonic behavior (which may consist of severe and extended withdrawal or of agitated behavior--see the description of catatonic schizophrenia below).

Schizophrenic patients may be said to have psychotic episodes (or attacks), meaning that from time to time they dissociate from reality, possibly in passivity, in confusion, or in violent agitation. In the vernacular, they "go off" or "lose it." When the literature refers to depression as a psychosis, the connotation might be that the lack of emotional responsiveness to events constitutes a withdrawal from reality.

SUBTYPES OF SCHIZOPHRENIA

According to the DSM-IV, the general criteria for schizophrenia are as follows:

1. Two or more characteristic symptoms showing for the greater part of a month, or more. These are listed as delusions, hallucinations, disorganized speech, grossly disorganized or catatonic behavior, and negative symptoms (flat affect, speechlessness, and lack of volition).
2. A compromise of social or occupational function.
3. Continuous presentation of signs over six months.
4. The ruling out of other disorders (e.g., substance abuse disorders, mood disorders, or a general medical condition).

Based on the tendency of certain symptoms to occur in combination, the DSM-IV delineates several major subtypes of schizophrenia:

Paranoid schizophrenia is marked by delusions of persecution or grandeur, or fierce delusional jealousies, with related hallucinations. Emotional responses in general may be normal, and gross behavioral disorganization is rare, but there may be unfocused anxiety or anger, or doubts about sexual identity. A key characteristic that marks the schizophrenia in this case is the presence of confused and disordered thought processes. There is a separate condition called paranoid disorder in which subjects entertain similar delusions, but with the distinction that they remain lucid and rational. They may lead highly structured lives based on elaborate delusional systems (e.g., the belief that they are being spied on and conspired against by the CIA, the KGB, or extraterrestrials). One patient imagined that it his old high school acquaintances were hunting him. In paranoid disorder, daily functioning may survive unimpaired, and sufferers rarely seek treatment.

Disorganized schizophrenia typically begins with a deterioration of grooming, hygiene, and overall functioning. Sufferers begin to exhibit peculiar behavior, like collecting garbage or talking to themselves, and their speech becomes abnormal in its metaphors and vagueness. Odd ideas and perceptions come on, like the feeling of presences. Social contact and communications break down. Friends may perceive a personality change and describe the person as "not the same." Disorganized schizophrenia is marked by incoherence; by bland, incongruous, or silly emotions; and by grimaces, mannerisms, and other odd behaviors. Patients may laugh and smile without cause and do things like take showers ostentatiously with their clothes on. Extreme social impairment, social withdrawal, and hypochondria may also be present. Delusions and hallucinations are only fragmentary.

FIGURE 15.1 Catatonic patients such as this may remain in fixed positions for many hours at a time.

In catatonic schizophrenia, one of several characteristics usually predominates: the patient may (1) adopt and maintain a rigid posture for hours at a time, (2) willingly assume bizarre postures, (3) go into a stupor, seemingly oblivious to the external world, (4) display a blind resistance to all instructions to be moved, (5) become excited and run amok, or rapidly alternate between excitement and immobility. Patients adopting odd postures may be manipulated as though they were wax statues, a state referred to as waxy flexibility (see Figure 15.1). One can move their semi-stiff limbs into new positions, and they will remain that way for hours or even for the greater part of a day.

A number of disorders closely related to schizophrenia are designated in the DSM-IV. For the most part, these consist of schizophrenic symptoms that do not quite meet the criteria for schizophrenia. Examples include a disorder equivalent to schizophrenia but of shorter duration (*schizophreniform disorder*), a schizophrenia-like disorder featuring prominent mood disturbances (*schizoaffective disorder*), a disorder consisting mostly of non-bizarre delusions (*delusional disorder*), and another involving brief psychotic episodes (*brief psychotic disorder*).

Typically, schizophrenia occurs in roughly 1% of a population, with a somewhat lower percentage affected at any one time (Mueser & McGurk, 2004; Walker et al., 2004). It is found equally in both sexes, but in women the onset is usually later and the course of the illness more benign. The prognosis is worse if the subject is poor, male, or an urban dweller, if onset is early or gradual, if there is a family history of the disease, and if functioning was poor before the diagnosis was made. Onset usually occurs in adolescence or young adulthood, and may come on rapidly or gradually. The first stage is marked by social withdrawal and a decline in performance, the second by the active manifestation of symptoms. These might then subside into a third, residual stage displaying entrenched negative symptoms. Some patients recover completely, while others may cycle between the residual stage and the second, active stage. About 10 percent of those diagnosed commit suicide (Freedman, 2003).

ETIOLOGY OF SCHIZOPHRENIA

> *People suffering from high fevers also sometimes suffer from hallucinations and delirious thinking, but I have yet to hear anyone suggest that understanding the content of such delirium could bring down the fever. (Vonnegut, 1975, p. 210)*

What causes schizophrenia? Numerous hypotheses have been put forth. Psychosocial models ascribe the cause to psychological or social factors in a person's environment. On the other hand, a range of biological and organic causes have been proposed: that schizophrenia may involve the overproduction of a natural opiate (endorphins); that it may be due to a deficiency of the hormone prostaglandin, of the pineal product melatonin, or of zinc; that it may reflect a sensitivity to wheat or consist of some other allergic reaction (Horrobin, 1979). All of these theories rest on a variety of evidence. However, the recognition of a crucial organic dimension to schizophrenia is growing. The strongest current hypothesis suggests that either genetic or environmental factors (like infection by the flu) cause abnormalities in the maturing brain. These lead to vulnerabilities which may be actuated, spontaneously or in response to stress, as the symptoms of schizophrenia (Walker et al., 2004).

Much evidence backs the idea of a predisposition to schizophrenia that is biologically based. For example, a worldwide survey established a 5 in 1000 incidence of schizophrenia in ethnic groups as diverse as Swedes, Inuits (Eskimos), and West African Yoruba tribesmen (Murphy, 1976). This consistency suggests a common factor as the cause.

There is also strong evidence that schizophrenia is genetically linked. Clearly, the risk for developing it increases with genetic similarity; that is, the more genes one shares with a schizophrenic relation (viz., parent, sibling, cousin and so forth), the greater one's chances of being affected. This observation is borne out by studies that examine the concordance rate of traits among twins. The concordance rate is an index that describes the percentage of twins that share a given trait. For instance, if all pairs of twins in a sample population share a trait, the concordance is 100 percent; if half share it, it is 50 percent. The importance of this for schizophrenia should be evident. In 1946, Kallman reported that the concordance rate of schizophrenia in identical twins was 86 percent. While the incidence of schizophrenia in twins is not substantially higher than the general population, Kallman's finding indicated that among identical twins, if one had schizophrenia, there was an 86 percent chance the other twin would also have it. This points to a genetic component to the disorder. But the question is, How do we interpret the meaning of the concordance rate? Is it possible to estimate from it the degree of heritability of a trait such as schizophrenia? The answer is yes.

Identical (monozygotic) twins come from a single divided egg. Thus, they are identical copies of one of a single cell (the zygote, or fertilized egg). In them, the factors of heredity are identical, and any differences between them are a function of environmental conditions. Fraternal (dizygotic) twins, on the other hand, come from two separate eggs developing together in the womb. It can be reasoned that, whereas any differences between identical twins are environmental, differences between fraternal twins ought to proceed from both environment and heredity. It should be evident that the latter is also true of any two sisters or brothers, but dizygotic twins are preferred in scientific studies, in order to preserve as many similarities with the monozygotic group as possible.

Using the information above, we can make the following deduction. The concordance rate shows us the percentage of identical twins that share traits. We, however, are interested in pairs that do not match. These differences can be ascribed only to environmental factors, so that the mismatches in identical twins represent a degree of environmental influence. If 10 percent of the pairs do not match, that is a 10 percent environmental effect.

By the same token, we know that the differences between fraternal pairs result from both genetic and environmental variables. If 30 percent of the pairs do not match, this is due to both types of variables. How much of this difference is attributable to genetics alone? We reason as follows: Since we are able to determine what the environmental effect is on identical twins for a given trait, we can factor out this value from the fraternal rate simply by subtracting it. In our example, we subtract the 10 percent of environmental influence on identical twins from the 30 percent difference in fraternal twins, leaving 20 percent of the variation we can ascribe to genetic influence alone. The formula for this procedure looks like this:

Fraternal twins' (monozygotic) differences:		Environment plus heredity
Identical twins' (dizygotic) differences:	-	Environment
		-----------------------------------
		heredity

Let us apply this method to determine how influential genes are in causing schizophrenia. Consider the following data (Gottesman & Shields, 1976) on the concordance rates for severe and mild schizophrenia:

	MZ Concordance	DZ Concordance
Severe schizophrenia	77%	15%
Mild schizophrenia	27%	10%

To find the influence of heredity in severe schizophrenia, we examine the concordance rate in identical (MZ) twins. In a genetically perfect world, 100 percent of identical twins would share every trait, including this one. However, only 77 percent of the sample matches for schizophrenia. This means that the remaining 23 percent of the twins (100 percent minus 77 percent) differ due to environmental factors. The environmental influence is thus 23 percent.

The fraternal twins (DZ) show a 15 percent concordance, leaving 85 percent who do not share the trait. This 85 percent difference is the result of both heredity and environment. So our subtraction looks like this:

Heredity and environment	85%
Environment	23%
Heredity	62%

For severe schizophrenia, then, hereditary factors can be said to be responsible for 62 percent of the cases. You might notice, since the differences are derived from the concordance rates, that one can arrive more efficiently at this figure simply by subtracting the concordance rates themselves (77 percent minus 15 percent equals 62 percent). So, for mild schizophrenia, the hereditary factor calculated from the data above would be 27 percent minus 10 percent , which is 17 percent.

Some researchers debate the assumption that the contribution of the environment is the same for identical and fraternal twins. This would call deeply into question this mode of comparison. Modern gene studies, however, have helped to bolster the genetic connection (Javitt & Coyle, 2004). Scientists are starting to identify genes that correlate to an increased susceptibility to schizophrenia. Several appear to regulate synaptic transmission, especially at glutamate sites (Harrison, Law, & Eastwood, 2004). Another codes for COMT, one of the enzymes that degrade dopamine, especially in the frontal cortex; this implicates the gene in cognitive dysfunctions. Generally, work in this area is speculative, but promising.

Current thinking (the *diathesis-stress model*) is that a significant genetic contribution predisposes one to schizophrenia. However, the existence of a predisposition does not define exactly how the genetic factor is expressed. For instance, the predisposition could be toward a particular biochemical imbalance, the deficiency of an enzyme, or some other physiological characteristic. In addition, no single gene will be found to be the culprit; multiple genes have already been associated with the disorder. Another critical factor involves developmental processes in the maturing brain, both in the womb and in early adolescence. Spurts in brain development might actuate genetic factors to interfere with the growth of neural connections. This sets up vulnerabilities, which then work in concert with environmental factors like stress to determine whether or not symptoms will manifest. For example, a person might inherit an enzyme irregularity that confounds brain maturation in early adolescence and triggers the onset of symptoms. On the other hand, a non-genetic scenario might involve a fetus' being deprived of oxygen, disrupting the growth of neurons, and creating faulty connections that could lead to schizophrenia when coupled with social stressors in young adulthood. In any case, evidence (Walker et al., 2004) reveals that brain abnormalities are present before schizophrenia is detected.

The level of biochemical involvement is what most interests the psychopharmacologist, since biochemistry can be influenced by drug therapy. The following sections will explain several theories of schizophrenia in which psychopharmacology has played a role.

The Dopamine Hypothesis

The biochemical theory of schizophrenia that prevailed over the last thirty-five years is the dopamine hypothesis. It rests on a single key association: that schizophrenic symptoms can be correlated with an overactivity of, or oversensitivity to DA at certain brain sites, suggesting that DA overactivity causes schizophrenia. The hypothesis was drawn from a number of observations. Two of the key ones are these:

<u>Neuroleptic drugs quell the symptoms of psychosis</u>. Neuroleptic drugs like chlorpromazine (Thorazine) have a dramatic antipsychotic effect. Early research revealed only one consistent biochemical action that correlated with this effect: the drugs block DA receptors. Furthermore, the degree of blocking corresponds to the strength of the clinical effects. It follows that, if neuroleptics block DA and stop psychosis, psychosis might be the result of abnormal DA activity.

<u>Some compounds that raise DA functioning induce psychosis</u>. If DA overactivity causes schizophrenia, it should follow that DA enhancers can cause psychosis, a key schizophrenic symptom. One such substance was found in amphetamine. This stimulant is a DA-promoting compound that can induce positive symptoms of schizophrenia, including a psychosis (*amphetamine psychosis*) that is clinically indistinguishable from that seen in paranoid schizophrenia. Moreover, small amounts of amphetamines given to schizophrenics can worsen their symptoms dramatically. Conversely, amphetamine psychosis can be treated with antipsychotic DA-blockers. The inference, then, is that amphetamines cause psychosis by raising DA activity, and that neuroleptics counter the psychosis by blocking DA.

Another compound capable of producing psychosis through DA enhancement is found in the treatment of Parkinson's disease. Parkinson's is a movement disorder attributed to a deficiency of DA in the basal ganglia; the goal of treatment is to raise DA functioning. The drug L-dopa is given to increase DA in the basal ganglia, but because it distributes broadly in the brain, it raises DA activity at other sites as well, such as the mesolimbic area. When this happens, schizophrenic symptoms appear. The opposite is also the case.

Symptoms of Parkinson's and other side effects related to DA impairment are seen with the use of neuroleptic DA-blockers. These observations further the connection between schizophrenia and elevated DA action.

There is no doubt that dopamine-blocking drugs are effective in reducing the symptoms of schizophrenia, but they are far from ideal, and there is a shadow over the dopamine hypothesis. A number of objections have been raised, including the following:

DA-blocking neuroleptics do not cure schizophrenia. Antipsychotic drugs that block DA do not treat the root causes of schizophrenia. They do not even eliminate all its manifestations but only suppress certain symptoms. While it cannot be denied the effects are useful and benefit a number of patients, the overall response is disappointing. Modern studies note that only 50 percent of patients show an "average good response" to these drugs, which means that the remaining 50 percent show disappointing or poor results (Van Putten, Marder, & Mintz, 1990).

There is no definitive evidence that neuroleptics act directly to block DA. Studies have shown only that applying neuroleptics correlates with a decrease in DA activity. The DA-blocking effect of antipsychotic drugs has been compared to the action of a breaker in an electrical circuit: pulling the breaker switch and killing the power in the whole house does not mean that you have solved the problem at the site of origin (like a short circuit in a toaster). In other words, the stepping down of DA activity might not be a direct effect, but a sequel to other mechanisms. For instance, other transmitters, such as serotonin, can play a role as modulators of dopaminergic systems.

Also telling is the fact that antipsychotic drugs eliminate mania as well as psychosis. Because mania is believed to be mediated more by NE than DA, NE mechanisms may be implicated, directly or indirectly, in the alleviation of psychotic symptoms.

Certain signs of DA overactivity are lacking. A case in point: if DA activity is high in schizophrenics, they should have a high content of DA metabolites at certain sites. Studies of the breakdown products of DA in most subjects with schizophrenics indicate that their DA production and release fall within the wide range of normal values (Freedman 2003; Walker, 2004).

Defenders of the hypothesis put forth rebuttals to both these observations. Schizophrenics may have higher densities of DA receptors at certain key sites, or they could be more sensitive to normal amounts of DA without necessarily metabolizing more. And the results of the postmortem studies might be confounded by the fact that the subjects were typically undergoing treatment with antipsychotic drugs, which reduce DA functioning.

Certain effects one should be able to predict from DA overactivity do not occur. Amphetamine, despite its DA-boosting capability, fails in some cases to produce several of the core symptoms of schizophrenia, such as formal thought disorder and flattened affect, and might even improve the negative symptoms (Svensson, 2000). Moreover, antipsychotics block DA immediately, but the symptoms do not abate for days or weeks.

In rebuttal to this last point, defenders respond that the delay is caused by small doses given cumulatively, which take time to reach an effective level; only an exceptionally high dose would relieve the symptoms rapidly. Haloperidol, an antipsychotic, seems to be able to do that. Furthermore, there are changes in receptor function that may take days or weeks to occur.

The debate over the DA hypothesis leaves us with a clear indication that DA activity plays a significant role in the etiology of schizophrenia. In fact, we know now that all the effective, clinically approved neuroleptics antagonize the D_2 dopamine receptor subtype and that this action alone produces the antipsychotic effect (Svensson, 2000). However, it seems less and less likely, as more research is done, that the solution to this problem lies in dopamine alone.

In response to challenges to the DA hypothesis, several modifications have been proposed.

One suggestion is that the dopaminergic pathways in the brain abound with inputs from other systems, which modulate their activity. Because of this, it could well be expected that DA output in these pathways would vary considerably. DA is simply a key transmitter in a much more complex picture of interdependent systems involving a number of other neurotransmitters. Some of these relationships are coming to light, as we will see below.

A second hypothesis offered to explain the differential response to DA-blocking neuroleptics is that schizophrenia is a heterogeneous disorder--it might arise from a number of causes. Only one of these would involve the elevation of DA at certain brain sites, and patients with this particular imbalance would be those who respond well to conventional treatment. These good responders, in fact, are mostly people with positive symptoms, while the negative symptoms seem stubbornly entrenched and are notoriously difficult to treat. This brings us to our next model.

The Two-Factor Model: Positive and Negative Symptoms

The DA hypothesis is considered a single-factor model of schizophrenia, emphasizing DA hyperactivity as the primary consideration. However, the substantial challenges to the hypothesis point up its inadequacy, as do the limitations of antipsychotic drugs as treatments. Only a limited number of patients who display mostly positive symptoms respond robustly to DA-blocking neuroleptics and manage to function well. Patients with mostly cognitive and negative symptoms that come on gradually respond poorly (Javitt & Coyle, 2004). Because of this, researchers (Strauss, Carpenter, & Bartko, 1974; Crow 1980a, 1980b, 1985) have proposed that the positive and negative symptoms of schizophrenia might reflect malfunctions in separate brain regions, or might be distinct disorders, perhaps arising from unrelated neurological conditions.

Experiments have shown the positive symptoms of schizophrenia (disorganization, delusions, hallucinations) to be associated primarily with the overactivity of D_2 dopamine receptors in the mesolimbic DA tract, which originates in the ventral tegmental area and projects to regions in the limbic system and forebrain. As the argument goes, neuroleptic drugs block dopamine at these sites and so can treat the positive symptoms in a number of patients. However, patients with negative symptoms frequently do not respond to DA blockers. What of them?

To begin to understand this problem, we must consider data from modern brain imaging techniques, which reveal differences between the schizophrenic and the healthy brain. MRI studies show a notable enlargement of the lateral and third ventricles (fluid-filled spaces within the brain) in some schizophrenic patients. These expanded cavities are a sign of reduced brain matter, and accord with findings that the whole brain volumes of people with schizophrenia are smaller than normal. The reduced size of the hippocampus is the most consistently identified feature (Walker et al., 2004). Other areas also show lower tissue densities. In some affected areas, the neurons have disorganized connections and "mis-wirings" in circuits, suggestive of disturbances in their early formation. Such abnormalities have been detected in the hippocampus, the basal ganglia, the thalamus, hypothalamus, and cortex. All of this supports the notion that schizophrenia is a whole brain disorder. However, no one abnormality characterizes all schizophrenic patients nor, for that matter, is unique to the disease.

PET scans reveal another difference in the schizophrenic brain—functional deficiencies in the mesocortical DA neurons that project to the frontal cortex. These scans, which measure the metabolic activity of cells, show that the mesocortical DA neurons are not working as hard as other cells. This deficiency in the prefrontal cortex (the foremost region of the frontal lobe and the brain) is referred to as hypofrontality.

The suggestion has been made that the DA receptors in the frontal lobe may be mostly of the D_1 variety; schizophrenic subjects seem to have fewer of these receptors than normal subjects (Okubo et al., 1997). In any case, this deficit can be corrected with drugs that *enhance* DA functioning. (Note, this creates a dilemma, because it is the opposite of the effect one wants to achieve with antipsychotic drugs, which are typically used to *block* DA overactivity in the mesolimbic area). In further support, damage to the mesocortical circuits in normal people can induce both negative and cognitive symptoms of schizophrenia; however, it must also be noted that damage to other brain areas can also produce these symptoms.

It is strongly suspected, therefore, that hypofrontality may be responsible for negative and cognitive symptoms. The emerging picture is a profile of the schizophrenic brain that involves DA overactivity in the mesolimbic tract and DA deficits in the frontal regions. This points up the inadequacy of an antipsychotic drug that simply blocks dopamine throughout the brain and helps to explain why patients with frontal lobe deficits may fail to respond to conventional therapy. A better treatment might involve raising DA functioning in the mesocortical tract and frontal lobe, while blocking it down in the mesolimbic tract.

Questions remain about what might cause such brain changes in schizophrenics. All of them might be subordinate to a single cause. Some researchers (Barr, Mednick, & Munk-Jorgenson, 1990) have argued that a viral infection contracted in the second trimester of pregnancy (months four to six) can wreak havoc on early neural development in the brain of a fetus, disrupting the formation of connections and setting up the vulnerability to schizophrenia. A comparison of birth records with recorded outbreaks of the flu and the subsequent incidence of schizophrenia shows a striking correlation that supports this hypothesis (Barr, Mednick, & Munk-Jorgenson, 1990). For example, an inordinate number of schizophrenic births occur in the winter, a few months after the fall flu season (Walker et al., 2004). Other possibilities include chemical effects of stress on the mother during pregnancy, damage soon after birth, or head injury before the age of ten.

In summary, the two-factor model is useful for explaining what seems to be the partial validity of the DA hypothesis and the differing responses of symptoms to treatment. According to this model, the positive symptoms are related to DA hyperactivity in some parts of the mesolimbic pathway, and are often relieved by DA antagonists. The negative symptoms may be related to diminished DA activity in some areas of the frontal cortex, as well as changes in brain structure, which could represent a separate form of organic brain disorder, perhaps a chronic and irreversible condition. This would explain why negative symptoms respond poorly to conventional treatment.

As far as the dopamine hypothesis is concerned, two reminders we can carry away from this discussion are (1) that the idea of neurochemical involvement in schizophrenia, including dopamine as a significant player, remains active, and (2) that many patients do benefit from DA-blocking drug treatments, although, disappointingly, the number returning to full social functioning constitutes a minority of the group with prominent positive symptoms (Javitt & Coyle, 2004).

The Dysregulation Hypothesis

A richer and more complex model of the neurochemical basis of schizophrenia has arisen with the discovery of new antipsychotic drugs, most notably clozapine (Clozaril) and risperidone (Risperdal). These drugs have turned out to be especially effective medications, with an impact not only on positive symptoms but also on some negative ones. In addition, they avoid some of the undesirable motor side effects of the first-generation neuroleptics. Like the conventional agents, clozapine and risperidone generally block D_2 receptors. What, then, makes for the difference in their effects and side effects? Apparently, it is an additional action--a strong blocking of 5-HT_2 receptors. It seems that certain serotonergic systems act as modulators of DA systems, and through these modulatory systems, clozapine and risperidone are able to lower DA activity at some sites, while raising it at others, instead of simply and directly blocking it everywhere. This allows them to alleviate the negative symptoms and avoid certain adverse side effects. (We will treat this in somewhat more detail in the next chapter.) The full picture is quite complex and involves a number of other transmitter substances, so that a more intricate model of schizophrenic symptoms begins to emerge.

The dysregulation hypothesis moves away from the idea of DA as the only factor when it comes to the biochemistry of schizophrenia. Instead, it postulates a number of interlaced transmitter effects, with some systems regulating others. The results of influencing parts of these systems can, therefore, become a matter of great subtlety and complexity.

The PCP Model of Schizophrenia

PCP and a related compound, ketamine, were both introduced as anesthetics, but were found to induce hallucinations, along with several other unpleasant side effects. Ever since the late 1950s and early 1960s, researchers have taken an interest in the fact that the psychosis-like effects of PCP can resemble the full spectrum of schizophrenic symptoms (Javitt & Zukin, 1991) and are, in fact, often indistinguishable from acute schizophrenia. Given the discussion above, it should be apparent that any agent capable of producing all three categories of symptoms—positive, negative, and cognitive—is of scientific interest.

The psychosis-like reactions to PCP, observed in both drug treatment clinics and laboratory settings, include agitation, bizarre behavior, paranoia, and severe hallucinatory disturbances. At times, subjects on the drug exhibit a waxy flexibility like that seen in catatonic schizophrenia, or become withdrawn without losing consciousness. When PCP was administered to schizophrenic patients, it led to an exacerbation of disordered thinking, to depersonalization, and to disturbances of body image and mood. Further testing distinguished these effects from those of LSD and amphetamine (Javitt & Zukin, 1991). More recently, ketamine, a drug sometimes misused at the dance parties known as raves, has been shown to cause motor slowing, speech reduction, and a disruption of learning and abstract thinking identical to the negative symptoms and cognitive deficits seen in schizophrenia. Both compounds can induce social withdrawal and exacerbate hallucinations in schizophrenic subjects (Javitt & Coyle, 2004).

At the time of the early PCP observations in the 1960s, the ability of researchers to exploit them was limited by a lack of knowledge of PCP's mechanism of action. We now know that both PCP and ketamine are powerful antagonists of a subtype of glutamate receptors—the NMDA receptor. With this finding, attention shifted to glutamate and an array of intriguing data has emerged.

Experiments have shown that the blockade of glutamate at NMDA receptors by antagonists such as PCP and a compound called MK-801 causes schizophrenic symptoms (Javitt & Coyle, 2004). This seems to be occurring because the NMDA receptors are modulating the release of DA in related circuits. More specifically, circuits using glutamate, an excitatory transmitter, and others using GABA, an inhibitory transmitter, seem to be balanced to regulate the activity in DA pathways, like an accelerator and a brake. And there are more complex possibilities. For instance, if a number of glutamatergic neurons are hooked up to GABA neurons, blocking glutamate (the excitatory circuit) would compromise the GABA-ergic neurons, crippling the inhibitory circuit and letting the DA pathway become overactive enough to produce schizophrenic symptoms (Carlsson, Waters, & Carlsson, 1999). Given their dopaminergic connections, these descriptions are consistent with a dopamine hypothesis.

Schizophrenia is coming to be seen more and more as a brain-wide disorganization of neurons and dysfunction in information processing. It is therefore interesting that all brain cells contain glutamate, the majority of neurons use it, and most neurons have receptors to accept input from glutamatergic neurons (Harrison, Law, & Eastwood, 2003). Moreover, glutamate plays a significant role in neural processing. It amplifies signals, helps the brain to sort information, contributes to mental focus and attention, and is implicated in learning and memory. All of these functions suggest possible links to schizophrenic symptoms, including negative and cognitive ones. Harking back to the idea that schizophrenia might be an outcome of disease early in brain development, we find that glutamate assists in the formation of connections among neurons in the developing brain. Moreover, people with schizophrenia possess glutamatergic deficits. They have diminished activity at glutamatergic receptors in the hippocampus, thalamus, and prefrontal cortex (Walker et al., 2004). Postmortem studies of schizophrenic brains show fewer NMDA receptors and elevated levels of compounds that impair or are toxic to

NMDA receptors. All in all, the data on glutamatergic actions in the brain could be enough to explain all the classes of schizophrenic symptoms.

The story of the dopamine hypothesis is a good example of how pharmacology can drive our understanding of neural physiology. Once a drug like chlorpromazine is discovered to quell the symptoms of schizophrenia, and once it is realized that monoamines, in particular DA, are involved in the mechanism of action, it is logical to suppose that schizophrenia is the result of a DA malfunction and to try to pinpoint the DA brain circuits involved. Hypotheses must stand on the data one has, even if they are sparse. However, since we are aware generally of the astounding complexity of the brain, and as our knowledge of receptor systems and their pharmacology grows, it should come as no surprise that the biochemical models of schizophrenia are also becoming bewilderingly elaborate. In one sense, this is good news, because the more detailed our understanding becomes, and the more articulated our map of patterns of neurotransmission, the better chance we have of intervening more specifically, effectively, and safely with drug treatments.

ANTIPSYCHOTIC DRUGS

The drugs that are used to treat schizophrenia and the psychosis seen in some forms of mood disorders are referred to as *neuroleptics, antipsychotics,* or *major tranquilizers.* The term neuroleptic means "nerve grabber," from the Greek-derived prefix *neuro-* for "nerve" and *lepsis* for "take hold." It was coined to describe the effects of the first generation of antipsychotic drugs and has come to be primarily identified with these compounds. As D_2 receptor antagonists, they are highly effective for relieving the positive symptoms of schizophrenia and for reducing the agitation and psychomotor activity of psychosis and mania, but they pose a substantial risk of serious motor disturbances. We will refer to them as the first-generation neuroleptics.

The term antipsychotic is used more generally, and especially in the United States, as an umbrella term to refer to any of the drugs used to treat schizophrenia and psychosis. Accordingly, the first-generation neuroleptics are also referred to as *typical, conventional,* or *traditional antipsychotics.* The term atypical antipsychotics has come to be more narrowly associated with a newer, second generation of compounds characterized by a strong serotonergic receptor antagonism, and we will adopt this usage. Alternate terms are *novel* or *new antipsychotics.*

The term *major tranquilizer* is a touch misleading and of less use, because it suggests a connection with the ("minor") tranquilizing action of the benzodiazepines, when, in fact, the pharmacology of tranquilization and antipsychosis is very different.

The first generation neuroleptics, whose use prevailed from the 1950s until the end of the 1980s, are of two chemical families. The first, the phenothiazines take chlorpromazine (Thorazine) as their prototype. The second, the butyrophenones, resemble the phenothiazines in their mechanism of action and clinical effects, but differ chemically. They offer some advantages as an alternative treatment. Their prototype is haloperidol (Haldol).

The second family of compounds, the atypical antipsychotics has been gradually gaining in prominence over the first-generation neuroleptics since 1990. For the most part, these drugs are characterized by stronger serotonergic binding (at 5-HT_2 receptors) than dopaminergic binding (at D_2 receptors), which presents some significant advantages. The most prominent new antipsychotics are clozapine (Clozaril) and risperidone (Risperdal).

The History of Antipsychotic Drugs

Before the synthesis of the neuroleptics, from as far back as 2000 BC onward, the treatment of mental patients was an abomination. They were slaughtered, imprisoned, bound, sent into battle in the front ranks, whirled into unconsciousness on stools, dunked in icy water, injected with insulin until their dwindling blood sugar comatized them, electroshocked, lobotomized, and dosed with every conceivable preparation. One writer described the asylums early in the twentieth century:

> *The major problem was violence. It was the violence of beat-up patients, beat-up staff, rooms torn apart, windows broken, toilets stuffed, clothes torn off, excrement thrown around and the all-day dehumanization of everyone. It was a time when knives and forks could not be provided at meals--curtains, wall pictures, and anything but nailed-down furniture were not possible to use. There were the "pack" rooms with their row on row of slabs and tubs for what was euphemistically called "hydrotherapy." There were the seclusion rooms furnished with nothing but a mattress and an out-of-reach light bulb where a creature, nude or in rags, paced like a caged animal, shouting back at his hallucinations. There were the insulin suite, the lobotomy ward--and always the interminable locking and unlocking of every door in the place. (Cohen, 1975)*

Among remedies too numerous to mention that were tried over the centuries, by far the only significant discovery, and a fortuitous one at that, was made in the twentieth century by the French surgeon Henri Laborit.

Laborit was initially concerned with the shock caused by surgery on the human body and the muscle tension that rendered a patient difficult to operate on. He conjectured that inhibiting the autonomic nervous system might alleviate these problems, so he tried a new drug synthesized in 1950, a phenothiazine called promethazine (Phenergan). It turned out to have little autonomic inhibiting effect, but produced noticeable calming. Somewhat encouraged, Laborit urged the development of the drug he envisioned, and Specia Laboratories took up the case, with chemist Paul Charpentier spearheading the effort. In the course of the work, Charpentier spliced one chlorine atom onto the phenothiazine ring of a promazine molecule, yielding a compound low in sedation but high in autonomic blocking effects--chlorpromazine (Thorazine). Charpentier's chlorine atom was to have a phenomenal impact on Western society; it made him the father of the greatest modern revolution involving psychoactive drugs.

Laborit found that the new drug, when given the night before surgery, allayed the fears of patients without causing unconsciousness like a sedative, and it lowered the amount of anesthetic needed for the operation. This quieting of patients, and their indifference to external stimuli, suggested to Laborit that the drug might be useful in a psychiatric setting. But the psychiatrists of France, disenchanted by then with drug treatments, were highly resistant to his exhortations. In January, 1952, Laborit finally prevailed on his own colleagues at Val de Grace hospital to try chlorpromazine on Jacques Lh., 24, a patient in a severe manic episode. Twenty days later, Jacques Lh. walked out of the hospital. After centuries of bogus treatments, this manufactured molecule, chlorpromazine, was the first drug to block specific psychotic symptoms.

In March of 1952, the psychiatrist Jean Delay obtained chlorpromazine and began to test it. Convinced that the drug was not just calming patients, but alleviating psychosis in various disorders, he became the first to report its effects at a major conference, and championed its use (Delay, Deniker, & Harl, 1952). His work sparked the revolution in patient care made possible by chlorpromazine.

In 1954, chlorpromazine (Thorazine) reached the United States, and it appeared a year later on the market. By then, mental health care had begun to undergo profound changes. Before chlorpromazine, schizophrenia often meant permanent hospitalization. The patient population had continued to increase steadily following World War II, but now the duration of stays in hospitals dropped dramatically. Withdrawn patients became active, and wildly hallucinating ones calmed down. The hospitals emptied, and some large facilities actually closed. Moreover, when patients relapsed, it was mostly because they had failed to continue their medication.

Chlorpromazine brought on an explosion in neurotransmitter research, since its actions highlighted the roles of certain transmitters in mental illness. Intense research began on the part of the pharmaceutical companies to develop more efficient compounds and profit from the chlorpromazine breakthrough. The first nonphenothiazine compounds to be developed were the butyrophenones; these are chemically different from, but clinically equivalent to, the phenothiazines. Haloperidol (Haldol) assumed primacy among this later class of neuroleptics and became the prototype.

For thirty years after the invention of chlorpromazine, the dopamine hypothesis and dopamine-blocking drugs informed the treatment of schizophrenia. The initial impact on the schizophrenia wards had been dramatic; however, as time passed, clinicians' satisfaction eroded. The treatments mostly alleviated symptoms; they did not treat, nor help to illuminate, the causes of the disorder. In the 1970s, a few attempts were made to develop alternative drugs, like molindone (Moban) and loxapine (Loxitane). These varied in their molecular structures and showed some promising binding properties. Loxapine, for instance, was a strong DA-blocker like chlorpromazine, but also showed some serotonergic binding that anticipated the generation of drugs to come. On the whole, however, the effects of these drugs resembled the traditional neuroleptics, and none achieved widespread use.

The 1980s brought waves of change. Researchers began to make better assessments of the symptoms of schizophrenia, distinguishing the negative symptoms and recognizing the independence of cognitive symptoms from positive, psychotic ones. Inroads were made in understanding the varying responses of symptoms to drugs and the brain pathways and neurotransmitter systems that might be involved. Playing a key role in these efforts was the invention of new, atypical antipsychotic drugs like clozapine.

Clozapine (Clozaril), the first new antipsychotic, had been synthesized in the late 1950s in an effort to develop a new benzodiazepine. It did not work; it failed to reduce anxiety. However, it did prove to be an effective antipsychotic, more effective in some respects than conventional agents, and low in motor side effects. Unfortunately, when it was put into clinical use in Finland in the 1970s, several patients died from complications after developing agranulocytosis (a condition involving a lowered white blood cell count, which compromises the immune system). For a time, clozapine was restricted and testing stopped, but then researchers discovered that the condition would reverse if the drug was discontinued, which could be done at the first signs of a problem. Because clozapine held so much promise for treating patients whom conventional treatment failed, it was brought back into use. The day of its re-introduction in 1989 marked the beginning of the decline of the first-generation neuroleptics.

The source of clozapine's superior efficacy seemed to be its antagonism of 5-HT_2 receptors. This shifted the research focus to serotonergic involvement in schizophrenia and led to attempts to develop drugs that blocked 5-HT_2 receptors as well as D_2 receptors. The first of these agents, risperidone (Risperdal), arrived on the market in 1994, and was followed over the next ten years by a half dozen similar agents. By 2004, risperidone was the most-prescribed antipsychotic medication.

FIRST GENERATION NEUROLEPTICS

Pharmacokinetics

The gastrointestinal absorption of the first-generation neuroleptics from the oral route is quirky and incomplete, but effective nonetheless. Oral administration is common because it is convenient and serves well enough, considering that many use chlorpromazine for long periods of time. On the intramuscular route (the deltoid muscle is preferred), neuroleptics may be three to four times as potent as on the oral route, and too rapid an injection may pose hazards to blood pressure. The intramuscular route is used mainly when agitated patients have to be rapidly tranquilized, because absorption is fast, and when outpatients are being medicated weekly instead of daily for long-term treatment, since intramuscular injection allows more accuracy in dosage.

Most of an oral dose of neuroleptics, with some exceptions, is absorbed in 30 to 60 minutes. Distribution is rapid, with as much as 90 to 95 percent of a dose binding to tissues. (In addition, neuroleptics may bind in the stomach to antacid and antidiarrhea medications, impeding absorption.) These compounds concentrate in the liver, lungs, adrenal glands, and spleen, with brain tissue levels low compared to other sites. Some of the behavioral effects are observed after several doses, implying a cumulative effect, and psychotic symptoms may not begin to abate for days or weeks, implying more involved changes in transmitter systems. This, recall, was submitted as one of the challenges to the DA hypothesis.

Metabolism occurs in the liver, where neuroleptics induce microsomal enzymes. The metabolism of chlorpromazine is known to be slow and complex, but the exact process is unclear. Over 160 metabolites have been postulated, some of which are clinically active, and these may have their own side effects, such as sedation and low blood pressure, requiring patients to shift to another drug. In addition, some chlorpromazine metabolites have been found in the urine as long as a year after the drug is stopped; even active, unmetabolized chlorpromazine has been found after a year. This suggests a long, tardy drug action. When treatment is discontinued, psychotic symptoms may not return for three months, due to the persistence of active drug molecules and active metabolites.

The kidneys eliminate most neuroleptics, and the bile a small part. As for dosage, there are wide variances, and amounts can range from 8 to over 2,000 milligrams.

Pharmacological Effects

The first generation neuroleptics have been found to block several transmitters: ACh, NE, DA, and 5-HT, as well as the hormone histamine. In this section, we will concern ourselves primarily with the dopaminergic actions related to the neuroleptic effect. We will take up the other transmitter actions as they become pertinent in the discussions on clinical applications or side effects.

Dopamine is prevalent in three brain areas: (1) the mesolimbic pathway (which extends to the nucleus accumbens, the amygdala, the hippocampus, and the frontal cortex), (2) the hypothalamus, and (3) the basal ganglia, which receive inputs from the dopaminergic nigrostriatal pathway (see Figure 9.5). Each of these regions has important implications for neuroleptic effects and side effects. The relief of the positive symptoms of schizophrenia is associated with the blockage of the D_2 receptors in the mesolimbic pathway; D_2 receptors are those that do not involve cAMP and a second messenger system. (The possibility remains open that other transmitters, such as the peptides found in close conjunction with DA at certain synapses, are involved.) Neuroleptic D_2 blockage in the frontal cortex is associated with a slowing of EEG patterns and manifests as sedation in normal subjects. In schizophrenic subjects, this might assist with the disappearance of hallucinations and confused thinking, without undue sedation. However, as we have seen, it usually fails to alleviate the negative symptoms.

Upon administration of a neuroleptic drug, there is an immediate blockage of D_2 receptors and a partial antipsychotic effect. Over the next six to eight weeks, more therapeutic effects manifest, and these correlate with a decreased release of dopamine (Freedman, 2003). Patients become quieted, showing a lack of initiative, less impulsive behavior, and a disinterest in the environment, with no agitation, anxiety, or aggression. They move slowly and become emotionally inexpressive. Early in treatment, they may be drowsy and slow to respond to their surroundings, yet they can be aroused by mild stimuli such as questions, and their insight and intellect remain intact. Agitated patients are aroused, while those who are withdrawn become more responsive. Delay, the first clinical tester of chlorpromazine, drew this portrait of the neuroleptic effect in humans:

> *Sitting or lying, the patient is motionless in his bed, often pale and with eyelids lowered. He remains silent most of the time. If he is questioned, he answers slowly and deliberately in a monotonous, indifferent voice: he expresses himself in a few words and becomes silent. Without exception, the response is fairly appropriate and adaptable, showing that the subject is capable of attention and of thought. But he rarely initiates a question and does not express his anxieties, desires, or preferences. He is usually aware of the improvement induced by the treatment but does not show euphoria. (Delay & Deniker, as cited in Marholin & Phillips, 1976)*

It should be noted that the neuroleptic effect is not especially pleasant for patients, nor is it experienced as a calming or tranquilizing effect in the manner of the benzodiazepines.

Clinical Applications

Phenothiazines counter the symptoms of schizophrenia, and they clearly work better than a placebo. Some patients may respond to one phenothiazine, but not to another, for reasons unknown. The mental disorders commonly treated with neuroleptics are schizophrenia and bipolar disorder (a mood disorder). Hallucinations, delusions, panic, hostility, confusion, withdrawal, emotional tension, and motor agitation--all are alleviated by most of these agents with about equal success. However, deeply ingrained paranoid delusions may resist neuroleptic treatment. In fact, paranoid patients may blame deleterious side effects on feared entities like Martians and the C.I.A., extending their illness to embrace the treatment.

Another use of phenothiazines is the long-term maintenance of patients outside the hospital. Fluphenazine enanthate (Prolixin), a phenothiazine given intravenously, may last two weeks or more, and fluphenazine decanoate (also Prolixin) can be given subcutaneously with an effect that stretches to ten-week intervals, with the added advantage of low interactions with other drugs--an important factor outside the hospital. But they have the disadvantage that patients cease to take the treatment seriously after a while--it seems so insubstantial--and they relapse. Relapses among schizophrenic patients are estimated at 30 percent (Freedman, 2003); most of those among outpatients are caused by a failure to take medication.

The first-generation neuroleptics have increasingly come to be displaced by the newer, atypical antipsychotics. The drug treatment for schizophrenia today involves trying an atypical antipsychotic drug like risperidone or ziprasidone first. At the first signs of a severe side effect, the patient will be switched to a first-generation drug.

In addition to having antipsychotic effects, first-generation neuroleptics make effective antiemetic (antivomiting) medications, because they block DA receptors in the chemoreceptor trigger zone of the medulla in the brain stem. In other words, they inhibit the vomiting center. The phenothiazine prochlorpromazine (Compazine) is often used, but may show side effects, like parkinsonian symptoms; the butyrophenone haloperidol (Haldol) may be given as well.

Phenothiazines have diverse other applications. They can be used for calming patients before an operation, the purpose for which Laborit first intended them. They can be used to delay premature ejaculation in males. They relieve severe itching and stubborn hiccups, and the drug trifluoperazine (Stelazine) is used for *chorea*, a condition involving uncontrollable movements of the limbs. Phenothiazines are also used to treat acute alcoholics, agitated older patients with dementia, and patients with depressive psychosis. Often, neuroleptics are given in combination with other drugs--primarily those used to treat mood disorders, and those used to treat neuroleptic side effects.

Side Effects

Some patients respond to neuroleptics almost as to a cure; about 20% have a complete remission of symptoms (Freedman, 2003). However, most do not return to full normal functioning and must take antipsychotic drugs for many years, perhaps a lifetime. Unfortunately, the first-generation neuroleptics are clumsy drugs with a multiplicity of fairly serious side effects. All of them are preferable to psychosis, but they are much to be feared and guarded against.

In general, first-generation neuroleptics have a wide safety margin between therapeutic and toxic doses, but since individuals respond differently, and since treatment frequently proceeds at large dosages for extended periods of time, some side effects must almost always be tolerated. These are more a function of a patient's susceptibilities than of drug dosages. Because most of the available agents rank about equal in antipsychotic properties, none standing out as superior, the choice of a drug for a given patient hinges on what side effects prove more or less severe for a particular neuroleptic. Finding the right drug for a patient might therefore involve some trial and error.

The most serious side effects arise because the neuroleptics distribute throughout the brain; it is impossible to limit their action only to the dopamine receptors in the mesolimbic pathway. Instead, they penetrate to other brain sites where they also block DA. This intrusion in the basal ganglia causes motor disturbances, and in the hypothalamus, hormonal irregularities.

Motor disturbances are a great concern in neuroleptic therapy. One serious motor side effect is parkinsonism. To be effective, neuroleptics must be given in doses high enough that, as a side effect, they block 70 percent to 85 percent of the D_2 receptors in the striatal area of the basal ganglia (Wolkin et al., 1989), which is a key site of the extrapyramidal motor system. This motor system is compromised by the high level of DA blockage, leading to what are known as extrapyramidal side effects. Parkinsonism, so called because it resembles the symptoms of Parkinson's disease, is prominent among them.

Parkinson's disease is associated with a loss of DA activity in the basal ganglia; in this case, the loss is a result of drug actions. The disease has been described as follows:

> *. . . [it is characterized by rigidity and tremor. The rigidity is essentially the same in all muscles; it is accompanied by poverty of movements. . . . From a standing position, the patient has difficulty in starting to take his initial steps. The subject also has the same problem in arresting the movement. During forward locomotion, short, shuffling steps are taken. The masked face has a fixed expression accompanied by no overt spontaneous emotional response. The tremor with its regular frequency and amplitude occurs while the subject is at rest; it is lost or reduced during a movement. (Noback & Demarest, 1972, p. 186)*

Patients describe the odd sensation of finding it difficult to turn will into movement; it helps, they say, to think, "I will reach that door," rather than "I want to take a step." In early stages, fine motor disturbances may first appear in handwriting, and they may worsen to the point of bodily immobility. Postural instability can be so bad that patients will walk backwards, a symptom that is sometimes mistaken as psychotic. Many readers may recognize Parkinson's disease in the head movements of the elderly: short, rotating movements of the head that seem to be almost voluntary movements from the upper neck. (You could roughly mimic this movement by drawing, in the air, a circle about the size of a dime, using the tip of your nose.) In later stages, patients appear to be rigidifying into statues, a stiff shaking and trembling in the limbs the only movement left to them.

The basal ganglia run on a balance between dopamine and acetylcholine. Most neuroleptics block both transmitters, but tend to block dopamine more. It is really the supremacy of ACh that causes the extrapyramidal symptoms of parkinsonism. To correct for the symptoms then, additional anticholinergic (muscarinic) agents are given to block the ACh activity down to where it will again balance with the low dopamine activity. Phenothiazines like thioridazine (Mellaril), which block both transmitters equally, tend to have fewer motor side effects.

A second extrapyramidal motor disturbance seen with neuroleptic drug use is akathisia. Unlike the locked and frozen hold of parkinsonism, this is a compulsive restlessness, a desire to move. The term comes from Greek for "not" (*a-*) "sitting down (*kathisia*)." The earliest case on record is a chamberlain in the court of Napoleon III, who breached the rules of etiquette continually because he couldn't stay still. Patients describe a jittery feeling in the abdomen and abnormal muscle sensations that movement relieves. Seated, they may shift legs, tap their feet, fidget, rock forward and back, and finally get up to move around, unable to sit through a meal or movie. Standing, they may march in place. "It feels as if ants were running up and down my bones," one patient remarked (Ekbom, 1960). These symptoms, sometimes mistaken for anxiety, may seem worse to the patients than the original psychotic ones and can inspire resistance against medication; even suicides due to this effect have been reported (Rotrosen & Adler, 1995). Akathisia, too, is an extrapyramidal condition and responds to antiparkinson medications. It is more likely in younger patients, and parkinsonism in older.

A third form of extrapyramidal side effects is dystonias. These are sudden, jerky movements that can occur in the first four days of treatment, or after dosage increases. They consist of continuous, involuntary writhings caused by massive and sustained muscle contractions. Patients' necks may arch severely backward, and their eyes pull uncontrollably upward. The mouth puckers so the tongue protrudes, and this can interfere with swallowing or breathing. Patients sweat profusely. If dystonias are severe enough, they can affect breathing and be lethal. This condition too is treated with antiparkinson agents.

Another neuroleptic motor effect is akinesia, a condition of reduced movements. Tremors, shuffling steps, and stiffness of posture show. Muscular rigidity may advance to a catatonic waxy flexibility. Patients may become withdrawn in a state that has the appearances of depression. Akinesia is more likely with potent, low anticholinergic drugs and is reversible.

Tardive dyskinesia is a movement disorder that typically appears after years of neuroleptic use but has been known to begin after mere months. Its causes are poorly understood. *Tardive* means "with a delayed onset" or "late-blooming." *Dyskinesias'* are poorly coordinated movements. The beginnings of tardive dyskinesia are insidious; usually the first sign is slight worming motions of the tongue on the floor of the mouth. Other symptoms include fluttering eyelids, a trembling upper lip, lip smacking and puckering, protrusions and dartings of the tongue, holding of the tongue in the cheek, and puffing and blowing the cheeks. The head may arch backward, twisting to the side. Patients may rock, thrust their pelvises forward, twist, worm, and writhe around. They may fling or flail their limbs, rotate their ankles, or make quick, dancing movements of their heads or toes (*chorea*). Dystonias (jerky movements) may also be present. Because of tardive dyskinesia, a group of mental patients on an outing may appear to the casual bystander to be deranged or suffering from some physical complication, rather than from the long-term side effects of their own medication. Upon reduction of the drug, the symptoms show more prominently. Increasing the dosage can block symptoms, but it also establishes the potential of worsening them. The condition can be irreversible.

Tardive dyskinesia generally affects more than 10 percent and as much as 45 percent of some hospitalized populations of psychiatric patients (Woerner et al., 1991).

The prospects for managing it well were slim in the past, but have recently improved. Symptoms can be avoided in the first place with careful dosing that remains at a minimum for the desired effects. Physicians may remove the offending drug and switch to another, perhaps to a newer compound with a low incidence of side effects such as this. One may also medicate the symptoms separately. It has been recognized that tardive dyskinesia is caused in part by cell damage resulting from neuroleptic treatment, which can be favorably treated with antioxidants like vitamin E.

The neuroleptic blockade of DA in the hypothalamus causes a number of autonomic side effects and hormonal imbalances. The one of greatest concern is neuroleptic malignant syndrome. This condition is rare but potentially fatal. Some of the symptoms resemble severe parkinsonism (catatonia and tremors), and instabilities of autonomic function can cause pulse rates, blood pressure, and temperature to go haywire. The body may heat and cool itself at inappropriate times, and temperatures can surpass 104 degrees, resulting in brain death. DA agonists may be given to help reverse the DA blockade.

Other hypothalamic effects include weight gain, which may follow from a stimulation of the appetite centers, and constipation. Furthermore, sexual disruptions may occur due to hormonal changes, especially with thioridazine. Erection and ejaculation in males and ovulation in females may be blocked, and menstrual irregularities may occur. Females may give fluid (*colostrum*) or milk from their nipples, and even the breasts of males may enlarge, the result of prolactin released from the pituitary by order of the hypothalamus.

As a result of all of these undesirable DA effects, one is put in the awkward position of having to weigh alternatives. If DA-blockers are given to treat psychosis, they can lead to parkinsonism. Conversely, if L-dopa is given to raise brain DA activity in the treatment of Parkinson's disease, it can lead to schizophrenia-like reactions. There is no easy choice of a specific drug treatment; all options involve a calculated decision based on how much the relief of one warrants a risk of the other.

First-generation neuroleptics block acetylcholine as well as dopamine; consequently, they are capable of producing the anticholinergic syndrome, which includes dry mouth, dilated pupils, blurred vision, and constipation. Dry mouth may be prolonged, causing pain for patients with dentures. It is also believed to be responsible for water intoxication; in this condition, patients may confuse dry mouth with thirst and drink constantly from hospital water fountains. This can lead to a state of irritability, lethargy, confusion, and, if it proceeds far enough, to seizures, coma, and death. Some drugs, like trifluoperazine (Stelazine), are advantageous for their low anticholinergic effects. As we saw, drugs that strongly block DA in the basal ganglia but do not block ACh enough can cause parkinsonism. However, if antiparkinson agents are given to further reduce ACh at these sites, they can add to the overall anticholinergic side effects of neuroleptics.

Another transmitter blocked by neuroleptics is norepinephrine. Blockage in this case causes antiadrenergic effects. Blood vessels can dilate, and blood pressure can drop. The effects of lowered blood pressure (*hypotension*) may be felt more when the individual rises from sitting or lying down. Some people experience this normally, on occasion, as a tingling of the head and obscuring of the vision when they stand up suddenly. The condition is called orthostatic hypotension.

Another serious neuroleptic side effect is agranulocytosis (a lowering of the white blood cell count), which in turn means a lowered resistance to infection. This condition is rare, but can often lead to death. Other damage to blood cells is also possible early in treatment. Chlorpromazine and promazine show a high probability of producing a temporary jaundice, a sign of possible liver dysfunction (or allergy), usually in the second to fourth week of treatment.

An unusual side effect produced mostly by phenothiazines is a sensitivity to sunlight. Upon brief exposure to the sun, phenothiazines stored in the skin, chlorpromazine in particular, cause pigment alterations that result in grayish-purple blotches. This can be treated with sun screens and lotions, but in the eyes the problem is more serious. When the eye of someone on high doses of chlorpromazine is exposed to sunlight, pigment deposits can appear as white, gray, and brown opacities in parts of the cornea, causing an overall brown discoloration of vision, night blindness, and permanent visual impairment.

One advantage offered by first-generation neuroleptics is that they produce no euphoria, and therefore no psychological dependence. Likewise, physical dependence and abuse seem not to develop. Withdrawal is unlikely because of the neuroleptics' year-long excretion rates, and their low tolerance is fortunate and ideal, allowing use to continue over extended periods.

The effects of neuroleptics at toxic doses vary, but generally they are exaggerations of the effects noted above: low blood pressure, temperature irregularities, seizures, extrapyramidal and anticholinergic signs, and sleepiness. Generally, the safety margin is wide. Suicide on neuroleptics is difficult and rare, since massive doses cause no respiratory depression.

Neuroleptic effects may be compromised by interactions with substances that induce cytochrome P-450 in the liver, among them barbiturates, and the sedatives phenytoin and carbamazepine, both of which are sometimes prescribed for mania.

As can be imagined, facing side effects so severe and possibly numerous, many unhospitalized patients discontinue their medication and relapse. It is regrettable that these compounds, so well adapted to treat psychosis, should carry such grave qualifications. When they are the only agents available, the only solution is to use them judiciously and to monitor patients closely. Hope, however, lies in the development of the atypical antipsychotics and other drugs that do not have such a strong D_2 blocking action.

BUTYROPHENONES

Because they structurally resemble the analgesic meperidine (Demerol), the butyrophenones were synthesized by Eisleb in 1938 as potential painkillers. In the wake of the excitement over chlorpromazine and the search for even better antipsychotics, Janssen discovered the neuroleptic properties of haloperidol (Haldol) in Belgium in 1958. The same year, it was introduced into therapy in Europe, but it did not arrive on the United States until 1967. There are currently about seven butyrophenones on the U. S. market, at least four of which are indicated for the treatment of schizophrenia. Haloperidol (Haldol) was the traditional alternative to the phenothiazines. Droperidol (Inapsine) is an antiemetic (anti-vomiting agent), but is also used for rapid calming in acute psychosis, to subdue agitated patients.

The butyrophenones are rapidly absorbed through the gastrointestinal tract, reaching peak blood levels in 2 to 6 hours; these levels remain high for about 3 days, then show a slow decline. Metabolism and excretion proceed even more slowly than with the phenothiazines. Full excretion takes several days after withdrawal of the drug; however, even after a small dose, traces may be found in the system for weeks afterward. More potent than the phenothiazines, butyrophenones are usually given in 6 mg to 20 mg doses orally, or in extreme cases, doses up to 100 mg. Two mg to 25 mg is the IM dose.

Although the butyrophenones differ structurally from the phenothiazines, their clinical effects are similar, probably because they share the same mechanism, blocking dopamine and norepinephrine receptors. In humans, they produce some sedation, an indifference to stimuli, and a decrease of initiative and activity, as well as a decrease of anxiety. Were it not for the phenothiazines, the butyrophenones would be the drugs of choice for treating psychosis. Generally, they make an effective alternative, but they are not the marked improvement that was hoped for.

Primarily used in the treatment of schizophrenia, the butyrophenones have other applications as well. They seem to be useful specifically for depressions involving psychosis. Furthermore, in psychiatric emergencies caused by agitated patients, or in cases of surgical delirium, droperidol is used for rapid calming. This low-toxicity compound is given only intravenously or intramuscularly, with IM absorption almost as rapid as IV, quelling excitement in minutes.

The butyrophenones are also useful for Gilles de la Tourette's syndrome. This is a disorder involving patients in sudden involuntary movements, mimicry, expostulations, and obscenities; noises like yelps, grunts, and barks; and other motor and verbal tics. Haloperidol treats about 90 percent of those affected.

Lastly, butyrophenones are potent drugs that inhibit vomiting (for other than motion sickness, as during morning sickness in pregnancy and after surgery).

The severity of certain side effects is the main reason that the butyrophenones cannot compete with the phenothiazines. On the whole, serious side effects are rare at therapeutic dosages, although they may appear in the elderly. The perilous toxicities of the phenothiazines--jaundice and blood abnormalities--are absent, and orthostatic hypotension is less, but the extrapyramidal involuntary movements are more pronounced. This is due to the butyrophenones' low blockage of acetylcholine, which causes a high acetylcholine-to-dopamine ratio in the basal ganglia, and, hence, serious extrapyramidal manifestations. The butyrophenones show some sedative side effects, but fewer than the phenothiazines. Other effects include insomnia, depression, delirium, and confusion. As with other neuroleptics, abuse potential is low, and overdosing does not lead to respiratory depression.

ATYPICAL ANTIPSYCHOTIC DRUGS

Between 30 percent and 50 percent of psychiatric patients respond poorly to first- generation neuroleptics, due either to adverse side effects, inadequate therapeutic response, or poor compliance. Thirty to sixty percent on first-generation drugs develop extrapyramidal symptoms (Ereshefsky, 1995, p. 285). Moreover, the best expectation is a partial response, since negative symptoms are not affected. This situation is far from ideal. It is fortunate, therefore, that newer drugs present some improvements.

Although they differ in their pharmacokinetics (like varying half-lives), almost all of the atypical antipsychotics share a characteristic profile of therapeutic and side effects. It includes the following elements:

- Like the first-generation neuroleptics—in fact, like all antipsychotic drugs—they block D_2 receptors in the mesolimbic pathway, which alleviates the positive symptoms of schizophrenia. However, they bond at these sites at a lower rate and more weakly than the first-generation neuroleptics, and are rapidly released.
- They show a stronger affinity for 5-HT_2 sites than D_2 sites. This additional action characterizes almost all of these compounds. Given that the schizophrenic brain shows an overactivity of DA at some sites (like the mesolimbic pathway) and an underactivity at others (like the frontal cortex), it has been hypothesized that a modulatory action by serotonergic systems might lead to corrective effects in both pathways, allowing some control over both positive and negative symptoms.
- Atypical antipsychotics are low in the incidence of extrapyramidal motor side effects (like tardive dyskinesia) and parkinsonism, a great relief to patients. Two hypotheses are offered for this, one attributing the effect to weaker D_2 binding, one attributing it to 5-HT_2 modulation (Walker, Kestler, Bollini, & Hochman, 2004).
- Most of them have a less disruptive influence on cognitive symptoms, such as those involving memory and clarity of thinking.
- They are able in some cases to alleviate the negative symptoms of schizophrenia, which traditional neuroleptics cannot do. However, there is still no agreement that the data on this are conclusive (Kane, 1999, p. 1402). There is some evidence that the atypical antipsychotics may improve cognitive symptoms as well (Freedman, 2003).
- Because some of the severe side effects are lessened, patients are more likely to stay on drug treatment and are less likely to relapse.
- Their use often results in the side effect of weight gain. This is of concern, since weight gain is these cases, after several years of treatment, seems to be associated with an increase in diabetes, high blood pressure, and hyperlipidemia (excess fat in the blood, which can in turn lead to diabetes) (Baldessarini & Tarazi, 2001).

A number of atypical antipsychotics have appeared on the market since the debut of clozapine in 1989. Some of the more successful agents have included: risperidone (Risperdal), quetiapine (Seroquel), olanzapine (Zyprexa), ziprasidone (Geodon), and amisulpride (Solian); the newest arrival is aripiprazole (Abilify).

Clozapine (Clozaril)

Clozapine was the first atypical antipsychotic drug to be introduced. It was of great interest because it not only relieved the positive symptoms of schizophrenia, but had a beneficial influence on some of the negative symptoms as well. Perhaps its chief asset, however, is the reduction of serious neurological side effects like tardive dyskinesia, which had plagued users of the first-generation drugs. In this respect, it promised a new era in treatment. Moreover, it showed some success with patients who failed to respond to the conventional neuroleptics. Finally, possibly because it presents fewer dreaded side effects and more benefits, clozapine decreases the rates of relapse (often from patients discontinuing their medication) and suicide.

As we have seen, however, early trials revealed a serious threat in the form of agranulocytosis in the first year of treatment. Current estimates place the degree of risk lower than was first thought—at 0.4 percent. The condition reverses if clozapine is discontinued when the first signs appear (Kane, 1999), but proper management of the drug requires frequent monitoring. Consequently, the use of clozapine is limited to patients who respond badly or not at all to phenothiazines and butyrophenones.

Clozapine is administered orally in daily doses amounting to 200-400 mg, with low initial doses to avoid sedation and low blood pressure. After a 200 mg dose, peak blood levels are reached in about 2.5 hours. It is metabolized by the enzyme CYP3A4 into two major inactive metabolites, which are excreted through the urine and feces. The elimination half-life varies; it averages about 12 hours but may take as long as 30. The onset of its therapeutic action may not occur for weeks or months.

Clozapine shows a conventional neuroleptic effect, blocking D_2 receptors, which is associated with the alleviation of positive symptoms receptors, but it has a stronger blocking effect on 5-HT_2 receptors in the frontal cortex and the striatal system. It proves superior to first-generation neuroleptics in relieving a number of both positive and negative symptoms of schizophrenia. Clozapine also acts at D_4, adrenergic, muscarinic ACh, and histamine receptors.

At effective dosages, clozapine produces few, if any, extrapyramidal motor disturbances (except for some akathesia-like effects in some patients); it shows no tardive dyskinesia and no release of the hormone prolactin. Aside from agranulocytosis, the greatest concern over the side effects is weight gain, which is experienced by a majority of users. Probably because of clozapine's antihistamine effect, sedation is not uncommon. It has been observed that patients on this drug smoke less--nicotine and clozapine both promote the action of acetylcholine.

Risperidone (Risperdal)

When the action of clozapine was first discovered, efforts began to develop antipsychotics with a similar atypical profile—weak binding at D_2 receptors and stronger action at 5-HT_2 receptors. Risperidone (Risperdal) was the second such drug to reach the United States market, in 1994, the first new compound in twenty years to be recommended as a first-line treatment for schizophrenia--that is, not as an adjunct or alternative to other drugs. In 2004, it was the most prescribed drug for schizophrenia (*New York Times*, 2004).

Risperidone is well-absorbed orally and binds heavily with plasma proteins (90 percent). The average effective dose range is 4 to 8 mg daily. It is preferentially metabolized (that is, it will be chosen first over other substances) by the liver enzyme CYP2D6 to a major active metabolite as potent as risperidone, so that both contribute to the clinical effect. Risperidone reaches peak plasma levels in one hour, its metabolite in 3 hours. The average half-life of both is 22 hours.

Unlike clozapine, risperidone is a very strong binder at D_2 receptors. This makes it effective for relieving positive symptoms of schizophrenia, but also means it can induce extrapyramidal motor disturbances like the phenothiazines. However, these tend to be minimal when the drug is used at low dosages. Risperidone also has a strong affinity for 5-HT_2 and histamine receptors.

The use of risperidone leads to some weight gain, but not as much as clozapine, and preliminary evidence suggests the need for some concern over diabetes. The most frequent side effects of risperidone are sedation (from its anti-histamine action), agitation, anxiety, insomnia, headache, nausea, orthostatic hypotension, rapid heartbeat, and an increase in prolactin levels.

Overall, at proper dose ranges, risperidone is more effective than conventional agents against both positive and negative symptoms of schizophrenia, shows a quick onset of effects, and is safer than clozapine—all factors that recommend it as a first-line treatment for schizophrenia superior to the typical neuroleptics and clozapine. In addition, clinicians have begun to use it to treat depression.

Other Atypical Antipsychotics

A number of other atypical antipsychotics have been introduced in the wake of risperidone. Quetiapine (Seroquel), marketed in 1999, presents a profile that should be familiar by now. It binds more strongly to 5-HT_2 than to D_2 receptors and shows few extrapyramidal side effects. It is a good oral drug, readily absorbed. Like risperidone, it produces less weight gain than some of the atypical antipsychotics, but it may worsen chances of an onset of diabetes and cause high blood pressure and hyperlipidemia. There is also developing concern about adverse effects on the eyes.

Olanzapine (Zyprexa), introduced in 1996, is structurally similar to quetiapine, with similar therapeutic and behavioral effects. It, too, is well absorbed on the oral route. Extrapyramidal side effects are rare, but prominent weight gain is cause for concerns about diabetes and high blood pressure.

Ziprasidone (Geodon) is among the best of these agents for avoiding weight gain. Its antagonism of 5-HT_2 and 5-HT_{1A} receptors, similar to the action of buspirone, holds some promise for antianxiety and antidepressant actions in addition to antipsychotic effects.

Aripiprazole (Abilify) is a new compound that acts as a partial agonist at dopamine receptors; possibly, this allows it to moderate DA function in overactive systems, while augmenting it in underactive circuits like the frontal cortex. It also offers less weight gain at recommended dosages.

Amisulpride (Solian) challenges the definition of an atypical antipsychotic in its lack of binding to 5-HT_2 receptors and its high affinity for D_3 receptors in the limbic system. It also presents less weight gain and the promise of applications for treating depression.

Sertindole (Serdolect), developed in 1996, was withdrawn from the market for possible negative cardiovascular effects.

CONCLUSION

The development of newer, safer antipsychotic agents is changing treatment strategies for schizophrenia. Current thinking focuses on four areas, all of which are in early developmental stages:

1. Choosing the right drug. We do not yet have the data to predict the responses that would help a clinician prescribe one drug over another, so that, clearly, work is needed in this area. Eventually, it might be possible to recognize a genetic profile that predicts the toxicity of drugs in certain patients and to tailor medications accordingly.
2. Beginning treatment earlier. Since atypical antipsychotics have lightened concern regarding the long duration of antipsychotic drug treatment and the damage of extrapyramidal side effects, the possibility arises to begin pharmacotherapy at the early signs of onset, in adolescence and young adulthood.
3. Combining agents. Clinicians are beginning to recognize that, since the treatment of schizophrenia is predominantly symptomatic and designed to eliminate discomfort, patients may benefit from using several compounds to relieve a number of the symptoms.
4. Improving drug performance. In addition to matching drugs to patients and combining agents, new work is being done on determining optimal doses; some point out that insufficient attention had been given to this in the era of the neuroleptics.

Although antipsychotic drugs have been our focus in this chapter, it should be said that they are not yet the answer to schizophrenia and are often not the sole mode of treatment. They invariably play a role and are a great aid, but on the whole, it has been found that the best treatment is a combination of drug therapy, psychotherapy, and a supportive social environment. Real improvements occur in environments that shape healthy behaviors which can endure without support from drugs.

One of the disadvantages presented by the antipsychotics is that, while they do not effect a cure, they make patients docile. In hospital settings, it is not uncommon for more patients to be given drugs than actually benefit from them, because the drugs makes the patients manageable. In other cases, the prescribing of these drugs might be too hasty and routinized to be well-considered. Paranoid symptoms, for instance, might abate anyway due to the security of the hospital or to changes of wards.

In addition, patients with schizophrenia may be turned onto the street simply because their symptoms are not a threat or problem to anyone. Yet only 20 to 30 percent of patients diagnosed with schizophrenia can be expected to live and work independently (Walker et al., 2004). The ethical issue this observation raises is valuable for reminding us that we still cannot treat the root cause of schizophrenia, and that drug treatments used solely to produce the clinical effect of manageability, while they are certainly an improvement over the violent wards of the fifties, are not an end to responsibility.

Chapter 16

Mood Disorders and Their Treatments

Here, where men sit and hear each other groan:
Where palsy shakes a few, sad, last gray hairs,
Where youth grows pale, and spectre thin, and dies:
Where but to think is to be full of sorrow
And leaden eyed despairs.

John Keats, *Ode to a Nightingale*

A mood disorder is an illness that has a disturbance in mood as its primary feature. Mood, or affect, can be thought of as a prolonged emotion that colors the whole psychic life, with elation as the peak and depression as the pit.

GENERAL SYMPTOMS OF MOOD DISORDERS

The mood disorders are characterized by two major features: depression and mania. Their occurrence is often episodic. A person might experience an episode of depression or mania, after which the symptoms go into remission, but then recur at a later time. States of depression alone, or states of depression and mania, may come and go in rhythmic cycles, interspersed with periods of normalcy.

A **major depressive episode** is characterized by many symptoms. As the episode develops, there may be a painful inability to experience pleasure and a consequent loss of interest in customary activities. Sadness and indifference grow, while the sex drive shrinks. The subject may develop delusions of worthlessness, guilt, and self reproach. Sleep disturbances, such as getting too much or too little sleep, are common. So are fatigue and a decreased energy level. The patient has no stomach for even the smallest task and may speak, if at all, only to answer questions, after silences of several minutes, in low, slow, monotonic, one syllable words, consistent with slowed up thought processes. Appetite changes lead to weight losses or gains. Motor behavior may be markedly slowed (psychomotor retardation); those affected may be seen sitting on the side of the bed in the morning, taking hours to rise and dress. They cannot concentrate; they complain, and become brooding and tearful, plagued by thoughts of suicide. In other cases, there may be fear of death, and anxiety attacks. Nihilistic delusions and hallucinations may appear, as well as periods of agitation, during which patients cannot sit still; they pace, pull, or rub things, and wring their hands.

When considering depression, readers should keep in mind that sorrow is a natural part of a human's emotional terrain. Depression can be part of a normal reaction to a major life stressor, such as the death of a spouse or friend. According to the DSM-IV, in order to be diagnosed as having a major depressive episode, one must meet the following criteria:

1. For nearly every day of a two-week period, one must show a depressed mood or a loss of interest in pleasure, plus four of the other characteristic symptoms: significant weight change, sleep abnormalities, motor agitation or retardation, loss of energy, feelings of guilt or worthlessness, loss of concentration, or recurrent thoughts of suicide or death.
2. One must show significant distress, or impairment of social or occupational function.
3. Mania does not appear.
4. Other conditions are ruled out, including medical conditions, substance abuse, and the normal process of grieving (bereavement).

In the majority of cases, if a major depressive episode goes untreated, it will persist about six months, and then go into complete remission. The most serious health threat of such an episode is suicide. While depression reigns, motivation is at such a low ebb it deters patients from injuring themselves. Most suicides occur during early recovery, when rising energy levels and clearer concentration restore the power to act.

There are significant gender differences in the occurrence of depressive episodes, which are twice as frequent in women as in men (American Psychiatric Association, 1994, p. 325).

Mania is the counterpart of depression. Mild mania (*hypomania*) resembles normal high spirits, but full mania is clearly a disorder. Occurences, which may last from days to months, usually come suddenly and escalate over a few days. In a manic episode, people display an expansive, elated, irrepressible mood, cheerful and infectious, with an unceasing and undiscriminating enthusiasm; if crossed, however, they may show just as energetic an irritability. Speech may be loud and rapid, proceeding in an uninterruptable stream with wild flights of ideas and incoherent shifts of topic, and interspersed with jokes, theatrics, and bursts of song, or, in a negative phase, with complaints and hostile tirades. Manics show an inflated sense of self esteem, perhaps with delusions about having a special relationship with some celebrity, or with God. The environment constantly distracts them; they engage in intense activity of all sorts: exercise, hypersexuality, and grandiose scheming. They may plan to initiate many activities or projects simultaneously, regardless of the risks involved (e.g., in business ventures or investments). Eager to act, they may ignore the ethical concerns of their profession. Frenetically sociable, they commonly call friends at all hours of the night with no sense of imposition; they renew old acquaintances and give money to strangers. They may smash furniture out of sheer energy, go on buying sprees, make foolish investments, and drive recklessly. Days of no sleep may pass, yet they are fraught with energy until they have exhausted themselves and everyone around them.

The criteria for a manic episode are as follows:

1. One has an abnormally elevated or irritable mood for at least a week, plus three of the other characteristic symptoms: inflated self-esteem, a decreased need for sleep, talkativeness, flights of ideas, increased involvement in activities or motor agitation. If irritability is present, four other symptoms must also appear.
2. The symptoms are not closely mixed with a depressive phase.
3. One shows social or occupational impairment, requires hospitalization, or shows psychosis.
4. Other causes and conditions are ruled out (medical conditions, substance abuse, etc.).

Manic episodes of lesser severity are referred to as **hypomanic** ("below manic"). *Hypomania* is an expansive or elevated state of shorter duration and with fewer symptoms than full-blown mania. It is defined as uncharacteristic of a person's customary behavior, but not causing severe impairment of functioning. In some cases it may even result in increased productivity.

CLASSIFICATION OF MOOD DISORDERS

The classification of mood disorders simply describes and labels patterns in which manic and depressive symptoms occur. There are primarily two patterns: conditions involving depression alone (called **unipolar** because only one pole, or extreme of mood, is encountered), and conditions in which both manic and depressive symptoms are found, mixed or in alternating phases (**bipolar disorders**).

A **major depressive disorder** is marked primarily by a recurrence of major depressive episodes, without mania. A lesser grade of depression of longer duration (two years), with fewer symptoms and no impairment of functioning, is recognized as **dysthymic disorder.**

Most individuals who have manic episodes will eventually have a major depressive episode. This bipolar pattern is less prevalent than unipolar depression. In one type of bipolar disorder, mania is identified as the salient feature; in the other, depressive episodes are the salient feature, accompanied by hypomania. An extended bipolar mood disorder of less severity and longer duration is recognized as **cyclothymic disorder**.

The DSM-IV discusses other features that may appear with depression. Subjects may show psychotic or catatonic symptoms. (In fact, depression is often a significant feature in cases of schizophrenia.) Some depressive states are seen to arise from a number of identifiable causes, such as medical conditions, substance abuse, seasonal patterns, bereavement (grief over loss of a loved one), and birthing. These may or may not be a factor in the diagnosis.

HISTORY: THE ETIOLOGY AND TREATMENT OF DEPRESSION

Until the mid-1950s, the primary treatment for depression, one used mainly because it was found to work, was **electroconvulsive shock therapy** (ECT), which consisted of shocking the brain with an electrical current. However, ECT was used irresponsibly and developed a justified bad reputation. Frequently, it was set up as a punishment, or it was administered without proper precautions or muscle relaxants, so that patients might suffer burns or wrench muscles in the convulsions induced by the shocks. For some, it still carries the barbaric stigma of the days of lobotomies and insulin comas.

However, it is generally recognized that ECT continues to be an effective treatment for depression, and may serve better than the best antidepressant drug. The current version of the procedure, when administered properly in small, targeted doses, is relatively harmless and inexpensive. It is indicated when antidepressants do not work or are persistently refused, and it is preferred in cases of high suicidal risk, because its effects can be immediate. Drug treatment takes a week to a month to show results, a luxury that cannot be afforded when patients are resolving to do themselves in. The procedure is not without drawbacks, however. Some evidence associates it with possible short-and long-term memory impairments.

In the 1950s, the accidental discovery of drugs that relieve depression seemed to offer a safer and more humane alternative to ECT. Most of our understanding of the action of these drugs, and their development, centers around a hypothesis formulated at that time—the **monoamine hypothesis** (Hirschfeld, 2000). It asserts that depressive states result from a deficiency of one or another of the monoamine transmitters DA, NE, and 5-HT. A corollary of the hypothesis holds that an antidepressant drug relieves depression by restoring or promoting the action of one or more of these transmitters.

The research that led to this idea focused on the monoamines serotonin (5-HT) and norepinephrine. Early evidence of a neurotransmitter related to mood pointed to serotonin. It was known in the mid-1950s that LSD, a hallucinogen then under investigation, blocked 5-HT receptors in the periphery and produced pronounced behavioral changes. Scientists considered that, if LSD also acted on 5-HT receptors in the brain, it might be involved in the regulation of mood (Hirschfeld, 2000).

A further connection was suggested by investigations with reserpine, an extract of the plant *Rauwolfia serpentina,* used to control blood pressure. Reserpine had two important features. It antagonized the 5-HT-blocking effect of LSD (a mechanism of action that would promote 5-HT activity) and produced a sedation resembling depression in lab animals. These actions also pointed to a possible 5-HT connection to mood.

In 1951, a key development for the monoamine hypothesis came by accident. At that time, an antibacterial drug called iproniazid (Marsilid) was being tested to treat tuberculosis. It was found to have little therapeutic effect on the disease, but it produced noticeable improvements of mood. During the iproniazid trials, patients in the tuberculosis wards, typically depressed and despairing, became more active and resistant to fatigue. Even the terminally ill patients waxed cheerful and optimistic, despite the fact that their lungs showed no improvement. Zeller established that iproniazid produced these effects by blocking MAO, the enzyme that degrades the monoamines DA, NE, and 5-HT, and thereby increases levels of these transmitters in the synapse, presumably promoting their activity. Iproniazid became the prototype of the class of antidepressants known as MAO inhibitors, or MAOIs, and strengthened the monoamine connection: low mood, low monoamine functioning; improved monoamine functioning, improved mood.

A second class of antidepressants superior to the MAOIs surfaced soon after. These were the **tricyclic antidepressants** or **TCAs**, so called because of the triple ring in their molecular structure. The earliest of these was imipramine, followed later by amitriptylene. However, the action of the tricyclics puzzled scientists at the time. They did not inhibit MAO, and they showed some sedative rather than stimulant effects.

Julius Axelrod and his co-workers were in a good position to try to explain this.

They were using a new technique of radioactively tagging substances to trace their location and movements in tissues. Using this method with NE in synapses of the sympathetic nervous system, they had discovered the cellular re-uptake mechanism, work which earned Axelrod a Nobel Prize in 1970.

When Axelrod and his colleagues labeled imipramine, they found that the tricyclic antidepressants interfere with the re-uptake mechanism in adrenergic (NE) neurons. When re-uptake is blocked, more transmitter is available to act on post-synaptic receptors. This effect fit nicely with the going theory: while MAOIs increase the amount of transmitter in the synaptic gap by preserving it from degradation by the enzyme MAO, the tricyclics increase it by interfering with its re-uptake. The mechanisms differ, but the results are functionally equivalent. Later studies showed that imipramine produces a similar effect at serotonergic sites.

Following Axelrod's work with imipramine, and as more evidence came in, attention shifted to NE as the primary neurotransmitter implicated in depression, and to the construction of a **catecholamine hypothesis**—that is, one focusing more narrowly on NE and DA. It was found, for instance, that reserpine, which was suspected earlier of causing depression by promoting the action of 5-HT, actually works by depleting NE. It seems to interfere with the neurons' ability to store monoamines in the pre-synaptic terminal. The transmitters leak into the synapse and are metabolized by enzymes, leaving little in storage in the vesicles for release (Hirschfeld, 2000).

Further support for a catecholamine hypothesis came from the fact that administering the NE precursor DOPA (dihydroxyphenylalanine), which increases the amount of NE synthesized by the cell, reverses the depression caused by reserpine, but the SE precursor 5-hydroxytryptophan does not have a similar effect. Moreover, investigation showed that NE synapses seem to be under-functioning in depressed patients. At their NE synapses, the activity of both synthesizing and destructive enzymes was found to be low, their urine contained lower-than-normal levels of the primary metabolite of NE (MHPG), and, as could be expected, high levels appeared in manic patients (Schildkraut, 1965). In addition, the depressed group was found to respond well to drugs that enhanced NE activity. All of these data suggested that moods rise and fall with levels of NE activity.

Further support was evidenced by a procedure known as the dexamethasone suppression test. This test involves a brain system called the hypax (hypothalamus-pituitary-adrenal axis), which regulates a cascade of hormone release in response to stress. The end result of hypax activity is an increased concentration of cortisol in the blood, a substance which is needed for the optimal metabolism of carbohydrates in response to stress and infection. As blood levels rise, cortisol shuts off its own release through a feedback mechanism, a chemical "brake" that relies on NE. Researchers are able to test this shut-off—and NE function—by activating it with a cortisol-like drug called dexamethasone. When given to a normal subject, dexamethasone acts like a cortisol overload and triggers the NE shut-off, dropping normal cortisol levels. However, when it is given to depressed subjects, who are low in NE and have no shut-off to speak of, cortisol levels remain intact. In the clinical setting, this simply means that one can administer dexamethasone, then test a few hours later for cortisol levels. If they haven't changed, it is a sign of an NE deficit (a faulty braking mechanism) and maybe a neurochemical basis for a mood disorder as well.

Although there was strong evidence such as this for the involvement of NE in depression, and evidence as well that seemed to point to NE as the primary culprit rather than 5-HT, it must be said the catecholamine hypothesis was far from perfect, and critics offered compelling objections. Some of these were as follows:

Point: It takes weeks for the therapeutic effects of antidepressants to appear. At first, it was thought that the re-uptake process or modulatory effects on other systems would match the time span of the therapeutic effects. But findings showed that catecholamine re-uptake is blocked within an hour, and changes in the number and configuration of receptors can occur within half an hour. Why, then, the long delay in visible results? Clearly, the boost ing of catecholamines alone did not explain the situation.

Point: Some other drug actions belied the hypothesis. Cocaine, for example, was shown to block the re-uptake of catecholamines, the same mechanism as the tricyclics, but it does not have a true antidepressant effect. On the other hand, some drugs (like mianserin and iprindole) were found to have no effect on monoamines, including NE, yet they serve as effective antidepressants. Such data suggested a more complex mechanism than the hypothesis accounted for.

Point: No one has ever been able to show a convincing correlation between the inhibition of MAO and the relief of depression. Simply increasing catecholamine levels as a mode of treatment has never had much success. This suggests that a successful antidepressant action does not work by catecholamines alone.

Similarly, there seems to be no clear correlation between catecholamines and mania. If antidepressants behaved as they should and raised catecholamines, and catecholamines behaved as they should and raised mood, we should expect a higher incidence of mania in medicated patients, some of it mediated by drug actions. It is produced in some cases. However, in 1985, Jules Angst showed that the rate of alternation from depression to mania in bipolar patients had for the most part remained consistent over decades, and had not been affected by the introduction of imipramine (Healy, 1997, p. 158).

Point: In the 1950s, Shepherd and Davis had conducted the only clinical trial relating the use of a drug to depression and suicidal thinking. They administered reserpine and found that it relieved depression better than a placebo (p. 92). This contradictory finding had never been given much play.

Point: Further study of the re-uptake process revealed that blocking re-uptake can lead not only to an increase of transmitters in the synaptic gap, but also to their depletion, by exposing them to enzymes.

In summary, the catecholamine hypothesis has never been adequately confirmed, nor even properly understood, yet it has never been refuted. Almost certainly, it will take its place as part of a more complex picture. Healy conjectures that its value lay in the fact that it was a constructive theory which tried to account for the action of antidepressants, during a period when the idea of chemical transmission between nerve cells was struggling to gain prominence over the theory of electrical transmission. For doctors and patients, it provided a convenient device, the image of a broken system one could try to correct, and for the pharmaceutical industry it provided a clear purpose, to develop drugs that would raise catecholamine levels (p. 160).

All along, evidence for the abnormality of 5-HT action in depression had paralleled the evidence for NE; however, 5-HT had usually lagged behind because the chemical tools for manipulating it were not developed until later. Serotonin was known to be connected to mood changes; it increased catecholamine levels; it had a similar re-uptake mechanism that was affected by imipramine; and giving tryptophan, its precursor in synthesis, enhanced the effects of MAOIs. Consequently, a parallel hypothesis had been proposed for

5-HT as early as 1967. However, the findings for NE were strong, and other evidence had suggested that 5-HT actions were peripheral to the action of antidepressants, and so they were treated.

Up to that point, theorizing about the action of antidepressants had taken place in the absence of an understanding of receptors. But as the 1970s dawned, receptor knowledge was growing, more findings about 5-HT appeared, and more specific drugs to selectively manipulate 5-HT were being developed. It was noted, for example, that depressed patients had lower levels of the main 5-HT metabolite (5-HIAA) in their cerebrospinal fluid, a sign of low 5-HT activity. Studies correlated these levels at the time with suicidal thinking and impulses. It was also found that patients testing low for the metabolite responded well to 5-HT enhancers. Studies of imipramine binding showed that depressed subjects had fewer-than-normal 5-HT binding sites on their blood platelets.

Strong support came with the arrival of the first antidepressants to selectively inhibit 5-HT re-uptake without influencing catecholamine systems. These were named **selective serotonin re-uptake inhibitors**, or **SSRIs**. They clearly had antidepressant effects and furnished researchers with better tools for studying 5-HT actions. However, the first SSRI (zimelidine), produced in Europe, caused serious adverse side effects. Because of that, together with the fact that there was no commercial drive at the time to invest in antidepressant research, the development and marketing of the SSRIs lagged for a decade. Fluoxetine (Prozac), which was to become the flagship antidepressant of the nineties, had been synthesized in 1972, but thirteen years passed before clinical evidence for its antidepressant properties was produced, and only in 1987 was it finally licensed in the United States. Two other popular antidepressants soon followed, sertraline (Zoloft) in 1992 and paroxetine (Paxil) in 1993. As a result of all these developments, 5-HT moved to center stage in antidepressant research, and became the glamor transmitter of the 1990s.

Researchers have continued to add to the evidence for the role of 5-HT in depression. There are the obvious facts that SSRIs work as antidepressants, and that every successful antidepressant enhances the action of 5-HT in some way. Moreover, serotonin regulates sleep, appetite, biorhythms, mood, aggression, and anxiety, and irregularities in all of these functions can be seen across the spectrum of cases of depression. In the brains of depressed subjects, there is reduced 5-HT binding at some sites. In other areas, a high density of 5-HT2 receptor sites indicates that neurons are up-regulating and constructing more receptors to compensate for a 5-HT transmitter deficiency. Also, the blood plasma of depressed subjects shows reduced amounts of tryptophan, which is needed for 5-HT synthesis.

In the general scheme of things, however, there is no more convincing evidence to confirm or refute a serotonin hypothesis than a catecholamine hypothesis. Observations of a variety of antidepressant actions indicate that 5-HT re-uptake blockade is neither sufficient nor necessary to relieve depression. In terms of pure efficacy for most mood disorders, the tricyclics remain the best drug treatment; the SSRIs are preferred, however, because they are much more convenient to administer. Electroconvulsive shock therapy, with the least specificity of all, may be the most effective approach, especially in severe cases (Healy, 1997). Specificity in drug action might not be the answer, and some of the newest compounds on the market try to exploit this principle by targeting the interconnections between NE and 5-HT systems, employing a dual action that affects both.

The monoamine hypothesis is the object of a growing dissatisfaction. Researchers and drug developers have clung to it because it does explain to some extent the action of antidepressants and provides a program for the development of new drugs. However, the clinical success of the MAOIs, TCAs, and SSRIs is still less than ideal and does not lead us to explore other systems and basic mechanisms that might be involved in the pathology of depression. Some clinicians feel that the hypothesis is outgrowing its usefulness.

In general, all the observations bolster the notion that alterations in monoamine systems play a role in depression. But the manipulation of NE and 5-HT levels, while clearly useful, seems to be only a partial solution. It is most likely that depression and its treatment involve a number of disordered systems, as well as modulatory and downstream effects that progress over time.

Similarly, no one factor has been demonstrated to "cause" mood disorders. Quite a bit of data supports the idea that a genetic predisposition may be involved. Twin studies have shown a 58 percent concordance among identical twins and a 17 to 18 percent concordance among fraternal twins (Berritini, 1993). Also, there is a higher risk in persons who have family histories of these disorders. As genetic research on the human genome proceeds, chances are we will find, not one or two factors, but a range of biological elements that code for depression, as has already been found in cases of some diseases. In general, heredity, early environment, and complex interpersonal relations might each contribute, so that a full understanding may call for a biopsychosocial perspective.

Akiskal and McKinney moved in this direction in 1973 when they proposed a hypothesis to integrate the psychosocial and biochemical models of depression. Previous explanations of depression had ranged from aggression directed toward the self (Freud) to loss of reinforcement (behaviorists) to the monoamine hypothesis, but none of these hypotheses was capable of explaining both endogenous and reactive depression. Endogenous depression was typically seen to originate biologically in low monoamine levels, whereas reactive depression was explained environmentally in terms of psychological responses to a precipitating event like the loss of a loved one. Considering that the symptoms do not differ between these two conditions, Akiskal and McKinney suggested that depression might be seen as a psychological state corresponding to lowered monoamine levels in the reward system. They pointed out, however, that these lowered levels can be the result of a variety of inputs. They can be the result of biochemical changes, like an injection of reserpine, or of environmental changes, like stressful life events. For instance, animals exposed to inescapable shocks at first react strongly and try to escape, but eventually they stop responding. Even when the opportunity to escape is presented to them, they do not avail themselves of it because they have learned to be helpless (learned helplessness). Animals in this condition become depressed, and if measured, they show lowered brain levels of monoamines. In short, they have a neurochemical condition that was environmentally induced. Therefore, both biochemical and environmental factors can result in low monoamine levels, which means that both endogenous and reactive forms of depression have a common mechanism, a "final common pathway" underlying depressive symptoms (Akiskal & McKinney, 1973; Akiskal, 1983).

THE TREATMENT OF DEPRESSION: ANTIDEPRESSANTS

The antidepressants are a class of drugs with a relatively selective action that elevates the mood of the depressed at therapeutic dosages. This action is distinct from that of stimulants, so it cannot be said that these drugs simply excite the depressed into normalcy. Stimulants themselves have been used for some aspects of depression, but their success has been limited.

In order to better understand the classifications of the antidepressant drugs, it is helpful to recognize that they are based on five distinct mechanisms of action:

1. They block the enzyme MAO, promoting the action of all the monoamines (DA, NE, and 5-HT).
2. They specifically block the reuptake of DA.
3. They specifically block the reuptake of NE.
4. They specifically block the reuptake of 5-HT, by acting on the 5-HT1A receptor.
5. They stimulate or antagonize the 5-HT2 receptor.

The earlier antidepressants worked primarily by blocking MAO or the reuptake of serotonin (5-HT). Some of the more recent agents, however, work through combinations of these effects, and are classified accordingly.

Antidepressants are named and categorized as follows:

The **MAO inhibitors** are so called because they increase NE by interfering with monoamine oxidase. Since MAO is the enzyme that degrades DA and 5-HT as well as NE, it can be seen that the MAOIs are not selective in their effect, but raise all monoamine levels. The prototype of the MAO inhibitors is tranylcypromine (Parnate).

The **tricyclic antidepressants** are named after the triple rings central to their molecular structure. These compounds promote NE activity by interfering with the reuptake of NE into the presynaptic terminal. They also block the reuptake of serotonin. For many years, the tricyclic antidepressants (TCAs) have been the standard for the treatment of depression. The prototype is imipramine (Tofranil), and the second most commonly used compound is amitriptyline (Elavil).

A third, heterogeneous class of antidepressants is known as **second-generation antidepressants**. They were discovered and developed in an effort to improve on the tricyclics, the first generation of widely employed compounds. Generally, the second-generation compounds are more convenient in terms of administration and side effects, although they have not been shown to be superior to the tricyclics for relieving depression. They are of various chemical classes and mechanisms of action and, therefore, are also referred to as atypical antidepressants.

One type of second-generation antidepressant proved to be especially successful. These were the **SSRIs, the selective serotonin reuptake inhibitors,** which specifically promote the action of serotonin by blocking its reuptake. The most well-known drug in the class is fluoxetine (Prozac).

In response to the limitations of the single monoamine hypotheses regarding NE and 5-HT, researchers developed modern **dual-acting antidepressants** that have actions at two different types of synapses. Although the successful TCAs already exhibited a dual action like this to varying degrees, an action these researchers had well in mind, the term **dual-acting antidepressants** is used to describe only the newer drugs designed to avoid some of the limiting side effects of the classic first-generation antidepressants. Most of these drugs to date act at NE and 5-HT synapses; these compounds are often referred to as **SSNRIs, or selective serotonin and norepinephrine reuptake inhibitors**. Venlafaxine (Effexor) is a key drug in this class.

Other new drugs with mechanisms of action that are of interest in the treatment of depression include:

- a class of second-generation atypical antidepressants that inhibit the reuptake of NE and DA without affecting 5-HT, called **dopamine and norepinephrine reuptake inhibitors (DNRIs)**; bupropion (Wellbutrin, Zyban) is a unique drug in the vanguard of this class
- drugs that selectively inhibit the reuptake of NE (atomoxetine [Strattera] and reboxetine [Vestra]), also known as **SNRIs**, and
- dual-acting drugs that promote NE and 5-HT transmission but also specifically block the 5-HT_2 receptor (mirtazepine [Remeron]).

As can be seen, the categories of antidepressants are based on the five actions listed above, or combinations thereof.

MONOAMINE OXIDASE INHIBITORS

Even though the antidepressant properties of iproniazid were recognized in the tuberculosis wards in 1951, the compound was shelved until 1957, when Nathan Kline reported the drug's effectiveness in the treatment of depression. However, iproniazid was implicated in 54 deaths four years later, and since new MAO inhibitors with less toxicity were being developed, it was retired. The MAO inhibitors in general proved to be inferior to the tricyclics, and they dropped out of use until the late seventies, when they were revived to treat phobias and atypical depressions with extreme anxiety

The **monoamine oxidase inhibitors (MAOIs)** fall into two categories. The earlier types, like iproniazid, were derived from hydrazine, an ingredient in rocket fuel. However, these proved high in liver toxicity. Safer derivatives were developed, but unfortunately they did not work as well. Of the four MAOIs currently on the U.S. market, two of them are hydrazines: phenelzine (Nardil) and isocarboxazid (Marplan). Later, **nonhydrazine** compounds were developed, with less liver toxicity and a quicker action. The only one of these on the U.S. market is tranylcypromine (Parnate), the prototype of all the MAOI antidepressants. Tranylcypromine was derived from stimulants--the amphetamines-- although it has the same action as the other MAO inhibitors. The newest MAOI, selegiline (Emsam), is designed to be administered transdermally via a skin patch.

Pharmacokinetics

The usual administration of MAOIs is oral. They are lipid-soluble. Rapid and full absorption occurs through the gastrointestinal tract, although they are absorbed readily by any route. MAOIs pass the blood brain barrier, and they accumulate in the liver and heart as well as the brain. Their passage through the system is relatively quick. Soon absorbed, they reach peak blood levels in about one hour. Biotransformation occurs in the liver, and within 24 hours, 98 percent of a dose is excreted, mostly through the gastrointestinal tract, and to a lesser extent through the kidneys. Their long latency of effect, therefore, is not a result of the direct presence of the drug, but of the cumulative destruction of MAO in the synapses throughout many successive doses. Eventually, after about 10 days, enough MAO has been lost to allow NE levels to rise, producing a manifest therapeutic effect. The duration of action is long, a result of the crippled enzyme supply, which has to be replenished. By the same token, when the drug is stopped, the therapeutic action continues for 1 or 2 weeks, while the body resynthesizes the enzymes and resumes normal metabolism.

The average dosage of tranylcypromine is 20 mg a day, one dose in the morning and one at night, continued for 2 weeks. If there is no toxicity, the dose can be raised to 30 mg per day.

Pharmacological Effects

For the most part, MAO inhibitors bind irreversibly to MAO molecules and put them out of commission. From the actions described above, it can be seen that the MAOIs increase levels of NE, 5-HT, and DA (also epinephrine), but the role of these transmitters in depression remains murky. To further confuse matters, the degree of MAO inhibition does not correlate to the degree of effectiveness. Nevertheless, it is clear that MAOIs reverse reserpine depression in a manner that has been well studied. Reserpine causes the artificial release of DA, NE, and 5-HT from the vesicles, and their consequent destruction by MAO, resulting in depression. MAO inhibitors, however, block the enzyme threat, saving these neurotransmitters, despite their state of "exile" from the protecting vesicles and their exposure to the enzyme.

Clinical Applications

Before the introduction of the serotonin reuptake inhibitors in the late 1980s, the tricyclics were the drug of choice for depression. They worked well; however, treatment failed about a third of the time. In those cases, MAOIs, which were less safe and less effective, were used.

Currently, their primary use is for atypical depressions, types that do not fit the main DSM-IV categories. These are mild, variable depressions with such symptoms as phobic anxieties, hysteria, somatic complaints, and oversleeping or overeating. The MAOIs seem to work better in some of these cases, whereas the tricyclics excel for unipolar depression.

Side Effects

The fact that only four MAOIs have survived screening in the U.S. attests to their many and severe toxicities. They are loner drugs with batteries of vicious interactions, and if you prowl the drugstore shelves you will see warnings against combined effects with MAOIs on many and sundry packages. In 1964, Parnate (tranylcypromine) was withdrawn from use for several months because it killed several people with a dangerous effect that became known as the cheese syndrome. When the mechanism of the syndrome became clear, Parnate was reintroduced, but restricted only to hospitalized patients with depression, whose diets could be supervised.

It is known that MAOIs produce their therapeutic effect by inhibiting type-B MAO in the central nervous system. However, they also inhibit type-A MAO, found widely in the gastrointestinal tract. This action suppresses the metabolism of certain foods, those containing the substance tyramine. As a result, unmetabolized tyramine rises to higher-than-normal levels and causes a release of stored NE. Add this to the flood of NE already sponsored by the MAOIs, and you get an adrenergic overload in the periphery that raises blood pressure levels to killing heights. This is accompanied by severe headache, a rise in body temperature, and intracranial bleeding.

Tyramine is present mostly in foods containing fermented (aged) proteins. It is critical, then, for MAOI users to abstain from such delicacies as aged cheeses (cheddar, Camembert, gruyere, Stilton), aged wine (Chianti, even sherry or beer), pickled herring, sardines, lox, chicken livers, figs, raisins, pickles, sauerkraut, coffee, chocolate, soy sauce, sour cream, snails, broad beans, yogurt, avocados, and licorice an uncouth menu containing moderate to high amounts of tyramine. In fact, an average meal of natural or aged cheese alone contains enough tyramine to cause a marked rise in blood pressure due to NE release. Hence, *the cheese syndrome*. Enzyme activity in the gastrointestinal tract does recover from the dangerous influence of the MAOIs, but the period of susceptibility may last from 2 to 3 weeks (Hollister & Claghorn, 1993).

At therapeutic dosages, it is possible for MAO inhibitors alone, especially tranylcypromine, to cause high blood pressure (hypertension) by raising catecholamine levels in the periphery. With tyramine rich foods and a number of other drugs, this danger is augmented. Some risky companions include amphetamines, epinephrine, ephedrine (found in many cold medicines), and tricyclic antidepressants.

On the other hand, the MAOIs can also cause low blood pressure (hypotension). In this case, the effect comes through the central stimulation of NE neurons, which inhibit peripheral sympathetic activity and cause blood pressure to drop. One result of this is orthostatic hypotension, the experience of dizziness upon standing up. Other effects include dry mouth, blurred vision, an abnormal intolerance of light, decreased gastrointestinal movement, rapid heartbeat, sexual dysfunctions (delayed ejaculation, impotence), and dry skin.

Although they elevate the mood of the depressed, MAOIs apparently do not affect-nor mal subjects; therefore, abuse is unlikely. They do not lead to physical dependence, abuse, or withdrawal. However, accidental overdoses can be fatal. And an unforeseen side effect, suicide, may occur as antidepressants return patients' initiative to them. If the patient has been suffering from negative ideation, dwelling on suicide, antidepressants may restore enough resolve to make that escape attainable.

Signs of acute toxicity with MAOIs may not appear for 11 hours after ingestion because of the long latency period. Poisoning starts with headache, nausea, and vomiting. The heart races; the pupils dilate, and the subject shows an intolerance of light (photo**phobia**). Signs of central nervous system stimulation may appear. But the greatest risk is from hypertension, which may lead to stroke. Hyperactivity and confusion proceed to hallucinations and delusions, and finally to convulsions and death. The best treatment is to acidify the urine to speed excretion, to maintain blood sugar and temperature balance, to keep blood pressure down, and to watch that too low a pressure doesn't develop.

Reversible MAO Inhibitors

The huge disadvantage of the irreversible MAOIs is that they inhibit both types of MAO, impairing the metabolism of tyramine in the gastrointestinal tract and making possible a crisis of high blood pressure. The ideal MAOI would be one that inhibits only MAO-B, relieving depression without affecting MAO-A and tyramine metabolism. Such a drug is not yet on the horizon; however, there are improvements in sight. The problem with current MAOs is that MAO-A is damaged permanently, leaving one susceptible to the "cheese syndrome" for two or three weeks until gastrointestinal enzyme activity recovers.

A new class of MAOIs, the reversible MAOIs, show a reversible, short-acting MAO-A inhibition that allows gastrointestinal enzymes to recover in a matter of hours, greatly reducing the time window for a severe hypertensive crisis. Selegiline, the newest MAOI to be approved for the U.S. market, has a relatively selective and irreversible effect on MAO-B, and so relieves depression, but it is a weak, reversible inhibitor of MAO-A and suppresses the catecholamine release caused by tyramine, reducing the risk of a hypertensive crisis. In addition, it can be administered via a skin patch. Improvements like these may lead to wider use of MAOIs.

TRICYCLIC ANTIDEPRESSANTS

The parent compound of the tricyclic antidepressants, iminodibenzyl, dates back to 1889. In the mid-fifties, this compound was resurrected, and a number of its derivatives went through broad screenings for various uses. The derivative imipramine, because of its similarity to the phenothiazine molecule, left animal testing as an antipsychotic, but when it was given to schizophrenic patients suffering from depression, it was found to improve their mood, so it went into wide clinical use as an antidepressant. On the whole, the tricyclics proved more effective than the MAO inhibitors, with fewer toxic side effects. Consequently, imipramine (Tofranil) and the related compound amitriptyline (Elavil) became the main treatments for depression at that time.

Pharmacokinetics

Quite lipid soluble, the tricyclic antidepressants are well absorbed through the gastrointestinal tract, reaching peak plasma levels in half an hour to an hour, and they distribute rapidly (see Figure 20.1). Animal studies show accumulations in the brain, liver, and kidneys. The extent of binding to blood proteins varies widely among the compounds, but some bind in large amounts, 80% to 90%, although they generally remain free for about half an hour after absorption. These affinities make for a long latency period; it takes 5 to 10 days to reach steady plasma levels, and the therapeutic antidepressant effect may not begin for 1 to 4 weeks. This is a crucial consideration. It is one reason that, in some highly suicidal patients, electroconvulsive therapy may be preferred.

Metabolism of the tricyclic antidepressants is an individual matter, so much so that one person's blood level may be 40 times that of another's. Because of this, dose requirements differ and can pose difficulties. Typically, eighty percent of the original full dose is metabolized by the liver. In excretion, half of the dose goes to the bile, and about two thirds of this re-enters through the intestine, but is eventually reabsorbed and passed through the urine.

Due to blood affinities, metabolic factors, and the chemical properties of the several agents, the half lives of the tricyclics may range anywhere from 5 to 126 hours, but on the average, the half lives are long. Some of these drugs also show a treatment pattern known as a **therapeutic window**, where only a certain dose range produces therapeutic effects. Too high or too low a dose, and you miss the window—no benefits. Blood levels are not hard to monitor, so the window can be found and maintained, but the frequent drawing of blood samples makes for an inconvenience.

Average doses of imipramine (Tofranil) and amitriptylene (Elavil), the two most commonly used tricyclics, are 150 to 300 mg. Three to six months of treatment usually suffices.

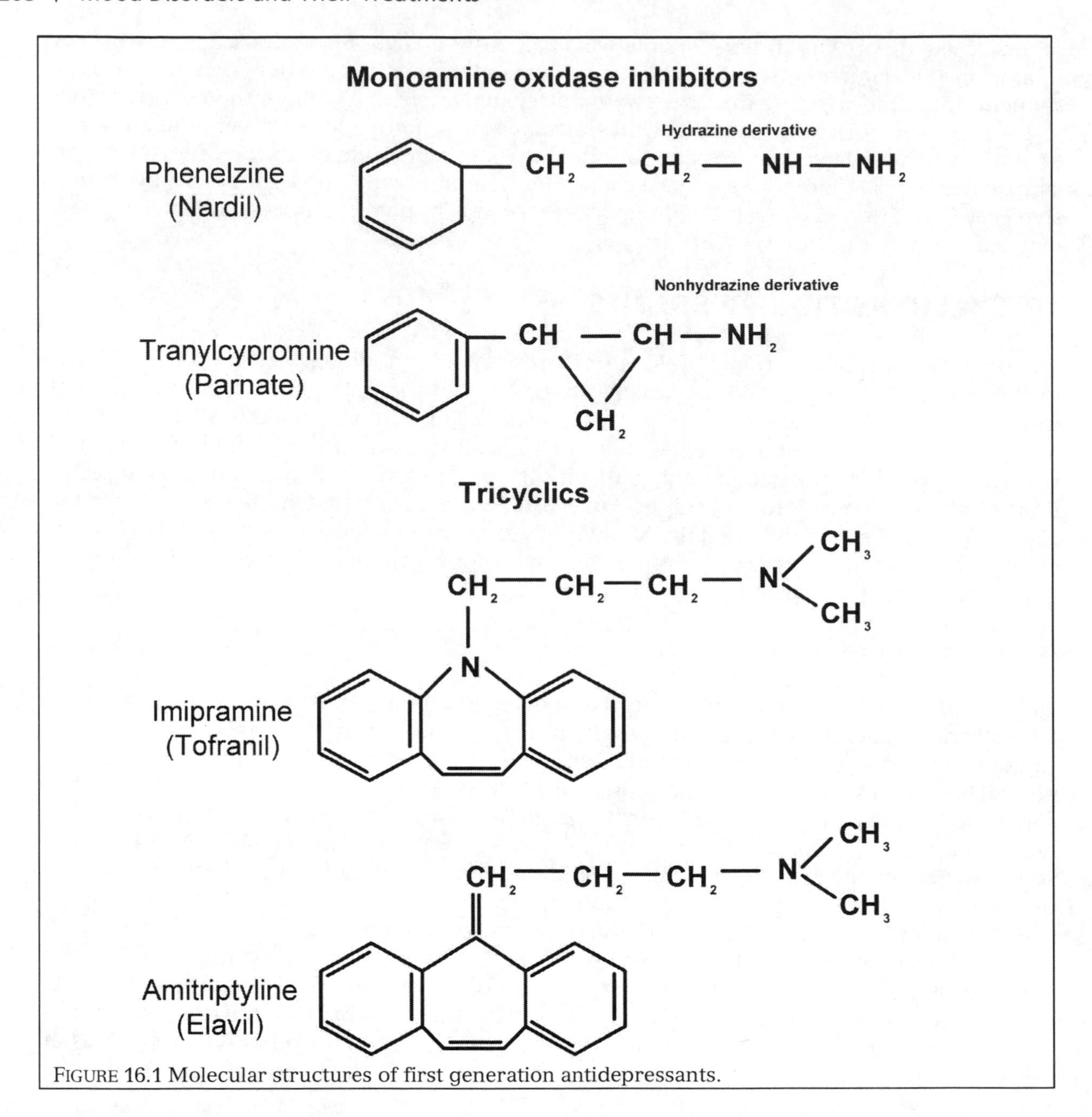

FIGURE 16.1 Molecular structures of first generation antidepressants.

Pharmacological Effects

The tricyclics have five distinct actions. The first two are therapeutic: They inhibit the reuptake of NE and 5-HT, contributing to the improvement of mood. Key distinctions among agents in this class are based on how differently they affect the reuptake of NE as opposed to that of 5-HT. The other actions consist of antagonistic effects at three receptors. They antagonize ACh receptors at muscarinic sites; they antagonize noradrenergic receptors at alpha-1 sites; and they antagonize histamine receptors. Each of these actions produces a familiar battery of side effects, which we will discuss below.

The hypothesis usually advanced for the antidepressant action of the tricyclics is that they block the reuptake of NE into the presynaptic terminals. They also appear to increase the amount of NE released at each nerve impulse. This is somewhat counterbalanced by a decreased sensitivity in the receptor, but the overall effect is an increase of NE activity, which relieves depression. The tricyclics also block the reuptake of 5-HT, augmenting serotonergic activity as well. However, newer drugs like bupropion (Wellbutrin) and atomoxetine (Strattera) show antidepressant effects not linked to either of these mechanisms. We must return, then, to the possibility of several types of depression with several mechanisms, since no model accounts for all of the facts. Furthermore, imipramine has binding sites that seem so specific as to raise questions about the likelihood of natural antidepressants being present in the brain.

The tricyclics show strong, even stronger, anticholinergic effects at the muscarinic synapses than the phenothiazines, which they resemble. In general, the involvement of ACh in the action of the tricyclics suggests that, at least indirectly, it might have a modulatory effect on NE or 5-HT activity. Newer compounds such as trazodone (Desyrel) offer fewer anticholinergic reactions and cardiovascular effects.

Normal subjects who try imipramine report the effect to resemble the feeling one has when one is tired but cannot sleep because the fatigue is driven by a sense of inner restlessness. Only in the presence of depression does imipramine have an antidepressant effect. Then it increases activity, alertness, and appetite, and it allows patients to sleep.

Clinical Applications

Until the late 1980s and early 1990s, tricyclic compounds were the most widely prescribed drugs for unipolar depression. Now, however, due to their potentially severe side effects at relatively low doses, the tricyclics are usually given only when two or more newer-generation antidepressants fail (DeVane, Grothe, & Smith, 2002).

All of the tricyclics are about equally effective, but some differentiations may be made. Imipramine (Tofranil) is used for depressions with psychomotor retardation, because its mood elevating properties lead to more active behavior. It has also shown some usefulness for panic attacks, agoraphobia, phobic anxiety, and obsessive-compulsive disorder. If agitation occurs with the depression, amitriptyline (Elavil) suits better because it has sedative effects. And desipramine (Norpramine), with a stimulatory action, serves best in subjects presenting a lack of drive.

Antidepressants in general are becoming the drugs of choice for treating panic disorders, obsessive-compulsive disorder, and some phobias. They are also being used to treat the craving associated with cocaine dependence.

Side Effects

As we mentioned above, the tricyclics produce three distinct constellations of side effects, based on their antagonism of three receptors. Adrenergic side effects present the most concern. The most severe and frequently reported are cardiovascular, especially for amitripyline. These come from antagonism of the alpha-1 receptors, which accept NE molecules near the synapse as a mechanism to shut off release of the neurotransmitter. Consequently, blockading these receptors in the periphery can cause adrenergic stimulation. Symptoms of this include a racing heartbeat, arrhythmia, and, more rarely, heart failure, and sudden death. A lesser, but still influential cardiovascular complaint, is orthostatic hypotension due to decreased blood pressure, and a number of patients must be taken off tricyclics due to this. Less severe adrenergic effects are dizziness and drowsiness.

A second constellation of side effects comes from the antagonism of muscarinic cholin ergic receptors. Anticholinergic actions might also be responsible for some cardiovascu lar side effect, such as racing heartbeat and dangerous arrhythmias. Other symptoms of the anticholinergic syndrome include psychomotor slowing, loss of concentration, muscle weakness, dry mouth, fatigue, headaches, tremors, constipation, blurred vision and dizzi ness. Older patients seem more susceptible to these effects.

These actions can lead to a considerable risk of additive anticholinergic effects with other drugs. A threefold threat can arise in the treatment of depressive psychosis. First, neuroleptics are given, and these have some anticholinergic action. Second, to correct for some of the transmitter imbalances caused by these drugs in the basal ganglia, and attendant motor problems, antiparkinson drugs may be given, and these augment the an ticholinergic action of neuroleptics. Third, in psychoses exhibiting depressive symptoms, it would not be unusual to prescribe a third, antidepressive agent as well, adding even more anticholinergic action, to make a triple dose, subjecting the system to much stress. The neuroleptic thioridazine (Mellaril) and the antidepressants imipramine (Tofranil) or amitriptyline (Elavil), both high in anticholinergic actions, are a particularly bad combination. Tolerance to these effects does develop, however, and if doses are managed carefully and raised slowly, these drugs can be used to maximum advantage. Sometimes, drugs like physostigmine or pyridostigmine can be used to counteract a severe anticholinergic syndrome. These block enzymes and promote ACh. However, they may have their own deleterious side effects, such as slowed heartbeat, bronchoconstriction, and low blood pressure.

A third constellation of TCA side effects comes from the antagonism of histamine receptors, which is characterized primarily by drowsiness (sedation) and weight gain.

The tricyclic antidepressants are not appreciably toxic, but acute toxicity and lethal overdosing are possible, and this may occur at doses not far above the therapeutic dose. This factor is especially weighty under the circumstances, because tricyclics are being prescribed to depressed patients who are no strangers to thoughts of suicide, and who may elect to take all of their medicine at once. Physicians must take care to avoid prescribing a lethal dose.

As noted before, patients vary widely in their sensitivity to tricyclics, even up to toxic levels. Delirium is one signal that the dosage is too high. The symptoms of poisoning are reduced reflexes, seizures, arrhythmias, dilated but sluggish pupil movements, raised pulse, lowered body temperature, and respiratory arrest followed by cardiovascular collapse. Many of these symptoms follow from anticholinergic stresses. A mitigating circumstance of poisoning is that, by slowing movement through the intestines, tricyclic antidepressants slow their own absorption. This allows one to address the matter in the stomach and apply immediate measures such as inducing vomiting, pumping the stomach, and administering activated charcoal. Besides these, however, management is difficult due to threats to the heart, and recovery may be long because of rapid and extensive tissue binding. One to 1.2 grams of imipramine is the toxic dose, and 2.5 grams is commonly fatal.

The tricyclics do not cause addiction, but they do induce a mild withdrawal syndrome marked by malaise, aches, vomiting, anxiety, and restlessness. This can be alleviated at the end of treatment by tapering off the dosages over a few days.

The most notable drug interactions occurring with tricyclics involve exaggerated anticholinergic effects. This can occur with alcohol, benzodiazepines, antiparkinson drugs, and all of the neuroleptics. Because of competition for liver enzymes, antidepressant effects may decrease in the presence of alcohol, lithium, barbiturates, chloral hydrate, pro pranolol, smoking, and oral contraceptives.

In some cases, tricyclics reduce parkinsonism, but in others they cause it; the mechanism is confusing. Tricyclics have some other phenothiazine-like side effects as well: tremors, jaundice, photosensitivity, and sedation (especially with amitriptyline). Amoxapine, a heterocyclic antidepressant, is particularly phenothiazine like, in that its primary action is DA blockage. Consequently, it can produce tardive dyskinesia, extrapyramidal reactions, and other neuroleptic side effects.

Additional antidepressant side effects include profuse sweating in the upper extremities (cause unknown), anorexia, insomnia, nausea, vomiting, and heartburn. Paradoxical anxiety and depression, mania, and psychotic symptoms can occur in some cases. Tricyclic antidepressants seem safer than most drugs in the first trimester of pregnancy; this is hopeful, but not cause enough to relax all suspicions.

SECOND-GENERATION ANTIDEPRESSANTS

The **second-generation antidepressants** are a heterogeneous group of agents that were developed to improve on the shortcomings of the MAOIs and the tricyclics. They have various mechanisms, so their naming is a historical convenience. Some compounds in this category, the heterocyclics, were developed with the tricyclics in mind, but have more rings in their chemical structures. Other compounds are "crossover" drugs from other chemical classes, like certain benzodiazepines, which were found to be useful in countering depression, and which showed fewer side effects. A number of drugs in this class have been subsumed under later classifications, depending on their mechanisms of action.

In general, these drugs show comparable, but not superior, actions to the TCAs in relieving depression. For the most part, the primary advantage they offer over their predecessors is that they show fewer or less troublesome side effects, especially in regard to anticholinergic effects, heart effects, and toxic overdoses. The low occurrence of heart effects in some of these compounds makes them good medications for elderly patients with cardiac problems, who may be put at risk by tricyclics. Orthostatic hypotension, an undesirable side effect of the tricyclics, is absent in many of the second-generation antidepressants. Furthermore, several of these compounds show an onset of action that is somewhat shorter than the two-week average of the tricyclics, and they are more convenient to administer.

It is not important for our purposes to present a detailed account of the differences among all these drugs. However, it is good to understand that, while they all show useful antidepressant actions, they are not more or less all the same. They have significant differences in chemical structure, mechanisms of action, and profiles of effects (see Table 20.1). For instance, while some are heterocyclic variants of the tricyclics, alprazolam (Xanax) is a modified benzodiazepine, and amoxapine (Asendin) was derived from a neuroleptic (loxapine).

The pharmacological profiles and the transmitter actions of these drugs differ as well. Many agents, similar to the tricyclics, inhibit the reuptake of NE to varying degrees.

TABLE 16.1 Comparison of Second-Generation Antidepressants

Drug	Chemical class	Transmitters affected	Half-life
Amoxapine (Asendin)	Dibenzoxazepine	NE+ DA-	8-10 hrs (major metabolite 30 hrs)
Maprotiline (Ludiomil)	Tetracyclic	NE+	27-58 hrs
Trazodone (Desyrel)	Triazolopyridine	5-HT+ NE	6-13 hrs
Fluoxetine (Prozac)	(unrelated to other antidepressants)	5-HT+	24-96 hrs
Bupropion (Wellbutrin)	Aminoketone	NE+/- DA+ 5-HT	14 hrs
Clomipramine (Anafranil)	Dibenzazepine Tricyclic	NE+ 5-HT	19-37 hrs
Alprazolam (Xanax)	Benzodiazepine	GABA+	11 hrs

Application	Side effects/ comments	Dosage mg/day
Depression Anxiety	Neuroleptic-like effects Drowsiness Dry mouth Risk of tardive dyskinesia after extended use	200-300
Depression Antipsychotic/ antimanic	Dry mouth Drowsiness Nervousness (infrequent)	75-100
Depression Anxiety Agoraphobia*	Priapism Drowsiness	150-400 600 for inpatients
Depression Obsessive-compulsive disorder Attention deficit hyperactivity disorder* Bulimia*	Insomnia Anxiety Nervousness Sexual dysfunction	20-80
Depression Seasonal affective disorder*	Weight loss Agitation, restlessness Seizures	200 (days 1-3) 300 (day 4 on)
Depression Obsessive-compulsive disorder	Seizures (infrequent)	25-100
Depression Anxiety	Dependence	3

* Application not approved by the FDA
(Source: Data from *Physician's GenRx: The Complete Drug Reference* (5th ed.). 1995. Riverside, CT: Denniston Publishing Co.

Among them are maprotiline (Ludiomil) and nomifensine (Merital). Amoxapine likewise shows a strong NE action, but because of its neuroleptic pedigree, it has significant DA effects as well; one of its metabolites is a DA-blocker as strong as haloperidol. This action makes amoxapine particularly suited to depressions that occur in conjunction with psychoses, but it also means that it shows neuroleptic-like side effects (akathisia, dystonias, and dyskinesias). By the same token, it is the worst of these drugs for anticholinergic side effects and can compound these effects if given with neuroleptics, which also produce them. Sedation and orthostatic hypotension are also a problem. Tolerance may develop to its therapeutic action, and, unlike most of this group, it is toxic in overdose, capable of causing seizures and death.

Some second-generation antidepressants, such as fluvoxamine (Luvox) and bupropion (Wellbutrin), show little or no NE actions. This is evidence that transmitters other than NE are involved in the mechanism of depression. Bupropion, in contrast to amoxapine, promotes DA activity by blocking reuptake and may have a direct agonistic effect at the DA receptor. Consequently, this drug, instead of treating psychotic symptoms, can cause them at high doses. Orthostatic hypotension doesn't show for bupropion, since it is an NE meditated side effect. There is a very low risk of overdosing, and bupropion has been put to good use in the treatment of bipolar affective disorder.

Fluvoxamine is an antidepressant that inhibits the reuptake of 5-HT; it shows no NE actions. Alprazolam (Xanax), like the benzodiazepines, has primarily GABA-ergic actions. effects. It has shown itself to be a drug with high abuse potential and has seen some ilicit use.

As a whole, the second-generation antidepressants are more convenient drugs than tricyclics, but they present a bewildering array of pharmacological actions, all of which are evidently involved in relieving depression. Some of these drugs became the harbingers of later categories of agents, as more drugs with similar actions were developed. For example, fluoxetine (Prozac) and fluvoxamine (Luvox) were to be included in the growing class of drugs that selectively inhibit the reuptake of serotonin.

SELECTIVE SEROTONIN REUPTAKE INHIBITORS

Eventually, out of the field of second-generation antidepressants emerged a number of compounds of great pharmacological interest. These substances were effective antide pressants, but were highly selective in promoting the action of 5-HT, with little effect on DA or NE systems.

The exact mechanism of action for the antidepressant effects of the SSRIs has not been confirmed. Clearly, they block the reuptake of 5-HT into the presynaptic terminals, and in so doing promote 5-HT activity. However, this effect alone might not be the primary-connection to the therapeutic response, but may trigger a sequence of adaptive changes in transmitter systems. The onset of therapeutic effects, for instance, does not occur for three to eight weeks after the start of administration (Stahl, 1998, p. 9).

As of 2007, six SSRIs are in use: fluoxetine (Prozac), sertraline (Zoloft), paroxetine (Paxil), fluvoxamine (Luvox), citaprolam (Celexa), and escitaprolam (Lexapro). Fluvoxamine is approved only for obsessive-compulsive disorder, the other five for depression.

SSRIs provide significant advantages over previous treatments for depression. Given their high selectivity for serotonin, they are free of troublesome anticholinergic effects.

With low NE involvement, they are less toxic to the heart and, as a result, are much safer in overdose, that is, harder to use to commit suicide, a factor that appeals hugely to pre scribing physicians. Since the side effects are milder, patients are less likely to stop taking the pills, as often happens otherwise (Stahl, 1998, p. 8). Furthermore, although the onset of therapeutic effects may not occur for six weeks, the dosage schedule is convenient and simple: a pill a day. Ease and safety, therefore, give the SSRIs their clinical edge.

But there is another advantage. The SSRIs are not only worthy for their treatment of depression, but they relieve atypical depression, and panic disorder as well. They are the first drugs to alleviate obsessive-compulsive symptoms and show some promise for treating other behavior disorders with elements of compulsion (e.g., exhibitionism). Furthermore, it appears that they can help with eating disorders like bulimia. These broader applications have bolstered their sale and reputation.

Nevertheless, the SSRIs are not without their problems. While the stimulation of 5-HT_2 receptors in some areas may be responsible for therapeutic effects, in others, it seems to produce a number of undesirable side effects (Stahl, 1998, p. 10). Early in treatment, anxiety might manifest from stimulation of 5-HT_2 receptors in hippocampal and limbic circuits; however, in the long term, SSRIs can relieve anxiety. In the hypothalamus, this effect may lead to reduced appetite, nausea, and weight loss. In neural pathways related to sleep, 5-HT_2 stimulation can cause insomnia. It also appears that 5-HT_2 neurons play a role in regulating DA release. Stimulating 5-HT_2 release in the basal ganglia might be responsible for suppressing DA there and causing neuroleptic-like side effects like akathisia and agitation.

A characteristic side effect of the SSRIs, which is often of concern, is the inhibition of sexual functioning. This might result from the fact that 5-HT_2 neurons mediate the release of DA in some circuits, a connection also exploited by some of the newer antipsychotic medications. In this case, the stimulation of 5-HT_2 receptors in reward areas may inhibit the activity of DA to affect sexual functioning. Males may experience impotence and delayed ejaculation; women, the inability to have an orgasm. However, since SSRIs are usually put to use in severe cases of depression, they bring on welcome, if not life-saving, improvements of mood, and this trade-off with a curtailment of sexuality does not possess the tragic or alarming cast that it might have under other circumstances. In less severe cases of depression, and long-term treatment, it becomes more of an issue.

Another battery of SE side effects is gastrointestinal, most likely due to a large number of 5-HT_3 receptors in the GI tract, in the wall of the gut. These can mediate effects like nausea, gastrointestinal distress, cramps, and diarrhea.

Given their serotonergic side effects, it is possible for the SSRIs, when used with other 5-HT enhancers, to produce a serotonergic syndrome involving high body temperatures, high blood pressure, seizures, and possibly death. Consequently, one must be careful when switching from an MAOI, or any other serotonin enhancer, to an SSRI, to be sure that the effects of the previous drug have cleared sufficiently to avoid additive 5-HT effects.

Paradoxical effects have been noted with SSRIs, namely, the sudden emergence of an intense suicidal preoccupation, but there is a debate over the statistical significance of the data. Some studies have shown the incidence to match that of the tricyclic antidepressants, and in some cases, a placebo. Nevertheless, paradoxical reactions can and do occur.

Other prominent side effects of SSRIs include headache, nervousness, insomnia, sweating, dizziness, and tremor.

Fluoxetine (Prozac), among the first in this class, emerged as the celebrity among all antidepressants, and proceeded to carve itself a niche in American drug history beside Miltown and Valium. It became a favorite not because it is a superior treatment for depression, but because of its convenience of administration and its favorable profile of side effects. It gained further play as the first successful treatment for obsessive-compulsive disorder. And, finally, it took on the mantle of other widely prescribed "social" drugs, because, in its ability to shape mood, it has begun to be seen in some quarters of psychiatry as a chemical tool for altering people's psychological destinies--not just the clinically depressed, but the anxious in danger of becoming depressed, and the sad with low self-esteem who would benefit from a cosmetic mood lift.

Fluoxetine, the first SSRI to see broad clinical use, came onto the market as a second-generation antidepressant in 1987. By 1988, prescription sales for fluoxetine matched the sales for all antidepressants two years earlier. Like other second-generation compounds, fluoxetine is not superior to the tricyclics for relieving depression; its appeal lies in its convenience of administration and in its broader range of applications. The tricyclics must be administered over several weeks in progressively larger doses, and blood levels must be carefully monitored to hit the therapeutic window without overdosing. Fluoxetine, on the other hand, can be given at a flat dose of one 20 mg capsule daily (or two daily doses totaling to more than 20 mg). Blood monitoring is unnecessary, and there is no danger of a toxic overdose. One rare suicide that did go on record occurred at a dose of 7,000 mgs (Cowley et al., 1990). The abuse potential seems to be low. In addition, fluoxetine not only treats depression, but is also being prescribed for anxiety, addictions, eating disorders (bulimia and obesity), and obsessive-compulsive disorder. Herein lies its appeal. However, as a treatment for depression alone, it proves to be 60 percent effective, as compared to the tricyclics' 80 percent effectiveness rate (Cowley et al., 1990).

Fluoxetine shows a highly specific action for blocking the reuptake of 5-HT. It has no NE or anticholinergic effects, shows no sedation, no severe toxicity, and no birth defects in animals. It is absorbed through the gastrointestinal tract, reaching peak plasma levels in 6 to 8 hours. About 94 percent of a dose binds to blood proteins. Metabolism occurs mostly in the liver, where fluoxetine induces cytochrome P-450. Its half life is 2 to 3 days, but its chief active metabolite (norfluoxetine) persists for 7 to 15 days. As a result, it may take weeks to achieve steady blood levels. Excretion takes place mostly through the kidneys.

Fluoxetine displays the side effects typical of SSRIs. Among its hallmark effects are anxiety, insomnia, and anorexia (loss of appetite). Anxiety and insomnia may appear with a caffeinelike syndrome, along with jitteriness and tremors. Loss of appetite can lead to weight loss; accordingly, fluoxetine has been prescribed as a diet pill. Decreased sexual functioning has been reported, and there have been scattered incidents of severe reactions, such as seizures or attacks of suicidal mania (an exuberant impulse to kill oneself). In general, because fluoxetine is so new, its long-term side effects in humans are not known. There is cause to be concerned over its widespread prescription before the full implications of its effects on humans become clear.

One issue raised by fluoxetine concerns the pharmacology of social engineering. Because it can improve mood and self-esteem, an SSRI is capable of turning a brooding, low-achieving person into a cheerful, productive one. On one level, it can serve as an antidepressant medication, like a tricyclic or MAOI. On another, it presents itself as a safe and convenient preventative to alleviate ongoing anxiety that could develop into depression. On a third level, it could be used for what Peter Kramer, author of the bestselling *Listening to Prozac*, calls "cosmetic psychopharmacology." If a pill can free you from your undesirable biochemical fate, why not use it? Why sit alone at home in a slough of despond, when you are one pill away from a productive and thriving work and social life, and a mood upswing free of guilt and fear and low self-esteem? Questions like these are bound to confront us more and more as biochemistry and genetics intrude on our current conceptions of mood, personality, identity, and behavior. It has been noted, for instance, that an intact serotonin system is associated in animal studies with the control of aggression. If human criminal acts were able to be associated with low serotonergic functioning could a mandatory prescription become part of a court sentence?

Sertraline (Zoloft) is a SSRI of a different chemical class from fluoxetine, more potent and specific in its inhibition of serotonin reuptake. To its advantage, it has a shorter half-life than fluoxetine, but like other SSRIs, it induces P-450 enzymes and can produce a serotonergic syndrome when taken with MAOIs. Its characteristic side effect is diarrhea.

Paroxetine (Paxil) is the most potent of the SSRIs. As effective as other antidepres sants, it is superior for its lack of anticholinergic side effects. Its characteristic side effects are drowsiness and dry mouth.

Fluvoxamine and citaprolam are roughly similar to other members of this class. They have been used successfully in Europe for the treatment of depressive disorders, but have yet to be released in the United States.

On the whole, the SSRIs prove to be effective not only for depression, but for obsessive compulsive disorder and possibly eating disorders. They are convenient and safe. They do, however, cause GI discomfort, sexual dysfunction, and central nervous system side effects, and must be used cautiously with other psychoactive medications. There may, too, be infrequent paradoxical reactions of increased depression and suicidal mania.

SELECTIVE SEROTONIN AND NOREPINEPHRINE REUPTAKE INHIBITORS

The term *dual-acting antidepressants* is applied to a fairly recent class of drugs that act at two synaptic sites. Several of these drugs inhibit the reuptake of both NE and 5-HT. It should be noted that the early first-generation tricyclic antidepressants also inhibit both NE and 5-HT reuptake, but with their serious anticholinergic, adrenergic, and antihistaminergic side effects, they are considered to be of a different era. The new selective serotonin and norepinephrine reuptake inhibitors (SSNRIs) show a less problematic profile in this regard. The two approved for use in the U.S. are venlafaxine (Effexor) and duloxetine (Cymbalta).

In addition to their use in major depressive disorder, both venlafaxine and duloxetine have proved to be effective in treating anxiety, which may be associated with depression, and in relieving chronic pain that is not associated with depression. Both pose a risk of suicidal thinking and behavior. Upon cessation of treatment, as with the SSRIs, dosages should be gradually reduced.

Venlafaxine was introduced to the market in 1994 to treat major depressive disorder, as well as generalized anxiety disorder, panic disorder and social anxiety disorder. Low dosages produce a strong inhibition of 5-HT reuptake and higher doses a strong inhibition of NE reuptake as well. The effect on DA reuptake is less significant. Venlafaxine is rapidly metabolized in the liver, with a very short elimination half-life, which has occa sioned the development of an extended release form to avoid frequent dosing. The drug shows no P-450 enzyme inhibition, so that it is low in interactions with other drugs. To a large extent, venlafaxine avoids severe negative side effects originating from the blockade of cholinergic, adrenergic and histaminergic sites. Nevertheless, some anticholinergic effects might be seen, such as dry mouth, sleep irregularities (somnolence or insomnia) and sexual dysfunction; and increased blood pressure, an adrenergic effect, has been observed. Other side effects include nausea and nervousness. Weight gain and sedation are not a problem.

Duloxetine (Cymbalta) is a dual-acting serotonin and norepinephrine reuptake inhibitor approved for the treatment of major depressive disorder and generalized anxiety disorder. It is also prescribed to treat chronic neuropathic pain (viz., pain originating in neural dysfunction) associated with diabetes. Duloxetine binds highly with blood protein and has an elimination half-life of 12 hours. Metabolized by P-450 in the liver, it poses a risk of liver injury for heavy users of alcohol. The most common negative side effect is nausea; other side effects include dry mouth, constipation, decreased appetite, fatigue, somnolence, increased sweating and sexual dysfunction. Newborns who have been exposed in the third trimester of pregnancy have presented with respiratory and other problems. Moreover, interactions with MAOIs are a danger, so that, upon switching medications, two weeks should be allowed to clear the drug before an MAOI is given.

THE TREATMENT OF MANIA

Lithium

The drug of choice for the treatment of mania is lithium. Though taken as a drug, it is actually an element, an alkali metal like sodium, potassium, or cesium. It is the lightest metal, in fact, since it falls third in the periodic table of elements, after hydrogen and helium. As such, no company can patent it. Lithium occurs naturally in mineral waters, and in trace amounts in sea water, plants, and animal tissue. In their antimanic effects, lithium salts are remarkably specific.

Earliest records of the use of lithium date to ancient Greece, when mineral water was prescribed for the treatment of mania. After that, its use was lost, and mania was treated with narcotics or depressants. Opium and camphor were used briefly in the late eighteenth century, ether and chloroform in the nineteenth, and bromides and barbiturates in the early twentieth. None of these really worked.

Meanwhile, lithium enjoyed a short resurgence in the nineteenth century as a treatment for gout and in the 1920s as a sedative hypnotic, but fell out of favor due to its side effects. Lithium and mania did not meet again until the late 1940s in Australia, and then by a matter of chance.

John Cade, an Australian psychopharmacologist, was testing the theory that mania might be a form of intoxication caused by an active metabolite in the circulation. The natural place for Cade to begin his search for a suspect metabolite was in the urine, so he injected guinea pigs intraperitoneally with the urine of manics and normals. The manics' urine produced more toxic effects in the guinea pigs. Next, Cade tried to narrow the possibilities, hypothesizing that urea or uric acid might produce the same result. But instead of injecting with urine, Cade chose a soluble uric acid salt, which happened to be lithium urate. With these injections, all of the manic effects were blocked, and the guinea pigs be came placid and unresponsive to stimuli. Further investigation proved that the lithium ion, and not the urate, was responsible for the calming. By the wildest chance, in an attempt to induce mania in guinea pigs, Cade had administered not the cause, but the treatment.

Cade first tried lithium on humans on March 29, 1948:

> *There was a little wizened man of 51 who had been in a state of chronic manic excitement for 5 years. He had lived on a back ward during that time and was restless, dirty, destructive, mischievous, and interfering. He was started on lithium citrate. . . On the fourth day of treatment, his therapist noted a change but the nursing staff did not agree. However, on the fifth day he appeared quieter, tidier, less disinhibited and less distractible. His progress was rapid and at the end of three weeks he was on a convalescent ward. He remained well and left the hospital on July 9, 1948. . . and returned to his old job. (Mason & Granacher, 1980, p. 255)*

Unfortunately, lithium chloride had been tried as a salt substitute in the United States the preceding year, and three articles and a letter appeared in the *Journal of the American Medical Association* attributing several deaths to its use. After that, resistance was up against lithium. Cade's findings had to go the long way around, through clinical trials in Denmark and acceptance in Europe, before the FDA approved it 20 years later, in March of 1970. The only clinical form currently available in the States is lithium carbonate (Li2CO3) (Eskalith).

The lithium salt is a highly water-soluble molecule that is rapidly absorbed from the oral route via the intestine. Blood levels peak between 30 and 100 minutes, but there may be a lapse of a week or more in the therapeutic response. That is because the drug molecules, despite the fact that they are unbound in the blood, are slow to cross cell membranes. They may enter the cell as a sodium replacement, a little bit with each action potential, slowly accumulating in the neuron. It may take three weeks or longer to achieve maximum effects (Post & Chuang, 1991). Except for this lag time while lithium is being absorbed, the degree of effect as a rule corresponds to blood levels. Twin studies show that distribution in tissues may vary according to genetic differences (Mason & Granacher, 1980, p. 257).

Lithium is excreted through the kidneys. Blood levels drop rapidly for about 24 hours, while approximately half of the dose is excreted; for 4 or 5 days thereafter, excretion continues at a moderate pace, and then trails off over the course of two weeks. The pace of excretion may be qualified, however, by the whole balance of lithium and sodium levels. If the body's sodium level is low, from low salt diets or heavy sweating, it tends to conserve lithium as well as sodium, drawing it back from the kidney tubules into active circulation. Side effects or intoxication may result from doses reabsorbed in this way. Therefore, lithium is ill advised for those on low sodium diets, and users should also take care about sweating heavily in hot weather. Conversely, when sodium levels are high, the body eliminates lithium more quickly.

Lithium's mechanism of action is uncertain, but it is likely to be complex. It is known to reduce levels of NE and 5-HT, perhaps by inhibiting their release or by speeding their reuptake. Since low bioamine levels correspond with depression and high ones with mania, this reduction of bioamines would make sense. It has also been hypothesized that lithium may replace sodium during the action potential.

Hypotheses about lithium's mechanism of action are complicated by observations of its effects on bipolar disorder. When given during a manic episode, it is ineffective, because its action is too slow. When given during a depressive phase, it may worsen the depression. However, when given for prevention, it dramatically stabilizes mood, normalizing both the manic and depressive poles. The question is this: How can lithium regulate both excitatory and inhibitory systems? The effects cannot be explained by simple and direct changes of bioamine levels, but suggests the involvement of other systems. One suggestion is that lithium is known to inhibit adenylate cyclase in the brain, which is a compound involved in second-messenger systems. Post and Chuang (1991) have postulated that lithium may affect G-proteins in second-messenger systems. Since second-messenger systems mediate cell responses in a variety of transmitter systems, lithium could thereby dampen both excitatory and inhibitory pathways. However, this would not explain why lithium has such a negligible effect outside the brain. Furthermore, lithium has no noticeable effect on people without mania. At therapeutic dosages, there is no sedation and no euphoria—only a remarkable reduction of mania in manics.

Lithium is also used for recurrent unipolar depressions and for mood disturbances associated with schizophrenia (*schizoaffective disorder*). When patients in manic episodes are treated, they are given haloperidol for rapid calming until lithium levels rise.

Lithium can cause skin reactions during use. Less common are possible toxic effects on the kidneys, and thyroid disturbances. Pregnant women using lithium should be advised that it can cause heart and other birth defects, and can pass to a newborn via breast milk.

The great danger of lithium treatment is toxicity. At therapeutic doses it is generally safe, but, as we saw, factors like low-salt diets and heavy sweating can intrude to cause toxic imbalances, making lithium overdoses all too frequent. Fortunately, blood levels are easily monitored. Once-a-month checkups are routine in outpatients, but once, or even twice a week would be preferable, if somewhat inconvenient. With careful planning, doses can be kept low enough so that side effects do not appear. The average dosage schedule is two 56 mg tablets taken three times a day for a week, and then a drop to 2 to 4 tablets a day.

The first signs of lithium toxicity are subtle and insidious. Toxicity may begin with nausea, fine tremors in resting hands, muscular weakness, fatigue, slurred speech, unsteady balance, ataxia, excessive urination, and thirst. Other signs include dizziness, sleepiness, blurred vision, parkinsonism, and weight loss. These progress gradually to coarse tremors, twitching, grayish discoloration of the skin, rigidity, seizures, and coma. Lithium, needless to say, should be discontinued, although signs of acute toxicity may not appear for as long as two days after the overdose because of slow absorption. Correcting the sodium balance of the blood helps excretion.

Alternative Treatments for Mania

While lithium is quite remarkable in terms of its therapeutic action, in terms of its side effects, it leaves much to be desired. Furthermore, it is ineffective in some cases, especially in cases of rapid cycling, where manic-depressive mood swings occur four or more times a year. The most frequent alternative treatment is carbamazepine (Tegretol), a compound resembling the tricyclics, which is used also as an anticonvulsant medication. Carbamazepine proves as effective as lithium in preventing a relapse of bipolar symptoms, and is superior in treating rapid-cycling forms of mood disorder. It also serves well for patients unable to tolerate the side effects of lithium. Carbamazepine may be used alone, or in combination with lithium. Little is known about its mechanism of action.

The most common side effects of carbamazepine are allergic skin reactions, nausea, drowsiness, ataxia, vertigo, blurred or double vision, and slurred speech; many of these symptoms can be avoided with the proper adjustment of dosages. Some side effects are rare, but dangerous. One is a potentially fatal syndrome that is marked by blisters on the skin. The carbamazepine metabolite, carbamazepine-10, 11-epoxide, is potentially toxic. And carbamazepine can cause birth defects if taken by pregnant women. Like lithium, this is a drug that requires watchfulness.

Valproate is another treatment for mania. However, it is less effective than lithium and does not relieve depression. Less desirable compounds that have been tried are clozapine, some benzodiazepines (clonazepam and lorazepam), MAOIs, tricyclic antidepressants, and SSRIs. Each of these is limited in its effects on mania or depression, and each presents significant drawbacks.

REFERENCES

Akiskal, H. S. (1983). Dysthymic disorders: Psychopathology of proposed chronic depressive subtypes. *American Journal of Psychiatry*, 140, 11-20.

Akiskal, H. S., & McKinney, W. T. (1973, October 5). Depressive disorders: Toward a unified hypothesis. *Science*, 182, 20-29.

American Psychiatric Association. (1994). *Diagnostic and statistical manual of mental disorders* (4th ed.). Washington, DC: American Psychiatric Association.

Berretini, W. H. (1993). The molecular genetics of bipolar disorder. In J. J. Mann & D. J. Kupfer. (Eds.). *Biology of depressive disorders (Part A): A systems perspective. The depressive illness series, Vol. 3* (pp. 189-204). New York: Plenum Press.

DeVane, C. L., Grothe, D. R., & Smith, S. L. (2002). Pharmacology of antidepressants: Focus on nefazadone. *Journal of Clinical Psychiatry, 63*(suppl. 1), 10-17.

Healy, David. (1997.) *The antidepressant era*. Cambridge, MA: Harvard University Press.

Hirschfeld, R. M. A. (2000). History and evolution of the monoamine hypothesis of depression. *Journal of Clinical Psychiatry 61*(Suppl. 6), 4-6.

Hollister, L. E., & Claghorn, J.L. (1993). New antidepressants. *Annual Review of Pharmacology and Toxicology, 32*, 165-177.

Kramer, P. D. (1993). *Listening to Prozac*. New York: Viking.

Post, R. M., & Chuang, D.-M. (1991). Mechanism of action of lithium. In N. J. Birch (Ed.). *Lithium and the cell: Pharmacology and biochemistry* (pp. 204-234). New York: Academic Press.

Schildkraut, J. J. (1965). The catecholamine hypothesis of affective disorders: A review of supporting evidence. *American Journal of Psychiatry*, 122, 509-522.

Stahl, S. M. (1998). Basic psychopharmacology of antidepressants, part 1: Antidepressants have seven distinct mechanisms of action. *Journal of Clinical Psychiatry, 59*(Suppl. 4), 5-14.

Chapter 17

Amphetamine and Cocaine

The stimulants are an extensive family of compounds that excite the central nervous system, although they do so through different chemistries and mechanisms. On the whole, they stimulate behavior or cause arousal, ease depression, induce euphoria, increase alertness, suppress the appetite, and banish fatigue. In high doses, they may cause irritability and excitement that can rise to psychotic pitches. Paradoxically, several stimulants are also known to calm some forms of hyperactivity.

The class of stimulants falls loosely into four subgroups. The first consists of amphetamine and cocaine, both of which are considered protoypes of the stimulants. A second group is the xanthines, or methylxanthines, made up of three fairly mild CNS stimulants that are chemical cousins: caffeine, theobromine, and theophylline. A third group is the convulsants, powerful stimulants known mostly for their induction of seizures (e.g., pentylenetetrazole [Metrazol] or strychnine). And, as a fourth group, some sources would count the antidepressants.

Amphetamine and cocaine, the focus of this chapter, have a history of prominent abuse that overshadows their applications in medicine.

AMPHETAMINE

History

The first amphetamine was synthesized in 1887 in a search for a substitute for the naturally occurring stimulant ephedrine. However, it wasn't until 1927, the year dlamphetamine was made, that their major effects became apparent. The amphetamines were found to stimulate the central nervous system, heighten blood pressure, reverse anesthesia, and enlarge the bronchial passages. With the marketing of Benzedrine in the 1930s, they entered medical use as a treatment for asthma, narcolepsy, depression, and hyperactivity in children, and as appetite suppressants.

It was during and shortly after World War II that social problems with the amphetamines began. Unlike cocaine, amphetamine can be fairly well-absorbed on the oral route, and it has a duration of effect of about seven hours. This made it a useful means of keeping soldiers alert in combat. After the war, amphetamines were prescribed as safe euphoriants and energizers—cures for depression and fatigue. In 1945, *d*-amphetamine (Dexedrine) came onto the market as an appetite suppressant. It was during this period that these agents began to be severely abused.

The first outbreak of abuse occurred in Japan, which hadn't had a severe drug episode since tobacco in the 1600s. During World War II, the Japanese had used methamphetamine to maintain production, and when the war ended, it was sold without a prescription to reduce stockpiles. Many students, nightworkers, urban delinquents, and people affected by postwar dislocation began to inject these "wakeamines" or "awakening drugs" for their euphoriant effects. The abuse epidemic spread for ten years, until multiple efforts at control caught up with it. In 1954, 2 million out of 88.5 million people, mostly teenagers and young adults, were abusers. In a concentrated effort, however, the Japanese government reversed the problem with an effective three-pronged attack that consisted of (1) tight controls on amphetamine production, importation, and sale, (2) penalties for abuse, and (3) education of the public. Some abuse shifted to other substances, but in the late sixties the problem subsided, only to resurge again in the early seventies (Masaki, 1956, p. 15; Brill & Hirose, 1969, p. 181; Kato, 1969, p. 592).

Widespread abuse also took place in Sweden, where amphetamines went on sale in 1938 under the slogan, "Two pills beat a month's vacation." The following year they were made prescription drugs, and prescribing was extensive, but still within sensible bounds. However, more rigid restrictions instituted after the war may have had the effect of publicizing amphetamine effects. Oral misuse spread among the arts subculture. When it reached the morphinists, IV use began, and from there it moved into the criminal underworld and other asocial groups, and a black market sprang up. By 1959, Preludin and Ritalin were on the menu as well. Smuggling was a problem, and abuse was evident among young male arrestees. Bans only increased home production and stoked the black market.

During this distressful period, a group of physicians tried an unprecedented measure in the history of drug control. They secured permission from the government to legally prescribe amphetamines to users (ten or fewer clients to each physician). However, the project failed after two years when two physicians grossly exceeded prescription limits. In 1966 and 1967, the epidemic peaked. Only restrictions of increasing stringency and the dissemination of information brought the situation under control by 1970, when use stabilized.

Americans had been aware of the alerting effects of amphetamines since the early 1930s, when black market prices became cheap, but as in other countries, concern over misuse did not mount until the postwar years. Students switched from caffeine tablets to amphetamine pills, and truck drivers took the new drugs to stay awake and alert on long hauls. Both groups patronized the black market, where 75 cents could get you 1,000 tablets. They joined the ranks of athletes and businessmen who had been using amphetamines since before the war. This growing misuse boomed in the fifties and sixties, with many users getting drugs by deceiving physicians with fake names and false prescriptions. Truck stops in the early sixties became major distribution centers for both illicit uppers and downers—amphetamines to keep the truckers sharp, and barbiturates to slow them down at the end of a run. Billions of doses of these agents were circulating by 1962. Some companies pulled amphetamines off the legitimate market, and amendments to federal food and drug laws led to the closer documentation of shipments so that supplies were harder to divert. Then, however, home laboratories began making supplies at higher prices. Another problem was that IV use, which had begun among American servicemen in Korea and Japan (who would mix heroin and amphetamine), began to spread. Public crackdowns tended only to carry the word beyond the heroin subculture.

However, by the late sixties and early seventies, government actions had successfully put pressure on all the channels of supply for illicit amphetamines. They were made Schedule II drugs. Admonitory articles in medical journals led to a decline in prescriptions. The black market supplies had been reduced by new policies, and illicit labs were busted. Public campaigns were mounted. And the speed freaks themselves, prominent on the West Coast drug scene by 1967 and undesirable even to the drug subculture, were walking advertisements against speed (Brecher, 1972, p. 302). The net effect was that amphetamine abuse declined and has not been a major problem since. But, unfortunately, this was not a case of society successfully obliterating the abuse of a drug, because as pressure on amphetamines grew, importers switched to cocaine, which was becoming an evident problem by 1970. During their heyday, cheap and available amphetamines had all but driven cocaine off the black market, but at this point the trend reversed. The problem with uppers continued, therefore, except that over the next ten years, the speed freak came to be supplanted by the crackhead.

The late eighties and early nineties saw a resurgence of amphetamine use in the form of *crystal meth,* also known as *ice* or *crystal.* This is a smokable, crystalline form of methamphetamine that gives a high lasting hours, compared to crack's few minutes, and it is addicting.

Pharmacokinetics

Amphetamine molecules occur in both right-handed and left-handed forms; in other words, forms making up optical mirror images of each other. To differentiate such types of molecules, the prefixes *d* for *dextro* ("right") and *l* for *levo* ("left") are used. Accordingly, *d*-amphetamine is the right-handed molecule, and *l*-amphetamine is the left. Another type of amphetamine molecule consists of the *d* and *l*-types combined, giving *dl*-amphetamine, and still another variation is achieved by attaching a methyl group to the amphetamine molecule. Methamphetamine, the methylated *dl* form, produces effects similar to those of *d*-amphetamine. On the market, the most common amphetamines are *dl*-amphetamine, or just *amphetamine* (Benzedrine), *d*-amphetamine (Dexedrine), and methamphetamine (Methedrine and Desoxyn). Usually, the salt is prepared with sulfuric acid, yielding *amphetamine sulfate.*

Amphetamine is absorbed well and quickly from the oral route, unlike cocaine. On a normal stomach, effects may begin in 30 minutes and peak within 2 to 3 hours. The intravenous route is used mostly by abusers, who call the injection of amphetamine *mainlining.* With this method, the onset of effects is under five minutes.

Amphetamines are lipid-soluble and cross the blood-brain barrier. Metabolism takes place in the liver, and a good portion of a dose, somewhat less than half, is excreted in the urine unchanged. A full dose is usually gone in about 72 hours.

Pharmacological Effects

Catecholamines (DA and NE) are the keystone of amphetamine's central nervous stimulation. The actions proposed can be summarized as follows:

1. Amphetamines release newly synthesized catecholamines (DA and NE) from presynaptic terminals.
2. They release larger quantities of catecholamines than usual at the synapses.
3. They block catecholamine reuptake at the synapse.
4. They inhibit MAO.

In effect, amphetamines stimulate the release of large quantities of transmitter, then keep it active by blocking reuptake and guarding it from degrading enzymes. The result is a formidable adrenergic response at both peripheral and central nervous synapses. One of the distinctions between amphetamines and cocaine is that cocaine's predominant action seems to be to block the reuptake of catecholamines, whereas amphetamine has the important addition of releasing them from the presynaptic terminals as well. In drug screening and classification tests, a key sign that characterizes amphetamines and other stimulants is their ability to counteract the effects of CNS depressants.

One of the most sought-after effects by users and misusers of amphetamines is mental alertness and arousal, which can be had at a 5 to 25 mg dose. This is probably a result of a stimulated reticular formation and a boost of NE, bestowing a sense of wakefulness and decreased fatigue. EEG patterns show signs of arousal, enabling users to sustain their attention and concentration for a long time. Tiredness from lack of sleep may seem to dispel magically under amphetamine's influence, and the need for sleep may be postponed. Research has shown that mental performance improves, but only on simple tasks; the user can get more work done, but the number of errors remains normal (Hoffman & Lefkowitz, 1990, p. 211). Complex intellectualizing (e.g., problem solving) in normal, well-rested people is not helped by amphetamines, but users in general do report less mental clouding, better concentration, and clearer thinking. Steady use of these drugs, however, may result in overarousal. Insomnia may develop as amphetamines change the sleep pattern, markedly reducing dreaming sleep and overall sleep time. Upon cessation, users may experience a rebound effect of prolonged sleep and may take two months to recover their usual patterns.

As well as banishing fatigue, amphetamines inspire one with an exuberant sense of physical energy and can improve athletic performance—another adrenergic effect. Any kind of physical task impaired by fatigue or boredom, or requiring stamina, may also be improved. However, as with mental arousal, this effect may reverse with overdosage or overuse, and other types of performance, such as those involving dexterity or fine motor skills or those requiring long-term high energy output, may suffer. An especial danger is when the dose wears off and the user "crashes" (experiences a heavy torpor and falls asleep). This can be as counterproductive as the continued alertness was productive. The steady use of large doses may be followed by a rebound depression.

Another spur to amphetamine abuse is the euphoria and elation that are typical responses to the drug and that may be courted by some users at low doses without undue danger of becoming psychologically dependent. In the low dose range, these effects are mild. At high doses, however, amphetamine is a strong euphoriant. Five minutes after an IV injection of large doses, users feel an orgasmic "rush". Some believe this to be related to the speed with which the drug enters the brain. In seasoned users, the rush may occur immediately upon injection. In their case, they are conditioned to the drug effect, and the conditions of administration act as a stimulus to trigger transmitter release in the brain, even before the drug arrives. The rewarding effects of amphetamine are associated with catecholaminergic neurons in the brain, especially the dopaminergic mesolimbic pathway extending from the ventral tegmental area to the nucleus accumbens.

Generally, amphetamine euphoria shows tolerance, requiring increasing doses for continued effect, but it has been noted that modest quantities can produce mild euphoria consistently without an increase in dosage. Few street users are content with that, however, so their use escalates to excessive dosages.

At normal oral doses, amphetamine can directly affect the synapses of the sympathetic nervous system in the periphery and cause a release of NE that results in a strong sympathetic reaction. Because of this mimicking of a sympathetic reaction, amphetamine is referred to as a sympathomimetic drug, and in fact is one of the most potent. The drug-induced sympathetic response is felt by users as an anxiety state or a panic attack, their pupils and air passages widening, their systems mobilized for an emergency that doesn't exist.

Stimulant abusers strive for the greatest possible central stimulation and euphoria with the least possible amount of peripheral stimulation and sympathetic response. Methamphetamine (Methedrine), known in the drug subculture as *meth* or *speed*, is a choice drug in this respect, and the amphetamines as a rule are preferred to cocaine.

In addition to the CNS effect of euphoria, amphetamines at moderate dosages (5 to 50 mg) produce other signs of NE stimulation in the CNS, such as a loss of appetite, increased motor activity (like fidgeting), and slight tremors. An increase of meaningless repetitive behavior (stereotyped behavior) has been attributed to DA actions.

Amphetamines suppress the appetite by stimulating satiety-signaling neurons in the hypothalamus (that is, those indicating, "We've eaten enough"), and they may cause weight loss, not only by reducing the desire for food but also by increasing the body's general activity level and metabolic rate. In addition, there may be some loss of smell and taste, which diminishes the appetite. However, the anorexic effects show tolerance, so that people using amphetamines to lose weight shortly regain their appetite. To continue, these dieters must then raise the dosage into the realm of side effects such as insomnia and euphoria.

At normal oral doses, amphetamine increases blood pressure (which slows the heart rate by reflex). This effect shows tolerance sooner than CNS arousal and euphoria. That is why abusers can achieve such phenomenal doses before suffering threats to the heart. In one case, a user injected 15,000 mg in 24 hours without acute illness, while new users have died at 120 mg done by rapid IV injection (Brecher, 1972, pp. 287-288). At higher doses with no tolerance, the heart rate increases as a result of an overall sympathetic effect.

Although amphetamine stimulates the respiratory center in the medulla, breathing rate and volume do not increase appreciably in humans. But amphetamines (like theophylline, an antiasthma medicine) do cause the bronchial muscles to relax, expanding the caliber of the lung passageways and making breathing easier.

Clinical Applications

Although at first the amphetamines were prescribed freely for many conditions, they never reached their original clinical promise, due to the problem of dependence and the development of better chemical agents. Eventually, in 1970, the FDA limited their use to three conditions: attention deficit hyperactivity disorder in children, obesity, and narcolepsy.

The only current and fully accepted medical use for amphetamines is to treat attention deficit hyperactivity disorder (ADHD) in children. This is a poorly understood disorder, formerly known as *hyperactivity, hyperkinesis,* or *minimal brain dysfunction.* The condition is characterized by difficulty in concentrating, impulsive behavior, poorly regulated activity (over- or underactivity), memory problems, and academic difficulties. The use of stimulants to treat the disorder began in 1937, in the wake of an epidemic of viral encephalitis, when Dr. C. Bradley, a pediatrician, used Benzedrine successfully to treat convalescing children who were hyperactive and distractible (Silver, 1992, p. 103). After that, it became routine to treat such behaviors with stimulants. When some children with ADHD are put on small doses of stimulants, they become less restless, impulsive, and distractible, with a longer attention span. They are better able to organize their thoughts, and they perform better on tasks involving short-term memory. In general, their use of learning strategies improves, leading to better performance at school. A similar calming effect has been seen in adults in certain anxiety states, such as before a test.

The stimulant effect in these cases was once considered paradoxical, because one would expect an increase in restlessness and agitation from a stimulant. Current thinking, however, is that the symptoms of ADHD may be attributable to a deficiency of DA and NE in brain systems, which is corrected to some degree by stimulants. Metabolite and enzyme measures in the blood, urine, and extracellular fluid of children lend support to this idea. Serotonergic mechanisms do not seem to be involved. Nonetheless, as it stands, the staunchest support for the use of stimulants for ADHD is tradition. In at least two-thirds of the cases, it works.

The three stimulants commonly prescribed in the U.S. for ADHD are methylphenidate (Ritalin), dextroamphetamine (Dexedrine), and pemoline (Cylert). Methylphenidate is by far the most prescribed, with an average dose of 15 to 30 mg a day, in divided doses. Due to rapid metabolism, as many as 4 or 5 doses a day may be required. Interestingly, the dose does not relate to body weight, so that a child and an adult might require the same amount (Silver, 1992, p. 108). The most frequent side effects are loss of appetite and difficulty falling asleep at night. Both effects may subside over 2 to 3 weeks. Since the duration of action is short, appetite effects may be manipulated by timing the doses, so that a 3 to 4-hour suppression of appetite may end with a rebound hunger closer to mealtimes. Sleep difficulties may be countered with mild sedatives. The appearance of stomachaches, headaches, or motor tics (usually of the head or neck) may require a shift to another medication.

There is concern that stimulants may have an adverse impact on growth and development in children. However, some argue that the clinical significance is negligible (less than 3 percent variance in adult height, about 1 to 3 centimeters) (Silver, 1992, p. 116). It was suggested that this effect was due to the suppression of growth hormone, but recent findings show that growth hormone is released at night when the medication is not acting.

Drug holidays are another issue. Some physicians argue that these drugs should be used as meagerly as possible and should be stopped on vacations, or even on weeknights and weekends. This would guard against the formation of tolerance and against the deterioration of performance, should long-term use be stopped. Others feel that drug holidays are unnecessary if one is careful in prescribing.

When stimulants fail, a second line of treatment for ADHD is tricyclics and other antidepressants, such as imipramine (Tofranil), desipramine (Norpramin), bupropion (Wellbutrin), and the antihypertensive drug clonidine (Catapres). These drugs also foster catecholaminergic actions. A third line of treatment calls for low doses of drugs with neuroleptic (thioridazine [Mellaril]), sedative (carbamazepine [Tegretol]), and antimanic (lithium) effects.

Amphetamines have been tried in short-term weight-loss programs for obesity, but most agree that they are more a liability than a help. An obese person, by medical definition, is 20 percent or more over ideal body weight. As a health risk, obesity involves an increased chance of cardiovascular disease, of adult-onset diabetes, and of sickness and mortality in general. *D*-amphetamine and methamphetamine are the best drugs for appetite suppression, but they have a high abuse potential. Therefore, the FDA approves as weight-loss aids only a limited number of anorexics. Phenylpropanolamine (Dexatrim) is the best known of these; 50 mg is equivalent to a strong mug of coffee (200 mg of caffeine), and it can have possibly severe side effects, such as raised blood pressure and nervousness.

Another problem with amphetamines as appetite suppressants is that, even at moderate doses, tolerance develops within 2 to 6 weeks, at which point dieters can recover their appetites and start to regain weight. Higher doses might overcome this block, but at the risk of dependence. Also, it becomes a temptation for dieters whose programs are failing to medicate their disappointment with drug euphoria. Consequently, many euphoriant stimulants have masqueraded as "diet pills." Insomnia can also be a problem if diet pills are taken in the latter part of the day.

A further consideration is that drug therapy for obesity is too superficial and mechanical a treatment, since overeating likely has psychological and genetic roots that the drug cannot address. The dieter still needs a strict eating regimen when the drug regimen ends. For all of these reasons, many disapprove entirely of amphetamines as appetite suppressants, and some states have banned them. At best, the amphetamines are tolerated for this purpose, being of questionable value, of short-term effectiveness, and possibly of dangerous consequence.

Another condition for which amphetamines have been used is narcolepsy, a condition of severe and uncontrollable sleepiness due to abnormal neural functioning. Narcolepsy was the first condition which amphetamines were found to treat effectively. At a dose of 5 to 60 mg, the drugs produce no tolerance for the effect of warding off sleep. However, in light of the dangers of euphoria and dependence, this use is no longer deemed advisable.

Side Effects

Amphetamines have a battery of side effects related to their stimulatory action. These include agitation, confusion, palpitations, raised blood pressure, tremors, dizziness, headache, delirium, fatigue, and insomnia. Users may become talkative. Some experience a paradoxical drowsiness. Sweating, blurred vision, and dry mouth may appear. Effects like these can occur at low doses and vary widely among individuals. Only some people experience them, usually at manageable levels, with tolerance developing over the course of a few days.

Tolerance varies for different amphetamine effects. It comes on quickly for appetite suppression. On the other hand, children with attention deficit disorder and some individuals with narcolepsy have remained effectively on the same low doses for years, with no tolerance at all.

Acute toxicity from the amphetamines is idiosyncratic and unpredictable. Toxic signs may appear in some persons after as little as 2 mg, but they are more frequent after 15 mg. Toxicity is more likely in beginners, since they have no tolerance to effects like cardiovascular irregularities and raised body temperature, to which chronic users are inured.

Chlorpromazine can be used to treat amphetamine poisoning because it antagonizes many effects, stopping tremors and lowering blood pressure. Diazepam can be used to stop convulsions, and acidifying the urine with ammonium chloride helps to speed excretion. Toxic signs usually vanish in about a week. However, the rebound depression from withdrawal can last months and may require treatment.

Deaths resulting directly from an overdose of amphetamines are uncommon. In this sense, the old slogan, "speed kills" is misleading. Subjects with no tolerance have survived doses as high as 400 to 500 mg, and chronic abusers have reported doses as high as 1,700 mg daily, without deleterious effects, partly because they develop tolerance to the cardiovascular threat. When speed does kill, it probably does so in a severe depression that follows an amphetamine binge, when the user has depleted the transmitters responsible for normal mood. Or it may come in general from the stresses and conditions of the speed freak's lifestyle. Abusers may grow scrawny from appetite suppression and poor eating habits; they may have skin sores and mortal infections from neglected health and dirty needles; and they may run risks from destructive and aggressive behavior.

One of the most marked and severe side effects recognized with amphetamines is a condition referred to as *amphetamine psychosis*. Dosages of 60 to 300 mg a day of *d*-amphetamine can produce, within a week, a typical paranoid psychosis with hallucinations and disordered thinking, alternating with periods of mania. This condition is associated mostly with injection rather than oral use, and, as expected, is found most frequently in chronic users. However, it can also occur in the uninitiated after a single large dose or a short period of intake. It seldom occurs under 50 mg, usually appears between 36 and 48 hours after a single large dose, and frequently it vanishes completely upon cessation of the drug. In the early stages of the psychosis, the patient acts euphoric, loquacious, and overconfident. This mood soon turns to suspicion, fearfulness, and aggressiveness. Vivid tactile and auditory hallucinations manifest, along with paranoid delusions and a loosening of associative thinking. Users are often aware, though, that the hallucinations or other conditions are drug-induced (pseudohallucinations). They may grind their teeth, show repetitive behavior, suspicion, fear, antisociability, and aggression. In full blossom, amphetamine psychosis is clinically indistinguishable from paranoid schizophrenia. The subject's sense of time and body may change. Parasitosis (or formication), the feeling that bugs are crawling all over or under one's skin, can occur, causing the patient to pick or excoriate the skin. This effect is most likely a rebound effect of the drug on peripheral nerve endings.

The hallucinations of amphetamine psychosis can be treated with antipsychotic DA antagonists, usually haloperidol. Upon cessation of the stimulant, recovery slowly begins. Often, the condition is gone in about a week, but in some cases it has been known to linger for years.

Amphetamine Abuse

Let's issue a general declaration to all the underground community, *contra speedamos ex cathedra*. Speed is antisocial, paranoid making, it's a drag, bad for your body, bad for your mind, generally speaking, in the long run uncreative and it's a plague in the whole dope industry. All the nice gentle dope fiends are getting screwed up by the real horror monster Frankenstein speed freaks who are going around stealing and bad mouthing everybody. (Ginsberg, 1965; as cited in Brecher, 1972)

Amphetamine first appeared on the market in 1932 as Benzedrine. Benzedrine inhalers, a drug form marketed as a bronchodilator to relieve asthma, provided a convenient form of abuse. The core of the inhaler consisted of a paper strip saturated with a good dose of amphetamines—about 250 mg. One needed only extract the paper strip and chew it or soak it in beer or coffee. Eventually, these inhalers were banned in 1959 by the FDA. Much more drastic abuse, in the great incidence in Sweden and Japan, however, occurred in IV form. "Speed freaks," IV shooters of methamphetamine (speed), typically procure the drug as tablets or crystals and prepare it as a solution for IV injection.

Some amphetamine abusers begin by procuring the drug, licitly or illicitly, for practical reasons: to lose weight, to recover from hangovers, to relieve boredom, or to provide stamina on long work shifts. Many learn to raise the dose to achieve euphoria, and they become psychologically dependent, with depression on withdrawal. More commonly, users buy street amphetamines specifically to get high; however, the street drug is often caffeine or contains some other over-the-counter stimulant as well. Because of their abuse potential and the danger of moderate to severe addiction, amphetamines were rated Schedule II drugs in 1970 by the Controlled Substances Act.

Typically, users move from low oral doses taken several times daily to high oral doses, until they can tolerate a gram or more a day. Then they may switch to intravenous use. At this stage, it is typical to graduate to a run, a shooting binge extending over several days. Veteran speed freaks may inject themselves up to 10 times around the clock and average up to 2 grams a day for 4 to 6 days. The allure of this drug marathon is the climactic rush or *flash* immediately after each hit (IV injection). Users describe it as an ineffable experience, ecstatic, exalting, and orgiastic—a whole-body orgasm.

After a rush, a milder euphoria sets in, and the users experience many of the positive effects we have described, such as vigor and clear headedness. Whenever the rush, euphoria, and hyperexcitability fade—after three or four hours—it is time for the next hit. Over the course of the run, users do not eat or sleep, but grow more shaky, tense, irritable, and paranoid.

When the run ends, a few hours pass before the users suffer the symptoms of withdrawal. Then they rebound into a profound depression and sleep lasting up to two days, to awake ravenous, on a rebound from long appetite suppression and fasting. Much of the paranoia may be gone, but the heavy lethargy may persist for days. This is *crashing* in street lingo. At this point, a user may start another run. But if not, depression is the worst of it, and suicidal thinking is possible. Withdrawal symptoms are usually gone within a week, but the depression may linger.

Amphetamine abusers frequently try to maintain euphoria and knock out the toxic symptoms of speed by mixing it with depressants (barbiturates or alcohol) or narcotics. A *speedball* is speed (cocaine or amphetamine) taken with an opiate. Speedballs give the quick awakening of speed with the dreamy drift of opium, and some report that the rush is followed by a lengthy euphoria. With amphetamine/barbiturate use, aggression is more likely, due to the barbiturate disinhibition. As one user said, "Barbiturates make you want to get out on the street and start kicking asses. Speed gives you the energy to get up and do it" (Brecher, 1972, p. 287). Similarly, if abusers use barbiturates to try to ease themselves off a run, they may be moved to unprovoked violence.

The chronic IV use of heavy doses of methamphetamine, such as those taken by speed addicts, can lead to anorexia, paranoia, and other familiar symptoms, and even to some degree of catatonia. It is possible for users to stay awake most of the time for weeks, if they can manage maybe an hour a day's sleep, so that some of the chronic effects are undoubtedly from sleep deprivation. In addition to paranoid psychosis, these conditions can precipitate schizophrenia, especially in borderline users who are already unstable.

The prognosis for complete recovery is good for even the most disorganized high-dosers, provided they can abstain for six months. However, the fatigue felt during a crash can persist for months and drive users back to the drug.

The speed freaks, whose heyday occurred around 1967, were considered the lowest rung of the drug subculture at the time (see Ginsberg quotation at the head of this section). Most were white with middle-class values, education, and family attitudes, but no skills for operating in the criminal drug underworld. They stood in contrast to the heroin subculture, which consisted of highly skilled individuals who could function in the black market, which was integrated into a web of other illegal and legal enterprises. Furthermore, the junkies' drug calmed them, but the speed freaks acted suspicious and paranoid, looked like "dope fiends," and had the jitters. For instance, they would try to pass a bad check to a bank teller, then panic and bolt in the middle of the transaction. In *Licit and Illicit Drugs* (1972, pp. 287-288), Brecher writes,

> *. . . the speed freak survives by sponging on others and by dealing in drugs. Lacking skills and standards, he cheats. And the victims of his cheating are generally speed freaks like himself, paranoid like himself, on the verge of violence like himself. The violence that ultimately emerges . . . arises when the direct drug effect, the paranoia, occurs in a chaotic community where almost everybody is simultaneously engaged in sponging on everybody else, cheating everybody else—and suspecting everybody else. This is the*

scene that leads even confirmed drug users to conclude that "speed is the worst."

COCAINE

Sherlock Holmes took his bottle from the corner of the mantelpiece, and his hypodermic syringe from its neat morocco case. With his long, white, nervous fingers he adjusted the delicate needle, and rolled back his left shirt-cuff. For some little time his eyes rested thoughtfully upon the sinewy forearm and wrist, all dotted and scarred with innumerable puncture-marks. Finally, he thrust the sharp point home, pressed down the tiny piston, and sank back into the velvet-lined armchair with a long sigh of satisfaction.

Arthur Conan Doyle
The Sign of Four

Cocaine has effects like those of amphetamine, but of a shorter duration; while the effects of methamphetamine may last for hours, those of IV cocaine last only minutes. abusers describe the euphoric effects of both drugs in almost identical ways, and cocaine users have been shown to be unable to distinguish between the effects of cocaine and *d*-amphetamine at matching dosages. Some, however, claim that cocaine has subtler effects than amphetamine, and it is probable that cocaine sniffed differs from amphetamine shot up intravenously. Cocaine poisoning is almost identical to amphetamine poisoning, because they share similar catecholamine (DA and NE) mechanisms. Therefore, much of what was said of amphetamine above likewise applies to cocaine.

Clinically, cocaine is classified as a local anesthetic, along with its related synthetic compounds procaine (Novocain) and lidocaine (Xylocaine). Of this class, however, cocaine has the most prominent effects on mood and behavior. Due to this, it has assumed much more importance on the street than in the clinic, and became the drug of abuse of the eighties.

History

Cocaine is found in significant quantities in only two species of the coca shrub, which grows in moist, tropical climates. It originates in the leaves of *Erythroxylon coca*, a tree native to the slopes of the Peruvian and Bolivian Andes at an altitude of 1,000 to 3,000 feet, where the annual rainfall surpasses 100 inches a year. *Erythroxylon novogranatense* grows in the drier mountainous regions of Colombia and the Caribbean Coast. Many of the coca-growing regions are unsuitable for other crops, so the economic incentives are high for growing coca for exportation.

In its native regions, the indigenous use of the shrub is well-documented, and the highlanders' practice of chewing or sucking on the coca leaves goes back at least 5,000 years, to predate the Incas. Some small cultivated patches are believed to be 1,000 years old. It is clear that, by A.D. 1000, the coca shrub was broadly cultivated. The natives frequently chewed the leaves (which contain 0.6 percent to 1.8 percent of the alkaloid) and praised them for the sense of strength and wellbeing that they bestowed. The drug eased long mountain journeys, which travelers measured by the number of "chews" they took, and it eliminated cold and hunger on the trails.

When the Spanish conquistadors arrived in the sixteenth century, they found coca deeply entrenched in the Inca social structure. Its use was controlled by the ruling classes, who disbursed the right to use it to their social inferiors. One could approach the throne of the emperor only with coca leaves held in the mouth, and casual use of "the greatest of all natural productions" was a sacrilege. Exploiting its value, the conquering Spaniards employed coca as currency to recruit the Incas for labor.

Cocaine use did not catch on quickly in Europe because the leaves were in poor condition on arrival and had little effect. The Europeans even accused the Peruvians of having overactive imaginations. But a turning point came in the mid1800s, when two developments occurred. First, in the 1840s or 1850s (accounts vary widely about who and when), the chief alkaloid of the coca leaf was first isolated; Albert Niemann reported on it in 1859, noting its bitter flavor and its numbing effect on the tongue, and he named it *cocaine*. The second development was that Angelo Mariani, a French chemist and entrepreneur, took a fancy to the drug and mixed coca extract into many of his products, such as teas and lozenges, which he marketed in Europe. His crowning achievement, though, was the phenomenally successful Vin Mariani, a concoction of coca and wine. It had many faithful and famous devotees and advocates: President McKinley, Thomas Edison, the Czar of Russia, and, eminent among them, Pope Leo XIII, who issued Mariani a gold medal and cited him as a benefactor of humanity.

Soon after its isolation, cocaine aroused interest as a substance that countered depressants, so it was studied as a treatment for alcohol and morphine addiction, and was shown to have analgesic properties, able to numb a pinprick. In 1884, it was first used medicinally in dentistry and eye surgery. At that time, the dangers of physical dependence were still unsuspected.

In the 1880s, two popular figures spread the news of the new drug and its effects. Sometime early in the decade, Sigmund Freud heard about it, either through his teachers or published accounts, and it is clear that he procured some in 1884. The young, harried neurologist tried about 50 mg, and it cheered him wonderfully. Shortly after, he wrote,

> *In my last severe depression I took coca again and a small dose lifted me to the heights in a wonderful fashion. I am just busy collecting the literature for a song of praise to this magical substance. (Jones, 1953, p. 80)*

Two months later, Freud published *Ueber Coca*, his "Song of Praise" for cocaine, in which he described its effect on himself and others, lauding it for inducing "exhilaration and lasting euphoria, which in no way differs from the normal euphoria of the healthy person." The article aroused interest in medical circles. Freud sent samples to his friends, sister, and fiancée, recommending cocaine as a safe exhilarant, and to his colleagues for anesthesia, psychiatry, and the treatment of morphine withdrawal. He added to his other claims that cocaine increases self-control and vitality, bestows the capacity for more work, has no after effects like alcohol and leaves one with no craving, but a curious aversion to continuing use. Generally, cocaine came to be touted as a wonder drug, which is how the Parke-Davis Pharmaceutical Company advertised it in 1885. It was prescribed for opium, morphine, and alcohol dependence, and was used as a general tonic and favorite ingredient in medicine, soda, and wine.

However, after Freud's advocacy, attacks followed based on observations of the dependence and mental disturbances caused by cocaine, and Freud was accused of unleashing a third scourge on humanity, the first two being alcohol and the opiates.

Freud's reversal came after he had given some cocaine to his friend Ernst von Fleischl-Marxow, a morphine addict with a nervous disease. Fleischl-Marxow gradually increased his dosage, within a year, to twenty times the initial level, until he was taking a gram daily, and he developed cocaine psychosis. Freud, who nursed Fleischl-Marxow through the harrowing nights, changed his position toward cocaine and retracted his former endorsements.

The medical community, however, maintained an interest in cocaine as a local anesthetic, because of its temporary and reversible effects. It was Carl Koller, a friend of Freud, who made the first connection between cocaine's anesthetic properties and its use in surgery (eye surgery). It was also one of the first alkaloids to be chemically synthesized in 1923.

A second celebrity to broadcast the news of cocaine in the 1800s was none other than Arthur Conan Doyle's fictional sleuth, Sherlock Holmes, an unapologetic cocaine addict who rhapsodized on the virtues of cocaine at the beginning of *The Sign of Four*, part of which is quoted in the epigraph to this section. Doyle is said to have confused the effects of cocaine with those of morphine in depicting Holmes's behavior, which for the most part is sedate and dreamy.

Between 1885 and 1905 came the Great Cocaine explosion, a boom time for the drug. Widely available in Europe and America, it was used for recreation, and it was also the secret ingredient in many patent medicines. Both sniffing and injection spread down the social ladder. In 1885, John Styth Pemberton of Georgia introduced French Wine Cola—Ideal Nerve and Tonic Stimulant, which was based on a syrup containing products of the coca leaf and the African kola nut (which contains about 2 percent caffeine). This led to Coca Cola, "the intellectual beverage and temperance drink," being introduced in 1888 amid much fanfare, as a headache remedy and a tonic for the elderly. It soon came to be known as *dope* in slang. Later, Coca Cola came under attack by the Pure Food and Drug Law (1906), and the coca leaves were decocainized, though still allowed. Pemberton carbonated the drink and added caffeine, which is one of the reasons that soda fountains became associated with drug stores. Today, in fact, pharmaceutical coca is imported from South America, processed to extract cocaine for medical use, and the remaining leaf material is prepared for Coca Cola.

In the latter 1800s, in dry states, cocaine replaced liquor; in others, bars added it to whiskey, and peddlers even sold it door-to-door. But it did not take long before the abuse potential and the psychosis-inducing properties were plain, and when the 1890s came in, the trend was reversing.

Through the first decade of the 1900s, restrictions tightened, although the boom continued. In 1906, the Food and Drug Act eliminated cocaine from medicines and soft drinks, and almost all states regulated its use. Still, in 1902, 90 percent or more of the use was nonmedical, and in 1906 there were as many users as there were in 1976, with only half of the population. A year later, use peaked, with cocaine ten cents a gram where legal, and five dollars where not. It wasn't until 1914 that the Harrison Act drove the drug underground into the realm of musicians and bohemians.

The Harrison Act classified cocaine as a narcotic, but instead of prohibiting use or possession, it functioned as a revenue statute, enforcing the monitoring of supplies, trafficking, and sales. It is generally recognized that the support for this act came mostly from unsubstantiated gossip. In the American South, attitudes against cocaine took a distinctly racist tone. In the wake of Reconstruction, a fear had arisen of drug-stimulated blacks rebelling against the new segregated social order. The original "dope fiends" of popular culture and folklore were African-American workers and prostitutes. Myths circulated that cocaine improved pistol marksmanship and gave demonically overstimulated blacks a zombielike imperviousness to .32 caliber bullets, due to temporary immunity to shock. For this reason, some police departments actually switched to .38 caliber bullets. Whites possessed by a paranoia of mass murders by dope fiends faulted the drug as "a potent incentive in driving humble negroes all over the country to abnormal crimes." The fact is, there is little evidence of widespread use of cocaine by African-Americans, and by 1914 most may not have been able to afford it. Nonetheless, the stereotypes forged during these years have continued to haunt the users of illegal drugs ever since, whether the pharmacology fits or not, so that even modern barbiturate and marijuana abusers have been characterized as maniacal dope fiends in the grip of an involuntary homicidal mania. Although generally the treatment of drug users has become more enlightened, these images continue to serve as useful propaganda for mobilizing public opinion in favor of law enforcement, so they persist. Unfortunately, they also contribute to miseducation about the effects and dangers of particular drugs.

By the 1920s, cocaine prices were up, due to tighter controls on illicit dealing and dispensing. At thirty dollars an ounce, cocaine was restricted to the bohemian and jazz cultures. By the thirties, when the cheaper and longer-acting amphetamine became available, cocaine all but vanished from the scene.

We have seen that when successful law enforcement and public education dried up much of the amphetamine market around 1968 to 1970, prices rose. As a result, cocaine once again became economically competitive and came back into favor, flooding the speed market (1968). Into the mid-seventies, the view of cocaine was still that of an expensive and glamorous upscale treat—the "champagne of drugs." However, as the demand became known and South American producers drew more profit, the network of growing, processing, smuggling, and distributing developed, and prices began to drop consistently.

The growth of the cocaine industry accelerated moderately through the 1970s, but the first half of the 1980s saw a boom as the purity of the product increased and the price plummeted. From 1974 to 1985, the number of people who said they had ever used cocaine increased from 5.4 to 22.2 million (Kozel & Adams, 1986, p. 973). All other indicators—seizures of illicit drugs, dealers' prices, and so forth—support that finding.

In addition to market demand, smugglers found cocaine much easier and more profitable to smuggle than marijuana, without significant increases in penalties if caught. Consequently, most of the system went over to coke, and Brazil, Venezuela, and Ecuador joined Peru, Bolivia, and Colombia in production. The Reagan administration responded with a War on Drugs, passing a 1981 amendment to the Posse Comitatus Act. This allowed military participation in order to stop smuggling, and organized the South Florida Task Force.

One peculiarity of the rise in cocaine abuse was its impact on the 26yearold and older bracket of the population. As a rule, most new drug users are adolescents, but the at-risk population for cocaine in the last two decades was young working adults. The popular image of the cocaine abuser in the seventies centered on the glitter people: Hollywood actors, athletes, artists, jazz musicians, designers, ad executives, and models (although the drug was in all social classes to some extent. And the image in the eighties centered on the yuppie—a young, urban professional holding a white collar job. In 1985, the average user was a 30yearold white male earning $25,000 or more a year (Black, 1985).

The year 1986 was a turning point, bringing another surge in use. It was in the first quarter of this year that a leap in the practice of smoking was reported, and the slang terms *crack* and *rock* began to appear in the media. Actually, crack had been familiar to the drug scene as early as 1981 and 1983 in New York, Miami, and Los Angeles (Inciardi, Lockwood, & Pottinger, 1993, p. 9). Crack is a freebased form of cocaine. In making it, the original, purer alkaloid (base) is freed from the cocaine hydrochloride by treating the crystals with a basic solution--usually water and baking soda. The result is small, white chunks of cocaine that resemble pieces of crumbled soap and that make a crackling sound when smoked. This turned out to be a great marketing innovation, and a vast improvement over the previous form of freebasing, which involved vaporizing the cocaine with hot, potentially explosive gases, such as ether, in a device known as a base pipe. With crack, the freebase could be sold ready-made in small, plastic vials containing one or two rocks (65 to 100 mg), costing 10 to 20 dollars. This brought the street prices down; instead of buying a gram for $100, users could come to the "crack house" more frequently with less money—an important development because it brought crack to the inner city in a big way. The small rocks could also be easily hidden or disposed of in the event of a police raid.

Surveys of freebasing among cocaine users show an increase from 1 percent in 1977 to 5 percent in 1981, and to 18 percent in 1984. Since crack smoking yields an effect that is 5 to 10 times more intense than cocaine sniffing, there was also an alarming rise in the need for treatment and emergencies, and in deaths. The prices and mode of administration that had kept cocaine problems down were now removed. The increased bioavailability of crack to brain tissue and resulting intense euphoria made it virtually a new drug. Dependence, the occurrence of which had still been under debate when sniffing was in, was certainly a danger, if not an inevitability, with crack.

By 1989, the cocaine business had become a highly organized global industry commanding billions of dollars, and the user problem had surpassed the ability of treatment centers and law enforcement to control it. In the producing countries, drug barons have become towering political forces. For instance, in 1985, the Bolivian cocaine trade brought in 2 billion dollars, three times the amount of official Bolivian exports (Andersen et al., 1985), and the same year Colombian overlords almost as powerful as the government offered to help pay off the $13 billion dollar national debt if the government would agree not to extradite them to the United States (Whitaker, Shannon, & Moreau, 1985, pp. 19-22). In fact, lucrative profits easily draw in participants at all levels of the business, right down to the inner city preteens, some of whom can make hundreds of dollars in a day transporting and selling drugs.

The first half of the 1990s has seen a stabilization of cocaine abuse. A study in Manhattan showed a decline in use among youthful arrestees in Manhattan between 1987 and 1993 (Golub & Johnson, 1994). This may be due to drug-abuse prevention efforts and to the new generation of potential users learning by witnessing the errors and suffering of the previous generation. In general, however, the incidence of use is still high, with about 1.3 million abusers reported in 1992, three times the number of people addicted to heroin. As such, cocaine use remains visible as a serious drug and social problem (Withers et al., 1995). In general, however, the incidence of use is still high, with an estimated 6 million abusers (Blum et al., 1996). As such, cocaine use remains visible as a serious drug and social problem.

Pharmacokinetics

The most common means of administering cocaine are by chewing the coca leaf or stuffing it into the cheek, by sniffing (*snorting*) the crystals and absorbing the drug through the nasal membranes, by injecting it, and by smoking it in the form of crack. The typical processing procedure is to extract the alkaloid from the coca leaf, producing an intermediate byproduct known as coca paste. From this, the cocaine is stabilized as a salt using hydrochloric acid. The result is cocaine hydrochloride, a white, crystalline powder, which can be sniffed, or injected in solution.

The intranasal user usually puts the crystals on a smooth surface (e.g., a glass mirror), chops them finely with a card or straight edge, and combs them into lines, which are then inhaled through a straw, tube, or rolled-up piece of paper (e.g., a fifty-dollar bill). As we have seen, smokers purify the cocaine by freeing it from the hydrochloric salt in the presence of a base (freebasing) and smoke it in the form of crack. Some officials fear that a byproduct of the extract—coca paste or coca base—which is 80 percent cocaine sulfate and smokes as well as freebase, may become a cheaper form of abuse, as it has in some of the producing countries.

The only legitimate preparations of cocaine are those designed for SC application as local anesthetics.

Unlike amphetamine, cocaine shows poor absorption on the oral route. However, chewing the coca leaf and absorbing the drug through the mouth lining lengthen the absorption time and the duration of effect. The Incas added ashes (containing $CaCO_3$, the carbonate of lime) to the leaves to intensify the effects. The ashes may have alkalinized saliva, causing the cocaine to become less ionized and more readily absorbed through the membranes of the mouth. The presence of an alkaline substance is found to increase blood plasma levels by a factor of ten. Today, the Andean Indians still add lime.

Cocaine shows no special affinities for tissues. Intravenous use yields extremely potent effects, with blood concentrations peaking soon after injection. After a 10 to 25 mg dose, onset of effects occurs within two minutes and peaks within five to ten. These include increased heart rate and blood pressure. The user feels a rush of intense euphoria followed by a crash and an intense craving for more cocaine. Crack smokers experience a similar pattern—an intense rush after about ten seconds, but then a sharp letdown after only a few minutes, followed always by a hunger for more of the drug.

With intranasal administration, the effects of cocaine are moderate compared to injecting or smoking. Contrary to popular lore (that the nose is a short hop to the brain), this is a fairly long route, with the drug traveling for 3 or 4 minutes through the circulation and being diluted before hitting the brain. One hundred milligrams shows an onset of effects within 2 minutes that peak in about 15 to 20 minutes, and are gone in less than an hour. Twenty-five to one hundred milligrams may increase the heart rate by 8 to 10 beats per minute and raise the blood pressure. Higher doses (140 mg) can cause a slight temperature increase and perhaps dilate the eyes. Unlike the shooter and smoker, the sniffer may not experience a crash. It is worth noting that before 1986 and the spread of crack smoking, emergencies and deaths were considerably fewer, and the addictiveness of stimulants (by laboratory definitions) was not established. In the case of the street drug, high prices and adulteration were also undoubtedly factors in tempering dependence.

Cocaine is rapidly metabolized by enzymes in the blood (plasma esterases) and in the liver. A moderate dose may remain active for only 5 to 15 minutes in the body before it is degraded. This quick metabolism is one of the chief differences between the effects of cocaine and those of amphetamine. The plasma half-life after oral or nasal administration is approximately one hour. Excretion takes place via the urine, which may contain metabolites for 24 to 36 hours after use. These substances serve as markers in drug testing for cocaine abuse. One of the more interesting developments in drug testing over the past two decades is a method that uses hair samples to detect drug use. Drug or metabolites distributed to and preserved in hair can be identified and used to assess, not only whether one has used cocaine (or a number of other substances), but also how long ago drug use took place (Staub, 1993).

In determining the intoxicating dose of cocaine, the route is an important factor. Ten-milligram doses taken intranasally have no effect, but, as we saw, doses of 100 mg produce a high that peaks in 15 to 20 minutes and lasts under an hour. A habitual sniffer takes about 30 mg doses at regular intervals. Injected doses run about 10 to 25 mg. The toxic dose for a 150-pound person is considered to be 1.4 grams, but it is much lower for freebased cocaine like crack.

Pharmacological Effects

Cocaine causes its main effects by blocking the reuptake of DA, NE, and 5-HT. At one time, the rewarding effects of cocaine were attributed to the release of NE, but it was shown that destruction of the DA terminals on the mesolimbic pathway running from the ventral tegmental area to the nucleus accumbens halted the self-administration of cocaine in lab animals. This circuit is now thought to be critical to the rewarding effects of stimulants and other drugs. Pathways extending to other brain areas, including the thalamus and brainstem, also appear to be important (Withers et al., 1995), as do 5-HT, enkephalin, GABA, and glutamatergic systems.

In the periphery, cocaine produces sympathetic responses through NE actions, like the amphetamines. When applied locally, cocaine causes anesthesia by blocking the initiation and conduction of the action potential in all nerve fibers, especially small ones. This anesthesia causes the numbing of the gums and nasal membranes familiar to cocaine abusers. This numbing, cocaine's minty cooling sensation, and its flaky white crystalline texture may be part of the reason that its initiates call it *snow*. An advantage is the fact that, when cocaine is applied locally in clinical use, it constricts blood vessels, retarding its own absorption and helping to localize itself at the desired site of anesthesia.

Low doses of cocaine slow the heart rate by stimulating the vagus nerve (see Otto Loewi's experiment), but moderate doses increase it and can lead to a prominent increase of blood pressure in conjunction with constricted vessels. At high dosages (such as with the use of crack), in addition to an adrenergic stimulation that drives the heart hard, there is a massive contraction of the heart muscle. Cardiac failure and death may follow, which many believe may be from severe spasms of the coronary arteries or from cardiac arrhythmias.

Cocaine makes breathing easy and pleasant by constricting the nasal vessels, stimulating respiratory centers, and widening the bronchi (lung passages). However, when the drug wears off, nasal vessels relax; over time, this causes habitual users to develop stuffy noses.

The euphoria from cocaine is closely linked to brain concentrations, and it seems to correlate to the rate of change of plasma levels rather than to a simple increase in quantity. The euphoria is most pronounced shortly before the plasma concentration has begun to fall. An intranasal dose of 25 to 100 mg produces a peak euphoria in 15 to 30 minutes, followed in 45 to 60 minutes by anxiety, fatigue, depression, and the desire for more cocaine. With smoking or injecting, effects are much more intense, producing a rush. Heart rate, blood pressure, and respiration shoot up, and restlessness and irritability may manifest after a few minutes.

After the dose wears off, the sense of energy deflates; fatigue, sedation, dysphoria, and anxiety appear. This is called *coming down* or *crashing* in street slang. An especially important factor at this stage is that brain levels may deplete while the plasma concentration is still high. This means that the user may start coming down and feeling discomfort well before blood levels have hit zero. With smoking or injection, the discomfort may come when plasma concentrations have fallen only to half. Part of this acute tolerance may derive from a drop in the sensitivity of occupied receptors. The result is that the user feels moved to take another dose while a significant part of the first is still present and active. This greatly increases the chance of an overdose. Crashing is less common with sniffing than with smoking and injecting.

There are no major physiological disruptions when the cocaine user crashes, but the intense fatigue and depression that follow smoking or injection have come to be considered a withdrawal symptom, and after withdrawal, a craving for more drug may develop. Nonetheless, the effects of cocaine are reversible and full recovery follows. With crack, however, the fatigue and depression of the crash, and the craving, are especially severe.

The current idea is that crack causes a marked increase of catecholaminergic activity. The neurons compensate by lowering the number or sensitivity of their receptors, and because of this, the user is unable to reach the previous level of stimulation from normal levels of biogenic amines (DA, NE, and 5-HT). Consequently, there is an overwhelming urge to regain normal mood by using the drug again. This is a physiological event that constitutes a withdrawal symptom.

Cocaine fever, or the pyrogenic effect of cocaine, is a rise in body temperature that occurs for several complex reasons. An increase in muscular activity from motor stimulation could contribute, as could conservation of body heat from the narrowing vessels in the periphery, similar to the mechanism the body uses to conserve heat in cold weather. Moreover, cocaine might have a direct action on temperature centers in the hypothalamus. The chill that portends the fever may be a symptom of the body readjusting its temperature regulation to a higher level. Indians in the Andes who chew coca leaves walk around comfortably in shirt sleeves at 10,000 feet above sea level, in temperatures of 30 degrees Fahrenheit.

Clinical Applications

The only clinical application of cocaine is as a local anesthetic. Local anesthesia is defined as the loss of sensation without loss of consciousness and without impairment of central vital functions like circulation or respiration. Cocaine, as we have seen, can be a good drug for this. It blocks the action potential along axons and prevents the sensation of pain from leaving the area. Numbing occurs in 2 minutes, and effects peak in 15 or 20. The half-life is about an hour, due to rapid metablolism by enzymes in the blood (plasma esterases). Because of this rapid metabolism, cocaine is not the drug of choice for prolonged dental work such as a root canal. Novocain, with a longer action, is preferable.

In medical procedures, physicians commonly use cocaine on membranes of the nose, pharynx, mouth, and throat, for example, to pass a tube through the nose or throat. At one time, the drug was applied extensively in eye surgery and other ophthalmological procedures, but the restricted blood flow was found to cause sloughing of the corneal skin.

By far the prevalent use of cocaine is its illicit, nonclinical one as a euphoriant, to give a sense of power, energy, and wellbeing to the user.

Side Effects

The adverse effects of cocaine became apparent when the drug became more popular, available in quantities large enough to cause dependence and toxicity, and as it became more potent in the form of crack.

The central nervous system side effects of cocaine are similar to those of amphetamine, including increases of respiration and blood pressure, restlessness, mania, and paranoid psychosis. Vomiting is a possibility from stimulation of the emetic center. Chronic use of cocaine can produce dependence, with withdrawal symptoms such as irritability, a craving for the drug, sluggishness, sleep, and so on.

An interesting effect that has been noted is that with repeated use, cocaine appears to increase the sensitivity of the nervous system to its effects. For example, psychomotor stimulation increases upon repeated injection. This might be in keeping with an effect known as *kindling*, the fact that after chronic use, a small dose may suddenly become as toxic as a large one. Similarly, repeated small doses in animals can cause convulsions.

When sniffed, cocaine can damage the nasal membranes in several ways. Due to vasoconstriction, blood supplies to membrane tissues are lowered, and oxygen needed by cells is depleted. This can lead over time to swelling, tissue death (*necrosis*), and delays in the healing of wounds. Another factor is the drying out of tissue by the drug in its salt form, which in itself may cause cracking and bleeding. Furthermore, adulterants, such as sugar, baking soda, baby laxative, or even household cleansers, are used by dealers to cut street cocaine (a process akin to watering down beer to stretch profits). Incompletely absorbed, these often contribute to tissue damage as well. The consequence is that chronic cocaine users bring ruin upon their noses, which become stuffy or perpetually runny, with itchy, inflamed, and bleeding membranes. They will frequently touch, blow, or rub their noses, further irritating the tissue. In advanced cases, lesions and holes can develop in the septum, the wall dividing the nostrils. More cocaine affords relief, but worsens the problem later. Coke abusers used to be known as *horners* ("horn" = nose) because police would check for cocaine use by squeezing the suspect's nose, eliciting an agonized scream from heavy users.

Other modes of administration pose problems, too. Smoking the freebase can cause chronic chest congestion and irreversible lung impairment. Injection invites deterioration of the veins in the muscles, kidneys, and heart. Needles add the risk of blood poisoning, hepatitis, and AIDS. That is another reason that many prefer crack smoking to shooting.

The fact that cocaine diffuses across the placental barrier has raised a great deal of concern about *crack babies,* children exposed to high doses of cocaine in the womb. As many as 50 percent of the pregnancies seen at inner city hospitals in New York City show exposure to cocaine (Dow-Edwards, 1991). Animal studies have shown the drug to be associated with serious complications in pregnancy--premature births and the separation of the placenta from the uterine wall; some studies have shown retardation of growth in the womb. After birth, disturbances of neurological function have been noted in humans, such as tremors, seizures, motor and EEG abnormalities; these are usually passing and resolve within about six months. Because newborns cannot metabolize the drug well, they may show signs of intoxication: dilated pupils, rapid heartbeat, high blood pressure, and seizures. Moreover, cocaine may remain in breast milk for 48 hours after use. There is ample evidence that the children of cocaine-using mothers are likely to be at risk for developmental and behavioral problems. Though some deformities have been observed, cocaine does not appear to be a major teratogen, and in general, exposed infants are not born drug-dependent. Many of these observations (Dow-Edwards, 1991), and inferences from animal studies, are complicated by other factors, such as poverty, the abuse of multiple drugs, poor health, poor prenatal care, and sexually transmitted diseases.

Acute intoxication and poisoning are the worst dangers of cocaine. Cocaine toxicity resembles that of amphetamine. Grinding of the teeth is one notable characteristic, and the first stages of hallucination are marked by *snow lights* (a whiting out of the visual field). In the final stages, *parasitosis,* the feeling of bugs crawling under the skin, may be pronounced, giving this sensation the slang name of *cocaine bugs.* Patients may scratch and pick the skin into open sores, or even gouge themselves with a knife to cut out the imaginary insects.

We have seen several factors that contribute to the danger of cocaine overdose: the availability of purer drug, the powerful forms of administration (IV injection and crack smoking), the decrease of subjective effects in conjunction with the craving to take another dose while blood levels are still significant, and the puzzling effect of kindling—a sudden sensitivity to a small dose after prolonged use. Death from overdose usually follows from cardiac arrest, due to the direct effect of cocaine on the heart muscle, to arrhythmias, or to severe vasoconstriction (*vasospasm*) that raises blood pressure. It can result, also, from stroke and seizures. In cases of severe poisoning, there may be respiratory depression, a rebound effect when the stimulation wears off. Common management is to support vital functions and treat the various symptoms: diazepam for convulsions (too high a dose of barbiturates is needed), propranolol for sympathetic hyperactivity, and after stabilization, chlorpromazine or haloperidol for any remaining psychosis. DA antagonists tested in nonhuman primates have shown a promising ability to block the convulsive and lethal effects of cocaine.

Cocaine Abuse

> *You see people looking at the floors, looking at their chairs, picking up little things and putting them in a pipe and smoking them and turning green and coughing because its not crack, and people falling on the floor and untying their shoes, and people hiding in closets and getting paranoid, peeking out windows and looking out the doors.*
>
> (Description of a crack house, as cited in Inciardi, Lockwood, & Pottieger, 1993, p. 61)

In most respects, cocaine as a drug of abuse is more like than unlike amphetamine. Animal subjects with round-the-clock access to the drug show weight loss, self-mutilation, and death within two weeks. Among humans, light recreational users who snort about once a week show no problems. But heavy users, those who take the drug periodically in heavy binges and stay intoxicated for days, are like speed freaks and suffer the same chronic effects.

The question of the addictiveness of stimulants is problematic and demonstrates how complex the idea of addiction can be. In this case, the dependency is tied to the dosage level and the mode of administration. It is clear that the chewing of coca leaves does not cause dependence. They have been used by natives of the Andes for untold generations for their pleasant effects (decreased hunger and fatigue, and a sense of wellbeing), but there is no evidence of dependence or tolerance, as is the case with cocaine. Acute overdoses, chronic toxicity, psychosis, neglect of responsibilities, and an obsession with drug use are exceedingly rare. These users have no trouble discontinuing use if they move to lower altitudes, where the coca shrubs do not grow. Schultes reports that he used coca leaves daily for eight years without becoming addicted (Brecher, 1972, p. 271). Of especial interest is the fact that with chewing, a user can achieve blood levels comparable to those of sniffing (Van Dyke & Byck, 1982).

At sniffing doses, the issue of dependence is controversial. Cocaine does not seem addictive, in the sense that the same small dose every day can achieve the same effect without tolerance. Less than 20 percent of intranasal users become dependent (Withers et al., 1995). In addition, the physical signs of withdrawal are not dramatic, including the effect on the EEG and sleep patterns. On the other hand, cocaine does seem addicting in that it produces a profound psychological reaction in the form of depression and craving, and in that it is severely habit-forming. Monkeys, rats, and humans will self-administer it (Koob & Bloom, 1988), and animals show the same pattern as with amphetamines. When daily access is limited to several hours, the animals reach a stable level of intake and no physical dependence. But with continuous access, animals will self-administer in long binges, and a significant number will self-administer a lethal overdose after several days (Koob & Bloom, 1988). Rhesus monkeys deprived of food for several days prefer to self-inject cocaine rather than to eat.

Part of the problem in assessing these seemingly contradictory effects is due to the fact that dependence had been defined in terms of the withdrawal syndromes of opiate and depressant dependence. These models put an emphasis on physiological withdrawal signs. However, with powerful stimulants, much weaker physiological signs are superseded by a deep pharmacological depression and craving for the drug. These can lead to continual consumption and drug-seeking behavior, and are pronounced in the cases of IV injection and crack smoking. This has been noted, too, in the urban areas of Peru with the smoking of coca paste. As a result, a shift to accommodate these patterns occurred in the criteria for dependence.

One effect unique to chronic cocaine users is that they seem fascinated with their own thoughts, with concern over meanings and "essences." Repetitious behavior (stereotyped behavior) is common. Many patients with full-blown toxic psychosis exhibit a compulsion to disassemble and reassemble mechanical objects, like a toaster or a car; usually, they are too disorganized to reassemble the objects.

Typically, dependence is signaled when users acquire access to a large and continuous supply of cocaine and when they switch from sniffing the powder to smoking crack. Estimates of the time span from first use to the seeking of treatment vary from about 4 to 11 years (Withers et al., 1995). In some samples, a significant number of abusers have been diagnosed with depressive or other psychiatric illnesses, or personality disorders (Withers et al., 1995). Endogenous depression may complicate the picture of cocaine withdrawal during treatment, which is normally marked by a rebound depression of its own. Cocaine use correlates with previous abuse of marijuana; that is, the probablility increases with the frequency and recency of marijuana use. This does not mean that marijuana use causes cocaine use, but indicates that if you are in the class of marijuana smokers (and alcohol and nicotine users), there is a higher statistical chance that you may enter the class of cocaine users. This observation is the basis of a recent idea, referred to as the "reward deficiency syndrome," which assumes that compulsive substance abuse may have a genetic basis (Blum et al., 1996).

Cocaine dependence usually begins with casual use and progresses to high-dose, compulsive use in a pattern of 1 to 7 binges a week, with each ranging from hours to days, and followed by a lull in use. Positive effects diminish with tolerance, while negative effects increase. The pattern resembles that seen with amphetamines. Cocaine abusers frequently abuse other substances as well, and may use alcohol and sedatives to relieve insomnia after a binge. Some will also abuse opioids when they are available.

Several withdrawal patterns have been observed (Withers et al., 1995), involving variables such as in- and out-patient settings, and IV use versus smoking. In inpatient settings, symptoms are mild enough not to warrant medication and decrease gradually over a month. In outpatient settings, a three-phased pattern has been observed. First, there is a crash in mood and energy lasting up to four days, similar to an amphetamine crash. Second comes a period of 1 to 10 weeks of dysphoria, loss of pleasure, lack of motivation, and increased craving, during which the risk of relapse is high and may be triggered by environmental cues or avoidance of withdrawal. Third comes an indefinite phase of episodes of craving, and their gradual extinction. After the initial crash, some users experience a "honeymoon" period when they are overjoyed at being drug-free, but this gives way in the second phase to a "wall of anhedonia," an inability to feel pleasure or reward. If patients can pass this without relapsing, there is a reasonable chance of remaining abstinent, especially if they leave the previous drug-taking environment.

Environmental cues associated with the condition of abuse play a prominent role in cocaine withdrawal and the triggering of a relapse. It has been hypothesized that the reward systems involved in cocaine use may especially sensitize the user to the act of drug taking and its associated stimuli. Because these systems also mediate the biological incentives and motivation that ensure survival (e.g., seeking food), these motivations may be redirected to drug-seeking behavior. In short, environmental cues evoking memories of cocaine euphoria may activate powerful drives. It is very important in treatment to remove the individual as much as possible from the environment associated with drug use. Reports of relapse among cocaine abusers run from 20 percent to as high as 80 percent (Withers et al., 1995).

The treatment of cocaine dependence focuses on disrupting the cycle of binging, on keeping the patient in treatment, and on preventing relapse. Pharmacological intervention has been aimed mostly at the early stages of withdrawal and attempts to lessen the withdrawal syndrome and reduce the craving. Results have been mixed. Among the most promising agents are the following:

1. Desipramine, an antidepressant used to reduce craving and prevent relapse. It has the disadvantage of a 2 to 3-week delay of onset.
2. Bromocriptine and amantadine, DA agonists that have proved effective in some studies for reducing the craving, presumably by countering the undersensitivity of DA reward systems during abstinence.

Current studies suggest that a combination of pharmacological and behavioral or cognitive therapies prove most effective (Withers et al., 1995). Among the nonpharmacological treatments are many of those used to quit alcohol and nicotine. They include inpatient services (*detox*), psychotherapy, family therapy, vigorous exercise (to raise endorphin levels), aftercare such as programs modeled on Alcoholics Anonymous, and contingency contracting.

OTHER LOCAL ANESTHETICS

Procaine (Novocain) and lidocaine (Xylocaine) are both stimulants and local anesthetics that work by a mechanism similar to that of cocaine. Licitly, they are found frequently in dental work; illicitly, they may be found as adulterants in street cocaine, along with amphetamines or simple carbohydrates like milk sugar (lactol) or mannitol ($C_6H_{14}O$, a sweet crystalline alcohol found in many plants and used to test kidney function). Both procaine and lidocaine are capable of inducing euphoria. Intranasal lidocaine has been reported to be indistinguishable from cocaine, although pharmacologically it shows weaker central actions and longer peripheral ones in matching doses. Procaine, synthesized in 1905, is only one-tenth as potent as cocaine and is rapidly metabolized. One difference between these substances is that animals will self-administer procaine but not lidocaine. Neither is said to give as clean a high as IV cocaine.

OTHER STIMULANTS

Smokable Methamphetamine (Ice)

Until the 1980s, methamphetamine abuse was perceived in the context of other amphetamine abuse. After the resurgence of illicit cocaine use, it was no surprise that drug users would rediscover methamphetamine. It is competitive, if not superior, as a euphoriant in terms of its strength and its much longer duration of action. In the 1970s, the black market developed a smokable, freebased form of *d*-methamphetamine, called *ice* or *crystal*. Use probably originated in Korea and the Phillipines and spread east to Hawaii and the West Coast of the United States in the early 1980s. Late in the decade, methamphetamine became a prominent drug of abuse in southern California, although the smoking of ice as a general practice is more recent (Beebe & Walley, 1995).

Ice smoking yields effects similar to IV amphetamine use (Beebe & Walley, 1995). One-tenth of a gram gives a high that peaks in 30 minutes, and the effects may last up to 15 hours, due to the drug's long half-life. The effects, in general, are similar to those of the classic stimulants. Major concerns are exposure to the fetus, cardiovascular effects, and high temperatures. The toxic psychosis associated with ice may last much longer than that seen with cocaine, as long as several weeks.

Ephedrine

The genus *Ephedra* comprises a variety of desert shrubs. The horse-tail plant *Chinease ephedra* from this genus contains a naturally occurring crystalline alkaloid, ephedrine, used in China for 2000 years before it was introduced into the West in 1924. It causes the release of NE and may also have direct effects on receptor sites. Generally, ephedrine shows a profile of effects similar to the amphetamines.

The cardiovascular actions of ephedrine are tenfold those of epinephrine ($C_9H_{13}NO_3$), which it vaguely resembles ($C_{10}H_{15}NO$); although of lower potency, ephedrine shows more CNS action than epinephrine, but less than amphetamines. Tachyphylaxis can develop to its peripheral actions.

Ephedrine has many clinical applications as a mild stimulant and can be found in over-the-counter medicines. It is used to treat bronchospasms. Its power to relax the bronchial muscles is less prominent but more sustained than epinephrine's, and is good for milder cases of asthma. It is also used for nasal decongestion, allergic disorders, narcolepsy, and as a pressor agent (to increase blood pressure) during spinal anesthesia. Ephedrine appears in a number of herbal and natural health preparations, and is an active ingredient in many illicit preparations passed off as amphetamines. Although it has not been closely controlled, high-dose use of ephedrine can result in dependence. In December 1993, Congress restricted sales by mail and limited over-the-counter distribution to ten pills per bottle.

Khat

Khat (*Catha edulis*) is a shrub that grows in East Africa. The fresh leaves contain the active ingredient (-)-cathinone (also called *norpseudoephedrine*), which induces effects similar to those of amphetamine, but less potent. Many inhabitants of East African countries (such as Ethiopia, Somalia, Kenya) and of Arabia chew the leaves, brew them as a tea, or mix them into soft drinks or alcohol. The vitamin-rich khat leaves also have some nutritional value. Psychological dependence seems evident, but no proof of physical dependence has been shown.

Methcathinone (Cat)

Methcathinone, called *cat*, was synthesized in Germany in 1928, and was used as an antidepressant in the Soviet Union in the 1930s and 1940s. In 1957, it was tested and patented as an appetite suppressant in the United States, but was shelved because of its abuse potential. The effects resemble those of methamphetamine. Cat surfaced as a drug of abuse in 1987 in Michigan's upper peninsula, when a student interning at Parke-Davis, assigned to destroy the unmarketed samples, stole them instead and circulated them where they caught the attention of an illicit drug designer. Cat is relatively easy to make with ephedrine and a number of household chemicals like Drano, epsom salts, and battery acid. Several dozen labs were soon operating, on and beyond the peninsula, inspiring a crackdown. Anecdotal reports of heavy use mention an apparently anticoagulant side effect of bleeding from mucous membranes--eyes, ears, nose, penis, and anus--possibly an effect of adulterants in the preparation. Widespread use has not yet become a problem in the United States. In Russia, however, cat competes aggressively with the illegal cocaine market (Hettena, 1995).

Convulsants

Convulsants are a class of compounds that cause general CNS stimulation and are capable of producing violent seizures, but they often act more in the brain stem and spinal cord than in the cortex. The actions, which largely involve stimulation through blockage of inhibitory systems, are not NE-mediated. Agents included here are strychnine, picrotoxin, pentylenetetrazol, and bicuculline. They are used mainly in research and have no therapeutic or recreational value.

The action of convulsants is general, but several anticonvulsant agents are able to block their effects, barbiturates being the most prominent. If sedatives are given, however, they can deepen the already profound depression that follows the convulsions during recovery, and they can cause death by respiratory depression and cardiac arrest.

Strychnine ($C_{21}H_{22}N_2O_2$), a convulsant and a virulent poison, is an alkaloid from the seeds of the Indian tree, *Nux vomica*. It is used in rodent poisons and, surprisingly enough, in some "bitters" for mixed drinks. It may also be used to cut street drugs. Let the buyer beware, for the LD may be as low as 30 mg. Strychnine acts by inhibiting the Renshaw cells and allowing continuous play of the spinal motor neurons. This causes contraction of all of the voluntary muscles, so that the slightest stimulus triggers convulsions powerful enough to defeat breathing and cause suffocation.

Chapter 18

Stimulants: Amphetamine Analogues and Designer Drugs

DESIGNER DRUGS

Around 1984 and 1985, the media first took notice of a series of new street drugs. Smart home chemistry was making it possible to manufacture analogues, drugs with chemical structures and effects similar to those of tried and true psychoactive molecules. The most workable parent compounds were amphetamine, from which numerous analogues were made, and synthetic drugs resembling heroin (*opioids*), from which a group of synthetic analgesics called fentanyls was being made. These analogues might have slightly less, slightly different, or even more powerful effects than the parent substance. Chemically, hundreds of thousands of such analogues are possible. Furthermore, since an amphetamine analogue is technically not amphetamine, chances were that it was not covered by drug laws. The result was a *legal* street trade in powerful psychoactive compounds, many with untested effects, along with potentially toxic agents if the manufacturers were not rigorous enough in their laboratory methods.

These analogues became known popularly as *designer drugs* after the fashion of designer blue jeans. For years, the basic design of blue jeans had remained unchanged until famous brand name designers like Calvin Klein began to modify them in distinctive ways. This became compared in popular literature to the modification of an amphetamine or heroin-like molecule. The term supposedly originated with Gary Henderson, professor of psychopharmacology at the University of California at Davis, who was involved in the early investigations of deaths caused by unknown street drugs.

In 1984, to deal with the problem of the legal home manufacture of psychoactive substances, Congress was given special emergency powers to ban drugs that are a potential threat to public health, with a year to establish justification of the ban. Previously, this was a six-month process. In any case, the efficacy of stopping smuggling at the borders is a moot point when such capabilities exist for making illicit drugs at home. In a further effort to keep up with home chemists, Congress passed a law called the Analogues Act in 1986. It allowed the DEA to ban drugs "substantially similar" to those already banned and to ban drugs that have effects "substantially similar" to or greater than already illegal drugs. The original makers of methcathinone (see previous chapter), assuming that the drug was legal, ordered ephedrine in bulk from drug supply houses under their own names. They were apprehended and prosecuted under the Analogues Act, based on the fact that cat and its effects resemble methamphetamine, an existing controlled substance. However, the Act has been criticized for its vagueness, because it calls into question substances like household nutmeg. (From oil of nutmeg or oil of sassafras, the stimulant MMDA can be derived.)

MDMA

A prominent drug of abuse that surfaced in the 1980s was MDMA, a methylated amphetamine molecule known chemically as 3,4methylenedioxymethamphetamine and known by users as Ecstasy, XTC, Adam, Essence, Clarity, and a host of other terms. MDMA was first synthesized in Germany in 1914 as a parent compound for further drug development and was patented by the Merck Company. The drug, however, was never marketed and was generally ignored until its illicit nonmedical use in the United States in 1968.

When the German patent expired, MDMA became valueless to the pharmaceutical houses, so manufacture stopped. It entered psychotherapy on a small scale because MDA, which psychiatrists had been using as an adjunct to therapy (for reasons to be seen), was made a Schedule I drug by the Controlled Substances Act of 1970. MDMA, having an analogous action, was unscheduled at the time, so it was adopted as a substitute. Street use, reported during this intermediate phase in Boston and Chicago, continued to spread in California, Texas, Florida, and New York. In 1978, the psychological effects were first reported. In 1980, California psychiatrists took advantage of a legal prerogative permitting physicians and pharmacists, under certain specifications, to manufacture licit drugs not commercially available. This meant that limited supplies of still-legal MDMA came into restricted psychiatric use. However, through reports and studies, word began to spread. A leak into the drug culture followed, and use gained momentum in 1984. In 1985, unregulated use boomed in Texas, where MDMA could be purchased at bars and convenience stores. Meanwhile, the media had noticed, and soon the whole country was aware of Ecstasy, the latest love drug, at just about the time the term *designer drug* was becoming generally known. Texas senator Lloyd Bentsen petitioned the FDA to restrict the compound on an emergency basis, and it was placed on Schedule I. In response, some members of the psychiatric community objected to this scheduling status, which marks MDMA as having a high abuse potential and no accepted medical use, and which removes it from use as a psychiatric drug. However, based on its continued popularity as a drug of abuse and evidence of selective damage to serotonergic neurons in rats, Schedule I it remains. When the threat of an epidemic subsided, the situation proceeded to the next familiar step, the establishment of clandestine labs. Though still a problem, illicit MDMA use is seldom excessive, limited by its side effects and by its price tag, which is about $25 a tablet (McDowell & Kleber, 1995).

In the 1990s, MDMA became associated with social gatherings known as *raves*. The rave phenomenon began in Europe in the 1980s and soon spread to the West Coast of the United States. Marathon, all-night dance parties powered by the rapid, cybernetic beat of "techno" rock, raves are staged in marginal locations like warehouses, basements, or unused tenements or schools, and are open to a select public for a fee. For example, the owners of a local music club might rent the site at a minimal rate and promote the event through their regular patrons and friends. Participants surreptitiously bring or buy drugs at the rave. The favored drugs, like MDMA and methamphetamine, are those conducive to hours and hours of dancing, though LSD, mushrooms, and marijuana are also seen. Since many participants are underage drinkers, alcohol use is not salient. The aesthetic of the rave is provided by the atmosphere of the fringe location, and by the extended drug experience, coupled with the cold, hard beat of the music and hours of vigorous dancing. Sponsors have been known to distribute handbills discouraging drug use and warning of adverse drug effects under these conditions, which may involve overcrowding, exhaustion, and dehydration (Millman & Beeder, 1994).

Most MDMA use is oral. The average initial dose ranges from 70 to 150 mg, with smaller supplementary doses of about 40 mg commonly taken at thirty-minute intervals. With this pattern, however, a second supplementary dose tends only to worsen side effects without increasing subjective ones.

MDMA acts on a number of transmitter systems, but its primary mechanism of action appears to be to release 5-HT and block its reuptake (McDowell & Kleber, 1995). However, some antagonistic serotonergic effects have also been noted: Moderate to high dosages have decreased tryptophan hydroxylase activity at certain brain sites of rats, which suggests that the synthesis of 5-HT is impaired. High acute doses deplete brain 5-HT in the hippocampus, and the fact that experimental monkeys stop sleeping is another sign of serotonin loss.

The effect of MDMA that has drawn the most attention is the subjective effect of inducing positive mood changes. Most of what is known comes from two or three human studies, particularly one done by Greer on 29 patients (Shulgin, 1986). MDMA seems to affect the mood of subjects and, in particular, how they relate to others. Subjects report that they feel an intimacy with those present during use, and this fosters easy communication, one of the attractions for psychiatry. Affective changes have been variously reported as follows:

- MDMA makes the user more accepting and patient after use and brings about positive changes in self-image, in relationships to others, and in attitudes and feelings in general.
- The user feels more alive, euphoric, and living, feels more self-confidence and self-acceptance, feels grounded, blessed, and at peace.
- MDMA induces a sense of emotional closeness and bonding with others, but does not increase sexual desire or enhance sexual performance.
- It brings expanded mental perspectives, insight, and better presence of mind.
- It facilitates communication, empathy, and understanding, and produces a sense of euphoria and ecstasy, and even of transcendental religious experience.

- It evokes an easily controlled, altered state with emotional and sensual overtones.

These claims seem to indicate that MDMA is a unique drug in its selectivity for inducing positive emotional effects. Some have suggested that it be considered the prototype of a new class of drugs to be called empathogens (or entactogens) after these effects. The reasons should be obvious for psychiatric interest in a drug that would lower defenses, aid communication, and improve the users' self-image and positive emotional involvement with others. Although little pharmacological work has been done with MDMA, limbic actions are strongly suggested.

There is some disagreement over the production of perceptual effects by MDMA. Some studies report no effects, or mild ones--less than users expected. Others report definite psychedelic effects typical of the classic hallucinogens--very mild at low doses (Siegel, 1986). These include visual displays of geometric patterns, usually of black and white lines, points, and curves. At 300 mg, these take on faded blue, yellow, and red coloration and appear to be located about two feet in front of the eyes, changing slowly. Other reported effects are perceptual afterimages, vibratory movements in the visual field, the sensation of objects moving in peripheral vision, and pseudohallucinations (see glossary) appearing with the eyes open or closed. Complex mescaline-like imagery (of faces, animals, landscapes, etc.) have also been seen, but lack the vivid colors encountered with other hallucinogens. Objects may appear duplicated or distorted in size, perceptions that are characteristic of an incipient toxic psychosis induced by mescaline and cocaine. Other hallucinatory effects include a sense of lightness or floating, of falling through tunnels, or of disembodiment.

MDMA may also produce increased sweating, blurred vision, nausea, the dilation of pupils, and nystagmus (quick, jerky movements of the eyes up and down or back and forth). Sympathetic effects are encountered as well. The pulse rate and blood pressure rise over the first hour of use in just about all cases (sometimes strong enough to constitute a threat to those with cardiovascular disease), then they decrease and may go slightly below normal by the sixth hour (Downing & Wolfson, 1985). There may be mild analgesia and anesthesia, and appetite suppression. Many users find the initial effects of MDMA to be unpleasant, although they report that the experience as a whole is rewarding.

Although MDMA was originally developed as an appetite suppressant, the only clinical use to which it has been put is as an adjunct to psychotherapy, and that unofficially. As one source puts it, the practice of psychotherapy is treated with "benign neglect" by the medical community, and no drug is officially accepted as an adjunct to treatment. However, psychotherapists have claimed that MDMA is an effective aid in (1) breaking through psychological defenses, (2) integrating identity, (3) disabling self-hatred and enabling interpersonal contact and intimacy, (4) facilitating communications between people involved in a significant emotional relationship, and (5) psychologically alleviating the dependence on other drugs, perhaps by easing some of the motivating stress. Furthermore, to date, use seems safe in therapeutic settings, although much work remains to be done.

A prominent concern with MDMA use is evidence of significant neurological damage to serotonergic systems (Barnes, 1988; Miller & Gold, 1994). This is shown to some extent in studies of rodents, but is much clearer in studies of primates, which are more predictive of effects in humans. In humans, studies show reduced 5-HT metabolism (Miller & Gold, 1994), implying damage like that seen in animal studies. This selective destruction of serotonergic nerve endings remains the key point of concern regarding MDMA use; it is unknown whether or not this effect is reversible.

One of the salient and consistently mentioned side effects of MDMA is tension and stiffness in the jaw, and the symptoms of teeth clenching and grinding seen with amphetamine and cocaine are common. The jaw clenching may persist for days, or in some cases, for weeks after use. This is consistent with a general increase of tension, tremor, and achiness and tightness in muscles.

Another side effect that is almost universal in users is nausea, beginning about a half hour after administration and lasting about a half hour. Vomiting is rare. Other side effects are appetite suppression during use, headaches, sweating, ataxia, a feeling of slight coldness, and tingling or numbing of the extremities. There is a distinct hangover, and pronounced negative side effects on the second day after use.

Consistent with other stimulants, MDMA may cause insomnia as a common after effect, but of an especially persistent sort. Similarly, some subjects report residual effects of anxiety and nervousness (during or after use), and of fatigue and depression. The tenacity of some of these effects is noteworthy and may continue a week or more. The emotional aftermath in some cases may be unpleasant, involving loneliness, sadness, fear, paranoia, vulnerability, rage, racing thoughts, and a sense of emotional imbalance. Some have reported this as an impression of emotional "crud" remaining from thoughts and feelings dredged up during the drug sessions. Certain studies have found no serious side effects (Shulgin, 1986).

MDMA has a reasonable safety margin. Death is rare, but is a possibility in cardiac cases. Overdosing is possible and may be fatal. Similar to the kindling effect noted with cocaine, toxicity is possible at previously tolerated doses. But acute reactions are rare and are noted mostly with doses of 100 mg or more or in sensitive individuals, and usually after repeated doses. Toxic symptoms include numbness and tingling in the extremities, a luminescence seen around objects, an increased acuity to cold and color perception, vomiting, apparent movement of the floor, ataxia, crying, visual hallucinations, racing heartbeat, high temperature, increased muscle tone, hypertension (high blood pressure) progressing to hypotension (low blood pressure), kidney failure, and liver damage. Psychosis may appear at doses of 200 mg or more; this may involve severe anxiety, paranoid delusions and ideas of reference, threatening hallucinations (both visual and auditory), dissociative reactions, and semicatatonic states that last up to three days. These symptoms are resistant to haloperidol, which is usually effective for psychosis. Confused states have also been noticed for other amphetamine analogues: MDA, MMDA, HMDA, and HMDMA. Residual symptoms may persist for hours or even weeks, and the release of sensitive emotional material may later bring users into a clinic to seek counseling.

The abuse potential of MDMA is limited, since the desirable effects decline with increased dosage or repeated use, and the undesirable side effects increase. On the other hand, baboons and rhesus monkeys have been shown to self-administer the drug, which is a common indicator of abuse potential (Shulgin, 1986). In keeping with MDMA's empathic effects, most misuse has occurred in social situations; the type of alertness caused by MDMA does not seem to be conducive to studying or other solitary tasks.

MDMA is less toxic than MDA but more so than mescaline. The LD50 is 97 mg/kg in mice and 22 mg/kg in monkeys. The human LD is unknown. In 1992, several deaths were reported at raves in England. These appear to have been connected with overexertion; hot, crowded conditions; and dehydration from lack of water, possibly in a combined effect with MDMA use (McDowell & Kleber, 1995).

Another amphetamine analogue, MBDB is a nonhallucinogenic compound that produces empathic effects similar to those of MDMA. It is a potent blocker of 5-HT reuptake and a moderate blocker of NE reuptake, but does not block DA reuptake at all (unlike amphetamines, MDA, and MDMA).

OTHER SUBSTITUTED AMPHETAMINES

Although they are considered amphetamine analogues, the drugs in this section also bear a close structural resemblance to the hallucinogen mescaline. Consequently, some sources consider them to be mescaline derivatives.

MDA

MDA is methylenedioxyamphetamine. There are two isomers, both active, with different effects; the *d* isomer, the more active, has amphetamine-like effects. The *l* isomer is more like LSD. However, MDA is not hallucinogenic, but has reported effects resembling those of MDMA (the N-methyl derivative of MDA)(see Figure 18.1). Like MDMA, it is a potent 5-HTreleasing agent.

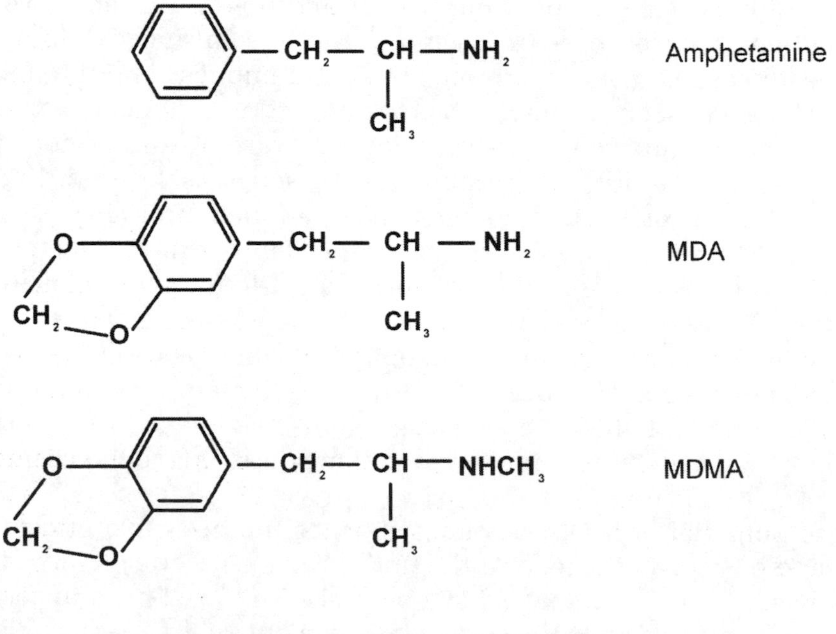

FIGURE 18.1 Molecular structures of amphetamine and two of its analogues.

At a 75 mg oral dose of MDA, subjects report no perceptual alterations, but a sense of amplified emotions, feelings of peace and tranquility, feelings of tenderness and gentleness, openness, an emotional closeness to companions, peace, calm, serenity, increased awareness of the importance of interpersonal relationships, an enhanced response to music, and a moderate shift in time perceptions. Effects begin in 1 hour, peak in 2 hours, and some effects may still be felt after 8 to 12 hours.

Side effects include an increase in blood pressure, dilated pupils, dryness of mouth, unsteadiness of gait, and difficulties in concentrating on tasks. Some amphetamine-like effects have been noted. These include mild insomnia, appetite suppression, and, late in the drug session, some overactivity and overstimulation. Some users mention chills, a numbing or tingly feeling, or physical weakness at some point during use.

Because of its empathic effects, MDA was in use as an unofficial adjunct to psychotherapy until 1970, when it became a controlled substance. It has also appeared in street use.

MMDA

MMDA (3methoxy4,5methylenedioxyamphetamine) is another substituted amphetamine, synthesized in 1962. It has never been reported occurring in nature, but it closely resembles the natural hallucinogens myristicin and elemicin, which are found in nutmeg and mace. Seventy-five milligrams is the threshold dose for subjective effects, and 150 mg orally is the average dose. Onset of effects occurs in 30 to 60 minutes and may consist of minor dizziness, pupil dilation, and fleeting nausea. Psychological effects begin about 90 minutes after ingestion, peak an hour after that, and are usually mostly gone 2 hours after they begin. These effects are mild and easily manipulated. They consist of minimal sensory distortions but an intensification of mood, drowsiness and relaxation with dreamlike imagery upon the closing of the eyes, and an overestimation of elapsed time. Currently, MMDA is a Schedule I drug.

DOM

DOM (or 2,5 dimethoxy-4-methyl-amphetamine) is an amphetamine analogue and designer drug that also bears a resemblance to mescaline. At low doses, it induces an amphetamine-like stimulation, while at somewhat higher doses, it produces hallucinations like mescaline's. Its mechanism of action differs from that of amphetamine and does not seem significantly to involve blockage of the reuptake of NE, DA, or 5-HT. DOM is discussed at greater length in the chapter on adrenergic and serotonergic hallucinogens (Chapter 25).

As far as designer drugs are concerned, the amphetamine analogues are only part of the story. The other significant designer drugs of abuse are the fentanyls. These are more appropriately discussed later with the opiate agonists and antagonists (see Chapter 23).

Chapter 19

Stimulants: Xanthines

The xanthines, or methylxanthines, include three mild stimulants that are chemical relatives: caffeine, theophylline, and theobromine. *Xanthine* is a term derived from the Greek word for yellow, because if these compounds are heated until dry with nitric acid, a fairly routine laboratory procedure, they leave a yellow residue. As a whole, the xanthines claim a delicious and voluminous history, and we all know them well, since they make up the active ingredients in coffee, tea, chocolate, and cola drinks.

COFFEE

Of the two commercial species of coffee plant, the first to come to light was *Coffea arabica* (*Arabica* for short), a glossy—leafed shrub with fragrant white flowers and red, cherry-like fruit, native to Ethiopia. The species—our favorite drinking coffee—now encompasses thirteen varieties of plants. Chances are that it was chewed or brewed as far back as Paleolithic times, but the legend of antiquity most frequently told is that of Kaldi, an Arabian goatherd. One day, Kaldi saw his goats exuberantly gamboling on the hillside. He traced the cause to berries of a plant on which the goats were browsing. Kaldi sampled the berries, and soon he, too, had joined his herd in its frolics. Later, he took some specimens to a holy man, who saw in the drug an aid to prolong the stamina of dervishes in their prayers.

From this Arabian tale about an Ethiopian plant, it is clear that coffee crossed the Red Sea early in its history. There is evidence of its cultivation in Ethiopia as early as A.D. 575, and in Yemen in the fourteenth century. By that time the Yemenis apparently knew of the roasting and grinding process, whose secret they guarded carefully. The first creditable date in coffee's history is 1450, when legend marks Sheik Gemaleddin with bringing it into Arabia to cure himself of an illness. The early Arabs fermented the berries and made a sort of wine drunk hot, called *qahwah*, the same word used for grape wine. This eventually became Turkish *kahveh*, French *café*, and English *coffee*.

Coffee first spread through the Muslim world as a devotional drink, completing its pilgrimage to Mecca a little before 1500. By 1510, it was a ritual part of all religious festivals in Cairo. A year later, however, a long chronicle of coffee controversies began in force. Khair Bey, acting governor of Mecca for the Sultan of Egypt, became outraged when he saw Meccan dervishes drinking coffee in a mosque, fueling up for evening worship. He had never heard of coffee, but mistook it for wine, since it was called by the same name. So the governor caused a public upheaval by banning coffee and punishing its drinkers. But when Bey's overlord the Sultan got word, the ban was repealed, since coffee drinking was already accepted in Egypt.

The great age of the coffeehouse began when houses first opened in Constantinople in 1554. In the Ottoman Empire, they successfully weathered all religious restrictions and government bans, to develop into luxurious schools of wisdom where readers and orators entertained the quietly lounging patrons.

Not long thereafter (1582), Rauwolf of Augsburg, the first European to mention coffee, reported its use throughout Asia Minor, Syria, and Persia. It arrived in England in the early 1600s as a medicine, but it was not long after its arrival that coffee was being drunk purely for pleasure. The first English coffeehouse opened in Oxford in 1650, and others in London soon after. This was a time of political turmoil. As popular gathering places where talk was freely exchanged, the coffeehouses quickly evolved into institutions of historic import. The Royal Society and Lloyd's of London (the largest insurance firm in the world), both began in the coffeehouses of that time. The 1670s saw colorful pamphleteering pro and con over coffee drinking and the public image of the houses. Charles II managed to shut them down as hotbeds of seditious talk—but for only eleven days. A pattern was emerging: where coffee brewed, so did revolution.

During this period, the coffeehouses continued to grow as "penny universities" (the price of a cup of coffee), where the most influential figures of England could be found trading witticisms and debating morals, politics, and literature. It has been said that "England's great struggle for political liberty was really fought and won in the coffee house" (Ukers, 1935/1978, pp. 69-70). Meanwhile, the government watched, planning suppressions and heavy taxes on coffee. In 1676, when the monarchy established a monopoly on news, the coffeehouses served as a grapevine to leak information to the public. Eventually, all suppressions failed, and by 1690, coffeehouses were firmly established in English life. They helped perceptibly to reduce drunkenness during the gin epidemic of the early 1700s and continued to grow in stature, peaking between 1715 and 1750, when over 2,000 establishments flourished in London. On the continent, between the debut of the Western coffeehouse in Italy (1645) and the mid1700s, much the same happened.

Throughout the seventeenth and eighteenth centuries, Europeans carried coffee and its cultivation to their colonial landholdings. The Dutch brought it to Ceylon, Java, and New Amsterdam in the American colonies. (The American coffeehouses, too, were political centers for revolutionary philosophy.) In 1723, the French managed to transport a single tree to Martinique, from which almost all of the South American plantings came.

In 1820, Runge isolated caffeine from green coffee beans in Germany, although other researchers were also isolating it around the same time and calling it by other names. The word *cofeina* first appeared in a French medical dictionary in 1823. Toward the end of that century, *Coffea robusta* (or just *Robusta*), a second type of commercial coffee, was discovered in what was then the African Congo. Robusta has twice the caffeine of Arabica, with a harsher flavor.

Coffee is prepared by two different methods. In the wet method, the berries are handpicked and sorted by floating them in sluices of water. The outer coverings are removed, and the green beans are dried for storage and shipment. This is the more selective of the two methods, the sorting being more uniform. In the more common dry method, the berries are stripped right from the trees, raked out on the ground and let dry; then the hulls are stripped off by machine, and the beans bagged. The beans are roasted to taste, then cooled, ground, and vacuum-packed soon after grinding. A can of coffee from the supermarket has a shelf life of about two weeks before it goes stale. Unground green beans stay in reasonable shape for about a year.

Much modern research is dedicated to decaffeination methods. This is done by applying a solvent to hot, steamed, swollen beans to draw off the caffeine, but unfortunately, some flavorful oils and waxes go with it. Some of the solvents initially used—methylene chloride, formaldehyde-dimethylacetal, acetone, propane, benzyl alcohol—were harsh substances that left slight residues, not enough to be unsafe, but still undesirable. Alternatives like the Swiss method use natural extracts of the beans themselves, and today even safer solvents, like water, are being used. The extracted caffeine is then used in soft drinks. In fact, soft drink companies are the nation's largest decaffeinators for this reason.

Instant coffees are produced by percolating a thick aqueous extract, then dehydrating it. Usually the harsher-tasting Robustas are used because the manufacture softens the taste a little. Arabica oil is then added for flavor. The dehydration process called *freeze-drying* involves freezing the coffee, placing it into a vacuum, and allowing the ice to evaporate as a gas without first melting into water (*dessication*).

Coffee connoisseurs should note that fine paper filters used in the drip method of coffee making at home can strain out flavorful colloids from the drink. A flannel or muslin bag (a *quador*), or even a clean white sock, is preferable. Hard water, which is usually associated with alkalinity, can partly neutralize the flavor. However, when water is softened using the ion-exchange process, the result is worse, since excess ions form soaps with fatty acids in the roasted coffee. The demineralization process is preferred. Chlorine in tapwater, too, can affect the taste adversely.

The 1990s saw a resurgence of coffeehouses in Europe and America. In 1995, America had about 4,500 nationwide (Marriott et al., 1995). Several factors contributed. Starting in 1980 and accelerating through the nineties, the consumption of gourmet and specialty coffees grew, and cappucino stands and espresso bars sprouted up in major cities along with the coffeehouses. Take note, however, that according to National Coffee Association estimates, the consumption of coffee decreased from an average of 3.1 cups per day for every adult in 1960 to 1.75 cups per day in health-conscious 1991 (Yang & Siler, 1991). While three-quarters of the adult population drank coffee in the 1960s, by 1991 only about half indulged (Yang & Siler, 1991). The gourmet coffee craze, therefore, merely displaced other patterns of consumption, but the appeal of exotic coffees as an affordable luxury supported the renaissance of the coffeehouse. Other contributing factors were the growing emphasis on healthy lifestyles and sobriety, and the need for nonalcoholic social settings. Alluding to the fact that coffee remains one of the few acceptable drugs, a Washington public relations executive remarked, "Coffeehouses are middle-class crackhouses" (as cited in Marriott et al., 1995).

TEA

Tea by definition can mean infusions made from the bark, leaves, flowers, or stems of many plants, as with herbal teas, but here we specifically mean the brewing of leaves from *Camellia_sinensis,* the tea plant, to get the familiar infusion that produces a pleasant, tangy astringency in the mouth. Tea contains not only caffeine but significant amounts of theophylline and traces of theobromine. The oldest caffeine beverage, native to China, India, Burma, Thailand, Laos, and Vietnam, tea enjoys a worldwide consumption that ranks second only to water.

Chinese legend attributes the gift of tea to Shen Nung, the Divine Cultivator, first tiller of the soil, who supposedly wrote of it as a medicine in 2737 BC. Another legend tells of Daruma, the Indian saint and founder of Zen, who came to Nanking, China, in 520 AD. Daruma sat and faced a wall to meditate. This he did for several years until, one day, he fell asleep. When he awakened and realized what had happened, for penance he cut off his eyelids. But from the spot where they fell, the first tea plant sprang up, an aid to keep one awake at prayers. (Sound familiar?)

The first creditable date in the history of tea is provided by Kuo Po's dictionary, which mentions it as a medicine in 350 AD. In the 400s it is described as an article of trade. And in 780 AD, leading merchants commissioned Lu Yu (orphan, poet, and scholar, who dodged monastic training to run away with the circus as a clown) to write the three-volume *Ch'a Ching,* a lyrical treatise on the horticulture and manufacture of tea, a book which greatly popularized the beverage and laid the Taoist foundations of the tea code that evolved into the Japanese tea ceremony. In Lu Yu's time, tea was ground up and whipped in water rather than brewed.

Tea traveled to Japan around 600 AD, but it did not evolve into the Zen tea ceremony until the fifteenth or sixteenth century, when it became a symbol of savor, simplicity, and the perfection of the ordinary. The ceremony still stands as an epitome among rituals. The tea house and the implements surrounding the ritual developed into a magnificent aesthetic, accessible to the common man. It came to be that the insensitive man was said to have "no tea" in him, the decadent or overemotional to have "too much tea."

Soon after Europeans first got wind of tea as a medicine for fever, headaches, stomachaches, and pain in the joints, the Dutch East India Company sailed the first shipment from Java to the Netherlands. The first public sale of tea in England was in 1657, and it soon joined coffee, sherbet, tobacco, and chocolate on the coffeehouse menus. It may have already arrived in the colonies by that time. By 1700, all of Europe had tasted tea, but only the English and Russians had adopted it as part of their national characters. The Russians hauled it overland in lengthy caravans brewed it in 40cup hot water heaters called *samovars.*

The tea trade in the East came to be dominated by the English East India Company. It held a world monopoly on all the tea in China, which remained the main exporter for a number of reasons, among them cultural isolation, control of the preparations, and lack of demand. The powerful company, delegated by England to dispense British law in the East, was in fact the imperial government of India. In the late 1700s, it ran an ad campaign that, combined with a high tax on alcohol, turned England into a nation of tea drinkers. The British word *tea* came from the Fukien word, *t'e.* By the 1850s, the drink was a fixture of British life. The aristocracy took *low tea,* afternoon tea with pastries and sandwiches, while the middle class had *high tea,* tea with lunch leftovers (cold cuts, bread, and cheese) after work at dinner time.

"Taxation without representation" was the great tea issue of the late eighteenth century. To keep the East India Company solvent, the Crown granted it the right to carry on its tea trade monopoly with the American colonies tax-free, allowing company agents to sell cheap tea and bypass the American merchants. This was a blatant act of favoritism in trade and in effect allowed the company to pocket the tea tax directly from the colonists, without their permission. The company thought the Americans would be pleased to get cheap tea, but to the contrary, the Boston Tea Party showed the colonists' indignation. When the first shipment of tea arrived in Boston, the colonists came disguised as Native Americans and dumped cargoloads of it into Boston Harbor on the night of December 16, 1773. This was one of the precipitating events of the American Revolution. Tea drinking then became politically incorrect in America, which is how Americans became a nation of coffee drinkers.

When Britain's trade monopoly with China expired in the early 1800s, the East India Company tried growing Chinese tea in India, but to no avail. Meanwhile, the Dutch were trying to plant Java. But neither crop took, until it was discovered that the tea native to Assam in Southern India would grow better than the Chinese varieties. India subsequently developed into one of the world's strongest producers. Sri Lanka (Ceylon) followed suit in the 1880s when planters brought in tea to replace the coffee crop, which had been devastated by a leaf blight. Ironically, the dead coffee trees were stripped and sent to England to make legs for tea tables. Most American breakfast tea still comes from India, Sri Lanka, or Indonesia.

From 1958 on, all species of tea plants have been considered a single species containing many varieties. Normally, *Camellia sinensis* would grow into a thirty-foot evergreen tree, but in cultivation it is pruned back to a bush, and as it leafs out, the leaves are plucked. These "tiny little tea leaves" are of the highest quality and full of caffeine, since the content is higher at the top of the plant. The term pekoe on boxes of tea bags refers not to a type of tea, but to the stage at which the leaves were plucked. *Flowering orange pekoe* describes the leaf in the bud, *orange pekoe* is the unfolding of the second leaf, and *pekoe,* of lower quality, is the unfolding of the third leaf from the bud. The ideal plucking is at "two and a bud"--that is, two young leaves and a bud of new growth at the tip of the stem.

After picking, the fresh, unbruised leaves are withered with warm air, crushed with rollers to expose the cell mass, then oxidized (fermented) by exposure to the air in a cool, dark place for up to 3 hours, which turns them a bright copper red. This *black tea,* which is simply oxidized tea. *Green tea,* the kind served in Chinese restaurants, is the same, except that it is dried without oxidation. *Oolong tea* is only partially oxidized.

In the next stage, the tea is dried, winnowed (impurities such as stems are blown away), and graded. Some teas may require additional steps. Earl Grey tea, for instance, is black tea sprayed with oil from the peels of bergamot, a citrus fruit. Lapsang souchong is a Chinese black tea flavored with smoke. In the final stage, the teas are shipped in airtight boxes.

A few innovations occurred to give us tea as we know it today. The tea bag first appeared in 1904 when a New York merchant shipped out samples in small, hand-sewn silk bags instead of tins. Today, they are the most popular form of tea usage. Also in 1904, iced tea was served for the first time at the Louisiana Purchase Exposition in St. Louis. Now, about 75 percent of tea in the United States is drunk this way. Instant tea made its appearance in the 1950s, and iced tea mix in the 1960s. A recent marketing development, as with coffee, is decaffeinated tea.

CHOCOLATE

Chocolate, which comes from the cacao tree, is believed to have originated in the forests of the Amazon and the Orinoco rivers, and was cultivated by both Aztecs and Mayans. The Aztecs believed it was given to man by Quetzalcoatl, god of the air, as a gift from paradise, a legend perhaps recalled later by Linnaeus in 1720 when he named the cacao tree *Theobroma cacao*, "food of the gods." Theobroma cacao is one of twenty species of Theobroma, an evergreen with brilliant dark foliage that prefers a low altitude and a warm, humid climate and grows beneath the shade of larger trees. It is always in flower, just as chocolate lovers might imagine, and hung with 6- to 10-inch pods that each hold two to four dozen cacao beans.

The Aztecs prepared chocolate as *chocolatl* ("warm beverage"), a thick, frothy, somewhat indigestible liquid eaten with a spoon and flavored only with vanilla, since the ancient Mexicans knew nothing of sugar cane. Montezuma (early 1500s) was said to have eaten nothing but 50 goblets of chocolate a day, making him the earliest documented "chocoholic."

The first mention of chocolate in Western literature occurred in 1502 when Columbus, during his fourth voyage, intercepted a trading ship off the coast of Yucatan and brought cacao beans to Spain. However, no one knew what to do with them until about 1528, when Cortez became interested enough in chocolate to learn the recipe, as well as the details of cacao tree cultivation, from the Aztecs. Western use spread slowly, and the Spaniards succeeded in keeping the preparation a secret for the next hundred years. Still, its spread was inevitable. The early 1600s brought chocolate to the aristocracies of Italy, France, and England, who sweetened it with sugar, and by mid-century it was on German apothecary lists as a stimulant and on the menus of established coffeehouses in England. Chocolate houses then sprang up all over Europe. With use, its cultivation also began to spread to countries within 20 degrees of the Equator—to the West Indies, Venezuela, Asia, and the Gold Coast of Africa. Africa is today's largest producer.

The real history of chocolate, however, is rooted in its manufacture. Cortez's recipe probably resembled the modern process: As with coffee, chocolate beans are left for about a week to ferment with the sweet and sour pulp that covers them. The plump, moist beans, reddish-brown inside, are then sun or oven-dried, cleaned, roasted, cooled, broken into bits, and shelled. Then the nibs are ground and processed into *chocolate liquor* or *cocoa mass*, what we call baking chocolate. This fairly indigestible substance is the starting point of all chocolate products.

In 1828, C.J. van Houton of the Netherlands patented a way to alkalinize chocolate liquor and remove two-thirds of the fat to get cocoa powder, the forerunner of today's breakfast cocoa. The drawn-off fat was called *cocoa butter*. This prepared the way for the chocolate bar (1847), which is a mixture of cocoa butter, cocoa powder, and sugar. Dark, sweet chocolate consists of chocolate liquor, sugar, and added cocoa butter, with flavorings like vanilla, salt, spices, and essential oils. Bittersweet chocolate is similar, but has more liquor and less sugar. *White chocolate* is made from cocoa butter, with sugar, milk fats, and milk solids added in prescribed proportions. Due to loose regulatory guidelines in the past, a number of products have been marketed as white chocolate that can't properly be called chocolate at all.

The white powder that appears on chocolate, giving it a gray appearance, is called *fat bloom*. It is a result of high temperatures (78 degrees or more) causing the cocoa butter to rise to the surface. *Sugar bloom*, similar in appearance, can appear due to condensation, which forms droplets on the chocolate, making the sugar dissolve and rise to the surface. These blooms do not affect the quality and flavor of the chocolate. Nevertheless, to avoid them, you should store chocolate in a cool, dry place (65 to 70 degrees, with less than 50 percent humidity).

The final flourish in the manufacture of chocolate came in 1876 when M.D. Peter in Switzerland mixed milk solids into chocolate to get milk chocolate (defined by the FDA as 12 percent to 24 percent milk solids). This sent the drug on its way to widespread popularity.

Chocolate is not rich in caffeine so much as in theobromine, a less potent xanthine stimulant. Cacao is the main natural source of theobromine. One serving of commercial cocoa mix averages about 4 to 15 mg of caffeine and 65 to 250 mg of theobromine.

OTHER XANTHINE SOURCES

Cola drinks are another common source of caffeine. A 360 ml can of cola may contain almost 70 mg of caffeine. Other sources include cola nuts from Sudan and mate, guarana, and yoco from South America. In addition, caffeine may be found mixed with many other drinks and over-the-counter drugs, including stimulants, analgesics, and cold medicines.

CAFFEINE

Caffeine (1,3,7trimethylxanthine) is the world's most popular drug. Just about everyone in North America ingests it in some form. The daily U.S. intake is 200 mg or more per person, most of which (about 90 percent) comes from coffee. Generally, caffeine is classified as a psychomotor stimulant--that is, capable of increasing the behavioral activity of an organism through actions in the central nervous system.

Pharmacokinetics

Most alkaloids are insoluble in water, but caffeine, as well as theobromine and theophylline, is slightly water soluble. Its lipid solubility is high. After oral administration, absorption through the stomach is rapid and complete. The absorption of caffeine from soft drinks may be delayed because of their pH and because the sugar may be absorbed first. Significant brain and blood levels have been observed as soon as 5 minutes after ingestion, and peak plasma concentrations are reached between 30 and 60 minutes

(Sawynok & Yaksh, 1993). Maximum central nervous effects occur in 2 hours. Any immediate buzz from a cup of coffee is most likely an effect of sugar or a placebo effect from previous conditioning with the beverage.

Caffeine distributes in almost equal concentrations throughout all body fluids and tissues, passing both the placental and blood-brain barriers, with a low percentage of binding and no affinities for particular organs. Metabolism takes place almost completely, in the liver, and involves cytochrome P-450. Xanthine metabolism in general is influenced by a number of factors: diet, smoking, pregnancy, oral contraceptives, age, and disease. Due to genetic variation, some people are fast and others slow metabolizers; the ratio in a population varies over ethnic groups (Sawynok & Yaksh, 1993). Metabolism has also been found to vary between males and females, with females metabolizing more rapidly during the first hour (Callahan et al., 1983). Normally, the half-life of caffeine is 3 to 5 hours. In women in the later stages of pregnancy and in the presence of the chronic use of oral contraceptive steroids, the fate is about twice as long. All the xanthines show cross-tolerance to one another.

Excretion proceeds through the kidneys, with only about 1 percent to 5 percent of a dose passing unchanged. Toxic signs appear at about 1 g (5 to 6 cups at 200 mg per cup), and the lethal dose has been placed at about 10 g—about 50 cups of coffee.

Table 19.1 indicates the dosages of caffeine contained in a number of familiar drinks and preparations.

TABLE 19.1 Caffeine Content of Popular Beverages

Beverage	Caffeine (mg)	Theobromine (mg)
Chocolate milk	5	58
Cocoa	4-15	250
Bittersweet chocolate bar	20	130
One ounce of chocolate	20	44
Five-ounce cup		
of brewed coffee	80-150	
of drip coffee	110-150	
of instant	60-100	
of decaf	1-6	
Tea	25-75	3-4 (0.4-0.8 theophylline)
Five-ounce cup with teabag		
1-min. brew	9-33	
3-min. brew	20-46	
5-min brew	20-50	
decaf	3	
Instant tea	28	
Iced tea		
regular	12-28	
decaf	4	
canned	22-36	
Twelve-ounce colas	15-60*	
Diet colas	1-29	
Twelve-ounce soft drinks		
Mountain Dew	54	
TAB	46.8	
Coca-Cola (Diet Coke)	45.6	
Shasta Colas	44.4	
Dr. Pepper	39.6	
Pepsi Cola	38.4	
Diet Pepsi	36	
Pepsi Light	36	
RC Cola	36	
Canada Dry Diet Cola	1.2	
Drugs		
No Doz	100	
Vivarin	200	
Anacin	32	
Excedrin	65	(prescription)
Dristan	16.2	
Triaminicin	30	
Dexatrim	200	
Darvon Compound	32.4	

Pharmacological Effects

Several important mechanisms have been proposed for the effects of caffeine. The most significant appears to be its antagonism of adenosine receptors.

Adenosine may be considered a naturally occurring depressant in the body, and has its own receptors. It inhibits the release of a number of transmitters in the central nervous system, including NE release from autonomic nerve endings. It slows the firing rate of central nervous neurons and pacemaker cells (which keep the heartbeat steady). In addition, it enhances the contractions of smooth intestinal and blood vessel muscles. The xanthines antagonize adenosine at every juncture. Caffeine competes to occupy the adenosine receptor and causes a partial block; for example, where adenosine was suppressing NE release in the sympathetic nerves, NE begins to flow, causing a slight sympathetic excitation. Where adenosine was acting to constrict blood vessels, caffeine dilates them.

It is known that chronic administration of caffeine increases the number and sensitivity of adenosine receptors in the brains of rats, by way of compensation. It is not clear whether or not this is the mechanism for tolerance. On the other hand, if the adenosine response becomes too high, the number of receptors then decreases (down-regulation). This self-regulating mechanism limits the severity of withdrawal that you might experience with caffeine.

The most important pharmacological effects of caffeine are cardiovascular. Caffeine simultaneously affects a number of systems that regulate circulatory functions, even to contradictory ends. They may be summarized as follows:

Caffeine stimulates heart action. By dilating the arteries of the heart muscle, caffeine increases the blood flow and oxygen available to the heart. It also increases the strength of the heart muscles in contraction. Both effects contribute to more work by the heart, a higher output of blood per pump, a more complete emptying, and an increased blood flow in general. Of the three xanthines, caffeine produces the most cardiac stimulation. Tolerance for this effect is rapid, however; the stimulation tends to be short-lived and is unlikely to produce abnormal stresses, although some individuals may be more sensitive than others. In normal individuals, the heart action may increase briefly, then fall below its original level.

Caffeine affects the peripheral blood vessels by acting on them in two opposing ways. Acting centrally in the medulla, caffeine stimulates the autonomic nuclei that *constrict* peripheral vessels. At the same time, acting directly on the vessel muscles in the periphery, it *dilates* them. The usual outcome is a slight dilation, a net action of these and other effects.

While caffeine dilates the peripheral vessels, it constricts those in the brain, most likely by antagonizing adenosine at these sites. This action can relieve headaches that originate from the vasodilation of blood vessels in the brain. (On the other hand, caffeine can sometimes cause headaches through CNS stimulation.)

Blood pressure changes may follow from these cardiovascular actions. Oral use usually produces a moderate increase in blood pressure, while intravenous injection results in an initial fall, and then a rise in blood pressure.

In addition, the patterns of cardiovascular response are dose-related. Low doses slow the heart through autonomic stimulation of inhibitory systems in the medulla, then may speed it up. Higher doses drive the heart rate and may produce irregular beats.

On the whole, the observed cardiovascular effects of caffeine result from a number of factors whose interaction presents a blurry picture. Dosage and the routes of administration are to be considered, as well as such mechanisms as direct actions on tissues (like the release of calcium or adenosine antagonism), the stimulation of centers in the brain stem, and the release of catecholamines from the sympathetic nerve endings and the adrenal medulla.

This last effect, the release of NE from sympathetic nerve endings and the release of epinephrine from the adrenal medulla, manifests as a sympathetic reaction. The NE release, however, shows tolerance in two or more days. These effects may be the result of adenosine blockage.

Another peripheral action of caffeine is that it causes skeletal muscle to contract and smooth muscle to relax. At doses well above therapeutic ranges, caffeine causes a contraction of the skeletal muscles, which may be due to adenosine antagonism or to the liberation of calcium from storage sites. Calcium facilitates the release of ACh at the synapse and the neuromuscular junction; this in turn causes a sustained activation of the skeletal muscles. On the other hand, caffeine relaxes smooth muscles, especially the bronchial muscles, which makes breathing easier. The xanthine compound theophylline, related to caffeine, is more potent in this respect, and is used as an anti asthmatic medication.

Other peripheral effects of caffeine include increased secretion of acids and pepsin in the stomach (although decaffeinated coffee and cereal beverages have been shown to cause almost as much), the elevation of free fatty acids in the blood plasma, and an increase in the basic metabolic rate. An increase of urine output is another major effect, cause unknown; possibly increased blood pressure causes more blood flow in the kidneys, and more filtration through the glomeruli.

Caffeine also produces considerable central nervous stimulation. It stimulates the respiratory center in the medulla, increasing the respiratory rate, and at a high dose this can lead to respiratory failure, because neurons shut down when they are overdriven.

At normal dosages (100 to 500 mg, 1 to 3 cups of coffee) caffeine stimulates the cortex. The EEG shows an arousal pattern. For the user, this results in wakefulness and a loss of fatigue, an increase in mental alertness, rapid and clearer thinking, an enhanced sensitivity to stimuli, better physical coordination, and some restlessness. It can allow sustained intellectual effort. It is thus no coincidence that the coffeehouse has traditionally been a place with intellectual overtones.

It has been shown that caffeine can increase performance in various ways. Its cortical arousing properties counteract fatigue, prolong stamina, and improve thinking; at the same time, the skeletal muscles increase their capacity for work. Attention, alertness, and reaction time improve. Typists type better, racers run better, and cross-country skiers ski better. Boredom fades and vigilance improves at monotonous tasks. Mood also improves. However, on the down side of performance effects, 1 to 3 cups of coffee have been shown to disrupt delicate coordination, accurate timing, and arithmetic skills (Curatolo & Robertson, 1983). Also, some coffee may improve driving skill, but danger rears its head when the dose wears off, vigilance drops, and a slight rebound depression sets in.

Caffeine promotes wakefulness via the reticular formation. It does not interfere with dreaming (REM) sleep, but it does change the sleep stages, decreasing the time one spends in deeper sleep. As a result, one sleeps less soundly. Furthermore, it can prolong the time it takes to fall asleep. About 200 mg can accomplish this, and no tolerance shows for the effect. Conversely, upon removal of an accustomed dose of caffeine, the subject becomes very heavy-lidded.

While caffeine is noted to increase spontaneous locomotor activity in animals at low doses, chronic exposure or high doses may lead to a dramatic reduction of activity (Sawynok & Yaksh, 1993). The mechanism of adaptation involved is not clear.

Clinical Applications

Caffeine has no specifically useful clinical applications, but it does appear in pharmacotherapy. For one thing, it may be found in many over-the-counter analgesics, diuretics, weight control aids, allergy relief preparations, and alertness drugs, but there is little or no therapeutic justification for such use. Some headache medications feature mixtures of caffeine and aspirin; this, too, is weakly justified, although caffeine is used clinically with ergot to treat migraine headaches. Both caffeine and ergot relieve headache, apparently by constricting brain vessels.

As a respiratory stimulant, caffeine finds some use in the treatment of apnea when it occurs in premature infants. *Apnea* is a breathing disorder consisting of lapses in breathing of 15 seconds duration or more, with the causes often being unclear. Likewise, caffeine may be administered as a respiratory and cardiac stimulant in cases of alcohol, barbiturate, and opioid overdoses. (As we saw, however, it can be a problem in the presence of rebound excitations.)

Lastly, caffeine has been suggested as a substitute for Ritalin in the treatment of attention deficit hyperactivity disorder in children, since it produces less dependency.

Side Effects

Over the years, caffeine has been suspected as a culprit in many diseases, but as it stands now, there is little evidence to link it to any serious consequences. Many of the previous studies were found to be invalid because the experimenters did not control for smoking, and coffee drinkers tend to be smokers as well. Therefore, the studies failed to differentiate between the two drugs, and suspicions linking caffeine to pancreas, kidney, bladder, and benign breast cancer have had to be put aside until better studies can be designed. Likewise, there are only tenuous links, if any, with cardiovascular disease, high blood pressure, ulcers, and birth defects. In fact, at this point, it appears that caffeine taken in moderation is fairly safe. Only a few reservations are in order. First, there is slight evidence of birth abnormalities in animal teratogenic studies, and at very high doses caffeine causes chromosome breakage in non mammals. Although it has been recognized that high dosages in animal studies do not appear to apply to humans, these two examples are suggestive. In 1980, the FDA issued a warning to pregnant women, voicing suspicions about developmental toxicity—damage that shows up only at a later stage of growth (Rall, 1985, p. 596), and caution seems in order for any drug use during pregnancy, especially in the first trimester. Nursing mothers would do well to avoid it, since it can make babies irritable, cause colic, and interfere with sleep.

A second concern is the possibility of caffeine's raising cholesterol levels, which can lead to clogged arteries (atherosclerosis) and coronary disease (Thelle, Arnesen, & Ford, 1983).

Third, caffeine is directly related to fibrocystic breast disease (involving certain kinds of breast lumps). Such lumps may often disappear when caffeine ingestion stops. (Abstaining may also reduce premenstrual symptoms.)

Heartburn is a major side effect of caffeine and probably the main reason people give up drinking coffee. This is not due to an overdose of stomach acid as one would at first suspect. It is more likely related to the reduced muscle tone caused by caffeine in the esophageal sphincter. If for some reason a person's esophageal muscle tone is already low, bad heartburn may result with caffeine use. It is true, however, that caffeine can cause acid indigestion in the stomach through the stimulation of gastric acid secretion, and that it can cause other gastrointestinal discomforts, such as abdominal pains with pressure over the midriff, diarrhea, and symptoms due to gas or constipation. It can have either constipatory or laxative effects on the intestines, depending on the dose and preparation. However, it is likely that some of these effects are attributable to other ingredients of coffee, not just to caffeine.

Caffeine is remarkable in that it is not considered addicting, although it produces psychological dependence, physical dependence, tolerance, and a mild withdrawal syndrome. Part of this distinction is based on the fact that in experiments with rats and baboons, the animals did not sustain self-administration of the drug when given the opportunity. This indicates a low abuse potential. However, a condition known as *caffeinism* is applied to describe people who feel compelled to drink 6 or more cups a day.

At low levels of overindulgence in caffeine, side effects occur that are extensions of the drug's main actions. These are central nervous stimulations that are normally seen at higher doses but may be present at lower doses in more sensitive persons (or in children who drink a lot of cola). They include jitteriness, restlessness, insomnia, nervousness, irritability, a racing heart with irregular rhythms, and hand tremors. The caffeinist shows further exaggerations of these signs as well as others, such as muscle tics, rapid breathing, palpitations, flushing, diuresis, and sensory disturbances. Coffee oils may cause gastrointestinal irritation and diarrhea, and the tannin in large amounts of tea can cause constipation. Effects on the endocrine system can result in stress-like reactions through the release of epinephrine and NE and cause a state indistinguishable from anxiety disorders.

At normal doses, little tolerance builds to the effects of caffeine, but some builds at prolonged high dosages. When a heavy coffee drinker abstains, slight withdrawal symptoms may occur, the most familiar of which is headache. The caffeine withdrawal headache may develop in users accustomed to drinking about 5 cups of coffee a day. It begins about the eighteenth hour of abstinence and may last for one or two days, accompanied by a runny nose and aching muscles. Other aspects of withdrawal may mimic the symptoms of caffeinism: anxiety, irritability, restlessness, stomach upset, and cold sweats. However, lethargy may also manifest. Muscles may become tense due to catecholamine levels that have been increased to compensate for reduced adenosine sensitivity. After withdrawal, it takes about two months to lose tolerance to caffeine.

Fatal poisoning from caffeine is rare. High doses usually produce vomiting and convulsions. One gram (4 to 9 cups) induces untoward reactions of the central nervous and circulatory systems. Again, these are excitations of an even higher pitch than the caffeinist knows. They may involve mild delirium, ringing in the ears, flashes of light, muscle tension, and tremor. At massive dosages only (2 to 5 g), caffeine affects the spinal cord, exciting the spinal reflexes. At dosages of 10 g (about 30 to 100 cups of coffee, depending on strength), it produces shaking, convulsions, and death. Central nervous system depressants can be used to counteract the toxic excitement.

In its interaction with alcohol, caffeine sobers the user by compensating for drunkenness through other actions, not by lowering blood alcohol levels. In effect, you're just as drunk, only more aroused. In some cases, it might seem better to let sleeping drunks lie, but there is evidence to suggest that coffee may improve driving in drinkers. That is not to guarantee that they will drive well enough to be out on the road. Smoking stimulates the elimination of caffeine and may shorten the plasma half-life by half (Sawynok & Yaksh, 1993), probably through the induction of other liver enzymes. In general, caffeine does not affect the metabolism of other drugs.

The worst that can be said of caffeine is that there is slight evidence against it regarding blood cholesterol levels and fibrocystic breast disease, although newer, more valid studies may reveal other causes for concern. Likewise coffee drinking is not recommended for cardiac patients because it is capable of inducing heartbeat irregularities, nor for ulcer patients because it has been shown to speed ulcer formation in animals, due to gastric irritation from increased acid in the stomach. Light sleepers and the very young or old, because of the excitability of their nervous systems, would do well to avoid it, as would pregnant women. Barring that, caffeine seems a less evil drug than most, and caffeine eaters seem more likely to die in a political revolution than in an excess of stimulation.

THEOBROMINE AND THEOPHYLLINE

Theobromine is a xanthine found mostly in chocolate and cocoa. Samples of chocolate milk average about 58 mg of theobromine and 5 mg of caffeine per serving; a 1ounce chocolate bar contains about 44 mg of theobromine and up to 6 mg of caffeine. A cup of cocoa has about 250 mg, and a cup of tea 3 to 4 mg of theobromine. Aside from its ingestion in chocolate products, theobromine is of no pharmacological significance. Its actions, which are analogous to those of caffeine, are so weak that they have no therapeutic uses, nor even recreational ones.

In 1888, theophylline was discovered in tea leaves, its only significant source. One cup of tea contains 0.4 mg to 0.8 mg. This xanthine, whose actions also resemble those of caffeine, is notable for three effects: bronchodilation, and heart and central nervous system stimulation.

Theophylline is superior to other xanthines in its ability to relax smooth muscles in the periphery. This includes the respiratory muscles that control the caliber of the air passages in the lungs, the same muscles that spasm painfully in asthma attacks. Theophylline thus has an important use as an antiasthmatic treatment, because it relaxes these muscles and reduces the paroxysms. At the same time, it stimulates respiration from the medulla and may be applied, like caffeine, for prolonged apnea. Theophylline is available in oral sustained-release forms for chronic asthma, and in rectal and injectable forms.

Theophylline is capable of significant heart stimulation, and at therapeutic dosages it may cause a modest increase in heart rate. Like caffeine, only more potently, it augments the contractile force of the heart, emptying it more completely and frequently, and sending more blood to most organs. For these reasons, it may be used to stimulate the heart in cases of congestive heart failure (that is, blockage of the heart by too much blood, e.g., due to a faulty valve). Theophylline also produces more central nervous stimulation than caffeine, making serious toxicity, as well as lethal poisoning, more frequent. As a result, because theophylline is the only truly useful xanthine, most of the pharmacological work in this class of drugs has been devoted to synthesizing safer asthma medications. Aminophylline, a soluble theophylline salt, is one of the most widely used agents. Enprofylline is a good bronchodilator, five times as effective as theophylline, with less reduction of adenosine.

It is worth a caution that, unlike adult livers, the fetal liver converts theophylline to caffeine in the course of metabolism.

Chapter 20

Nicotine

Nicotine is classified as a *ganglionic stimulant*. This refers to its stimulation of the sympathetic chain of ganglia in the autonomic nervous system. It is known almost exclusively from the use of the tobacco plant (*Nicotiana tabacum*). Related compounds are nornicotine, also found in the tobacco leaf, and lobeline, which is found in the lobelin plant (*Lobelia inflata*).

HISTORY OF TOBACCO

The first users of tobacco were probably the Mayans, whose civilization was at its peak in Central America from 1500 to 1600 AD. The earliest depiction of a tobacco smoker is from an early Mayan temple relief, circa 300 AD (a detail of which is shown in Figure 20.1). Eventually, cultivation of the tobacco plant spread northward, and tobacco assumed a prominent place in rituals throughout the Native American peoples. Native American legends claim that a hungry wood nymph, in return for feeding her, gave the tribes corn, beans, and tobacco.

FIGURE 20.1 Representation of a smoker from an early Mayan temple relief.

Columbus was the first Westerner to encounter tobacco. On Christmas of 1492, halfway between Santa Maria and Fernandina, he saw a canoeist with a load of the leaves, and the natives brought him some at San Salvador. Two weeks later, they showed Columbus how it was smoked: by twisting the leaves into rods and inserting them up into the nostrils. The early observers, however, didn't understand the Indians' actions; they thought the Indians were "drinking smoke" or perfuming themselves. Despite this, it didn't take long for the sailors to catch on and carry the "smoke stick" habit back to Europe by the early 1500s.

Tobacco began its colorful European tour partly as a medicine—for everything—and soon after became an object of controversy, widely and vigorously praised and condemned. Rodrigo de Jerez, an early *tobacco drinker,* as smokers were then called, blew smoke from his nostrils and was arrested and jailed for demonic possession. In 1559, tobacco traveled to France when Jean Nicot, sent to Lisbon to negotiate a royal marriage, brought some back to Catherine de Médicis, the French queen mother. Its reputation for curing her migraines sparked a court fashion, where it became known as *nicotiane,* and in 1570 the plant was called *nicotiana tabacum.*

The late 1500s saw tobacco widely spread from Portugal to China. Sir Francis Drake carried it to England in 1573, and the gallant Sir Walter Raleigh glamorized pipe smoking at the English court, where it soon became a fad. As a medicinal "holy healing herb" and a panacea, tobacco found a place in the Vatican garden. By the turn of that century, however, it was becoming known as an evil pagan plant, and as quackery in medicine that produced frenzy, delirium, trance, and stupefaction. Kings were horrified and disgusted by the fog banks of poisonous and immoral air staling their courts. A familiar pattern of tobacco use was beginning, to be repeated individually in many different nations: first, the phase of medicinal use and praise; second, the phase of glamour use and faddism accompanied by an unsuspecting acceptance; third, the beginning of outcry against the weed as unhealthy, irreligious, smelly, and likely to cause fires, and in the East, against tobacco houses as seditious gathering places; fourth, a period of repression, taxation, and government monopolies; fifth, a realization of the government's dependence on revenues from tobacco as a trade item; and finally, its acceptance.

Pipe smoking became popular in the seventeenth century, and tobacco assumed an ambivalent cultural position. On one hand, its use spread to the aristocracies and beyond, while on the other, the Pope and Eurasian kings and governments banned or restricted it, only to find that their efforts were ineffective or that the tax revenues and trade monopolies were too sweet to relinquish. John Rolfe managed to introduce tobacco successfully into Virginia in 1613; it subsequently became an important commodity and a form of currency in the colonies. King James once planned to supply a London tobacco monopoly from the Virginia plantations, but the plan failed due to smuggling. Later, Ben Franklin turned the economic tables by promising Virginia tobacco to France in return for financing the American Revolution.

Throughout the first half of the seventeenth century in Europe, smoking continued to spread. Two great events that hastened its progress were the plague of 1614—when people believed that smoking could ward off the evil—and the Thirty Years' War (1618-1648), which carried the habit to Eastern Europe. Smoking did not have to walk to China, however; Portuguese traders had already brought tobacco there in the mid1500s.

If the seventeenth century was the age of pipe smoking, the eighteenth was the age of snuff. Patched and bewigged courtiers would inhale pinches of ground tobacco from rococo snuff boxes and absorb the nicotine through the mucous membranes of the nose. The habit began with the continental courts, nobility, and clergy in the 1620s and was carried to England by the courtiers of Charles II around 1700. Compared to smoking, snuff taking was a clean and inoffensive habit, although by this time much of the smoking controversy had subsided.

The next significant developments in tobacco's history came in the nineteenth century. First, in America, a new mode of administration rose to popularity—chewing—to many, a disgusting habit that filled the saloons with spitoons. Second, in the 1820s, Possalt and Reiman isolated the active ingredient and named it nicotine, in memory of Jean Nicot. Third, flue curing, a new method of preparation, was invented. In this process, which takes 4 to 6 days, the tobacco leaves are heated, and any damaging smoke and gas are drawn off through flues. The leaves come out aged and dried, and afford a milder smoke. This was the first step in a major leap forward for tobacco.

Another nineteenth century development was the invention and spread of cigarettes, which began appearing in the 1850s. They spread rapidly through Europe and America and were being rationed in the Civil War, although chewing was still more popular. Finally came the biggest thrust: the invention of the cigarette machine. In the late 1850s there were cigarette factories, but the cigarettes were handmade at a rate of about 200 a minute. In 1881, when the cigarette machine came in, the rate rose to 5,000 a minute. With the cigarette (which gives close to a pharmacologically ideal dose), with the milder, flue-cured tobacco; and with mass production, the habit began its climb to stupendous popularity among men, women, and children. A period of protest followed. Nicotine was dropped from the *U.S. Pharmacopoeia* in the 1890s, and fourteen states had banned cigarettes by 1925. This was the familiar rejection phase of the drug, and, true to form, it soon abated because of tax revenues. The bans were repealed, and by World War II, smoking was in.

The cigar began growing in popularity around the turn of the twentieth century and had its peak around 1920. Technically, a cigar is tobacco rolled in a leaf instead of in paper.

In 1938 came the first study linking smoking to lung cancer, and evidence continued to mount. In 1954, startling statistics were released implicating smoking in lung and heart disease (Austin, 1978, p. 42), yet sales continued to increase, and state taxation measures in the sixties were offset by bootleggers. A crisis point was reached in 1964 when the Surgeon General's Advisory Committee ascertained that smoking shortens life and advised that warning *labels (CIGARETTE SMOKING MAY BE HAZARDOUS TO YOUR HEALTH)* appear on cigarette packages. Consumption then dropped—for two months. In 1966 when the labeling practice started, consumption still rose.

In 1971, when tobacco ads were banned on radio and TV, package warnings were changed to read *CIGARETTE SMOKING IS DANGEROUS TO YOUR HEALTH*, and cigarette prices rose. During this period of labeling, however, there was no dramatic decrease in consumption. New opponents then entered the field on the side of the government—nonsmokers who demanded the right to breathe clean air at the worksite and in other public places. The Public Health Smoking Act of 1970 established laws restricting public smoking, not a very novel idea in the history of tobacco. Court cases have since affirmed the claim that nonsmokers have the right to a smokeless environment.

The anti smoking movement was further buoyed by Surgeon General C. Everett Koop's 1986 report on passive smoking, presenting evidence that nonsmokers may be at a health risk by breathing others' smoke. A particularly ominous knell for the future of nicotine was rung by Koop's 1987 report, which made a strong case for nicotine as an addicting substance.

How is it that such a questionable drug has held up against these governmental onslaughts? Some factors are the tobacco companies' well-funded promotional campaigns, vigorous lobbying in Congress, and effective defenses against cancer and other liability suits in the courts. In addition, the tobacco industry has the political support of libertarian interests, which oppose government regulation on principle as a curtailment of individual freedoms.

Nevertheless, the image of tobacco products and the stance of the tobacco industry is being gradually eroded by government policy, media efforts, and the public perception of smoking and its consequences. Tobacco companies have been criticized for the aggressive marketing of cigarettes in developing countries, for allegedly pitching ads to the young (in the guise of Joe Camel), and for enhancing the nicotine content of cigarettes with additives and plant breeding research, and the public relations representatives of major companies have been called to account for their ethics in the press.

The current climate and its progress seems to be to educate smokers and encourage them to quit, to castigate and sour the image of tobacco dealers, and, as unobtrusively as possible, to squeeze this major and costly national health risk out of the picture. In a hearing over the issue of Brown and Williamson (marketers of Kool, Raleigh, Belair, and Viceroy cigarettes, among others) genetically enhancing the nicotine content of their tobacco plants, a government official remarked that, if the FDA came to perceive that cigarette makers intended people to purchase their products to satisfy an addiction to nicotine, it would consider regulating tobacco as a drug (Leary, 1994).

Over the last two decades, as the medical message becomes clearer and factors that encourage smoking are curtailed (the glamorizing of smoking in the media, role models smoking, peer pressure), the habit has begun to decline. Still, 50 million Americans smoke; 6 million have died from smoking-related causes since 1964; 17 million try to quit each year; and 1.3 million manage to succeed (Fiore et al., 1992).

NICOTINE

Nicotine, isolated from tobacco in 1828, is a colorless, volatile alkaloid, one of the few that occur naturally in liquid form. The world's most widely used drug after caffeine, it has no therapeutic action or application, and in fact, it is one of the most powerful poisons routinely ingested by Americans. The molecule exists in two mirror-image forms (*isomers*). One form has a positive charge, and the other is neutral; the neutral form is more easily absorbed through mucous membranes. Both are present in tobacco smoke.

Pharmacokinetics

Inhalation of tobacco, smoking, is by far the most prevalent means of administering nicotine. Tobacco smoke is an *aerosol*, a colloid system consisting of a liquid dispersed in a gaseous medium, as in a fog or disinfectant spray. In tobacco smoke, liquid, water-soluble nicotine is suspended in the watery portion, and it enters the lungs in this form. Inhalation of a pinch of the ground leaves (snuff) leads to absorption through the mucous lining of the nose rather than the lungs.

A common form of oral administration is chewing a plug of tobacco leaves; this involves absorption through the mucous lining of the mouth, as does snuff dipping, tucking a pinch of tobacco in the cheek, which enjoyed an upsurge during the cigarette scare of the 1970s. Another oral form is nicotine gum, which is designed to wean smokers from cigarettes by substituting a safer means of administration. Topical absorption has been known to produce poisoning. It is most often seen in cases of tobacco croppers and users of nicotine-containing insecticides.

Absorption of nicotine through the lungs hinges on a number of factors: the number and duration of puffs, the volume of smoke taken in, the length of the cigarette, and the number of cigarettes smoked in a certain amount of time. So many variables are involved that establishing a standard intake is a perpetual problem in smoking research. An average cigarette contains about 0.5 to 2.0 mg of nicotine, 10 percent of which is actually inhaled and absorbed. The speed of absorption through the lungs is faster than intravenous injection. The absorbed dose reaches the brain in about 10 seconds, and 90 percent crosses through the blood-brain barrier. This amounts to a small peak in the nicotine dose after every puff, although peak blood levels are reached about the time the smoker is stubbing out a cigarette. Smokers who do not inhale get a significantly lower dose than inhalers. When taken on the oral route, nicotine (a base) ionizes in the stomach and is taken up much better by the intestine. In general, passive diffusion is the only mechanism involved.

Nicotine distributes quickly and widely, concentrating in the brain at up to five times the blood level, as well as in the sympathetic ganglia, adrenal medulla, parotid glands, stomach, thyroid, pancreas, and kidneys. Movement out of the blood is rapid, with half a dose gone into redistribution in about 5 minutes and 99 percent after an hour. It has been shown that after 70 minutes, various means of administration—cigarettes, noninhaled cigars, and nicotine gum—reached about equal blood levels of nicotine (Balfour, 1984, p. 3). This means that the absorption of nicotine by these means is effectively the same; however, one should keep in mind that smoke contains thousands of other compounds.

Eighty to 90 percent of a dose of nicotine is biotransformed rapidly in the liver. This acts as a safeguard against poisoning on the oral route, since the intestinal vessels lead to the liver, where a good deal of a dose is nullified on the first pass before it ever reaches the brain. The oral route is thus rather inefficient. Some metabolism occurs in the lungs and kidneys as well. The half-life is two hours. Due to enzyme induction, smokers are found to metabolize the drug more rapidly than nonsmokers, and noted also is the fact that individuals vary in the types of metabolites formed (Ashton & Stepney, 1982, p. 34). It is likely that someone who smokes one cigarette an hour may get a slow, cumulative effect.

Excretion of nicotine and its metabolites occurs through the kidneys. The pH of the urine is an essential factor in whether or not the drug is reabsorbed into circulation. If the urine in the nephron tubules is acidic, with a pH under 6, nicotine is ion-trapped and excreted; otherwise, it passes back into circulation. Alkalinizing the urine can thus be a means of retaining nicotine in the circulation, and diets that accomplish this have been proposed as a means of reducing smoking behavior in people who wish to cut down on their habit; it allows them to keep the nicotine for a longer time on their receptors, which leads to less smoking. Some alkaline foods include molasses, raisins, dried figs, lima beans, spinach, kidney beans, brewer's yeast, bean sprouts, almonds, brussel sprouts, and carrots. Furthermore, since stress can cause the urine to become acidic, nicotine elimination may accelerate, and this may be a factor in why smokers feel that they need a cigarette when they are anxious. (It has been pointed out, however, that the urge for a cigarette is almost immediate and does not correlate with the physiological effects of stress.) Elderly people, as a rule, excrete nicotine more slowly.

Nicotine is one of the deadliest drugs known, with an LD of only about 60 mg, able to kill in minutes. If you could fully absorb all of the nicotine in just two cigars, you would die. Inhalation, however, does not provide enough of the drug quickly enough to be fatal. The body also has several protections against poisoning, at least on the oral route. One is the first pass metabolism by the liver; another is activation of the vomiting center when blood levels get dangerously high.

Pharmacological Effects

Pharmacologically, nicotine is classified as a stimulant; it excites the central nervous system, yet it clearly has some calming properties. Many people under stress reach for a cigarette to soothe themselves, a time when their psychological dependence is most apparent; yet others, weary and working late, may smoke to alert themselves. Nicotine is recognized to do both. In animal studies too, arousing or calming effects may be unpredictable, possibly depending on the state of the animal at the time of administration. In general, nicotine's stimulation and calming can be shown to be dose-response effects, and it has been supposed that a smoker may attain either effect—stimulation or calming—in a given situation by accurately but unconsciously adjusting smoking behavior to give the right dose (a process called titration).

A two-phased (biphasic) action is evident at the cholinergic synapses where nicotine works. The reader may recall that cholinergic receptors are divided into two classes: those responding to muscarine (*muscarinic*) and those responding to nicotine (*nicotinic*). The nicotine molecules attach directly to the nicotinic receptors and stimulate them at first, but then, after exerting a powerful depolarizing effect on the postsynaptic membrane, the molecules remain on the receptors and block further action. Thus, they go from exciting to blocking the cholinergic receptors, from an initial, short-lived excitation to a depression of neurons. Part of this effect, the antagonism of ACh at the neuromuscular junctions, may be responsible for the reduced muscle tone and sense of muscular relaxation that come from smoking.

Like most stimulants, nicotine is associated with an increase of NE at adrenergic synapses and with the release of epinephrine and NE from the adrenals. This is responsible for the drug's sympathetic reaction.

As part of this sympathetic reaction, nicotine increases both the heart rate and blood pressure. A first puff (or the first cigarette of the day) carries greater cardiovascular effects (increasing the pulse rate) because receptors have been clean and unoccupied for a while, and it carries a greater subjective response. After five minutes of smoking, the heart rate increases from about 75 to 90 beats a minute. This is a summation of many possible effects: the excitation of sympathetic cardiac ganglia or the inhibition of parasympathetic ones; the direct stimulation of vasomotor centers in the medulla, which can influence the heart indirectly through blood pressure changes; and the release of E and NE from the adrenal medulla. With tolerance in seasoned users, the increase in heart rate may be negligible. Other noticeable changes in the heart at fairly low dosages are an increase in the output of blood at each stroke, a more forceful beating, more blood flow to the heart muscle, a higher consumption of oxygen, and rhythmic irregularities. Most of these are transient, short-term effects. One negative consequence of smoking is that nicotine tends slightly to deprive the heart of oxygen by increasing the heart rate and the need for oxygen, while the blood becomes oxygen-poor because of carbon monoxide from the smoke.

Nicotine increases the flow of blood to the skeletal muscles, but the vessels of the skin constrict, causing less blood flow there and giving smokers cold hands and feet. Their skin temperature may also be low. On the whole, dilatational and constricting effects on the circulation are localized, and the pattern is somewhat confusing. Blood changes include an increase of free fatty acids and an increased tendency to clot.

In the gastrointestinal tract, nicotine causes increased muscle activity in the bowel, which may result in diarrhea. The drug initially stimulates then inhibits salivation and bronchial secretions. Some salivation may additionally be caused by the mouth's attempt to cope with the dryness of tobacco smoke. It could be a conditioned effect as well.

The central nervous system is markedly stimulated at all levels by nicotine, but as with the cholinergic synapses, depression soon follows the excitation. The EEG patterns in the reticular formation show an arousal pattern that is indistinguishable from that of a person working and concentrating hard. Nicotine improves vigilance in tasks that involve listening and seeing, and users remain sensitive to target stimuli longer than others. Nicotine also improves rapid information processing and has a beneficial effect on mental performance and memory. These improvements in mental efficiency may be sustained, and they may be one motive for smoking. However, learning under nicotine's influence is state-dependent. Nicotine may reverse some of the deficits caused by alcohol use.

In the brain stem, nicotine in relatively low doses stimulates both vomiting and respiratory centers. Vomiting may come, too, from the stimulation of sensory pathways in the periphery; this and nausea are effects frequently occasioned in green smokers having their first serious encounters with tobacco. Respiration increases may either be due to a direct stimulation of neurons in the medulla, or an indirect effect due to oxygen receptors in the carotid arteries and aorta. These receptors detect the lowered oxygen conditions of the blood due to carbon monoxide, and they may trigger a compensatory increase in breathing. On the other hand, nicotine in high doses overstimulates and consequently blocks neurons in the medulla, suppressing respiration and leading to asphyxiation.

Nicotine increases NE and DA levels in the hypothalamus; it also causes the hypothalamus to release ADH (antidiuretic hormone), which in turn signals the kidneys to reabsorb water.

Some of the sedative effects noted from smoking may come from 5-HT release in the brain. A sense of stress relief might be a result of short spells of tranquility in the cortex, as nicotine first stimulates, then blocks receptors. There is other calming also, in that nicotine reduces aggression and decreases spontaneous motor activity (an effect that varies at low dosages).

Trembling hands in heavy smokers is a frequently observed phenomenon. As dosage increases, these can develop into muscle tremors and eventually convulsions and respiratory depression.

Clinical Applications

Although once tried as a medicine for what seems nearly everything, nicotine now has no accepted therapeutic uses. Its primary function is as a poison: concentrated extracts of tobacco are used as an ingredient in insecticides and fungicides.

Side Effects

The side effects of nicotine are in some respects difficult to separate from those of tobacco smoke, since the two are so closely intertwined in use, and since tobacco smoke contains many more substances than just nicotine.

Nicotine increases the risk of coronary heart disease 5 to 19 times in smokers, and even more if they have high blood pressure. This happens because it can reduce high density lipoproteins, which regulate cholesterol levels. The result is that high cholesterol can cause atherosclerosis and pose a coronary risk.

Until a few years ago, nicotine was not generally regarded as an addicting drug. One reason for this was that the strict measures of dependence applied to opiates and sedatives were not applied to nicotine until the late seventies. In 1987, however, Surgeon General C. Everett Koop compiled a report demonstrating that "cigarettes and other forms of tobacco are addicting in the same sense as are drugs such as heroin and cocaine" (U.S. Department of Health and Human Services, 1988). The report amassed large amounts of data to show that nicotine produces dependence according to criteria established by the World Health Organization, the APA, and the NIDA, as follows:

1. Nicotine produces tolerance.
2. It shows psychoactivity and the users' need to maintain a desired level of nicotine.
3. It shows compulsive patterns of use, in that smoking becomes a regular day by day activity and people who would like to quit cannot.

4. It is a reinforcing substance that leads to further ingestion: Studies indicate that animals will self-administer nicotine, although under more restricted circumstances than cocaine or amphetamine.
5. It produces withdrawal symptoms: a craving for the drug, restlessness, nervousness, irritability, difficulty in concentrating, and sleep disturbance.

For a drug to be considered addictive, there must be withdrawal symptoms with a demonstrated physiological basis. The physiological changes with nicotine use are recognizable, but not as dramatic as those of cocaine or heroin. They include a decreased heart rate, decreased basal metabolism, decreased cortical arousal, CNS hypersensitivity, a decrease in blood pressure and respiratory rate, an increase of skin temperature, and a longer total sleep time. An increase of appetite, eating, and weight gain are also noted. Some of these are identifiable as rebound effects, and their magnitude is dose-related. Furthermore, administration of nicotine (e.g., nicotine gum) reverses the withdrawal symptoms.

The report also extensively compared patterns of nicotine abuse with those of narcotics and stimulants. Like "harder" drugs, nicotine shows repetitive patterns of use, continued use despite harmful effects, recurrent cravings, and relapses following abstinence. In short, it fits the behavioral patterns of other substance abuse.

There are many reinforcing effects that may lead to a psychological dependency on nicotine: alertness, muscle relaxation, memory improvement, sharpened attention, lowered irritability, and a lessened appetite, although slight euphoria may be a more important lure. Animals will self-administer nicotine to help cope with an unpleasant stimulus and will even prefer it to the tranquilizer diazepam. Nicotine does not reinforce behavior in animals as much as cocaine or amphetamine do, however.

Toxicity from nicotine ingestion is most common from sprays like pesticides or from children eating tobacco products. A toxic dose of nicotine, at only 10 mg, first induces nausea, salivation, abdominal pain, and vomiting. This last is an effective way of removing the danger as well as slowing absorption. Other symptoms are diarrhea, cold sweat, headache, dizziness, disturbed hearing and vision, mental confusion, weakness, faintness, lowered blood pressure, labored breathing, and a weak pulse that is rapid and irregular. Tremors may lead to convulsions and collapse. Death then follows in a few minutes from both central depression of respiration and from the inhibition of ACh in the peripheral muscles, both of which contribute to suffocation. The best treatment is to induce vomiting or pump the stomach. Activated charcoal is given, and respiration supported. Alkaline solutions are ill-advised because they promote the reabsorption of nicotine from the urine.

The most significant drug interaction with nicotine occurs with women on oral contraceptives. Smoking increases their chance of coronary heart disease by a factor of ten. As a stimulant, nicotine can counteract the effect of minor tranquilizers. And through the induction of microsomal enzymes, it can reduce the effectiveness of theophylline, lessening its half-life from 7 to 4 hours in smokers and causing a need for higher doses to relieve asthma.

SMOKING

There's more to smoking than simply inhaling nicotine. The chemical makeup of smoke, the method of inhalation, and the type of tobacco are all variables that affect the body. Studies of smoking, therefore, go beyond examining the mere fact of administering nicotine; in fact, so many factors are involved that studies have even been done to ascertain that smoking is a drug-seeking activity.

There are as many as 4,000 compounds in burning tobacco and paper, some in the form of gases, some present as fine particles, and none of them beneficial to health. Among the more undesirable gaseous components of cigarette smoke are carbon monoxide (CO), carbon dioxide (CO_2), ammonia, cyanide, and formaldehyde. The particulate portion of the smoke consists of water droplets, nicotine, and tar. Chemically, tar is made of polycyclic aromatic hydrocarbons (PCHCs), which include some documented carcinogens, some metallic ions, and some radioactive compounds. Of all these substances in smoke, the most hazardous are tar, nicotine, and carbon monoxide.

The nicotine released from the tobacco into the smoke rides into the lungs suspended on miniscule particles of tar. It is found in smoke as neutral molecules and as positively charged ions. The neutral form seems to be preferred by smokers, being absorbed more readily and bestowing more pleasure, and it has been shown that smokers will increase the dose to increase the intake of neutral nicotine.

People smoke to get nicotine onto their receptors, or to replenish it. Smoking is a faster route even than IV injection; as we saw, the dose hits the brain in about 10 seconds. In general, being acidic, cigarette smoke is not well absorbed, especially from the mouth membranes. Cigar and pipe smoke are somewhat less acidic and somewhat better absorbed orally, so one can achieve a satisfactory dose without drawing smoke into the lungs.

Despite all the variables of smoking behavior and the different styles of smokers, among them such things as the number and strength of draws and the burning temperature, studies have shown that most smokers (especially heavy smokers) seem to target a particular dosage range for nicotine and adjust their smoking accordingly.

With cigarettes, users can accurately control the dosage (titration). The general tendency is to smoke at a consistent rate of 1 to 2 μg/kg of nicotine per puff, at 1 to 2 puffs per minute. Several factors may be responsible for this rate. It may give a good dose for cortical arousal, or it may reflect a dose-response range wherein the smoker can slightly manipulate the biphasic effects of the nicotine molecule to get an excitatory or inhibitory effect. Or the rate may be dictated by the rapid decline of brain effects between puffs.

Since there is a clear dose-response relationship between exposure to cigarette smoke and the risk of disease, modern low tar and nicotine (T/N) cigarettes are preferable to regular ones. For the last 40 years T/N levels have been dropping steadily, and low-tar sales have been increasing. Low T/N cigarettes may contain as little as 15 mg of tar or less and 0.1 of nicotine. Ultralows have less than 4 mg of tar. The advantage of these is that they reduce exposure to two of the three most dangerous substances in tobacco smoke. However, the process of self-titration described above can counteract some of the benefits. Dedicated smokers may readjust their behavior and oversmoke to up their nicotine intake. They may take more and larger puffs, inhale more deeply, or smoke to a shorter length and thereby gain back as much as two-thirds of the nicotine lost from a low T/N cigarette. Smoking is such an individual matter to begin with that T/N levels vary in smokers from the outset. In fact, the averages of T/N reported on the packages are derived from smoking machines, which lack the flexibility and individuality of human smokers, who may even change smoking styles for different types of cigarettes.

Another problem in evaluating the health benefits of low T/N cigarettes lies in the character profile of those who tend to smoke them. In the U.S., low T/N smokers start later in life as smokers, which reduces their risk; furthermore, choosing a "less dangerous" cigarette may reflect a stronger health consciousness, which may extend into other areas like diet. These variables confuse assessment of the actual benefits derived from the cigarettes. In general, low T/N smokers do seem to benefit from somewhat less exposure to tar and nicotine. On the other hand, because they tend to smoke more, they have more exposure to smoke, and consequently to the risk of disease.

Smoking causes the inhibition of hunger through several mechanisms. One cigarette can inhibit hunger contractions in the stomach for up to an hour. A slight increase in blood sugar and some deadening of the taste buds from smoke in the mouth also lower eating motivation.

A smoker who kicks the habit is in danger of gaining weight, because smoking increases the metabolic rate (heart rate and oxygen consumption), and stopping reduces it again. As the consumption of oxygen is reduced, more fat storage takes place by comparison. Therefore, if a reformed smoker continues to eat his or her customary amount, some of it will then convert to extra pounds. In addition, because the sense of taste sharpens again, the reformed smoker is tempted to eat more.

Smoking is the greatest health hazard in the United States, and it is the nation's largest preventable cause of death. Most deaths proceed from the several forms of cancer linked to cigarette smoking, from heart attacks, from coronary artery disease, and from chronic lung disease (bronchitis and emphysema). Over 300,000 die annually from smoking-related causes. All of this correlates with the amount of exposure to cigarette smoke. Forms of smoking that involve less inhalation, like cigar and pipe smoking (where smoke may be held in the mouth rather than fully drawn into the lungs) show only a slight increase over normal mortality rates. However, it should be remembered that these statistics do not directly incriminate nicotine, but cigarette smoke and its thousands of components.

Because most smokers inhale the smoke, the impact on the lungs is direct. Tar and other irritants in smoke constrict the airways and cause an undue secretion of mucus. Bronchoconstriction may be acute after even a single cigarette. Furthermore, the lung's natural clearance mechanisms are impaired. The inner surfaces of normal healthy lungs are covered by a microscopic deep-pile carpet of waving cilia that move foreign material up and out. Smoke can inhibit or kill these cilia in places, breaking the chain of transportation out of the lungs. All of these mechanisms—blockage, bronchoconstriction, and the destruction of the cilia—impede elimination, contribute to the collection of further irritants (including more cigarette smoke and environmental pollutants like asbestos), and may lead to chronic lung obstruction. Tar, for example, takes a long time to clear out, and, as it accumulates, it can damage lung cell nuclei. In young adults, impaired respiratory function may appear after only a few years of use.

Vitamin A has been shown to protect the life of lung cilia and lower the risk for lung cancer. Smokers should also keep their supply of vitamin C up, because smoking can deplete levels by as much as 25 mg per cigarette.

Chronic bronchitis may develop with habitual smoking. This is an inflammation of lung passages, with enough increase of mucus to cause expectoration (removal by spitting). Emphysema is an irreversible increase in the size of the lungs' air spaces by dilation or destruction of their walls. Not all smokers develop it, which leads researchers to suspect other factors (like environmental pollutants). Low T/N cigarettes don't seem to help here.

In addition to respiratory ailments in the lungs, smoking can compromise the oxygen-carrying potential of the blood. Oxygen is normally carried by hemoglobin, but carbon monoxide (CO) entering the blood from smoke in the lungs has 200 times an affinity for hemoglobin than oxygen, with a half-life of 3 to 4 hours in the body. As much as 10 percent of all hemoglobin may be found occupied by CO in the form of carboxyhemoglobin, unable to carry oxygen. This may explain the shortness of breath that smokers experience after exertion. It can also constitute a threat to a fetus, which depends on the mother for its oxygen. This problem is augmented by the fact that smoking also decreases blood flow in the placenta. All told, one pack of cigarettes is more dangerous for its 260 mg of CO than for its nicotine alone. The long-term attrition of oxygen can cause increased risk of atherosclerotic diseases at sites such as the aorta and the coronary arteries; this can result in conditions like chest pains (angina pectoris) or heart attacks.

Considerable evidence links smoking to heart disease. Several factors may be involved. One is the boosted blood pressure and heart rate and the lessened oxygen supply we have mentioned, which stress the heart. Smoking can affect cardiac rhythms. And, as we saw, it increases the susceptibility to high cholesterol in the blood, which can lead to atherosclerosis and heart attack. Another factor might be enhanced clotting of the blood. In the periphery (along with local NE release), this may contribute to vascular disease. All of these factors can eventually lead to sudden cardiac death. In the U.S., where mortality from coronary heart disease is double that of other countries, smoking is a prime suspect. On the bright side, though, is the fact that cholesterol problems, reduced oxygen levels, and heart risks all reverse rapidly (in one or two months) when you quit.

Smokers will not want to hear it, but they are probably already well aware of the strong link between smoking and cancer. Smoking is recognizably the major cause of lung cancer (from which more women die than from breast cancer). In addition, it contributes to cancers of the mouth, larynx, esophagus, throat, bladder, and pancreas. Again, these are not directly attributable to nicotine or tar (which itself has over 2,000 compounds), but are more likely due to a synergistic action of several smoke constituents, such as benzpyrene or arsenic, or an interaction with environmental pollutants as well. A genetic factor is another possibility, since cancers can develop after a few years in some smokers and not at all in others. Snuff dipping increases mouth and pharynx cancer. With the addition of alcohol consumption, the risk of esophageal cancer is increased. Quitting smoking, however, can reverse precancer signs.

The fetus, too, does not fare well on cigarette smoke. Smoking has been linked to a higher rate of spontaneous abortions, stillbirths (twice as likely), early infant deaths, and significantly lowered birth weights. At no point during a pregnancy is smoking advisable, and the period of breast feeding is best included under this warning as well.

In drug interactions, smokers show a more rapid metabolism of many drugs (e.g., theophylline, caffeine, imipramine). Opiates produce less sedation for them, and benzodiazepines less tranquilization, though not all of these are metabolic effects.

The issue of smoking has become politicized only in recent years, when studies showed that not only is the habit harmful to those doing it, but also to nonsmokers in the vicinity who inhale the smoke, which is called passive smoking. Passive smokers may have an increased risk of lung and urinary tract problems and of cancer of the pancreas and liver. The adverse side effects of passive smoking form the basis for the arguments of anti smoking lobbyists, which led to banishment of smoking from the workplace and finally from all public places (January, 1989). Their claim is that smoking is a mild form of assault and a public health hazard.

Why do people smoke? And what are the reinforcements that maintain smokers' habits? We know that smoking is a learned behavior, and surveys show that the most influential teachers are adolescent peers, who provide the strongest motive to start. This is despite the fact that one-third of smokers report becoming sick on the first try. Role models among family and teachers, in the media, and in commercial ads likewise contribute to the force of "desirable imitation." Puberty is the critical time for most.

Reaping the effects of nicotine is a primary reinforcement for smokers. We have seen how there is only about a 10-second interval between a puff and a mild stimulation in the reward systems of the brain from NE and DA release; thus, there is a reinforcement at every puff. Studies have also shown that when nicotine content in cigarettes is reduced, smokers increase smoking behavior to get more, which indicates that "tobacco drinkers" smoke to get nicotine, and taste is probably not of primary importance. Inhalation is another indicator of this, and the fact that people continue to use high T/N cigarettes, although tar does account for a certain amount of flavor, aroma, and other sensations.

Another reinforcement from nicotine comes from using it as a psychological tool for arousal or relaxation. Animal studies show that nicotine reduces the effects of anxiety on performance. This arousal, sustained attention, and improved performance function as a reward, as does the relaxation derived at a different dosage. In these respects, certain brands of cigarettes stand out as especially needed or rewarding.

In addition to the primary reinforcements of the drug effect, there are secondary reinforcements that smokers become attached to, such as the pure activity of smoking, the sight, taste, and aroma of the cigarettes, oral gratification, and the displacement activity (such as smoking under stress). Some dedicated cigar and pipe smokers do not even absorb significant amounts of nicotine when they simply hold smoke in their mouths; nevertheless, they become habituated to all the pleasant accompaniments of smoking. In one study, smokers deprived of tobacco still preferred to smoke lettuce-leaf cigarettes, with none of nicotine's rewards (Balfour, 1984, p. 167).

Lastly, as with many habituating and addictive drugs, avoidance of the rigors of withdrawal is a factor contributing to an ongoing habit. As drug withdrawals go, the effects of nicotine withdrawal are comparatively mild, and a few people experience none at all. Others can easily abstain for periods without inconvenience. It appears to be an individual matter, with the dosages that cause dependence remaining unestablished, and the mechanisms of withdrawal not fully explained.

In general, withdrawal begins within 24 hours of cessation and shows a profile of both stimulatory and depressant rebound effects. Symptoms include irritability, anxiety, restlessness, depression, a loss of concentration, drowsiness, headaches, tremors, palpitations, sweating, hunger, insomnia, and gastrointestinal complaints. Some of these symptoms may persist for weeks or months. The craving to smoke peaks in a day or two, and is generally more severe in the evening; in some unfortunate habitués, this can last for a year. Moreover, there is no difference in the severity of these effects for lighter smokers. And, be advised, cutting back does not seem to be a good idea, since partial abstinence can produce a withdrawal more severe than quitting outright. Quitters also show a low arousal EEG, a decline in performances that require vigilance, an increase in hostility, lowered heart rate and blood pressure, and an increase in peripheral blood flow. They commonly gain weight.

Along with dieting, kicking the cigarette habit is one of America's national obsessions, especially with the antismoking campaigns that have been gaining in strength and frequency since the Surgeon General's warning first went on cigarette packages. As Mark Twain once said, "Quitting smoking is easy. I've done it many times." What are your chances of quitting smoking successfully? For all of the conventional methods, the average success rate is about 20 percent, and the real challenge is not so much getting off the weed, but staying off. Relapse is the major pitfall. Your chances are better if you have any of these factors (Balfour, 1984, p. 172):

1. are of the male sex
2. have had a higher education
3. are an extrovert
4. are emotionally stable
5. have a low cigarette consumption
6. have spent fewer years smoking
7. are a noninhaler
8. have a low consumption of coffee and alcohol.

(Balfour, 1984, p. 172)

As for the methods, however, none seems preeminent.

One of the highest ranking, and definitely the cheapest, programs for kicking the habit is plain old self-motivation and self-control. Smokers with good intentions frequently enroll themselves in programs to assuage their health consciousness without a total commitment to quitting (and bring all the success statistics down), but someone devoted and sworn to quitting stands the best chance. Self-control can be strengthened by visualizing the consequences of smoking when the craving is on, by using a "buddy system" and not quitting alone, or by signing a contract with another party to pay a stiff penalty in the event of failure (*contingency contracting*).

Two pharmacological aids to quitting have come into use since the 1980s, nicotine gum and the nicotine patch. Both forms have been designed to deliver lower doses of nicotine by safer routes, to help reduce the symptoms upon cessation of smoking, and to help wean smokers from the drug. If nothing else, these modes of administration eliminate the damage caused by smoke in the lungs, a considerable advantage, since the administration of smoke, not nicotine, is the primary hazard.

Nicotine polacrilex gum, available in 1 mg, 2 mg, or 4 mg sticks, can produce blood levels of nicotine up to 64 percent of what smokers get (Fiore et al., 1992). Overall, the gum has shown varied results, and seems to be largely ineffective when used alone, in the absence of a counseling or support program. Patients may use the gum incorrectly, mistiming its use, chewing it too fast (like chewing gum), or pairing it with acidic foods or drinks that impede absorption (Fiore et al., 1992). Some find the taste aversive. Moreover, the gum relieves only some of the unpleasant symptoms of withdrawal. Signs like depression, insomnia, hunger, anxiety, tremulousness, and the craving for the drug continue, indicating that these may be effects due to other components of tobacco smoke, or to conditioning. One advantage is that nicotine gum can be used like smoking to cope with stressful situations, delivering a helpful dose of nicotine, but this may reinforce the habit of using the gum, so that people may continue to use it longer than is recommended (Fiore et al., 1992). In general, the success of nicotine gum seems to be limited.

The nicotine patch (officially, the *nicotine transdermal delivery system*), introduced in 1992, consists of a small round patch, resembling an adhesive bandage, designed to be attached (one a day) to the skin; this topically delivers a controlled, steady, low-level dose of nicotine into the bloodstream. As with nicotine gum, the strategy is for short-term use to reduce the symptoms of withdrawal, especially the craving for nicotine, but this method does not affect the hunger or weight gain that typically accompany cessation of smoking (Fiore et al., 1992). Neither does it provide the little kick of reinforcement that can come from smoking, or even from chewing nicotine gum. Success rates of abstinence at six months after quitting range from 22 to 42 percent with the patch (Fiore et al., 1992). This is not as effective as was first anticipated, but still makes this device superior to other smoking cessation aids. Despite the advice of the package inserts, studies show that using the patch for 6 to 8 weeks works as well as using it for 10 to 18 (Fiore et al., 1992; Kolata, 1994). The most commonly reported side effects are local skin reactions, insomnia, and abnormal dreams. The "patched" who continue to smoke increase the risk of toxic effects from nicotine, and this is not a good idea at all for those with cardiovascular problems. It is not clear whether counseling programs in conjunction with the patch improve the results (Fiore et al., 1992; Kolata, 1994). In general, the patch is easy to use, if a little pricey (8 weeks' treatment at about $224 [Kolata, 1994]), and justifies a modest expectation of success.

Besides pharmacological aids to quitting smoking, there are smoking clinics that use a variety of other techniques. Behavioral techniques include controlled smoking (not quitting), stimulus control (eliminating situations in which one smokes), relaxation training, contingency contracting, social support, and aversion training. Other methods involve psychotherapy and group therapy, acupuncture, hypnosis, and sensory deprivation. Some of these techniques show promise, but more work needs to be done. Most effective are various combinations of these techniques: pharmacological and behavioral. The success rate of clinics is only 12 to 28 percent (Balfour, 1984, p. 190). Of the 41 million ex-smokers in the United States, 90 percent say they quit without formal programs (U.S. Department of Health and Human Services, 1988).

What it seems to come down to is that the perilous consequences of smoking are, in the main, mere abstractions to the average smoker. They are postponed and not even inevitable (after all, heavy smokers have survived to be octogenarians) and therefore not awe-inspiring. On the other hand, the inconveniences of quitting and withdrawal are discomforts enough to the average smoker that it does not seem to be worth investing even a small amount of suffering to avoid a distant, statistical evil that might never materialize. And the positive health boons, the disappearing cough, reordered metabolism, and reversal of lung dysfunctions often do not seem incentive enough. The cognitive split between rationally knowing the dangers of smoking while continuing to smoke are summed up in Graham Hemminger's ditty, "This Smoking World" (p. 128):

Tobacco is a dirty weed:

I like it.

It satisfies no human need:

I like it.

It makes you thin, it makes you lean,

It takes the hair right off your bean,

It's the worst darn stuff I've ever seen:

*I like it.**

From Graham Lee Hemminger,
"This Smoking World," in the *Penn State Froth*.
Reprinted with permission of Pennsylvania
State University Archives.

Hair loss, it should be said, is not associated with tobacco use.

Chapter 21

History of Opiates

FIGURE 21.1 *Papaver somniferum* (opium poppy).

Boasting a 6,000-year history, the opium poppy, *papaver somniferum*, once indigenous to Asia Minor, is the source of opium. It is an annual plant, three or four feet high with large four to five-inch flowers in red, white, or purple (Figure 21.1). In the few days between the dropping of the petals and the maturation of the seed pod (capsules), the harvesters come in the evening, wearing masks to avoid drowsiness from the fumes, and lacerate the capsule, causing it to exude slowly a white liquid like thick milk. This dries in the seasonal breeze until it is a brownish, gummy resin by morning. The workers come and scrape off this sap, rolling it between thumb and forefinger into small balls or loaves; these are wrapped in leaves and set out to dry and thicken, and they may be further dried and powdered. In some cases, the poppy juice may be boiled and filtered. The result of the process is raw opium, source of the most powerful pain killers known.

Crude opium extract contains about 0.5 percent codeine and 10 percent morphine, along with resins, oils, sugars, and proteins. Purified from crude opium, morphine, codeine, and papaverine are known as opiates. Compounds like heroin, which come from alterations of the morphine molecule, along with other synthetic painkillers unrelated to morphine or heroin by structure or potency, are called opioids. This distinction, however, is often ignored, and we will refer to all of these drugs as *opiates*. Sometimes, especially in law enforcement, opiates are referred to as narcotics, a term that has come to mean all illegal drugs. The reference is legitimate in the case of opiates, since it means "sleep-inducing." However, in legal and government parlance a stimulant like cocaine may be considered a narcotic, too, a misnomer that derives mostly from its association with the Harrison Narcotics Act and the Federal Narcotics Bureau, which suppresses the smuggling and sale of controlled substances.

HISTORY

Ancient references to opium are scattered throughout the cultures of the eastern Mediterranean. It is possible that the *joy plant* mentioned in a Sumerian tablet of 4000 BC was *papaver somniferum*. Images of opium poppies ornament Cyprian vases of 1100 BC as well as the tombs of the pharaohs (1600-600 BC); and the Ebers papyrus (1300 BC) suggestively mentions a "remedy to prevent the excessive crying of children," which some researchers take to be the first reference to medicinal use. The scraping and collecting process is recorded on Assyrian cuneiform tablets of 700 BC. Apparently, from Assyria and Sumeria the poppy traveled to Egypt, where the most potent variety, *opium thebaicum*, the only good source of medicinal black opium up to 1200 AD, was cultivated near Thebes. This variety, with a high percentage of thebaine, was difficult to grow and export. It made famously good medicine, but the high thebaine varieties are low in euphoriant effects, so medicine it remained. *Papaver rhoas* proved more profitable to ship, and Egypt conducted a brisk opium trade with the Phoenicians and Minoans, which is how it came to Greece.

Opium is evident in many facets of Greek culture. One of the earliest possible references (1000 BC) is Helen's care-drowning drug from the *Odyssey* (see page xx). Another possibility is the drug that Aesculapius (the Greek demigod credited as the founder of medicine) used to resurrect Hippolytus, son of the hero Theseus (from a legend circa 600 BC). Statues of Aesculapius are crowned with poppies, and the great hospital at Cos was dedicated to him. On the first night of their visit to this hospital, patients received an infusion of opiates and possibly belladonna, and the resident doctors would interpret their dreams. The legendary physician Hippocrates (born 420 BC), was educated there and was known to use opium to treat various ailments. However, the first indisputable reference occurs in Theophrastus in the third century BC, who mentions the juice of the poppy. Our word *opium* comes from the Greek word *opios*, which means "a little vegetable juice."

The poppy abounds in Greek legend and myth. Demeter, whose daughter was given to the god of the underworld, was said to have created the poppy to sleep and to escape the misery of her loss. Another legend has it that Hypnos, the god of sleep and the Greek version of our Sandman, lived with his mother Nyx (*night*) on the Isle of Lemnos in a cave surrounded by poppies. He was said to lull mortals to sleep by pouring poppy juice into their eyes. Death (Thanatos) was the brother of Hypnos, and Dreams (one of whom was Morpheus) were his sons.

At the time of another key Greek physician, Galen (born in Asia Minor circa 140 AD), cultivation of the poppy was spreading, opium cakes and candies were selling in the Greek streets, and dependence was common throughout the classical world. But as the Roman Empire grew, the use of opiates in Western medicine declined. About 300 AD, opium made the journey east, carried to Persia and India by Alexander the Great and by Arab merchants. The seeds didn't arrive in China, a land now associated with opium, until 600-700 AD. Originally it was employed there, as elsewhere, as a constipative agent against diarrhea.

The advanced Arab civilization of the first millenium wrote in scientific detail of opium, summarized the opium lore of Galen and other learned men, catalogued its medical uses, and enumerated its various forms of preparation in formularies and encyclopedias.

It was the Arabs who returned opium to the West in medieval times. In the ninth century, Muslim physicians founded the School of Salerno in Sicily, which promulgated the use of opium up to the twelfth century in the form of the *spongia somniferum*. Opium in this period could also be obtained in the forms of topical pastes and poppyhead tea. To all indications, no widespread abuse developed—quite the opposite. With the coming of the plague and the shutdown of intercourse with the East, historical references to opium vanish until the mid-sixteenth century, when Paracelsus revived it.

Paracelsus (1493-1541, actually Phillipus von Hohenheim) brought opium back into medicine in the form of a recipe he called the *Anodyne Specific*, which contained opium, orange and lemon juice, cinnamon, cloves, musk, juice of corals, and a dash of pearl and gold. He also dispensed pills, which he called laudanum, whose chief active ingredient was undoubtedly opium. His followers called laudanum the *Stone of Immortality*, alluding to the precious Philosopher's Stone of the alchemists, and praised it as a cure for every disease save leprosy, boasting with Paracelsus himself that it could revive the dead. In retrospect, who could blame such enthusiasm? Opium had more legitimate, dramatic, sometimes even relevant, medical effects than most other compounds that had been tried at random. Because of its toxicity, however, the idea of laudanum lapsed for another century.

Only by the mid 1500s and early 1600s did clear evidence of the awareness of opium dependence and withdrawal begin to show up in the West, some of it noted by travelers (like Rauwolf of Augsburg) who described the abstinence symptoms suffered by Eastern dervishes. In seventeenth century Europe, opium was just beginning to appear in apothecary shops, its modern medical uses being fairly well-perceived by then, while in England, Thomas Sydenham was reviving a vague relative of Paracelsus' formula. In 1680, he introduced the public to Sydenham's Laudanum, a sumptuous blend of opium, sherry wine, saffron, cinnamon, and cloves, initiating what would evolve into the patent medicine industry. Copycat compounds soon appeared and proliferated, such as the potent Dover's Powder (concocted by sea captain and self-proclaimed doctor Thomas Dover). This was a mixture of opium, ipecac, licorice, saltpeter, and tartar that was widely traded overseas. Opium use was at this time gaining acceptance in Asia as well as in the West. Still presented as medicines, these preparations were nonetheless cheaper than beer or wine for convalescents who continued using them as intoxicants.

In 1803, a 16yearold pharmacist's apprentice in Germany, Friedrich Serturner, convinced that opium had a single active ingredient, succeeded in precipitating tiny white crystals out of the gray, powdered opiate, (a project noted by some as the beginning of alkaloid chemistry). He called the substance *morphium* (morphine) after Morpheus, the Greek god of dreams. Physicians embraced the new medicine, praising it in the continental journals of 1817 as purer *and safer* than opium. The isolation of codeine from opium followed in 1832 and of papaverine in 1848, by which time the use of opium alkaloids had spread throughout the medical world.

In the early 1800s, opium was in use enough in England that domestic cultivation had begun, but the significant surge of awareness on the part of the public was marked by two "media events." The first was the anonymous serialization in *London* magazine of Thomas De Quincey's *Confessions of an English Opium Eater* (1821/1981), a spellbinding and stylistically potent exposé of the author's addiction and the pleasures and pains of opium use. The article was a public sensation and brought the unexamined practice of opium taking in England into the limelight, giving addiction a name, so to speak. Ironically, what De Quincey claims he intended as an examination of the power of dreams and imagination and a caution against opium use was so literarily evocative, exotic, and fascinating (and still is), that he was blamed for luring many readers to experiment with the drug. In his defense, the work also spurred the first scientific studies of addiction.

It is important to note that at this time opium was as cheap and easily had at the druggist as aspirin is today, and that addiction was viewed with about the same mild disapproval as drunkenness. This is plain from De Quincey's accusation that the poet Samuel Taylor Coleridge continued using opium for pleasure (after his toothache was gone), whereas he paints his own abuse in the light of a chronic gastric ulcer whose treatment had mired him in dependency. He faults Coleridge for sensual and recreational indulgence, the point being that loss of moral restraint, not dependence, was the sin. In this sense, alcohol, more apparent in its effects at this time, was seen as a worse problem than opium, despite the fact that opiates were prescribed at the merest indication, and more and more people were becoming involved with them. As with tranquilizers over a century later, it was a temptation for physicians to prescribe for their patients' guaranteed satisfaction rather than for a specific ailment.

A second stir was caused by the discovery in the 1830s and 1840s of the massive use of opiates by entire communities in the Fenlands, low-lying marshy districts in the north of England. Prone to ague, rheumatism, and neuralgia, the north country inhabitants turned to opium for relief, to such an extent that it replaced alcohol and became part of the social fabric, tolerated and controlled by informal social mechanisms. It was said that pounds of the best Turkey import loaded the market stalls. In Ely, "the sale of laudanum was as common as butter and cheese" (Latimer & Goldberg, 1981, p. 60). Opium defenders and libertarians of the time pointed to the successful functioning of the north country societies as evidence that drugs could be used harmlessly on a wide scale.

By mid-century, both the medical and recreational use of opium was widespread. Although many people did not become abusers, opium was beginning to be seen as a social problem. Then, in 1855, the matter was raised to a higher octave. This was the year that the hypodermic syringe, which had been invented by Dr. Alexander Wood two years prior, was made available. Doctors took to injecting patients subcutaneously, first with opium solutions, because they believed that injection sidestepped addiction, and then with morphine, because they believed morphine to be purer and safer than opium. Intravenous injection soon followed.

Compounding the trend was the fact that mass production, made feasible by industrial growth, meant narcotics (and needles) for anyone who wanted them. By the 1860s, use was phenomenal, with opiates so accessible that severe withdrawal was virtually unrecognized. Usually, the onset of withdrawal was read as a return of whatever ailment one was being treated for (or as a related problem), which indicated a need for more opiates at higher doses; of course, that solved the problem and reinforced the diagnosis. In other cases, patients mistook withdrawal symptoms for flu or intestinal problems.

Nevertheless, between De Quincey and the new potency of injectable morphine, awareness of addiction grew, legal measures were passed to limit the sale of opiates to druggists, and in the 1870s the habit-forming properties of morphine were first noted. Addiction cures sprang up, and religious temperance movements brought anti opium sentiment to a head. Patent medicines were marked "Poison." The foreign trade in opium was hotly contested, and in 1908 opiates were placed among the more severely restricted drugs.

The British opium experience is intimately bound up with the use of the drug in Asia. The drug may have come to China via Arab traders by 600 AD. Opium dens first appeared in the late seventeenth century, when Portuguese traders in the South Seas brought the smoking habit in from the Americas. The British first became involved, however, in 1757, when the British East India Company took control of most of India, along with the opium crop, and opened the supply route to China. Opium became the solution to the problems that Britain was having with its China trade.

Except for certain coastal contact points like Canton and other river deltas, China remained a closed book to foreign powers. Remarkably self-sufficient, it wanted few commodities from Europeans; in the main, it exported goods and took in silver. Opium, however, it wanted, more and more ravenously, much to Britain's advantage; moreover, it was willing to pay. And pay heavily it did, until it was being economically bled by foreign powers. The situation worsened with crackdowns on China's part to try to stanch the outflow of currency, and with an increase of trade on Britain's part. In fact, every attempt by China to repress smuggling helped business. Stricter laws only increased the amount of bribes, and destroying large supplies only motivated competing smugglers, who rushed in to fill the gap. At one point, opium sales to China made up 14 percent of the official revenue of British India.

Tensions eventually came to war, the first from 1839-1842, and then another under a new Emperor (1856-1860). The British and other European powers involved were victorious in both cases. It is generally recognized that the motive on the part of the West was not only to maintain a lucrative drug market, but to pry open the doors of China to

Western diplomacy and commerce. As spoils of victory, Hong Kong was ceded to the British as a Crown colony, and Canton and Shanghai were opened for trade. The second war cost China twenty million pounds sterling, the opening of the remaining ports (which irreparably weighted the balance of trade in Britain's favor and amounted to an economic collapse), and legalization and regulation of the opium trade, which lasted until 1906.

America, too, ran a vigorous opium commerce in competition with the British in China. America's opium experience in general ran parallel to Britain's. The use of opium in the U.S. began medicinally, mostly in the form of laudanum, and spread during the nineteenth century. During this period—a drug experimenter's paradise—opium, and later morphine, were cheap and available without a prescription, and most users were respectable, white, middle-aged middle-class females or white Southern males, who used the drugs medicinally (at least at first) and procured them legally. As in Britain, addiction still wasn't seen as a problem, only as somewhat reprehensible.

The 1850s were a time of expanding use, when morphine was on apothecary shelves competing with laudanum, when patent medicines were beginning to appear, and when the impact of Wood's invention, the hypodermic syringe, was felt on the American side of the Atlantic, intensifying the problem of substance abuse. Although some authorities ascribe the boom in compulsive morphine use to the treatment of soldiers wounded in the Civil War, others dispute the connection. There is little doubt that the war did play a role in introducing many of the wounded to "soldier's joy," as morphine was known. The Prussian-Austrian War (1866) and the Franco-German War (1870) in Europe are similarly cited.

After the Civil War, there was a shift to more censorious attitudes toward opium and morphine. This was precipitated by many factors: the potency, availability, and overprescription of the new drug morphine; its use in the Civil War; the temperance movements against alcohol; a growing awareness of overdosing and habituation; the negative image of African-American drug users (cocaine); and the later development of alternative, nonaddictive analgesics. Not the least among these factors was the Chinese drug problem in the American West.

After the gold strike (1848), great numbers of Chinese immigrants were brought in as cheap labor for the grueling and perilous work of digging mines and shipping out the ore. This work completed, the whites drove the Chinese out of many areas in the 1850s, and the 1860s found them settled in boom towns building railroads, again doing the most undesirable labor. In this way, Chinatowns sprang up throughout the West—small, encapsulated villages and neighborhoods where Chinese culture and institutions throve largely intact, including the venerable institution of the opium den. The dens spread the technique of smoking, which contributed to the upswing in use at the time.

The Chinese coolies had already been the targets of racist resentment, accused of stealing jobs from white laborers (in fact, jobs white labor didn't want). But with the opium-smoking habit spreading to young men and women of respectable families who visited the opium dens as tourist attractions in places like San Francisco's exotic and picturesque Chinatown, and with the bottom dropping out of the American economy in 1873, making times tough all over, anti-Chinese sentiment turned vicious. In the media, the Chinaman became the Yellow Peril, a threat to white labor and home industry. In San Francisco, ordinances were aimed against opium den owners, and soon the California legislature passed a state anti opium law, forbidding the importation of opium by Chinese—but not by Americans. These measures and others were all clearly to vex "Heathen Chinese" by targeting smoking opium, leaving unscathed the white middle and upper class drinkers and injectors. They were the first nonalcohol drug measures taken against consumers.

By the 1870s, morphine sulfate could be had at any pharmacy and general store in laudanum, syrups, and candies, and its use was still socially acceptable. Addicts, mostly upper and middle class women, were not stigmatized and not identifiable from their morphine habit, and alcoholics were seen as more likely to commit crimes. In some places, drug users switched from alcoholism to morphinism to salvage their good reputations. The error of treating the flu-like symptoms of withdrawal with more opiates was becoming evident, but withdrawal was still not well understood, and tolerance was laid to other factors (perhaps other alkaloids) besides morphine. The self-injection of morphine boomed in the late 1860s and peaked in the 1870s. Overdosing increased as people attempting SC injections hit veins. As a safety device for physicians, Dr. J. H. Kane introduced the use of the tie-cord. This was, in effect, a tourniquet, used to tie off a limb. If the injection missed, the drug could still be gradually and safely released at intervals into general circulation by loosening the cord every few minutes. This cord has come to characterize the modern heroin abuser, who uses it to raise veins for injecting.

By the latter 1800s, addiction was recognized as a national problem, but the patent medicine craze (circa 1870-1880) was just under way, a period when thousands of unlabelled preparations laced with opiates, with names like Winslow's Soothing Syrup, Darby's Carminative, and Godfrey's Cordial, were urged on consumers by entrepreneurs. Cocaine hydrochloride was debuting at this time, and many other psychoactive preparations (chloral hydrate, ether, and tinctures of cannabis) stood unprohibited on the apothecary shelves.

By the turn of the century, public opinion had begun to swing toward less libertarian attitudes. Addiction cures and local legislators were fighting morphinism and patent medicines, and morality declaimed against untoward drug use. But then a new and more potent twist was added to the story, when heroin came onto the market in 1898.

Heroin (diacetylmorphine) is a synthetic derivative of morphine, first made by London chemist C. R. Alder Wright in 1874. The heroin molecule is fundamentally a morphine molecule with two acetyl groups affixed to it between the matching alcohol and phenylhydroxyl groups. Wright used the process of boiling morphine with acetic anhydride (a compound related to table vinegar), which produced a number of compounds, heroin among them. Some time later, Heinrich Dreser of Friedrich Bayer and Company (who is sometimes mistaken for the synthesizer of heroin) reported on his experiments with the drug and named it from the German *heroisch*, meaning "a small, potent unit." He endorsed it as a nonaddictive analgesic, a good remedy for coughs, chest pains, and pneumonia, with an LD 100 times the ED. It went on the market as Bayer Heroin in 1898 as a medicine for coughs, bronchitis, and tuberculosis, in lieu of codeine. Contrary to some beliefs, heroin was not introduced as a morphine cure, although it was employed that way in some places. Unmistakably, it was the most potent narcotic yet. Although each heroin molecule is biotransformed into a morphine molecule, heroin's higher lipid solubility and more rapid absorption into the brain add to its effect.

Four or five years after heroin's introduction, due to Dreser's advocacy and wide availability, its clinical popularity had spread, and the question of heroin addiction was cropping up. In 1911, however, Dr. J.D. Trawick was still capable of remarking in the *Kentucky Medical Journal,* "I feel that bringing charges against heroin is almost like questioning the fidelity of a good friend" (as cited in Trebach, 1982, p. 40). At the same time, evidence of heroin addiction in New York City, the key site of abuse, began to grow. There were 149 heroin-related admissions to Bellevue Hospital in 1914, compared to one in 1910 (Trebach, 1982, p. 43).

The first quarter of the twentieth century brought the formation of the social attitudes toward drugs that still inform the 1990s to some degree. The boundaries between drug use, misuse, and abuse became clarified, and morality gravitated toward the control of opiates and alcohol. These values can be stated in terms of three norms: (1) that individuals are responsible for their actions, and therefore drug misuse is a punishable loss of self control; (2) that legitimate pleasures are earned, unlike drug taking, which is an illicit and unearned pleasure; and (3) that repressive legislation was the best way to attack the problem (Zentner, 1975, p. 102). Indeed, the government set out with irrational vengeance to eradicate habit-forming drugs and what it called the crime, poverty, and insanity associated with addiction. For the first time, and increasingly thenceforth, addiction became heavily linked with criminality in the public mind. Since the underworld smoked opium, their loose morals were blamed on the pharmacology of the drug. Well-meaning advocates for federal legislation demonized addicts, promulgating the "dope fiend" myth, and the law itself eventually made substance abusers into criminals.

In 1902, the United States, having acquired the Phillipines as a result of the Spanish American War, became concerned with the opium problem there and in the Far East. Dr. Hamilton Wright, "the father of American narcotics laws," was appointed to the International Opium Commission. Nonmedical importation was banned in the Phillipines, and China, Britain, and the United States made a pact to restrict the opium trade. During the first decade of the century, legislation of all sorts was passed to control habit-forming drugs. The Pure Food and Drug Act of 1906, a key piece of drug legislation, prohibited the importation of dangerous drugs, required that drug ingredients and quantities be stated on labels, and required that compounds meet official standards of identity and purity. This actually served to safeguard addicts from impure preparations. Of course, once reliable labeling appeared, many people avoided drugged products. It is estimated that 50,000 patent medicines were on the market at the time and that sales plummeted by a third (Musto, 1973). Another significant law was passed in 1909, prohibiting the importation of opium for smoking or nonmedical use (recognized as an anti-Chinese measure).

The Harrison Narcotics Act

During this period, Hamilton Wright, in an aggressive drug-slur campaign, was pressing the urgency of the situation on the public, hyping the myth of the drug fiend and demon drugs. Religious interests and the media crusaded with shameless propaganda to spread among the populace a fear of drugs and addicts—an effect, it would be safe to say, that has only begun to wear off. These efforts came to fruition on December 17, 1914, when President Wilson signed into effect the Harrison Act, the first federal antinarcotic legislation. Because nothing in the Constitution assigns government the right to control drugs, debates raged over the constitutionality of dictating moral behavior to the public and of interfering in policies better left to the medical profession. Consequently, the act was passed as a tax action, ostensibly as a law to fulfill our commitment to the Hague Opium Convention (1912), when 34 nations signed an agreement to tighten domestic controls on the manufacture and distribution of opium, cocaine, and other drugs. In practice, the Harrison Act was the dawn of a troubled era for drug users and stands as the cornerstone of narcotics laws to this day.

> *On the surface, the Harrison Act was not a prohibition, but an act to provide for the registration of (with collectors of internal revenue), and to impose a special tax upon, all persons who produce, import, manufacture, sell, distribute or give away opium or coca leaves, their salts, derivatives, or preparations, and for other purposes. (Trebach, 1982, p. 118).*

The idea was to disallow the nonmedical flow of drugs (e.g., in grocery stores) and to monitor and document their movement through legitimate medical channels. Druggists and physicians were to register with Internal Revenue. For a one dollar fee and registration with the district collector, physicians could obtain a license to prescribe opiates, provided they acted "in good faith" or "in the legitimate practice" of their profession. The proponents of the act saw it as a controversial but much-needed control for America's rampageous drug habit. A House of Representatives report (1913, June 24) noted that America's population of 90 million was importing and consuming 400,000 pounds of opium a year (as cited in Trebach, 1982, p. 21). Some legislators saw this act as an amendment to the ban on the importation of smoking opium of 1909 and saw its purpose as a move to eliminate recreational abuse of narcotics, while leaving their medical applications untouched: "Nothing contained in this section shall apply to the dispensing or distribution of any of the foresaid drugs . . . by a physician registered under this Act in the course of his professional practice only." However, as it turned out, law enforcement had a radically different interpretation.

Ham Wright, amid the anti drug frenzy and public fears that his propaganda had whipped up, saw the act "designed to place the entire interstate traffic in habit-forming drugs under the administration of the Treasury Department," and the Treasury Department went ahead with its own agenda to enforce the act with repressive zeal. The ambiguous phrases "and for other purposes" and "the legitimate practice of his profession," which allowed medicine its say, were taken by the enforcement agency *not* to mean maintaining addicts in their habits (viz., prescribing nondiminishing doses). For users, this meant that the act itself cut off all nonmedical channels for procuring drugs, while the Treasury Department "read" the act to shut down the medical channels as well. In effect, all legal supplies of narcotics were instantly cut off, throwing addicts on the dangers of the black market. And by addicts, remember, we still mean many respectable people from the previous century who had become dependent through medical treatment and who had been able to acceptably maintain themselves with some dignity through doctors and druggists.

The Harrison Act, then, "changed drug dependency from a misfortune into a national disaster" (Zentner, 1975, p. 103). Granting doctors no latitude in their policies toward addiction, the Bureau of Internal Revenue started prosecuting those who prescribed for addicts, without regard for what constituted good or bad faith. Between 1915 and 1938, 25,000 physicians were reported in violation (Coffee, 1938). Such blatant intimidation pushed many doctors away from the prescribing of opiates in marginal or even legitimate cases, and supplanted medical policies with government ones; namely, that cutting off the drug supply and inflicting strict penalties would lead to a national cure. The upshot was that one and all, upstanding turn-of-the-century dowagers and young joybangers, went underground, scouting for contraband connections or for doctors who would risk prescribing.

The Treasury Department was flooded with applications for "registration permits" by users hoping not to become criminals, but no such permits existed. Some physicians, solicitous of longstanding patients and friends, continued supplying drugs out of humaneness, while the unscrupulous sold prescriptions, but all were now accountable to drug inspectors for their opiate prescriptions and were liable to prosecution. Under these conditions, the roots and channels of today's addict subculture grew. The possession and use of narcotics became increasingly associated with immorality, criminality, insanity, and death. By way of a loose analogy, you could appreciate the social consequences if cigarettes were declared addictive (as they indeed have been, by the Surgeon General), if all legal supplies were shut down, and if doctors could not prescribe them to people who were dependent on them. The black market would boom, and users would become criminals overnight, not by a criminal act, but by a legislative one.

Soon after enforcement of the Harrison Act began, cases of physician violations began to percolate up to the Supreme Court. However, the court's decisions in several key cases still left doubts about the interpretation of the act, which kept valid the arbitrary rulings of enforcement agencies. Ironically, during this whole period, no case of responsible maintenance, clear of other factors like the selling of prescriptions, was ever ruled on. Finally, in the 1919 decision of *U.S. v Webb*, in a discussion tangential to the case, the court made a definitive ruling that regular prescriptions could be made only in diminishing doses.

In light of America's nineteenth century drug experience, most of the antidrug furor of this time was aimed at morphine, the predominant opiate of abuse. Heroin was a different story. It was a new agent with no criminal record as yet; its abuse and addiction potential were still being ascertained through the first decade of the century; and it was still defended by some physicians. Therefore, it had leeway to gain ground before public knowledge caught up with it. The heroin subculture was already forming in Manhattan around 1910, due partly to Ham Wright's verbal assassination of morphine and the 1909 ban on smoking opium. This was the main site from which abuse radiated south and west to other urban centers, where it tended to remain concentrated. Most new users were healthy, intelligent, white, urban males 15 to 25 years old, who ganged in unruly social clubs at dance halls, movies, and vaudeville shows, and who sniffed heroin occasionally for fun. Heroin at this time was very easy to use. With the pressure of the Harrison Act on morphine, the heroin black market was growing. Heroin was cheap, compact, easy to smuggle, easy to adulterate, easy to carry, simple to sniff, and it cropped up casually on social occasions, much as cocaine did in the seventies and eighties. As a matter of fact, the cocaine supply at the time was running low, and many users crossed over to heroin.

Soon heroin was publicly demonized along with the other opiates. Anxiety increased at the outbreak of World War I, when draftees and other soldiers were discovered using it, and heroin became visible as a national problem. In 1916, the Surgeon General declared it a menace to public health, and in 1920 the AMA pronounced against it, by which point users were beginning to shoot it intravenously. The public mythologies that had developed around cocaine were visited on it: that it obliterates social responsibility, excites users to cold-blooded crime, and bestows superhuman reflexes. Heroin was linked to Bolshevism, anarchy, and terrorism. In 1924, then, Congress amended the 1909 Smoking Opium Act to prohibit the importation of crude opium to manufacture heroin (Statutes at Large, 1924), in effect outlawing all domestic use of the drug. This measure, however, didn't stop trafficking. By the 1930s, heroin had largely superseded morphine for abuse, and by the 1940s heroin addiction was the dominant addiction in the underworld. In contrast, international efforts influenced by American policy caused the world production of legal heroin to drop from a 9,000 kg peak in 1926 to 101 kg by 1979 (96 of which were consumed by Britain) (Trebach, 1982, p. 54).

The narcotics scene in America remained fundamentally unchanged during the *Anslinger Era*, the period from Harry Jacob Anslinger's appointment as U.S. Commissioner of the Federal Bureau of Narcotics (established within the Treasury Department in 1930), to his resignation in 1962. This period was marked on one hand by the developing underground of morphine and heroin users seeking connections through dealers and doctors, and on the other by Anslinger's austere position paralleling that for liquor control; that drug use was absolutely immoral and that it could be squelched by criminal sanctions and harsh policies (implemented sometimes by immoral and unethical methods).

Several developments took place during this time. One was the end of Prohibition and the transfer of mobsters' energies to narcotics. This process took some years. Unlike alcohol, which was simple to manufacture and distribute, heroin required the construction of a global network, from the growing fields in Turkey to the processing sites in Europe to the smugglers and pushers in the New York streets. After World War II, abuse shifted to minorities in the slums and began to spread.

The end of the Anslinger era came when Anslinger resigned from the Federal Bureau of Narcotics in 1962, most likely under pressure from the Kennedy administration. This marked a relaxation of repressive policies and a more humane vision of addiction. Another major factor in the change of attitudes at this time was the availability of methadone, a synthetic opiate that could be used rationally and successfully in addiction treatment. From this time on, rehabilitation expanded and was increasingly adopted as an alternative by official policy makers.

Methadone, which is itself addicting, is an acceptable treatment for opiate dependence. It relieves the anxiety, depression, and craving for heroin; it occupies opiate receptors and blocks the euphoric effects of heroin if users try to go back on their habit; and it is cheap.

The sixties began with a brief heroin shortage in New York City due to law enforcement (Brecher, 1972, p. 94). Prices inflated tenfold when dealers found that demand held steady, and they remained high. The mid- to late sixties saw a boom in heroin abuse. It began to penetrate into African-American and Latin populations, and then to spread among white, middleclass suburban youth, who were reported to be mainlining it by

1970 to 1971. A factor here was the open attitude toward drugs entertained by the sixties counterculture. Already outlaws by using marijuana and LSD, the flower children and hippies were tolerant of other drugs as well.

Another concern of the time was the use of heroin among soldiers in Vietnam (which resurrected the specter of morphine and the Civil War), who had access to a cheap and pure supply of the drug from Burma, Laos, and Thailand. Dr. Norman E. Zinberg, on a fact-finding mission in Vietnam for the U.S. Department of Defense and the Drug Abuse Council, noted, "I saw one young man who had just returned to base after thirteen days in the field pour a vial of heroin (approximately 250 mg) into a large shot of vodka and drink it" (Zinberg, 1971). The usual New York City bag (an average dose for one IV shot) is 10 mg, so this soldier was drinking a street addict's supply for about a week—and wasting it, because heroin is poorly absorbed from the oral route. Military crackdowns against marijuana only tended to drive the soldiers to heroin; then a crackdown on heroin drove the prices up, and many soldiers started injecting it to use their drug supply more efficiently. Estimates of South Vietnam abuse range from 5 percent to 25 percent of the military population (Brecher, 1972, p. 188). Very few soldiers, however, brought the habit back, as was feared. And those who did had methadone to come home to.

With Kennedy and Anslinger, drug policy became a matter of presidential politics. The policies of the Nixon White House reflected the crosscurrent of trends in the latter half of the sixties. Declaring war on drugs, Nixon upped the budget considerably, mostly in areas of prevention and treatment, emphasizing methadone. At the same time, in light of an increase in all sorts of drug abuse, more powerful sanctions were put into place, and the Drug Enforcement Administration (DEA) was founded. In 1970, a watershed year, the Comprehensive Drug Abuse Prevention and Control Act was passed. This was the most complete single drug enactment ever made by Congress and was designed to collect, summarize, and define all federal policies relating to drugs of abuse. It sought to codify all narcotics laws and amendments since 1887, and it established the schedules of control and licensing, listing heroin as a Schedule I substance, with high abuse potential and no accepted medical use (a controversial point). As the law of the land for drug abuse, the act put a closing bracket on the era dominated by the 1914 Harrison Narcotics Act. Like the earlier act, it, too, made criminal provisions for possession, sale, and trafficking of drugs and came at a time when public opinion was stirred up over drug abuse by the counterculture, minorities, and the hard drug underworld.

Around 1972 and 1973, there was a drop in heroin abuse. Nixon was quick to point to his drug policies, but a large factor undoubtedly was Turkey's agreement to ban poppy cultivation in 1972 (a practice partly revived two years later under stricter controls). The effect of this was merely to cause a lag while the sources of supply shifted. Most of America's opium had come from Turkey at this time and was processed through the "French connection" at Marseilles. At this point, the Turkish trade dropped, to be replaced by "Mexican mud," heroin from Mexican poppies, processed from morphine hydrochloride rather than from morphine base (which gives it a brownish color). Another primary supplier of opium in the 1980s was (and still is) the Golden Triangle of Southeast Asia, a district embracing parts of Laos, Burma, and Thailand.

The latter seventies continued the uneasy balance between government recognition of and support for maintenance programs and stricter enforcement. On one hand, President Carter made unprecedented moves in encouraging a review of the therapeutic potential of heroin and marijuana, and he advocated other drug policies, such as decriminalizing possession of less than an ounce of marijuana. On the other hand, the proportion of the drug abuse budget devoted to enforcement (compared to treatment) rose noticeably (Trebach, 1982, p. 241).

These trends have continued, the two great social drug themes being rehabilitation and enforcement. On the whole, although heroin maintains its place in the drug scene, and new generations of users continue to discover it (possibly unaware of its particular dangers), the trend in general seems to be a decline in use. In New York City, as of 1994, the majority of heroin injectors were those who had started injecting during the period of heroin's widest popularity in the 1960s and early 1970s, and are now aged from their late 30s to 50s (Golub & Johnson, 1994).

Chapter 22

The Opiates

The history of the opiates is especially elaborate; not only does it extend back to prehistory, but also it involves four substances (opium, morphine, heroin, and methadone), each of which has had a significant impact on human societies. Now we will examine these drugs with a psychopharmacologist's eye to see what pharmacological effects form the basis of their historical importance.

PHARMACOKINETICS

Opiates may be taken orally, by injection, or by inhalation (sniffing or smoking), depending on the drug. Generally, the oral route is inferior, with slower and less complete absorption. If opiates are swallowed, they must wait to reach the intestines to enter circulation because of their alkalinity, so absorption is unpredictable and erratic. Blood and brain levels are then only a fraction of what they would be if the same dose were taken intravenously. Morphine is the least lipidsoluble of the opiates and the best of a bad lot for oral absorption.

The IV, IM, or SC injection of opiates yields better effects than the oral route, but presents the danger of an accidental overdose, especially if an intended IM or SC injection unwittingly hits a vein. Subcutaneous use is called skin popping (or *skinning*) by abusers, and IV injection mainlining. The latter provides a much more rapid onset of effects. However, morphine resists dissolution in the blood as well as in the stomach and reaches the brain only in small amounts, about 20 percent of what circulates in the periphery. An IV injection of some opiates can take 30 to 60 minutes to achieve significant brain levels, due to the blood-brain barrier, but heroin enters more efficiently. Despite this, seasoned users report instant euphoria following self-administration. This immediacy is most likely a conditioning effect which may be due to a placebo response that mobilizes the brain's natural opiates (endorphins). In other words, the brain starts the rush (euphoria) to some extent in anticipation of the arrival of the drug.

Besides drinking and injection, which figure prominently in the history of opiates, inhalation has also been significant. Opium smoking, as we have seen, was most popular among the Chinese and led to China's financial oppression. Heroin, too, can be smoked, with a rapidity of effect comparable to IV injection. In addition, the crystals of heroin can be sniffed, as was done by soldiers during the war in Vietnam, and in 1910 in New York City, where the drug was abundant and cheap.

Morphine reaches all body tissues. At therapeutic concentrations, about a third binds to blood proteins, while the other portion accumulates in the kidneys, liver, lungs, and spleen. It crosses the placental barrier, and the fetus can show dependence and withdrawal when birth removes it from its drug supplier, the mother.

The liver rapidly metabolizes opiates, biotransforming a significant amount on the first pass, although this tends to vary widely among people. The half-life in a young adult is only 2.5 to 3 hours, and 24 hours after administration tissue concentrations are low. Consequently, morphine's duration of action is only 4 or 5 hours. This is a matter of great importance to the drug dependent, who must seek another "fix" three or four times a day to avoid withdrawal symptoms. Heroin acts largely by being biotransformed into morphine, and about ten percent of a dose of codeine is metabolized into morphine as well. Consequently, morphine is the key to most opiate activity.

Ninety percent of a dose of morphine is excreted in 24 hours through the kidneys, with most of it metabolized. Traces may be found in the urine, however, well after two days. Another 7 to 10 percent of the dose enters the bile and passes out through the gastrointestinal tract.

Morphine is prepared as *morphine sulfate*, a water-soluble salt stabilized with sulfuric acid. The optimal dose for analgesia is between 5 mg and 15 mg, and 10 mg is the standard effective dose for most patients.

OPIATE RECEPTORS

> *It cannot be much wondered at, considering our Active principles are a Sal-Volatile-Oleosum and that Opium is such, and that we naturally carry an Opiate within us, that in some cases our ordinary Sal-Volatile-Oleosum . . . being by some accident exalted towards the Nature of Opium, may have the effect of an Opiate upon us.*
>
> Dr. John Jones,
> *The Mysteries of Opium Reveal'd*, 1700
> (as cited in Latimer & Goldberg, 1981, p. 53)

The discovery of natural receptors for morphine in the 1970s opened a field of research that has become one of the richest in pharmacology.

From 1955 to 1971, psychopharmacological research was following hot on the invention of chlorpromazine and its dramatic relief of the symptoms of schizophrenia. Experimentation focused on the role of monoamines (5-HT, DA, NE, E) in neural transmission and in schizophrenia. Then, in 1973, opiate receptors were discovered almost simultaneously by Eric Simon's laboratory at New York University and Solomon Snyder's lab at Johns Hopkins. The technique they used was to radioactively label morphine molecules, in the hope that, like monoamines, morphine would bind specifically with biological tissue; that is, it would have its own receptor, and the labeled substance would then make the binding sites detectable. The idea of receptors for neural transmission was not a new one, but the idea of specific receptors for morphine was. Candace

Pert at Johns Hopkins, working with this technique, was able to map the opiate pathways in the brain. She found that the highest concentration of receptors was in pathways for chronic pain and in the limbic system. These neural paths, had been thought to be dominated by monoamines, so the existence of the opiate receptors came as quite a surprise and added a new dimension to monoamine research. Pert also noted the existence of opiate receptors in other vertebrates, notably the hagfish, one of the oldest vertebrates known.

The hagfish certainly had no access to poppies and was not developing receptors in hopes that humans would come along and discover morphine. The implication was clear: there must be an undiscovered natural opiate that used the receptors and acted as the body's own painkiller. Because such a substance would be of immense pharmacological importance, the research race was on.

From the receptor characteristics, scientists could make some predictions about the properties and structure of the molecules that might use it. Hans Kosterlitz in Scotland and Lars Terenius in Sweden located a promising large molecule that seemed a likely candidate. Peptides then entered the picture. These are molecules made up of sequences of amino acids, like long sentences in which particular amino acids appear like recurring words. It was Hans Kosterlitz and John Hughes who isolated the first of these peptides, from an extract of pigs' brains. They were pentapeptides, sequences of five amino acids. Hughes and Kosterlitz named them enkephalins.

In fact, enkephalins had already been discovered in 1964 by Dr. Choh Hao Li of the University of California. Li found in the pituitary a large peptide, a 91-amino acid sequence, which he called *beta-lipotropin,* but it exhibited no pharmacological activity that was detectable by the testing techniques of that time. It seemed to be a mysterious "hormone without a function." However, peptides were known to have implications in behavior. In light of this, finding a role for Li's hormone was just a matter of time.

After Hughes' and Kosterlitz's discovery in Scotland, the Johns Hopkins team began mapping the binding of enkephalins in calves' brains on Pert's opiate receptor pathways. They found enkephalins to have a complex relationship to other transmitters. The strategic location of enkephalin opiate receptors on the monoamine pathways for chronic pain suggested that somehow enkephalins are involved in modulating the entire system.

Dr. Li put the remaining key pieces into place. When he heard of the enkephalins, he realized that they were familiar. They were embedded in his large beta-lipotropin molecule, and were part of its long amino acid sequence. Then came one of those unlikely leaps that appear in the history of so many scientific discoveries. Li had an Iraqi grad student who called attention to the fact that, as a rule, camels seemed especially hardened to pain; you can stick them with a knife, and they will not respond. The student subsequently sent Li 200 camel pituitaries on his next visit home. From them, Li extracted a new, somewhat smaller hormone: beta-endorphin. This was a very active analgesic, with a potency 100 times that of morphine and 40 times that of either of the two known enkephalins. It was also noted that in test rats it induced catatonia (Figure 22.1). The full significance of beta-endorphin began to become clear with the realization that within Li's original beta-lipotropin molecule, with its 91 amino acid sequence, there appears the shorter sequence of 30 amino acids that is beta-endorphin, and this in turn contains the 5-amino acid sequence that makes up met-enkephalin.

As they are now understood, the peptides--or neuropeptides, so-called because they act in the central nervous system--fall into three families, each descended from a precursor substance, which is itself the product of a gene. The first precursor, found mainly in the pituitary and hypothalamus, gives rise to beta-endorphin. The second, found throughout the central and peripheral nervous systems, is the chief (but not exclusive) source of the enkephalins. The third gives rise to a type of neuropeptide known as dynorphins.

Beta-endorphin has turned out to be a molecule of fundamental significance. It may be produced from ACTH, a pituitary hormone released during stress. And it can be reduced to alpha and gamma-endorphin, which have opposite effects: Alpha-endorphin produces a short-term analgesia and tranquilization like the enkephalins. On the other hand, gamma-endorphin, given to test animals, has caused violent behavior, irritability, and oversensitivity to pain. This suggests that betaendorphin might be used to dull or enhance the perception of pain. If so, it could be the central substance in the body's pain sensing system. Animals will self-inject it, which indicates that it has positive reinforcing effects.

FIGURE 22.1 Rats injected with beta-endorphin exhibit catatonia. They remain in stiff, unnatural postures such as those depicted here.

Neuropeptides are believed to produce the natural analgesia seen in many situations: the obliviousness of wartime victims to terrible injury; the imperviousness to pain evidenced in religious trance states, like those that make self-stabbing possible in some rituals; resistance to pain in natural childbirth; and analgesia in acupuncture and in placebo studies. Further support arises from the fact that the same antagonists that block morphine block these types of analgesia as well, presumably because they block the body's natural opiates.

Current research focuses on the molecular structures of natural and synthetic opiates, the variety of receptors they activate, and the natural opiates that use the receptors. By the late 1970s, researchers had concluded that there must be more than one type of opiate receptor. Evidence now supports the existence of three types, which have been named with the Greek letters mu (μ), kappa (κ), and delta (δ). Work is being done to discover whether specific kinds of receptors can be associated with specific effects; already there appear to be receptors dominant in analgesia, in dysphoria or psychotomimetic effects, and in the alteration of feeling and mood. Roughly, an assignment of effects can be made as follows (Jaffe & Martin, 1990, p. 488):

mu (μ)	supraspinal analgesia, respiratory depression, miosis (pupil constriction), reduced gastrointestinal movement, euphoria
kappa (κ)	spinal analgesia, less intense respiratory depression and miosis (pupil constriction), dysphoria,psychotomimetic effects
delta (δ)	analgesia and positive reinforcement shown in animal studies

A subtype called the sigma receptor has also been proposed. This receptor, however, does not bind with the opiate antagonist naloxone, one indication that it may not be a true opiate receptor. Sigma receptors are distributed widely in the central nervous system and at many sites in the periphery. Instead of being found on pre- or postsynaptic membranes like most transmitters, they are found on the membranes of the structures within cells (e.g., the nucleus and endoplasmic reticulum) (Garner et al., 1994). Selective sigma agonists induce psychosis-like behavior, and drugs like PCP have been associated with actions at these receptors. Chlorpromazine and haloperidol bind to these sites as well, which suggests that sigma receptor antagonism may be part of their antipsychotic action (Contreras et al., 1987).

The binding patterns and affinities of the various neuropeptides to the various receptors are complex and still under avid investigation, but one of the hopes of the future is to develop drugs that can target specific receptors and effects, drugs that can achieve analgesia without euphoria and dependence.

An interesting touch to this story is that, in 1986, the brain was found to have the ability to synthesize morphine itself (Donner et al., 1986), validating, after over 300 years, Dr. John Jones's hypothesis that "we carry an Opiate within us."

PHARMACOLOGICAL EFFECTS

Morphine is the prototype of the opiates. It is the chief active ingredient of opium and the predominant active metabolite of heroin. Accordingly, the opium eater or smoker, the morphinist, and the heroin shooter all are experiencing, for the most part, morphine effects.

The major effects of morphine occur in the central nervous system and the gastrointestinal tract. In the CNS, euphoria and analgesia are the most significant effects, and in the GI tract, constipation. In medicine and in abuse, the entire history of opiates can be written in terms of these three effects. Pharmacologically, euphoria and analgesia are closely linked, although there has been some success with synthetic opioids in separating them. Analgesic and constipatory actions are the main therapeutic actions and are discussed below under clinical applications.

The mechanism of opiate euphoria is not understood. This effect, however, is eloquently described by several authors who were addicts. Chief among these is Thomas De Quincey (*Confessions of an English Opium-Eater*), mentioned earlier, who took laudanum to varying degrees for over 50 years in the nineteenth century. Also prominent are Jean Cocteau, a French filmmaker and writer of the 1920s who smoked opium, and William S. Burroughs, a pre-Beat writer and American morphinist of the Anslinger Era in the forties.

Opium euphoria frequently manifests in conjunction with an intensification of the twilight states between waking and sleep, where dreams and visions of extraordinary complexity and detail are experienced with conscious lucidity. De Quincey describes an increase of "the creative state of the eye," a sympathy between the waking and dreaming states of the brain. On one hand, like normal dreams, the opium dreams fascinate the subject with their exoticism, like the Emerald City of Oz (with its fields of poppies) and Xanadu of Kubla Khan; on the other hand, their nightmarish phantasmagoria are enhanced, terrifying the dreamers with presences and falls into abysses, and oppressing them with threatening or melancholy images. After ten or twelve years of use, De Quincey described a frightening change in the character of his visions (brought on perhaps by personal circumstances), which became "accompanied by deep-seated anxiety and gloomy melancholy, such as are wholly incommunicable by words" (De Quincey, 1821/1981). During this period, De Quincey presented a classic example of a nineteenth century English opium dream:

Under the connecting feeling of tropical heat and vertical sun-lights, I brought together all creatures, birds, beasts, reptiles, all trees and plants, usages and appearances, that are found in all tropical regions, and assembled them together in China or Indostan. From kindred feelings, I soon brought Egypt and all her gods under the same law. I was stared at, hooted at, grinned at, chattered at, by monkeys, by paroquets, by cockatoos. I ran into pagodas: and was fixed, for centuries, at the summit, or in secret rooms; I was the idol; I was the priest; I was worshipped; I was sacrificed. I fled from the wrath of Brama through all the forests of Asia: Vishnu hated me: Seeva laid wait for me. I came suddenly upon Isis and Osiris: I had done a deed, they said, which the ibis and the crocodile trembled at. I was buried, for a thousand years, in stone coffins, with mummies and sphinxes, in narrow chambers at the heart of eternal pyramids. I was kissed, with cancerous kisses, by crocodiles; and laid, confounded with all unutterable slimy things, amongst reeds and Nilotic mud. (p. 109)

This dream is characteristic of opium dream literature in its intricacy, its colorful detail, its exotica and heavy atmosphere, its mythic motifs, and its movement between cosmic heights and abysses. However, the most-cited instance of opium dream literature—if not of drug literature as a whole—is "Kubla Khan" by Samuel Taylor Coleridge, a fragmentary poem inspired by an opium dream. In the imagery they experienced, both De Quincey and Coleridge (who were contemporaries) were undoubtedly influenced by their own imaginations as well as the predilections of intellectual society. As De Quincey wrote, "If a man 'whose talk is of oxen,' should become an opium eater, the probability is, that . . . he will dream about oxen" (p. 33). Or, to quote an old Talmudic saying, "We do not see things as they are. We see them as we are."

In Xanadu did Kubla Khan
A stately pleasure-dome decree:
Where Alph, the sacred river, ran
Through caverns measureless to man
Down to a sunless sea.
So twice five miles of fertile ground
With walls and towers were girdled round:
And here were gardens bright with sinuous rills,
Where blossomed many an incense-bearing tree
And here were forests ancient as the hills,
Enfolding sunny spots of greenery.
But oh! that deep romantic chasm which slanted
Down the green hill athwart a cedarn cover!
A savage place! As holy and enchanted
As e'er beneath a waning moon was haunted
By woman wailing for her demon-lover!
And from this chasm, with ceaseless turmoil seething,
As if this earth in fast thick pants were breathing,
A mighty fountain momently was forced,
Amid whose swift half-intermitted burst
Huge fragments vaulted like rebounding hail,
Or chaffy grain beneath the thresher's flail:
And 'mid these dancing rocks at once and ever
It flung up momently the sacred river.
Five miles meandering with a mazy motion
Through wood and dale the sacred river ran,
Then reached the caverns measureless to man,
And sank in tumult to a lifeless ocean:
And 'mid this tumult Kubla heard from far
Ancestral voices prophesying war!
The shadow of the dome of pleasure
Floated midway on the waves;
Where was heard the mingled measure
From the fountain and the caves.
It was a miracle of rare device,
A sunny pleasure-dome with caves of ice!
A damsel with a dulcimer
In a vision once I saw:
It was an Abyssinian maid,
And on her dulcimer she played,
Singing of Mount Abora.
Could I revive within me
Her symphony and song,
To such a deep delight 'twould win me,
That with music loud and long,

I would build that dome in air,
That sunny dome! those caves of ice!
And all who heard should see them there,
And all should cry, Beware! Beware!
His flashing eyes, his floating hair!
Weave a circle round him thrice,
And close your eyes with holy dread,
For he on honey-dew hath fed,
And drunk the milk of Paradise.

Kubla Khan
Samuel Taylor Coleridge

Many opium users report lying passively in a half-waking state, while lucid visions parade in front of them:

> *I lay down and closed my eyes. A series of pictures passed, like watching a movie. A huge, neon-lighted cocktail bar that got larger and larger . . . a waitress carrying a skull on a tray; stars in a clear sky. (Burroughs, 1953, p. 7)*

> *. . . at night, when I lay awake in bed, vast processions passed along in mournful pomp; friezes of never-ending stories, that to my feelings were as sad and solemn as if they were stories drawn from times before Oedipus or Priam . . . . (De Quincey, 1821/1981, p. 103)*

Changes of mood reported by opium users (e.g., the affective states associated with their opium visions) are mediated by actions in the limbic system. Likely, these are important in morphine's analgesic action of altering the emotional response to pain.

Another often-mentioned positive opium effect is a sense of expanded intellect. The literary users speak clearly of this as one of the incentives for taking the drug. De Quincey says, "[T]he opium eater feels that the diviner part of his nature is paramount; that is, the moral affections are in a state of cloudless serenity; and over all is the great light of the majestic intellect" (p. 75). Elsewhere, he claims that opium introduces the most exquisite "order, legislation, and harmony" among mental activities and "communicates serenity and equipoise to all the faculties" (pp. 7374). Other accounts agree. However, De Quincey also complained that opium hung a millstone on his ability to act on intellectual summons and hampered his ability to compose.

In the past, the opiates have been employed as calming and sleep-inducing drugs. Hence, their classification as narcotics. However, sleepiness and sedation are not their most characteristic effects. These effects are seen, but not always. In fact, the opiates are clinically valued more for their ability to dull pain without knocking patients out. If patients do sleep, they can be easily wakened.

With morphine, despite the fact that some sedation is expected, a paradoxical effect occurs in some species of animals (pigs, horses, cows, bears, sheep, tigers, goats, and lions) by which the animals show excitement and high fever (hyperthermia).

In its cardiovascular actions, morphine causes the vessels in the skin to dilate, making the user feel flushed and warm. This produced the sensation of "traveling prickly heat" reported by shooters in the nineteenth century when they released the tie-cord after an injection. But even at anesthetic dosages, the opiates effect no major heart changes, and so make good drugs for recovery from heart surgery. Recumbent patients show no major blood pressure or heart changes; however, because of dilated veins and arteries, blood pressure may drop when the patient rises (orthostatic hypotension), and more so in the presence of phenothiazines. For such reasons, people with low blood pressure should not take opiates.

People using morphine therapeutically claim that their extremities feel weighty and their bodies warm. Their faces or noses may itch and their mouths dry out. In pain-free users, nausea and vomiting are common, They experience dysphoria—anxiety, fear, mental clouding, an inability to concentrate—and they slow physically, becoming drowsy and apathetic. Their vision may blur. Such effects may be related to the setting in which the drug is used. However, most users feel euphoric, generally upon repeated exposure. This includes a sense of warmth and wellbeing, of serenity coupled with infinite energy and strength, or for some it may be of a different style: a pleasant, calm, half-sleep of inward gazing. There are people, too, who find the encounter with opiates an ordeal much to be avoided, and they fail to see the charms that addicts extol so highly.

CLINICAL APPLICATIONS

Although still called narcotics, opiates are rarely, if ever, prescribed to induce sleep. Barbiturates and the anxiolytic sleeping pills are better and safer. The opiates are chiefly painkillers: the only time they would be prescribed would be if pain were the cause of insomnia.

For analgesia, nothing has been found superior to this class of drugs. The attempts to synthesize more specific, effective nonaddicting agents, of comparable potency but without euphoria, have not succeeded greatly. And since the laboratory synthesis of morphine is difficult, it is still derived from poppies.

The painkilling action of morphine is complicated by the fact that the mechanisms of pain perception are elaborate and poorly understood. It is apparent that several CNS sites and different neurotransmitters are involved. Some of these sites include the spinal pathways that transmit sensory input upward to the brain, the periventricular area (the brain's "punishment" system), and the thalamus. Neuropeptides like the enkephalins and endorphins, and the various types of opiate receptors are involved in these systems, as well as at other sites, suggesting complex interactions. Furthermore, pain itself is not a simple entity, and different types may be handled by the systems in different ways.

One distinction useful in understanding the analgesic action of morphine is the difference between pain and suffering, with *pain* being the sensory input carried to the brain via the neural pathways, and *suffering* the patient's cognitive response to it. Suffering involves the patient's emotional reactions, expectations, and previous experience with pain. The hallmark of morphine analgesia is that patients know pain, but do not suffer from it. Morphine does alter the pathways that carry the sensory input, but it more strongly alters the patient's awareness of and emotional responses to the signal. In other words, users report feeling pain, but not the suffering and displeasure that are associated with it. Some patients may not even recognize a painful stimulus until it is pointed out. Then they perceive it, but their appreciation of its unpleasantness is curtailed.

Because it does not dim other subjective effects, morphine excels as a painkiller. Vision, hearing, and touch remain clear. At analgesic doses, patients remain awake and do not become sedated or silly, as with barbiturates, ether, or nitrous oxide, and severe respiratory depression does not occur.

Morphine works on most types of pain, but it serves better for the continuous dull kind rather than for the stabbing, intermittent kind. In the lab, it raises tolerance to pain, but you must grant the distinction between laboratory pain and real pain, especially in regard to a patient's expectations. Real pain may not be so controlled. Medically, morphine should be regarded only as a last resort for severe pain, because it is so addictive and because there are alternatives for moderate pain. A combination of codeine and aspirin can provide good relief, with fewer side effects. Only in ranges where the side effects become a problem should you switch to morphine.

Of course, morphine is good only for the symptomatic treatment of pain; it does not cure it at the source. Consequently, as an analgesic after operations, it has the fault of possibly masking pains that could indicate complications; in other cases, it may confuse the subject about the location of the pain or hide the progress of a disease. Pain, after all, is a message about the condition of tissues, a message that morphine shuts off.

Morphine is widely used for terminal illness. Not only does it give strong analgesia, but its euphoriant effects can help to ease a sufferer's days. Tolerance and physical dependence develop, but these are not an issue when life looks tenuous. Terminal patients on morphine are not legally considered addicts. Nevertheless, although dosages may be held the same possibly for weeks or months, sometimes tolerance can become a problem with massive use. Some physicians are of a mind that morphine should be given in maintenance doses before pain develops, rather than just alleviating the pain once it is present.

Generally, theories about the treatment of pain are changing. Previously, undertreatment of pain was the norm, but it is becoming more widely recognized that when narcotics are applied in the presence of pain, they produce only temporary physical dependence, and most patients can't wait to get off them. In some hospitals, acute pain services have opened, staffed by "pain specialists" equipped with new approaches in pain control. One of these is a computerized, patient-controlled pump, enabling sufferers to intravenously administer their own medication as desired. The pump is programmed to prevent administration patterns that would lead to an overdose. Epidural techniques use an implanted catheter to access areas of the spinal cord rich in opiate receptors. Through it, tiny doses of morphine can be placed just outside the spinal cord. Only very small amounts even reach the bloodstream this way, and a small dose can last a day. Furthermore, previously unattainable amounts of analgesia can be reached.

Because of their peripheral effects on the gastrointestinal tract, the opiates have had a primary use for the relief of diarrhea and dysentery. Although they increase some sorts of intestinal contractions, they can help to treat diarrhea by blocking peristalsis, the movement of food through the bowel, and by inhibiting the entry of digestive juices to the intestines. Paregoric is a traditional medicine containing opium tincture mixed with benzoic acid, camphor, and anise oil, and is still available. The recipe survives only as a social convention; there are no therapeutic reasons for this combination.

In cases of opiate dependency and extended use, these gastrointestinal actions lead to a rather unpleasant side effect. With peristalsis inhibited as well as the digestive juices, the dry, slow-moving fecal matter undergoes even more drying as water is absorbed, which causes it to harden, slowing the movement further. As if that were not enough, morphine has been observed to tighten the anal muscle, and its subjective effects may distract the user from internal signals to defecate. All of these factors together cause a colossal case of constipation, which, because of slow tolerance, is a constant problem for long-term users. Even on this delicate subject, the writers are not silent. Coleridge wrote,

> *The dull quasi-finger on the Liver, the endless Flatulence, the frightful constipation when the dead Filthe impales the lower Gut—to weep & sweat & moan & scream for the parturience of an excrement. . . O this is hard, hard, hard! (as cited in Latimer & Goldberg, 1981, p. 79)*

The opiates have also been used effectively for cough suppression, because they suppress the "cough center" in the brain stem. The opiate derivative, codeine is particularly effective, and superior to morphine for this action. The full mechanism of coughing is not clear. There seem to be sites in the CNS, as in the cough reflex center of the medulla, where part of codeine's action takes place. In the periphery, there may be special stretch receptors in the bronchial muscles, and there may be other sites as well. The dosages of codeine required to suppress coughing are lower than those for analgesia, and dependence is therefore not a problem. However, newer nonopiate agents, like dextromethorphan (Delsym), a cough suppressant with fewer side effects, have been developed. Like pain, coughing is a practical, sometimes necessary, mechanism and should not be casually eliminated unless it is clearly a problem--for example, if it leads to insomnia.

SIDE EFFECTS

Constipation, just discussed, is the main peripheral side effect of morphine. The central nervous system side effects include respiratory depression, nausea, a slight drop in body temperature, imbalances in the hypothalamus, and low hormone output from the pituitary. The release of histamines may cause itching. Subjective side effects include dysphoria, dizziness, and mental clouding.

The most significant side effect of morphine, a CNS effect, is respiratory depression. This comes partly from morphine's direct action on respiratory centers in the medulla and pons, where high concentrations of opiate receptors can be found. Slowed breathing can be discerned even with small dosages, and changes and irregularities may persist for 4 or 5 hours. At larger doses, breathing becomes slow and shallow. In morphine or heroin overdoses, respiratory depression is the effect that kills in morphine or heroin overdoses. Morphine also enhances the danger by deadening the ability of brain stem receptors to respond to increasing amounts of CO_2 in the blood, which is the body's cue to breathe faster and take in more oxygen.

Given in pregnancy, morphine can prolong labor, overdrug the mother, and cause respiratory depression in newborns. The latter effect may be present at low dosages, since an infant's blood-brain barrier is undeveloped.

Nausea and vomiting are well-observed side effects of opiates. Nausea results from direct stimulation of the chemoreceptor trigger zone in the medulla. Vomiting is the result of the direct induction of contractions in the upper gastrointestinal tract. Mostly, these effects are seen with first use of opiates, and there is much variability among individuals. Some people vomit every time from the drug, some never at all. Bed ridden patients seem to have much less difficulty, leading to the supposition that the vestibular mechanism that mediates movement and balance may be involved. Some abusers claim that vomiting seems of no consequence on morphine, because the euphoriant effects are so powerful. That would explain why many street users persist through initial unpleasantness. On the other hand, there are those who experience vomiting as a salient effect and never try opiates again.

Changes in body temperature regulation are another characteristic side effect of the opiates. Cocteau alludes to them as follows:

> *Opium is a season. The smoker no longer suffers the changes in the weather. . . . He suffers only from the changes in drugs, doses and hours, in everything in fact which influences the barometers of opium. (1929/1958, p. 74)*
>
> *Opium has its colds, shivers and fevers which do not coincide with cold and heat. (1929/1958, p. 74)*

These passages register the fact that opiates reset the body's thermostat in the hypothalamus. After one therapeutic dose of morphine, body temperature drops to a slightly lower level, and the thermostat maintains it at the new setting, as it would normal body temperature. Chronic high doses, on the other hand, raise body temperature.

Opiates depress pituitary functions, which can result in changes like decreased blood levels of testosterone, leading to a decreased sex drive. Tolerance can show for this effect, however. Cocteau reports that opium smoking does not cause impotence, but it removes all sexual obsessions and replaces them with "others which are somewhat lofty, very strange and unknown to a sexually normal organism" (p. 75). He calls opium "the negative of passion" (p. 72).

Several side effects are important in determining clinical dosages. Tolerance and physical dependence can follow from repeated daily administration. For fear of dependence, it is good to avoid euphoria, although some practitioners hold that euphoria is a valuable therapeutic aid in combating the depression brought on by incurable illness. When dependence does occur, the suppression of withdrawal symptoms becomes a consideration. Furthermore, long-term use can bring on a syndrome resembling acute morphine poisoning, involving sedation, chronic constipation, decreased respiration, and pinpoint pupils.

This last action, constriction of the pupils, is a conspicuous side effect of morphine in overdose. It is an autonomic effect originating from a brain action of unknown origin. No tolerance shows.

In cases of overdose, the subject usually arrives in the emergency room asleep, stuporous, or in a deep coma. The key diagnostic signs are the coma, the pinpoint pupils, and the respiratory rate, which may be as low as 2 to 4 breaths a minute. The skin is cold and clammy from low body temperatures, the skeletal muscles are flaccid, the jaw relaxed, and the tongue may block breathing. Falling blood pressure may lead to capillary damage and shock, and the skin may turn blue from lack of oxygen. Needle marks (*tracks*) on the arms are another sign the physician may check for. Overdosing may sometimes be the result of injecting opiates into chilled skin areas. Lack of circulation in cold tissue may prompt a second dose, but if the skin warms up, both doses go into play. People in shock or with low blood pressure may also overdose the same way, if circulation resumes.

Opiate overdoses are handled by administering antagonists to reverse respiratory depression. However, some compounds are not complete antagonists, but possess some capacity to stimulate the opiate receptors themselves, so they may further threaten respiration. Moreover, the antagonist may wear off before the opiate does, so patients should be monitored.

All of the opiates show cross-tolerance. None shows with sedative-hypnotics, however, so that in combination, accidental death can result. Opiates and alcohol can cause an additive depression of respiration. Moreover, mixtures of opiates with depressants like alcohol and barbiturates can make overdose treatment chancy.

HEROIN

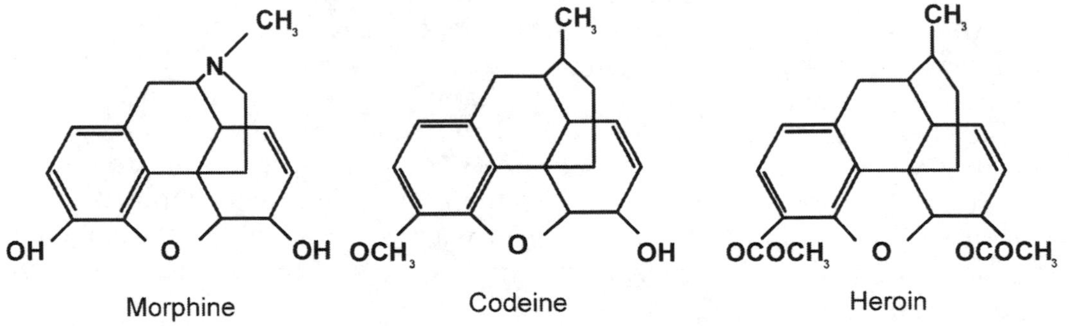

FIGURE 22.2 Molecules of morphine, heroin, and codeine.

Heroin (diacetylmorphine) is active through its biotransformation into morphine (see Figure 22.2). Logically, then, given in equipotent doses, both agents have the same effects. However, injected IM or IV, heroin is about three times as potent. This may be because its lipid solubility is higher than morphine's, allowing it to penetrate the blood-brain barrier faster. In the brain, each heroin molecule is then hydrolyzed into a morphine molecule.

CODEINE

Codeine, one of the natural alkaloids derived from opium, has a low affinity for opiate receptors. Its analgesia (120 mg equal to 10 mg of morphine) may come from its partial biotransformation—about 10 percent—into morphine. This biotransformation seems to be the reason that its oral efficacy is relatively high compared to its IV efficacy—about two-thirds—probably due to morphine production in the first pass metabolism in the liver. Abuse liability is low, although some adolescents have been known to try cough medicines for a thrill, and desperate abusers may resort to them to fend off withdrawal.

Codeine is primarily a cough suppressant (antitussive agent) because of its particular affinity for the opiate receptors that mediate coughing. The mechanism is still not clear.

Dextromethorphan (Delsym) is a synthetic relative of codeine with no analgesic or addictive properties, which is capable of elevating the cough threshold. Equal in potency to codeine, it has effects that persist for 5 to 6 hours, with fewer subjective and gastrointestinal side effects and very low toxicity. High doses may produce some CNS depression. It is found in many cough medications and in over-the-counter syrups and lozenges.

Chapter 23

Opiate Agonists and Antagonists

A variety of synthetic agents that show a full spectrum of interactions with opiate receptors was first developed during the 1930s and 1940s. These agents are called opioids. They include as subcategories morphinelike agonists, which stimulate specific opiate receptors, and antagonists (e.g., naloxone), which block specific receptors. More complex in their actions are a group of mixed action opioids, including partial agonists (buprenorphine, propiram) and agonist-antagonists (nalorphine, pentazocine). Overall, these substances show a set of complex interactions with the various opiate receptors. Some important distinctions to keep in mind are that these agents may:

1. Stimulate certain opiate receptors and not affect others (morphinelike agonists).
2. Inhibit certain opiate receptors and not affect others (antagonists).
3. Only partially stimulate certain receptors, producing effects similar to, but much weaker than, the opiates (mixed action opioids: partial agonists).
4. Stimulate or partially stimulate some receptors and antagonize others (mixed action opioids: agonist-antagonists).

The last category, the mixed action opioids, may also induce partial stimulations that amount to blocking or antagonistic effects. For instance, pentazocine is not as powerful a euphoriant as morphine, but it stimulates the appropriate receptors enough to qualify it as a drug of abuse, and its use can cause withdrawal. On the other hand, if it is given to a morphine abuser who is detoxifying, it cannot produce enough stimulation to stop morphine withdrawal. The partial stimulation is experienced then as a lack of stimulation, or antagonism.

In general, action at the mu receptor produces euphoria and some types of analgesia. Consequently, it is the strength of an opioid's mu receptor action that determines how well it will serve as a satisfactory substitute for heroin in the treatment of narcotics dependence.

MEPERIDINE

Meperidine (Demerol, Pethadol), the first analgesic to be synthesized, was produced by Eisleb and Schaumann in 1939 (Table 23.1 and Figure 23.1). Chemically unlike morphine, it is well absorbed orally, but about 50 percent of the dose is lost in first-pass metabolism. Injected, it shows onset of action in 10 minutes, with a 2 to 4-hour duration of effect. Therefore, it must be administered more often than morphine's 4hour intervals. Because IV administration can induce an alarming increase in heart rate, meperedine is usually given IM, although there may be erratic absorption and some tissue irritation. Upright patients may experience a fall in blood pressure, which passes if they lie down. An injection of 75 to100 mg is equivalent to 10 mg of morphine.

Meperidine produces a profile of effects somewhat like those of morphine, including analgesia, sedation and, in some patients, euphoria and nausea. Clinically, meperidine is used as an analgesic and is most widely prescribed for hospital patients. It is preferred to morphine during labor because it can cross the placental barrier in two minutes and has milder side effects—particularly less respiratory depression in the infant.

Other side effects, like constipation, biliary spasm, and urinary retention occur, but again to a lesser degree than with morphine. One visible difference is that meperidine dilates rather than constricts the pupils.

At first, meperidine (like many opiates) was mistakenly thought to be nonaddictive. Tolerance develops slowly, probably due to its short duration of action, which makes continuous depression of the nervous system harder to sustain. As tolerance to respiratory depression progresses and doses increase, excitation, hallucinations, and seizures may appear, probably due to an accumulation of the metabolite normeperidine. Withdrawal shows fewer autonomic effects than morphine, and starts and ends sooner. The most frequent abuse is by hospital staff, since the hospital is the setting where it is mostly used.

FENTANYL

Fentanyl (Sublimaze) is an analogue of meperidine, a synthetic analgesic with 80 times the potency of morphine. This does not mean it alleviates greater pain, but that it produces the same effect in lower doses. It is used regularly as an anesthetic in major surgery, often co-administered IV with droperidol. Given its potency, only infinitesimal doses (20 to 80 micrograms) are needed to induce euphoria. At surgical doses, fentanyl is safe, but higher doses suppress respiration and can be lethal. Some users, however, seem to be able to sustain massive doses, for reasons that are not understood.

DESIGNER DRUGS AND CHINA WHITE

In 1975, drug designers on the West Coast produced and marketed on the street a drug they were calling *China White*. (This was actually the street name for the finest Southeast Asian heroin.) The new drug caught the attention of the authorities when several deaths were attributed to it. In fact, the drug turned out to be a street version of fentanyl—

alpha-methyl-fentanyl—which the makers were trying to peddle as real China White. Fentanyl and its analogues are prime designer drugs: they are of high potency, manageable and cheap to make, and can be sold as heroin at a premium rate. However, it is easy to kill yourself with fentanyl, which is apparently what happened in this case.

Several years later, the so-called China White struck again. In December of 1979, the staff at several California drug clinics were mystified by the appearance of a number of fairly young admissions affected by severe, advanced, and irreversible cases of parkinsonism. Advanced Parkinson's disease is almost always associated with the aging process, as the passage of time gradually leads to the loss of over three-quarters of the dopaminergic cells of the substantia nigra. These cases, however, were found to be casualties of a street drug that users were again calling China White. This latest version was clearly something that no one had seen before.

As it was subsequently discovered, the makers of this designer drug had been trying to craft an analogue of meperidine called MPPP, which they were pushing under the name of *new heroin,* but which street users identified with China White. However, the makers overcooked the ingredients in the MPPP recipe, producing a high percentage of a side product called MPTP. Investigators found that MPTP, nontoxic in itself, is converted by MAO in the brain to MPP+, a substance that selectively destroys dopaminergic cells in the substantia nigra and causes parkinsonism severe enough to incapacitate and immobilize those affected. In effect, when the bad batches of new heroin reached the brain, they aged the substantia nigras of the users by 80 to 100 years, freezing their bodies as stiff as statues.

Ironically, the discovery of MPTP and MPP+ provided researchers with a laboratory model for Parkinson's disease, making advancements possible in a research area that had been at a virtual standstill. It also sparked investigations into environmental exposure to MPTP, which is found in some herbicides; early exposure to MPTP and partial damage to dopaminergic functioning might hasten the appearance of Parkinson's disease by augmenting the normal course of DA cell loss over time. To put it simply, there is some evidence to support the idea that, if you live in a rural area where crops are sprayed with herbicides containing MPTP, you may exhibit signs of Parkinson's disease earlier in your aging process.

By 1984, at least five other fentanyl analogues were circulating (as many as 200 have been made). One of them, para-fluoro fentanyl, had never been written up in the pharmacological literature, which has led to the supposition that the illicit labs are in expert hands. One such lab, it is said, could produce the equivalent of the world's heroin supply without getting within sniffing distance of a single poppy.

MIXED ACTION OPIOIDS

Although the mixed action opioids are narcotics, they may be thought of as weaker, in some respects, than morphine and heroin. Taken by normal people, they are hard drugs that can activate opiate receptors and produce dependence. But taken by recovering abusers, they are about as well-received as carob by chocolate lovers. Opiate receptors may receive weaker stimulations, and the drug may bind to the various types of opiate receptors in patterns different from those the abuser is used to. The result is that the same spectrum of effects (analgesia, euphoria, constipation, etc.) appears with individual elements expressed to different degrees, greater or lesser than with morphine.

Some drugs included in this class are nalorphine, pentazocine, nalbuphine, buprenorphine, and cyclazocine. Generally, these drugs have enough of an analgesic action to make them viable substitutes for morphine, and a low enough abuse potential to make them medically acceptable, although they are known to be abused at times. In other effects, however, they differ.

Used as a detoxification agent, nalorphine (Nalline) produces a morphinelike withdrawal, only milder and with no craving. However, it was removed from the market for producing side effects of anxiety and hallucinations.

Pentazocine (Talwin) produces analgesia by a different mechanism from morphine and is only one-fourth as potent. It can stimulate receptors enough to qualify for abuse (Schedule IV), but not enough to stop morphine withdrawal in progress. Also, it causes respiratory depression.

Nalbuphine (Nubain) produces analgesia by stimulating kappa receptors, but can precipitate withdrawal symptoms by strongly blocking mu receptors. It produces respiratory depression with a ceiling at 30 mg and has low abuse potential.

Buprenorphine (Buprenex), is 25 to 30 times as potent as morphine for analgesia. As a partial mu agonist, it shows promise as a drug to be used in the treatment of opiate dependence, to suppress withdrawal symptoms and to help prevent relapse.

METHADONE

Methadone, a petroleum-based synthetic analgesic and morphinelike agonist (see Figure 23.1), was developed in Germany near the end of World War II as a substitute for diminishing supplies of morphine. It was named Dolophine, some think, after Adolf Hitler. Following the surrender of Germany in 1945, a U.S. Department of Commerce intelligence team was rooting through the records of I.G. Farbenindustrie in search of Nuremberg indictment material, when it discovered the documentation for methadone and appropriated it as spoils of war. Methadone does not chemically resemble morphine, but it bears certain molecular configurations that allow it to bind to opiate receptors. It is a good analgesic. Because it mimics the actions of morphine in many respects, but is a much weaker euphoriant, it has become the drug of choice for the treatment of morphine withdrawal and a saving grace for the narcotics police.

Methadone is absorbed well orally. About 90 percent binds in the blood tissues, and some binds in the brain. The half-life is long—a day to a day and a half. With repeated administration, therefore, it may gradually accumulate in tissues. Methadone is equal in potency to morphine as an analgesic (5 mg to 15 mg), although heroin abusers have reported the reappearance of pains when they were put on methadone maintenance. This is not so much a disadvantage, since for many users it means a return to a more normal perception of pain. Doses of 60 to 100 mg are more effective than 20 to 40 mg, which is of note because some physicians have moral qualms about prescribing too high a dose of narcotics to patients (Jaffe, 1995).

Methadone mimics morphine enough to qualify itself as a drug of abuse; this is one indication why abusers consider it a tolerable, if disappointing, substitute for their street habits. For those unexposed to morphine or heroin, it is an addicting narcotic, something authorities did well to remind themselves of shortly after its introduction. It is nonaddicting for heroin or morphine abusers, however, in the sense that, if dosages decrease, abusers feel a desire to return to heroin, not to higher doses of methadone.

Because of its binding properties, its active metabolites, its accumulation in tissues, and its gradual release upon discontinuance, methadone produces a withdrawal mild enough to sometimes go unnoticed. As a result, recovering abusers can be switched from opiates to methadone without a crushing sense of loss, anxiety, or depression, and in some cases can be weaned comfortably from methadone without severe withdrawal. Unfortunately, when methadone doses are reduced to a 20 to 40 mg range, frequently the craving for heroin returns, like a permanent reminder left in the nervous system that methadone is only able to mask. So for some, methadone maintenance is indefinite.

The advantages of methadone for the treatment of opiate dependence can be summed up as follows:

1. It's oral and easy to administer.
2. It has a long action, with effects that persist through repeated use.
3. The effective dosages remain stable.
4. It costs relatively little.
5. It blocks opiate euphoria, so addicts can't return to heroin easily.
6. It prevents opiate withdrawal and has a milder withdrawal of its own.

In light of these properties, methadone's two clinical uses have become to alleviate opiate withdrawal and to maintain recovering abusers in a heroin-free condition.

Although methadone is addicting on its own behalf, many who use it orally show no behavioral effects. Some of its effects, like sedation, respiratory depression, and constriction of the pupils, fade due to tolerance. It does moderately depress male sexual functioning.

Propoxyphene (Darvon, Dolene), one of the four stereoisomers of methadone, has analgesic actions and other CNS effects comparable to those of codeine. About half to two-thirds the potency of oral codeine, propoxyphene is used therapeutically for analgesia when aspirin does not suffice, or it may be combined with aspirin as codeine is. As a Schedule IV drug, and less desirable for recreation than codeine, propoxyphene has nonetheless suffered about the same amount of abuse (Jaffe & Martin, 1990, p. 510).

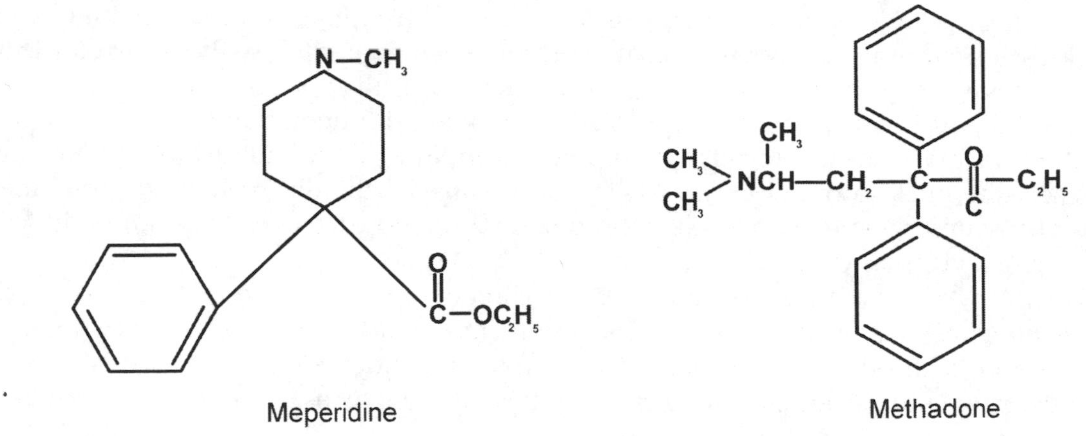

FIGURE 23.1 Synthetic opioids.

LAAM

LAAM stands for L-alpha-acetylmethadol (trade name: Orlaam). This is a synthetic opiate similar to methadone, and was approved by the FDA in 1993 as a treatment for opiate dependence. LAAM is not a potent mu agonist like methadone, but works through two active metabolites that have mu agonist actions. Consequently, the onset of action is slower than with methadone, but the active metabolites have a half-life of 2 to 6 days. This means that LAAM can be given orally to patients only three times a week, which is much more convenient than the daily regimen of methadone, especially in many programs where the drugs can be taken only at the clinic. LAAM has been shown to be as effective as methadone in reducing heroin use, although some patients request methadone instead. The treatment dropout rate is also slightly higher (Jaffe, 1995). The side effects of LAAM are similar to those of methadone, although methadone is advisable over LAAM for females pregnant or of child bearing age.

NALOXONE

Naloxone (Narcan), a pure antagonist that completely blocks receptors, is the prototype of the opiate antagonists and one of the most important synthetic opiates. It has a higher affinity for the receptors than morphine, which means that it is a competitive antagonist. It binds strongly to all sites, but ten times more to the mu (μ) receptors (for euphoria and analgesia). If a person dependent on morphine is injected with naloxone, the naloxone immediately usurps morphine activity at the receptors. Any analgesia, euphoria, or respiratory depression vanishes, and the person suffers prompt withdrawal. It is interesting, however, that when naloxone and a similar agent, cyclazocine, were tested on heroin-dependent subjects, it was found that anxiety, depression, and craving for heroin did not diminish with the other effects. With such a profile, naloxone is not very useful for detoxification, since it exacerbates withdrawal and seems not to alleviate the depression or craving from loss of the drug. Furthermore, although it blocks morphine's action, it does so for only a few hours, at which point users can easily return to their habits. Needless to say, they dislike naloxone, which in itself is nonaddicting.

Small SC doses (0.5 mg) of naloxone given to abusers immediately cause a moderate to severe withdrawal similar to abrupt stoppage of opiates. One milligram given IV can block the effects of 25 mg of heroin. An important use of this is for testing individuals who report to clinics for therapy, to see how badly hooked they are. This can be judged from the severity of withdrawal symptoms.

In normal people, with doses up to 12 mg, naloxone has no effects at all. Slight drowsiness occurs at 24 mg. Generally, its actions are noticeable under only two conditions: if morphine has been previously taken, or if the body's natural opiates (endorphins) have been mobilized to kill pain. In both of these cases, naloxone dramatically reverses analgesia.

The opiate antagonists are of importance for several reasons. First, they are a lifesaving remedy for opiate poisoning, since they immediately reverse respiratory depression and the threat of asphyxiation. This obtains not only for overdosed users, but also for newborn babies, when opiates have been given to the mother during labor. Furthermore, they are capable of restoring blood pressure to normal and reversing gastrointestinal effects and sedation. Second, as we saw above, the synthetic opiate antagonists play a role in the diagnosis of opiate addiction. And third, they are a crucial tool in research, helping to define the relationships of the various opiates and endorphins with the known types of receptors. In this connection, opiate antagonists currently play a role in the investigation of how natural opiates like endorphins work in connection with eating behavior and obesity and with the "high" that runners experience during training.

Another research application is that naloxone can be used to elucidate the role of the body's own opiates. As well as antagonizing morphine, naloxone curtails the natural analgesic systems by keeping endorphins off the opiate receptors, leaving an organism totally unbuffered to pain. Endorphins are believed to be released under certain conditions and procedures, like stress, acupuncture, and electrical stimulation. Naloxone reverses the analgesia under all of these circumstances. It even blocks analgesia that can be produced psychosomatically through the use of a placebo. And people with strong natural resistance, who can normally tolerate a great deal of pain, are sensitized by naloxone.

Because it does not stimulate the opiate receptors to which it binds, naloxone itself produces no withdrawal syndrome. Nevertheless, by unmasking the body's compensation to morphine, it can lead to rebound effects. For instance, the body pushes respiration to compensate for chronic morphine depression. When naloxone displaces the morphine, respiration goes into overdrive.

NALTREXONE

opiate antagonist

Naltrexone (ReVia) is a pure competitive opiate antagonist, similar to naloxone, which acts at mu receptors. Like naloxone, naltrexone will precipitate withdrawal in opiate-dependent patients. Fifty milligrams is capable of blocking the subjective effects of 25 mg of IV heroin for as long as 24 hours. Tripling the dosage can achieve this for a period as long as three days, but at high doses naltrexone poses a risk of injury to enzyme functions in the liver. Once back on the street, users may attempt to override the competitive blockade of receptors with high doses of narcotics, which can be done. Needless to say, this could have serious consequences.

In 1995, the FDA approved naltrexone as a medication for alcohol dependence, to be used as an aid in a clinical setting. Such use is based on findings that naltrexone can reduce alcohol intake and relapse rates in the alcohol-dependent. This is likely due to the involvement of opiate receptors in intoxication or other positive-reinforcing effects of alcohol. It is not clear, however, exactly how naltrexone intervenes: it may augment intoxication or lessen the rewards of drinking (Franklin, 1995).

OPIATE ABUSE

> *He asked the question they all ask. "Why do you feel that you need narcotics, Mr. Lee?"*
>
> *When you hear this question you can be sure that the man who asks it knows nothing about junk. (Burroughs, 1953, p. 98)*

Unmedicated withdrawal (going *cold turkey*) from a large narcotics habit is an ordeal. The symptoms, abusers say, are not unlike an atrocious case of the flu, protracted over four to seven days. They include gooseflesh (hence the term *cold turkey*), hot and cold flashes, and a running of body fluids—profuse runny nose, sniffles, teary eyes, and sweating:

> *The last of the codeine was running out. My nose and eyes began to run, sweat soaked through my clothes. Hot and cold flashes hit me as though a furnace door was swinging open and shut. . . . My legs ached and twitched so that any position was intolerable, and I moved from one side to the other, sloshing about in my sweaty clothes. (Burroughs, 1953, p. 27)*

Mighty bouts of yawning and violent fits of sneezing are common too. De Quincey (1821/1981, p. 123) describes sneezing fits of 2 hours duration occurring two or three times a day. Twitching in the limbs, particularly the legs and feet, is believed to have given rise to the expression *kicking the habit*. Muscle tremors may appear, and joints and muscles may ache, making movement uncomfortable. On the other hand, restlessness, insomnia, tension, and anxiety keep the sufferer from remaining relaxed and still. Nightmares may accompany sleep. Stomach cramps, strong vomiting, and explosive diarrhea appear as rebound effects from the relaxation of muscles in the GI tract due to a high-dose habit. One observer reports the unsettling effect of seeing a patient's abdomen move from intestinal contractions, as though it were filled with writhing snakes. Writes Burroughs, "The addict is aware of his visceral processes to an uncomfortable degree" (1953, p. 127). Increased respiration manifests as panting. The abuser may feel ravaged by weakness, or irritable and hypersensitive to stimuli. In males, sexual functions return with spontaneous orgasm and ejaculations.

One important symptom that seems to come from a distinct pharmacological action on certain receptors is that described as *the craving*. It has been mentioned that, when prolonged treatment with methadone is dropped below a certain dosage (20 mg to 40 mg), the craving for heroin returns. A few lucky recovering abusers manage to escape the craving, but many do not, and these have to remain on methadone indefinitely, or they will feel the physiological compulsion to return to their habit. Compounding this craving are a sense of cognitive grief and mourning for the loss of the state of euphoria.

The degree and character of withdrawal depend on the habit: namely, on the dosage and frequency of use, the type of drug, and the duration of the dependence. Seldom is narcotics withdrawal fatal; in this respect, alcohol withdrawal is much more dangerous. The worse the habit, the sooner the signs appear. Small-scale users (60 mg a day) suffer a mild withdrawal, which can nevertheless be uncomfortable, involving dysphoria, insomnia, tension, a craving for heroin, and cognitive deficits.

Secondary conditioning, which also operates in the case of alcohol and stimulants, is another factor working against the alcohol-dependent. Not only are they conditioned to the effects of the drug, but also to the apparati and environment of use. The classic case is that of the "needle freak," who may be reinforced by injecting and only acting out the life of an abuser. Needle freaks may report to a clinic convinced they are dependent, but when given naloxone, they react mildly or not at all, which shows that they are not, in fact, dependent on opiates. In the absence of heroin, abusers may sometimes resort to shooting water (or worse), to assuage these secondary needs, like a smoker who will settle for herbal cigarettes just to keep smoking, even though nicotine cannot be had from them.

To demonstrate these effects, researchers have conditioned withdrawal in rats. In this procedure, a stimulus is presented to animals suffering from withdrawal. Later, after recovery, when they are presented with the stimulus, the animals will manifest withdrawal symptoms and feel driven to self-administer opiates. In addiction treatments with humans, therefore, it is a good idea that abusers not return to the old scenes of the addiction, where euphoria and withdrawal have become associated with smells, sights, and sounds in the environment. Furthermore, experiments with lobotomized dogs (Latimer & Goldberg, 1981, p. 282) have shown that other sites in the body—the spine, stomach, pancreas—are capable of "learning" and responding to an injection schedule, a fact that raised early theories that tolerance and conditioning could occur on the cellular level.

Heroin is currently the most abused opiate. Although it has been said with good cause that it is the most addictive of all illicit drugs, this does not mean that most of those who try it get hooked; it refers more to the difficulty of abusers getting off once they are on it. Getting hooked is a highly individual matter, depending on social factors as well as on an individual's psychology and physiology. And, of course, there is no reliable way to project how many people try heroin compared to how many become dependent. Informal evidence indicates that many more people try or chip heroin (use it occasionally) than eventually become dependent. For example, 98 percent or more of the Vietnam vets left their habits in Southeast Asia. Some people try heroin a few times and are repelled by the nausea or vomiting that is characteristic of early use, while others apparently get enough euphoria to carry them through to tolerance of brainstem effects. Some people, the writer Sir Walter Scott among them, have found the entire experience unpleasant; to them, opiates are just another medicine to be endured.

Other users, however, are not so fortunate. De Quincey describes how, at his very first use of opium for rheumatic pains, after an initial revulsion, an "abyss of divine enjoyment" was suddenly revealed. On the average, it is recognized that dependence takes some time: regular daily use over a period of weeks. The problem is that it is easy to begin as an occasional user—a *chipper*—who might only sniff or shoot up on weekends (De Quincey had an early phase of use once every three weeks for the opera). Usually the chipper feels in control, while the habit slowly creeps up, sometimes over the course of many years.

Four factors can be identified that lead to dependence. The first is medical use that leads to a habit, which is largely unnecessary these days due to synthetic analgesics but is still known in cases of terminal illness.

The second factor concerns patterns of social circumstances. The users might be part of a social substratum and embrace heroin along with a constellation of other illegal or antisocial behaviors (e.g., unregistered firearms). They may move to heroin on a continuum of other drug use, or they may feel compelled to use it to relieve psychological stress and pain and, like the Vietnam vets, escape an ugly reality.

A third factor that hooks users is the instant, intense euphoria that some feel in early use and try to court without addiction. In IV use of morphine or heroin (mainlining), the euphoria is intensified to a *rush*. Abusers have described this concentrated blast of pleasure in sexual, ecstatic terms as a whole body orgasm that may persist for five minutes or more, followed by a spell of tranquility. The rush seems to be related to the speed with which the drug enters the brain, which would explain the preeminence of heroin for abuse, it being more lipid-soluble than morphine.

The fourth hook is that, once withdrawal symptoms manifest, they are unpleasant enough (in conjunction with the loss of euphoria) to warrant staying on the drug. Unlike all of the historical suspicions, the purity of the preparation and the means of administration have no bearing on the addictiveness of a narcotic. And no one can predict who the abusers are going to be. (You takes your dose and you takes your chance.)

The preferred method among abusers is to mainline morphine or heroin. The shooter buys the powdered morphine or heroin crystals in a *bag*, a packet containing one or two doses (*hits*). These are dissolved in water by heating in a spoon or a bottle cap (*cooking up*), then drawn through a cotton swab with an eyedropper to filter out impurities. The user then ties off the arm below the shoulder with a cord, piece of rubber tubing, or whatever is at hand, like a necktie or scarf. This causes the veins of the arm to expand for easier shooting. Usually care is taken to disguise or hide this telltale paraphernalia (*works*), in the event of a narcotics search.

Death from opiate abuse occurs most frequently from overdoses leading to respiratory depression and consequent suffocation. Overdosing is a constant concern for abusers, since they are never quite sure what they have in a new batch of street drug. Sometimes a recovering addict who has been through detox or who has been separated from the drug, and whose tolerance has been lowered, will return to a reunion shot at the old pre-detox dosage and will overdose. Another type of overdose might occur from conditioned tolerance. In this case, part of the tolerance that leads to the need for higher dosing is believed to be connected to environmental cues--namely, the atmosphere of familiar surroundings. Strange as it may seem, simply by injecting in a new and unfamiliar place, the user may lower the dosage needed to get high, or to produce respiratory depression. If the usual dose is taken, then, an overdose might result. This hypothesis has been advanced to explain some otherwise mysterious deaths by overdose (Siegel et al., 1982).

In addition to overdosing, the abuser's lifestyle can result indirectly in death through association with the underworld, neglect of proper nutrition, the inability to sense the painful warning signs of some diseases because of constant analgesia, or an increased susceptibility to disease.

Because of the use of unsterilized water, the failure to clean the skin, and repeated or shared use of needles, it is not uncommon for abusers to be afflicted with hepatitis, tetanus, abscesses, or AIDS. Many deaths follow from hepatitis as a result of septic injections, and abusers are often recognized by the *tracks* (needle scars) on their arms, due to unclean punctures. Too many injections can lead to the collapse of veins. Furthermore, needle sharing among abusers is a significant factor in the spread of AIDS. And heroin abusers frequently show a disregard for hygiene, nutrition, and other aspects of personal care.

Despite all of this, there are no necessarily bad medical effects attached to the actual opiate dependence itself, and it is a myth that simply using the drug over a long period of time will lead to a serious deterioration of health. This impression stretches back to De Quincey, who structured his *Confessions* to progress from the pleasure to the pains of opium, while at the same time he discusses a deterioration of health, most likely from other causes, which darkened his opium experiences and his mood in general (Ward, 1966). In fact, pure heroin, clean use, and judicious dosing do not cause problems. The dangers are mostly from overdoses, adulterated drugs, and secondary problems like health care and the criminal status of the abuser's lifestyle.

TREATMENT OF OPIATE ABUSE

Two types of long-term treatment for opiate dependence are prevalent: methadone programs and therapeutic communities. Of all current programs, none is very successful at returning recovering addicts to a complete drug-free existence; all show about the same moderate degree of success. Britain allows a third type of program: maintaining addicts over the long-term on heroin, prescribed in conjunction with psychotherapy.

The treatment of opiate dependence ideally has three phases: (1) detoxification, (2) short-term maintenance, and (3) long-term treatment.

Detoxification (*detox*) is a short period of treatment focusing on getting abusers off their street habits and through withdrawal. In preparation, the narcotics dosage is gradually decreased over 1 to 2 weeks, while benzodiazepines are given for calming, and then an opiate antagonist, naloxone or naltrexone, is given in increasing dosages. This speeds up the withdrawal process to minimize discomfort and blocks euphoria to reduce the temptation to relapse. Sometimes clonidine (Catapres), an agent used against high blood pressure, may be used to alleviate the aspects of withdrawal linked to NE activity. Because it is not an opiate agonist, however, clonidine alone does not help with craving, insomnia, or aching muscles; it does not shorten the period of withdrawal, which remains the same as going cold turkey; and it shows no direct effect on relapse rates (Jaffe, 1995).

One approach to short-term treatment after detox is to continue to prescribe opiate antagonists to ward off temptation, and to break the link of associations with narcotics' rewarding effects. This seems to work for a limited number of patients; most bail out after a few weeks (Jaffe, 1995).

More commonly, patients are maintained on methadone, whose safety and effectiveness in reducing illicit heroin use and keeping patients in treatment has been well demonstrated. The usual procedure is to have patients report to the clinic once daily to receive an oral dose of methadone, generally mixed with orange juice. A 100 mg dose can prevent heroin withdrawal and block the euphoria of several bags (as much as 80 mg) of street heroin. In conjunction with pharmacological treatment, counseling and other psychosocial treatment services have also been shown to be of significant help. An added incentive for all involved is the reduced risk of contracting HIV for patients who stay in treatment.

However, some abusers are not too happy with this single legal alternative. Methadone is a barely satisfactory surrogate, after all, if what you'd prefer is legal heroin, and many choose it simply as an alternative to being sent to prison. Some patients may drop because they find it inconvenient to report to a clinic once a day, which federal regulations require to avoid the dispensing and possible redistribution of drugs on the street. In some cases, low doses of methadone prescribed by clinics do not suffice to overcome the abusers' craving for heroin, so they relapse.

Originally, the strategy behind the use of methadone was to transfer users to methadone and then wean them from that, in which case withdrawal would be far less severe, sometimes even negligible. Unfortunately, as we have seen, it was often found that even after a protracted period of time, when the methadone dosage was reduced below a certain point, the craving for heroin would return and drive abusers back to their habits. Hence, these programs evolved to some extent into methadone maintenance programs, rather than transitional programs back to a drug-free life. Sustained abstinence from drugs seems to occur in only 10 percent to 19 percent of cases, a statistic that holds for methadone as well as other modes of treatment (Maddux & Desmond, 1992). The majority of patients who discontinue methadone maintenance return either to methadone or heroin.

Consequently, methadone is far from being a cure, but is undeniably a great social expediency. As a rule, the longer that one remains in methadone treatment, the greater are the odds of achieving social stability. One might even point to methadone's chief benefit being the fact that it is a legal narcotic—it offers abusers enough of an effect to mollify their craving, while removing the threat of imprisonment and the economic pressures of the black market that lead to crime. Moreover, these programs can be implemented economically on a large scale.

While long-term maintenance on methadone is better than a heroin habit in the eyes of society, some object on the principle that methadone, too, is a narcotic drug. Another mode of treatment, the therapeutic community, strives for rehabilitation in a completely drug-free atmosphere.

Therapeutic communities (TCs) are the second most used treatment for narcotics dependence. Even though methadone maintenance is recognized as the most successful and viable treatment, cheap and possible on a wide scale, it is clearly only a stopgap, handling, but not curing, addiction.

Therapeutic communities are founded on premises prefigured in the Shreveport Clinic, a notably humane, successful, and controversial government clinic that operated for a period in the early 1900s. The first TC was Synanon, founded in 1959 by Charles Dederich to treat alcoholics, but it slowly shifted to heroin abusers, while maintaining some Alcoholics Anonymous-like principles that have come to characterize TCs. These include (1) the belief that there is no such thing as an ex-abuser (only an abuser not using a drug at the moment), (2) a reliance on mutual support (patients helping patients; even the staffs are ex-abusers), and (3) the use of continual confession and catharsis.

TCs have evolved to include a well-disciplined schedule in a live-in setting, with a system of rewards and punishments. Rather than the friendly and supportive atmosphere of AA, however, the leaders of TCs have adopted a model of challenge and confrontation in treatment. The goal is to detox abusers and keep them off heroin by providing a disciplined and stable existence with strong community support and group encounters, and by helping them win back their dignity and self-respect. Faith is put in the willpower of the individual to stay off heroin, while relapses are expected and minimized. The philosophy is to become drug-free, so methadone does not play a large part; it is rejected as an addicting narcotic.

TCs clearly have economic limitations; they cannot handle the large numbers of abusers that the methadone clinics can. Moreover, many abusers are poorly socialized to begin with and cannot function in a community setting, and the open door policies of most communities allow them to walk out. Then there is the opposite problem of those who become so reliant on the community that they never leave. Is it legitimate therapy, critics ask, if it only works in the artificial context of the treatment facility and its subcommunity? The general verdict is that TCs can work, but only for the limited number of people who can adapt to them and who can remain for a longer period—or permanently.

A third type of treatment, heroin maintenance, is an idea that has been considered and tried to some extent in England with limited success. Today, the practice of prescribing to confessed abusers has been all but eliminated; there seems to be little to recommend it.

Considering treatment as a global problem, we might note that certain laws and principles hold true for the heroin (and cocaine) network that seem endlessly baffling to societies trying to stem the abuse of drugs. First, the consumers remain loyal, and the pharmacological demand at the cellular level keeps the market humming. No treatment plan has yet been invented to make a satisfactory dent in this demand. Second, law enforcement does not seem to affect the available supply; it frequently works against itself by driving prices up, increasing the profit margin of the suppliers and increasing addict crime. This case was apparent when China outlawed opium in Canton. There was no better news for the smugglers; the import taxes vanished, and the value of the product soared. It's no less true for America today. The last thing the drug lords want is to see heroin become a legal medical problem and lose the status of contraband, which is the third point—that the profits are phenomenal.

The heroin and cocaine black market functions like the demonic alter ego of corporate consumer culture. It involves an unethical multinational organization, astronomical profits, a potentially toxic product that can socially incapacitate the user, a market compelled to bleed itself dry to keep itself supplied, and a system that in some respects gains strength from opposition. In addition, it has the power to penetrate and weaken its opponent's forces, by bribing police and government officials or offering exorbitant bounties for narcotics officers' lives.

A fourth principle of the global narcotics network is that it pivots on steady demand, while the conditions of supply are flexible enough to adapt to radical change. When America broke the French Connection with Turkey and Southeast Asia (through the fall of Saigon), the cultivation moved to Mexico. When the U.S. contrived with Mexico to spray the poppy crop with Agent Orange in 1978, growing moved to the Golden Triangle (Laos, Burma, Thailand). When drought struck there, the source became the Golden Crescent (Iran, Afghanistan, Pakistan), and a new flood of high-quality Persian Gold hit the United States in 1980. Needless to say, the economic stress on the peasant farmers in these developing countries makes the possibility of a cash crop like opium a lifesaving boon.

So, from the grower (who is tempted to grow opium by being economically disenfranchised) to the crime barons who process and transport the drug, to the pusher (who can retire before the age of 30), to the users (the poor, the adolescent, the bored) who are willing to risk drugs because they feel they have nothing to lose by it, the whole system is driven by social alienation and the lure of lordly profits.

Lastly, the fifth principle involves the fact that the United States borders are too extensive to seal. There will always be an easy ingress for smugglers, despite the colossal amounts of heroin, marijuana, or cocaine that we have seen intercepted on the news. What's more, the entire heroin supply could be replaced by a few home labs manufacturing synthetic opiates.

Chapter 24

Anesthetic and Cholinergic Hallucinogens

Hallucinogens (also known as *psychotogens*, *psychotomimetics*, *phantasticants*, and *psychedelics*) are drugs that can produce hallucinations, disturb cognition and perception, and sometimes cause states resembling delirium or the psychotic episodes of schizophrenia. Chemically, hallucinogens are the most heterogeneous class of psychoactive drugs, embracing both natural and synthetic compounds, and differing radically in their molecular structures, their mechanisms of action, and the neurotransmitters they affect. In this chapter and the next, we will be discussing the key hallucinogens in all of their variety. We will begin with the *anesthetic hallucinogens* ketamine and phencyclidine (PCP), two synthetic sedatives used as anesthetics, which have some hallucinogenic characteristics. The rest of the compounds are arranged according to the transmitters they resemble structurally, which is one of the most convenient ways to classify them. Of these, we will first consider the *cholinergic hallucinogens*, involving ACh systems.

In general, the anesthetic and cholinergic compounds included here produce hallucinatory experiences which are accompanied by states of confusion, delirium, and disorganization, and which one is often unable to recall.

Most of the history of the hallucinogens predates modern times, and much of it comes from ancient cultures that were familiar with naturally occurring psychoactive substances. Only about 6 species of hallucinogens are used over most of the planet, except in the Americas, where about 100 species have been recorded in use.

Our word *hallucination* comes from the Latin *alucinatio*, meaning a wandering of the mind or the attention, or idle talk or prating. Medically, it is defined as a sensory perception in the absence of an actual external stimulus, which may occur in any of the senses.

Several distinctions are drawn among hallucinatory events. True hallucinations consist of experiencing things or events that are not there (*positive hallucinations*) or of the failure to experience things and events that are (*negative hallucinations*). In both cases, the perceivers would believe that what is perceived is reality. This is not the case with pseudohallucinations. Here the perceivers know they are "seeing things," or otherwise sensing things which are not in actuality there. Another permutation is an illusion, in which actual stimuli are present, but are misperceived or distorted.

It is worth remembering that the term *hallucination*, as used in the context of Western psychiatry, suggests a pathological condition. Psychiatry does not acknowledge or encourage visions *per se*, but recognizes that visionary experience is prized in the beliefs of some other cultures. One person may see Christ, and it is considered a hallucination; another sees Christ, and it is considered divine illumination. Cultural context is a key factor in interpreting such experience.

Many older cultures, such as the Aztecs and Greeks, used and valued visions as information of a higher order than daily reality and put them to cultural use in art, religion, and domestic life. In modern scientific cultures, there is no basis for interpreting such experience as utilitarian or as "a message from the gods"; it is considered disordered, or, at best, irrelevant. Individuals tend to be isolated by the experience instead of enriched, and the imagery remains cryptic and unsupported by a communal interpretation. To judge a shaman (holy man or sorcerer) by our own concept of hallucinations, therefore, would be a misapplication of cultural standards. Of course, it should be said that pathologies are recognized in primitive cultures. When the visions control the shaman rather than vice versa, he is considered a madman.

ANESTHETIC HALLUCINOGENS

The hallucinogens ketamine and PCP are sedative compounds used as anesthetics. Because of its side effects, PCP has been restricted to use in animals; ketamine continues to be used on humans. Both drugs have been abused, but PCP has attained more notoriety because it falls within the means of illicit drug makers to produce it. Both drugs induce states involving extensive cognitive and sensory disorganization, in which hallucinations may play a part.

Ketamine

Ketamine (Ketalar, Ketaject) is a rapidly acting general anesthetic that was the most widely used battlefield anesthetic in Vietnam. Its action is characterized by a profound analgesia, by an enhanced tone in the skeletal muscles, and by cardiovascular and respiratory stimulation. Sometimes a slight transient respiratory depression has been noted.

In surgical procedures, ketamine is administered IV. It has a 10 to 15 minute half-life, corresponding to its short anesthetic effect. The drug action ends via redistribution and metabolism in the liver, although the major metabolite is active and is one-third as potent as ketamine. Ketamine crosses the placenta, but its safety for use in pregnancy has not been ascertained. Two mg/kg, administered slowly, is the dose for surgical anesthesia. The drug resembles no known transmitter.

An IM dose of 1.0 to 2.0 mg/kg of ketamine produces an intense experience lasting about an hour. The effects include a sense of floating and dissociation, stimulation, hallucinations, and increased mental associations.

As for side effects, ketamine increases the blood pressure and pulse rate and can cause arrhythmia. Low blood pressure (hypotension) is a possibility as well. With rapid administration at high doses, there may be severe respiratory depression or apnea instead of respiratory stimulation. Other side effects include nystagmus, muscle twitches resembling convulsions, anorexia, ataxia, dizziness, slurred speech, nausea, and vomiting.

Some patients show a reaction upon emergence from ketamine anesthesia. Symptoms include pleasant, dreamy states, vivid imagery, hallucinations, confusion, excitement, and irrational behavior. This condition may last a few hours, and recurrences of up to 24 hours are known. There are no residual effects.

Phencyclidine (PCP)

PCP (phencyclidine), a derivative of ketamine, is also a sedative, but it shares the properties of drugs in several other classifications. Though it is not considered a true hallucinogen, it can induce pronounced sensory distortions, with some hallucinatory effects. In addition, PCP has effects much like cocaine, and the hallucinatory effects may be related to those experienced in psychotic states associated with stimulant use. PCP has also been a drug of abuse, a popular homemade street drug since the 1960s.

Phencyclidine, the prototype of the phencyclidine compounds, goes by many names. Its chemical name is *l*-phenylcyclohexyl-piperidine; its trade name is Sernyl, and it has known on the street as *PCP, angel dust, hog, super weed, busy bee, mist, goon, tic,* and *tac*. It was synthesized in 1956 by Parke Davis, in its search for better surgical anesthetics and analgesics.

When first synthesized, PCP was found to work as a potent analgesic in animals (with considerable species differences), and as an effective short-acting IV anesthetic in humans. It was released in 1963 for use in major surgery. Of particular interest was its stimulation of respiration, blood pressure, and heart rate. However, human subjects reported bizarre effects after waking: agitation, excitement, disorientation, and delirium, and a significant proportion of subjects hallucinated severely. Consequently, in 1965, PCP was diverted to use only in veterinary medicine, under the name Sernylan. This may be the reason it was later sold as *horse tranquilizer*, although it is, in fact, an anesthetic and analgesic, not a calming agent. Two years later, PCP had become available to the San Francisco flower children as *PeaCe Pills*, and toxic cases began to show up in emergency rooms. This contradicted early researchers' judgments that the adverse effects would deter abuse. It is true, however, that it turned out to be not much of a peace pill and vanished for a year, only to reappear in New York City, where it had another limited run. Media coverage continued to spread its popularity, so that in 1970 it was taken off the market, and use declined.

Nevertheless, PCP use continued to spread geographically, since it is cheaply and simply made with some basic knowledge of chemistry, some accessible equipment, and less than $100 worth of chemicals. In addition, one home lab can produce millions of dollars worth of the drug. It is also easy to ingest by several forms and routes. Street use resurged in 1975, especially in California, and the number of emergency admissions diagnosed as schizophrenic increased, very probably misdiagnoses of PCP reactions. It was only after a report on the popular news show *60 Minutes* that the National Institute on Drug Abuse officially recognized PCP as a problem (1977), and the following year, the FDA made it a Schedule II controlled substance. By 1980, it had been moved to Schedule

I, making everything about it—production, possession, and sale—punishable by law. However, this still left many of the analogues legal: TCP, PCE, PCPY, PCC, and *l*-phenylcyclohexylamine hydrochloride. All of these substances are now under federal control. Still, in 1986, PCP was the problem drug of choice in Washington, DC.

Now completely illicit, PCP comes under more names and colors than all other street drugs combined. Early on, it was sold under the name of more familiar and acceptable compounds (for example as pure THC, the active ingredient in marijuana) until its own effects and names became known, and it gained many users through this masquerade. The substance itself is most commonly a granulated or crystal powder of varying shades of white. The routes of administration may be oral, by snorting, or smoking. Originally PCP came in oral tablets or capsules (called *tic* and *tac*). These sometimes contained a lethal dose. The crystal, powdered like table salt, could be snorted like cocaine, but it was also sold in one-gram lumps that could be dissolved in fluids and drunk. Drinking, however, is the easiest way to overdose. A more popular technique that came into use around 1979 was to sprinkle the crystals over marijuana and roll them into a marijuana cigarette (*reefer*); this afforded much better dosage control. A variant of this was *pinwheel joints*—smaller than reefers—made of parsley, mint, oregano, tobacco, or other leaf mixtures. These forms made PCP acceptable and available to many marijuana smokers.

A number of creative uses have been found for solutions of PCP. Instead of sprinkling the crystals into joints, the leaf mixtures or joints may be soaked in PCP, dried, and then smoked. To disguise the drug, some users have soaked string in the solution and threaded it through regular cigarettes. It also has been smuggled into prisons by soaking objects in it, such as letters, tissues, dental floss, or wrapping paper. The solution can be injected or even put into the eyes with an eyedropper.

On the most common route, inhalation by smoking. only about 30 percent of the drug enters the lungs. About five minutes after the first puffs, the high begins, peaking in 15 to 30 minutes. Peak blood levels occur somewhere between 1 and 4 hours. The user stays intoxicated for 4 to 6 hours, and it may take a day or two to return to normal. On the oral route, 2 to 10 milligrams bring effects on in 30 to 60 minutes, which peak in 2 to 5 hours, followed by a 12hour recovery period.

PCP is a weak base with high lipid solubility. It stores in fat tissue and shows an affinity for the brain and liver. The liver biotransforms it by hydroxylation, producing some active metabolites whose effects are unknown. The half-life is 45 minutes at low doses, but may be as long as 3 days in the case of overdoses. A rat's brain still shows low levels of PCP after 48 hours, and it can be found bound to melanin (a black pigment) in the substantia nigra for at least 21 days. There is potential for cumulative effects, which may explain long-term deficits after prolonged or acute administration. The drug concentrates in the urine, where high doses may be detected for up to a week. Acidifying the urine hurries excretion.

Five milligrams is considered a low dose, but as few as 20 mg can produce a short coma. The margin between 5 and 20 milligrams is significant in light of the purity of street doses, which can vary from 10 percent to 100 percent pure. Seventy to 1,000 mg produce a prolonged coma.

Though it resembles no known transmitter, PCP has been shown to interact with several receptors and most neurotransmitter systems. Evidence points to interactions with ACh, DA, NE, and 5-HT systems (Contreras et al., 1987) In addition, two binding sites for PCP have been identified. One is the sigma opiate receptor, to which are attributed some of the psychosis-like effects of PCP intoxication. A second binding site is a receptor specific to PCP, which is located in the ion channel associated with the NMDA receptor and the action of excitatory amino acids. By binding in the ion channel and blocking the movement of ions through the membrane, PCP noncompetitively antagonizes the channel-opening action of excitatory amino acids at the receptor. The result could be some of the inhibitory effects seen with PCP use--anticonvulsant actions and ataxia (Contreras et al., 1987).

PCP has pronounced dose and species-dependent effects. In rodents, it produces dose-dependent psychomotor stimulation like that of amphetamine and cocaine, with incoordination. In lower primates, it produces effects ranging from mild ataxia and sedation to prolonged stupor and catalepsy. Dogs yelp and have seizures. In humans it produces a puzzling mixture of stimulant, depressant, and hallucinogenic effects. At low doses (below 5 mg), stimulation, euphoria, confusional states, and memory impairment occur. At moderate doses, PCP produces conceptual disorganization, delusions, stereotyped movement, and violent behavior. At high doses, symptoms include extreme agitation and violent behavior, unresponsiveness, delusions, hallucinations, and eventually anesthesia. In general, peripheral effects include increased salivation, sweating, increased blood pressure and heart rate, and muscle rigidity.

Originally developed for anesthesia, PCP is unique among anesthetics in that there is no significant depression of respiration or blood pressure at effective doses. It produces complete anesthesia and an unresponsive state, but the subjects seem awake with fixed stares (*doll's eyes*), and they report a sense of dissociation from both the environment and themselves. Analgesic effects may be mediated by the thalamus (the sensation processing nuclei), as is indicated by the impairment of touch and the sensory distortions that accompany the reduction of pain. It has also been noted that subjects show reduced PCP effects when put into a quieter environment (Linder, Lerner, & Burns, 1981, p. 22), which again suggests changes at the thalamic level of sensory input. Numbing of the extremities and mild analgesia may occur at low doses (5 mg), while moderate doses completely ``waste" the subject and cause body-wide numbing; however, this is accompanied by a supersensitivity to other sensory stimuli like sights and sounds.

Though not considered a true hallucinogen, PCP does induce perceptual distortions that seem to be related to the alteration of sensory input. On the other hand, there is documentation showing that PCP intoxication mimics some of the primary symptoms of acute and paranoid schizophrenia (e.g., incoherent thought processes, hallucinatory voices, self-destructive impulses), as well as those of mania and depression.

The typical PCP high lasts 4 to 6 hours with return to normal 24 to 48 hours later (Contreras et al., 1987). PCP intoxication is often mistaken for the effects of other drugs, which is a problem because mismanagement of PCP abusers can be dangerous. The key distinguishing symptoms are the occurrence together of elevated blood pressure and tiny, jerking eye movements (*nystagmus*), a combination which is not seen with any other drug. Doll's eyes are often mentioned. Subjects on low to moderate doses may seem excessively drunk on liquor (from depression of the CNS), with motor disturbances, incoordination, a staggering gait, incoherence, and slurring of speech or stuttering. Unlike alcohol, however, PCP has the stimulatory effects of increasing reflexes and muscle tone, thereby producing stiff or unusual postures. Subjects may appear to be in a wide-eyed stupor, disoriented, rigid and unable to communicate, though still conscious, and they report feelings of loneliness and isolation. This is seen as catalepsy at higher doses. Grimacing and jaw-clenching have been noted, and excited PCP abusers may bite. There may be a loss of bowel or bladder control.

One of the trademark effects of PCP is distortions of body image. Users report feeling "like a rubber doll," in a state in which their limbs seem to elongate or shrivel in a plasticized condition. This may be an effect of distortions in the feedback from musculoskeletal systems. Feelings of dissociation and alterations of time and depth perception have been reported.

Although quite a few experimenters report the effects of PCP to be bizarre and unpleasant, chronic users describe the experience (even their first) to be happy and euphoric. Although they feel wired, time seems to stop. They feel light and are able to absorb music; they experience floating sensations, and a sense of oneness and of omnipotent strength. Some describe hallucinatory interactions with religious figures. Their bodies feel rubbery. And none of this, they report, is like what LSD does.

One of the frequently mentioned—and dramatic—effects of PCP is that it increases aggression, violence, and antisocial behavior in humans. Abusers have a reputation for becoming irritable and assaultive. This is a delicate and controversial area in light of some of the misrepresentations of stimulant users propagated by authorities in the past. Media and police reports perhaps should be viewed skeptically, especially in cases where forceful police actions have been taken against offenders. Nevertheless, the literature and accounts of PCP abusers are filled with grotesque episodes of sometimes elaborate violence, more so than for other substances. There are accounts of abusers mutilating themselves, impetuously injuring others, and reacting to situations with energetic aggression. Treatment facilities know well that PCP abusers should never be left unattended in waiting rooms. Typical of such reports is this one:

> *A 17-year-old New Jersey boy and his girlfriend decided to rob a nearby summer home at the seashore. Instead, the youth chose to bludgeon to death the elderly woman who lived in the cottage. He awoke the next morning covered with blood and with no recollection of his brutal act. (Clark & Agrest, 1978, p. 34)*

Is it possible that under the effects of PCP we have finally found the mythical dope fiends of the thirties, with their dead, fixed gaze, invulnerability to bullets, and indiscriminate assaultiveness? Certain PCP effects would seem to point to this: the doll's eyes and nystagmus, the sense of invulnerability, the analgesia and disinhibition of aggression. And there is no doubt that PCP abusers respond more unpredictably and brashly than do many other substance abusers. But it is important not to jump to conclusions. Many users do not experience such effects at all; many claim they do not connect PCP with feelings of aggression; many claim to be too disoriented to fight. Much of the documented violence involves property damage, and panic reactions to being restrained may also play a role. Moreover, many users may have previous histories of antisocial acts, possibly, for example, the couple above who "decided to rob" a summer home.

Side Effects

Some of the effects of PCP are strange enough that what some users consider desirable, others may count as unpleasant. Early reports of anesthesia subjects reflect the kinds of side effects that led to the discontinuation of PCP as a human medicine:

> *My legs are a mile away...I feel huge and spongy one moment and tiny the next. . . Everyone's voice is really loud . . . This is like being in a submarine . . . I'm floating...I am now two people watching each other...I'm scared. I feel like I'm going to die. (Linder, Lerner, & Burns, 1981, p. 4)*

Other effects that manifested in recovery from anesthesia were grimacing, arm flailing, stiffening of the legs, shouting, muscle tension, nausea and vomiting, persistent confusion, anxiety and insomnia of 4 to 5 days' duration, mood changes, and—at high doses—convulsions. Memory loss of the recuperation period was common, and younger patients had hallucinations. Positive effects were more common among older male patients, while older female patients could become aggressive and violent (Linder et al., 1981).

Tolerance to the use of PCP shows in animal research. Self-administration experiments reveal that it is a potent reinforcing drug, another distinction from hallucinogens like LSD, psilocybin, or THC, which do not reinforce self-administration. When animals are trained to self-administer cocaine, PCP can be substituted with similar results. It is possible that the two drugs may act on common transmitters or brain systems.

So far physical dependence has not been reported with PCP, but it is evident that abusers are often unable to quit. And, while there is no conclusive evidence of brain damage from chronic exposure, the psychosis that can follow from use implies that something can go wrong. In addition, PCP does pass to the fetus.

PCP often mimics mental illness, causing organic brain syndromes that can last from days to months or longer. Psychotic symptoms are more likely in novices and in those with a history of schizophrenia. Accidental use may pose dangers because it may be difficult to convince patients that they are not having a mental breakdown. Depression is a common sequel to the psychosis, but PCP abusers should not be entrusted with tricyclic antidepressants, since a suicidal overdose is possible. The entire process of recovery may extend over two months in some cases.

The greatest dangers of PCP (besides the danger of escalating to chronic use) are, in fact, from its secondary effects. The confused and uncoordinated users may fall, drown in an inch of water, burn themselves, invite violence from others, drive recklessly, fall from high places, or suffer from other effects of impaired perception and delusions. Suicide is possible from depression. Sometimes classic schizophrenia has developed as an aftermath of the drug psychosis, cause unknown. In 1978, during the last resurgence of PCP use, 100 deaths and 4,000 hospital admissions were reported (Clark & Agrest, 1987). Treatment at that time consisted of large doses of vitamin C given to acidify the urine and hasten excretion.

Because PCP abusers show unpredictable behavior, suspicion, and hostility, traditional management techniques do not work (e.g., talking quietly and reassuringly does no good with incommunicative patients). Periods of cooperation may alternate with periods of imbalanced behavior, so it is very important to monitor patients closely, even if they seem calm. Moreover, subjects are hypersensitive to stimuli of all sorts, and these seem to trigger agitation and violent responses. Police controls like armlocks, mace, and firing a warning shot, or crowded hospital waiting rooms and confrontational therapies can produce exactly the opposite of the intended effects and precipitate agitated responses or attacks, since PCP abusers may not be intimidated by guns or other threats. In treatment, therefore, stimulation should be reduced as much as possible, in a dark and quiet room.

Most abusers procure their PCP from illicit labs, which are extremely dangerous because of the volatile chemicals kept there. Hydrogen cyanide gas often kills the workers, and a number of the labs discovered by the law disclose their presence by blowing up.

CHOLINERGIC AGONISTS

↑up

Some hallucinogens are cholinergic agonists; namely, they stimulate ACh receptors. You may recall some effects mediated by these receptors. In the periphery they constrict the pupils and bronchii, contract bladder and intestinal muscle, govern salivation and sweating, cause a drop in blood pressure, slow the heart, and increase muscle tone (even to the point of paralysis). In the brain, their locations and functions are not well understood, but observed effects include anxiety, restlessness, dreaming, nightmares, delirium, and insomnia. High doses of cholinergic agonists may cause any one of the above effects, as well as depression, drowsiness, confusion, incoordination, ataxia, slurred speech, convulsions, paralysis, and coma. All of the cholinergic agonists discussed here are found in nature and so have rich cultural and historical backgrounds.

Muscarine

Muscarine, a key ACh agonist, is found in the fly agaric mushroom (*Amanita muscaria*). The name of the mushroom comes from the fact that it was once supposedly mixed with milk and set out to attract and stupefy flies. In Russian, it is called *mukhomor.* Specimens of the two species *muscaria* and *pantherina* vary in hue from a vibrant yellow or orange to a brilliant crimson, and are usually flecked distinctively with the white fragments of their own outgrown and broken veils. The agaric grows typically in northern climates, in the company of birches and pine trees, most notably in Scandinavia and Siberia.

The fly agaric contains a number of active ingredients, not all of which have been identified, but muscarine, ibotenic acid, and muscimol are known to be of importance. Muscarine acts by directly stimulating certain ACh receptors in both the CNS and periphery, and it is of such pharmacological distinction that these receptors, you will remember, are called *muscarinic receptors,* as opposed to those agonized by nicotine. Muscarine, however, occurs in the fly agaric in only small amounts. Muscimol, a GABA-like substance, appears to be the principle psychoactive ingredient.

The brunt of the literature about amanita use dates back only to the seventeenth century, although scholars have suggested that the Greek rites of Dionysus may have used a solution of amanita, and the ethnobotanist Wasson cogently argues that the fly agaric is the *soma* spoken of in the *RigVeda,* a ``food" taken in Indian rituals dating back to 2,000 BC (Wasson, 1971). Wasson also provides a number of accounts, from travelers of the last three centuries, describing amanita use by tribesmen of northeastern Siberia--the Koryaks, Chukchi, and Kamchadals. The variety of reports provides a picture of intoxication by amanita.

The Siberians usually collect and dry the mushroom. Wasson's observations led him to suspect that this might be a requisite for its psychoactivity. The dried pieces may be chewed, but usually are swallowed at a gulp, supposedly because of their nauseating taste. Some observers have seen them chewed by a woman and then given to a tribesman, who immediately swallows them. Often, water is taken with the mushrooms. It may be drunk cold with the dried specimens, or the agarics may be soaked or boiled in it. Sometimes water or berry juice is drunk off from a mushroom marinade. Three mushrooms are the usual dose, but up to ten may be taken.

The effects of the fly agaric and their order vary among individuals. A typical pattern is that, within an hour, the user shows some pulling and twitching of the muscles, often of the face, and trembling of the hands. Some mushroom eaters vomit, but this does not impede the course of the intoxication. Next comes a stage of pleasant excitement, and a sense of greatly increased bodily agility, lightness, and strength. Some observers claim to have witnessed remarkable physical feats performed by the users. In most cases, there is a period of excitement, agitation, and pronounced gaiety when users sing, dance, talk garrulously, beat drums, or run about almost involuntarily, and, it is said, may bolt into ditches, ponds, or streams and injure themselves if they are not looked after. Their actions at times have been described as frenzied or raving, their limbs moving strangely and seemingly out of control.

One of the characteristic symptoms of agaric intoxication is *macropsia*, a condition of visual distortions in which objects seem to be inordinately large:

> *A small hole appearing to them as a great pit, and a spoonful of water as a lake. (Krasheninnikov, 1775)*
>
> *If one wishes to step over a small stick or straw, one steps or jumps as though the obstacles were tree trunks. (von Langsdorf, 1809)*

For the user, this period of agitation phases into hallucinatory transports. These involve voices and visions, and may be ecstatic and intensely enjoyable, or infernal. Subjects may at first retain a consciousness of the surroundings and can continue to interact with others present, but eventually they are drawn into visionary worlds and lose contact. Some tribes believe that the agaric will reveal one's future during the session.

At some point, most mushroom eaters lapse into a deep slumber. In many cases, the visions are encountered as dreams in this stage. If sleep occurs early in the intoxication, users may waken to the hallucinatory and ecstatic effects. If later, they may waken in low spirits. Most reports hold that the hangover and headaches seen with a drug like alcohol are absent, although some mention weakness, headaches, and vomiting. The user may recall nothing of the intoxication.

In laboratory studies, the peripheral effects of both the *muscaria* and *pantherina* species of amanita have been observed to be deeply unpleasant. They consist of profound sweating, increased salivation, pupil constriction, increased bladder tone, decreased heart rate and blood pressure, and muscle spasms that show as twitching of the limbs. The effects are dangerous, but fatalities are rare. According to the anecdotal evidence, overdoses can produce convulsions and death. There also is a condition resembling dependence depicted among the Siberian tribesmen.

It is noteworthy that the hallucinogenic principle of the fly agaric is excreted unchanged and remains active in the urine. This is exploited by tribes like the Koryaks, who recycle the hallucinogen by collecting their urine and drinking it. Those who have not eaten the mushroom can become intoxicated in this way, and a judicious user, by carefully deploying a small supply of mushrooms with a supply of hallucinogenic urine, can remain intoxicated for days. Some accounts mark the limit of effects at two "passes," while others claim that the drug may remain effective after being recycled through as many as four or five drinkers (Wasson, 1971).

The Siberian tribesmen are rivaled in their love of the agaric by the reindeer of the region, who display a taste for both the mushroom and the urine of those who use it. When either the fly agarics or human urine are available, reindeer kept by the tribes may become excited and unmanageable and fight with each other. It is said that by eating the flesh of a freshly killed reindeer which has browsed on the mushroom, one can become intoxicated (Wasson, 1971).

Some writers have linked the agitating effects of amanita to acts of extravagant self-injury, aggression, and violence. And Scandinavian writers have attributed the killing frenzy of the Norse *berserkers* to the influence of the agaric. The evidence for these claims, as shown by Wasson, is thin or nonexistent, and often relies on hearsay and speculation.

The next drugs we will discuss promote cholinergic action, not by stimulating receptors directly, but by inhibiting acetylcholinesterase, the enzyme that degrades ACh. The effects, of course, are similar to those of the cholinergic agonists.

Physostigmine

Physostigmine, a natural compound, was the first AChE antagonist to become known. It was found in the mid1800s in the Calabar bean (*Physostigma venenosum*), a climbing liana found in swampy coastal areas of West Africa, particularly around the Calabar coast of Nigeria, near the mouth of the Niger. The powerful secret societies there used it as an ordeal to test for guilt:

> *The accused was made to drink a toxic potion made from eight seeds of the Calabar bean, ground and mixed with water. In such a dose, physostigmine acts as a powerful sedative of the spinal cord, and causes progressively ascending paralysis from the feet to the waist, and eventual collapse of all muscular control, leading to death by asphyxiation. The defendant, after swallowing the poison, was ordered to stand still before a judicial gathering until the effects of the poison became noticeable. Then he was ordered to walk toward a line drawn on the ground ten feet away. If the accused was lucky enough to vomit and regurgitate the poison, he was judged innocent and allowed to depart unharmed. If he did not vomit, yet managed to reach the line, he was also deemed innocent, and quickly given a concoction of excrement mixed with water [to induce vomiting] . . . .*
>
> *Most often, however, given the toxicity of the Calabar bean, the accused died a ghastly death. . . .* (Davis, 1985, p. 37)

Upon investigation in the West, physostigmine was found to be of some use in the treatment of glaucoma (a build up of pressure inside the eye) and in the treatment of *myasthenia gravis* (a heaviness of the muscles resulting from compromised ACh action at peripheral synapses). Side effects were many and toxic, however, and physostigmine has been supplanted by modern synthetics.

New anti-acetylcholinesterase agents include DFP (diisopropyl fluorophosphate), malathion, parathion, sarin, and soman. These drugs irreversibly impair AChE and are used mostly as insecticides. Human poisoning from these compounds has occurred among field workers, but some antidotes are available in hospital emergencies. Sarin and soman are among the most toxic and lethal synthetic agents known. They have been stockpiled as nerve gases for chemical warfare, and have sometimes been used in terrorist attacks (such as the Tokyo subway gassing in 1995, in which sarin was used to kill commuters).

ANTICHOLINERGIC HALLUCINOGENS

Muscarine, because it directly stimulates ACh receptors, and physostigmine, because it enhances ACh activity through enzyme inhibition, are both ACh agonists that produce hallucinations. This next class of agents does the opposite—it produces hallucinations through the *antagonism* of ACh receptors.

The anticholinergic hallucinogens cause many of their effects by blocking muscarinic cholinergic receptors in the brain. There are three of importance: hyoscyamine, atropine, and scopolamine. Chemically, hyoscyamine is *l*-hyoscyamine. Atropine is *dl*-hyoscyamine. And scopolamine is *l*-hyoscine. These three substances are found widely distributed in nature in four genuses of *Solanaceae*, the potato family: Datura, Atropa, Hyoscyamus, and Mandragora. Many hallucinogenic Datura species are found worldwide; the other three genuses are mostly indigenous to Europe.

Since these drugs block cholinergic receptors, it is to be expected that they induce many symptoms of the anticholinergic syndrome. Rapidly absorbed through the GI tract and through mucous membranes, they block the secretion of many body fluids. They block perspiration and salivation (causing dry mouth) and block mucus in the nose and throat; these effects have a clinical application—atropine and scopolamine can be found in some decongestant cold medications. Body temperature may soar to fever levels, and heart rate can increase by as much as 50 beats a minute. The pupils dilate markedly even at moderate doses. These drugs produce loss of muscle tone in the bladder and GI tract and inhibit the secretion of acid into the stomach (although, as an ulcer treatment, they have many side effects).

In large doses, the ACh antagonists produce symptoms like those of toxic psychosis: delirium, confusion, drowsiness, and loss of attention. They furthermore lack charm as recreational hallucinogens because they produce no vivid sensory effects; instead, they cloud consciousness, impair sensory perception, and obliterate recent memories, so the user cannot even recall the intoxication. Their pronounced peripheral symptoms, such as dry mouth and increased heart rate, may also negatively color psychological effects. Their noxious side effects and toxicity make these drugs of low abuse potential. In poisoning, death may come from respiratory paralysis.

Deadly Nightshade (Atropine)

The deadly nightshade (*Atropa belladonna*) was a favorite of medieval poisoners; about a dozen of the berries did the trick (see Figure 24.1), although as few as three may kill a child who eats them off the plant. It is the source from which atropine was first isolated in 1831, and it also contains scopolamine. The name *belladonna* ("beautiful woman") may come from the fact that Egyptian and Roman women applied the juice to their eyelids or conjunctival sacs to dilate their pupils, which made their eyes look larger and more amorous. (Modern studies using photographs have shown that women with dilated pupils are considered to be more friendly and attractive, even though differences in pupil size are not consciously detected by viewers.)

FIGURE 24.1 Deadly nightshade.

Early descriptions of poisoning from the berries report that victims become cheerful and talkative with an inclination to sing or dance. This is followed by a confused state marked by a loss of speech. Then the victim begins to act disordered, exhibiting mania and delirium. The crisis may involve violent convulsions followed by sleep, or death by respiratory depression.

In some cases, anti-ACh alkaloids confer a floating sense of lightness and wellbeing, and one of their peculiar attributes is that they induce a sense of flight, which may be the reason that medieval witches rubbed themselves with creams and ointments of belladonna, mandrake, and henbane. Moreover, the vaginal route is an especially effective means of administration, and witches are known to have applied the cream with a stick—possibly a broom handle. If so, tales of flight astride a broomstick may not be as far from fact as one might imagine. The excitations of the Witches' Sabbath and other documented witch behaviors fall within the scope of the pharmacological effects of the anti-ACh drugs.

Atropine, the chief psychoactive ingredient of deadly nightshade, is named after Atropos, the Greek Fate who cuts the thread of life. It is a prototype of the anti-ACh hallucinogens. At low doses, it does not seem to affect behavior or the EEG; at moderate doses, it produces some excitement and delirium and blurry vision from dilation of the pupils. In fact, opthalmologists use atropine as eyedrops to widen the pupils for eye examinations.

Atropine antagonizes AChE inhibitors and may be given in hospital emergencies if someone is poisoned by an AChE-inhibiting insecticide. It is only a partial antidote, however. The AChE inhibitors act by impairing enzymes and allowing ACh to act unchecked. Atropine corrects this by blocking receptors and guarding them from ACh overuse, although this does not do anything to restore the enzyme's action. Conversely, physostigmine (an AChE inhibitor) can be given as an antidote for anti-ACh poisoning (for example, if children eat deadly nightshade berries). In this case, the atropine blockade occurs first, then physostigmine knocks out the enzyme and allows an increase in ACh to override the blockade. However, physostigmine has a much shorter duration of action than atropine, so one has to monitor patients to be sure the anti-ACh effect does not gain ground again.

Atropine can also be given as an antidote for fly agaric mushroom poisoning, since it acts against the cholinergic agonist muscarine and has a higher affinity for the receptors. In some cases, however, atropine has been reported to intensify and prolong the suffering, so care must be taken to identify the substances involved. It is good to remember to carry a sample of any toxic agent to the hospital, if possible, should you suffer from or attend a case of poisoning.

Mandrake

The mandrake (*mandragora officinarum*), which grows wild in the Near East and in warm countries around the rim of the Mediterranean, is another medieval witch drug, containing atropine, scopolamine, and hyoscyamine (Figure 24.2). The plant appears variously in the Bible and in ancient Egyptian and Greek sources as a medicinal, a sleeping potion, an aphrodisiac, and a fertility drug (Thompson, 1975).

FIGURE 24.2 *Mandragora officinarum*, the mandrake, has a root that reputedly resembles the human form, in this case feminine.

It was part of common medieval lore that hanged men frequently had erections and ejaculations. Supposedly, this is because the sudden snapping of the neck by the coils of the noose sends an impulse down the spinal cord, which jolts the reflexes of the lower spine, causing these effects. Popular myth had it that where a hanged man's semen fell, there grew a mandrake, with its forked foot-long root resembling a vegetal effigy of a human being. The plant supposedly shrieked when uprooted, driving anyone within earshot mad. Witches used it to make flying potions and to induce prophetic mutterings. High doses are capable of causing prolonged and vivid hallucinations, but they virtually paralyze the subject by blocking ACh synapses in the periphery, the ones that control muscle movement. (This suggests that the root has other ingredients besides muscarinic blockers.)

At low doses, mandrake alleviates tension and fosters sleep, and medieval commonfolk employed it as a sedative-hypnotic for nervousness and pain.

Henbane

Henbane was the principal drug used in medieval sorcery. It is native to parts of Europe, India, western Asia, and North Africa, and is found in the northern and northwestern United States and Canada. It is toxic to deer and most birds, which can die from eating the seeds; hence its name meaning "harmful to hens." Pigs, however, can eat it, which is probably why Dioscorides, a Greek physician, named it *hys cyamos*, or *hog's bean*.

Henbane was a folk remedy for many conditions and was part of the *spongia somniferum* used as a medieval sedative and anesthetic. The seeds were smoked for toothache. In the United States, it was used to control urinary spasms, but it no longer has official applications. In Europe, it is used to treat earache and rheumatism.

Henbane contains scopolamine, hyoscyamine, and some atropine; its stimulatory actions are modified by the central depressant effects of scopolamine, which is an effective hypnotic. Poisoning is not uncommon because people often confuse the root with parsnip or chicory root. Toxic symptoms include atropine-like effects, as well as diarrhea, abdominal pains, and salivation (instead of dry mouth). Some subjects have reported that all objects appeared scarlet for 2 to 3 days following poisoning. Smoking henbane can produce convulsions and mania.

Datura

Datura is a genus of plants of the family *Solanacea*, which includes about 20 species. Daturas are found distributed round the globe and play a significant role in the practices of many cultures. The main psychoactive principles are scopolamine and hyoscyamine. Atropine and other alkaloids may be present in smaller amounts. The plants are highly toxic; nevertheless, they have seen wide use as medicines and ritual hallucinogens. The various preparations generally involve mixing the pulverized seeds into fermented drinks or steeping the leaves and twigs in water.

Datura produces a condition that has been compared to a psychotic delirium, involving disorientation and profound confusion. Early in the intoxication, subjects may become violently agitated and require restraint. They then pass into a phase of hallucinations and sleep, and afterwards do not recall the experience.

The uses of Datura are many, and not all are righteous. The name, for instance, comes from *dhatureas*, bands of thieves in India who used datura to drug their victims into a stupor. Similarly, it has been used the world over by malefactors, thieves, prostitutes, and adulterers to incapacitate their victims or anyone who would interfere with their machinations.

The many species of Datura play widespread and various roles in primitive ritual. In ancient Greece, the virgins in the temple of Apollo may have used it to prophecy at Delphi (Schultes, 1970). One West African tribe feeds *Datura stramonium* to beetles and then uses their poisonous dung to execute unfaithful lovers. Some African tribal users also recognize physostigmine (the Calabar bean) as an antidote. In the initiation of the Algonquin Indians of the eastern United States, the amnesia-inducing properties of datura played a symbolic role. Adolescent males were confined for a period of two to three weeks while they fed on nothing but *wysoccan* (datura). The delirium, disorientation, and amnesia induced by the plant would make the initiate forget boyhood--literally--and learn manhood (Schultes, 1970).

The *wysoccan* of the Algonquins is the most prominent species of Datura--*Datura stramonium*. It is believed to have originated in North America, but now grows in temperate and subtropical regions around the world. It is a large, bushy plant with toothed, ill-smelling leaves. Because of this, in some places it has been called *stinkweed*. Its large, trumpet-shaped flowers, in shades of white to lavender, give off a strong scent, and it bears a small prickly fruit, which has inspired the names *thorn apple*, or the *devil's apple*. Although all parts of the plant are toxic, the scopolamine-laden leaves have been rolled and smoked like marijuana.

The European-American experience with *Datura stramonium* appears to have begun in the 1960s, when some English troops, coming to quell an uprising at Jamestown, Virginia, gathered the plant for a salad and ate it (Furst, 1976, p. 141). Eventually, *Datura stramonium* became known as *Jamestown weed*, which was later elided to *jimsonweed*.

In Haiti, *Datura stramonium* goes by the name of the *zombie's cucumber*. The reference, it turns out, is more than a product of idle fancy. In 1982 and 1983, ethnobotanist Wade Davis traveled to Haiti and unearthed one of the most interesting uses of Datura. His mission was to discover whether or not a poison lay at the heart of the zombie myth, and, if so, what poison. His journey was inspired by the reappearance of one Clairvius Narcisse on his sister's doorstep, eighteen years after being pronounced dead at a modern hospital and buried. Davis summed up his findings concerning the creation of zombies in his book, *The Serpent and the Rainbow*:

> *. . . the bokor in creating a zombi cadavre may cause the prerequisite unnatural death not by capturing the ti bon ange [one of the souls] of the living but by means of a slow-acting poison that is applied directly to the intended victim. Rubbed into a wound or inhaled, the poison kills the corps cadavre slowly, efficiently, and discreetly. That poison contains tetrodotoxin, which acts to lower dramatically the metabolic rate of the victim almost to the point of clinical death. (Davis, 1985, pp. 226-227)*

Once the victim has been drugged and is to all appearances dead, Davis goes on to explain, he or she is buried alive. Sometimes the person may in fact die of the poison or suffocate in the coffin, but when the plan is successful, the *bokor* is able to return within a short period of time and retrieve the living body from the grave. The traumatized victim is led before a cross, baptized, and given a new name, and is then drugged once more with a paste made from the *zombi's cucumber*, a powerful psychoactive agent that produces a state of confusion and amnesia. Davis postulates that this paste, made of sweet potato, corn syrup, and *D. stramonium*, relieves certain symptoms of tetrodotoxin poisoning. The "zombie" is then led away to begin a hellish new life in a remote district, laboring on a work farm under a zombie master, where more psychoactive drugs may be used to keep the condemned convinced they are dead, buried, and eternally enslaved. Clairvius Narcisse was in such a situation for 18 years, until his zombie master died, at which time he made his way home. This process, Davis discovered, is part of a highly structured penal system, run by secret societies, with both judicial and religious overtones, and with unofficial recognition by the rural populace.

Chapter 25

Adrenergic and Serotonergic Hallucinogens

ADRENERGIC HALLUCINOGENS: MESCALINE

The adrenergic hallucinogens appear to work through the neurotransmitter NE. Mescaline is the compound of primary significance here. DOM, a structurally related substance, is known mostly as a low level drug of abuse.

The drug referred to as mescaline is found in the peyote cactus (*peyotl*), which is common to Mexico and the Southwest United States (Figure 25.1). The cactus (*Lophophora williamsii*) is small, spineless, and carrot-shaped. Most of the plant grows underground, except for its green-gray pincushion crown or *button*. Although the whole plant is psychoactive, the spheroidal crown is generally used. It is sliced into discs and dried, and these segments are known as *peyote buttons* or *mescal buttons*.[1]

Peyote has been used since pre-Columbian times by the Aztec, Huichal, and other Mexican Indians. According to surviving Aztec codices, it was one of the offerings made to the gods in the Aztec temples and was eaten ceremonially. Its use was reported by the Spanish chronicler Hernandez as an aid to divination, and Christian missionaries noted its sacred application. From time to time, Western notables and writers have reported on self- experiments with the cactus. Lewin investigated the plant in the 1880s, and it bore his name for a time (*Anhalonium lewinii*); the Parke-Davis pharmaceutical company sold a tincture of the drug. Havelock Ellis wrote of his use of peyote in 1902, Aldous Huxley in 1954 (*The Doors of Perception*), and Carlos Castaneda in 1968 (*Teachings of Don Juan: A Yaqui Way of Knowledge*). On the whole, peyote has remained the curiosity of a few, rather than spawning an epidemic of abuse. This is probably because, as an early investigator Dr. Weir Mitchell reported, "These shows are expensive." Ingestion of the buttons can cause vomiting, hangover, headaches, and considerable nausea (if one has not fasted). Some users, such as philosopher-psychologist William James, may experience no visions and thus become flatly disenchanted.

FIGURE 25.1 Peyote cactus, from which peyote (mescal buttons) and mescaline are derived.

Peyote has had a unique status among American hallucinogens in that it has an accepted sacramental use in the Native American Church of North America. By the late 1800s, the tribal culture of the Plains Indians had disintegrated, and the ground was fertile for the reception of rituals such as the Ghost Dance, which helped consolidate the remaining native culture. It was into this context that Quanah Parker introduced peyotism. His white mother had been taken by the Comanches and had borne him in captivity. After the Indian wars, however, many whites came looking for captured children, and Quanah's grandparents retrieved him and took him to Texas. There he fell ill but couldn't be nursed on white man's food, so his grandmother got him a Mexican Indian *curandera*, who dosed him with peyote and healed him. Under her tutelage, Quanah learned the secrets and rules of this healing herb and took them back to the Comanches (Marriott & Rachlin, 1971).

The use and rituals of peyotism spread rapidly. They traveled north by rail and were exchanged in various places in the government boarding schools that collectivized the members of many tribes, until now they are found from Washingon state to North Carolina. Current Church membership is estimated at 250,000. Controversial even among Indians, the cult justified itself as a form of Christianity, adopting as its object the fostering of moral Christian values: generosity, hard work, cleanliness, self-respect, sobriety, and helpfulness to others. But by 1900, resistance was building, and the first drug charges were brought against users in 1909. By and large, however, with effort, peyotism cults managed to defend themselves and elude the passing of government sanctions. The issue was brought before the Congress in 1918 during the antidrug furor of that time, but the cults were ultimately validated and chartered as the Native American Church. Another threat came with the drug crackdowns of the late sixties, but a case decided in Dallas, Texas, allowed the Church to own, transport, and use peyote in its natural state. However, in 1990, in another strong national antidrug climate, the Supreme Court ruled that individual states have the right to legislate against the use of peyote in religious ritual. Around 1996, the membership of the Church had become large enough that the cactus was in short supply for the ceremonial meetings

Near the end of the nineteenth century, peyote was studied by German pharmacologists. Over thirty psychoactive alkaloids were identified, but mescaline was determined to be responsible for the visual effects. In 1918, its chemical structure was described as being similar to NE and the amphetamines. However, the mechanism behind the visual hallucinations is unknown. Mescaline displays are usually clear and vivid, unaccompanied by delirium, amnesia, or clouding of consciousness. Amphetamine produces such effects only at chronic high doses. Synthesis was first accomplished in 1919, making mescaline the first hallucinogen to become available in pure form. Many synthetic derivatives of both mescaline and NE are possible, some of them psychoactive.

Mescaline is rapidly and completely absorbed orally, but passes poorly through the blood-brain barrier, so that high doses are needed. It takes half an hour to 3 hours to reach significant brain concentrations. The half-life is 6 hours, but vestiges may persist in the brain for 9 or 10. It is excreted mainly in the urine, mostly unchanged, and leaves no psychoactive metabolites. Three mg/kg produces euphoria, and 5 mg/kg is the usual oral hallucinogenic dose. The LD50 in rats is 370 mg/kg. In peyote rituals, when the buttons are eaten, the usual dose is 4 or more whole buttons, but the potency of the plants varies from location to location and from season to season.

It would stand to reason that, as an adrenergic enhancer, mescaline would have some of the effects of cocaine and amphetamine. This is true. It can cause a sympathetic reaction consisting of widened pupils, increased heart rate and blood pressure, raised body temperature, EEG arousal, and behavioral arousal. There may be jumpiness and tremors in the limbs. Some of these symptoms can appear at hallucinogenic doses (5 mg/kg).

Mescaline produces profound sensory and psychic distortions that may last half a day to a day, without impairing intellect or insight. In 1926, Heinrich Klüver in Chicago conducted a laboratory investigation of mescaline hallucinations and identified forms characteristic of many hallucinogenic states: LSD intoxication, migraine headaches, trance states, etc. (Klüver, 1966). He classified four constants among visual forms:

1. Gratings, latticework, fretwork, filigree, honeycomb, chessboard
2. Cobweb figures
3. Tunnels, funnels, alleys, cones, vessels
4. Spirals

Klüver noted that the hallucinations appeared localized at reading distance, but differed greatly in apparent size and proceeded beyond conscious control. All had varied and saturated colors, intense brightness, and involved symmetrical geometric configurations. The hallucinations could be seen with eyes open or closed. Subjects were unable to view a blank wall without seeing it tattooed with projected hallucinations. Time and space distortions were common. Klüver did not examine what Siegel (1985, p. 251) calls second-stage imagery, which includes faces, scenes, landscapes and other complex forms, encountered after the more abstract geometrical visual patterns. These we will discuss in more detail under LSD hallucinations.

Death from high doses of mescaline follows from convulsions leading to respiratory arrest. Tolerance shows more slowly than to LSD, and there is cross-tolerance between the two drugs despite the evidence of separate mechanisms. Chlorpromazine (Thorazine) blocks the intoxication.

DOM (STP)

The letters DOM are derived from the chemical name of this drug: 2,5 dimethoxy4methylamphetamine, which marks it as an amphetamine, but, unlike amphetamine, DOM shows almost no ability to block the uptake of DA, NE, or 5-HT. The molecule is also closely related to mescaline. The street name STP is reported to mean *Serenity, Tranquility, Peace,* and the name has also been connected with the popular fuel additive STP (scientifically treated petroleum).

DOM was developed in 1964 by Dow Chemical. In early 1967, the formula was released to the scientific community for reasons unknown. Augustus Owsley Stanley III, probably the most renowned of all home chemists (famous for his LSD of the purest quality at the height of LSD use), decided to try his hand at it. It debuted in the hippie community of Haight Ashbury at the Summer of Love solstice celebration in 1967, and as a result, the emergency wards filled up with users fearing that their trips would be eternal; it was rumored that some tripped for three days. DOM earned a reputation as a megahallucinogen. In fact, it is 100 times as potent as mescaline, but only one-thirtieth as potent as LSD.

Low oral doses of DOM (2 mg) produce an amphetamine-like arousal with no euphoria or excitement, but with signs of sympathetic excitation. At low doses, animals show periods of stupor and catatonia and signs of hallucinations. Intoxicating doses (5 to 10 mg) produce an excitement similar to mescaline, with more marked euphoria. DOM has been passed off as mescaline on the street. High doses can produce motor dysfunctions and convulsions.

It has been claimed that if chlorpromazine is administered to inhibit a DOM trip, as is done with LSD, it only potentiates the effects. However, this has not been substantiated by animal studies, although chlorpromazine will block the low dose sympathomimetic signs.

SEROTONERGIC HALLUCINOGENS: LSD

> *. . . this is not half as good as the peaceful ecstasy of simple Samadhi trance. . . .*
>
> Jack Kerouac (after his first trip)

> *We were just insane. We were out of our heads.*
>
> John Lennon (after his first trip, having been slipped LSD in a drink unaware)

> *I have never recovered from that shattering ontological confrontation. I have never been able to take myself, my mind, and the social world around me seriously.*
>
> Timothy Leary (reflecting on his first trip)

> *No good, no* bueno.
>
> William S. Burroughs (after his first trip)

LSD (lysergic acid diethylamide) is the most well-known of the 5-HT hallucinogens, a class of agents that also includes psilocybin, psilocin, DMT, bufotenine, and conceivably the MAO inhibitor harmaline. These drugs are credited with producing experiences of tremendous sensory, emotional, and psychological impact, without the behavioral excitement of mania or the psychosis of amphetamine.

LSD was not synthesized until 1938, and the first human LSD trip did not occur until March 19, 1943, which some consider the birth of the psychedelic era and the first significant use of hallucinogens in modern Western culture. Yet arguments can be made for a much earlier history. LSD belongs to a class of agents called *ergot alkaloids*. These are derived from ergot (*Claviceps purpurea*), a poisonous fungus that infects rye and other grains and wild grasses in Europe and America. The fungus yields the parent compound lysergic acid, which has many derivatives. In the form of moldy grain, then, a toxic version of LSD was available to our ancestors.

In Greece, the Mysteries of Demeter, the goddess of grain, were celebrated once each fall and involved *kykeon*, a drink of ultimate illumination made of pennyroyal mint and water sprinkled with purple grass rust (*Claviceps paspali*). The ethnobotanist Wasson calculates this to be about one-twentieth as potent as LSD and sufficient for a 4hour trip (Latimer & Goldberg, 1981, p. 24). Plato, Aristotle, and Socrates were all veterans of this ritual.

Historically, most occurrences of ergot ingestion were among populations who unwittingly ate infected rye or other grains and suffered accidental toxic outbreaks of a condition called ergotism. This condition may have affected grazing animals as far back as the Mesozoic Era 250 million years ago, but more recent outbreaks are recognizable in chronicles of the Middle Ages. In medieval Europe, moldy grain was usually destroyed, but in times of famine it was retained to make bread. During one episode in 944 C.E., 40,000 deaths were said to have occurred. For a long time, the connection between such unheralded episodes and ergotism remained obscure.

Ergotism occurs in two forms. The *gangrenous* type is marked by vasoconstriction due to a direct action on blood vessels, and continued exposure leads to circulatory damage. The consequence is reduced blood flow at first, then complete stoppage; the tissues of the extremities die, and the affected parts fall away. *Convulsive* ergotism is the second form. It has symptoms of tingly fingers, crawling sensations in the skin, vertigo, ringing in the ears, insomnia, vomiting, diarrhea, and headaches, and is accompanied by disturbances of sensation, disordered thinking, and hallucinations. Muscle spasms lead to powerful contractions and convulsions. Involuntary muscle fibers also are stimulated. Delirium, psychosis, mania and depression may appear.

The medieval sufferers of ergotism may have experienced hallucinations or feverish deliriums of flames and devils, which led to the name *ignis sacer* ("holy fire"). The condition was also called *St. Anthony's Fire*, perhaps because the shrine of St. Anthony was near the hospital that treated the disease, or because it was the monks of the Order of St. Anthony who cared for the afflicted. Ironically, the pilgrimage to the shrine and the accompanying change of diet may well have worked many cures that appeared to be supernatural.

Some argue that the Salem witchcraft records of the seventeenth century reflect the behavioral symptoms of convulsive ergotism, but this remains a matter of debate. Any evidence of psychedelic hallucinations is absent from the reports, and these would presumably be distinctive enough to be recognized, if ergotism were the case. The last great ergotism epidemic was recorded in Russia from 1926 to 1927.

Ergot is of pharmacological interest because it can be used to precipitate birth by inducing labor contractions. The first recorded use of this sort appears in a Frankfurt herbal of 1582. Ergot entered academic medicine in 1808, but it was recognized as dangerous because of its ability to cause uterine spasms. Therefore, it was confined to the treatment of bleeding after birth, since it also stops blood flow. The modern history of LSD began when the common nucleus of the ergot alkaloids—lysergic acid—was isolated by Jacobs and Craig in the 1930s, and W. A. Stoll of Sandoz Laboratories obtained the first ergot alkaloid in pure form (ergotamine), which opened the door for wider therapeutic use.

Several years later, when other labs discovered a new, water-soluble ergot alkaloid and threatened Sandoz's commercial lead in the ergot market, Albert Hofmann, who worked in the same lab as Stoll at Sandoz, decided to return to alkaloid chemistry. The ergot field was an uncharted realm of research and an exciting prospect for Hofmann. During his intense involvement in it, he made Methergine, a leading drug that gives muscle tone to the uterus, stops bleeding, and stabilizes the blood flow during birthing. Hofmann continued to synthesize other lysergic acid compounds that promised interesting pharmacological properties. In 1938, he synthesized number 25 in the series of new molecules (see Figure 25.2). Hofmann was hoping for an analeptic, a circulatory and respiratory stimulant like nicotinic acid diethylamide. What he got instead was a revelation.

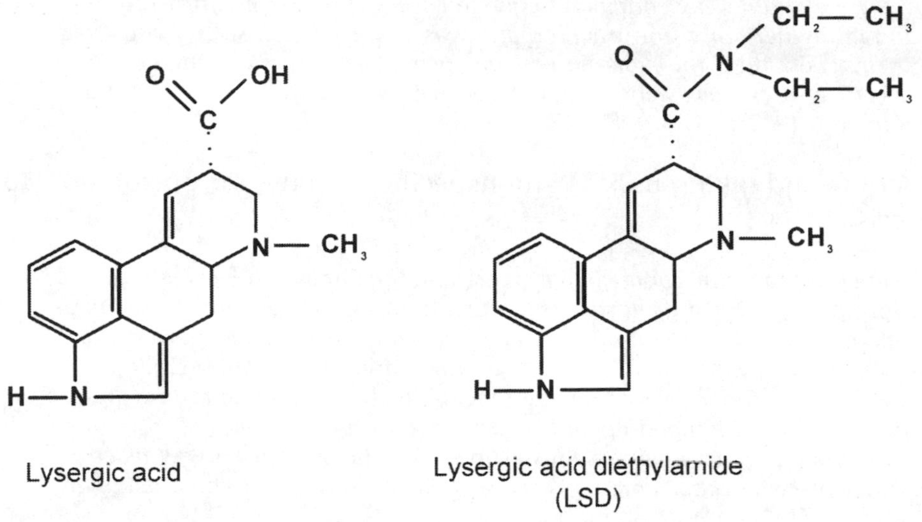

FIGURE 25.2 Molecular structures of lysergic acid and its derivative LSD.

LSD_{25} showed a strong uterine effect, and animals became stuporous, but restless. In general, there seemed to be nothing of special interest, so tests were discontinued, and Hofmann went on with his ergot research. But he claims that LSD_{25} stayed on his mind; he felt it might have promise still. So, five years later, in 1943, he decided to make a new batch and send it back to be retested. This was an unusual breach of protocol, since LSD_{25} had previously been stricken from the list. It was during the preparation of this batch, on March 16, 1943, that Hofmann was first affected

> *by a remarkable restlessness, combined with a slight dizziness. At home I lay down and sank into a not unpleasant intoxicated-like condition characterized by an extremely stimulated imagination. In a dreamlike state, with eyes closed . . . . I perceived an uninterrupted stream of fantastic pictures, extraordinary shapes with intense, kaleidoscopic play of colors. After some two hours this condition faded away. (Hofmann, 1983, p. 15)*

Hofmann had been working with LSD tartrate and had been taking meticulous precautions against toxicity, but he surmised that he must have absorbed the minutest amount through his fingertips. That seemed hardly possible, since no drug was of such a potency. But in light of his remarkable experience, he decided to self-experiment.

Hofmann administered 0.25 mg (250 micrograms) of LSD tartrate to himself on April 19, 1943. This dose, reasoned Hofmann, was the minimum that would produce an effect, based on his current knowledge of the ergot alkaloids. What he could not anticipate was that LSD, effective at 0.03 mg to 0.05 mg, was different from anything that he, in all his years of alkaloid chemistry, had encountered. Hofmann had given himself a massive "hit," quintuple or more the usual street tripper's dose.

First, Hofmann ascertained that LSD was indeed the cause of the disturbance of the previous Friday. But soon the distortions threatened to become so intense that he had his lab assistant escort him home by bicycle.

> *On the way home, my condition began to assume threatening forms. Everything in my field of vision wavered and was distorted as if seen in a curved mirror. I also had the sensation of being unable to move from the spot. Nevertheless, my assistant later told me that we had traveled very rapidly. (Hofmann, 1983, p. 17)*

Arriving home and taking milk as a nonspecific antidote for poisoning, Hofmann entered a dark crisis:

> *. . . Everything in the room spun around, and the familiar objects and pieces of furniture assumed grotesque, threatening forms. They were in continual motion. . . . every exertion of my will, every attempt to put an end to the disintegration of the outer world and the dissolution of my ego, seemed to be wasted effort. A demon had invaded me, had taken possession of my body, mind, and soul. I jumped up and screamed, trying to free myself from him, but then sank down again and lay helpless on the sofa. . . . I was taken to another place, another time. . . . at times I believed myself to be outside my body. . . . (Hofmann, 1983, pp. 17-18)*

A doctor had been called, but by the time he arrived, the worst had passed, and he found no cause to prescribe medication. Hofmann then entered a more beneficent phase and began to enjoy the visual phenomena.

> *Kaleidoscopic, fantastic images surged in on me, alternating, variegated, opening and then closing themselves in circles and spirals, exploding in colored fountains, rearranging and hydbridizing themselves in constant flux. It was particularly remarkable how every acoustic perception, such as the sound of a door handle or a passing automobile, became transformed into optical perceptions. Every sound generated a vividly changing image, with its own consistent form and color. (Hofmann, 1983, pp. 18-19)*

By late evening, the "breakdown" was ending. Exhausted, Hofmann slept, to awaken tired but clearheaded, with a sensation of wellbeing and renewed life. "The world was as if newly created. All my senses vibrated in a condition of highest sensitivity, which persisted for the entire day," wrote Hofmann. He was intrigued by the potency and spectacular effects of the new drug. Despite such a strong intoxication, there was no hangover, and he could lucidly recall every detail of the hallucinatory experience. These were unusual effects for known hallucinogens.

With such interesting psychic effects entering the picture, LSD passed back into further investigation with animals at Sandoz. Mostly pharmacological properties were established, since cognitive effects were impossible to detail from animal studies. The first scientific report about LSD appeared in Zurich in 1947, and two years later the first human studies in North America began.

In the 1950s, LSD came to the United States in two guises. First, Sandoz Laboratories was supplying independent investigators who wished to experiment with the drug. Notable among these was Dr. Humphrey Osmond. He was a British psychiatrist working in Canada, studying psychosis and mental illness, and was the first to draw attention to the similarity between mescaline and adrenaline, implying that schizophrenia could be caused by the result of the body's ability to produce its own hallucinogens through some metabolic abnormality. Investigating LSD as a producer of a model psychosis, Osmond noted ecstatic experiences among his subjects.

It was through Osmond's work that Aldous Huxley came to first take mescaline in 1953, which he did under Osmond's supervision. Huxley recorded his experience in his famous essay *The Doors of Perception*. In a correspondence with Huxley several years later, Osmond coined the term *psychedelic* and subsequently proposed it to the New York Academy of Sciences. By the time Sandoz applied to the FDA (1953) for investigational new drug status, rumors were already out about the perceptual fireworks produced by lysergic acid, and the international media were beginning to respond with articles like "My Twelve Hours as a Madman," run in *MacClean's Canada National Magazine* in 1954.

Meanwhile, below boards, LSD was being tested as a potential incapacitating agent by the Army Chemical Corps and was studied and used by the CIA as an aid to interrogation or a truth drug. It was the Army scientists who coined the term *trip* to describe the period of intoxication. Eventually, LSD was found to be too disorienting and unpredictable in interrogation (even for friendly agents to incapacitate themselves with if captured), and the Army abandoned it in the early sixties in favor of more potent hallucinogens, like BZ (quiniclidinyl benzilate), which has a 3day duration of effects and a 6week aftermath of disorientation and hallucinations.

The FDA, CIA, and independent researchers were intricately intertwined in the fifties. The CIA helped fund research at the same time that it was monitoring orders through the FDA and following research projects in hopes of discovering uses for the drug.

The real kickoff year for LSD in the United States was 1960. This was the year that Timothy Leary first discovered psychedelics by tripping on magic mushrooms (which contain the 5-HT hallucinogen psilocybin) in Mexico; he was to become the popular spearhead of the movement on the East Coast and the key figure identified with LSD. In that year, also, Ken Kesey volunteered to be dosed with LSD in medical experiments; he was the symbolic figurehead of the West Coast movement. The year before, Allen Ginsberg, too, had first experienced a somewhat paranoid LSD trip at the Mental Research Institute in Palo Alto.

Timothy Leary was first involved with psilocybin before LSD. A promising clinical psychologist, he had not long been a lecturer at Harvard when he had his first psychedelic experience in Mexico. He carried his experience back to the university, where he and another professor, Dr. Richard Alpert, began to use psilocybin mushroom pills in legitimate experiments to study the effects of set and preparation on users, who were chosen from among convicts, theologians, clergy, and artists. In his famous Good Friday experiment, Leary gave psilocybin to ten theology students at a Good Friday service, and nine reported an intense religious experience. This precipitated a debate about mystical experience and whether drug states constitute false mysticism.

From Leary, psychedelics (via Allen Ginsberg) made their way to the New York jazz scene and to the Beats, the countercultural movement of the preceding generation. There are also indications that psychedelics made their way to Washington through friends of Leary. The CIA was well aware of Leary almost from the beginning, and was concerned, since in its view psychedelics were a potential weapon and nothing but a danger. When Leary published in the *Journal of Atomic Scientists* a suggestion that because Russians could dose the water supplies with LSD, the government should do so itself to prepare the public, the CIA was alarmed.

Soon, the heat was on Leary--from the government, from his peers, and from the University administration, who connected his experiments with the illicit campus drug supply. The upshot was that he had to surrender his experimental drugs and was subsequently dismissed (May 1963). Alpert soon followed, dismissed for violating an agreement not to administer LSD to students. Leary's and Alpert's advocacy of LSD by this point was far more freeform, provocative, and messianic than sober scientific investigations allowed.

By that time, psychedelics and Leary's situation were high profile in the public eye. Furthermore, soon after the turn of the decade, bestselling books like *Exploring Inner Space* by Jane Dunlap and *My Self and I* by Constance A. Newland were on the U.S. market. Such claims as Newland's, that her experiences under LSD cured her of frigidity, heralded the wave that was about to hit. In 1963, the Sandoz production patents expired, which removed the hindrances from manufacture by others, and LSD began to appear on the streets, still legal.

In the summer of 1963, Leary and Alpert founded the IFIF (International Foundation for Internal Freedom) in Mexico and soon relocated with thirty members to the estate of William Hitchcock in Millbrook, New York, a scene which has been described as "Psychedelic Central for the whole East Coast" (Lee & Shlain, 1985, p. 102). The enterprise had an intellectual bent to it, emphasizing controlled sets and settings and using texts like *The Tibetan Book of the Dead* as guides to achieving spiritual goals with the drug.

If there was a "Psychedelic Central" for the West Coast, it was Ken Kesey's place at La Honda, California. In 1960, Kesey, a graduate creative writing student at Stanford, participated in a study of hallucinogenic drugs to make some money. A few weeks later he found himself a job as a night attendant on the psychiatric ward. Soon, drugs were circulating among his friends. Out of these experiences, Kesey authored *One Flew Over the Cuckoo's Nest.*

In the years from 1964 to 1966, publicity about LSD peaked, both good and bad. Hofmann calls them years of "veritable hysteria" and laments the rash of uncontrolled self-experimentation that so frequently came to bad ends and had the social consequence of doing in his promising creation. The first surge of street acid hit the college scene in 1965, and the Haight Ashbury hippie and drug scene was forming. Psychedelic art was born from San Francisco music posters for the first great "happenings," or psychedelic gatherings.

By the next year, tensions about the psychedelics were high, and rumors, distortions, and misconceptions about LSD were rampant. Leary gave a notorious interview for *Playboy* magazine, expatiating on the special delights of sex on acid, which he claims gave the drug a huge popular boost. Bogus, peril-ridden, and adulterated substances were circulating. Soon this public circus surrounding LSD led Sandoz to recall the drug and withdraw its sponsorship. A Senate subcommittee was examining the case of psychedelics, and stricter regulations went into effect. Manufacture and sale of LSD was made a misdemeanor, and researchers without special exemptions had to relinquish their supplies.

Nonetheless, the cat was out of the bag, and use peaked during 1967 to1968. In January of 1967, forty thousand "acidheads" turned out for a Tribal Be-In in San Francisco's

Golden Gate Park. In reporting it, Herb Caen, a columnist for the *San Francisco Chronicle,* coined the term *hippie.* In the following months, a newspaper prediction that "100,000 will invade Haight Ashbury this summer" turned out to be a self-fulfilling prophecy; the rumor itself brought young people in from all over the country. That summer—the Summer of Love—the Monterey Pop Festival sparked the national acid rock era.

From 1968 on, use of LSD declined. Law enforcement, bad trips, bad street drugs, unstable users, polydrug problems, increased use of mescaline and peyote, and the exaggerated reports of possible chromosome damage all played a part. LSD was made a Schedule I drug, its possession a misdemeanor and its sale a felony. The freshness of the Haight Ashbury scene had been glutted by the influx of newcomers, and most of the original residents scattered to the country. Back east, Millbrook had closed due to police harassment, and Leary's psychedelic career went into retrograde when he was charged for narcotics violations and sentenced to San Luis Obispo minimum security prison.[2] By 1970, harder drugs were coming in, and the psychedelic culture was fading. It effectively came to an end by the mid-seventies.

Interestingly, LSD began to reappear in the 1980s due to the trial of Richard Kemp in Britain. Kemp had found a cheap and easy means to manufacture acid and had a large distributing organization in the United Kingdom. At his trial in 1977, Kemp was required to reveal his formula, which went on the public records and became accessible to anyone who cared to seek it out. Epidemiological surveys show an increase in LSD use in the early 1990s, and an increase of hallucinogen use in general (Gold, 1994). Like MDMA, LSD has become a part of the rave scene. The 1990s dose of LSD appears to be lower than that of the 1960s--20 to 80 micrograms as opposed to 100 to 200 micrograms; this may make it seem more appealing and safer to young users (Gold, 1994).

Pharmacokinetics

Although some researchers injected it, LSD (Delysid) leaves the bloodstream so rapidly that injection is unnecessary. It is usually taken orally as an odorless, colorless, tasteless solution. GI absorption is easy and complete, and distribution is rapid and efficient, with the drug easily crossing the placental and blood-brain barriers. Peak concentration occurs in body organs 10 to 15 minutes after injection, except for the small intestines, which take 2 hours. Contrary to what one would expect, the largest amount of LSD concentrates in the liver, the site of metabolism, and the lowest concentration is in the brain. Within the brain, the pattern of distribution shows the highest levels in the visual areas (especially the lateral geniculate body), in parts of the limbic system (emotional centers), and in areas of the reticular formation. That is to be expected, judging from the effects.

The metabolism of LSD is rapid, with blood levels halving every 3 hours. Biotransformation takes place in the liver, and 80 percent of the drug is excreted through the intestines and bile, with 1 percent to 10 percent passing unchanged. The half-life is 3 hours, and a whole dose is fully gone in a day. The effective dose of LSD is miniscule, about 50 micrograms. It shows an onset of action in 30 to 90 minutes and a duration of effect (a trip) of 5 to 12 hours.

Given the rapidity of its metabolism in contrast with its slow onset (2 hours), and given the long duration of its effect, it seems likely that LSD produces its action by imbalancing a natural system--for example, by blocking 5-HT at the synapse, which is followed by a rebound of serotonergic overactivity or receptor hypersensitivity. The exact mechanism, however, is not clear.

LSD is not very lethal in humans. Although the LD in humans is not known, if we compare it proportionally to the ED and LD in rabbits, we could estimate it would take a 300- to 600-fold overdose to kill a person. In monkeys, the LD 100 is 5 mg/kg, an enormous dose. The potency is so high, however, that even a 600-fold overdose does not amount to much of the drug. The effective dose for psychedelic effects in humans is 0.03 to 0.05 mg, and is about the size of the period at the end of this sentence. To aid in handling, street distributors usually dissolve LSD into a sugar cube or soak it into small bits of absorbent paper (called *blotter* in this form). Only the tiniest amount penetrates to the brain, but that is enough.

Tolerance to LSD develops rapidly in daily users, with consistent doses becoming ineffective in 3 to 4 days, but upon cessation, tolerance drops quickly. Doses at weekly intervals remain effective. Cross-tolerances develop with mescaline and psilocybin. The effects of all three of these drugs can be reversed with chlorpromazine; fifty milligrams IM rapidly reverses negative LSD effects.

No physical dependence or addiction has been demonstrated for LSD, nor for any other hallucinogen.

Pharmacological Effects

Three pharmacological actions of LSD are of interest, although their relation to the behavioral effects is not yet clear (Aghajanian, 1994). LSD shows a potent inhibitory effect on the $5\text{-}HT_{1A}$ subtype of serotonin receptor, a large concentration of which is found in the raphé nucleus of the brainstem. LSD shares this affinity with DMT and psilocybin, but not with mescaline. This action is probably not the basis of the hallucinogenic effects, since buspirone also inhibits these neurons, but it is not a hallucinogen. A second action of LSD is an affinity for $5\text{-}HT_2$ receptors, which it does share with mescaline. Many $5\text{-}HT_2$ receptors are found in the cerebral cortex; they are implicated in perceptual and cognitive functions and in the neurochemistry of schizophrenia--the same receptors that are blocked by the atypical antipsychotics clozapine and risperidone. This might be the basis of some of the profound perceptual and cognitive distortions produced by LSD, and it is interesting in light of the resemblance of some LSD effects to psychosis. In fact, it is reasonable to expect that clozapine and risperidone may be useful in blocking some effects of LSD, and might serve as treatments for LSD intoxication or for bad reactions.

A third action of LSD is activation of the NE neurons of the locus coeruleus through $5\text{-}HT_2$ modulations. The locus coeruleus consists of a dense concentration of NE neurons that receive an extraordinary amount of sensory input from all regions of the body and relay it to other parts of the brain. It is believed to serve as a detector of changes in both the body and the environment. Animal studies show that LSD enhances the responsiveness of the locus coeruleus to stimuli. Paradoxically, at the same time it decreases spontaneous motor activity in rats (Aghajanian, 1994). The behavioral effects that might proceed from these actions are not clear.

It should be noted that the types of hallucinations seen with LSD intoxication are not unique to this drug. There are many states in which LSD-like hallucinations can be evoked, among them twilight states between sleeping and waking, insulin hypoglycemia, fever delirium, epilepsy, psychosis, advanced syphilis, sensory deprivation, extreme hunger or thirst, sensory bombardment, electrical stimulation, crystal gazing, dizziness, and migraine headaches. Similar hallucinations have been produced by long slow distance running , along with dizziness, dissociation and stupor (Morgan, 1978). The relationships between these states and LSD mechanisms remain to be clarified.

Some perceptual changes may come from the fact that LSD increases the size of the sensory signals delivered to the cortex, although it does not act directly on sensory pathways, except for the brain's visual systems. These alterations possibly come from the sensitizing of the sensory collaterals that activate the reticular formation, which in turn modulate the sensory input in the cortex. The EEG shows arousal.

Tripping

LSD inebriation (as Hofmann calls it), apparently inevitable once the drug has been taken, occurs over a span of 6 to 12 hours and involves a sequence of changes. This was soon dubbed a *trip*, since subjects seemed to journey through a progression of mental and emotional experiences. Each LSD trip is unique, even for one person. In addition, set and setting can exert strong influences on the character of the trip: such factors as previous experience with psychedelics, attitudes toward illicit drugs, the motivations for use, and the people present during intoxication. Nevertheless, cutting across all the variations, investigators have found certain basic patterns and motifs.

To begin with, a latency period follows administration, with onset occurring in about 2 hours.

When effects do appear, the first are usually subtle autonomic signs arising from stimulations of the sympathetic nerve centers. These include slightly raised body temperature, dilated pupils, a slight increase in heart rate and blood pressure, increased sugar levels and increased salivation. Somatic changes may include sweating and chills, tremors, blurred vision, weakness, dizziness, and sometimes numbing, goose bumps with creeping or tingly skin, headaches, nausea, and vomiting. In general, none of the physiological effects are severe, another reason that LSD did not attract attention during animal tests. Only later tests and more careful observations led researchers to infer the induction of hallucinations in higher mammals like dogs, cats and chimpanzees (Hofmann, 1983, p. 24). In spiders, low doses caused the building of more well-proportioned webs, but at high doses, the webs were rudimentary and disorganized.

After about 20 minutes, autonomic signs wane, and over the next 30 or 40 minutes, they are superseded by alterations of sensation, perception, and mood. In the first phase of perceptual alterations, the subject may experience mood changes, abnormal body sensations, a decrease in sensory impressions, abnormal color perception, space and time disorders, and visual hallucinations. Some of the visual effects reported are objects seeming to become luminescent, to assume auras, to leave trails as they move, or to vibrate with emphatic reality. Colors may be synaesthetically heard, and sounds may be experienced as lights and forms.

Scientific investigations of LSD hallucinations reveal an early phase involving the types of simple form constants discussed in Klüver's mescaline experiments. Siegel and Jarvik (1975) found that hallucinations in the first phase appeared like a movie or slide show projected in front of the eyes and involved many geometric forms. There was typically a bright light in the center of the visual field obscuring the details there, but permitting peripheral imagery to be seen, the whole creating a tunnel-like perspective. The forms tended to pulsate and move toward or away from the central illumination, interacting with great rapidity. All colors were reported, but red increased in proportion to the dose.

Siegel notes that the hallucinatory episodes would begin with black-and-white forms moving randomly, then taking on blue hues, pulsating and organizing themselves. There would follow an increase of lattice, tunnel, and kaleidoscopic forms (the point Hofmann probably hit on April 19 in the midst of his bicycle trip home). From 90 to 120 minutes into the trip, the lattice tunnels would shift to red, orange, and yellow coloration, and explosive and rotational patterns would begin to develop.

Well after the lattice-tunnel shift comes a second phase of hallucinations involving complex imagery. This second phase is seen by users as the most significant part of the trip, with its awe-inspiring release of personal material, ego disruptions, and apocalyptic emotional changes.

Typical forms included small animals, human figures (caricaturish but often friendly), cartoonish objects, and religious symbols and images. These figures begin in the periphery and may seem to be overlaid on a background of active geometric shapes. Recognizable scenarios and childhood scenes with strong emotional content were common, but were often embellished into fantastic aerial or submarine perspectives. A likely theory is that these phenomena represent the spontaneous release of stored memories.

At the peak of the experience, subjects pass from pseudohallucinations to true ones, themselves becoming part of the imagery and losing their critical perception of its unreality. To the subject, the "dream" becomes real. A tremendous rapidity of imagery can occur, transmuting in fantastic combinations at a rate of ten images a second—beyond any ability to report what is happening. Subjects may seem to become separated from their bodies and see themselves from outside.

Far from being objectively observed by a detached hallucinator, the imagery of a trip is accompanied by profound, spontaneous, emotional changes that may vary from horror and panic to beatific transcendences and an oceanic sense of merging with the cosmos. Ideas that occur in this state may seem invested with an importance that defies utterance. Mood changes may be large and rapid, and thinking is difficult. Major ego disruptions, if they occur, come near the end of the second hour (Krippner, 1970). These consist of a sense of loss of body, loss of self, loss of behavioral control, and depersonalization. One may have a sense of flying, of visiting other worlds or dimensions, of reliving ancestral memories and unlocking deep secrets, or of being hypomanically possessed of grandiose creative powers. In a bad trip, the reaction to this phase is negative, consisting of paranoid and persecuted feelings and reduced movements, and the user may end up huddling traumatized in a corner.

J. Houston (1969) has classified the types of alterations that LSD users experience into four categories or levels. First, sensory distortions can lead to a new understanding of basic experience. Second, recollective/analytical experiences can bring to a new perception of one's personality. Third, symbolic images can lead to new mythical and archetypal interpretations of experience, and, fourth, integral experiences resembling religious conversions can cause a renewed sense of unity with God, spirit, or universe.

In some cases, the tripper may have difficulty readjusting to normal reality afterwards, and experienced users allow a period of recuperation before any further experiments. Some users instinctively take time to assimilate what they have learned or experienced before proceeding.

In terms of dosage, there seems to be a threshold for tripping. Low doses of LSD produce only autonomic effects and some perceptual distortions, with no euphoria and no sense of displaced realities. There is a general range of 0.05 mg to 0.2 mg for 6 to 9 hours of psychedelia—hallucinations, mood changes, depersonalization, and the reliving of repressed memories. The depth and length of the trip is dose-related. A moderate dose, for example, might reach only to the first phase of geometric pseudohallucinations.

Clinical Applications

By the mid-seventies, LSD was officially recognized to be of little therapeutic use. The ergot alkaloids, however, are still used to induce birth labor and to treat migraine headaches, in which 5-HT plays a role.

In clinical studies in the 1950s, it was thought that LSD might be used to produce a model psychosis by imitating the mechanisms of schizophrenia. If so, it would have been a valuable research tool for the study of psychosis and the reversal of its symptoms by antipsychotic drugs. However, research soon showed LSD intoxication and genuine psychosis to be two different entities. For instance, the following differences have been enumerated (Lipton, 1970):

	Schizophrenia/Psychosis	LSD
1.	true hallucinations	pseudohallucinations
2.	primarily auditory	primarily visual
3.	threatening	sometimes pleasant
4.	seen with open eyes	best seen in dark
5.	characterized as disrupting, disorienting	sometimes an integrated, superorganized state of awareness
6.	subject resistant	subject suggestible
7.	subject withdrawn	subject will communicate, albeit poorly

In fact, amphetamine or PCP in high doses mimics psychosis better than LSD. A positive LSD state shows more resemblance to the early pre-psychotic stages of schizophrenia (Cohen, 1985, p. 291).

LSD was also employed in the treatment of alcoholics, but it was found not to be significantly better than *d*-amphetamine (Hollister, Shelton, & Krieger, 1969). Sometimes psychotherapists used it to provide insights in patients or to improve morale in terminal cancer cases. It seemed to have the effect of relieving pain, not through pharmacological analgesia, but probably through dissociation, ecstasy, or other mental effects.

Four models have been proposed (Smith & Seymour, 1985, p. 297) to represent the perceptions of LSD over its brief history. These are (1) as psychotomimetic, a drug to mimic psychosis, (2) as hallucinogenic, a drug to study the organization of perception, (3) as therapeutic, a healing drug, and (4) as psychedelic, a consciousness-expanding drug with positive cultural implications. However, not having emerged as clinically useful in any particular setting by the time it achieved notoriety, LSD was soon lost to consideration as a licit drug for any reason. A 1962 regulation requiring that the safety and efficacy of a new drug had to be *proven for the condition for which it was marketed* eliminated research that might have demonstrated therapeutic value. As one source later complained, "Meaningful research at the clinical level has been blocked by a governmentally sanctioned and legally enforced climate of fear" (Smith & Seymour, 1985, p. 303).

Side Effects

As psychoactive drugs go, especially ones with effects as dramatic as these, LSD is comparatively safe. It is not addictive, and no human deaths proceeding from pharmacological effects are on record. When deaths have occurred, they have been either from psychological repercussions or the actions of adulterated compounds. The human LD is unknown. The LD50s in other species fluctuate widely; mice log in at 50 mg/kg to 60 mg/kg (IV) and rabbits at 0.3 mg/kg, with death following from respiratory arrest.

In addition, current research has shown infrequent complications and no clear, demonstrable danger to physical health. Several studies and reports that emerged during the sixties became highly politicized and were often exaggerated. For example, some well-publicized findings showed a higher incidence of chromosome damage to the white blood cells of users. But it was deemphasized that the experience did not directly concern reproductive cells. Findings with actual reproductive cells were ambivalent, and many other reports showed nothing. Furthermore, other substances and conditions break chromosomes, among them X-rays, caffeine, aspirin, and fevers. Since then, larger studies have shown no connection between chromosome anomalies and LSD (Hofmann, 1983).

Fetal deformities were another issue, since studies showed that high doses given to mice during gestation led to increased stillbirths and deformities. Again, no such connection has been corroborated. Even harmless substances at such dosages are problematic, and the human data on LSD and pregnancy are not clear. Nonetheless, LSD should be avoided during pregnancy because it crosses the placenta easily, and the incidence of fetal abnormalities in the children of mothers who use LSD has proven to be higher than for the population at large. No causes can be assigned, and no miscarriages or deformities have been reasonably attributed to LSD.

In addition, there are no cases on record of permanent brain damage due directly to use of the drug. During the government's campaign against LSD in the 1960s, the Army Chemical Corps ran tests to duplicate findings on damaging side effects, but was unable to report any success (Lee & Shlain, 1985, p. 32). In regard to the politicizing of LSD effects and side effects, one is tempted to recall Timothy Leary's ironic remark: "These drugs apparently cause panic and temporary insanity in many officials who have not tried them."

What are the dangers of LSD then? Besides bad trips, which may be experienced by healthy users, four types of chronic reactions (Smith & Seymour, 1985, p. 299) have been well-documented, some of which may be serious enough to be lethal. These are prolonged psychotic reactions to tripping, life-threatening depression, exacerbations of existing mental illness, and flashbacks. A fifth reaction has also been observed (Smith &

Seymour, 1994), a persistent distortion of sensory perceptions (posthallucinogen perceptual disorder).

Bad Trips

A bad trip occurs when the psychedelia experienced during LSD intoxication take a dark turn, in which case the psychological impact of the trip is traumatizing, the imagery is phantasmagoric, and the insights are appalling rather than creative or ecstatic. This can occur in a healthy user, although the risk is higher for mentally unstable or marginally adjusted individuals. In certain cases, the bad trip can precipitate suicide, a prolonged psychotic reaction, or a permanent mental disorder. Generally, negative set and setting are the key contributing factors.

Bad trips most often occur in novice users, who may likewise experience distress from the strangeness of the perceptual distortions and feel out of control or trapped because of the inevitability of the trip once the drug has been taken. They may yearn to be rescued from the drug state and may try to flee. Such an unpleasant start can precipitate a 1 to 6hour nightmare. The subject may experience disturbing imagery leading to panic, paranoia, and suspicion. In other cases, there may be cognitive shifts and poor judgment, leading people to throw themselves from windows or walk out into the ocean. In earlier phases, the user may have a fear of the trip's being eternal, while in later phases, the user may forget the drug has been taken and become absorbed in the atrocious realities of the trip, where philosophical insights, ideas, and dark moods may be overwhelming.

In most cases, the seasoned staff at the Haight-Ashbury Free Medical Clinic in San Francisco (ground zero for America's drug problems of today and tomorrow) found that most patients could be talked down from a bad trip. The typical procedure is to put the subject in a quiet, lit place (since darkness spawns hallucinations), and to focus attention on a voice or visual stimulus. One should bolster the patient's confidence rather than analyze the psychological reasons for the loss of reality. It is not advisable to hamper the patients' movements; rather, one should let them sit, stand, walk, or lie. One should not move quickly, and should speak in a relaxed, conversational tone. Some sleep, or tranquilizers or sedatives may help; usually 25 mg of chlordiazepoxide or 10 mg of diazepam are given. In the second stage (visual hallucinations) or third stage (insights) of intoxication, communication may be lost. If the patient is out of control and refuses tranquilizers, medication is recommended, usually 2 mg to 4 mg of intravenous haloperidol, and the patient may be hospitalized. But treatment with major tranquilizers may not be successful if the LSD was a street dose mixed with other agents.

Bad trips have been reported with other psychedelics besides LSD, such as mescaline.

Psychotic Reaction

A severe bad trip can lead to a prolonged psychotic reaction that requires hospitalization. It is apparent, however, that in the majority of cases, these proceed either from mental instability in the user or from adverse circumstances in the use of the drug. Contributing factors that have been recognized are: preexisting character structure, insecurity, negative experiences (panic), mood and stress level, insufficient preparation, negative set or setting, high doses of the drug, frequent use, and reentry problems (depression) attending return to normal reality. The most high-risk types are unstable, immature, or rigid personalities; paranoid, depressed, or schizoid persons; and the relatives of schizophrenics. Chronic users, too, may show serious long-term personality disruptions, especially if they are already pre-psychotic or psychotic personalities. Of course, healthy, prepared, well-adjusted users, therefore stand a much better chance of avoiding unpleasantness. In laboratory settings, one study using 5,000 subjects and 25,000 trials of use logged only 1 per 1,000 adverse reactions of 24 hours or longer duration, and the sample included emotionally ill patients (Cohen, 1985). Another study showed 0.8 per 1000 reactions of 48 hours or longer duration, and 1.8 per 1000 in mental patients (Smith & Seymour, 1985, p. 298). These findings justify Albert Hofmann in his disappointment that LSD has been anathematized because of irresponsible use.

Psychotic reactions to LSD have been seen to mimic forms of schizophrenia (catatonic, undifferentiated, and schizoaffective). The most frequent long-lasting adverse reaction is a schizophrenia-like paranoid response, but most problem cases recuperate in a week with tranquilizers and supportive psychotherapy. Manic depressive episodes and dissociative reactions have occurred, as well as hallucinosis (visual hallucinations with no thought disorder). A psychotic reaction may also develop from flashbacks.

Finally, problems may develop from the inadvertent use of LSD. Stable people who are slipped doses of the drug can remain permanently disorganized, presumably because they think they are genuinely disordered and begin the trip in panic, with no assurance of its impermanence. In some cases, the released psychological material—otherwise of potential use—has a powerful negative valence that leads to panic or psychosis, and the extremity of fear obliterates its value and makes impossible any kind of rational assimilation.

Flashbacks

A flashback is the spontaneous recurrence of a trip after a period of normalcy. Occurrences of flashes of varying frequency and duration may take place over a period of weeks or months after drug use. They are more common after multiple ingestions of LSD. For example, in the following case, a 29-year-old graduate student had taken two 700-microgram doses 45 minutes apart.

> *For a week following ingestion, I was in a state of digesting what I had experienced. Then, on the night of the full moon, I reexperienced many of the visuals and feelings I had encountered on the acid trip. These kept me awake throughout the night and left me exhausted and somewhat shaken in the morning. For a period of months thereafter, I experienced a variety of what appeared to be spontaneous psychedelic happenings. . . . These included shifts in color and form perception; slides appearing to be movies with bodies of water and people in motion; buildings leaning inward as though I looked down streets through a fisheye lens. Every evening at twilight, the walls of my cottage moved in and out as though the room were breathing. Most trying, however, were nights of the full moon. I seemed to slip back into the acid trip at the height of its intensity. (Smith & Seymour, 1985, p. 300)*

This person soon learned to accept these episodes without fear, until they gradually abated, which is typically the case if LSD is discontinued.

The mechanism of flashbacks is unknown. Theories have been proposed linking them to psychological processes and to physiological ones (such as the belated release of some drug residue). Frequent users have reported lightbursts and the prolongation of afterimages in peripheral vision for days or weeks after a trip. Flashbacks are not intrinsically pathological: some consider them surprise little bonus trips; it is a matter of one's outlook. They also have been known to occur following marijuana use (Smith & Seymour, 1985), and similar states have been described in the absence of any psychedelic drug use. Alcohol intoxication, marijuana, barbiturates, and antihistamines may similarly precipitate LSD-like flashbacks.

Post-hallucinogen Perceptual Disorder

This disorder has been noted in long-term studies of adverse psychedelic drug reactions. It is an infrequent condition consisting of chronic and disturbing changes in perception. Individuals have reported a sense of dissociation "like living in a bubble under water," and trails of light and images that follow the movement of their hands. Some have described a discoloration of the visual field, like a "purple haze" (Smith & Seymour, 1994). Sufferers often feel they have become permanently brain-damaged, and so may display symptoms of anxiety, depression, or a phobic reaction similar to agoraphobia. The disorder has appeared in those without any previous psychiatric history, and also after a single dose (Smith & Seymour, 1994).

In summary, as far as toxicity and deleterious effects on individuals and societies go, there are other substances with more caveats than LSD. But there are three things for potential users to remember: it is illegal, it is frequently mixed or treated with agents (like strychnine) that justify the utmost caution, and it can bring a budding mental disorder into full blossom.

PSILOCYBIN AND PSILOCIN

With LSD, Hofmann's career as father of the modern hallucinogens had only begun. Records of the existence of "magic mushrooms" in the New World first appeared in chronicles of the early Spanish writers after Cortes (1529-1590). They were used ceremonially to obtain visions of one's future. In El Salvador, Guatemala, and environs, archaeological evidence in the form of 30-centimeter-high carvings of pileate mushrooms with godlike or animal-like figures at the base may be connected with magic mushrooms, indicating magical, medicinal, and religious ceremonial use dating back to at least 500 B.C.E., and possibly much earlier. The mushrooms were called *teonanacatl* ("god's flesh") in the Aztec. Their existence remained so in doubt, however, that in 1915 Saffold argued against it, claiming that the mushrooms were really a misreading of mescaline. Around 1936 to 1938, Weitlander and Schultes verified the ceremonial use of the mushrooms. It was not until 1953 that investigators Valentina Pavlovna Wasson and her husband R. Gordon Wasson were able to gain the confidence of the cultists and use and study the mushrooms in detail (Wasson, 1957). The Wassons reported that the cult of the teonanacatl in Mexico is heavily interlaced with Christian motifs, the mushrooms being said to grow where a drop of Christ's blood has fallen to earth. One early Spanish writer reported its being administered as the bread of the Eucharist. Usually the ceremony takes the form of a consultation, a petitioner seeking advice from a soothsayer. Bad experiences are guarded against by an insistence on the petitioner's being ceremonially "clean," which involves a period of celibacy and other requirements before ingesting the drug; nonobservance is believed to lead to death or madness.

To help them, the Wassons enlisted mycologist Roger Heim from Paris, who found that the agents in question were gilled mushrooms from the family *Strophariaceae,* of a dozen to fifteen species, mostly of the genus *Psilocybe,* which are found in Central America and in the southwestern United States. Heim (in 1957) sent samples for chemical analysis to Paris and the United States, but when the Paris research turned up fallow, Hofmann's aid was sought. Heim sent him 100 grams of *Psilocybe mexicana,* which was especially suited for laboratory cultivation, and which became "the magic mushroom" as far as the West was concerned.

Hofmann was unable to determine a hallucinogenic principle from animal studies, so he swallowed an average dose of the mushrooms (2.4 grams or 32 specimens), which he estimated from the Wassons' reports. Thirty minutes later, "everything assumed a Mexican character," which Hofmann found impossible to dismiss. At 90 minutes, says Hofmann, "the rush of interior pictures, mostly abstract motifs rapidly changing in shape and color, reached such an alarming degree that I feared that I would be torn into this whirlpool of form and color and would dissolve." The "dream" lasted 6 hours. "I felt my return to everyday reality to be a happy return from a strange, fantastic but quite real world to an old and familiar home" (Hofmann, 1983, p. 113).

Hofmann eventually isolated the active principle by having himself and volunteers from the lab sample tiny doses of the separations to see if they contained the hallucinogen. Finally, the next year, Hofmann reported the discovery of psilocybin and psilocin.

Psilocybin and psilocin are serotonin-like and LSD-like indole compounds. Psilocybin is the only phosphorus-bearing indole compound in nature, which means that the molecule is more stable. In metabolism, phosphoric acid is removed, and psilocybin is biotransformed into psilocin; the two agents are thus virtually identical. Like LSD, they block 5-HT activity, but they are considerably less active, with shorter effects. A mushroom trip lasts from 4 to 6 hours.

The amount of active ingredient varies from species to species of mushroom (in *P. mexicana,* 0.2 percent to 0.5 percent of psilocybin). Consequently, doses may vary from 2 to 40 mushrooms (for *P. cyanescens,* 2 to 5; for *P. semilanceata* [Liberty Caps] 10 to 40). Because of the lower potency, doses and effects are easier to control than with LSD.

The psychological effects of psilocybin are dose-related. Low doses (4 mg to 5 mg) yield a pleasant, relaxed experience with some body sensations. Fifteen milligrams can produce perceptual distortions of time and space. Higher doses cause perceptual and body image changes and possibly hallucinations. Depending on the dose, a sympathetic reaction may appear. CNS effects may come from the metabolism of psilocybin into psilocin, which is more lipid soluble and 1 to 1.5 times more potent (although in the mushroom it is found only in trace amounts in the mushroom).

In addition to Hofmann, the Wassons and others describe a "Mexicanization" of perception under the influence of magic mushrooms. At first, they attributed this to the setting or the user's expectations, but it has led to the interesting suspicion that the style of Aztec art may be derived from the perceptual distortions caused by the hallucinogen.

MORNING GLORY SEEDS

Ololiuqui is the Aztec name for the psychoactive seeds of a species of morning glory vine (*Rivea corymbosa*). In 1651, the Spanish chronicler Hernandez described Indian priests who ate of this plant to have fantastic visions, to obtain divinations, and to communicate with the gods. The use of ololiuqui in magic and medicine extends back to pre-Columbian times, and is still practiced by isolated tribes in Southern Mexico. Hernandez also mentioned *tlililtzin*, the seeds of *Ipomoea violaceae*, a different psychoactive species, found in all temperate zones. This is the blue morning glory of the gardens of Europe and the United States.

In 1959, Albert Hofmann undertook to isolate the active ingredients of *ololiuqui*, obtaining a small sample of seeds from R. Gordon Wasson in Mexico City. Hofmann began with the unlikely hypothesis that another indole compound was involved. To his disbelief, he found the guess correct. The active ingredients were lysergic acid amide, lysergic acid hydroxyethylamide, and related alkaloids. Lysergic acid amide, 10 to 20 times less potent than LSD, had only been known previously as a synthetic compound (LA111) produced by Hofmann and others in ergot alkaloid chemistry, yet here it was in nature. It was unusual, too, in that similar substances had only been known in primitive plant life such as fungi.

The hippies of the sixties were active and thorough researchers into all forms of psychedelic compounds. When they discovered that effective doses of an LSD-like hallucinogen were growing in their backyards, orders to seed companies boomed. Morning glory seeds proved to be inferior inebriants, however. They taste bad and are almost indigestible. They have less psychic clout than LSD and can cause a sense of mental emptiness, anxiety, and depression. The side effects that occur with other 5-HT psychedelics—nausea, vomiting, headaches, raised blood pressure, dilated pupils, and weariness—may be intense. In any case, nowadays, commercially sold seeds are coated to cause sickness and vomiting if you eat them.

BUFOTENINE

Bufotenine is another hallucinogenic indole compound. It is found in the skins and parotid glands of certain species of toads (such as *Bufo marinus*), in seeds of the tree *Piptadenia peregrina* (found in Haiti and Venezuela), and in miniscule amounts in the fly agaric mushroom. It is toxic, but prepared carefully, it may have hallucinogenic properties.

At Mayan sites, icons and the remains of bones of *Bufo marinus* leave a doubt whether the toads were consumed for their psychoactive properties or were stripped of skin and parotid glands to be eaten as food. In Europe, toad venom was prized for intrigue and warfare, and *Bufo marinus*, indigenous to the New World, quickly found a use there. The knowledge that the skins of some toads are psychoactive also provides a basis for thinking that witches included toads in their recipes for psychopharmacological reasons.

The toxicity of bufotenine alone casts doubts on its usefulness as a ritual hallucinogen. Timothy Knab, another student of Professor Schultes at Harvard, managed to get an old *curandero* in the mountains of southern Vera Cruz to allow him to sample a small bit of paste elaborately prepared from the toads. The old man himself wouldn't touch it. Knab reported an intoxication marked by sensations of fire and heat, convulsive muscle spasms, a headache, dreadful hallucinations, and delirium. For six hours he lay stricken (Davis, 1985, p. 131).

In a 1950s experiment with IV injections of bufotenine, subjects reported a prickling sensation at low doses, along with nausea and breathing difficulties. These increased at higher doses and purpled the lips and faces of the subjects from lack of oxygen. At even higher doses, their faces turned eggplant purple.

Bufotenine is definitely used hallucinogenically by the Indians of the upper Orinoco valley of Venezuela, who take it as an active ingredient in a form called *Cohoba snuff*, made from the pulverized seeds of the *Piptadenia peregrina* tree. Cohoba snuff contains other alkaloids as well, which we will discuss in the next section.

Other side effects reported with bufotenine (similar to the side effects of other serotonergic agents) include raised heart rate and blood pressure, blurry vision, increased muscle tone, motor deficits, staggering, muscular rigidity, and minor paralysis. All in all, it is rougher than many other hallucinogens, such as psilocybin and DMT.

DMT

DMT, or N,N-dimethyltryptamine, is another serotonin-like hallucinogen. It was synthesized in 1931 and found to be hallucinogenic in 1956. It is not widely used in the United States, but it is found in many genera of plants (*Acacia, Mimosa, Piptadenia, Virola*) and is used in many other locales.

DMT is a key active ingredient in a number of psychoactive snuffs of South America. It is seen often in this form because it cannot be absorbed orally; it must be injected or inhaled. Two fairly well-documented preparations are Virola snuff and Cohoba snuff.

Virola snuff, used by peoples of the northwest Amazon and the headwaters of the Orinoco, is known variously as *paricà, yakee, epena,* and *nyakwana*. It is prepared by boiling the blood-red resin out of the bark of several species of jungle trees (Virolas), and drying and powdering it. The resin contains several tryptamine alkaloids. The hallucinogenic snuff is used by shamans and medicine men to diagnose illness, and in some tribes of Brazil and Venezuela is used recreationally (Schultes, 1976, p. 76). Virola intoxication involves a period of excitability followed by a numbness of the limbs, twitching of the face, a lack of motor coordination, nasal discharges, nausea, and frequently vomiting. Macropsia, the apparent magnification of objects, has been noted.

Cohoba snuff, used by South American tribes of the Orinoco river basin, is also referred to as *paricà* in some locales, as well as *yopo*. It is derived from the seeds of the pods of *Piptadenia peregrina,* or *Anadenanthera peregrina,* a tree of the bean family. The snuff contains DMT and other tryptamine alkaloids, as well as bufotenine. Often the powder is mixed with an alkaline substance (ashes or the lime from snail shells). It is not clear whether this is to assist absorption, as it is in the case of similar material being chewed with coca leaves. The effects, almost immediate, involve muscle twitches, slight convulsions, and lack of motor coordination, followed by nausea, visual hallucinations, and a troubled sleep. Macropsia commonly occurs, as with Virola snuff.

In North America, DMT, taken in purer form and not as a plant product, is also inhaled. It is unusual in its rapid onset and the short duration of its trip. It was jokingly referred to in the sixties as *businessman's LSD* because it could theoretically be taken over a lunch hour. Thirty milligrams inhaled shows an onset of effects in 10 seconds, with full intoxication in 2 to 3 minutes, and the effects ending in about 10 minutes. Thirty milligrams injected shows pupil dilation, rapid heartbeat, and increased blood pressure within 5 minutes. Full intoxication occurs in 10 to 15 minutes. Subjects show difficulty in concentrating and expressing their thoughts, display euphoria, mirth, and behavioral excitement, and they hallucinate with eyes open or shut. In some cases, an opposite condition of paranoia, anxiety, and feelings of panic may appear. Most symptoms are gone in an hour, although some residual effects may carry over into the second hour. There is no evidence of psychological or physical dependence.

HARMALINE

Harmaline was isolated from plants in 1841 and first synthesized in 1927. Another anciently known hallucinogen, it occurs in a number of plants with psychoactive uses. In the Middle East, it is the principle alkaloid of Syrian rue (*Perganum harmala*), which is taken as an intoxicant. In South America, it is found in several species (especially *caapi* and *inebrians*) of the genus *Banisteriopsis*, which are used to make *ayahuasca*. *Ayahuasca* (known also by *yajé* and several other names) is a bitter, nauseating drink extracted from the bark of these two species of gigantic jungle lianas bearing tiny pink flowers. Although this is probably the most extensive form in which harmaline is taken, the chief active ingredient is harmine, a related compound. The natives of the western Amazon in Brazil, Colombia, Peru, Ecuador, and Bolivia use Cohoba snuff in puberty rituals, in the initiation of shamans, in cures, and in mythic ceremonies. High doses of *ayahuasca* produce a sense of reckless abandon and nightmarish visions and hallucinations. At regular doses, vividly colored hallucinations are seen. The drug does not impair consciousness or motor control, and dancing is often a feature of the rituals that involve it.

An effective dose of harmaline is 70 to 100 mg IV or 300 to 400 mg taken orally. After oral administration, onset comes in 1 hour, with a duration of action of 6 hours. First symptoms are unpleasant. Burning or prickling of the hands, feet, or face—followed by numbness—almost always occur with onset. There may also be a feeling of pressure in the head or chest, nausea, vomiting, dizziness, and general malaise. Because of general discomfort and anxiety, subjects usually withdraw into a dark, quiet place. Harmaline may induce hallucinations of geometric patterns and of vivid images manifesting in meaningful, dreamlike sequences.

An MAO enzyme inhibitor, harmaline may prolong and alter the effects of drugs like MDA, LSD, and mescaline, and it may do the same for other ingredients in *yajé* (like DMT).

Ibogaine

Ibogaine is the most prominent of about a dozen indole alkaloids found in the iboga plant (*Tabernanthe iboga*), a member of the dogbane family that grows in equatorial Africa. Its use has been documented among the Bwiti tribe, whose sorcerers claim to use it to speak with spirits and ancestors, and whose hunters use it to stay awake all night. Initiation into the tribe hinges on one's having a vision of the god plant Bwiti, which is achieved through iboga intoxication (Schultes, 1976, p. 54).

Scientific studies show that ibogaine, as well as being a hallucinogen, produces stimulation and anxiety in humans. In large doses, it is a strong central nervous system stimulant that can lead to convulsions, paralysis, and the arrest of respiration.

Until recently, ibogaine was a minor hallucinogen of passing interest. New discoveries, however, indicate that it may be useful in the treatment of opiate (heroin), stimulant (cocaine), and alcohol dependence. Animal studies show that ibogaine can disrupt some of the psychological or physiological aspects of addiction. Two effects are of particular interest (Sweetnam et al., 1995). Ibogaine can decrease the self-administration of morphine by animal subjects, and it can attenuate certain DA effects induced by morphine and cocaine. Findings like these raise the hope that ibogaine may block some of the reinforcing effects of addictive drugs, and may help withdrawal and recovery. At the time of this writing, however, all that is known is that ibogaine affects a broad range of receptors, many of which are associated with opiate and cocaine abuse. Possible mechanisms underlying the observations are under investigation.

MYRISTICIN AND ELEMICIN

Myristicin and elemicin are hallucinogenic compounds found in nutmeg and mace, two common household spices. The molecules resemble mescaline. Nutmeg comes from the powdered seed kernels of *myristica fragrans*, the nutmeg tree, and mace comes from the seed coats. One or two teaspoons full, brewed as tea, can cause euphoria after a latency period of several hours and produce an intoxication that may be prolonged. The ingestion of large amounts of nutmeg can cause euphoria, hallucinations, and an acute psychotic reaction. The side effects are unpleasant and may be confused with those of atropine; they include flushing of the skin, increased heartbeat, and drymouth. But unlike atropine, nutmeg may constrict the pupils early in its effect (Payne, 1963; Weiss, 1960).

In general, myristicin and elemicin do not have much to recommend them for recreation and so are abused as a last resort when no other agents are available.

CONCLUSION

In this chapter, we have focused on a number of the key hallucinogens and their pharmacology, and on the natural forms in which they occur. We have by no means exhausted the subject. For instance, there are many other psychoactive snuffs and drinks in use by the peoples of South America, of which our knowledge is limited. There is *shanshi*, a poisonous cattle-killing plant of the Andes, used by the Ecuadorian peasants to become intoxicated and to induce a sense of flight. There is an auditory hallucinogen of central Mexico, *sinicuichi*, whose active ingredients appear to come from the chemical family of the quinolizidines. There are varieties of coleus and petunias that may be psychogenic. The list of such cases is a long one. What chemistry underlies the application of these plants and what therapies may dwell in their tissues, only further research can unveil.

ENDNOTES

1. Mescal buttons should not be confused with *mescal beans* or *mescal liquor*. These are psychoactive agents distilled from the fermented *agave* cactus (*Sophora secundiflora*). This cactus is poisonous due to a nicotine-like ingredient (cystisine) that can cause hallucinations, convulsions, and possibly respiratory failure.
2. Leary escaped overseas in September of 1970 and was apprehended in Afghanistan in January of 1973. In 1976, he was released for good behavior.

Chapter 26

Marijuana and Hashish (THC)

> *. . . I noticed that all the plants were in a perfect calm, not experiencing the least agitation, because of the extreme heat untempered by the slightest breath of wind. But passing by a certain plant covered with foliage I observed that, in that air, it was moving softly from side to side with a soft light movement, like a man dizzied by the fumes of wine. I began to gather the leaves of this plant and to eat them, and they have produced in me the gaiety that you witness. Come with me, then, that I may teach you to know it.*
>
> Hassan Mohammed ibn-Chirazi, A.D. 1260, "How Hashish was Discovered," (the monk Haidar is speaking) (Kimmens, 1977, p. 26)

THC (delta-9-tetrahydrocannabinol) is the primary active ingredient of both marijuana and hashish, which are derived from the hemp plant (*cannabis sativa*).

Cannabis, originally from Asia, now grows throughout the world's temperate and tropic zones, because it was widely cultivated to make hemp rope from its fibers. In fact, it is the oldest cultivated plant not used for food. It came to the western hemisphere in 1545 with the Spaniards, who brought it to Chile to cultivate it for its fiber. In the United States and Canada, it came to be regarded as little above the status of a weed, since it grows well without attention. Because of this, much later, in the 1960s, *weed* became a nickname for marijuana.

The cannabis plant contains as many as 426 chemical agents, including more than 60 cannabinoids (compounds unique to cannabis), which may interact with or work synergistically to produce the psychoactive effect (Dewey, 1986). Delta-9 THC, believed to be the chief psychoactive ingredient, was not isolated and synthesized until 1964. The task was difficult, since THC, containing no nitrogen, is not an alkaloid; consequently, its extraction from the plant is complicated and differs from the usual methods. The drug concentrates in the resins and is found distributed unevenly over the plant. Most is found in the flowering tops, some in the leaves, less in the fibers. The effects of a packet of street marijuana, therefore, depend on the potency of the resins and which parts of the plants are in the mixture. Both male and female plants are psychoactive, but usually the flowers of the female plant have the highest concentration of resins. Sinsemilla is a seedless version of cannabis, developed by home growers and users of marijuana in the United States in the 1970s. It has significantly higher concentrations of THC throughout the plant.

Three forms of cannabis preparations are prevalent: marijuana is a smoking preparation consisting of a dried mixture of crushed seeds, leaves, flowers, and fine stems of hemp. (Users usually pluck the stems and seeds out.) The name comes from the Spanish or Portuguese word for "intoxicant" or some say from Mexican for *Mary Jane,* a slang word for cheap tobacco. Other names are *weed, pot, hemp, bhang, ganja, charas,* and *kif.*[1] The THC content of marijuana varies anywhere from none to 5 percent, although for sinsemilla it is 6 to 14 percent.

Hashish is a concentrate of the resins of the flowering tops of female plants. The name comes from an Arabic word originally meaning "herbage" or "fodder," from the appearance of the dried stems and leaves. The THC content of hashish is from 5 to 20 percent.

Hash oil is an extract prepared by boiling hash in a solvent and straining out the oils. The THC content of hash oil is high, from 20 to 70 percent.

History

The documented history of cannabis is spotty but long, dating back to a first dubious reference in 2737 B.C.E. by the mythical Chinese Emperor Shen Nung, who supposedly mentions it both as a euphoriant and a medicine.

One of the more engaging stories of early cannabis use concerns an Islamic secret sect from Persia in the late eleventh century C.E. The sect was founded by Hassani Sabbah, who embarked on a militant crusade to spread the Ismaili philosophy throughout Islam. The Ismailis were considered ruthless, cunning, and unscrupulous, remaining fanatically loyal to their sheik, even under the severest torture. The earliest legends surround the leader of the sect in Syria, who was known as the Old Man of the Mountain. A version of his story is told by Marco Polo in his *Travels*. The Old Man had a palace in the mountain fastnesses, which he planted with splendid gardens, furnishing them with delights for every sense, including women beautiful enough to be taken for the houris of the Mohammedan paradise promised in the Koran. Then, writes Polo, The Old Man takes those who wish to become his men at arms, drugs them, and has them conveyed to his palace gardens. Upon awakening, they believe themselves to be in paradise. The Old Man holds court there, masquerading as a great prophet. Then, later, whenever he wishes to have one of his enemies killed, he drugs one of his chosen and has him removed from the garden. The young man wakens outside in disillusionment and disappointment. The Old Man summons him and asks him where he has been, and the man says, "Paradise," describing the gardens for all to hear, so that those who know nothing of the deception would die to go there. And the Old Man tells them that if they will fulfill his mission and kill such-and-such an enemy, he will have his angels carry them to paradise. So, of course, they obeyed his every order, scornful of their own wellbeing for the promise of eternal delights. Such was the tale told to account for the fabulous loyalty and ferocity of the Syrian Ismailis (Kimmens, 1977, pp. 18-21).

The drug used by the Old Man was hashish, and his followers came to be known as *hashishi, heississini,* or *assassini,* which is the origin of the English word *assassin.*

Archaeological searches in Syria have failed to turn up evidence of gardens in the dwelling places of the assassins, and some have supposed that the drug state itself was used to suggest paradise. But it seems pharmacologically unlikely, as others claim, that cannabis mixtures and preparations were used to incite the assassins to a killing frenzy. For one thing, THC is not a stimulant, although its actions do include some excitatory effects.

The oldest written mention of hemp intoxication appears in Herodotus, a Greek historian of the fifth century B.C.E. He describes in detail how the Scythians, who lived in central Asia and the Crimea (north of the Black Sea), cleansed themselves after a funeral. They set up a tripod-like tent covered with woolen mats, dug a pit in the center, and threw red-hot stones into it. They then crept under the mats and threw hemp seeds on the hot stones, bathing themselves in the vapor that arose and "howling with joy" (Kimmens, 1977). Some speculate that the whole hemp plant may have been involved in these ceremonies, since the seeds are not very potent. The Scythians' joy, as we shall see, was more than a matter of simple vapor or steam.

In the Near and Middle East, it seems that cannabis has been used much more as an intoxicant than as a medicine. It was a controversial substance in orthodox Islam, vilified as an instrument of the devil. What little we know survived in places that eluded the purge of the great Islamic conquest. However, the Koran never mentions it, leaving its legitimacy ambiguous, and many accounts were written, pro and con. In 900 C.E., Muhammed Ali ibn Washiya listed it in his *Book of Poisons.* Nevertheless, its social use in the Moslem world and North Africa spread until the middle of the eleventh century, when it appears suddenly in Middle Eastern records as a full-blown drug menace, and over the next 100 years it became the favorite intoxicant of undesirables of all sorts. In the well-known *Tales of the Arabian Nights* (tenth century C.E.), the hashish eater appears as an object of ridicule.

Hashish first came to Europe as a result of Napoleon's Egyptian expedition from 1798 to 1799. It is said that Albert Sonnat, the principal physician on the campaign, was the first to introduce the drug into France, but a competing claim has it that many homesick soldiers used it in Egypt against orders and brought it back with them. This campaign, which was intended to make the French imperial presence felt in Egypt and Syria, was a success; it led to an intense interest in the eastern Mediterranean, and trade and travel boomed. By the 1830s and 1840s, cannabis had become a romantic rage in Europe, and some pharmacists stocked hashish in the form of an oil-based extract. Travelers, too, could easily fetch it back from the East, since there were no laws restraining them.

By far the most renowned users of this time (1840s) were the Club des Hachichins (an intended pun on hashish eaters and assassins). The Club consisted of a clique of Paris bohemians who met at the posh Hotel Pimodan on Île Saint-Louis in the Seine. (This wasn't a hotel as we understand it, but more a luxurious apartment house.) It was a time, writes Theophile Gautier, "when decamerons of poets, artists and beautiful women came together to talk of literature, art, and love." Gautier does not disguise the fact, either, that they came together to down heavy hallucinogenic doses of hashish, well beyond the euphoriant doses of typical American users (1846/1977).

The Club is remembered particularly for its literary lights, who also documented some of its activities, among them Theophile Gautier, Gerard de Nerval, Alexander Dumas, and later, Charles Baudelaire. Unknown at the time, but later to accede to the stature of giants, they shared a passion for romanticism, sensation, orientalism, and intoxication.

In general, the Club used high doses of hashish in a concentrated paste that came from the tops of hemp, boiled in butter and water, strained, and mixed with sweeteners and flavorings like vanilla, cinnamon, or pistachio (which gave the paste the greenish color they refer to).

In America, cannabis never aroused much attention until the mid-twentieth century. The colonists grew hemp for its fiber in order to make rope, and it aroused some countercultural irony in the 1960s among those arrested for possession, that George Washington had grown it in his garden. However, the psychoactive principles of the plant did not attract attention for quite some time. Hashish saw some fashionable use in the hashish houses of the late 1800s. But it was only with a proliferation of use in the late 1920s that the first serious notice was taken of it as a problem drug linked with the underground and crime.

In the 1930s, cannabis was included in the antidrug climate fueled by the Federal Bureau of Narcotics under Harry Anslinger. With little documented support, the drug was built up in the public mind as a menace directly linked to crime. By 1936, all states had regulated against it in some way, and by 1937, it was seen as a paramount public danger and became the focus of Congressional hearings. In these, trumped-up reports by police claiming that marijuana (the killer weed) increases sexual excitement and violent aggression were played out against rational appraisals of what the drug in fact does. It was the cocaine myth all over, as the vision of armed, manic, drug-crazed minorities (African- and MexicanAmericans this time) was conjured to raise public furor. That same year (1937), the Marihuana Tax Act was passed, another attempt (as with alcohol and opium) to achieve regulation through taxation. By this law, growers, distributors, buyers, and sellers were taxed.[2]

This trend continued through the 1940s and 1950s. In 1941, cannabis was dropped from the *U.S. Pharmacopoeia* and the *National Formulary*. Indicative of the climate of the times is a report commissioned by Mayor LaGuardia of New York City. Titled "The Marihuana Problem in the City of New York," the study was designed to provide a clear, substantiated look at the issue, free of emotional politicking. It claimed that marijuana impairs the intellect and reduces physical activity, but that it does not cause violence. When the results became known, La Guardia was condemned by the American Medical Association for condoning the use of marijuana. It was the era of Reefer Madness.

Throughout the 1950s, marijuana remained a drug of minorities and subcultures like the Beat (beatnik) and jazz communities. The next development came in the 1960s, when it entered the middle and upper classes via the youth culture. Unlike LSD, use spread more slowly and steadily and grew to such extents that serious bids for its decriminalization were, and still are, being made.

The 1970s saw a boom in use, especially from 1974 on, with most users being 18 to 25 years of age. Tens of millions of people experimented with the drug. Use peaked in 1979, then began to decline. In the 1980s, the foreign trade diminished, partly because cocaine became more profitable and more convenient to smuggle, and smuggling was replaced by illicit domestic production, centered mostly in northern California. This shift was aided by the fact that homegrown sinsemilla is over 100 times more potent than imported marijuana. In 1970, a typical reefer (marijuana cigarette) might have had 10 to 15 mg of THC (1 percent by weight). Today, a reefer may have 150 mg, and if it is laced with hash oil, as much as 300 mg. The effects of such potent varieties of cannabis have never been thoroughly studied, which has raised some concern. At present, the use of marijuana is less of a subcultural or political statement and appears to be more casual and widespread among all social classes.

Pharmacokinetics

In present day America, THC is taken in the form of marijuana or hash (hashish). The dried, crumbled leaves are usually cleaned of seeds, hand-rolled into a small cigarette (a *reefer, joint, doobie,* or *bone*) and smoked, the aim being to inhale the smoke (which can be somewhat irritating to a novice), hold it, and absorb it through the lungs. Smoking this way is rather wasteful, however, so users who have expensive pot will smoke it in a pipe or water pipe. A water pipe (*bong*) is a cross between a pipe and a carafe of water. The smoker sucks on a long hose or tube, which pulls the smoke from the bowl and draws it bubbling through the water before being inhaled; this cools the smoke and filters it and may dissolve a portion of the water-soluble components from the smoke. Hash oil is usually administered by placing a drop on a joint and smoking it. For eating, hash or marijuana is often baked into foods and confections such as chocolate brownies or other desserts. Fitzhugh Ludlow describes similar forms of administration in the East in the nineteenth century:

> *Sometimes it appears in the state in which it exudes from the mature stalk, as a crude resin; sometimes it is manufactured into a conserve with clarified butter, honey, and spices; sometimes a decoction is made of the flowering tops in water or arrack. Under either of these forms the method of administration is by swallowing. Again the dried plant is smoked in pipes or chewed, as tobacco among ourselves. (Ludlow, 1857/1979, p. xi)*

Because of the variability of administration and different smoking styles, the amount of THC absorbed may vary widely. Experienced smokers (and this is true of tobacco, too) can hold the smoke in their lungs longer and absorb more. Generally, only about 60 percent of the THC in a marijuana cigarette is absorbed.

Because it is highly lipid soluble, THC is rapidly and completely absorbed via the lungs, showing peak plasma levels and the onset of psychological and cardiovascular effects in 5 to 10 minutes. Physiological and subjective effects peak in about half an hour, and the duration of action is 2 or 3 hours, unless one smokes again.

Generally, THC is three times less effective when eaten rather than smoked. The oral route is slow and incomplete, with little of the drug reaching the brain. The onset of action occurs later than with smoking and may take up to an hour. Peak plasma levels and peak effects are reached 2 to 3 hours after administration, with a duration of action of 3 to 5 hours or more. Administration by injection is not very safe, since the drug is not water-soluble and could be dangerous in the bloodstream.

After peak plasma levels are achieved, THC redistributes in minutes into fat tissues and parts of the central nervous system. It passes the placental and blood-brain barriers and accumulates in the liver, kidneys, spleen, lungs, and testes. Brain levels match those of other tissues. Metabolism takes place in the liver, where THC is rapidly biotransformed to an active metabolite with identical effects. Some have hypothesized that the action of THC depends on its conversion into this metabolite (11hydroxydelta 9THC). This in turn is converted almost completely to inactive metabolites. Some biotransformation can occur in the lungs.

After redistribution, THC has a half-life of about 30 hours. The half-life of inactive metabolites may be as long as 50 hours, with traces still present after weeks. These inactive metabolites may accumulate, whereas the active metabolites probably do not. Evidence shows that chronic smokers metabolize the drug more rapidly, and chronic use can alter the metabolism of alcohol and the barbiturates.

The excretion of THC takes place about equally in the urine and feces, and not through the lungs. Since THC is released slowly from tissues because of its fat solubility, the process of metabolism and excretion are slow. At the end of a week, a quarter to a third of the drug and its metabolites may remain, and some feel that complete elimination may not occur for a month.

Most THC used in the West is taken at fairly low "social doses," nothing like the potent hallucinogenic doses of many nineteenth century users. An average joint (1 to 2 grams of plant material) may have about 15 mg of THC, half of which (7.5 mg) is available to the smoker. However, the manner of use (passing the joint around, for instance) usually lowers the dose. Experienced smokers can up the dose by holding the slightly irritating smoke in their lungs longer. Sinsemilla, however, is significantly more potent.

Effects are clearly dose-related. Low doses (2 mg smoked, 5 mg eaten) produce mild euphoria; moderate doses (7 mg smoked, 17 mg eaten) produce perceptual and time distortions; and high doses (15 mg smoked, 25 mg eaten) produce hallucinations, delusions, and distortions of body image.

Pharmacological Effects

In 1964, Raphael Mechoulam delineated the structure of delta-9-tetrahydrocannabinol and identified it as the chief active agent in marijuana. It was twenty-four years, however, before Allyn C. Howlett (who, we feel compelled to mention, was once a student of the principal author) used radioactively labeled THC to locate a receptor for cannabinoids--the CB1 receptor. As was the case with opiates, once a drug receptor is discovered in a situation like this, researchers begin to inquire after the endogenous substance for which the receptor evolved. In 1991, Mechoulam recognized the natural agonist, the body's own cannabinoid, a small fatty acid which he named *anandamide*, after the Sanskrit word *ananda*, meaning bliss. A short time later, researchers discovered a second natural agonist, or *endocannabinoid*, known in short as 2-AG (2-arachidonoyl-glycerol). The CB1 receptor and these two endocannabinoids are of principal concern here. A CB2 receptor has been identified, but it operates only in the immune system and has no known psychoactive associations. There also seems to be a CB3 receptor, but it is not responsive to THC.

runners high

The CB1 receptor turned out to be something of a surprise, and it helped explain a puzzling phenomenon. Brain scientists studying the principal cells of the hippocampus (the pyramidal cells) had found that when calcium levels in these cells rise, incoming inhibitory signals from GABA neurons decline, which has the net effect of increasing activity in the pathway. What is striking about this is that the target cells seem to be signaling in reverse to the sending cells. The same pattern of neurotransmission was found to be occurring in the cerebellum. If this indeed were happening, it violates a tried and true principle of neural signaling, which is that, outside of the original development of neurons, signals only move forward from one cell to the next. Researchers named the phenomenon *depolarization-induced suppression of inhibition*, or DSI. As far as they could tell, the depolarization of the target cell was causing the release of an unknown messenger, which traveled backward across the synaptic gap to inhibit (suppress), the sending neuron.

The mystery transmitter remained unknown for years, until 2001, when researchers in California and Japan independently linked DSI with the CB1 receptor. They found that interfering with the receptor put an end to DSI, and that mice lacking the CB1 receptor lacked DSI as well. The molecule 2-AG proved an ideal candidate for the unknown substance, and it was subsequently shown that endocannabinoids were responsible for the suppression of inhibition and the phenomenon of backward signaling.

This finding helped to explain some other puzzling aspects of the endocannabinoids and their action. The CB1 receptor was first located on specific sub-populations of GABA-ergic neurons in the hippocampus, but unlike typical receptors for neurotransmitters, it was not located on the post-synaptic membrane but on the pre-synaptic knob. This is the location one would expect if transmitters were crossing the synaptic gap contrary to the usual direction and suggests modulatory or co-transmitting activity. Furthermore, while most neurotransmitters are water-soluble and stored in the synaptic vesicles, the endocannabinoids are fat-soluble and are not stored in neurons.

The picture that emerged, as best we can currently understand it, is as follows. When certain GABA-ergic neurons in specific hippocampal pathways fire, they release GABA, as we would expect, which binds to its receptors on the post-synaptic membrane. Since the effect of GABA is inhibitory, this helps to block the firing of the target cells. However, when endocannabinoids are present, five to ten firings of the GABA neurons, and the accompanying hyperpolarization (inhibition) of the target cells, causes the rapid synthesis of endocannabinoids from components on the post-synaptic cell membrane. These travel back, bind to their receptors on the sending neuron, and inhibit the flow of GABA from the vesicles. The endocannabinoid molecules are then quickly degraded by enzymes. The net result is a delay in the inhibition of the neural pathway and a temporary facilitation of its action (Nicoll & Alger, 2004). This is an important feature, for instance, in systems involving learning, where the increased firing of neurons promotes the storage of information.

The action of the endocannabinoids is brief and localized among fairly small groups of neurons, partly because of their rapid synthesis and degradation, and partly because their lipid solubility prevents them from diffusing widely in the brain's extracellular fluid.

The CB1 receptor seems to be present in all vertebrate species, which indicates it has been in existence for about 500 million years (Nicoll & Alger, 2004). It seems likely that, of the three types of CB receptors, CB1 receptors mediate all endocannabinoid effects in the brain. The predominate regions in which they are found are the neocortex, hippocampus, brainstem, basal ganglia, cerebellum, amygdala, and hypothalamus. They are also located in the pain-mediating systems of the brain and spinal cord, and in the olfactory bulb. The neurotransmitter anandamide is found to dominate in some areas, 2-AG in others. Because the primary association of the endocannabinoids is not with any particular neurotransmitter, but with second messenger (G-coupled protein) systems shared by slow-acting neurons of various types, CB1 receptors have to date been found in glutamate, DA, and ACh systems as well as those involving GABA.

In the neocortex and the hippocampus, CB1 is found on sub-populations of slow-acting GABA-ergic neurons (namely, those with second messenger systems). In these regions, it also suppresses the peptide CCK, which is an antagonist to opiate effects. This possibly explains synergistic effects marijuana has with the opiates. In the cerebellum, endocannabinoids act in the manner described above, only there they suppress excitation instead of inhibition (*depolarization-induced suppression of excitation*, or DSE), by impeding the action of glutamatergic, instead of GABA-ergic, neurons.

THC resembles the endogenous endocannabinoids enough to produce psychoactive effects by binding to CB1 receptors. Its molecular structure is unlike that of any known transmitter, but it seems to be related to steroids (similar to testosterone and estradiol) that are associated with depression (Dewey, 1986).

The pharmacological effects of THC do not fit easily into any of the categories established for other drugs, but instead share characteristics of stimulants, sedatives, analgesics, and hallucinogens. The discovery of the widespread distribution of CB1 receptors in second messenger systems in the brain helps to explain this. Sites have been found in the hippocampus (memory), the neocortex (cognition and learning), the cerebellum and substantia nigra (motor centers), the mesolimbic DA pathways (reward), the amygdala (emotional response), and the hypothalamus (appetite). Sites have also been found in the brain stem and spinal cord (vomiting, analgesia), and in the lymphatic system (immune functioning).

The pharmacological effects of THC have been studied in several species, including mice, rats, cats, monkeys, and pigeons. These are reasonable predictors of effects in humans; however, some salient discrepancies have been observed. THC enhances appetite in humans, but decreases food intake in animals. It increases the heartbeat in humans, while slowing it in some animals. Researchers, therefore, have to be careful when extrapolating animal effects to humans.

THC intoxication in humans is interesting in that users seem to have to learn to be intoxicated. New users inhale the smoke and achieve effective blood levels, but seldom do they become "stoned." Researchers have postulated that one has to learn to focus attention on the correct set of internal signs that indicate intoxication (like trying to move a single muscle that you have never consciously moved before). But once you can find and perceive these signs as pleasant, intoxication can be felt. The set (frame of mind) is also important in the intoxication. Users taking the drug alone may merely fall asleep.

At low social doses in humans, THC is a mild sedative-hypnotic resembling anxiolytics, and sedatives like alcohol. First, it produces a stimulation experienced as mild tension, anxiety, or restlessness, which gives way to a calmer, more introspective state. Most users are familiar, early in the experience, with an exuberant feeling of pointless hilarity and irrepressible mirth. Bayard Taylor, a nineteenth century travel writer, describes this effect well in his 1855 essay, "A Slight Experience of Hashish," which is the first experience with the drug reported by an American:

> *. . . I found myself infected with a tendency to view the most common objects in a ridiculous light. . . . The turban worn by the captain next put on such a quizzical appearance that I chuckled over it for some time. Of all the turbans in the world it was the most ludicrous. Various other things affected me in like manner, and at last it seemed to me that my eyes were increasing in breadth. "Achmet," I called out, "how is this? my eyes are precisely like two onions." This was my crowning piece of absurdity. I laughed so loud and long at the singular comparison I had made, that when I ceased from sheer weariness the effect was over. (Taylor, 1855/1977, p. 142)*

This mirthfulness is accompanied by a sense of well-being, mild euphoria, and a relaxation of anxieties.

In higher dosage ranges, THC resembles LSD and mescaline in its ability to produce hallucinations. High-dose intoxication typically begins with a feeling of calmness or detachment, usually associated with a sense of lightness or loss of body (depersonalization). The individual enters a dreamy, carefree state, where space and time expand. Shifts in time perception are one of the most commonly reported psychological effects and can be found in almost all of the classic accounts. Gautier describes getting up to cross the large and ornately decorated drawing room of the Hotel Pimodan:

> *I got up with great difficulty and started toward the drawing room door, which I reached only after considerable time, for some unknown force compelled me to take one step backward out of every three. According to my calculation, it took ten years to cover the distance. (Gautier, 1846/1977, p. 100)*

Many reports identify an enhancement of perceptions, in the forms of both an acute body awareness and a glorification of external experience. Heightened body consciousness is often connected with increased cardiovascular activity. Fitzhugh Ludlow, who authored the classic American account of hashish use in 1857 (*The Hashish Eater*), describes how, in his first experiment with hashish, it was heart palpitations that finally sent him to a doctor for salvation:

> *By an appalling introversion, all the operations of vitality which, in our ordinary state, go on unconsciously, came vividly into my experience. Through every thinnest corporeal tissue and minutest vein I could trace the circulation of the blood along each inch of its progress. I knew when every valve opened and when it shut; every sense was preternaturally awakened; the room was full of a great glory. The beating of my heart was so clearly audible that I wondered to find it unnoticed by those who were sitting by my side. (Ludlow, 1857/1979, pp. 26-27)*

Ludlow, thinking he was about to die of heart failure, went to his room and measured his pulse at about 90 beats a minute, but he still could not shake the illusion of violent coronary activity.

At higher doses, not only is the sense of inner stimuli enlarged, but sensations of the outer world as well. The increase of sensation quickly shifts into distortions. Gautier says, "[T]he meat turned to raspberries in my mouth, and vice versa. I could not have told a cutlet from a peach" (Gautier, 1846/1977, p. 91).

At such doses, the user may experience mescaline-like fantasies with vivid hallucinations. Reports describe caricaturish alterations of reality and an intensification of time and space distortions. One experiences the voyaging into other times and places, the disorganized and confused thinking, and the extreme and fluid emotional changes of dreams while yet awake.

Many have argued in favor of THC as a drug that enhances creativity. Aside from the difficulties of defining and measuring creativity, the sense of creative enhancement is generally conceded to be a delusion, a result of the heightened sensation and personal expansion one feels, which lend ideas, colors, and music a peculiar charm.

Clinical Applications

As far back as the third century C.E. cannabis was used as an anesthetic, and it saw later uses as an anticonvulsant, muscle relaxant, hypnotic, analgesic, and rheumatism medicine. There is a pharmacological basis for some of these applications. THC has been known to produce both anticonvulsant and convulsant effects, which is in keeping with its mixed profile of stimulatory and depressant actions. Depending on the dose and the route (IV), it shows some analgesic action, but it is also known to increase the sensitivity to pain. This could come from the fact that it may act differently on different types of pain. As a hypnotic, it resembles depressants by reducing REM sleep; however, it produces a hangover and is generally inferior for this purpose. THC has some bronchodilating effect, although cases of bronchoconstriction have been reported.

Nevertheless, there are some conditions for which cannabis has been argued to be a therapeutic drug of choice. It suppresses the vomiting reflex, which makes it an effective agent to reduce the nausea and vomiting caused by cancer chemotherapy. It stimulates appetite, so that it could help to promote weight gain in AIDS and cancer patients. It reduces muscle spasms and spasticity, which could be of use to patients suffering from multiple sclerosis. It relieves a build-up of pressure inside the eyeball, which is a significant risk factor for developing glaucoma, a disease of the eye which can lead to loss of vision. And it relieves chronic pain.

One reason that cannabis has not held up as a significant clinical drug is that the subjective effects are a problem at therapeutic dosages, and reasonable alternatives are available for all of THC's possible applications. By far, it has received much more attention and use as an intoxicant. Consequently, the U.S. federal government has classified cannabis as a Schedule I drug—that is, a drug with high abuse potential and no medical application.

Nevertheless, derivatives of THC are used for several minor but specific medical conditions. Capable of suppressing the vomiting reflex, they have been used to reduce the nausea and vomiting caused by cancer chemotherapy, although current regulations prohibit such use. And they have been tried with some success as appetite stimulants to promote weight gain in HIV-positive patients.

Side Effects

It destroys the mind, cuts short the reproductive capacity, produces elephantiasis, passes on leprosy, . . . dries up the semen, . . . burns the blood, . . . riddles the liver with holes, inflames the stomach, . . . and leaves in its wake a bad odor in the mouth as well as a film and diminished vision in the eye and increased pensiveness in the imagination. . . . It turns a lion into a beetle and makes a proud man humble and a healthy man sick. If he eats, he cannot get enough. If he is spoken to, he does not listen. It makes the well-spoken person dumb, and the sound person stupid. . . . It produces gluttony, making eating the addict's preoccupation and sleep to him a characteristic situation. . . . (Latimer & Goldberg, 1981, p. 31)

This catalogue, abbreviated here, is an Islamic condemnation of hashish by Muhammed az-Zarkashi, written in 1350. Its mixture of recognizably valid facts (increased appetite and increased distractibility) with propagandistic exaggerations shows that the politics of drug use and the inflamed biases it produces (both pro and con) are not restricted to our time. Abused drugs always have attractive effects—if not, no one would abuse them. And they always have threatening effects—if not, societies wouldn't condemn them. There is always an array of facts that can be carefully selected, neglected, or distorted to suit one's point, either to persuade or allow people to take drugs, or to prohibit them.

As is the case with its clinical applications, demonstrating adverse side effects of THC has political implications, since it would justify current policy to discredit the drug, while proving it safe would benefit marijuana advocates. Unfortunately, while some current findings are suggestive of adverse effects, few are conclusive either way. Some known disadvantages might affect only a small number of users, while in other cases reliable experimental designs are difficult to construct, or the results are contradictory, flawed by poor sampling, or blurred by confounding variables and left open to question.

Three early field studies have been frequently cited for showing no significant abnormalities between chronic marijuana and hashish users and nonusers. The studies involved 60 marijuana smokers in Jamaica (Rubin & Comitas, 1975), 80 marijuana users in Costa Rica (Coggins, 1976), and 47 chronic hashish users in Greece (Fink, Volauka, Panayiotopoulos, & Stefanis, 1976). The results of the studies were impressive and surprising. The average Jamaican marijuana smoker, for instance, smoked 7 to 8 reefers daily, each with about 7 times the American dose of cannabis (at that time). The only significant abnormalities between such smokers and nonusers turned out to be effects that were also attributable to tobacco smoking in the test group.

However, these studies are open to question. The sample groups were small, and many of the subjects were unskilled laborers whose impairments may have shown up in finer work. Similarly, if we were to look to the United States for evidence of abnormalities, we might not find many adverse effects either, because most users to date have been healthy, young adults who smoke intermittently at fairly low doses. Further ambiguity in trying to assess possible problems arises from the fact that animal studies do not translate well to humans. Therefore, factors such as these, despite the indications of the studies, do leave open the possibility that chronic problems might appear in an aging generation of pot smokers, or that an increased use of sinsemilla, with a high THC content and a broader user population, could have adverse effects on newer generations of users.

In its short-term effects, THC, it turns out, is less threatening than many drugs. It has a wide safety margin. Its LD is unknown and no deaths are on record. Those that have been reported are not related to the direct action of the drug, but to its preparation, route of administration (injection), or the physical condition of the user. Two cases of acute toxicity in young children, who accidentally ate cannabis-laced cookies, resulted in coma, but not death (Boros et al., 1996).

Among the more well-documented and severe pharmacological side effects are cardiovascular ones. Cannabis increases the heart rate and, less so, the blood pressure. This heavier workload on the heart muscle calls for more oxygen, which can increase the risk of a heart attack in those with an impaired heart muscle or a compromised ability to supply it with oxygen. Cannabis can also exacerbate the cardiovascular side effects of other drugs, such as tricyclic antidepressants (Kalant, 2004). Orthostatic hypotension may occur. As we saw, exaggerated cardiovascular effects appear in some of the classic accounts. This is possibly a combination of increased cardiovascular activity with increased body awareness.

A typical short-term cardiovascular effect in users is a reddening of the eyes, due to dilation of the blood vessels in the cornea, One can often recognize a marijuana smoker by these characteristic bloodshot eyes, an effect that has also been noted with alcohol.

There are no permanent adverse cardiovascular effects caused by cannabis, but the stress-like effects on the heart and circulation, sometimes involving an increase of blood pressure, suggest that individuals predisposed to cardiovascular disorders may be put at risk. People with heart disease should clearly abstain.

A less serious, characteristic side effect of THC intoxication is the stimulation of appetite, probably attributable to action at the CB1 receptors in the hypothalamus. This usually manifests as a craving for sweets and snacks and is known in slang as *the munchies*.

Another possible hypothalamic effect is a tremendous thirst produced by hashish at hallucinogenic doses, which was described by several users of the nineteenth century. Their accounts often depict this in humorous and overwhelming terms. Sometimes the thirst manifests itself in hallucinogenic spells as images of being lost in the desert or being imprisoned without drink. Ludlow strains to find words expressive enough to communicate what a godly drink a glass of water seemed to him after "the unutterable thirst that characterizes hashish."

THC intoxication is capable of producing several adverse mental conditions. Panic reactions and terror might occur as a result of sympathetic stimulation. Paranoid delusions are also not uncommon. Ludlow points out that he "learned afterward, suspicion of all earthly things and persons was the characteristic of the hasheesh delirium" (Ludlow, 1857/1979, pp. 22-23). Nowadays, this paranoia may be shaped by the illicit status of the drug, and two common fears are that the police will burst in upon the scene, or that others (a boss, parents, etc.) will discover the intoxication in inappropriate circumstances. In some cases, anxiety centers on the fear that the drug state may be perpetual. Hallucinations may likewise inflict terror, but as these shift, other emotions may succeed them. Overall, despite what seem to be cataclysmic changes of perception and psychology to the user, the symptoms frequently go unnoticed. There are no prolonged bad trips with traumatic aftermaths, as with LSD, although flashbacks have been reported.

High doses of cannabinoids can produce a toxic delirium consisting of brief episodes of hypomanic, psychotic symptoms. However, such dosages are seldom ingested recreationally in the United States, and the condition is self-limiting and requires no specific treatment. Symptoms of depersonalization, though, may recur or persist.

Several types of cognitive impairments have been documented during cannabis intoxication. The processing of information into short-term memory is compromised, an effect that is consistent with the presence of receptors in the hippocampus, and this can interfere with learning and the performance of tasks when subjects try to recall sets of directions or sequences of facts. Also evident are a decreased attention span, decreased verbal facility, and difficulties with problem-solving, consistent with the presence of CB1 receptors in the neocortex. All of these deficits disappear when the intoxication is over. "Mild but significant" cognitive impairments may show up in the offspring of mothers who smoke cannabis during pregnancy (Kalant, 2004).

Motor impairments are another feature of cannabis intoxication, probably associated in part with CB1 receptors in the cerebellum and basal ganglia, both centers for motor coordination. (As noted above, cannabinoids in the cerebellum were found to suppress the excitation of neurons.) At low dosages, loss of motor facility and slowed reaction time are minimal: however, two reefers may be enough to impair driving, and alcohol can add to the impairment. Studies of cannabis intoxication and motor vehicle accidents are complicated, because THC is rapidly re-distributed into storage and then slowly released, so that the blood levels of THC are only very loose indicators of the level of impairment and cannot prove that the user was intoxicated at the time of an accident. Nevertheless, the current status of the connection between cannabis-smoking and driving is summed up by Kalant (2004) as follows:

On the basis of the present information, one may conclude with reasonable confidence that cannabis does have a demonstrated capacity for impairing driving skills, that it is found in the blood of impaired or accident-involved drivers with a frequency that appears to exceed the probable frequency in the general population, but that those who use it regularly are most often young risk-taking males, who are also more likely to drive under the influence of alcohol. Therefore, the causal role of cannabis cannot yet be regarded as completely proven, but is strongly suggested by the increasing probability of "at-fault" accidents with increasing plasma levels of THC.

Allegations that marijuana use causes aggressive outbursts leading to violence and even sexual assault have frequently been used by civil authorities and others to justify prohibition measures. A caricature of this popular strain of thinking is seen in the 1937 exploitation film *Reefer Madness*, in which the drug is shown to cause antisocial behavior, sexual assault, murder and insanity in high school students, and in cases like the courtmartial of Lieutenant. W. Calley for the massacre of as many as 500 unarmed civilians in the village of My Lai during the Vietnam War. At one point during Calley's trial, the defense claimed that his behavior was due to his having been in a room "where, hours before, others had been smoking marijuana" (Escohotado, 1999). Scientific research has consistently corroborated that aggressive violence of this sort is not a pharmacological effect of THC. In fact, if there is one word in the popular discourse of marijuana which by its prevalence characterizes the drug effect, it is *mellow*.

Animal experimentation has shown that endocannabinoids may play an important role in extinguishing the response to traumatic experiences. Normal rats that are conditioned to associate a warning bell with a shock will gradually diminish in their response to the bell once the shocking has been discontinued. However, rats bred without CB1 receptors will continue to respond with a full measure of fear. This suggests that an organism with a low number of CB1 receptors or low endocannabinoid release might be susceptible to anxiety disorders like phobias and post-traumatic stress disorder, as well as chronic pain. It also suggests that some cannabis-users might be self-medicating with the drug to release anxieties causing by bad memories (Nicoll & Alger, 2004, p. 74).

A well-documented long-term effect of cannabis smoking is chronic inflammation of the respiratory tract, which presents as wheezing, shortness of breath, the presence of phlegm, and persistent coughing, and might lead to bronchitis or asthma. This is due to the route of administration by inhalation and is also seen with other types of smoking. A single joint can have as much tar as two packs of cigarettes, so that heavy smoking may cause irreversible respiratory impairment. Based on a few suggestive studies, researchers are investigating whether cannabis smoke can produce changes in the respiratory tract that might lead to cancer (Kalant, 2004). Furthermore, the carbon monoxide in marijuana smoke produces all of the same problems that it does in tobacco smoke, lowering the oxygen-carrying potential of the blood and compromising the oxygenation of an embryo or fetus.

Another question that has concerned researchers and authorities is whether or not cannabis induces lassitude and lack of motivation in users (amotivational syndrome). Zarkashi's Arab tract says, "It . . . generates in those who eat it laziness and sluggishness." Baudelaire, too, expatiated against hashish as a destroyer of the will. He claimed that it draws the eater inward, to a fit of self-contemplative monomania, and it "makes the individual useless to other men and society useless to him." He criticized the productive revelations as a delusion that fades with the dose and ultimately saw the whole experience as an immoral lassitude that robs the users of their ability to act. It is ironic that Baudelaire, an opium abuser and coiner of the term *artificial paradises* should have authored some of the most eloquent, informed, and impassioned polemics against the use of a drug. However, as it turns out, there have been no convincing experimental data to support these accusations. The three field studies of the chronic use of marijuana and hashish in Jamaica, Costa Rica, and Greece failed to corroborate the syndrome. A number of more recent studies correlating cannabis use with poor social outcomes (e.g., failure to complete an educational degree) are blurred by the inability to separate drug use from other factors in the social environment.

When Moreau de Tours was experimenting with hashish in nineteenth century France, he suggested that the drug effects might be used as a model for studying schizophrenia. Now, some studies suggest that marijuana use is associated with the precipitation or worsening of schizophrenia. For instance, Zammit and colleagues (2002) studied 50,000 Swedish conscripts and found that a recruit who reported smoking marijuana upon entering the army stood a much greater chance of developing schizophrenia five or more years after leaving it.

There is some statistical evidence that cannabis may contribute to the development of major depression and panic or anxiety disorders, as well as poor psychosocial outcomes. However, it is difficult to show conclusively that cannabis use alone is influencing the problem, rather than vice versa, or to rule out other influences. Consequently, there is more evidence than previously that this is the case, but these studies remain suggestive at best (Kalant, 2004).

It is a complex issue whether or not cannabis produces tolerance, withdrawal, and dependence. Because new users seem to need to become accustomed to THC intoxication, it was believed that the drug caused a *reverse tolerance*, meaning that effects would strengthen rather than weaken with repeated exposure. However, it has been shown that tolerance does develop, albeit only to a minor degree (Rang et al., 1995, p. 662). Cross-tolerance has been shown among various cannabinoids and CNS depressants, including alcohol (Newman, Lutz, & Domino, 1974). None has been shown for mescaline or LSD.

The development of dependence to THC is an unresolved issue. If one's definition of dependence includes physical dependence, marked by a clear withdrawal syndrome upon cessation of the drug, the case is weak. A mild withdrawal syndrome has been demonstrated, beginning one to three days after cessation of the drug, lasting two to six days, and marked by irritability, agitation, sleep disturbances, nausea, vomiting, diarrhea, sweating, salivation, and tremors--symptoms which resemble those of opiate or alcohol withdrawal. However, to produce this requires about 30 mg of THC every 4 hours for 10 to 20 days, and it is difficult to distinguish these symptoms from preexisting or other anxieties. Some animal studies have failed to elicit signs of withdrawal, and reports of a syndrome in humans are rare. Consequently, by this criterion, physical dependence does not seem to be prevalent. The matter awaits the development of a pure THC receptor-blocker, which could clearly demonstrate a withdrawal syndrome, if one exists.

On the other hand, if we define dependence more in line with the DSM-IV--in terms of behavioral patterns involving preoccupation with the drug, interference with important social relationships, loss of control over using and refraining, the case for THC dependence has more weight. Using these criteria, findings vary widely, but statistical evidence from several surveys shows that dependence in young people from 14 to 26 seems to occur in a range of 2 to 20 percent in the general populations studied, and as much as 30 to 50 percent specifically among users (Kalant, 2004).

There is evidence that long-term marijuana use suppresses the immune system, which carries a tentative implication that users could be more susceptible to infections. CB2 receptors are found in the immune system, but the relationship to THC remains to be clarified.

Like sedatives, THC crosses the placental barrier, and for that reason it should be avoided during pregnancy. In males, chronic use has been shown to reduce testosterone levels and sperm counts, to the same degree perhaps as alcohol and other sedatives. The data here are controversial, but they do raise some concern for an increasing number of prepubescent users.

Additives and adulterants to marijuana have on occasion been a problem. Paraquat, a defoliant, was sprayed on Mexican crops for a time in the 1970s. The residue was capable of producing toxic effects in smokers. The practice has since been discontinued. Adulterants found in street ounces of marijuana have included catnip, stramonium leaves, LSD, insect spray, rat poison, and strychnine.

ENDNOTES

1. Definitions of *kif* vary. In northwest Africa, it is a mixture of chopped dried hemp and black tobacco.
2. *Cannabis sativa* was specified by this law. Consequently, for a time, based on technicalities in federal and state law, there were places where *C. indica* was not illegal. However, *C. indica* has since been reclassified as a subspecies of *C. sativa*.

Appendix A

Drug Development and Animal Testing

Because of the stringent regulations established by the Food, Drug, and Cosmetics Act and its amendments, when a pharmaceutical company embarks on the development of a new drug, it faces a project that may take from 2 to 6 years and cost between 50 and 70 million dollars. Regulations in the United States are more demanding than in European countries. In Britain, a new drug may hit the market in as short a time as six months. The time lag between development and marketing rankles many major drug companies. The reason for this is that, as soon as a new substance is identified, the company takes out a patent for it, even before testing begins. This guarantees the company exclusive rights to produce and market this drug for 17 years. After that, the drug is fair game for competitors to produce and market, also. However, the tests required by the government may eat up as many as 7 years of the drug's market life, and this closes the gap between costs and profits. Needless to say, no matter how effective a drug is, companies are not interested in it unless it can be patented and broadly marketed. The three major considerations in the development of a drug are its medical need, its commercial potential, and the feasibility of its mass production. Drugs that are used in the treatment of less prevalent diseases (with fewer than 200,000 people affected) and that have reduced profit potential are called *orphan drugs*. In 1983, the Orphan Drug Act was passed to offer special privileges and market incentives to companies willing to produce such drugs.

The government also conducts its own tests on new drugs and may order them to be recalled for any number of flaws: too many serious side effects, insoluble tablets, leaky vials, incorrect labeling, or whatever. On the other hand, when a drug is desperately needed, as was the case with Vidarabine, a treatment for viral herpes simplex encephalitis, the FDA gave it preferential treatment. Vidarabine was cleared through normal channels in six months.

The development of a new drug really begins with the search for a molecule. The motives for the search vary. A company may be seeking a drug for a specific medical condition; it may be following a lead from findings in other labs; or it may free its scientists to pursue a promising line of development. The company has two sources to which it can apply for material. One is the organic chemist, who can take known molecules and alter them slightly to give them new properties--maybe advantageous, maybe not. For instance, with the synthesis of chlorpromazine, Laborit knew the tranquilizing effect he wanted was related to that of antihistamines, and that it might be possible to achieve this effect by altering slightly the structure of an antihistaminic compound. The chemist Charpentier analyzed the problem and decided to try changing the promethazine molecule. He ended up with chlorpromazine, a molecule that fortuitously shifted the effect in the right direction. Using similar methods, a chemist can mimic the drug of a competing company by, say, shifting a hydrogen atom from one end of a molecule to the other, spawning what is legally a new drug, but which has effects close to those of the original molecule. Drugs like this (and others) that jump on the bandwagon of already successful products are known as *me too* drugs. On the illicit drug scene, this is the same principle behind the production of designer drugs.

A second source for drugs is the psychopharmacognosist. This is a person who seeks new drugs in the world at large. The psychopharmacognosist ("one who recognizes drugs"), a specialist with a broad knowledge of drugs and their actions, may visit native peoples to study their folk medicines, may study ancient literature and folklore for allusions to promising compounds, or may botanize in exotic quarters of the world. All of the samples, usually plant material, are submitted to the chemist; the plant is dried, and its active ingredient isolated and identified. Then, like any other compound, it is ready to be screened as a potentially therapeutic substance. A notable relationship between an organic chemist and psychopharmacognosists is that between Albert Hofmann, the "father of LSD," and the researchers R. Gordon Wasson and Valentina Pavlovna Wasson. The Wassons roamed the bye corners of Mexico in search of the sacred, hallucinogenic, *teonanacatl* mushroom, which they found and sent to Hofmann, who isolated its active ingredient, psilocybin. The team next tackled the Mexican *ololiuqui* plant, which they found to be a species of morning glory, and isolated other lysergic acid derivatives. Among them, they pioneered the synthesis of the key modern hallucinogens.

One estimate holds that about 175,000 substances are evaluated every year, and about 200 appear as new drugs (Leavitt, 1982, p. 67).

ANIMAL TESTS

Drug testing involves many phases (see Figure A.1). Animal testing is the first. On the whole, animal models are of great use in evaluating the properties of a drug and assessing its effects on humans. It must be noted, however, that animals are recognizably imperfect, and sometimes the discrepancies between animals and humans are wide. No one has clearly defined the relevance of animal testing, and there has been no clear agreement on the proper criteria for judging a drug as safe and effective.

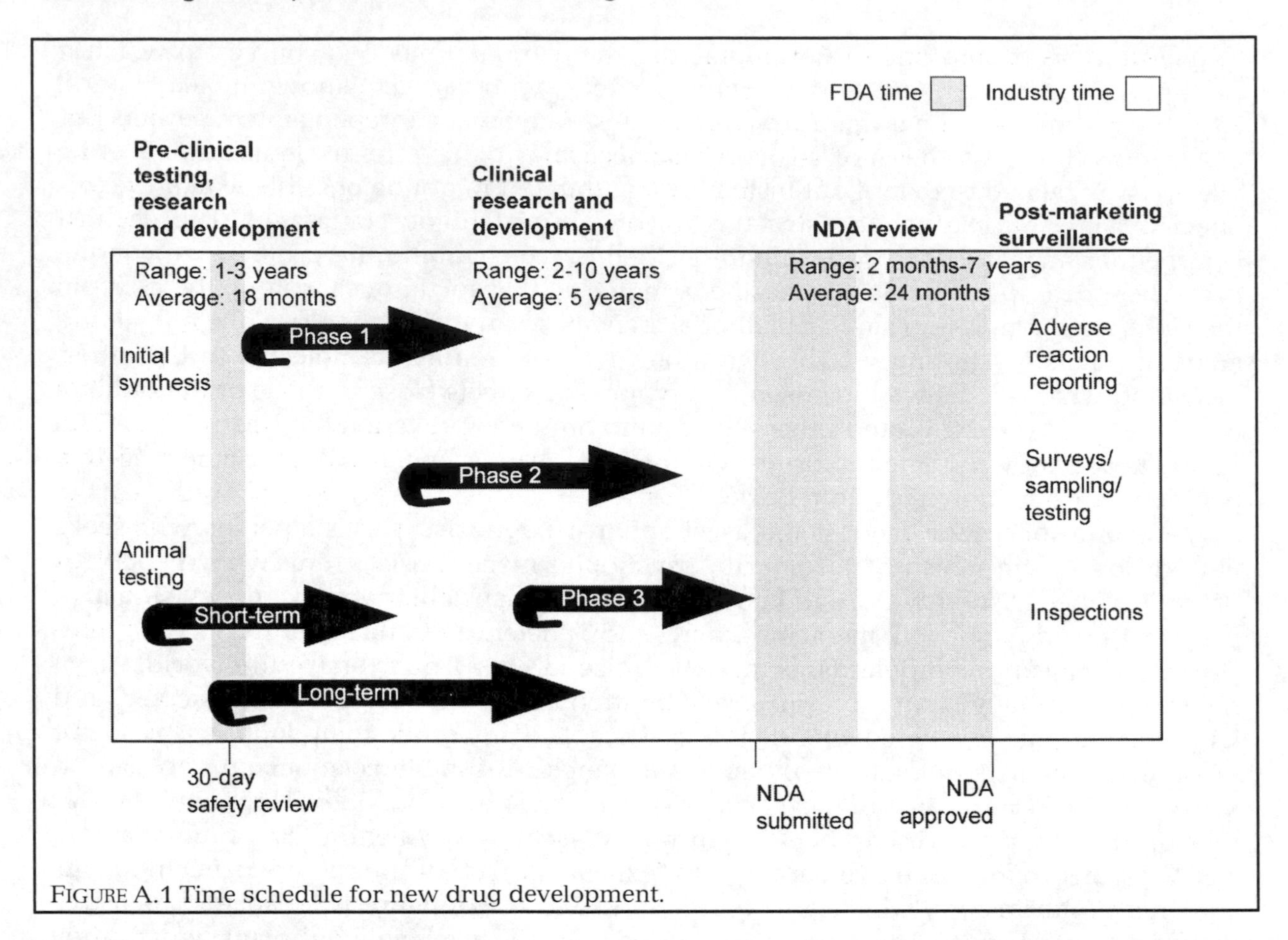

FIGURE A.1 Time schedule for new drug development.

Some drawbacks are apparent. Cats are good subjects because their nervous systems are similar to those of humans, but they sleep 65 to 80 percent of the time, and they are stimulated by some drugs that depress humans. Monkeys may suffer behavioral abnormalities from being confined. Rabbits possess an enzyme that metabolizes atropine and allows them to eat belladonna alkaloids (like tomato plant leaves), which are poisonous to humans. Furthermore, the drug thalidomide, which caused fetal abnormalities in thousands of humans, tested out safely on some animals.

An additional problem with psychoactive drugs is that there are no accurate ways to simulate mental disorders in animal models, since the mechanisms are not yet understood. Alternative indicators and approximations must be used.

On the other hand, some of the idiosyncratic attributes of animals are an advantage in certain tests. Because rabbits have no tear glands, they have been used as a model for testing irritant effects of eyedrops. Because rodents do not vomit, they have been used to test for toxicity on oral routes. Also, it is an advantage that many of these differences between animals and humans are thoroughly recognized. The laboratory rat is the most studied and understood animal this side of the featherless bipeds called humanity. And, despite the species gap, statistics have shown time and again that animals are valid indicators for predicting drug effects on humans.

TOXICITY AND METABOLIC TESTS

Since all drugs are potentially toxic, the first step is to discover their hazardous properties. Four types of toxicity tests are undertaken: (1) acute toxicity studies, for single doses, (2) subacute toxicity studies, for short-term use of the drug, (3) chronic toxicity studies, for long-term use, and (4) special toxicity studies for carcinogens and teratogens.

Acute Toxicity

Acute toxicity studies provide a rapid evaluation of some properties of a drug and give an indication of safe dosage ranges, as well as the first clues to some toxic mechanisms. In the tests, single increasing doses are administered by various routes to small groups of animals of two or more species. The cross section of animals chosen (male and female, young and old) is carefully designed. The animals are examined repeatedly for 24 hours and daily for a week thereafter. Information is collected about absorption from different routes, threshold doses, the ED50, duration of effect, the threshold dose for irreversible impairment, and other factors. Also during this phase the test for the LD50 is conducted. It usually involves about 60 mice and allows the therapeutic index to be calculated. Animals are autopsied for cause of death. Many drugs may be rejected at this point if the therapeutic index is unsatisfactory; otherwise, dosage guidelines are drawn up for future testing.

Subacute Toxicity

These studies test several drug routes over a 2- to 12-week period, depending on the intended use of the drug; they use three dosage ranges on small groups of two or more species of animals. The subjects are examined and tested extensively, and estimates of human dosages are formed. Possible cumulative actions are assessed, as well as liver and kidney toxicity and nervous system reactions.

Chronic Toxicity

Chronic toxicity studies differ from the subacute ones only in their duration, which can run from 3 months to 2 years. During this time, some animals are taken off the drug, and their recovery is observed. Organs are weighed, and body parts elaborately described and microscopically examined as well. These studies must be 6 months gone before any clinical testing may begin.

Carcinogenicity

In tests for carcinogenicity, which must be conducted for all drugs whose use is to exceed 6 months, 3 dosage ranges are administered to 2 species of animals by the same route intended for humans. They involve anywhere from 500 to 1,000 animals. The animals are weighed constantly during the study, an early detection method for tumor growth. After many months, all of the animals are sacrificed, and their tissues examined scrupulously for signs of cancer. Some false results may be obtained, since humans are exposed to many other carcinogenic factors in the environment than are the test subjects.

At high dosages, animals may excrete large amounts of a drug, but this is not cause enough to dismiss the results. One commonly hears remarks like, "So they gave 50 pounds of this stuff to a mouse and it got cancer, so now they say it's unsafe for humans. What bull spit." Although it is not entirely analogous to human testing, heavily dosing a mouse with a lifespan of 2 to 3 years is the closest reasonable approximation to how much drug a human might accumulate in a full lifetime. If the drug is not safe under these conditions, there is a decent chance that it is not safe enough for humans. Or, to put it another way, if the best indicator we have is fair at best, does that mean we prefer worse indicators, or none at all?

Teratogenicity

In these studies, which also involve about 500 rats and rabbits, the drug is administered to animals during pregnancy and lactation. All aspects of the reproductive process are observed: mating behavior, fertility, embryonic development, litter size, the health of offspring, and so forth. It has been noted that some well-known drugs like chlorpromazine, reserpine, and imipramine have damaging effects on animals, but not on humans.

PHARMACOLOGICAL TESTS

Pharmacological tests are objective measurements of behavioral changes in single traits of an animal during drug use. These are done when we already have some knowledge of drug effects. The testing profiles of the prototypical drugs in each class of behavioral drugs are well-defined, and new drugs are categorized by comparing and contrasting their test profiles against those of known drugs. Carefully looked for are modifications of behavior, changes in behavior (the elicitation of behavior not seen under normal circumstances), and alien behavior (like catalepsy, behavior not in an animal's normal repertoire). Some behaviors commonly examined in rats during these tests are exploration, sociability (submission, aggression), species characteristic behavior (sniffing, gnawing, licking), grooming, circling, emotionality (urination, defecation), motivation, pain, and catalepsy.

The criteria still used as guidelines for behavioral tests were set forth by V. G. Vernier. There are four:

1. The test should be sensitive at low dosages.
2. It should have qualitative specificity, meaning that it should be able to distinguish among already-known classes of compounds; if it couldn't tell an antidepressant from a stimulant, for instance, it would be of little use in specifying the character of an unknown drug.
3. It should be simple and easy to interpret.
4. It should have a general range and be applicable to a number of drugs in different dosage ranges.

It is also important to produce drug-response profiles that analyze the multiple effects of a drug simultaneously and to produce dose-response curves for both single-dose and chronic administration, since these normally differ.

Pharmacological tests are generally divided into two groups: direct and indirect.

DIRECT PHARMACOLOGICAL TESTS

A direct pharmacological test assesses the direct effect of a drug on a particular behavior or organic structure. Several instruments are used to do this:

Rating Scales

A rating scale is a simple way to codify the effects of a drug by observing the way an animal acts. There is a subjective variable in the sense that an observer is required to judge the degree to which behaviors occur. Irwin's rating scale for rats and mice, designed in 1968, is a common tool. This scale is used to rate a mouse's or rat's behavior. The observer has an 8point scale for each behavior and is required to score the animal, on the assumption that 4 points describes the normal degree of behavior. So, if a mouse walks normally at 4, it is creeping at 2 and sprinting at 8. Two or three independent judges rate the animals this way at varying dosages. Other traits looked for are awareness, motor activity, central nervous system excitation, posture, and so forth. Irwin's scales have proven sensitive enough to distinguish between classes of psychoactive drugs and between specific drugs within each category, between dosage levels, and even between the responses of different strains of mice. The tests are also simple, time-efficient, and useful as screening tools.

Objective Pharmacological Tests

There are thousands of these tests, so it will be enough to describe a few for each class of behavioral drug. They are objective assessments designed to evaluate single traits, in our examples, of rats and mice.

Tests for sedatives, depressants, and stimulants include the jiggle-cage, actophotometer, open field test, and hole-in-board test, all of which measure amounts of motor activity, a reliable indicator of whether an animal is depressed or excited. The jiggle-cage is a cage hung from a spring; when the rat inside moves even slightly, the motion is imparted to the spring and recorded. A rat that moves 1,000 times an hour normally may move 30,000 times an hour on amphetamines, or only 2 or 3 times an hour on depressants. The actophotometer test consists of a cage crossed by light beams. Whenever the rat moves and interrupts a beam, the movement is recorded and counted. The open field test uses a pen whose floor is marked off into areas like a hopscotch board. An observer counts the number of times a rat moves into or places both of its forepaws into a new area within a set time limit. The hole-in-board test is based on the inclination of rodents to poke their noses into holes, an exploratory trait. One wall of the rat's cage has a row of small holes. Whenever a rat nose protrudes through a hole, it trips a light beam and is counted, as in the actophotometer test.

Objective pharmacological tests for anxiolytics (some of which impair ACh function in the periphery) are aimed at the degree of muscle relaxation induced by a drug. These include the revolving cylinder and inclined screen tests. The revolving cylinder is just that. Rats are placed on a slowly rotating drum, where they have to balance like lumberjacks in a logrolling contest. They are timed for the period they are able to remain on the cylinder. Rats whose muscles are seriously relaxed, of course, fall right off. In the inclined screen test, rats are placed on a surface tilted at a specified angle, and they are timed for their ability to stay there.

The tests for neuroleptics (major tranquilizers) are of various characters. The test for muricide measures the ability of neuroleptics to reduce the inborn mouse-killing tendencies of rats. About 58 percent of a rat population are mouse-killers. Neuroleptics can reduce this percentage, whereas stimulants can raise it. The aggression test measures the ability of neuroleptics to reduce aggression in mice. Mice isolated for a week will fight other mice to death when they are returned to the group, but neuroleptics inhibit this behavior. Another test measures the degree to which neuroleptics produce catalepsy in an animal; this is a condition of immobility that "freezes" the limbs in position. In the lightest phase, the animal is awake, but it will not move unless it is prodded. In the intermediate phase, the animal cannot move. In the heaviest phase, the animal remains rigid in any posture in which it is placed. A rat made to sit up with its forepaws on a block will remain in that attitude when the block is removed, until the drug wears off. Even with its rear up, it will remain, if balance allows (see Figure 22.1). The same holds for humans. If you pick up the arm of a catatonic schizophrenic and place it behind the patient's head, the patient will not remove it for hours.

Antidepressants are tested by the swimming survival test. The mouse or rat is placed in a basin of water, and the amount of time it can tread water before its head first goes under from fatigue is noted. Then the animal is removed. Antidepressants raise an organism's ability to expend energy and increase the swimming survival time, while depressants reduce it. The mood of an animal, however, is impossible to measure with certainty.

Analgesics are tested with pain tests. The pain is usually inflicted in fairly innocuous ways. For instance, in the pain avoidance test, rats' tails are arranged to protrude through a hole in a partition. A tiny heat lamp about the size of a pencil flashlight is shone on the tail; the heat builds slowly until the rat gets a "hot foot," and the tail twitches to one side to avoid the heat. The time it takes the tail to twitch is recorded. An injection of endorphins can increase the rat's toleration of the heat four or fivefold. In another test, rubberized alligator clips graded in order of increasing pressure are clipped separately one by one onto a rat's tail. The lighter clips the rat ignores, but eventually one irks it enough so the rat tries to bite it off. Analgesics raise the degree of pinching the rat is willing to tolerate.

As can be seen, these tests translate characteristics of known classes of drugs into behaviors that can be objectively measured.

CONDITIONING STUDIES

Conditioning studies are designed to show the effects of the different classes of drugs on acquisition. Three main responses fall under study: the conditioned response, the unconditioned response, and autonomic responses. It is recognized that the acquisition of conditioned responses and the ability to generalize a stimulus are excitatory processes, while the extinction of conditioned responses and the ability to discriminate between conditioned stimuli are inhibitory processes. For example, an animal on stimulants readily acquires the conditioning response and jumps at anything even vaguely resembling the conditioned stimulus (that is, it generalizes); it has no patience to discriminate and maintains the response pattern, which is then difficult to extinguish. A sedated animal behaves to the contrary; it has trouble forming the response and cannot generalize well to other stimuli; it discriminates easily because it is slow to respond, and it relinquishes the learning in a short period. The first animal handles conditioning like a nervous wreck; the second is sluggish and could not care less.

Anxiolytics and neuroleptics are split in their conditioning effects. Anxiolytics have no effect on acquisition, but they inhibit the autonomic responses that go with it. For instance, a rat's brain may accept the conditioning, but its glands do not release adrenaline, and its heart will not race excitedly at the stimulus. Accordingly, brain waves may respond fully, but behavioral responses are selectively inhibited. Neuroleptics affect acquisition, but not the autonomic responses; namely, the rat has trouble responding, but shows the appropriate emotional reaction. Stimulants affect both.

Operant Conditioning Studies

The purpose of these studies is to evaluate the effects of drugs on learned but voluntary behavior. Both approach and avoidance studies are another facet of drug testing. The pole-climbing test poses an avoidance situation wherein rats must climb up a pole to avoid shocks from an electrified floor. The rats are warned by a buzzer that the shock is coming, which they anticipate and escape by climbing a pole. Drugs that reduce anxiety tend to impair anticipation but not the escape response; that is, despite the buzzer, rats will not bother to climb the pole until they are actually shocked.

The most general effects that can be reasonably summarized about operant conditioning are that stimulants, for the most part, increase operant responses, while sedatives and antipsychotics reduce them. However, it should be mentioned that a very high rate of response, like that of animals on high fixed ratio schedules, is impaired by the administration of stimulants. This is a case of the task variables qualifying a drug's effect and changing our evaluation of it.

Another noteworthy variable is that many drugs affect motivation, which sometimes makes the interpretation of results difficult. For example, amphetamines may seem to be reducing the approach response to a reward of food pellets, when actually they inhibit a rat's motivation to eat. The rat does not feel hungry, because the drug stimulates inhibitory areas in its hypothalamus, and its appetite is suppressed. In cases like this, tests must be used that involve other motivations, such as thirst or shock escape. And researchers must be scrupulously careful to insure the validity of the tests.

SITE OF ACTION STUDIES

Site of action studies are of two sorts: neurochemical, which investigate drug effects on transmitter levels or functions in parts of the nervous system, and electrophysiological, which study drug effects on brain waves, either through electroencephalographs (EEGs) or single nerve recording. In animals, neurochemical studies are done by administering a drug, which may be radioactively labeled, to a number of animals, which are then sacrificed and their brain parts analyzed for radioactivity and transmitter content. In this way it can be determined, for example, if a given sedative affects dopamine release in the basal ganglia, or whether there are special receptor areas in the brain where the drug binds. Thus, large amounts of data are collected regarding the classes of drugs, their affinities for the nervous system, and the transmitter levels in particular structures. These are of use because neurotransmitter fluctuations and actions in specific brain regions usually correspond to observed behavioral effects.

In electrophysiological studies, scientists use either large electrodes that monitor brain wave patterns over a general area or in a nerve bundle, or microelectrodes that monitor the activity of single neurons. Many intriguing effects are observed in the EEGs of nervous system structures during drug use. Atropine produces a strange effect by slowing the brain waves of the cortex, yet exciting the organism. Stimulants increase the frequency and reduce the voltage of the cortical waves; sedatives do the opposite.

Microelectrodes reveal unique effects in single neurons as well. These recordings are made by placing microelectrodes in or near a particular neuron, measuring its activity during drug administration. Some effects observed are that tricyclic antidepressants cause seizure-like discharges in individual neurons and that different drugs selectively inhibit areas of the medulla. Chlorpromazine inhibits the vomiting center there, which is why it is good for seasickness. Morphine inhibits neurons in the medulla's respiratory center, while amphetamine stimulates them, making amphetamine a possible antidote for a morphine overdose, at least in regard to respiration.

INDIRECT PHARMACOLOGICAL TESTS

How can you test an antidepressant on someone who isn't depressed, or an antiemetic on someone who isn't vomiting? You cannot. Indirect pharmacological testing, therefore, requires the artificial induction of a behavior, then an attempt to counteract it with drugs. It also puts us in the deplorable position of having to induce depression, vomiting, and other unpleasant conditions in lab animals as approximations of actual conditions. In addition, some prior knowledge of drug actions is required. For example, if we administer one drug to induce vomiting, followed by a chemical antagonist that attacks the molecules of the first drug, this would be no indication of the drug's action in an actual case of vomiting, since we have created a purely chemical interaction between two drugs. For this reason, the mechanisms have to be clear.

Laboratory models of convulsions can be produced with electroshock to the brain through electrodes, or by the administration of pentylenetetrazol (Metrazol), which produces brief episodes of convulsions by abnormally activating the motor neurons in the brain. Spinal convulsions can be induced with strychnine, which interferes with

Renshaw cell function, allowing spinal motor neurons to fire in excess. These effects can then be reversed with sedatives, neuroleptics, or anxiolytics.

The classic model for depression is the administration of reserpine, which releases DA, NE, and 5-HT from the vesicles and allows their destruction by MAO. The subject shows heavy eyelids, hypothermia, and diarrhea. This produces an ideal condition for testing any of the MAO-inhibiting antidepressants. Drugs like iproniazid block the action of MAO, prevent it from attacking the NE, and allow relatively normal functioning, even though the vesicles remain unnaturally opened. On the other hand, neuroleptics exaggerate reserpine depression by blocking NE receptors and further impeding the transmitter's action.

Among the most common indirect pharmacological tests is the amphetamine antagonism test. Amphetamines induce stereotypic (repetitive) behavior such as gnawing, grooming, or circling in rodents, which is taken as an indication of excessive dopaminergic activity, perhaps related to human psychosis. Neuroleptics block these effects and thus mark themselves as being potentially useful in the treatment of psychosis.

ETHICS OF ANIMAL EXPERIMENTATION

Tempers and emotions run high on both sides of the animal rights issue. Antivivisectionists paint pictures of Nazi-like atrocities perpetrated by negligent, callous experimenters on lovable pets. On the other hand, scientists denounce animal rights activists as naive, puppy-hugging vegetarians who would threaten medical research to let rats run loose. Yet, the fact is that some serious compromises are in the offing as more scientists hearken seriously to the issues, and even enlist as animal advocates, while animal lobbyists raise enough dust to bring about legislation like the Animal Welfare Act, passed in 1966 and amended in 1970, 1976, and 1985.

Much of the dilemma stems from metaphysical roots and depends on questions (like those surrounding abortion) which can be answered only according to a person's religious or philosophical convictions. The central question is: Are animals, as sentient beings like us, entitled to the same rights we would accord to humans, or are animals of less or different value than humans, available to be used as we deem fit? The status you assign to animal life is ultimately a personal decision based on beliefs, be they scientific or spiritual.

The extreme antivivisectionist view finds a focus in the book *Animal Liberation* by Peter Singer, which is the Bible of the animal rights movement. Singer coined the term *speciesism* to define the dictum that one species does not have the right to elevate itself above, or use, another. Such a statement, of course, is under fire from scientists on all sides. The core of the researchers' argument is cogently summarized in one doctor's remark, "If it comes down to a choice between saving my wife or my child and saving my dog, I have no doubts about what choice I'd make." Unfortunately, this is no false analogy. Since it is undeniable that animal experiments have saved hundreds of thousands of human lives, the question becomes this: What is humane? Would an animal rights activist refuse the use of a kidney dialysis machine and let a child die, on the grounds that the equipment exists only because of extensive animal experimentation? These are hard questions worth thinking about.

In their moderate aspects, animal rights issues are more manageable. Singer also posits in his manifesto that at the very least an animal has the right not to suffer. The question here is: Are we wasting animal life needlessly and causing unnecessary suffering? Over 60 million lab animals are killed every year in medical experiments that might not all be necessary. On this issue there is a vague consensus among antivivisectionists, researchers, and legislators alike that the needless killing of animals is at the least a waste of resources, time, and money, which in itself is undesirable. There is also an unformulated sense of moral persuasion supporting the feeling that, even if we use animals for our ends in great quantities, there is an air of unwholesomeness about causing them extended and agonizing pain.

The issue of laboratory atrocities is a wide open one that requires careful investigation. Animal rights literature cites case after case of mistreatments that would make any scientist we know cringe. The statistical incidence of these occurrences is unknown. The fact is that muckrakers going into laboratories to look for crucified animals are likely to be disappointed. Most facilities make an effort to use as few animals as possible and to ensure their proper and humane care. It is generally in the interest of an experiment that the animals be well-maintained. Furthermore, many researchers empathize with the animals they use. If animals must be killed, it is usually done without cruelty and without sentimentality.

Because of its obvious benefits, it seems unlikely that animal experimentation will end in response to cries of *speciesism*. On the other hand, it seems wise to conserve animal life and to guard against the mistreatment of animals, attitudes which recent legislation has moved to enforce.

CONCLUSION

About the end of its second year of testing, when most animal testing, except for the chronic studies, is finished, the drug company submits a full report in the form of a huge, section letter to the Secretary of Health, Education, and Welfare, informing him or her that the drug is in the Investigational New Drug (IND) Stage. The report includes details of the drug's composition, preparation, manufacturing, and conditions of use; the animal test results must be submitted, as well as evidence of the drug's therapeutic activity in animals and its promise and safety for human testing. The proposed clinical investigation must be strictly outlined and adhered to, and the physicians to be involved must be named. Although the chronic toxicity studies in animals continue throughout the entire testing period, the drug is now ready to move on to human testing.

Appendix B

Human and Clinical Research

Thirty days after the acceptance of an IND (Investigational New Drug) by the Food and Drug Administration, human investigations of a drug can begin. These investigations are divided into three phases (see Table B.1). Phase I consists of human pharmacological testing; this phase still focuses on the drug itself and studies its interaction with the human body in ways analogous to the animal testing. Phases II and III mark the clinical testing of the drug, the focus here being on how useful the drug actually is in the therapy of psychopathological conditions.

TABLE B.1 Phases of Drug Testing in Humans

	Number of patients	Length	Purpose	Percent of drugs successfully tested*
Phase 1	20-100	Several months	Mainly safety	70%
Phase 2	Up to several hundred	Several months to two years	Some short-term safety but mainly effectiveness	33%
Phase 3	Several hundred to several thousand	1-4 years	Safety, dosage, effectiveness	25-30%

* For example, of 100 drugs for which investigational new drug applications are submitted to the FDA, about 70 will successfully complete phase 1 trials and go on to phase 2; about 33 of the original 100 will complete phase 2 and go to phase 3; and 25 to 30 of the original 100 will clear phase 3 (and, on average, about 20 of the original 100 will ultimately be approved for marketing).

Source: U.S. Food & Drug Administration Consumer Special Report: New drug Development in the United States, January 1995, page 10. Washington D.C. Government Printing Office.

In all human drug experimentation, the subjects must give their informed consent before testing. They must sign a form accepting the fact that they will be receiving a compound under investigation. And they must be told the nature of the study, its purpose, risks, and benefits, to the extent that the results will not be compromised. At every juncture, care is taken that the subjects understand the implications of their involvement, that their consent is informed and voluntary, and that their legal rights are not preempted.

Different drugs by their nature require different courses of testing, and the procedures may also be affected by different regulations at the state level. However, the experimenters are firmly bound to report any adverse reactions to the FDA immediately.

PHASE I STUDIES

Phase I studies begin gingerly, since the effects of drugs on the human nervous system are difficult to predict from animal tests. They follow the same pattern as the animal studies. A small number of volunteers is chosen. They must be young, healthy, mentally stable, consenting adults, and intelligent enough to give an account of their experiences. Usual candidates are company employees, nurses, and medical students.

About the time that Phase I studies are beginning, process and manufacturing studies are also initiated, since the drug now stands a better chance of actually going into production. The purpose of these studies differs from the research studies in that they are designed to test a variety of processes and machinery by which a drug will be mass-produced. For instance, if there is a sticky procedure involving rare materials in the production of the drug, the process studies will seek a simpler alternative using more common materials. Or they will investigate several vehicles so that maximum (100 percent) absorption can occur.

Toxicity Studies

The main goal of Phase I testing is to establish whether or not a drug is safe for human use (since this cannot be infallibly deduced from the animal studies), to anticipate the variety of human responses, and to collect enough data to design future therapeutic trials. Toxicity studies begin with single doses given to each subject. The starting dose is usually 1/10 to 1/20 the expected ED, judging from the therapeutic index of the animal data. These doses are then increased until signs of toxicity appear. Acute toxicity studies run for a 24hour close evaluation period with a one-week follow-up. Physical exams are done, blood and urine samples taken, dosage-response curves drawn up, subjective testimony about drug effects evaluated, and side effects, hypersensitivities, and idiosyncratic responses scrutinized. Later, chronic studies and multiple dose studies (*loading doses*) for cumulative effects follow.

The classes of psychoactive drugs have batteries of well-documented side effects. Stimulants cause insomnia and racing heartbeat. Antidepressants cause heartburn, nausea, and headaches. The antipsychotic phenothiazines produce a purple-grey discoloration in skin exposed to sunlight, and a brown opacity of the cornea (loss of sight), possibly related to sunlight exposure as well. Because side effects like these are familiar, similar traits in new drugs are carefully observed.

Metabolic Studies

The purpose of these investigations is to identify the enzymatic pathways of a drug's metabolism in humans. These can often be determined through urine and blood analysis, or through radioactive labeling of the drug molecules and a scrupulous examination of the metabolites. The results are compared with what is known from the animal studies, and idiosyncrasies are sought out. Genetic factors may enter, as in the case of drugs like isoniazid, which is deactivated (acetylated) quickly by some individuals and more slowly by others; the slower deactivators frequently show side effects, since the drug remains in their systems longer.

Observation

Irwin's technique is the most prevalent method of establishing whether or not a drug is effective in humans. It uses an 8point rating scale to compare drugged with normal behavior in three areas: (1) psychomotor behavior, like arousal, wakefulness, activity, stimulus-response, drives, and endurance, (2) neurological behavior, like posture (can you stand up?), muscle tone (can you lift your arms?), equilibrium, gait, and reflexes, and (3) autonomic effects, like body temperature, sympathetic, and parasympathetic reactions.

Psychometrics

As with animals, thousands of objective measures are available for testing drug effects on humans. We will present an abbreviated menu to provide some conception of the differences between animal and human studies.

A common test for perception is the critical flicker fusion frequency test (CFF). If you look at a normal light bulb, you see it as a continuous light, although it is actually blinking at a rate of 60 cycles per second. Were the blinking to slow to 8 cps, you would notice it blinking; at 24 cps, you would be uncertain. The threshold point where you see the blinking first become a continuous effect is the *critical flicker fusion frequency*, the critical frequency at which the flicker fuses into continuous light. This is usually about 18 cps. Stimulants can raise the CFF to, let's say, 22 cps, while sedatives might lower it to 15 cps. Another perceptual test is the achromatic spiral aftereffect (SPIR). In this, the subject stares at a rotating Archimedean spiral. When the spiral stops, the eye sees it as continuing to rotate, in a visual echo of movement. Drug use affects the duration of this aftereffect, which is timed in the test.

Central and associative functions are tested by using word association time (WAT), paired association learning (PAL), and time estimation production (TEP). In the word association test, the subject must respond to a given word with the first associated word that springs to mind. This usually takes between 1 and 2.4 seconds, but drugs alter the interval. The paired association learning test requires the memorization and retrieval of learned pairs of words. Time estimation production simply requires the subject to estimate a time interval. For instance, how accurately can you estimate the passage of one minute, or five minutes? Many drugs alter your time perception. Other tests involve the solving of simple arithmetic problems, canceling out a particular character in rows of digits, repeating sequences of numbers forward or backward, or substituting symbols in cryptogram-like fashion.

Tests for motor function involve simple processes that are altered by drug use, such as reaction time (RT), which is measured by a motor response like pressing a button or a key to a visual stimulus, or tapping speed (TS), which measures how fast you can tap a pencil on a tabletop. Stimulants typically increase one's tapping speed and quicken reaction time. Sedatives have the opposite effect in all three tests, as one would expect. However, antipsychotics have variable effects, depending on the structure of the molecule.

In general, these measures are open to a wide number of subject variables (sex, age, diet, sleep habits, motivation, etc.).

Conditioning Studies

The most explored aspects of conditioning in humans are conditioned response formation, conditioned stimulus generalization and discrimination, and extinction of the orienting reflex. The typical model of conditioning in humans is eyeblink conditioning. A tone is sounded just before a puff of air is blown at the subject's eyelid, causing the eye to blink. After several pairings, the subject blinks at the sound of the tone alone. The drug effects on human conditioning as a rule tend to be the same as in the animal conditioning studies.

Correlation Studies

In humans, biochemical studies have to be made through blood and urine analysis, rather than dissection. Urine frequently carries the marks of drug use and behavioral states. For example, high levels of methylated catecholamines occur in the urine of people with some types of schizophrenia. And a variety of metabolites in the urine can betray the presence of drug abuse.

Blood chemistry is another marker of drug effect. Drugs and their metabolites in the blood inform us about the half-life, absorption, effective dosage, and other characteristics. Mescaline, LSD 25, and psilocybin increase the fat content of the blood by freeing fatty acids. High doses of barbiturates raise blood sugar levels. Also, blood effects might reveal the physical or emotional consequences of drug use.

Electrophysiological studies proceed with humans as with animals, since these can be done without injury. The three areas of interest are drug effects on the general brain EEG, effects on the spontaneous electrical activity of the cortex, and the effects on cortical evoked responses. Spontaneous effects are measured by observing the EEG as a drug is administered. For example, at low doses, barbiturates induce fast waves of the frontal lobes that spread to the occipital lobes. At a higher dose, large, slow, random waves appear, and as the dosage nears toxic levels, the wave amplitude increases and becomes interspersed with moments of electrical silence.

Evoked potentials are studied by applying a stimulus like a blinking light and noting its effect on the EEG during drug use. The brain waves that pulse in accord with the rhythm of a 5 cps light will change as drugs affect them.

PHASE II STUDIES

Phase II begins the clinical investigation of a drug, its therapy-oriented testing. Whereas the human studies asked, "How does the drug behave in the human body?" the clinical investigations ask, "Can the drug be used to treat a certain disorder?" Usually the disorder is already targeted, but investigators keep an open mind. For example, iproniazid was first administered as a tuberculosis treatment, but it did nothing for tuberculosis except make the patients feel better by relieving their psychological depression. Instead of a tuberculosis treatment, investigators had discovered an antidepressant.

A licensed doctor is appointed head of the clinical investigation of a drug. This person is responsible for notifying the FDA of all developments, progress, or mishaps. The FDA is especially concerned throughout Phase II with the safety data of the drug and with its therapeutic efficacy. The safety data include ECGs (electrocardiograms), EEGs, blood work, chest Xrays, observation of side effects, and bioavailability. The efficacy data uses two approaches: (1) self-rating of effects based on formal questionnaires and open-ended self-rating in response to unguided questions like, "How do you feel?" and (2) objective findings based on clinical observation and specific tests. The specific test booklet used, the *Early Clinical Drug Evaluation Unit* manual, is published by the National Institute of Mental Health.

Other interests of the clinical investigations are to define the clinical dosage, to further recognize adverse effects like possible dependency, to observe possible variables in a therapeutic setting (previous treatments, drug interactions, clinical environment), and to collect any more data which might optimize the use of the drug. Delayed effects may also be a factor; some antidepressants may require patients to remain on the medication for 12 weeks after symptoms have disappeared, then taper off slowly; this would be essential to the drug's clinical performance.

The early Phase II studies are broad, flexible observational studies in therapeutic settings such as hospitals. The trial is run uncontrolled on 10 to 20 patients, using free but safe dosage ranges and may last from 4 to 12 weeks, with daily clinical observation. Conclusions are then drawn from the test results on this limited group.

Late Phase II testing consists of more extensive, double-blind studies conducted on about 100 patients at several clinics. These are usually targeted for a specific illness and follow a strict protocol submitted by the pharmaceutical company to the FDA. The main FDA requirement is that there be two well-controlled studies with the drug. There are no further specifications than this. Well-controlled means placebo-control and positive control (tests against a good and accepted therapeutic drug), and it includes psychiatric studies that rigidly define the disorder to be treated (see discussion on the *Diagnostic and Statistical Manual of Mental Disorders*, page xxx). In short, two questions must be answered by these studies. First, does the drug have any value when administered for a limited time, at a certain dosage, to a well-defined group of patients? And, second, is this drug superior to existing, reliable drugs with the same purpose? If the answer to both of these questions is yes, the company is in business.

About the time that Phase II studies are beginning, stability studies are also started on the drug. These aim to design the chemical processes that can stabilize the drug molecule for storage, in hopes of giving it a shelf life of 2 years or more.

Psychopathological Profiles

To test the efficacy of drugs, especially on mentally ill patients, we must first know how each class of patients scores under normal conditions on the tests appropriate to their pathology. This adds up to an operational definition of each illness and allows us to judge the test differences produced by drug use. Suppose that we have a test to measure anxiety. First, we establish that a normal individual scores low on this test and that a psychopathologically anxious individual scores high. Now, using this test, we can objectively measure whether a certain sedative reduces the anxiety of the patient and shifts behavior toward normal.

Psychopathological profiles, then, consist of full descriptions of how members of each class of behavioral disorder, undrugged, respond to psychological tests. Another facet of the profile is the appraisal of the characteristic symptoms of a pathology, like the delusions and hallucinations that are the hallmarks of schizophrenia. These evaluations taken together provide an operational definition based on performance and on the appraisal of symptoms, which is in keeping with objective measures. The criteria for diagnosis of all mental disorders are delineated in *the Diagnostic and Statistical Manual of Mental Disorders*.

Since a psychoactive drug is designed to relieve the target symptoms of a certain disorder, the profiles are based on tests or checklists that address the salient features of each disorder. Thus, there are rating scales tailored for different illnesses. For instance, the LM Fergus Falls Behavior Rating Scale for anxiety is a 5point scale for nurses to complete; it covers 11 areas of behavior, like eating, cleanliness, verbal behavior, and interpersonal behavior. The Taylor Manifest Anxiety Scale is used to measure basic anxiety levels. Most scales of this sort consist of items (symptoms) to be marked on a checklist or of questions or statements (I am nervous) to be answered with simple true-false, yes-no, or never-sometimes-often responses.

The biochemical profiles of behavioral disorders are elaborated further, based on determinations about the biochemical correlates of the behavior disorders. The indices of telltale substances in the body are studied—levels for neurotransmitters, electrolytes (minerals), nitrogen, cholesterol, calcium, and steroids, among others. For instance, intracellular and bone levels of sodium have been reported to be elevated in the depressed. MAO levels appear to be lower in schizophrenics, and people with anxiety disorders tend to have higher levels of corticosteroids in their blood.

Likewise, electrophysiological profiles are based on the observed EEGs of the several pathologies. High amplitude EEGs, for example, are a recognized characteristic of depression. Imipramine appears to normalize (reduce) the amplitude of the waves for evoked responses at the same time that the patient is showing clinical improvement; however, imipramine increases the amplitude of these same waves in normal people, something that the researcher would not anticipate. With respect to these particular brain waves, the drug seems to normalize the depressed and depress the normal. Schizophrenics show fast wave activity or choppy slow wave activity, and sometimes the patterns that accompany the performance of mental tasks are absent.

In a word, the psychopathological profiles are definitions of mental disorders couched in observable, measurable, testable terms.

PHASE III STUDIES

By the time Phase III trials are begun, the long-term toxicity tests on animals are through. These studies now open up the test population to hundreds or thousands of inpatients and outpatients at a number of clinics and institutions. A considerable drawback to these experiments is the lack of uniform care, due to the multiplicity of institutional environments, so it is helpful to conduct these studies through organizations like the Veterans Administration Hospitals, which are broad-reaching facilities with a large hospitalized population but reasonably uniform in their procedures. It also helps to design the tests in such a way that data can be fed into computers in a uniform manner and easily collated. In general, an effort is made to agree upon the standards of the testing at this phase.

The Phase III studies are open label, or single-blind, studies, in which the drug is not concealed from experimenters. The goals of these studies are only to gather safety data on a large number of people. Are there adverse interactions with other drugs like alcohol and nicotine in the wider range of patients? How will geriatric and pediatric patients respond? These studies develop the dose regimens of the drug for each type of patient, provide more information on the mode of action, carve a niche for the drug in therapy, and buoy up the claims that will be made in the marketing of the drug.

Because of their breadth, Phase III studies are long and costly. If possible, doses near toxic levels are explored further. Fifty to a hundred patients will receive the drug for a year to test longer-ranging use. The tests involved are the same as those in Phase II.

Finally, when all testing is satisfactorily completed, the data are all assembled into a New Drug Application (NDA), a report as large as 100 large volumes, which is loaded into a van or small truck and packed off to Washington for approval. This document supports all of the claims made for the drug and all of the information given on the concise data sheet that will be included in drug shipments—information about diseases and treatments, methods of adminstration, dosages, contraindications, side effects, storage, and so on. At this point, the NDA is either approved or rejected for more development.

Even after the drug has been approved and is being marketed, post-marketing reports must be submitted to the FDA, quarterly in the first year, every six months in the second, and once a year thereafter. Clinical studies may continue. Furthermore, there are those who feel that there should be a Phase IV—worldwide studies of the drug in widespread use.

Glossary

acetylcholine (ACh) A neurotransmitter. One of its important functions is the activation of the skeletal muscles.

acetylcholinesterase The enzyme that breaks down acetylcholine.

ACh See **acetylcholine.**

AChE See acetylcholinesterase.

acid Slang for LSD.

action potential The nerve impulse or window of depolarization that travels along the axon when a neuron fires.

activated charcoal A form of charcoal made from organic matter with strong adsorptive properties; that is, substances attach to the surface of its particles. Used as an antidote in poisoning and overdoses to interfere with the absorption of toxic materials.

active transport The movement of materials across cell membranes by special protein carriers, as opposed to the unassisted movement by passive diffusion.

acute Having a short and severe course. Referring to single moderate to high doses of a drug, as opposed to **chronic** or long-term.

acute stress disorder A mental disorder resembling post-traumatic stress disorder but of shorter duration and accompanied by dissociative symptoms (**see dissociative disorder**).

addiction (drug) A condition of drug dependence marked by the compulsion to use a drug, a tendency to increase the dosage, physical and psychological dependence, withdrawal symptoms upon abstinence, and detrimental effects on the users, their relations, and society.

additive effect A combined drug effect in which doses of different drugs augment the effect as though they were doses of a single drug.

adenosine A substance that acts as a naturally occurring depressant in the body. Caffeine partially blocks its action.

ADHD See **attention deficit hyperactivity disorder**.

administration The giving or taking of a drug.

adrenal gland A gland near the kidneys that releases epinephrine and small amounts of norepinephrine into the blood. The inner core is called the *adrenal medulla;* the outer segment is called *the adrenal cortex.*

adrenergic Pertaining to norepinephrine (NE), which is also known as noradrenalin.

aerosol A suspension of colloidal particles in a gas.

affect A prolonged emotion that colors one's life and attitudes. Mood.

affinity The strength of the tendency of a molecule to bind to a receptor or tissue.

agonist A substance or molecule that contributes in any way to the activation of a receptor site (e.g., by attaching to it or by inhibiting an enzyme and allowing a neurotransmitter to stimulate it). See **antagonist.**

agonist-antagonist An opioid (synthetic narcotic analgesic) that stimulates some types of opiate receptors and antagonizes others.

agoraphobia Sometimes described as a fear of open spaces; fear of being alone and away from the safety of one's home.

agranulocytosis A symptom characterized by a marked decrease in the number of cells containing granules. The decrease involves white blood cells and consequently a lowered immune response.

akathisia A compulsive restlessness and desire to move--a side effect of neuroleptics.

akinesia A condition of reduced movements that may advance to a catatonic condition--a side effect of neuroleptics.

all-or-nothing response The property of a neuron to fire completely or not at all, but never to an intermediate extent.

amphetamine psychosis A drug-induced psychosis resembling a typical paranoid psychosis, with hallucinations and disordered thinking alternating with periods of mania.

amygdala (amygdalae) A set of limbic nuclei involved with aggression, odor, taste, exploration, and self-defense.

analeptics Same as **stimulants.**

analgesia Relief from pain.

analogue A chemical compound similar to another in most respects, but differing in one component; for instance, having an atomic group attached to a different place on a molecule.

anesthetics Depressants usually applied at high doses to induce a state of deep sleep with muscle relaxation and insensitivity to pain, for the purpose of performing surgery.

angina pectoris Pains in the chest due to arterial contractions caused by norepinephrine.

anhedonia An inability to experience pleasure. May be an insensitivity of the reward system due to drug actions.

anorexia Lack or loss of appetite for food, accompanied by a noticeable weight loss if it is chronic.

antagonist A substance or molecule that contributes in any way to the inhibition of a receptor site. See **agonist.**

anterograde amnesia Memory deficits for events following a trauma.

anticholinergic syndrome A battery of effects following from blockage of cholinergic receptors. Includes dry mouth, flushing, blurred vision, high temperatures, delirium, disorientation, agitation, and possible hallucinations.

antidepressants Drugs that relieve depression. They include the tricyclics and the MAO inhibitors.

antidiuretic hormone A hormone that signals the kidneys to reabsorb water rather than excrete it.

antipsychotics See **neuroleptics.**

anxiety A dissus emotional state resembling fear and characterized by apprehension of a vague future threat.

anxiolytics Minor tranquilizers. Drugs that relieve anxiety without causing drowsiness. The benzodiazepines are the major class of anxiolytics.

apnea Brief interruptions of breathing (loss of breath). The causes are generally unknown. Respiratory stimulants are of some use in treatment.

arrhythmia Irregular beating of the heart.

artificial hibernation A drug-induced state of low metabolism, muscle relaxation, and twilight sleep produced by inhibiting the central nervous system.

association areas Parts of the brain involved in the integration and evaluation of sensory experiences.

association neuron Also **interneuron.** A neuron that connects one neuron with another, found in the central nervous system.

asthma A condition marked by recurrent attacks of labored breathing and wheezing from spasms of the lung passages. Treated with stimulants and bronchodilators.

astrocytes Star-shaped cells that make up part of the glia. Their filaments end in the glial feet that constitute part of the blood-brain barrier.

ataxia Muscle incoordination that makes it difficult to walk and causes staggering.

atherosclerosis Narrowing and hardening of the arteries due to an accumulation of fatty material on the inner vessel walls.

attention deficit hyperactivity disorder Previously known as *attention deficit disorder, hyperactivity,* or *minimal brain dysfunction*--a behavioral disorder characterized inattention and impulsiveness. Treatment with stimulants produces paradoxical calming.

autism A withdrawal from reality--one of the symptoms of schizophrenia.

autonomic nervous system The nerves that control the organs and glands and maintain bodily processes.

axon The single long extension of the body of a neuron that carries the signal (action potential) to the next cell.

axon hillock The portion of an axon next to the soma--the little bump where the depolarization (firing) of the axon begins.

BAL See **blood alcohol level.**

barley malt A powder made from sprouted barley, a starchy cereal grain. The sprouted barley and the malt contain an enzyme that breaks starch down into sugar, so yeast can convert the sugar to alcohol in the fermentation process.

basal ganglia Two large forebrain structures involved in movement. Contain the key sites involved in parkinsonism. See **extrapyramidal system.**

basal metabolism The quantity of energy used by an organism at rest.

behavioral tolerance The ability to behave normally in spite of a drug's physiological effects.

behaviorism A branch of psychology that bases its observations and conclusions on definable and measurable behaviors and on experimental methods, rather than on concepts of ``mind.''

benzodiazepines The most significant class of minor tranquilizers, including diazepam (Valium), chlordiazepoxide (Librium), flurazepam (Dalmane), and triazolam (Halcion).

beta-endorphin See **endorphin.**

bioamines Nitrogen-containing compounds derived from amino acids. DA, NE, and SE are neurotransmitter bioamines.

bioavailability The degree to which a drug becomes available to the target tissue after administration.

biological equivalence The parity that results when two drugs affect the same biological systems to the same degree, even if they contain different active ingredients.

biorhythms Cycles of biological activity that may interact with environmental cycles (e.g., day and night). Sleep times, for instance, constitute a biorhythm.

biotransformation Alteration of molecules by natural mechanisms in the body. Most biotransformation involves the breakdown of nutrients in the liver; many drugs are deactivated by similar mechanisms.

bipolar disorder An affective disorder showing both extremes of mania and depression.

bizarre delusions Strange beliefs and convictions that are ungrounded in reality--a symptom of schizophrenia.

blood alcohol level (BAL) The percentage of alcohol in the blood. A BAL of 0.10 percent is considered intoxicated (while driving) by most state laws.

blood-brain barrier A set of factors that make up a tight seal around brain capillaries and prevent the movement of materials from the circulation into the brain. The factors are tight cell junctions in the brain capillary walls, a lack of pores, and the glial feet.

body compartment An area inside the body bounded by tissue: e.g., the blood vessels, peritoneal cavity, and extracellular fluid of the brain.

brand name Same as **trade name.**

bromide(s) Long-acting sedatives used widely in the nineteenth century.

bronchitis Inflammation of the larger air passages in the lungs.

bronchodilators Drugs that widen the air passages in the lungs.

bronchospasms Spasmodic contractions of the muscles of the larger air passages in the lungs.

butyrophenones A class of antipsychotic drugs. Less used than the phenothiazines.

cannabis Any preparation of *Cannabis sativa* that contains the psychoactive ingredient THC or other psychoactive cannabinoids. Used to refer to plant material or preparations as opposed to pure THC.

cardiac Pertaining to the heart.

cardiovascular Pertaining to the heart and blood vessels.

carotid artery The principal artery found in the neck, which supplies the brain with oxygenated blood.

catalepsy A condition of immobility in animals and man.

catatonia Muscle rigidity characterized by stiff unnatural postures in catatonic schizophrenia.

catatonic schizophrenia A form of schizophrenia marked by immobility (waxy flexibility) and dissociation from the environment.

catecholamine hypothesis The hypothesis that depression is linked to altered levels of NE in the brain.

catecholamines Bioamines containing a catechol ring. The neurotransmitter catecholamines are DA and NE.

cellular tolerance Same as **neuronal tolerance.**

central nervous system The neurons of the spinal cord and the brain.

chemical equivalence The parity that results when two drugs contain identical amounts of the same active ingredient.

chemical name The name of a drug molecule used by organic chemists, which often refers to the chemical structure of the molecule, and to its chemical class; e.g., lysergic acid diethylamide (LSD).

chemoreceptor trigger zone The center in the medulla, stimulation of which induces nausea.

chloral hydrate A sedative-hypnotic compound used in the nineteenth century. Unusual in that it does not suppress REM sleep.

chloroform An anesthetic similar to ether.

chocolate liquor The ground chocolate beans that are the starting point for all chocolate products. Also called *chocolate mass* or *baking chocolate.*

cholesterol A pearly, fatlike alcohol found in animal fats and oils.

cholinergic Pertaining to acetylcholine.

chorea Continual, jerky, involuntary movements--a side effect of neuroleptics.

chorionic villi The branching ends of the umbilical cord that dip into blood pools in the wall of the uterus. The site where most exchange occurs between the mother and the fetus.

chronic Over an extended period of time.

cingulate gyrus A limbic structure resembling a fold of the cortex, possibly involved in aggression, fear, and other emotions.

cirrhosis Liver damage caused by an increase of stored fat, which breaks free and damages the hepatic vessels, scarring and crippling the liver--caused by chronic, high alcohol use.

clinical equivalence The parity that results when two drugs produce the same overall therapeutic effect, even if they consist of different molecules affecting different systems.

CNS Central nervous system.

cocaine bugs See **parasitosis.**

collaterals Offshoots of an axon that carry the action potential to several other neurons.

colloid A substance consisting of one form of matter dispersed or distributed throughout a medium. A suspension is one form of colloid.

competitive antagonist A substance that has an affinity for a receptor, such that it competes with a neurotransmitters for occupancy of available receptors.

compulsion See **obsessive-compulsive disorder.**

compulsive substance abuse Drug dependence; drug addiction. The official classification for drug dependence in the fourth edition of the *Diagnostic and Statistical Manual of Mental Disorders.*

concentration gradient The degree of difference between two areas that contain a substance in unequal concentrations. Molecules in areas of high concentration tend to diffuse "down the gradient" into areas containing lesser concentrations.

concordance rate The frequency of occurrence of a trait occurring in both members of a pair of twins.

conditioned tolerance A form of drug tolerance resulting from an ongoing familiarity with the drug-taking environment. When the drug is later taken in unfamiliar surroundings, a loss of tolerance shows.

congener A chemical compound closely related to another. Used to refer to the additional chemicals found in alcoholic beverages: vitamins, amino acids, oils, and other alcohols.

convulsants Drugs that cause convulsions.

coronary Relating to either of two arteries branching from the aorta and supplying blood directly to the heart muscle.

corpus callosum The band of tissue that connects the two cerebral hemispheres and forms the bridge of communication between them.

cortical Pertaining to the neocortex of the brain.

cotransmitters Neurotransmitters that work in conjunction with other neurotransmitters to effect changes in neural functioning.

crack A freebased form of cocaine hydrochloride in the form of small crystallized "rocks." It crackles when smoked.

cranial nerves Nerves extending out of the brain.

crash A rebound depression following the euphoria and excitation of stimulant use.

cross-tolerance Tolerance produced for one drug by another drug. LSD, e.g., increases the tolerance for mescaline.

cumulative effects A combined drug effect in which drug doses are not fully deactivated before the next dose is taken, so that the drug accumulates and the effect increases.

curandera A Mexican Indian holy woman and healer.

cyclothymic disorder A mental disorder resembling bipolar disorder, with both manic and depressive episodes, but of milder intensity and longer duration.

cytochrome P-450 A liver enzyme (mixed function oxidase) that biotransforms alcohol, barbiturates, and many other substances. Readily induced, it is responsible for some cases of tolerance and for many drug interactions. See **inducibility.**

DA See **dopamine.**

delirium tremens (DTs) An effect of alcohol withdrawal consisting of profound disorientation, nightmares (the horrors), tremors, shaking, delirium, and hallucinations.

delusions Beliefs that are ungrounded in reality.

dendrites Treelike processes branching out from the body (soma) of a neuron.

depersonalization disorder A dissociative disorder marked by a sense of loss or distancing from one's body and by distortions of normal perceptions.

depolarization The reversal of the electrical potential across an axon membrane as channels open and sodium ions enter the axon.

desensitization A treatment for phobia that involves gradual exposure to an anxiety-inducing stimulus, while the patient is trained to relax. Tranquilizers or sedatives may be used.

dexamethasone suppression test A test using the cortisol-like substance dexamethasone to challenge an NE-dependent reaction in the hypax system. Used to implicate the role of NE in depression.

direct action The attachment of a drug molecule directly to a receptor site to produce an effect.

disorganized behaviors Symptoms of schizophrenia consisting of odd and incongruous actions, such as showering with one's clothes on.

disorganized schizophrenia A form of schizophrenia that is chronic with an early onset; it is characterized by disordered, incoherent behavior.

disorganized thinking A symptom of schizophrenia consisting of disordered thought processes. While the structure of speech may remain normal, the meanings are disjunctive, without logic, or apparently nonsensical.

displacement activity Engagement in an activity in place of another activity, e.g., a cock might scratch the ground instead of fighting.

disposition tolerance Tolerance due to the increased metabolism of a drug. See **metabolic tolerance.**

dissociative disorder A class of anxiety disorders, all of which involve a loss or partial loss of one's sense of identity. Symptoms include amnesia, changes of identity, alterations of sensory perception, distortions of body image, and a sense of detachment from self or world. The symptoms of depersonalization disorder in particular resemble the effects of some drugs.

dissociative reaction See dissociative disorder.

distillation The process of purifying a substance by evaporating it and collecting the condensation. In the distillation of wines, e.g., impurities are drawn off by evaporation and a liquid with a higher concentration of alcohol condenses and can be collected.

distribution The dispersal of a drug among the tissues of the body and the pattern of its concentration at various sites.

distribution half-life The time it takes for blood levels of a drug to drop to half (after equilibrium), due to the redistribution and storage of the drug (rather than due to its biotransformation and excretion).

disynaptic Involving two synapses (three neurons).

diuresis Increased urination.

dizygotic Coming from two separate eggs, as fraternal twins do.

dopamine (DA) A neurotransmitter that is both a bioamine and a catecholamine. Important in thinking, fine motor movements, and autonomic functions. Depletion of dopamine in the basal ganglia causes parkinsonism. DA overactivity is also believed to be a factor in schizophrenia.

dopamine hypothesis The hypothesis that schizophrenia is a result of DA overactivity in the brain.

dose-response curve A graph, for a particular effect, of dosages of a drug plotted against (1) the degree of effect on an individual (individual response curve) or (2) the number of individuals in a group showing the response (group response curve).

dose-response relationship The relationship between the amount of a drug given and the magnitude of the effect it produces. See **dose-response curve.**

double blind study A drug and placebo study where neither the experimenters who administer the treatment nor the subjects know that a placebo is involved. At the end of the experiment, the principal investigator decodes the effects.

down-regulation The process in which neurons reduce their functioning to maintain equilibrium through the desensitization of receptors, the reduction of the number of receptors, less production of neurotransmitter, or some other mechanism.

drug action The interaction of drug molecules with living tissue.

drug effect A perceptible change in the behavior of a tissue or organism elicited by a drug.

drug fate The mechanisms of the biotransformation and excretion of a drug.

drug holidays Brief, planned stoppages in a drug-taking schedule.

drug receptor Any tissue or biochemical structure able to receive and interact with a drug and participate in a drug response.

drug vehicle Any medium, usually an oil or aqueous solution in which drugs are dissolved or suspended for ease of administration, typically for injection.

dynorphins A type of neuropeptide, along with beta-endorphin and the enkephalins.

dysphoria Disquiet or malaise; "feeling bad." The opposite of euphoria.

dysthymic disorder A chronic mild depression.

dystonias Movements (e.g., massive writhings) caused by a disordered tension in the muscles--one of the side effects of neuroleptics.

E Epinephrine.

ECT See **electroconvulsive shock therapy.**

ED See **effective dosage.**

EEG Electroencephalogram. A tracing of the changes of electrical potential in the brain.

effective dosage (ED) The dosage at which a drug first produces a desired effect on an individual. In groups, the ED1 is the dosage that produces the effect in 1 percent of the population, the ED50 in 50 percent, and so forth.

electrical gradient The difference between an area with many electrons and an area with fewer.

electrical potential The potential for electrons to flow down an electrical gradient, from an area of more highly concentrated electrons to an area of less concentrated electrons. Same as **voltage**.

electroconvulsive shock therapy Delivery of a brief, high current, electric shock to the brain (that induces convulsions as a side effect). Still used in cases of certain kinds of depression.

empathogens A proposed name for drugs such as MDMA that have a prominent and positive emotional effect on users, including an increased empathy for others present.

emphysema A pathological accumulation of air in the lungs. May be caused by cell damage that creates air spaces due to smoking.

endocrine Secreting internally. Refers to glands that secrete substances such as hormones directly into the blood. The endocrine system involves internal chemical communications that are slower than those of the nervous system.

endogenous Originating internally.

endorphin A key neuropeptide that contains the enkephalin molecules in its structural sequence. Important in pain and reward systems in the brain.

enkephalin A neuropeptide associated with the mediation of pain and the action of opiates. Related to **beta-endorphin**. See **endorphin.**

entactogen Same as **empathogens.**

epidural Just under the surface of the skin.

epinephrine A catecholamine related to norepinephrine that is not a neurotransmitter but is capable of stimulating adrenergic receptors. Plays a key role in a sympathetic reaction. See **adrenal gland.**

equilibrium The state when concentrations of diffusing molecules have equalized. With semipermeable membranes, 50 percent of a substance is on either side, and diffusion occurring in both directions is even.

ergotism A condition resulting from poisoning by *Claviceps purpurea*, a fungus that infects rye and other grains, which contains a substance related to LSD. Accompanied by severe symptoms including gangrene, psychosis, hallucinations, and convulsions. Can be fatal.

esophageal sphincter Muscle fibers around the opening of the esophagus into the stomach.

ethanol Pure alcohol. Same as *ethyl alcohol, grain alcohol, grain neutral spirits,* and *absolute alcohol.*

ether A derivative of alcohol used as an anesthetic and intoxicant.

etiology The science of causes and origins of disease.

extracellular fluid (ECF) The body fluid around the cells. It is connected to the blood through the capillary pores and resembles the blood plasma. The brain ECF is a separate body compartment.

extrapyramidal system A network of nerve fibers that involves the basal ganglia and the substantia nigra. The extrapyramidal system mediates muscle tonus, posture, and movement coordination. It is also involved in parkinsonism.

fast action The action of a neurotransmitter that binds to a receptor and affects the functioning of an ion channel through a neural membrane. As opposed to a the slow action of a second messenger system within the membrane.

fate Same as **drug fate.**

fermentation Generally, the breakdown of complex organic molecules due to the action of a substance or organism. With alcohol, the breakdown of sugars by yeast.

fetal alcohol syndrome A variety of fetal abnormalities caused by the mother's chronic use of alcohol.

fibrocystic breast disease The growth of cystic spaces surrounded by fibrous tissue in the breasts. Cyst: an enclosed cavity lined by epithelium and containing a liquid or semi-solid material.

filtration The diffusion of molecules through the channels and pores of a membrane.

first generation neuroleptics DA-blocking drugs developed in the 1950s and used to treat schizophrenia.

first-pass metabolism The biotransformation of drug molecules as they first pass through the liver on their way from the site of administration to the site of action.

fluid mosaic model A description of a cell membrane as a double layer of phospholipid molecules with large protein globules embedded in it.

focus In reference to epilepsy, the point of origin of the neural discharges in the brain that are expressed as seizures.

forebrain All of the structures above the midbrain. Made up of the old brain and the new brain.

formication Same as **parasitosis.**

freebasing The process of purifying a drug by treating it with alkaloids (bases). For instance, treating cocaine hydrochloride with baking soda undoes the effect of the hydrochloric acid used to stabilize it and frees the cocaine in purer form.

frontal lobes The forward part of the cortex involved in learning, emotion, spatial organization, and motor functions. See **primary motor area.**

GABA See **gamma-aminobutyric acid.**

GABA shunt An alternate set of transformations in the Krebs cycle of a cell that allows it to produce GABA and glutamate.

GABA-T The enzyme that breaks down the neurotransmitter GABA.

gamma-aminobutyric acid (GABA) An important inhibitory neurotransmitter found only--but widely--in the central nervous system.

ganglion A cluster of nerve cell bodies in the periphery.

gastric emptying The emptying of the stomach into the intestine.

generalized anxiety disorder A diffuse state of anxiety that persists for a month or more and impairs performance of daily functions.

generic name The official, legal name of a drug for use by the public. Ex.: diazepam, amphetamine, aspirin.

Gilles de la Tourette's syndrome A disorder in which patients involuntarily yell, curse, grunt, or bark, and display a number of motor and verbal tics.

glia A gluelike supporting tissue surrounding the brain cells. Contains the astrocytes and glial feet contributing to the blood-brain barrier.

glomerulus The small bud that is the site where substances from the blood are filtered into the nephron tubules of the kidneys.

habituation A mild form of psychological dependence marked by a desire to take drugs for psychological effects, no increase of dosage, some psychological dependence, and consequences that affect primarily the users and not their relations or society.

half-life The time it takes for the blood concentration of a drug to drop to half. Measured from the point of equilibrium after absorption. May be due to metabolism, elimination, or redistribution. Same as **plasma half-life** (i.e., blood plasma).

hallucination A sensory perception in the absence of an actual external stimulus that may occur in any of the senses. May also occur as a failure to perceive stimuli that are present (negative hallucinations).

hallucinogens Drugs that cause hallucinations, psychosis-like effects, and distortions of perception and cognition. The class includes LSD, psilocybin, and mescaline.

hash oil An extract prepared by boiling hashish and straining out the oils. Consists of 20 percent to 70 percent THC.

hashish A concentration of the resins of the flowering tops of female cannabis plants. Has a THC content of 5 percent to 20 percent.

hemodialysis The artificial process of filtering the blood through a semipermeable membrane to clear it of impurities.

hemoglobin The oxygen-carrying component of the red blood cells.

hepatic Pertaining to the liver.

heroin maintenance programs Clinical programs, used to a limited extent in England, that treat recovering opiate abusers with prescribed doses of heroin.

heterocyclics A newer class of antidepressants containing more than three rings in their molecular structure. See **second generation antidepressants.**

hindbrain A three-inch-long extension of the spinal cord, including the medulla, pons, reticular formation--as well as the cerebellum.

hippocampus A limbic structure involved in memory and learning.

homunculus A "map" of the body located in the cortex and made of sensory or motor cells. Homunculus means "little man" or "dwarf." See **primary somatosensory area** and **primary motor area.**

hydrazines A class of compounds from which the MAOI antidepressants were first developed.

hypax The hypothalamic-pituitary axis. The hormone-releasing system that is affected by the dexamethasone suppression test, used to correlate low NE levels with depression.

hyperpolarization An increase of the electrical potential across the axon membrane by making the cell interior more negative.

hyperreactivity Reaction to a normal dose of a drug as though it were a large dose.

hypersensitivity Also **supersensitivity**. A response to a drug dose that would have no effect on an average individual.

hypertension High blood pressure.

hypnotics Depressants applied to induce sleep.

hypochondriasis An anxiety disorder consisting of a persistent unfounded fear that one has a serious disease.

hypoglycemia Low blood sugar.

hypomania Excited behavior that is greater than normal, but not enough to be considered full-blown mania.

hypopolarization The slight reduction of electrical potential across the axon membrane by making the cell interior less negative.

hyporeactivity Insensitivity to a normal dose of a drug. Tolerance is one form.

hypotension Low blood pressure.

hypothalamus A cluster of nuclei in the old brain (forebrain) that monitors the blood and signals the release of hormones that regulate basic biological drives and processes (eating, sex, body temperature, etc.). See **pituitary gland.**

hypothermia Low body temperature.

hypoxia A condition of lower than normal amounts of oxygen being supplied to tissues and organs.

idiosyncratic responses Incongruous or unexpected drug responses that are unique to an individual.

illusion A stimulus that is misperceived or mistaken for something else.

indirect action A drug action that doesn't involve the direct attachment of a drug to a receptor site, for example, the inhibition of an enzyme. See **direct action.**

individual response curve A graph of a drug effect on one individual, which plots varying dosages of the drug against the magnitude or intensity of its effect.

indolamine A bioamine containing an indole ring. The neurotransmitter indolamine is SE.

inducibility The capability of a drug to increase the supply of liver enzymes that biotransform it. Usually the result of chronic exposure to a substance.

interneuron Same as **association neuron.**

intra-arterial injection A route of administration involving injection into an artery.

intracranial injection A route of administration involving injection directly into the brain or its ventricles (fluid-filled spaces).

intramuscular Within the muscle tissue.

intraperitoneal injection A route of administration involving injection into the abdomen and into the fluid-filled sac that supports the intestines.

intrathecal Within the membrane that sheathes the spinal cord and brain.

intravenous Within the veins.

inverse agonists Substances that bind to a receptor and produce an effect opposite to that of receptor agonists.

ion A charged atom or molecule that has split off from a compound and in the process has gained or lost an electron.

isomer A molecule that is the mirror image of another molecule's structure.

Korsakoff's psychosis A form of alcoholic psychosis often associated with Wernicke's disease.

latency period The time between administration and the onset of a drug action, when the effect has not yet appeared.

laudanum A medicinal tonic that featured opium and contained a number of spices and possibly other psychoactive ingredients, such as wine.

LD See **lethal dosage.**

lethal dosage (LD) The dosage at which a drug kills one or more individuals in a sample. At LD2 it kills 2 percent, at LD50 it kills 50 percent, etc.

limbic system A set of old brain structures (amygdalae, septal region, hippocampus, cingulate gyrus, etc.) concerned with a number of functions, most notably, memory, emotion, and aggression.

lipid Pertaining to fat.

lipid-soluble Able to dissolve in fatty tissue. Lipid-soluble drugs can usually dissolve through biological membranes.

lithium An element (light metal) that relieves the symptoms of mania.

liver lobule The basic structural unit of the liver, the main site of biotransformation.

local anesthesia Loss of sensation without loss of consciousness and without impairment of vital functions like circulation and respiration.

locus coeruleus A nucleus in the reticular formation that governs the dreaming (REM) phase of sleep. Also the key center of NE neurons in the brain.

major depressive disorder A mental disorder characterized by one or more major depressive episodes, without mania. Criteria are two weeks or more of depressed mood or loss of interest, plus at least four other symptoms of depression.

major depressive episode An attack of depression marked by crushing sadness, fear, delusions of worthlessness, sleep and eating disturbances, and loss of motivation.

major tranquilizers See **neuroleptics.**

mania An affective disorder consisting of a hyperexcited condition involving an expansive emotional state, frantic activity, an inflated sense of self, hyperirritability, talkativeness, and impaired judgment.

MAO An enzyme that destroys the neurotransmitters DA, NE, and SE, and is found in all three types of synapses.

MAO inhibitors Same as **MAOIs.**

MAOIs A class of drugs that relieve depression by inhibiting the enzyme MAO and thereby raise bioamine levels. Noted for serious side effects.

marijuana A smoking preparation of marijuana consisting of crushed seeds, leaves, flowers, and fine stems of hemp.

mash The mixture of water, yeast, and starches or sugars that is the basis of the fermentation process.

maximum efficacy The dosage at which a drug produces its greatest possible effect in an individual or a group (the dosage at which 100 percent of the group shows the effect).

mechanism of action The specific biochemical process by which a drug produces its particular effect. Ex.: direct stimulation of a receptor or blocking the reuptake of neurotransmitters.

medial forebrain bundle A system of nerve tracts extending through the brain that mediates pleasure.

medulla oblongata A strip of tissue in the brainstem that contains many important centers for the control of autonomic functions. See **autonomic nervous system.**

meninges The series of membranes that enclose the central nervous system.

mesolimbic pathway One of the key dopamine pathways in the brain, originating in the ventral tegmental area of the midbrain and projecting to the corticolimbic system. Implicated in pleasure and reward and in drug dependency.

metabolic tolerance Tolerance resulting from the induction of liver enzymes. See **inducibility.**

metabolite A molecule that has been produced through the biotransformation of some other substance.

methadone maintenance programs Clinical programs that treat recovering opiate abusers with daily doses of the synthetic opiate methadone. The treatment is often long-term or indefinite.

methylation A metabolic process in which a methyl group is added to a molecule.

methylxanthines Same as **xanthines.**

microsomal enzymes Liver enzymes in the endoplasmic reticulum that metabolize nutrients, hormones, drugs, etc. (Microsomes are fragments of the endoplasmic reticulum that may be separated in a centrifuge.)

midbrain The short strip of tissue between the hindbrain and forebrain. Includes the tectum, tegmentum, and part of the reticular formation.

minor tranquilizers Same as **anxiolytics.**

miosis Contraction of the pupils of the eyes.

mixed function oxidases Enzymes that oxidize a wide variety of substances in the liver in the process of biotransformation.

monoamine oxidase inhibitors See **MAOIs.**

monosynaptic Involving one synapse (two neurons).

monozygotic Coming from a single divided egg--as identical twins do.

motor neurons Neurons that carry motor commands outward from the brain and spinal cord to the muscles.

multiple personality disorder The dissociative disorder consisting of the existence in an individual of two or more distinct personalities, each of which may dominate at different times and may or may not be aware of the others.

muscarinic Pertaining to muscarine. Used to describe the cholinergic receptors that respond to muscarine.

myasthenia gravis A disease that impairs the action of ACh at the skeletal muscle synapses, weakening the actions of muscles and making the limbs feel heavy.

mydriasis Wide dilation of the pupils of the eyes--an effect of some drugs.

myelin sheathing A fatty covering on axons that speeds up the transmission of the action potential.

narcolepsy A condition of severe and uncontrollable sleepiness due to neural dysfunction.

narcotic analgesics Drugs that are used to alleviate pain. They include all natural and synthetic opiates.

narcotics Drugs that cause sedation and drowsiness. In legal terminology, any illegal controlled substance.

NE See **norepinephrine.**

necrosis Death of tissue, usually in localized areas.

negative symptoms Symptoms of schizophrenia that manifest as the lack of behaviors seen in normal people, e.g., an absence of emotion or interest in the environment.

nephron Basic structural unit of the kidney; filters material out of the blood.

neural Pertaining to nerve cells (neurons) or their functions.

neuroleptic malignant syndrome A serious and potentially lethal condition linked to the use of neuroleptic drugs and associated with severe and unpredictable changes of body temperature.

neuroleptics Drugs that relieve the major symptoms of schizophrenia and produce waking states that resemble sleep. Also known as **major tranquilizers** and **antipsychotics**.

neuromodulation The process by which inputs to a neuron alter its sensitivity to other inputs or change its firing characteristics.

neuromuscular junction A junction between a neuron and a muscle fiber; a synapse.

neuron Nerve cell.

neuronal tolerance Adaptation of individual nerve cells to the presence of a drug.

neuropeptides Peptides that have an action on nerve cells. Some, like the enkephalins, are possibly neurotransmitters.

neurotransmitter A natural chemical released by one neuron to influence or communicate with another. Acetylcholine, dopamine, norepinephrine, serotonin, GABA, etc.

new antipsychotics DA- and 5-HT-blocking drugs developed after first generation neuroleptics. Used to treat schizophrenia.

new brain The large, convoluted neocortex (cerebrum) that constitutes the outer layer or covering of the brain.

New Glossary Items

nicotinic Pertaining to nicotine. Used to describe cholinergic receptors that respond to nicotine. See **muscarinic.**

NIDA The National Institute on Drug Abuse.

nigrostriatal pathway One of the key dopamine pathways in the brain; it runs from the substantia nigra to a region near the striatum of the basal ganglia. Implicated in the symptoms of parkinsonism.

noncompetitive antagonist An antagonist with a greater affinity for receptors than a neurotransmitter. It unseats the neurotransmitter molecules and blocks or inhibits the receptors.

nonproprietary name The official legal name of a drug for use by the public; e.g., iodine, sodium bicarbonate, diazepam.

nonspecific action A broad drug action that affects many organs and processes. E.g., alcohol depolarizes all nerve cell membranes and affects many systems.

nonspecific factors Factors in a drug effect that are not related to the pharmacology of a drug; e.g., the weight of the user or the environment in which the drug is taken.

noradrenergic synapses Synapses where norepinephrine is the neurotransmitter.

norepinephrine (NE) A neurotransmitter--both a bioamine and a catecholamine. Most important in mood regulation, reward systems, and the sympathetic reaction.

norepinephrine hypothesis The hypothesis that schizophrenia stems from the loss of NE in the reward system.

nucleus A cluster of nerve cell bodies in the CNS.

nucleus accumbens A nucleus that is part of the dopaminergic system of the brain. Implicated in reward and in the pleasurable reinforcing effects of cocaine and morphine.

nystagmus Rapid, involuntary movements of the eyeball (horizontal, vertical, or rotatory).

obsession See **obsessive-compulsive disorder.**

obsessive-compulsive disorder An anxiety state that involves obsessions or compulsions. Obsessions are repugnant but persistent notions that invade consciousness. Compulsions are senseless, repetitive behaviors that a person feels driven to perform; e.g., hand washing.

occipital lobe The part of the cortex governing vision.

old brain The part of the forebrain above the midbrain in the central area of the brain proper.

ololiuqui The Aztec name for the psychoactive seeds of *Rivea corymbosa*, a species of morning glory plant.

opiates As used in this book, any substance, natural or synthetic, that is related in action to morphine and binds to the same, or some of the same, receptors. Some writers use it just to mean opium, morphine, codeine, and heroin--the natural ingredients of the poppy and their derivatives, excluding the synthetic narcotic analgesics.

opioids As used in this book, the synthetic narcotic analgesics. Some writers use this term to refer to the whole class of compounds: the natural ingredients of opium, their derivatives, and the synthetic narcotic analgesics. See **opiates.**

oral administration Giving a drug by mouth. The route includes the mouth, esophagus, stomach, and GI tract.

orthostatic hypotension Same as **postural hypotension.**

osmosis The selective diffusion of a substance through a semipermeable membrane.

OTC drugs Drugs sold "over the counter" without the need for a prescription.

oxidation The most common means of biotransforming molecules (drugs) in the liver. The process uses oxygen.

pancreatitis Inflammation of the pancreas.

panic disorder An anxiety state involving sudden massive attacks of anxiety that trigger a strong sympathetic reaction without cause.

paradoxical response A drug response that is the opposite of the expected response; e.g., a stimulant that causes depression. May be experienced generally by many users.

paraldehyde A sedative-hypnotic used as a hypnotic and anticonvulsant (anesthetic?). Has a number of problematic side effects.

paranoid disorder A mental disorder in which the subjects have delusions of being persecuted. Differs from paranoid schizophrenia in that thinking remains rational, and daily functioning may not be impaired.

paranoid schizophrenia A form of schizophrenia marked by delusions of grandeur or of persecution, accompanied by disordered thought processes and loose associations.

parasitosis The tingly feeling that bugs are crawling all over (or under) one's skin. A result of the rebound stimulation of sensory neurons as a result of amphetamine or cocaine withdrawal. Known also as **formication** or **cocaine bugs.**

parasympathetic nervous system The part of the autonomic nervous system that maintains normal functioning of organs.

paregoric A traditional medicine for diarrhea, containg opium tincture mixed with benzoic acid, camphor, and anise oil.

parenteral routes Routes of administration other than oral. In most cases, this means injection, which is the predominant alternative to the oral route.

parietal lobes The parts of the cortex in the middle part of the skull, containing key sensory areas. See **primary somatosensory area**.

parkinsonism A condition that mimics the symptoms of Parkinson's disease and may arise from similar organic mechanisms.

Parkinson's disease A movement disorder arising from depletion of DA in the basal ganglia. Involves tremors and difficulty with willful movements, and progresses to stiff immobility.

partial agonist A substance that attaches to a receptor, but cannot stimulate it as much as its neurotransmitter and so produces a weaker action.

partially blind study A drug study in which the experimental staff are aware that both a drug and a placebo are being administered, but are not able to distinguish between them.

passive diffusion The movement of a given type of molecule or substance from an area where it is more highly concentrated to an area where it is less so. See **equilibrium.**

passive smoking Inhaling the smoke from nearby smokers while not actually smoking oneself.

peptides Any of a group of compounds formed by two or more amino acids by the linkage of the amino groups of one with the carboxyl groups of the other, through hydrolysis. See **neuropeptides.**

peripheral nervous system All the neurons outside the spinal cord and brain, branching to every organ and extremity.

peritoneum (abdominal wall) The tissue separating intestines and other entrails from the rest of the body.

periventricular area Fiber systems in the brain that cause fear and pain reactions when stimulated. Inhibition causes a mild high.

phantasticants Same as **hallucinogens.**

phenothiazines The main class of neuroleptic drugs.

phobia Unwarranted panic attacks upon exposure to a harmless stimulus, accompanied by avoidance behaviors that disrupt functioning.

photophobia An intolerance to light.

physical dependence A condition wherein the organism needs a drug to maintain normal physiological functioning.

pituitary gland The master gland of the endocrine system. Receives messages from the hypothalamus to release the hormones that mediate various functions; e.g., sex, fear, water regulation, etc.

placental barrier The membranous structure that separates the mother from the fetus. Works mainly by the passive diffusion of lipid-soluble material.

polarity A condition of having two magnetic poles. For example, a water molecule has a positive and a negative pole like a bar magnet.

polysynaptic Involving many synapses.

pons Part of the hindbrain that serves as a "bridge" to the midbrain.

positive symptoms Symptoms of schizophrenia that involve behaviors that do not appear in normal people, e.g., auditory hallucinations. See negative symptoms.

postnatal After birth.

postpartum Pertaining to the period following childbirth.

postsynaptic membrane Part of the surface of a neuron that contains the receptor sites, the place where the presynaptic knobs of other neurons "attach" and release their neurotransmitters onto the cell or its dendrites.

post-traumatic stress disorder An anxiety state that involves anxiety following a traumatic event, and possible avoidance of all reminders of the event.

potency The "strength" of a drug based on the amount required to produce a given effect, as compared to another drug. For example, if less of drug A than drug B puts you to sleep, A is more potent.

potentiation An effect whereby a drug that would be ineffective alone has an effect when taken with another drug.

prenatal Before birth.

presynaptic terminal The buttonlike end of an axon or collateral that releases neurotransmitters onto another cell. Also called synaptic knob.

primary motor area An area of the frontal lobe (cortex) that contains motor neurons integrating motor output to all areas of the body. A key site of epileptic seizures. See **homunculus.**

primary somatosensory area An area of the cortex in the parietal lobe that integrates sensory input from all over the body. A brain center for touch. See **homunculus.**

processes Extensions of the nerve cell body (soma). The dendrites, axon and collaterals are all processes.

proof A measure of the alcohol content of a beverage. The proof is double the percentage--86 proof is 43 percent alcohol.

propanediols An early class of minor tranquilizers, including meprobamate (Miltown), which was widely abused in the fifties.

protein-binding The binding of drug molecules to large proteins in the blood, which impairs their ability to leave the circulation.

pseudohallucinations Hallucinations that the subject knows are hallucinations. See **true hallucinations.**

psychedelia The experiences and imagery of LSD and other hallucinogenic intoxication.

psychedelics Same as **hallucinogens.** This term, coined by Humphrey Osmond, emphasizes the positive, "mind expanding" properties of drugs like LSD.

psychoactive drugs Drugs that produce behavioral effects by acting on the central nervous system.

psychological dependence A craving and compulsion to use a drug that is psychologically rather than physiologically based. E.g., compulsive gambling is a purely psychological dependence; a similar effect may come from drug use.

psychomotor Pertaining to motor effects of cerebral (psychic) activity.

psychopharmacology The study of psychoactive drugs and their effects.

psychosis A condition marked by loss of contact with reality, disordering of the personality, and often, delusions and hallucinations. May be applied to both schizophrenia and affective disorders (viz., the withdrawal from reality seen in severe depression).

psychotogens Same as **psychotomimetics** and **hallucinogens.**

psychotomimetics Same as **hallucinogens.** This term puts emphasis on the theory, now largely discredited, that hallucinogens mimic the effects of psychotic states. The same is true of the term **psychotogen.**

psychotropic Same as **psychoactive.**

pulmonary edema The accumulation of fluid in the lung cavities.

pyramidal system A key motor system in the brain, which is responsible for body movements and voluntary muscle control. Relevant here for its association with the extrapyramidal system, the latter being a site for many motor side effects of drugs, especially antipsychotics.

raphé nucleus A nucleus in the reticular formation that governs slow-wave sleep. A key center for the cell bodies of SE neurons.

rebound effects Withdrawal effects that are the opposite of drug effects. They are an unmasking of the body's compensation for the presence of a drug. Alcoholics, e.g., become hyperexcited when the depressant alcohol is withdrawn.

receptor sites Protein structures on neural membranes adapted to receive neurotransmitter molecules. In many cases, points from which nerve cells are stimulated (fired) or inhibited.

rectal (administration) Pertaining to the rectum, the last segment of the large intestine, and ending at the anal canal.

redistribution The process of drugs distributing into storage in tissues, then being released, often slowly, to become active again and then to be eliminated.

reefer A marijuana cigarette.

reflex A sensory-motor response that is mediated by the spine or the brain, without higher order elaboration.

REM Rapid eye movements. Movements of the eyes that often correspond with the dreaming phase of sleep.

renal Pertaining to the kidneys.

Renshaw cells Small interneurons in the spinal cord that control the firing of motor neurons. The firing of the motor neuron activates the Renshaw cell, which feeds the signal back to the motor soma and inhibits it from further firing.

repolarization The rebalancing of charges across the axon membrane following the action potential.

reserpine An antipsychotic ingredient of *Rauwolfia serpentina,* an Asian and Indian plant. Causes low blood pressure and possibly suicidal depression.

resting potential The biochemical condition of a neuron before firing.

reticular formation A network of fine fibers extending from the brainstem to the forebrain that governs alertness and arousal, sleep and waking.

reuptake The process of moving neurotransmitter molecules back into the presynaptic terminal after their release.

reverse tolerance An increase of sensitivity to a drug with repeated use. There are no experimental data to validate reverse tolerance as a physiological effect.

route of administration The method by which one administers a drug--orally, intravenously, topically, etc.

run A pattern of amphetamine abuse involving continual IV use over a period of several days to maintain euphoria.

rush A brief period of intense euphoria, especially following the injection of cocaine or amphetamine.

schizophrenia A severe mental disorder characterized by the symptoms of incoherent thought, blunted mood, ambivalence, and a split from reality.

schizophreniform disorder An emotional condition resembling schizophrenia that lasts two weeks to six months.

second messengers Substances that act within the cell to change its excitability. Their action may be initiated by neurotransmitters from another cell acting on receptor sites.

second-generation antidepressants A number of diverse compounds, developed after the tricyclics, that relieve depression through various mechanisms of action.

sedative-hypnotics Depressants that are useful for both sedation and the induction of sleep, usually at two different dosage levels.

sedatives Drugs that produce drowsiness and sedation through CNS depression. They include alcohol and the barbiturates.

selective serotonin reuptake inhibitors A family of antidepressants that affects (in most cases uplifts) mood by blocking the reuptake of serotonin; the resulting increase of serotonin has a regulatory effect on other transmitter systems involved in mood.

sensory neurons Neurons that carry sensory information from the periphery to the spinal cord and brain.

septum A limbic system structure whose removal can cause uncontrollable aggression (septal rage). Believed from this to have an inhibitory function.

serotonin (SE) Also **5-hydroxytryptamine** or **5-HT.** A neurotransmitter that is an indolamine. Important in movement, pleasure, temperature control, sensory perception, and deep sleep.

serotonin hypothesis The hypothesis that depression is linked to altered levels of 5-HT (serotonin) in the brain and that it can be treated by correcting 5-HT levels.

set The mental frame or expectations with which a drug is taken.

setting The physical and social environment in which a drug is taken.

side effects The drug effects that a user or experimenter is not primarily interested in. These are often undesirable effects, such as nausea, blurred vision, etc.

single-blind study A drug-placebo study where the experimenters know a placebo is involved but the subjects do not. See **double-blind study.**

sinsemilla A seedless variety of cannabis developed by home growers of marijuana in the United States in the 1970s.

site of action The place where a drug acts to produce its effect; e.g., synapses in the brain, synapses at skeletal muscles, all nerve cell membranes.

site of administration The location on or in the body where a drug is administered: mouth, lungs, rectum, skin, etc.

skin popping Also called **skinning.** Injecting a drug subcutaneously.

slope In a dose-response curve, relationship between the change in dosage of a drug and the magnitude of effect.

slow action A neurotransmitter action that initiates a series of enzyme changes in the postsynaptic neuron, altering its sensitivity to other inputs. See **neuromodulation** and **second messengers.**

social phobia Fear of situations in which one's performance will be evaluated by others (test taking, stage fright, public speaking).

sodium-potassium pump The active transport mechanism that restores Na^+ and K^+ to their places after an action potential.

solubility The capacity to dissolve.

soma The body of a nerve cell, containing the cell nucleus. The site where incoming signals are integrated.

somatic nervous system The nerves that go to the voluntary muscles. Made up of one-neuron links to the spinal cord.

specific action A drug action on a particular process or structure: a neurotransmitter, enzyme, receptor site, etc.

specific phobia An extreme unwarranted fear triggerd by a specific kind of stimulus, for example, cats, bridges, heights, dirt.

spinal nerves Nerves extending out of the spinal cord.

SSRIs See **selective serotonin reuptake inhibitors**.

state-dependent learning A type of learning acquired in a drugged condition, which can only be fully recalled or used if the same type of drug state is reinduced.

stereotyped behavior The persistent repetition of senseless acts or words.

steroids Any of a group of compounds (e.g., sex hormones) having the carbon atom ring structure of the sterols. A *sterol* is any of a group of solid, cyclic unsaturated alcohols, such as cholesterol, found in plant and animal tissue.

stimulants Drugs that excite the CNS, causing arousal and alertness, reversing CNS depression, abolishing fatigue, and possibly inducing euphoria. Include amphetamines, cocaine, the xanthines, and nicotine.

street name The unofficial name of a drug given to it by illicit users. Ex.: weed, bennies, ludes, crank, XTC.

striatum Part of the basal ganglia. A subcortical mass of gray and white substance in front of and aside the thalamus. See Figure 11.2.

structure-activity relationship The relationship between the molecular structure of a drug and its effect.

subcutaneous Under the skin, as in **subcutaneous injection.**

sublingual administration Administering drugs by placing them under the tongue and letting them dissolve on the mucous membranes of the mouth.

substance P A neuropeptide connected with the transmission of pain.

substantia nigra A nucleus in the midbrain where the somae of the brain's DA neurons are located. A component of the extrapyramidal motor system.

supersensitivity Same as **hypersensitivity.**

sympathetic nervous system The part of the autonomic nervous system that activates the organs in emergency or stress. Consists of a short neuron to a ganglion near the spine and a long neuron to the target organ.

sympathetic reaction Also **fight-flight-fright** response or **panic reaction**. Activation of the sympathetic nervous system by epinephrine and norepinephrine that prepares the body for an emergency. Marked by rapid heartbeat, panting, dry mouth, and movement of blood to the brain and muscles.

sympathomimetic An agent that mimics the action of the sympathetic nervous system. The most prominent action is the production of a sympathetic reaction through the release of NE in the periphery.

synapse The junction of an axon with any part of another neuron; includes the presynaptic terminal, the synaptic gap, and the postsynaptic membrane.

synaptic gap Also **synaptic cleft.** The fluid-filled space between the presynaptic terminal of one neuron and the membrane of another.

synergistic effect A combined drug effect wherein doses of two drugs multiply the effects of each other, so that each dose acts more potently than if it were taken alone.

tachycardia Rapid heart beat.

tachyphylaxis The swift development of tolerance within minutes or hours, often between the first two doses of a drug.

tardive dyskinesia An irreversible and severe movement disorder that involves lip smacking, dartings of the tongue, puckering and blowing of the cheeks, and a complex of chorea and dystonias--sometimes seen in conjunction with neuroleptic treatment.

tectum Part of the midbrain involved in vision and hearing.

tegmentum Part of the midbrain involved in motor functions. Location of the **substantia nigra**, where the somae of the brain's DA neurons are located.

temporal lobes The lobes of the cortex beneath the temples, governing visual and auditory memory.

teonanacatl The magic mushrooms of Mexico, which contain the psychoactive ingredient psilocybin.

teratogens Substances that cause birth defects and deformities.

thalami (thalamus) Two nuclei in the core of the brain that receive and relay all sensory input to higher brain centers. Part of the pain-sensing and arousal systems.

therapeutic communities (TCs) A mode of treatment for opiate-dependence involving community living, self-discipline, and mutual support among patients. No drugs are involved in treatment, and the goal is complete freedom from drug use.

therapeutic index A calculation of the safety margin of a drug gotten by dividing the LD50 by the ED50. See **lethal dosage** and **effective dosage.**

therapeutic window A limited dosage range of a drug that is the only available range for therapeutic effects.

threshold response The dosage at which an individual or group first exhibits a particular drug effect.

time course The time between the moment of administration and the end of a drug's effect.

titration In reference to smoking, the practice of controlling the dose of nicotine by slightly altering the way one smokes.

tolerance The adaptation of an organism to a drug, so that the same dose repeated produces less and less of an effect.

tonus The slight tension (contraction) in a resting muscle.

topical Applied locally. Applying drugs to the skin is a form of topical administration.

trade name The marketing name of a drug--invented by the drug company. Ex.: Prozac, Valium, Benzedrine.

tranquilizer A drug that produces tranquilization, which is a form of calming associated with the lessening of anxiety, in contrast to sedation, which is a form of calming associated with the induction of sleep.

transdermal (administration) Literally "across the skin." Refers to the administration of drugs by applying them to, and absorbing them through, the skin. Involves creams and ointments, and devices like the nicotine patch.

transmitters Same as **neurotransmitters.**

tricyclic antidepressants The most widely used group of antidepressant drugs. Contains a triple ring in its molecular structures--hence the name.

trip LSD intoxication--marked by a set of different kinds of experiences through which one progresses.

true hallucinations Hallucinations the subject believes are real. See **pseudohallucinations.**

unipolar depression An affective disorder showing only the extreme of depression and no mania.

up-regulation The process in which neurons increase their functioning to maintain equilibrium through the synthesis of more receptors, increased production of neurotransmitters, or some other mechanism.

vaginal (administration) The route of administration involving absorption of material through the membranes of the vagina.

variability A pharmacological factor consisting of the fact that individual responses to drugs vary.

variables Factors that influence the outcome of an experiment.

vascular Pertaining to blood vessels.

vasoconstriction The narrowing of blood vessels.

vasoconstrictor A drug that narrows (constricts) blood vessels by affecting their muscles.

vasodilation The widening of blood vessels.

vasodilator A substance that widens (dilates) blood vessels by affecting their muscles.

vasomotor Pertaining to the muscles that constrict or widen the blood vessels.

ventral tegmental area A part of the midbrain containing several nuclei. One of the key locations for dopaminergic somae in the brain.

vesicle A small membranous sac in the presynaptic terminal that holds a small supply of a neurotransmitter.

vestibular system A mechanism located in the middle ear that regulates balance.

voltage The potential for electrical current to flow. An electromotive force, whose strength is determined by the tendency of electrons to flow from an area of higher concentration into an area of lower concentration.

water intoxication A state of irritability, lethargy, and confusion that can proceed to seizures, coma, and death. Comes from drinking large quantities of water for extended periods of time, which may be a response to the dry mouth produced by neuroleptics.

water-soluble Able to dissolve in water and watery solutions. Water-soluble drugs often ionize.

waxy flexibility An immobile, statuelike condition that occurs in catatonic schizophrenia. Subjects adopt and maintain odd postures in a semistiff state, but their limbs can be repositioned, and they will hold the new posture for a long time.

Wernicke's disease A CNS disease related to beri beri, caused by a shortage of water-soluble vitamins, particularly thiamine. Seen in conjunction with alcoholism.

withdrawal symptoms The set of symptoms that manifest when a person dependent on a drug refrains from using it.

xanthines The class of stimulants that includes caffeine, theophylline, and theobromine, found in such beverages as coffee, tea, cocoa, and cola drinks.

References

Agarwal, D. P., & Goedde, H. W. (1986). Ethanol oxidation: Ethnic variations in metabolism and response. In W. Kalow, H. W. Goedde, & D. P. Agarwal. (Eds.), *Progress in Clinical and Biological Research, 214: Ethnic differences in reactions to drugs and xenobiotics* (pp. 99-112). New York: Alan R. Liss.

Aghajanian, G.K. (1994, March). Serotonin and the action of LSD in the brain. *Psychiatric Annals, 24* (3), 137-141.

Akiskal, H. S., & McKinney, W. T. (1973, October 5). Depressive disorders: Toward a unified hypothesis. *Science, 182,* 20-29.

Akiskal, H.S. (1983). Dysthymic disorders: Psychopathology of proposed chronic depressive subtypes. *American Journal of Psychiatry, 140,* 11-20.

Alper, J. (1983, December). Biology and mental illness. *Atlantic Monthly, 252,* 70-76.

American Psychiatric Association. (1994). *Diagnostic and statistical manual of mental disorders* (4th ed.). Washington, DC: American Psychiatric Association.

American Psychiatric Association. (1987). *Diagnostic and statistical manual of mental disorders--Revised.* (3rd ed.). Washington, DC: American Psychiatric Association.

American Psychiatric Association. (1980). *Diagnostic and statistical manual of mental disorders.* (3rd ed.). Washington, DC: American Psychiatric Association.

Andersen, H., Anderson, H., Shannon, E., Moreau, R., Contreras, J., Harmes, J., Margolis, M., & Smith, M. (1985, February 25). The evil empire. *Newsweek, 105,* 14-18.

Anderson, K. E., Conney, A. H., & Kappas, A. (1986). Nutrition as an environmental influence on chemical metabolism in man. In W. Kalow, H. W. Goedde, & D. P. Agarwal. (Eds.). *Progress in Clinical and Biological Research, 214: Ethnic differences in reactions to drugs and xenobiotics* (pp. 39-54). New York: Alan R. Liss.

Aranda, J. V., Brazier, J. L., Louridas, A. T., & Sasyniuk, B. I. (1981). Methylxanthine metabolism in the newborn infant. In L. F. Soyka & G. P. Redmond (Eds.). *Drug metabolism in the immature human* (pp. 183-198). New York: Raven Press.

Asberg, M., & Martensson, B. (1993). Serotonin selective antidepressant drugs. *Clinical Neuropharmacology, 16* (Suppl.3), S32-S44.

Aschoff, J., & Wever, R. (1981). The circadian system of man. In J. Aschoff. (Ed.). *Handbook of behavioral neurobiology, 4: Biological rhythms.* New York: Plenum Press.

Ashton, H. (1995). Protracted withdrawal from benzodiazepines: The post-withdrawal syndrome. *Psychiatric Annals, 25*(3), 174-179.

Ashton, H., & Stepney, R. (1982). *Smoking: Psychology and pharmacology.* New York: Tavistock Publications.

Austin, G. A. (1978). *Research Issues 24: Perspectives on the history of psychoactive substance abuse.* Rockville, MD: National Institute on Drug Abuse.

Baldessarini, R. J., & Tarazi, F. I. (2001). Drugs and the treatment of psychiatric disorders: Psychosis and mania. In J. G. Hardman, L. L. Limbird, & A. G. Gilman (Eds.). *Goodman and Gilman's The Pharmacological Basis of Therapeutics* (10th ed.) (pp. 485-520). New York: McGraw-Hill.

Balfour, D. J. K. (Ed.). (1984). *Nicotine and the tobacco smoking habit*. New York: Pergamon Press.

Barnes, C., & Eltherington, L. (1965). *Drug dosage in laboratory animals: A handbook.* Berkeley: University of California Press. As cited in Leavitt, 1974, p. 29.

Barnes, D. M. (1988, February 19). New data intensify the agony over ecstasy. *Science,* 239, 864-866.

Barr, Mednick, & Munk-Jorgenson. (1990). Exposure to influenza epidemics during gestation and adult schizophrenia. *Archives of General Psychiatry, 47,* 869-874. [Klein 478]

Baudelaire, C. (William M. Davis, translator.) In A. Flores, (Ed.). (1958). *An anthology of French poetry from Nerval to Valery in English translation* (p. 57). Garden City, NJ: Doubleday and Company.

Beebe, D.K., & Walley, E. (1995, February 1). Smokable methamphetamine ("ice"): An old drug in a different form. *American Family Physician,* 5(2), 449-453.

Berretini, W.H. (1993). The molecular genetics of bipolar disorder. In J.J. Mann & D.J. Kupfer. (Eds.). *The depressive illness series: Vol. 3. Biology of depressive disorders (Part A): A systems perspective* (pp. 189-204). New York: Plenum Press.

Black, M. (1985, February 25). Feeding America's habit. *Newsweek, 105,* 22-23.

Blackshear, P. J. (1979, December). Implantable drug delivery systems. *Scientific American,* 241, 66-73.

Blakemore, C. (1977). *Mechanics of the mind.* New York: Cambridge University Press.

Blue, E. (1979). Use of directive therapy in the treatment of depersonalization neurosis. *Psychological Reports, 45,* 904-906.

Blum, K. (1984). *Handbook of abusable drugs.* New York: Garden Press.

Blum, K., Briggs, A.H., Elston, S.F.A., & DeLollo, L. (1981). Ethanol preference as a function of genotypic levels of whole brain enkephalin in mice. *Toxicol. Eur. Res., 3,* 261-262.

Blum, K., Cull, J. G., Braverman, E. R., & Comings, D. E. (1996). Reward deficiency syndrome. *American Scientist, 84,* 132-145.

Boros, C. A., Parsons, D. W., Zoanetti, G. D., Ketteridge, D. and Kennedy, D. (1996, April). Cannabis cookies: a cause of coma. *Journal of Paediatrics and Child Health, 32*(2), 194-195.

Brecher, E. M. (1972). *Licit and illicit drugs.* Boston: Little, Brown and Co.

Brekke, J.S., DeBonis, J.A., & Graham, J.W. (1994, July/August). A latent structure analysis of the positive and negative symptoms in schizophrenia. *Comprehensive Psychiatry, 35* (4), 252-259.

Brill, H., & Hirose, T. (1969). The rise and fall of a methamphetamine epidemic: Japan 1945-1955. *Seminars in Psychiatry,* 1, 179-194. As cited in Austin, 1978, p. 185.

Bruce, R. L. (1977). *Fundamentals of physiological psychology.* New York: Holt, Rhinehart, & Winston.

Burroughs, W. S. *Junky.* (1953). New York: Penguin.

Calabrese, E. J. (1985). *Toxic susceptibility: Male/female differences.* New York: John Wiley and Sons.

Caldwell, A. E. (1970a). History of psychopharmacology. In W. G. Clark & J. del Giudice (Eds.). *Principles of psychopharmacology.* New York: Academic Press.

Caldwell, A. E. (1970b). *Origins of psychopharmacology: From CPZ to LSD.* Springfield, IL: Charles C. Thomas.

Callahan, M. M., Robertson, R. S., Branfman, A. R., et al. (1983). Comparison of caffeine metabolism in three nonsmoking populations after oral administration of radiolabeled caffeine. *Drug Metabolism and Disposition, 11,*211. As cited in Yesair, Branfman, & Callahan, 1984.

Cameron, N.A. (1947). *The psychology of behavior disorders: A biosocial interpretation.* Boston: Houghton Mifflin. As cited/adapted in Silverman, 1979, pp. 342-343.

Campbell, P. N., & Smith, A. D. (1982). *Biochemistry illustrated.* Edinburgh: Churchill Livingstone.

Carlsson, A., Waters, N., & Carlsson, M. L. (1999). Neurotransmitter interactions in schizophrenia—therapeutic implications. *Biological Psychiatry, 46,* 1388-1395.

Carlsson, A., & Serin, F. (1950). The toxicity of nikethamide at different times of day. *Acta Pharmacologica et Toxicologica, 6,*187-193.

Chance, M. (1946). Aggregation as a factor influencing the toxicity of sympathomimetic amines in mice. *Journal of Pharmacology and Experimental Therapeutics, 87,* 214-219.

Clark, M., & Agrest, S. (1978, March 13). The deadly angel dust. Newsweek, *34,* 3.

Cocteau, J. (1929/1958). *Opium: The diary of a cure.* New York: Grove Press, Inc.

Coffee, J. M. (Hon.). (1938, June 14). An investigation of the narcotic evil. *Congressional Record.* As cited in Williams, 1938, pp. xiii, xix.

Coggins, W. J. (1976). Costa Rica cannabis project: An interim report on the medical aspects. In M. C. Braude & S. Szara (Eds.). *Pharmacology of marijuana* (pp. 667-670). New York: Raven Press. As cited in Hollister, 1986.

Cohen, S. (1975, November). The major tranquilizers. *Drug Abuse and Alcoholism Newsletter, 10,* 1. Vista Hill Foundation.

Cohen, S. (1985, October-December). LSD: The varieties of psychotic experience. *Journal of Psychoactive Drugs, 17*(4).

Collins, W. (1859/1985). *The woman in white.* New York: Penguin.

Contreras, P.C., Monahan, J.B., Lanthorn, T.H., Pullan, L.M., DiMaggio, D.A., Handelmann, G.E., Gray, N.M., & O'Donohue, T.L. (1987). Phencyclidine: Physiological interactions with excitatory amino acids and endogenous ligands. *Molecular Neurobiology, 1,* 191-211.

Cooper, J. R., Bloom, F. E., & Roth, R. H. (1986). *The biochemical basis of neuropharmacology.* (5th ed.). New York: Oxford University Press.

Cowley, G., Springen, K., Leonard, E. A., Robins, K., & Gordon, J. (1990, March 26). The promise of Prozac. *Newsweek, 15,* 38-41.

Crow, T.J. (1985). The two-syndrome concept: origins and current status. *Schizophrenia Bulletin, 11*(3), 471-486.

Crow, T.J. (1980a). Molecular pathology of schizophrenia: More than one disease process? *British Medical Journal, 280,* 66-68.

Crow, T.J. (1980b). Positive and negative schizophrenic symptoms and the role of dopamine (Discussion, pt. 2). *British Journal of Psychiatry, 137,* 383-386.

Csaky, T. Z., & Barnes, B. A. (1984). Cutting's handbook of pharmacology. Norwalk, CT: Appleton-Century-Croft.

Curatolo, P. W., & Robertson, D. (1983). The health consequences of caffeine. *Annals of Internal Medicine, 98,* 641-653.

Davis, W. (1985). *The serpent and the rainbow.* New York: Warner Books.

Deadwyler, S. A., Hayashizaki, S., Cheer, J., & Hamson, R. E. (2004). Reward, memory and substance abuse: functional neuronal circuits in the nucleus accumbens. *Neuroscience and Behavioral Reviews, 27,* 703-711.

Delay, J., Deniker, P., & Harl, J. M. (1952). Utilisation en thérapeutique psychiatrique d'une phénothiazine d'action central élective (4560RP). *Annales Medico Psychologie, 110,* 112-117. As cited in Spiegel, 1989.

DeQuincey, T. (1821/1981). *Confessions of an English opium eater.* New York: Penguin.

Derringer, M. K., Dunn, T. B., & Heston, W. E. (1953). Results of exposure of strain C3H mice to chloroform. *Proceedings of the Society of Experimental Biology and Medicine, 83,* 474-479.

Dewey, W. L. (1986). Cannabinol pharmacology. *Pharmacological Reviews, 38,* 151-178.

Donner, J., Oka, K., Brossi, A., Rice, K., & Spector, S. (1986). Presence and formation of codeine and morphine in the rat. *Proceedings of the National Academy of Sciences, 83,* 456-467.

Dorrow, R., Horowski, R., Paschelke, G., et al. (1983). Severe anxiety induced by FG7142, a beta-carboline ligand for benzodiazepine receptors. *Lancet, 2,* 98-99.

Dow-Edwards, D.L. (1991). Cocaine effects on fetal development: A comparison of clinical and animal research findings. *Neurotoxicology and Teratology, 13,* 347-352.

Downing, J., & Wolfson, P. (1985). Clinical study of MDMA in normal subjects. Unpublished findings. As cited in Shulgin, 1986, p. 300.

Eccles, J. C. (1973). *The understanding of the brain.* New York: McGraw-Hill.

Ekbom, K. A. (1960). Restless leg syndrome. *Neurology, 10,* 868-873. As cited in Rotrosen & Adler, 1995, p. 308.

Ereshefsky, L. (1995). Treatment strategies for schizophrenia. *Psychiatric Annals, 25*(5), 285-296.

Ernster, V. L. (1984). Epidemiologic studies of caffeine and human health. In G. A. Spiller. (Ed.). *Progress in Clinical and Biological Research, 158: The methylxanthine beverages and foods: Chemistry, consumption and health effects* (pp. 377-379). New York: Alan R. Liss.

Eschenbrenner, A. B., & Miller, E. (1945). Sex differences in kidney morphology and chloroform necrosis. *Science, 102,* 302-303.

Escohotado, Antonio. (1999). *A Brief History of Drugs: From the Stone Age to the Stoned Age.* (K. A. Symington, Trans.) Rochester, VT: Park Street Press.

Eysenck, H. J. (1983). Psychopharmacology and personality. In W. Janke, *Response variability to psychotropic drugs* (pp. 127-154). Oxford: Pergamon Press.

Fink, M., Volauka, J., Panayiotopoulos, C., & Stefanis, C. (1976). Quantitative EEG studies of marihuana, delta-9-THC, and hashish in man. In M. Braude & S. Szara. (Eds.). *Pharmacology of marijuana* (pp. 383-392). New York: Raven Press. As cited in Hollister, 1986.

Fiore, M. C., Jorenky, D. E., Baker, T. B., Kenford, S. L. (1992, November 18). Tobacco dependence and the nicotine patch: Clinical guidelines for effective use. *Journal of the American Medical Association, 268*(19), 2687-2694.

Franklin, J. E. (1995, June 7). Addiction medicine. *Journal of the American Medical Association, 273* (21), 1656-57.

Freedman, R. (2003, October 30). Schizophrenia. *New England Journal of Medicine, 349,* 1738-49.

Frezza, C., Di Padova, C., Pozzeto, G., Terpin, M., Baraono, E., & Lieber, C. S. (1990, January 11). Higher blood alcohol levels in women: The role of decreased gastric alcohol dehydrogenase activity and first-pass metabolism. *The New England Journal of Medicine, 322*(2), 95-99.

Furst, P. T. (1976). *Hallucinogens and culture.* Novato, CA: Chandler and Sharp.

Garner, S. E., Kung, M.-P., Foulon, C., Chumpradit, S., & Kung, H. F. (1994). [^{125}(S)-*TRANS-7-OH-PIPAT*: A potential SPECT imaging agent for sigma binding sites. *Life Sciences, 54*(9), 593-603.

Gautier, T. (1846/1977). Le club des hachichins. In A. C. Kimmens. (Ed.). *Tales of hashish* (pp. 86-104). New York: Wm. Morrow & Co.

Gilman, A. G., Rall, T. W., Nies, A. S., & Taylor, P. (Eds.). (1990). *The pharmacological basis of therapeutics* (8th ed.). New York: McGraw-Hill.

Ginsberg, A. (1965, December). Interview with Art Kunkin. L.A. Free Press. As cited in Brecher, 1972, p. 292.

Gleitman, H. (1983). *Basic psychology.* New York: W. W. Norton.

Goedde, H. W., Agarwal, D. P., Eckey, R., & Harada, S. (1985). Population, genetic and family studies on aldehyde dehydrogenase deficiency and alcohol sensitivity. *Alcohol, 2,* 383-390.

Gold, M. (1994, March). The epidemiology, attitudes, and pharmacology of LSD use in the 1990s. *Psychiatric Annals, 24*(3), 124-126.

Goldstein, G., & Betz, A. L. (1986, September). The blood-brain barrier. *Scientific American, 255*(3), 74-83.

Golub, A., & Johnson, B.D. (1994). A recent decline in cocaine use among youthful arrestees in Manhattan, 1987 through 1993. *American Journal of Public Health, 84*(8), 1250-1254.

Goodman, L. S., & Gilman, A. (Eds.). (1970). *The pharmacological basis of therapeutics* (4th ed). New York: MacMillan.

Gottesman, I. I., & Shields, J. (1976). A critical review of recent adoption, twin and family studies of schizophrenia: Behavioral genetics perspectives. *Schizophrenia Bulletin, 2,* 360-398.

Greenberg, J. (1983, November 5). Natural highs in natural habitats. *Science News, 124*(19), 300-301.

Grilly, D. M. (1994). *Drugs and Human Behavior* (2nd ed.). Boston: Allyn & Bacon.

Grossman, S. P. (1967). *A textbook of physiological psychology.* New York: John Wiley and Sons.

Hammer, J. (1986, December). An alcohol antidote: In search of a better cup of coffee. *Esquire, 106,* 218-220.

Hand, P. J. (1981). The 2-deoxyglucose method. In L. Heimer & M. J. Robards (Eds.). *Neuroanatomical tract-tracing methods* (pp. 511-538). New York: Plenum Press.

Harber, M. H., & Jennings, R. B. (1964). Sex differences in renal toxicity of mercury in rats. *Nature, 201,* 1235.

Harrison Narcotics Act. (1914). P.L. 63-223, 38 Stat. 785.

Harrison, P. J., Law, A. J., & Eastwood, S. L. (2003). Glutamate receptors and transporters in the hippocampus in schizophrenia. *Annals of the New York Academy of Sciences, 1003*, 94-101.

Hemminger, G. L. This smoking world. In R. Baker. (Ed.). (1986). *The Norton book of light verse*. New York: W.W. Norton & Company.

Herodotus. *Histories* (IV:73-75). In A. C. Kimmens. (Ed.). (1977). *Tales of hashish* (p. 270). New York: Wm. Morrow & Co.

Hettena, S. (1995). Year of the cat. *Spin, 10*(11), 67-90.

Hoffman, B. B., & Lefkowitz, R. J. (1990). Catecholamines and sympathomimetic drugs. In Gilman, A. G., Rall, T. W., Nies, A. S., & Taylor, P. (Eds.). *Goodman and Gilman's: The pharmacological basis of therapeutics*. (8th ed.) (pp. 187-220). New York: Pergamon Press.

Hoffman, E. J., & Warren, E. W. (1993, September). Flumazenil: a benzodiazepine antagonist. *Clinical Pharmacy, 12*, 641-656.

Hofmann, A. (1983). *LSD: My problem child*. Los Angeles: J. P. Tarcher, Inc.

Hollister, L. E. (1986, March). Health aspects of cannabis. *Pharmacological Reviews, 38*(1), 120.

Hollister, L. E., Shelton, J., & Krieger, G. (1969). A controlled comparison of lysergic acid diethylamide (LSD) and dextroamphetamine in alcoholics. *American Journal of Psychiatry, 125*, 1352-1357. As cited in Ray, 1983, p. 393.

Hollister, L.E., & Claghorn, J. L. (1993). New antidepressants. *Annual Review of Pharmacology and Toxicology, 32*, 165-177.

Homer. *Odyssey*. Adapted from various translations.

Horrobin, D. F. (1979, March 10). Schizophrenia: Reconciliation of the dopamine, prostaglandin, and opioid concepts and the role of the pineal. *The Lancet, 1*(8115), 529-531.

Houston, J. (1969). Phenomenology of the psychedelic experience. In R. E. Hicks, & P. J. Fink. (Eds.). *Psychedelic drugs: Proceedings of the Hahnemann medical college and hospital symposium*. New York: Grune and Stratton, Inc. As cited in Ray, 1983, p. 388.

Inciardi, J.A., Lockwood, D., & Pottieger, A.E. (1993). *Women and crack-cocaine*. New York: Macmillan Publishing Company.

Jaffe, J. (1995, June). Pharmacological treatment of opioid dependence: Current techniques and new findings. *Psychiatric Annals, 25*(6), 369-375.

Jaffe, J. H., & Martin, W. R. (1990). Opioid analgesics and antagonists. In A.G. Gilman, T.W. Rall, A.S. Nies, & P. Taylor. (Eds.). *Goodman and Gilman's: The pharmacological basis of therapeutics* (8th ed.). New York: McGraw-Hill.

Javitt, D. C., & Coyle, J. T. (2004, January). Decoding schizophrenia. *Scientific American, 290*(1), 48-55.

Javitt, D. C., & Zukin, S. R. (1991). Recent advances in the phencyclidine model of schizophrenia. *American Journal of Psychiatry, 148*(10), 1301-1308.

Jellinek, E. M. (1952). Phases of alcohol addiction. *Quarterly Journal of Studies on Alcohol, 13*, 673-684.

Johnson & Johnson gets sub-poena on schizophrenia drug. (2004, January 24). *New York Times*, C4. Retrieved July 15, 2004 from Infotrac: New York State Newspapers.

Jones, E. (1953). *The life and work of Sigmund Freud, Vol. I (1856-1900).* New York: Basic Books. As cited in Brecher, 1972, p. 273.

Juliano, R. L. (1991). A new perspective for drug delivery research. In R. L. Juliano (Ed.). *Handbook of Experimental Pharmacology, 100: Targeted drug delivery* (pp. 1-9). New York: Springer-Verlag.

Kakuzo, O. (1928). *The book of tea.* New York: Duffield.

Kalant, H. (2004, August). Adverse effects of cannabis on health: an update of the literature since 1996. *Progress in Neuro-psychopharmacology and Biological Psychiatry, 28*(5): 849-63.

Kalant, O. J. (1966). *The amphetamines: Toxicity and addiction.* Toronto: University of Toronto Press.

Kallman, F. J. (1946). The genetic theory of schizophrenia. *American Journal of Psychiatry, 103,* 309-322.

Kalow, W., Goedde, H. W., & Agarwal, D. P. (Eds.). (1986). *Progress in Clinical and Biological Research, 214: Ethnic differences in reactions to drugs and xenobiotics.* New York: Alan R. Liss.

Kato, M. (1969). An epidemiological analysis of the fluctuation of drug dependence in Japan. *International Journal of the Addictions, 4*(4): 591-621.

Kay, S. R. (1991). *Positive and negative syndromes in schizophrenia: Assessment and research.* NY: Brunner/Mazel.

Kenakin, T. (1993). *Pharmacologic analysis of drug-receptor interaction* (2nd ed.). New York: Raven Press.

Kimmens, A. C. (1977). *Tales of hashish.* New York: Wm. Morrow & Co.

Kluver, H. (1966). *Mescal and mechanisms of hallucinations.* Chicago: University of Chicago Press.

Koester, J. (1981). Passive electrical properties of the neuron. In E. R. Kandel & J. H. Schwartz. (Eds.). *Principles of neural science* (pp. 36-43). New York: Elsevier/North-Holland.

Koester, J. (1981). Resting membrane potential. In E. R. Kandel & J. H. Schwartz. (Eds.). *Principles of neural science* (pp. 27-35). New York: Elsevier/North-Holland.

Kolata, G. (1994, June 22). Nicotine patch study sees 25% success rate. *The New York Times,* p. A14.

Kolata, G. (1978, November 17). Teratogens acting through males. *Science, 202,* 733.

Kolata, G. (1986, December 5). New drug counters alcohol intoxication. *Science, 234,* 1198-1199.

Koob, G. F., & Bloom, F. E. (1988, April 12). Cellular and molecular mechanisms of drug dependence. *Science, 242,* 715-723.

Kornetsky, C. (1976). *Pharmacology: Drugs affecting behavior.* New York: John Wiley & Sons.

Kozel, N. J., & Adams, E. H. (1986, November 21). Epidemiology of drug abuse: An overview. *Science, 234,* 970-974.

Kozikowski, A. P., & Barrionuevo, G. (Eds.) (1991). *Neurobiology of the NMDA receptor.* New York: VCH Publishers.

Kramer, P. D. (1993). *Listening to Prozac.* New York: Viking.

Krasheninnikov, S. P. *Description of the land of Kamchatka* Vol. 2. St. Petersburg, 1775. As cited in Wasson, 1971, p. 158.

Krippner, S. (1970). Psychedelic experience and the language process. *Journal of Psychoactive Drugs, 3*(1), 41-51. As cited in Ray, 1983, p. 387.

Laborit, H., Huguenard, P., & Allaume, P. (1952). Un nouveau stabilisateur végétatif (le 4560 RP). *Presse Méd, 60,* 206-208 (English and Spanish abstracts: *Presse Méd,* 1952, *60*(10). As cited in Caldwell, 1970b, p. 3.

LaGenia, B., Ward, M., & Musa, M. N. (1994). Clinical pharmacokinetics of benzodiazepines. *Journal of Clinical Pharmacology, 34,* 804-811.

Lang, R. M., Borow, K. M., Neumann, A., & Feldman, T. (1985). Adverse cardiac effects of acute alcohol ingestion in young adults. *Annals of Internal Medicine, 102,* 742-747.

Langer, R. (1986). Implantable controlled release systems. In G. M. Ihler (Ed.). *Methods of drug delivery* (pp. 121-137). Oxford: Pergamon Press.

Langsdorf, G. H. von. (1809). Einige Bemerkungen, die Eigenschaften des Kamtschadalischen Fliegenschwammes betreffend. [Some remarks concerning the properties of the Kamchadal fly-agaric.] Wetterauische Gesellschaft für die gesammte Naturkunde. *Annalen, 1*(2), 249-256. Frankfurt M. As cited in Wasson, 1971, p. 158.

Latimer, D., & Goldberg, J. (1981). *Flowers in the blood.* New York: Franklin Watts.

Leary, W.E. (1994, June 22). Cigarette company developed tobacco with stronger nicotine. *The New York Times,* pp. A1, A14.

Leavitt, F. (1974). *Drugs and behavior.* Philadelphia: W. B. Saunders, p. 241.

Leavitt, F. (1982). *Drugs and behavior.* (2nd ed.) New York: John Wiley and Sons, p. 236.

Lee, M. A., & Shlain, B. (1985). *Acid dreams.* New York: Grove Press.

Lee, T., Sokoloski, T. D., & Royer, G. P. (1981, July 10). Serum albumin beads: An injectable, biodegradable system for the sustained release of drugs. *Science, 213*(4504), 233-235.

Leslie, A. (1954). Ethics and practice of placebo therapy. *American Journal of Medicine, 16,* 854-862.

Lewin, R. (1980, December 12). Is your brain really necessary? *Science, 210,* 1232-1234.

Linder, R. L., Lerner, S. E., & Burns, S. R. (1981). *PCP: The devil's dust.* Belmont, CA: Wadsworth.

Lindes, M.C. (1985). *Nutritional biochemistry and metabolism.* New York: Elsevier.

Lipton, M. A. (1970). The relevance of chemically-induced psychoses to schizophrenia. In D. H. Efron (Ed.). *Psychotomimetic drugs.* New York: Raven Press. As cited in Ray, 1983, p. 374.

Little, R.C., & Little, W.C. (1987). *Physiology of the heart and circulation* (4th ed.). Chicago: Year Book Medical Publishers.

Longo, L. D. (1977, September 1). The biological effects of carbon monoxide on the pregnant woman, fetus and newborn infant. *American Journal of Obstetrics and Gynecology, 129*(1), 69.

Ludlow, F. (1857/1979). *The hasheesh eater.* San Francisco: City Lights Books.

Maddux, J. F., & Desmond, D. P. (1992). Ten year follow-up after admission to methadone maintenance. *American Journal of Drug and Alcohol Abuse, 18,* 289-303. As cited in Jaffe, 1995.

Malone, K., & Mann, J. J. (1993). Serotonin and major depression. In J. J. Mann & D.J. Kupfer. (Eds.). *The depressive illness series: Vol. 3. Biology of depressive disorders (Part A): A systems perspective* (pp. 29-49). New York: Plenum.

Marholin, D., & Phillips, D. (1976). Methodological issues in psychopharmacological research: Chlorpromazine--a case in point. *American Journal of Orthopsychiatry, 46*, 477-495.

Marks, R. G. (1979, July). Maternal paternal drug use now linked to birth defects. *Current Prescribing*. As cited in Ray, 1983, p. 93.

Marriott, A., & Rachlin, C. K. (1971). *Peyote*. New York: New American Library.

Marriott, M., Gegax, T. T., Shackleford, L., & French, R. (1995, February 13). Jiving with java. *Newsweek, 125*(7), 82-83.

Masaki, T. (1956). Amphetamine problem in Japan. *WHO Technical Report Series C, 102*. As cited in Austin, 1978, p. 185.

Mason, A. S., & Granacher, R. P. (1980). Clinical handbook of anti-psychotic drug therapy. New

York: Brunner/Mazel Publishers.

McDowell, D. M., & Kleber, H. D. (1995, March). MDMA: Its history and pharmacology. *Psychiatric Annals, 24*(3), 127-130.

McNamara, J. O., (1996). Drugs effective in the therapy of the epilepsies. In J. G. Hardman, L. E. Limbird, P. B. Molinoff, R. W. Ruddon, & A. G. Gilman (Eds.), *Goodman and Gilman's: The pharmacological basis of therapeutics* (9th ed.) (pp. 461-486). New York: McGraw-Hill.

Mello, N. K., & Mendelson, J. H. (1978). Alcohol and human behavior. In L. L. Iverson, S. D. Iverson, & S. H. Snyder. (Eds.). *Drugs of abuse: Vol. 2 Handbook of psychopharmacology*. New York: Plenum Press.

Miller, N.S., & Gold, M.S. (1994, March). LSD and ecstasy: Pharmacology, phenomenology, and treatment. *Psychiatric Annals, 24*(3), 131-133.

Millman, N. S., & Gold, M. S. (1994, March). LSD, Ecstasy, "rave" parties and the Grateful Dead. *Psychiatric Annals, 24*(3), 148-150.

Monroe, L. J. (1967). Psychological and physiological differences between good and poor sleepers. *Journal of Abnormal Psychology, 72*, 255-264.

Montgomery, R., Dryer, R. L., Conway, T. W., & Spector, A. A. (1983). *Biochemistry, a case-oriented approach* (4th ed.). St. Louis: C. V. Mosby. As cited in Lindes, 1985, pp. 47-49.

Moore-Ede, M. C., Sulzman, F. M., & Fuller, C. A. (1982). *The clocks that time us: Physiology of the circadian timing system*. Cambridge: Harvard University Press.

Morgan, W. P. (1978). The mind of the marathoner. *Psychology Today, 11*, 38-49. As cited in Siegel, 1985, p. 247.

Mueser, K. T., & McGurk, S. R. (2004). Schizophrenia. *The Lancet, 362*, 2063-72.

Murphy, J. M. (1976). Psychiatric labelling in cross-cultural perspective. *Science, 191*, 1019-28. As cited in Gleitman, 1983, p. 449.

Musto, D. (1973). *The American disease: Origins of narcotic control*. New Haven and London: Yale University Press, App. III (pp. 335-348). As cited in Austin, 1978, p. 201.

National Institute for Alcohol Abuse and Alcoholism (NIAAA) Clearinghouse for Alcohol Information. (1982, January).

Nemiah, J. C. (1980). *Neurotic disorders.* As cited/adapted in Roediger, 1984, p. 509.

Nestler, E. J. & Malenka, R. C. (2004, March). The addicted brain. *Scientific American, 290*(3), 78-85.

Network for Continuing Medical Education. (1984). *431: Implanted drug delivery systems: alternate paths* [Videocassette].

New York Times. (2004, January 24). Johnson and Johnson gets subpoena on schizophrenia drug. C4. Retrieved July 15, 2004 from Infotrac: New York State Newspapers.

Newman, L. M., Lutz, M. P., & Domino, E. F. (1974). Delta 9-tetracannabinol and some CNS depressants: Evidence for cross-tolerance in the rat. *Archives Internationale de Pharmacodynamie et de Therapie, 207,* 254-259.

Newman, L. M., Lutz, M. P., Gould, M. H., & Domino, E. F. (1972). Delta 9-tetrahydrocannibinol and ethyl alcohol: Evidence for cross-tolerance in the rat. *Science, 175,* 1022.

Nicoll, R. A., & Alger, B. E. (2004, December 1). The brain's own marijuana. *Scientific American,* 68-75.

Ninan, P.T., Insel, T. M., Cohen, R. H., et al. (1982). Benzodiazepine receptor-mediated experimental "anxiety" in primates. *Science, 218,* 1332-1334.

Noback, C. R., & Demarest, R. J. (1972). *The nervous system: Introduction and review.* New York: McGraw Hill.

Nutt, D. J., Glue, P., Lawson, C., et al. Flumazenil provocation of panic attacks: evidence of altered benzodiazepine receptor sensitivity in panic disorder. *Archives of General Psychiatry* (in press). As cited in Roy-Byrne, 1991, p. 12.

Okubo, Y., Suhara, T., Suzuki, K., Kobayashi, I., Inoue, O., Terasaki, O., Someya, Y., Sassa, T., Sudo, Y., Matsushima, E., Iyo, M., Tateno, Y., & Toru, M. (1997). Decreased prefrontal dopamine D2 receptors in schizophrenia revealed by PET. *Nature, 385,* 634-636.

Oldendorf, W. H. (1982, February). Some chemical aspects of the blood-brain barrier. *Hospital Practice, 2,* 143-164.

Olds, J. (1958). Satiation effects in self-stimulation of the brain. *Journal of Comparative and Physiological Psychology, 51,* 675-678.

Ostro, M. J. (1987, January). Liposomes. *Scientific American, 256,* 102-111.

Ottoson, D. (1983.) *Physiology of the nervous system.* New York: Oxford University Press.

Park, L., & Covi, L. (1965). Nonblind placebo trial. *Archives of General Psychiatry, 12,* 336-345. As cited in Leavitt, 1974, p. 200.

Payne, R. B. (1963). Nutmeg intoxication. *New England Journal of Medicine, 269,* 1085.

Pitts, F. N. (1969). The biochemistry of anxiety. *Scientific American, 220,* 69-75.

Post, R. M., & Chuang, D.-M. (1991). Mechanism of action of lithium. In N. J. Birch (Ed.). *Lithium and the cell: Pharmacology and biochemistry* (pp. 204 234). New York: Academic Press.

Prescribing tranquilizers called doctor's disease. (1960, February 6). *Science Newsletter,* p. 89. As cited in Smith, 1985, p. 24.

Rall, T. W. (1985). Central nervous stimulants. In L. S. Goodman & A. Gilman (Eds.), *The pharmacological basis of therapeutics* (7th ed.) (pp. 589-903). New York: MacMillan.

Rall, T. W. & Schleiffer, L. S. (1985). Drugs effective in the treatment of epilepsies. In L. S. Goodman & A. Gilman (Eds.), *The pharmacological basis of therapeutics* (7th ed.) (pp. 446-472). New York: MacMillan.

Rang, H. P., Dale, M. M., Ritter, J. M., & Gardner, P. (1995). *Pharmacology*. New York: Churchill Livingstone.

Rapaport, J. L. (1989, March). The biology of obsessions and compulsions. *Scientific American, 260*(3), 83-89.

Ray, O. (1983). *Drugs, society, and human behavior* (3rd ed.). St. Louis: C. V. Mosby Co.

Reed, C., & Witt, P. (1965). Factors contributing to unexpected reactions in two human drug-placebo experiments. *Confinia Psychiatrica, 8,* 57-68. As cited in Leavitt, 1974, p. 199.

Reisine, T. D. (1994). Synaptic transmission: Peptides. In A. Frazer, P. Molinoff, & A. Winokur (Eds.), *Biological bases of brain function and disease* (pp. 128-141). New York: Raven Press.

Reisine, T. D., & Pasternak, G. (1996). Opioid analgesics and antagonists. In J. G. Hardman, L. E. Limbird, P. B. Molinoff, R. W. Ruadon, & A. G. Gilman (Eds.), *Goodman and Gilman's: The pharmacological basis of therapeutics* (9th ed.) (pp. 521-555). New York: McGraw-Hill.

Roediger, H.L., III. (1984). *Psychology*. Boston: Little, Brown, & Company.

Roheim, G. (1955). *Magic and schizophrenia*. Bloomington, IN: Indiana University Press.

Rosenthal, E. (1990, February 13). Powerful new weapons change treatment of pain. *New York Times,* pp. C1, C12.

Rotrosen, J., & Adler, L. (1995). The importance of side effects in the development of new antipsychotic drugs. *Psychiatric Annals, 25*(5), 306.310.

Roy-Byrne, P. P., & Cowley, D.S. (1991). *Benzodiazepines in clinical practice: risks and benefits*. Washington, DC: American Psychiatric Press.

Rubin, E., Altman, K., Gordon, G. G., & Southren, A. L. (1976, February 13). Prolonged ethanol consumption increases testosterone metabolism in the liver. *Science, 191,* 563-564.

Rubin, V., & Comitas, L. (1975) Ganja in Jamaica. In *A medical anthropological study of chronic marijuana use*. Mouton: The Hague. As cited in Hollister, 1986.

Russell, E. S. (1955). Significance of physiological pattern of animal strains in biological research. *British Medical Journal,* 1, 826.

Sawynok, J., & Yaksh, T. L. (1993). Caffeine as an analgesic adjuvant: A review of pharmacology and mechanism of action. *Pharmacological Reviews, 45*(1), 43-85.

Schaefer, O. (1986). Adverse reactions to drugs and metabolic problems perceived in northern Canadian Indians and Eskimos. In W. Kalow, H. W. Goedde, & D. P. Agarwal. (Eds.). *Progress in Clinical and Biological Research, 214: Ethnic differences in reactions to drugs and xenobiotics* (pp. 77-83). New York: Alan R. Liss.

Schildkraut, J. J. (1965). The catecholamine hypothesis of affective disorders: A review of supporting evidence. *American Journal of Psychiatry, 122,* 509-522.

Schultes, R. E. (1970). The plant kingdom and hallucinogens (part III). *Bulletin on Narcotics, 22*(1), 43-46.

Schultes, R. E. (1976). *Hallucinogenic plants*. New York: Golden Press.

Searles, H. (1965). *Collected papers on schizophrenia and related topics*. New York: International Universities Press.

Zinberg, N. E. (1985, February 25). Brain power boosters. *Syracuse Post Standard,* B1. (Reprinted from Washington Post.)

Zinberg, N.E. (1971, December 5). *New York Times Magazine,* p. 122. As cited in Brecher, 1972, p. 191.

Zucker, R. S., & Lando, L. (1986). Mechanism of transmitter release: Voltage hypothesis and calcium hypothesis. *Science, 231,* 574-579.

Selzer, R. (1974, April). The drinking man's liver. *Esquire, 81,* 126-127.

Shulgin, A. T. (1986, October-December). The background and chemistry of MDMA. *Journal of Psychoactive Drugs, 18*(4), 291-303.

Shurley, J. T. (1970). Drugs, sensory and perceptual processes and variations in drug effects related to environments. In W. G. Clark & J. del Giudice. (Eds.). *Principles of psychopharmacology* (pp. 373-378). New York: Academic Press.

Siegel, R. K. (1985, October-December). LSD hallucinations: From ergot to electric kool-aid. *Journal of Psychoactive Drugs, 17*(4), 247-256.

Siegel, R. K. (1986, October-December). MDMA: Nonmedical use and intoxication. *Journal of Psychoactive Drugs, 18*(4), 349-354.

Siegel, R. K., & Jarvik, M. E. (1975). Drug-induced hallucinations in animals and man. In R. K. Siegel & L. J. West. (Eds.). *Hallucinations: Behavior, experience, and theory.* New York: John Wiley and Sons. As cited in Siegel, 1985, p. 251.

Siegel, S., Hinson, R. E., Krank, M. D., & McCully, J. (1982, April 23). Heroin "overdose" death: Contribution of drug-associated environmental cues. *Science, 216,* 436-437.

Silver, L. B. (1992). *Attention deficit hyperactivity disorder.* Washington, DC: American Psychiatric Press.

Silverman, R.E. (1979). *Essentials of psychology.* Englewood Cliffs, NJ: Prentice-Hall.

Smith, D. E., & Seymour, R. B. (1985, October-December). Dream becomes nightmare: Adverse reactions to LSD. *Journal of Psychoactive Drugs, 17*(4).

Smith, D. E., & Seymour, R. B. (1994). LSD: History and toxicity. *Psychiatric Annals, 24*(3), 145-147.

Smith, M. C. (1985). *Small comfort: A history of the minor tranquilizers.* New York: Praeger Publications.

Sokoloff, L., Reivich, M., Kennedy, C., et al. (1977). The (14c) deoxyglucose method for measurement of local cerebral glucose utilization: Theory, procedure and normal values in the conscious and anesthetized albino rat. *Journal of Neurochemistry, 28,* 897-916.

Spiegel, R. (1989). *Psychopharmacology.* New York: John Wiley & Sons.

Spiller, G. A. (Ed.). (1984). *Progress in Clinical and Biological Research, 158: The methylxanthine beverages and foods: Chemistry, consumption and health effects.* New York: Alan R. Liss.

Statutes at Large. (1924). 68th Cong. first sess., chap. 352.

Staub, C. (1993). Hair analysis: Its importance for the diagnosis of poisoning associated with opiate addiction. *Forensic Science International, 63,* 69-75.

Strauss, J.S., Carpenter, W.T., Jr., & Bartko, J.J. (1974). The diagnosis and understanding of schizophrenia: III. Speculations on the processes that underlie schizophrenia symptoms and signs. *Schizophrenia Bulletin, 11,* 61-76.

Suzdak, P. D., Glowa, J. R., Crawley, J. N., Schwartz, R. D., Skolnick, P., & Paul, S. (1986, December 5). A selective imidazobenzodiazepine antagonist of ethanol in the rat. *Science, 234,* 1243-1247.

Suzdak, P. D., Glowa, J. R., Crawley, J. N., Skolnick, P., & Paul, S. (1988, February 5). Is ethanol antagonist Ro. 15-4513 selective for ethanol?--response. *Science, 239,* 649-650.

Svensson, T. H. (2000). Dysfunctional brain dopamine systems induced by psychotomimetic NMDA-receptor antagonists and the effects of antipsychotic drugs. *Brain Research Reviews, 31,* 320-329.

Sweetnam, P. M., Lancaster, J., Snowman, A., Collins, J. L., Perschke, S., Bauer, C., & Ferkany, J. (1995). Receptor binding profile suggests multiple mechanisms of action are responsible for ibogaine's putative anti-addictive activity. *Psychopharmacology, 118*(4), 369-76.

Szasz, T. (1961). *The myth of mental illness.* New York: Hoeber-Harper.

Tallman, J. F., Paul, S. M., Skolnick, P., & Gallagher, D. W. (1980, January 18). Receptors for the age of anxiety: Pharmacology of the benzodiazepines. *Science, 207,* 247-281.

Taubes, G. (2001, November-December). UT Southwestern's Eric J. Nestler on the molecular basis of addiction. (Interview with Eric J. Nestler). Gary Taubes. ScienceWatch. Retrieved June 27, 2004, from http://www.sciencewatch.com/nov-dec2001/sw_nov-dec2001_page3.htm

Taylor, B. (1855/1977). A slight experience of hashish. In A. C. Kimmens. (Ed.). *Tales of hashish* (pp. 141-155). New York: Wm. Morrow & Co.

Thelle, D. G., Arnesen, E., & Ford, O. H. (1983). The Tromso heart study: Does coffee raise serum cholesterol? *New England Journal of Medicine, 308,* 1454. As cited in Ernster, 1984.

Thompson, C. J. S. (1975). *The mystic mandrake.* London: Rider and Company.

Thompson, J. H. (1983). Drug absorption, distribution and excretion. In J. A. Bevan & J. H. Thompson (Eds.). *Essentials of pharmacology* (pp. 23-35). Philadelphia: Harper and Row.

Trebach, A. S. (1982). *The heroin solution.* New Haven, CT: Yale University Press.

U. S. Food & Drug Administration. (1995, Jan). *FDA consumer: Special report: New drug development in the United States.* Washington, DC: U. S. Government Printing Office, pp. 8 &10.

U.S. House of Representatives. (1913, June 24). Registration of producers and importers of opium, etc.--"report."As cited in Trebach, 1982, p. 121.

Ukers, W. H. (1935). *All about coffee.* New York: The Tea and Coffee Trade Journal Co. As cited in Austin, 1978, p. 56.

United States Department of Health and Human Services. (1987, January). *Alcohol and health: Sixth special report to the United States Congress.* Washington, DC: U.S. Department of Health and Human Services.

United States Department of Health and Human Services. (1988). *The health consequences of smoking: Nicotine addiction. A report of the Surgeon General.* Rockville, MD: U.S. Department of Health and Human Services.

Van Dyke, C., & Byck, R. (1982, March). Cocaine. *Scientific American, 246,* 128-141.

Van Putten, T., Marder, S. R., Mintz, J. (1990). A controlled dose comparison of haloperidol in newly admitted schizophrenic patients. *Archives of General Psychiatry, 47,* 754-758.

Vanatta, J. C., & Fogelman, M. J. (1982). *Moyer's fluid balance* (3rd ed.). Chicago: Year Book Medical Publishers.

Vinar, O. (1969). Dependence on a placebo: A case report. British *Journal of Psychiatry, 115,* 1189-1190. As cited in Leavitt, 1974, p. 199.

Vonnegut, M. (1975). *The eden express.* New York: Praeger Publishers.

Vorhees, C. V., et al. (1979, September 21). Psychotropic drugs as behavioral teratogen *Science, 205,* 1220.

Walker, E., Kestler, L., Bollini, A., & Hochman, K. M. (2004). *Annual Review of Psychology, 55,* 401-30.

Ward, A. (Ed.). (1966). *Thomas De Quincey: Confessions of an English opium-eater and other writings.* New York: Carroll & Graf Publishers.

Ward, A. A., Jr. (1945). The anterior cingulate gyrus and personality. *Research Publications, Association for Research in Nervous and Mental Disease, 27,* 438-495. As cited in Grossman, 1967, p. 541.

Wasson, G. (1957). *Mushrooms, Russia, and history.* New York: Pantheon Books.

Wasson, R. G. (1971). *Soma, divine mushroom of immortality.* New York: Harcourt, Brace, Jovanovich.

Webb, S., & Webb, B. (1903). *The history of liquor licensing in England principally from 1700 to 1830.* London: Longmans, Green and Company. As cited in Austin, 1978, p. 71.

Weiss, G. (1960). Hallucinogenic and narcotic-like effects of powdered myristica (nutmeg). *Psychiatry Quarterly, 34,* 346.

Whitaker, M., Shannon, E., & Moreau, R. (1985, February 25). Columbia's kings of coke. *Newsweek, 105,* 19-22.

Williams, H. S. (1938). *Drug addicts are human beings.* Washington, DC: Shaw.

Withers, N. W., Pulvirenti, L., Koob, G. F., & Gillin, J. C. (1995). Cocaine abuse and dependence. *Journal of Clinical Psychopharmacology, 15*(1), 63-78.

Woerner, M. G., Kane, J. M., Lieberman, J. A., Alvin, J., Bergmann, K. J., Borenstein, M., & Schooler, N. R. (1991). The prevalence of tardive dyskinesia. *Journal of Clinical Psychopharmacology, 11,* 34-42. As cited in Rotrosen & Adler, 1995, p. 307.

Wolf, S. (1959). The pharmacology of placebos. *Pharmacological Reviews, 11,* 689-704. As cited in Kornetsky, 1976, p. 42.

Wolkin, A., Brodie, J.D., Barouche, F., et al. (1989). Dopamine receptor occupancy and plasma haloperidol levels. *Archives of General Psychiatry, 46,* 482-483. As cited in Rotrosen & Adler, 1995, p. 307.

Yang, D. J., & Siler, J. F. (1991, November 18). Fewer cups but a much richer brew. *Business Week,* issue 3240, 80.

Yeats, W. B. (1910/1962). A drinking song. In M. L. Rosenthal (Ed.). *Selected poems and two plays of William Butler Yeats* (p. 34). New York: Macmillan Company (Collier Books).

Yesair, D. W., Branfman, A. R., & Callahan, M. M. (1984). Human disposition and some behavioral aspects of methylxanthines. In G.A. Spiller. (Ed.). *Progress in Clinical and Biological Research, 158: The methylxanthine beverages and foods: Chemistry, consumption and health effects* (pp. 215-233). New York: Alan R. Liss.

Zammit, S., Allebeck, P. Andreasson, S., Lundberg, I., & Lewis, G. (2002). Self-reported cannabis use as a risk factor for schizophrenia in Swedish conscripts of 1969: historical cohort study. *British Medical Journal, 325,* 1199-1201.

Zentner, J. (1975). Prominent features of opiate use in America during the twentieth century. *Journal of Drug Issues, 5*(2): 99-108. As cited in Austin, 1978, p. 225.

Selzer, R. (1974, April). The drinking man's liver. *Esquire, 81,* 126-127.

Shulgin, A. T. (1986, October-December). The background and chemistry of MDMA. *Journal of Psychoactive Drugs, 18*(4), 291-303.

Shurley, J. T. (1970). Drugs, sensory and perceptual processes and variations in drug effects related to environments. In W. G. Clark & J. del Giudice. (Eds.). *Principles of psychopharmacology* (pp. 373-378). New York: Academic Press.

Siegel, R. K. (1985, October-December). LSD hallucinations: From ergot to electric kool-aid. *Journal of Psychoactive Drugs, 17*(4), 247-256.

Siegel, R. K. (1986, October-December). MDMA: Nonmedical use and intoxication. *Journal of Psychoactive Drugs, 18*(4), 349-354.

Siegel, R. K., & Jarvik, M. E. (1975). Drug-induced hallucinations in animals and man. In R. K. Siegel & L. J. West. (Eds.). *Hallucinations: Behavior, experience, and theory.* New York: John Wiley and Sons. As cited in Siegel, 1985, p. 251.

Siegel, S., Hinson, R. E., Krank, M. D., & McCully, J. (1982, April 23). Heroin "overdose" death: Contribution of drug-associated environmental cues. *Science, 216,* 436-437.

Silver, L. B. (1992). *Attention deficit hyperactivity disorder.* Washington, DC: American Psychiatric Press.

Silverman, R.E. (1979). *Essentials of psychology.* Englewood Cliffs, NJ: Prentice-Hall.

Smith, D. E., & Seymour, R. B. (1985, October-December). Dream becomes nightmare: Adverse reactions to LSD. *Journal of Psychoactive Drugs, 17*(4).

Smith, D. E., & Seymour, R. B. (1994). LSD: History and toxicity. *Psychiatric Annals, 24*(3), 145-147.

Smith, M. C. (1985). *Small comfort: A history of the minor tranquilizers.* New York: Praeger Publications.

Sokoloff, L., Reivich, M., Kennedy, C., et al. (1977). The (14c) deoxyglucose method for measurement of local cerebral glucose utilization: Theory, procedure and normal values in the conscious and anesthetized albino rat. *Journal of Neurochemistry, 28,* 897-916.

Spiegel, R. (1989). *Psychopharmacology.* New York: John Wiley & Sons.

Spiller, G. A. (Ed.). (1984). *Progress in Clinical and Biological Research, 158: The methylxanthine beverages and foods: Chemistry, consumption and health effects.* New York: Alan R. Liss.

Statutes at Large. (1924). 68th Cong. first sess., chap. 352.

Staub, C. (1993). Hair analysis: Its importance for the diagnosis of poisoning associated with opiate addiction. *Forensic Science International, 63,* 69-75.

Strauss, J.S., Carpenter, W.T., Jr., & Bartko, J.J. (1974). The diagnosis and understanding of schizophrenia: III. Speculations on the processes that underlie schizophrenia symptoms and signs. *Schizophrenia Bulletin, 11,* 61-76.

Suzdak, P. D., Glowa, J. R., Crawley, J. N., Schwartz, R. D., Skolnick, P., & Paul, S. (1986, December 5). A selective imidazobenzodiazepine antagonist of ethanol in the rat. *Science, 234,* 1243-1247.

Suzdak, P. D., Glowa, J. R., Crawley, J. N., Skolnick, P., & Paul, S. (1988, February 5). Is ethanol antagonist Ro. 15-4513 selective for ethanol?--response. *Science, 239,* 649-650.

Svensson, T. H. (2000). Dysfunctional brain dopamine systems induced by psychotomimetic NMDA-receptor antagonists and the effects of antipsychotic drugs. *Brain Research Reviews, 31*, 320-329.

Sweetnam, P. M., Lancaster, J., Snowman, A., Collins, J. L., Perschke, S., Bauer, C., & Ferkany, J. (1995). Receptor binding profile suggests multiple mechanisms of action are responsible for ibogaine's putative anti-addictive activity. *Psychopharmacology, 118*(4), 369-76.

Szasz, T. (1961). *The myth of mental illness.* New York: Hoeber-Harper.

Tallman, J. F., Paul, S. M., Skolnick, P., & Gallagher, D. W. (1980, January 18). Receptors for the age of anxiety: Pharmacology of the benzodiazepines. *Science, 207*, 247-281.

Taubes, G. (2001, November-December). UT Southwestern's Eric J. Nestler on the molecular basis of addiction. (Interview with Eric J. Nestler). Gary Taubes. ScienceWatch. Retrieved June 27, 2004, from http://www.sciencewatch.com/nov-dec2001/sw_nov-dec2001_page3.htm

Taylor, B. (1855/1977). A slight experience of hashish. In A. C. Kimmens. (Ed.). *Tales of hashish* (pp. 141-155). New York: Wm. Morrow & Co.

Thelle, D. G., Arnesen, E., & Ford, O. H. (1983). The Tromso heart study: Does coffee raise serum cholesterol? *New England Journal of Medicine, 308*, 1454. As cited in Ernster, 1984.

Thompson, C. J. S. (1975). *The mystic mandrake.* London: Rider and Company.

Thompson, J. H. (1983). Drug absorption, distribution and excretion. In J. A. Bevan & J. H. Thompson (Eds.). *Essentials of pharmacology* (pp. 23-35). Philadelphia: Harper and Row.

Trebach, A. S. (1982). *The heroin solution.* New Haven, CT: Yale University Press.

U. S. Food & Drug Administration. (1995, Jan). *FDA consumer: Special report: New drug development in the United States.* Washington, DC: U. S. Government Printing Office, pp. 8 &10.

U.S. House of Representatives. (1913, June 24). Registration of producers and importers of opium, etc.--"report."As cited in Trebach, 1982, p. 121.

Ukers, W. H. (1935). *All about coffee.* New York: The Tea and Coffee Trade Journal Co. As cited in Austin, 1978, p. 56.

United States Department of Health and Human Services. (1987, January). *Alcohol and health: Sixth special report to the United States Congress.* Washington, DC: U.S. Department of Health and Human Services.

United States Department of Health and Human Services. (1988). *The health consequences of smoking: Nicotine addiction. A report of the Surgeon General.* Rockville, MD: U.S. Department of Health and Human Services.

Van Dyke, C., & Byck, R. (1982, March). Cocaine. *Scientific American, 246*, 128-141.

Van Putten, T., Marder, S. R., Mintz, J. (1990). A controlled dose comparison of haloperidol in newly admitted schizophrenic patients. *Archives of General Psychiatry, 47*, 754-758.

Vanatta, J. C., & Fogelman, M. J. (1982). *Moyer's fluid balance* (3rd ed.). Chicago: Year Book Medical Publishers.

Vinar, O. (1969). Dependence on a placebo: A case report. British *Journal of Psychiatry, 115*, 1189-1190. As cited in Leavitt, 1974, p. 199.

Vonnegut, M. (1975). *The eden express*. New York: Praeger Publishers.

Vorhees, C. V., et al. (1979, September 21). Psychotropic drugs as behavioral teratogens. *Science, 205*, 1220.

Walker, E., Kestler, L., Bollini, A., & Hochman, K. M. (2004). *Annual Review of Psychology, 55*, 401-30.

Ward, A. (Ed.). (1966). *Thomas De Quincey: Confessions of an English opium-eater and other writings*. New York: Carroll & Graf Publishers.

Ward, A. A., Jr. (1945). The anterior cingulate gyrus and personality. *Research Publications, Association for Research in Nervous and Mental Disease, 27*, 438-495. As cited in Grossman, 1967, p. 541.

Wasson, G. (1957). *Mushrooms, Russia, and history*. New York: Pantheon Books.

Wasson, R. G. (1971). *Soma, divine mushroom of immortality*. New York: Harcourt, Brace, Jovanovich.

Webb, S., & Webb, B. (1903). *The history of liquor licensing in England principally from 1700 to 1830*. London: Longmans, Green and Company. As cited in Austin, 1978, p. 71.

Weiss, G. (1960). Hallucinogenic and narcotic-like effects of powdered myristica (nutmeg). *Psychiatry Quarterly, 34*, 346.

Whitaker, M., Shannon, E., & Moreau, R. (1985, February 25). Columbia's kings of coke. *Newsweek, 105*, 19-22.

Williams, H. S. (1938). *Drug addicts are human beings*. Washington, DC: Shaw.

Withers, N. W., Pulvirenti, L., Koob, G. F., & Gillin, J. C. (1995). Cocaine abuse and dependence. *Journal of Clinical Psychopharmacology, 15*(1), 63-78.

Woerner, M. G., Kane, J. M., Lieberman, J. A., Alvin, J., Bergmann, K. J., Borenstein, M., & Schooler, N. R. (1991). The prevalence of tardive dyskinesia. *Journal of Clinical Psychopharmacology, 11*, 34-42. As cited in Rotrosen & Adler, 1995, p. 307.

Wolf, S. (1959). The pharmacology of placebos. *Pharmacological Reviews, 11*, 689-704. As cited in Kornetsky, 1976, p. 42.

Wolkin, A., Brodie, J.D., Barouche, F., et al. (1989). Dopamine receptor occupancy and plasma haloperidol levels. *Archives of General Psychiatry, 46*, 482-483. As cited in Rotrosen & Adler, 1995, p. 307.

Yang, D. J., & Siler, J. F. (1991, November 18). Fewer cups but a much richer brew. *Business Week*, issue 3240, 80.

Yeats, W. B. (1910/1962). A drinking song. In M. L. Rosenthal (Ed.). *Selected poems and two plays of William Butler Yeats* (p. 34). New York: Macmillan Company (Collier Books).

Yesair, D. W., Branfman, A. R., & Callahan, M. M. (1984). Human disposition and some behavioral aspects of methylxanthines. In G.A. Spiller. (Ed.). *Progress in Clinical and Biological Research, 158: The methylxanthine beverages and foods: Chemistry, consumption and health effects* (pp. 215-233). New York: Alan R. Liss.

Zammit, S., Allebeck, P. Andreasson, S., Lundberg, I., & Lewis, G. (2002). Self-reported cannabis use as a risk factor for schizophrenia in Swedish conscripts of 1969: historical cohort study. *British Medical Journal, 325*, 1199-1201.

Zentner, J. (1975). Prominent features of opiate use in America during the twentieth century. *Journal of Drug Issues, 5*(2): 99-108. As cited in Austin, 1978, p. 225.

Zinberg, N. E. (1985, February 25). Brain power boosters. *Syracuse Post Standard,* B1. (Reprinted from Washington Post.)

Zinberg, N.E. (1971, December 5). *New York Times Magazine,* p. 122. As cited in Brecher, 1972, p. 191.

Zucker, R. S., & Lando, L. (1986). Mechanism of transmitter release: Voltage hypothesis and calcium hypothesis. *Science, 231,* 574-579.